MW01251510

Peter Norton's
Maximizing Windows 98
Administration

Peter Norton
Forrest Houlette

SAMS 201 West 103rd Street
Indianapolis Indiana 46290

Peter Norton's Maximizing Windows 98 Administration
Copyright © by Peter Norton

International Standard Book Number: 0-672-31218-2

Library of Congress Catalog No.: 97-69120

01   00   99   98   4   3   2   1

Interpretation of the printing code: the rightmost double-digit number is the year of the book's printing; the rightmost single-digit number, the number of the book's printing. For example, a printing code of 98-1 shows that the first printing of the book occurred in 1998.

Trademarks

Executive Editor
Grace Buechlein

Development Editor
Sunthar Visuvalingam

Managing Editor
Sarah Kearns

Project Editor
Mike La Bonne

Copy Editor
Keith Cline

Indexer
Chris Wilcox

Technical Editor
Paul Hinsberg
Dennis Teague
John Charlesworth
Susan Charlesworth

Production Team
Betsy Deeter
Becky Stutzman

Overview

Contents

About the Authors

Computer software entrepreneur and writer **Peter Norton** established his technical expertise and accessible style from the earliest days of the PC. His Norton Utilities was the first product of its kind, giving early computer owners control over their hardware and protection against myriad problems. His flagship titles, *Peter Norton's DOS Guide* and *Peter Norton's Inside the PC* (Sams Publishing) have provided the same insight and education to computer users worldwide for nearly two decades. Peter's books, like his many software products, are among the best-selling and most-respected in the history of personal computing.

Peter Norton's former column in *PC Week* was among the highest-regarded in that magazine's history. His expanding series of computer books continues to bring superior education to users, always in Peter's trademark style, which is never condescending nor pedantic. From their earliest days, changing the "black box" into a "glass box," Peter's books, like his software, remain among the most powerful tools available to beginners and experienced users, alike.

In 1990, Peter sold his software development business to Symantec Corporation, allowing him to devote more time to his family, civic affairs, philanthropy, and art collecting. He lives with his wife, Eileen, and two children in Santa Monica, California.

Forrest Houlette is a computer writer, trainer, and consultant who lives in Muncie, Indiana. He is president of Write Environment, Inc., a consulting firm that specializes in Visual Basic software development, custom documentation, training, and software for both education and business. Forrest holds a Ph.D. in linguistics and rhetoric from the University of Louisville. He began working with computers when he took a course in FORTRAN in 1979. Since then, he has programmed in BASIC, the Digital Authoring Language, C, C++, WordBasic, SQLWindows, and Visual Basic. During his career as a university professor, he taught linguistics and focused on usisV artificial intelligence techniques to improve software for writing. He has written computer-based education programs for the teaching of writing, one of which, Write Environment, won the Zenith Masters of Innovation competition. Forrest now focuses on writing about computers and creating custom software. He has taught courses on Windows 95, Windows NT, Office 97, and Visual Basic for Learning Tree International. He has authored or co-authored books for IDG, New Riders Publishing, Que, and Sybex. He is also a Microsoft Certified Product Specialist. Currently, he works as a programmer/analyst for AIMCO, in addition to his other interests. You may send him feedback on this book at `fth_we@iquest.net`.

Dedication (from Forrest)

To Judy and Alex, who have lived through this book with me; to John Craddock, for serving as a role model in teaching thinking about network administration; to Paul Hinsberg and the crew at Learning Tree, who forced me to learn more about troubleshooting than I ever wanted to; and to Sue, Sandra, Will, Christy, Don, and Nancy, who often don't get the recognition they deserve, but who were very helpful throughout the writing of this book. And to Peter Norton, who made this series possible.

Acknowledgments (from Forrest)

Many people have supported my work on this book. Thanks to David Fugate, an excellent agent; Grace Buechlein and Sunthar Visuvalingam at Macmillan for their patience and insight; the entire staff at Macmillan for their tireless effort; Dennis Teague and Paul Hinsberg, for their insight as technical editors; and to Paul Hinsberg for some excellent revisions. To all those I have missed in this brief listing, many thanks indeed.

Introduction

Windows 98 represents the next stage in the evolution of the Windows operating system, and a major step forward for system administrators. Many of us have been riding the crest of this evolution since some earlier version. Few of us worked with Windows 1.1 after its release in 1985. While Microsoft had brought a multitasking graphical user interface to the PC, both the PC and the software were not quite up to coping with such demands.

I joined the Windows bandwagon with version 2.11, when Windows was still unpopular with system administrators because it would not network well. One of my projects, however, required multitasking on a PC, and Windows was the only operating environment at the time that would meet my requirement. Windows evolved rapidly from this version, becoming network friendly and gaining robustness. Windows for Workgroups built networking into the operating system, and Microsoft considered Windows for Workgroups the ideal client for its Windows NT Server operating system.

Windows evolution slowed at this point. Microsoft had created Windows NT, a secure and scalable version of Windows employing new technology. Microsoft was also working on Chicago, the 32-bit incarnation of the desktop operating system. As a part of the Chicago effort, Microsoft created a new user interface to make working with your desktop computer easier.

During this period, Microsoft also pushed headlong into the networking market. Originally Microsoft licensed IBM's LAN Manager as its network operating system. With the advent of Windows NT, Microsoft tried to create a networking product that could compete with NetWare and UNIX. In the process, Microsoft took Windows NT through three revisions, which brought Microsoft networking into the market as a force to be reckoned with. All the while, the new 32-bit client operating system, code-named Chicago, promised a robust client for heterogeneous networks.

When Chicago (renamed Windows 95) was released—about a year later than planned—Windows again captured our imagination. We had a whole new environment to learn, and it contained many engaging features. Windows 95 brought us right clicking, a desktop with the features of Program Manager, a Task Bar, new buttons, new icons, and new neighborhoods. It was fun, and maddening to learn for those of us who had strong Windows 3.1 skills. Windows 95 was also network friendly, and fairly solid as a network client, especially with Windows NT as the server platform.

Windows 98 is not as major a revolution. If you have used both Windows 95 and a Web browser, you already know how to use Windows 98. This new Windows, however, has plenty of new features, especially for those who use the Internet or an intranet frequently. Windows 98 merges the desktop and the browser, as well as offering a host of technical enhancements that make it more useful for nearly every user. For those of us who must implement Windows 98 on business networks, the new operating system offers both a host of challenges and some interesting new tools to help us meet those challenges. Meeting those administrative challenges is what this book is about.

Who Should Read This Book?

The primary audience for this book is the system administrators, consultants, network analysts, and network technicians who have to keep Windows 98 clients on production networks running smoothly in a business setting. Over the last two years, I've taught Windows 95 to a number of such individuals. Their concerns have shaped the structure of this book significantly. I have tried to answer all of the recurring questions that came up in my training classes.

There is also a large secondary audience for this book. Lots of us want to go beyond the beginning books on Windows 98 and learn how to make our systems perform. No matter what anyone says, there are ways to make a 32 meg Pentium 200 crawl under Windows 98. Most of us would like to learn how to avoid such situations, and this book covers more about how to improve performance than most other books you will find.

Others among us want to learn how Windows 98 works, but we don't want to wade through the mountains of technical detail that Microsoft dumps into a resource kit. This book is your cheat sheet to help you focus the technical detail into meaningful chunks. It presents what you need to know and what you need to do to keep your systems going. Once you have this focus, wading back into all the detail is easier, because you have the framework that makes sense out of the details.

Others are ready to move from stand-alone systems to small networks, or need to move from some other side of computing into system administration. This book is designed to get you ready to administer systems and networks running Windows 98 in short order. You will get the basics and you will be ready to use other technical resources, like Microsoft's resource kits and knowledge bases, as you work with your systems.

What You'll Learn

When I planned this book, I wrote out the list of questions that I am always asked when I teach a class on Windows. The best way to show you what you will learn by reading this book is to share those questions with you. They represent the topics the book covers. And just in case you are scanning this list looking for a quick answer, the part or chapter that answers the question is listed following the question.

- How do I install Windows 98? (Chapter 1, "Reviewing Basic Installation")
- I have a 200 node network. How do I roll Windows 98 out to all those clients? (Chapter 2, "Preparing for a Rollout")
- I have Novell servers. How do I integrate Windows 98 with those servers? (Chapter 9, "Setting Up a NetWare Client," and Chapter 10, "Dealing With Multiple Client Hosts")

- I have Windows NT Servers. How do I integrate Windows 98 and Windows NT? (Chapter 8, "Setting Up a Microsoft Client," and Chapter 10, "Dealing With Multiple Client Hosts")

- I have several other types of servers. How do I integrate Windows 98 with these servers? (Chapter 10, "Dealing with Multiple Client Hosts")

- How do I install both local and network printers? (Chapter 3, "Reviewing Basic User Interaction")

- How do I secure files? (Chapter 18, "Securing the System," and Chapter 19, "Securing Shared Resources")

- How do I secure a computer? (Chapter 18, "Securing the System")

- How do I control user desktops on my network? (Chapter 17, "Securing the Desktop")

- Can I limit which programs can run on network clients? (Chapter 18, "Securing the System")

- How do I protect against viruses? (Chapter 18, "Securing the System")

- How do I install new hardware, and when should I upgrade? (Chapter 1, "Reviewing Basic Installation")

- How do I install new software and when do I need to upgrade my software? (Chapter 1, "Reviewing Basic Installation")

- Can I manage computer configuration centrally on my network? (Chapter 2, "Preparing for a Rollout")

- How do I manage Internet access? (Chapter 4, "Choosing the Active or Classic Desktop," and Part VI, "Participating on Intranets and Internets")

- How do I grant remote access to users? (Chapter 7, "Working with the WAN Connection")

- How do I support mobile users? (Chapter 7, "Working with the WAN Connection"

- What do I have to know about the architecture of the system? (Part II, "Understanding the Windows 98 Architecture")

- What is the network architecture of this system? (Chapter 6, "Understanding the LAN Connection")

- I have physically challenged users. How do I make Windows 98 accessible to them? (Chapter 15, "Configuring for Ease of Use")

- Do I need to have IntelliMouse? (Chapter 3, "Reviewing Basic User Interaction")

- What is this total cost of ownership issue? (Chapter 2, "Preparing for a Rollout")

- What is this zero administration issue? (Chapter 1, "Reviewing Basic Installation")

- What new hardware support is available? (Chapter 5, "Looking at the Core of the Operating System")

- What new software support is available? (Chapter 5, "Looking at the Core of the Operating System")

- How can we sensibly use multimedia in our setting? (Chapter 5, "Looking at the Core of the Operating System")

- How do I troubleshoot Windows 98? (Part VII, "Troubleshooting Windows 98")

- How do I communicate with Macs? (Chapter 8, "Setting Up a Microsoft Client")

How This Book Is Organized

This book is organized into seven functional areas, each representing a set of related topics that answer questions listed in the preceding section. These seven parts are ordered in the rough sequence that you would encounter the related questions if you have to implement Windows 98 as a desktop client operating system on a network.

Part I: Preparing to Run Windows 98

This section describes the basic installation procedure for a single system. It then describes ways of extending this procedure to allow multiple efficient installations on client computers attached to a network. It reviews the changes in the user interface, and then discusses how to build a desktop for client machines.

Part II: Understanding the Windows 98 Architecture

This part deals with architectural issues. It first describes the architecture of the core operating system services. It then describes both the local area network and wide area network architectures employed by Windows 98.

Part III: Configuring Windows 98 Clients

This part focuses on setting up network client computers. It shows how to set up Microsoft clients and NetWare under Windows 98. It then addresses the issue of multiple client hosts. Describing the advantages and disadvantages of using multiple clients on a single computer.

Part IV: Tuning Windows 98

This section addresses how to get the best performance out of Windows 98 systems. It describes performance tips that are relevant to any system, and then shows you how to use the System Monitor application to examine performance counters that Windows 98 tracks for you. It goes on to examine how to plan your monitoring, how to use Microsoft's Network Monitor to examine network traffic, how to configure a system to make it easy to use, and how to use scripts to simplify system maintenance. In addition, the accessibility options and the Windows Scripting Host are demonstrated, with good examples of how to use each.

Part V: Securing Windows 98

Because security is a major issue for many organizations, this part focuses on the areas of security that Windows 98 users need to address: physical security on the computer, file security, desktop security, security on shared resources, and data protection.

Part VI: Participating on Intranets and Internets

This section raises issues related to connecting a Windows 98 computer to either intranets, extranets, or the Internet. It shows how to create a Web server using Windows 98. It shows how to create Web pages using FrontPage Express and how to use them on the desktop. It describes how to use both VBScript and JavaScript, and then addresses special security concerns related to setting up an intranet or Internet connection.

Part VII: Troubleshooting Windows 98

Every operating system requires certain thinking skills for problem solving. This part focuses on building those skills for Windows 98 troubleshooting. It describes the Registry, the central database of configuration settings. It shows how to use the troubleshooting tools provided with Windows 98, as well as additional tools that Microsoft provides. It describes operating system level, application-specific, hardware and network-related troubleshooting procedures in separate chapters.

Icons

In the margins of this book, you will find several icons that help to identify specific kinds of information. You can use these icons to help you spot essential concepts as you skim through the text. The following paragraphs describe each icon and what it means.

Notes add to the basic text. They provide additional facts that are relevant, but don't necessarily fit the flow of the discussion at the moment. I've used them as asides that give you interesting facts that I've picked up from exploring Windows 98.

Tips are helpful hints about additional ways to use the operating system. Windows 98 provides at least two ways to do most things. Typically, I will describe the main or standard ones in the text, and offer tips that show you the alternatives that you might like better.

The dreaded warning icon alerts you to something you don't want to have happen to you. These usually represent the benefit of sad experience, so you will want to pay attention. Make sure you understand a warning thoroughly before you follow any instructions that come after it. You don't need to lose data accidentally or hose your system just so that you can learn the same lesson I did with the same pain.

I usually include a Peter's Principle to offer insight into how best to manage your Windows 98 systems. These recommendations are not hard and fast rules. They are however invariably based on my long personal experience with different ways of doing the same thing. Passages with this icon might also include ideas on where to find additional information. You might find shareware and freeware programs mentioned here.

Whenever you see a Looking Ahead icon, I'm providing a road sign that tells you where we're headed. That way, you can follow the path of a particular subject as I provide more detailed information throughout the book. When you talk about an operating system, sometimes you have to assume that the reader knows everything all at once. If I have to assume that you already know something, I will provide one of these pointers to the more complete discussion.

Knowing how the guts of the operating system and how the pieces fit and work together inside is particularly useful for administrators. Whenever you see the Architecture icon, I'm talking about the internal workings of Windows 98. Knowing how Windows 98 performs its job can help you determine why things sometimes don't work as they should. You'll appreciate these insights when you get to the part on Troubleshooting.

Whenever you change something as important as your operating system, there will be problems with older devices and applications that were designed for the previous version. The Compatibility icon clues you in to tips, techniques, and notes that will help you get over the compatibility hurdle.

Security is a crucial consideration of every facet of an administrator's role, especially considering that Windows 98 falls short of the stringent model offered by the Windows NT workstations in your enterprise. This icon draws your attention to the security implications—loopholes, work-arounds, additional tools—of the feature being discussed.

You'll almost certainly be running Windows 98 clients in a mixed environment with Windows NT, NetWare and even UNIX servers. This icon draws your attention to what works together and what does not, ensuring that your implementations can be readily ported between systems and environments. Compatibility also means connectivity across platforms.

I use the Performance icon to designate a performance-related tip. They cover a variety of monitoring and optimization techniques. The idea is to highlight the techniques you can use to adjust and improve the performance of your systems, particularly relating to the central processor, memory, disk caching, and network. You'll need to read them carefully and decide which ones suit your needs, and how best to apply them.

Standards have evolved since the introduction of Windows in order to define and regulate how computer systems should behave. Windows 98 has adopted many of the standards promulgated by ISO, IEEE, and other standards making bodies. I use this icon to help you find information about the standards Windows 98 conforms to, and also to let you know where Windows 98 has adapted the standard to its own purposes. Sometimes Microsoft conforms straightforwardly, at other times, as with the Java Virtual Machine, Microsoft capitalizes on the standard and adds its own functionality. Watch for these icons so that you can easily stay abreast of these issues.

Technical details can really help you localize a problem or decide precisely what you need in order to get a job done. They can also help improve your overall knowledge of a product. Sometimes they're just fun to learn. However, sometimes you just need an overview of how something works; learning the details would slow you down. I use the Technical Note icon to tell you when a piece of information is a detail. You can bypass this information if you need only an overview of a Windows 98 process or feature. This icon also gives you clues as to where you can look for additional information.

If there were no problems, there wouldn't be a need for administrators. At least, we'd have less of them around, and you might not need this book enough to want to pay for it. In addition, to the series of chapters entirely devoted to solving operating system, application, hardware and network problems, you'll easily find troubleshooting insights scattered through the rest of the book by watching out for the Troubleshooting icon.

Peter Norton®

I

Preparing
to Run
Windows 98

1

Reviewing Basic Installation

Peter Norton®

Microsoft, as it is wont to do, has come out with a new operating system: Windows 98. Your company has decided to go with it. You hear a lot of reasons why adopting Windows 98 is a good idea. Windows 98 is faster, supports newer hardware, makes work easier, merges the Web with the desktop, is easier for users, and does dishes to boot. Or you might have heard that a vice president with plenty of clout made the decision because his 12-year-old son liked the new interface better. Decisions about technology get made for lots of reasons. But the bottom line is that your job is to get Windows 98 installed throughout the company.

You have to set aside all debates and opinions and get to the task of doing installations and making sure that users can get their work done without interruption. This is no simple task. You have to come up to speed on a new operating system in short order, right about the time that most of the major training companies are struggling to get their Windows 98 courses released. If you're lucky, you got a chance to work with the beta version. But chances are somebody has handed you a CD and asked you to get to work.

The purpose of this book is to help you to get past the first hurdles in preparing to administer Windows 98 on your network. I have been testing Windows 98 on my office network since August 1997, and I will be sharing with you all the tips I've picked up. I can also save you some time by walking you through many of the procedures you will have to perform and by giving you overviews of how to resolve many of your administrative concerns.

Peter's Principle: Upgrade to Windows 98 or Wait for
Windows NT 5.0?

Should you upgrade to Windows 98? The answer depends on the type of operation you run. At home, my answer would be yes. Windows 98 contains several features to improve the kind of computing you are likely to do at home. Games have more support. Entertainment and multimedia hardware has more support. You can recover disk space on your large drives by using FAT32. You can multilink modems to your Internet service provider. You can do many of the cool things that home users like to do more efficiently with Windows 98.

If you are in business and are still on Windows 3.11, you should upgrade to Windows 98, so long as your hardware can support the operating system. You will like all the new features, and you will find Windows 98 to be a more stable networking platform. Windows 98 offers options for data protection not present in Windows 3.x; this alone is a good reason to upgrade.

Other businesses, however, may just have finished converting desktops to Windows 95. Having resolved all the issues related to such a rollout, they may not want to invest in yet another operating system. The question for businesses in this situation is whether there is enough new in Windows 98 to justify the cost of the licensing. If you have already converted to Windows 95, my answer is that you should not upgrade unless you have hardware that requires Windows 98. If you want to use the Universal Serial Bus or the IEEE 1394 Firewire, for example, you need Windows 98. Otherwise, you can download for Windows 95 most of the enhancements you would gain in Windows 98 from Microsoft's Web site.

Whether to deploy Windows 98 or Windows NT is a different question. Windows NT 4.0 lacks strong support for notebook computers. It lacks support for much of the hardware you might need to use. If you need to use existing hardware and do not want to upgrade memory, choose Windows 98. However, Windows NT 4.0 provides security. If you need security, choose Windows NT 4.0. Microsoft executives describe Windows NT 5.0 as a superset of Windows 98. It promises notebook support and many extra features to support efficient computing and data protection. The launch date for Windows NT 5.0 has slipped into 1999. You have a long wait if you are holding out for Windows NT 5.0.

The first task is to get Windows 98 installed somewhere so that you can see, first, how it installs and, second, how to plan installations throughout your company. As you and I both know, your first time through a setup routine can be filled with many surprises. In this chapter, I'm going to step you through the installation process so that you can save some trial-and-error learning.

This chapter covers single installations. If you need to read about scripted installations and rollout plans, skip to Chapter 2, "Preparing for a Rollout." Otherwise, this chapter covers the following topics:

- Preparing for setup
- Surviving the stages of setup
- Planning for zero administration
- Planning for multiple boot
- Getting back your former configuration
- Installing from scratch
- Installing new hardware
- Installing new software

Preparing for Setup

The first step in installing Windows 98 is to set the CD aside and spend some time checking the system. You have some maintenance you want to do, most of it preventive. You are also preparing for what might happen if installation fails. You want a clear path back to where you were if Windows 98 won't install, and you want to make certain that data can't be lost as you install the new operating system. In general, you want to take five separate steps:

Tip: Although this chapter assumes that you are installing over Windows 95, the installation program will install Windows 98 over Windows 3.x, using virtually identical steps.

1. Check the disk for free space and damage, and back up critical files.
2. Disable restrictive policies, those that prevent users from using a feature of Windows 95.
3. Upgrade third-party network clients.
4. Prepare for operating system differences.
5. Prepare for differences in hardware and software behavior.

Checking the Disk

When you check the disk, you want to carry out these steps:

1. Empty the Recycle Bin and delete all cached World Wide Web files.

Technical Note: The first four of these steps help you to prepare for the amount of disk space required by Setup. Nominally, Setup requires 90MB minimum of free disk space. However, this figure assumes the smallest possible cluster size on the disk and the choice to install only the minimum number of components. If you choose to install all components on a disk with the largest possible cluster size, you need 243MB of free space. In addition, if you direct Windows 98 to create an uninstall file during setup, you need up to 50MB of additional free disk space for the uninstall file.

2. Delete the contents of the TEMP directory, whether it is the directory C:\WINDOWS\TEMP or another directory that a TEMP environment variable points to.
3. Search for and delete all files matching the search strings ~*.tmp and Backup*.*. These files may not all be in the TEMP directory, because they are created by programs such as Microsoft Office in the current working directory.
4. Take note of any other temporary file naming conventions used by software that you have installed. Search for and delete these files.
5. If at all possible, relocate MS-DOS programs to a separate partition. If you choose to use FAT32 at any time after installing Windows 98, DOS programs located in the FAT32 partition will not be available to other operating systems that can view the drive.
6. Remark out any conflicting memory managers in the system configuration. These include EMM386 with highscan enabled or B000-C7FF included, QEMM, and 386MAX.

7. Back up all configuration files, Registry files, and critical data. (And verify this backup!! You may want a second backup just for safety's sake. Do a test restore just to make sure the backup media is good.)

8. Turn off software and hardware virus protection.

The last four steps help you to avoid headaches both during and after the install process. Step 5 protects the availability of critical DOS programs. Steps 6 and 8 prevent you from having to restart Setup after fixing a problem with memory management or virus protection. Step 7 prepares you to get back to the status of the system before starting Windows 98 installation if you have to.

Windows 98 Setup enables you to build an uninstall directory, so that you have a path back to your former operating system. This uninstall option works very well, and you should exercise it whenever you have a need to return to the former configuration immediately after a marginal installation of Windows 98. I have one laptop, a TI Travelmate 4000M, for example, that would not run reliably under Windows 98. The uninstall option got this machine back to Windows 95 in just a few minutes.

Tip: Windows 98 Setup enables you to specify where the uninstall file will be stored. It need not be on the same drive or partition where Windows 98 is installed.

Unfortunately, the best way to install Windows 98 is to back up the drive, and then to repartition the drive, destroying its former contents. Although risky, this procedure clears up many mysterious problems that are related to files from other applications remaining on the drive. The Web TV Viewer, for example, is software that always runs best if this procedure is used. Of course, you face reinstalling the applications and restoring the data, so you pay a penalty in time with this procedure. However, you are guaranteed the best installation.

Removing Policy Restrictions

Windows 95 introduced system policies for controlling the behavior of user systems. If you have not implemented policies known as restrictions, you need do nothing to prepare for Windows 98 setup. If you implemented restrictions for the default user, however, you need to clear them before you attempt Windows 98 installation. Restrictions can prevent Windows 98 from installing.

I sincerely hope that you used the default policy file location and automatic update when you set up policies, and therefore used a single, centralized policy file. If you did, clearing restrictions is fairly easy. Copy the policy file to a backup, edit the policy file to remove restrictions, and then reboot the machines to clear the policies. When you are finished, you can reapply the policies you need. Follow these steps:

1. Copy CONFIG.POL to CONFIG.OLD.

2. Use the System Policy Editor to edit CONFIG.POL and remove any restrictions.

3. Save CONFIG.POL.

4. Require users to boot their machines and log on twice (or do it for them). This action clears the old policies.

After you have completed installation, you must re-create your policy file by using the Windows 98 System Policy Editor. The policy file template has changed considerably, and you will want a fresh file.

Note: The default location for policy files on a Windows NT Server is the NETLOGON share \%SystemRoot%\SYSTEM32\REPL\IMPORT\SCRIPTS (if you are looking for the directory in the server's file system). For a NetWare server, it is the PUBLIC directory. %SystemRoot% is shorthand for "the directory where you installed Windows NT."

If you used manual policy updates and located your policy files in a single location, just locate your file and perform this same procedure. If you used multiple locations, you need to locate each policy file and perform this procedure.

Tip: Manual or automatic update for policies is set by using the Update policy under the Network book in the Computer Policies dialog box. See Chapter 17, "Securing the Desktop," for more information about system policies.

Preparing Your Third-Party Network Clients

Technical Note: If you are using third-party network clients, you want to visit that vendor's Web site and download the latest version. In the case of Novell's Client32, you need to have at least version 2.2 of the client software. In beta testing, earlier versions worked with limited functionality. You will, however, experience general protection faults and other system conflicts with older third-party clients.

Hardware will be the most frustrating of the problems you face in preparing to install Windows 98. You will probably encounter some hardware that is marginally compatible, or just plain doesn't work. You need to discover as much as you can about your company's hardware before you conduct installations. These are some of the problems I've encountered during setup. Although many of these issues may be resolved in the retail build of Windows 98, they are examples of the kinds of hardware problems you might face. The following network devices or software components will need your attention:

- 3COM Etherlink III PCMCIA—May fail to be identified. Get the up-to-date driver from 3COM.

- Xircom 10/100 or Intel 10/100 Cardbus—These cards may reject some data packets. Get the new driver from the manufacturer.

- Intel EtherExpress PRO/10+ and Intel 82595—These two devices use the default Duplex setting of Force Half Duplex. As a result, during Setup's second reboot, Setup cannot access the network. A dialog box offers the option of changing your network settings at this time. Accept this option, and change the setting to Auto Negotiate. Setup will continue normally.

- Windows 98 places the network username and password you specify in the Autologon setting. As a result, if you type the wrong password, you will not log on to the network and you will have no opportunity to change it. After installation is complete, use Regedit to search the Registry for the autologon key and delete the autologon value. Rebooting after making this change fixes the problem.

- If setting up on a brand new system or drive, you may see the error `Unable to find NETAPI.DLL during Setup` during the first reboot. Net Setup attempts to install the file, but it has not been copied into place yet. Setup should continue normally, however.

> **Tip:** Be aware that the set of problems you might face during setup changes each time someone attempts a new setup with a new configuration. Check the Windows Update Web site (select Windows Update from the Start menu) and the Microsoft Knowledge Base (at `www.microsoft.com`) for the latest information about setup problems.

Getting Ready for Operating System Differences

Windows 98 is a different operating system from Windows 95; as a result it has some differences in behavior, even when you are working with the classic interface. You need to anticipate these differences as you prepare to handle the new Setup program. You need to attend to these issues:

- If users have a My Documents or a Public Documents folder on their desktops, you should rename these folders. Windows 98 will install a new My Documents folder that is a shell extension, like the Printers folder or the Control Panel folder. The user can transfer the data back into the new folder after installation. Even though Windows 98 does not delete the existing folder, you do not want to risk losing data.

- If you cancel the Setup program from any dialog box, as in Windows 95, you must reboot and let the safe recovery routine restart Setup. You will have the option of starting over or of continuing where you left off. If you just rerun Setup, you will see a dialog box informing you that you must reboot.

- When you run Setup from the DOS prompt, you may see an error message that says your memory manager cannot be found. In this case, add DEVICE=HIMEM.SYS to the CONFIG.SYS file on the system and restart. Be sure to include the full path to the location of your HIMEM.SYS file in this line.

- On notebook computers that share a floppy and CD-ROM drive bay, you cannot make the emergency boot disk during setup. Swapping the drives will force the system to reboot. Cancel the boot disk operation at the first dialog box that enables you to do so, and make it after Setup has finished running.

- You cannot upgrade a non-English Windows 95 installation to an English Windows 98 installation. You must do a clean install of the English version in this situation.

- If you must troubleshoot and need to get to the Boot menu, pressing F8 no longer works. You need to hold the Ctrl key down during the power on self-test (or POST) to invoke the Boot menu.

Preparing for Software and Hardware Differences

With any new operating system release, everyone wonders what must be upgraded, replaced, or worked around on his or her system. You must deal with the following list of hardware options:

- You must have 16MB of RAM on any machine that will run Windows 98. Setup will not run if you have less memory. You get a message informing you that you must upgrade the amount of memory to install Windows 98.

- You must have a 486-based machine with a math coprocessor; otherwise Windows 98 will not install. Most 486 machines contain math coprocessors on the chip. Some models, such as a 486SX, will not.

- If you have a Number Nine Imagine 128 video card, either run Setup from MS-DOS or change your driver to the standard VGA driver before attempting setup. Otherwise the system will hang.

- If you run the Diamond InControl applet or the Aztech PnPchk applet, disable them before attempting setup.

- If you experience problems with a Gravis Ultrasound MAX sound driver installed, disable this driver using the System option in the Control Panel before running Setup.

- Sharp laptops with the APM BIOS were not supported during beta testing. Check the release documentation carefully for a possible workaround or solution.

- If you use a US Robotics Winmodem, boot in Safe mode and remove the modem by using the Control Panel's Winmodem Uninstall option. Reinstall the modem after setup. If you receive a `No dialtone` error, you should disable the sound card option. You are experiencing an internal conflict between the modem and sound card.

- Be aware that monitors and mice are easily misidentified. If functionality is not affected, do nothing. If functionality is affected, reinstall the manufacturer's drivers. If you have a Microsoft PS2 Mouse, you may need to add the following line to the [386Enh] section of the `SYSTEM.INI` file: `Mouse=*vmouse, msmouse.vxd`.

- On Compaq portables, if Setup hangs, reboot and let the safe recovery routine correct the problem. The problem usually occurs only when portables are docked.

- On IBM Aptivase, disable desktop effects before running Setup. The animated icons sometimes cause a conflict that generates a Trap 13 error. The effects will automatically be re-enabled when Setup finishes.

- You may have to manually reset performance settings in the System Control Panel after Setup is finished.

- On laptops with infrared ports, the ports may be detected and drives installed despite the fact that you have disabled the port in the BIOS. If you do not plan to use the infrared port, you can disable it later in the Control Panel.

- On some machines, you may have the opposite problems. IrDA ports are installed and available, but are not noticed by the setup routine. You will have to add these later, using the services of the Control Panel.

You need to attend to the following application issues:

- Do not use disk utilities designed for FAT16 with FAT32. Use updated utilities.

- DOS applications may not run well with Plug and Play sound cards. You may need to rerun the sound card setup utility to resolve the problem.

- DOS and 16-bit Windows applications may exhibit bizarre behavior—or not work at all—when you are using dual monitors under Windows 98.

- `SETVER` is not installed as a part of the default Windows 98 setup. If you run DOS applications that need `SETVER`, you need to add a line for it in the `CONFIG.SYS` file.

- MS-DOS `SHARE.EXE` is not supported under Windows 98. If you have an application that checks for the existence of this file, create a dummy file with this name in the `\WINDOWS\COMMAND` directory on your system.

- When you run Adobe Type Manager, Multi-Monitor is disabled. ATM causes appearance problems in the presence of Multi-Monitor.

- If the Ascend 97 Franklin Day Planner will not install, try renaming the `MFC42.DLL` file. Ascend 97 will copy its own version into place and complete the installation.

- If you use Chessmaster 4000, uncheck the Show window contents while dragging the check box in the Folder Options dialog box for any Explorer Window. The Folder Options item on the View menu invokes this dialog box. Click on the Advanced tab.

- If you use Agent 95, contact the manufacturer for an update.

- If you use Cheyenne Backup 2.0, contact the manufacturer for an update.

- Doom 95 will not work with a display adapter based on the S3 968.

- If you use Longbow AH-64D with an MS Sidewider Pro, download a patch from `http://www.ea.com/janes/news.htm`.

- If you use Macromedia Director 4.04, you must use a disk with less than 2GB of free space. You should plan to upgrade to the current version to resolve this problem.

- If you use MechWarrior 2 DOS 1.1, download the patch file `Mech2v11.exe` from `http:\\www.Activision.com`.

- If you use Microsoft Office Standard for Windows 95 version 7.0 with an ODBC driver, upgrade to version 7.0b to avoid errors with the ODBC driver. You can reach Microsoft's order desk at 800-360-7561. International sales are handled on 206-936-8661.

- If you use Microsoft Office 4.0, you must create a file named `SHARE.EXE` in the `\WINDOWS\COMMAND` folder. Office 4.0 expects this file to be present, and Windows 98 no longer includes it.

- If you are installing Microsoft Visual C++ version 4.2, do not copy older files over newer versions. You need the newer versions of the DLLs in place to keep Windows 98 and Visual C++ functional.

- If you use Netroom 3.04, do not run Customize. Also, make certain that `CACHECLK.EXE`, `NETROOM\STACKS.EXE`, and `NETROOM\SETCFG.EXE` are remarked out of the boot files and disabled. Windows 98 will hang during boot otherwise.

- If you use Norton Utilities, Anti-Virus, or Navigator, upgrade to the current version. Old versions will not work with FAT32, and some do not work with FAT16 under Windows 98. Be absolutely certain to check current release notes for details about how to use these utilities with FAT32 and Windows 98.

- If you use pcANYWHERE 7.0, you may see an error dialog box announcing that the modem would not initialize. Clear the dialog box; your call will complete normally.

- If you use Trend Micro's PC-cillin version 2.0, contact the manufacturer to check for an upgrade. Version 2.0 interferes with the operation of WordPad and Paint. You must reinstall these two applications to correct the problem.

- If you use PhotoShop 4.0, upgrade to PhotoShop V 4.01 by attaching to Adobe's Web site. Otherwise you will experience page faults.

- Do not run Reachout 95 version 7 on an ET6000 monitor with 256 or more colors if you wish to use Multi-Monitor. You will experience a general protection fault. You can safely run Multi-Monitor at 16 colors.

- The 32-bit version of Savage and the Trio64+ video card do not get along. You may experience hangs or double cursors. Rebooting helps, but installing the 16-bit version of the game solves the problem.

- Stacker 4.1 is not supported. Check with the manufacturer for possible solutions.

- If you use Winshield version 1.0.1, follow this procedure exactly when upgrading to Windows 98. First, run the setup program on the Winshield disks and uninstall Winshield. Do not do anything else at all before undertaking step 2. Second, immediately run Windows 98 Setup. Any other sequence may cause loss of all devices recorded in your Device Manager. Upgrade to Winshield version 1.5 to avoid the problem entirely.

- Zip-It 95 mistakes Windows 98 for Windows NT, and so refuses to install.

As I suggested earlier, these are just some of the problems that can occur. You may encounter others. The main reason is that Windows 98 takes a good-enough-is-best-left-alone strategy with driver upgrades. If you have a functional Windows 95 driver in place, it remains in place during setup. Your immediate response to any hardware issue arising from setup, either one which interrupts setup or one that appears after setup is complete, is to upgrade the driver for the device. Use Windows Update or the Update Driver button on the properties sheet for the device, accessible through the System icon in the Control Panel. Check the Knowledge Base at `www.microsoft.com` for the latest information on setup problems.

Surviving the Stages of Setup

After you have taken care of preparation, running Setup is a breeze. As with any program, you can use one of three methods: the AutoRun dialog box, the Add/Remove Programs icon in the Control Panel, or the Run dialog box to initiate the Setup program. Like many pieces of software, Windows 98 has an AutoRun program that runs and displays a dialog box when you insert the CD into the drive. Setting up the operating system is one of the options provided by buttons in this dialog box. Just click the appropriate button and you have started Setup.

Chapter 2 covers automated installations.

Note: Although you can run Setup from the Explorer, this is not a wise method. You should exit all Windows programs, including the Explorer, before running Setup. If you run Setup from Explorer, you have to close Explorer after Setup starts.

However, AutoRun is not entirely perfect; sometimes it does not run. To use the Add/Remove Programs icon, follow these steps:

1. Open the Start menu, choose the Settings option, and then select Control Panel from the cascading menu that appears.
2. Double-click the Add/Remove Programs icon.
3. Place the Windows 98 CD in the drive.
4. In the Install/Uninstall tab, click on the Install button and follow the directions.

To use the Run dialog box, follow these steps:

1. Open the Start menu and choose the Run option.
2. In the Run dialog box, enter D:\Setup, where D: is the drive letter designation of the CD-ROM drive.
3. Click on the OK button, and Setup runs.

After you have run Setup, the program takes control and almost automatically installs Windows 98. Setup needs user interaction at only eight points during the installation. In the several setups I undertook as a part of the beta program, a Pentium 200 with 32MB of RAM took between 36 and 45 minutes to complete the process.

When Setup starts, it displays an HTML page that provides information about the process (see Figure 1.1). Down the left side of the screen is a black panel that tells you what stage of setup you are in, approximately how much time remains in the process, and details about the setup process. In the panel with a cloud background, both dialog boxes and advertisements appear.

Figure 1.1.
Setup provides an informative screen that guides you through the process.

Setup occurs in five stages, each of which is described by one of the following five sections.

Note: If Setup is interrupted at any point for any reason, turn off the computer and then turn it back on. A Safe Recovery option restarts Setup at an appropriate point and works around whatever might have caused the interruption. Follow this procedure even if you canceled Setup yourself. Setup will not run unless you reboot the machine. You should power down to fully reset your hardware.

Preparing to Run Windows 98 Setup: Stage 1

The stage of preparing to run Setup has the following three steps:

1. A dialog box, shown in Figure 1.1, welcomes you to Setup, congratulates you on choosing Windows 98, and tells you about how long Setup will take. Click Continue to advance the Setup program. (You can exit Setup at this point if you need to by clicking Exit Setup.)

2. A dialog box appears, announcing that the Setup Wizard is initializing.

3. A dialog box appears, reminding you to close all running Windows programs (see Figure 1.2). While this dialog box is onscreen, you can use Alt+Tab to switch among Windows programs to execute exit commands. After you are done, click OK to continue with Setup. (You can exit Setup here by clicking Cancel.)

Figure 1.2.
Setup gives you an opportunity to close all Windows programs before continuing.

Tip: If you forget to close or disable a Windows program at this point, you can do so later during setup. Whenever the wizard pauses, you can use Alt+Tab to switch programs. If you need to disable a System Tray program, press the Windows key on the keyboard (or Alt+S or Ctrl+Esc if you have no Windows key) to open the Start menu and force the appearance of the task bar.

Collecting Information About Your Computer: Stage 2

After you have closed all Windows programs, you have entered the second stage of Setup, gathering information about your computer. This stage has the following five steps:

1. A license agreement dialog box appears. You must select the I accept the agreement option button to activate the Next button. Then click the Next button to continue.

2. A Checking Your System dialog box appears, as shown in Figure 1.3. Two progress bars reflect the completion of two processes. First, Setup checks for problems on your disk, running a version of ScanDisk. Second, it initializes the Registry database. If you are not installing on a clean system, Setup saves hardware detection time by carrying forward device settings from the existing Registry. Click Next to advance Setup.

Figure 1.3.
*Setup checks your
disk for errors and
initializes a Registry
for the new system.*

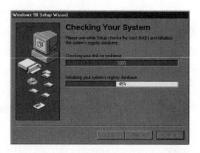

Warning: You may get an Unknown Error dialog box while checking the system, which suggests running Setup from the DOS prompt. Try powering down and using Safe Recovery first. Safe Recovery enables you to completely redo all you have done or to pick up at the last successfully completed step.

3. A Preparing Directory dialog box appears (see Figure 1.4). Two progress bars reflect the completion of two additional processes, checking for installed components (usually the dynamic link libraries present on the system) and checking for available disk space. Click on Next to advance Setup.

4. Setup offers you the chance to build an Emergency Startup Disk, as shown in Figure 1.5. You should take the opportunity to do so, unless you have a compelling reason not to— your CD-ROM drive is in the multipurpose bay of your notebook rather than your floppy, for example. Windows 95 Startup disks are not compatible with Windows 98. Click Next and follow the instructions in the dialog boxes to build the disk.

Figure 1.4.
*Setup checks installed
components and free
disk space.*

Figure 1.5.
*Setup enables you to
create a startup disk.*

Technical Note: The Windows 98 Emergency Repair Disk has a new structure. First, it is fairly full. Second, it has generic drivers for both IDE and SCSI CD-ROM drives onboard. Third, when you boot from it, the CONFIG.SYS and AUTOEXEC.BAT files onboard offer you a small menu, from which you can choose to install CD drivers or not. After you make your choice, these files install the RAMdisk driver, creating a virtual disk drive in memory. All your troubleshooting tools are copied to this virtual drive. You get many more tools than could fit on a single floppy, because the installation files are compressed on the floppy and expanded when the utilities are copied into the RAM drive.

5. A Wizard page announces that you are about to start copying files. Click Next to advance to the next stage of Setup.

Copying Windows 98 Files to Your Computer: Stage 3

The stage of copying files is one where you can take a coffee break for a few minutes. On the average system, you have about 20 minutes to kill. Microsoft provides animated advertisements, a progress bar, and an estimate of time remaining to keep you entertained while you wait (see Figure 1.6). In general, you will have no interaction with the Setup program because of the way the Version Conflict Manager works during Setup.

Figure 1.6.
Setup provides information about file copy progress.

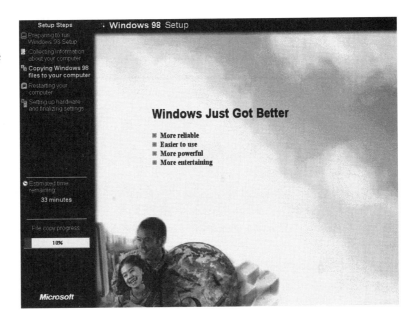

Restarting Your Computer: Stage 4

On completion of this phase, you may see a dialog box that announces copying is finished and Windows is ready to restart your computer. However, sometimes this dialog box does not appear. If it does, click on OK. You will then see a Restart Computer dialog box, as shown in Figure 1.7. You may restart at any time by clicking the Restart button, but the system will restart when the 15 second timer expires without your intervention. The restart is known as first reboot.

Figure 1.7.
Setup automatically restarts your computer.

Setting Up Hardware and Finalizing Settings: Stage 5

After first reboot, the final phase of setup begins. During the DOS-screen phase, Setup copies some network files into place and modifies configuration files. During graphical phase, Setup prevents all run-once and start-up programs from running. (Run-once programs run one time, and then their run entry is deleted from the Registry so that they do not run again.) You must log on as a user at this time on multi-user systems. Windows 98 initializes itself and scans for legacy hardware settings. You see a dialog box that announces Windows is setting up hardware and Plug and Play. The system then shows a Restart Computer dialog box like the one you saw before. This restart is known as second reboot.

After second reboot, the DOS-screen phase of the software load is normal. At the onset of the graphical phase, you must log on to multi-user systems. You then see a dialog box that announces Windows is setting up hardware and Plug and Play devices.

Warning: After setting up Plug and Play, Setup may ask you to insert disks or CDs for devices it finds on your computer. Normally, Setup copies the relevant drivers and sets up the device. However, some devices may have setup programs of their own. These can run in parallel with Windows 98 Setup, and they can interfere by opening existing files that Windows 98 Setup is attempting to copy over. Cancel such setup programs and install these devices and their related software after setting up Windows 98.

Next, you see a dialog box that lists six steps, and Windows cycles through them in sequence. First, system configuration (or system settings) are stored in the Registry. Second, the Control Panel applets are set up. Third, shortcuts are placed on the Start menu. Fourth, Windows Help initializes. Fifth, MS-DOS program settings are stored in the Registry. Finally, Microsoft FrontPage Express, a low-end HTML editor, is installed.

After FrontPage Express is installed, Windows 98 undergoes a third reboot. During the DOS-screen phase of the boot, you see configuration files being updated. Then you go into a normal graphical boot, and log on if necessary. You see a Welcome to Windows 98 dialog box that gives you access to a Registration Wizard, the Tune-up Wizard, and release notes. And of course, in true Microsoft style, plays you adult contemporary music.

Building the Emergency Startup Disk

The Windows 98 Emergency Startup Disk bears some further comment. First, Windows 95 Emergency Startup Disks are not compatible with Windows 98. You need to educate both users and administrators about this fact, or you may run into awkward situations in troubleshooting after Windows 98 is installed because someone used the wrong flavor of startup disk.

Second, the Emergency Startup Disk contains slightly different content from its Windows 95 cousin. Here is the directory listing for a freshly built disk:

```
Directory of A:\

AUTOEXEC BAT          1,103   02-16-98  12:16p  AUTOEXEC.BAT
CONFIG   SYS            629   02-16-98  12:16p  CONFIG.SYS
SETRAMD  BAT          1,416   02-16-98  12:16p  SETRAMD.BAT
README   TXT          4,419   02-16-98  12:16p  README.TXT
FINDRAMD EXE          6,855   02-16-98  12:16p  FINDRAMD.EXE
RAMDRIVE SYS         12,663   02-16-98  12:16p  RAMDRIVE.SYS
ASPI4DOS SYS         14,386   02-16-98  12:16p  ASPI4DOS.SYS
BTCDROM  SYS         21,971   02-16-98  12:16p  BTCDROM.SYS
ASPICD   SYS         29,620   02-16-98  12:16p  ASPICD.SYS
BTDOSM   SYS         30,955   02-16-98  12:16p  BTDOSM.SYS
ASPI2DOS SYS         35,330   02-16-98  12:16p  ASPI2DOS.SYS
ASPI8DOS SYS         37,564   02-16-98  12:16p  ASPI8DOS.SYS
ASPI8U2  SYS         40,792   02-16-98  12:16p  ASPI8U2.SYS
FLASHPT  SYS         64,425   02-16-98  12:16p  FLASHPT.SYS
EXTRACT  EXE         93,242   02-17-98   2:00a  EXTRACT.EXE
FDISK    EXE         63,900   02-16-98  12:16p  FDISK.EXE
DRVSPACE BIN         68,871   02-16-98  12:16p  DRVSPACE.BIN
COMMAND  COM         93,880   02-16-98  12:16p  COMMAND.COM
HIMEM    SYS         33,191   02-16-98  12:16p  HIMEM.SYS
OAKCDROM SYS         41,302   02-16-98  12:16p  OAKCDROM.SYS
EBD      CAB        303,471   02-17-98   2:00a  EBD.CAB
```

The differences from the Windows 95 disk are notable. One important fact about the utilities included on this disk is that they are FAT32 compatible. In addition, only these files will enable you to start Windows 98 if you boot from the Emergency Startup Disk. Notice as well that generic CD-ROM drivers are included (OAKCDROM.SYS, the ASPI*.SYS files, and the BT*.SYS files) so that you can access your Windows 98 CD if necessary when booting from this disk. In fact, the `CONFIG.SYS` file on the disk presents a menu that enables you to select CD support or no CD support. The `AUTOEXEC.BAT` file uses an environment variable to check whether CD support is installed, and loads `MSCDEX.EXE` if CD support is installed. All the recovery tools except FDISK are stored in a CAB file. They are expanded into a RAM drive as the Emergency Startup Disk loads.

Dealing with the New Version Conflict Manager

Another factor that you must deal with about the setup process is the behavior of the Version Conflict Manager. Microsoft introduced this tool some time ago to prevent applications from overwriting DLLs with older versions, thus causing the system to lose functionality because a component has dropped back a couple of versions. This utility so far has presented a dialog box that says you are about to overwrite a file with an older version. This dialog box suggests that you keep the newer file.

For Windows 98 Setup and Windows 98 Setup only, Microsoft has suspended this familiar behavior. The Version Conflict Manager (VCM) does not tell you that it is about to overwrite a file. The Version Conflict Manager now allows the Windows 98 file to overwrite the older file without notifying a user of the conflict in versions. The VCM backs up the old file in the `C:\WINDOWS\VCM` directory, and logs the change that it made in the `C:\WINDOWS\VERBACK.LOG` file. You therefore have a record of all such changes, and should suspected DLL conflicts occur, you have a means of investigating them.

After Windows 98 Setup has completed execution, the Version Conflict Manager reverts to its normal behavior.

Dealing With the Setup Log Files

Four log files appear in the root directory of the boot drive and can help you to troubleshoot if you are having problems with Setup. Probably the most important is `BOOTLOG.TXT`. It records the success and failure of each boot operation. The file contains lines such as the following:

```
[000A85FD] Loading Device = C:\WINDOWS\SYSTEM\IDECDROM.SYS
[000A8631] LoadSuccess  = C:\WINDOWS\SYSTEM\IDECDROM.SYS

[000A8731] SYSCRITINIT = VCACHE
[000A8731] SYSCRITINITSUCCESS = VCACHE

[000A8746] Dynamic load device mmdevldr.vxd
[000A8749] Dynamic init device MMDEVLDR
```

```
[000A8749] Dynamic init success MMDEVLDR
[000A8749] Dynamic load success mmdevldr.vxd

[000A8749] DEVICEINIT  = VCDFSD
[000A8749] DEVICEINITSUCCESS  = VCDFSD

[000A87EA] Initing esdi_506.pdr
[000A87F4] Init Success esdi_506.pdr

[000A87FA] INITCOMPLETE = VMM
[000A87FA] INITCOMPLETESUCCESS = VMM

LoadStart = system.drv
LoadSuccess = system.drv

Init = Final USER
InitDone = Final USER

Terminate = Reset Display
EndTerminate = Reset Display
```

Each block of lines represents the success of an operation undertaken during the boot process. In addition, with a little practice you can recognize the names of the components, or at least match them with files that you find in the Windows and system directories. If you have a problem, you want to search the file for the words *failure* and *error*. You also want to scan the file to find any set of lines that seems incomplete. Any such set of lines identifies the potential problem to you.

Knowing, however, that VMM (or the Virtual Memory Manager) failed to load does not necessarily explain *why* it failed to load. Looking into the three additional files might yield some cryptic clues. DETLOG.TXT, SETUPLOG.TXT, and NETLOG.TXT each records what happens during hardware detection, setup, and network initialization. Some lines from DETLOG.TXT demonstrate how cryptic this information can be:

```
ConfigMG device: ISAPNP\ROK4920\12345678: Status=620, Problem=20
RegAvoidRes: *ROK4920\0000
    IO=3e8-3ef(3ff:400:0)
    IRQ=5
```

However cryptic, these lines do identify a device (ISAPNP, or Industry Standard Architecture bus Plug and Play), its status code, its problem code, the I/O port for the device, and the IRQ assigned to it. Information such as this may not help you, but may help Microsoft Technical Support to assist you in identifying and correcting the problem. In addition, Microsoft Knowledge Base articles, searchable at the Microsoft Web site may identify which codes indicate a problem, and how to solve that problem.

Tip: The LOGVIEW.EXE program on the Windows 98 CD enables you to view all the logs in a single multiple-document interface program.

Planning for Zero Administration

Having worked through the basic installation procedure, you may have noted that you see several places where this procedure costs money. Chapter 2 shows you how to reduce some of these costs by reducing the amount of time and effort you have to spend on installations. Microsoft has prepared an entire strategy, called Zero Administration, however, to help you keep the Total Cost of Ownership (TCO) associated with operating PCs in a business setting as low as possible. The goal is to control costs associated with three kinds of activities:

- Installing and updating software
- Maintaining the configuration of both machine and software
- Controlling user modification of both machine and software

Microsoft's solution prior to Windows 98 has been to create a Zero Administration Kit that included components for each Windows operating system to implement these goals. The System Management Server, for example, can be used to centrally install both software and upgrades from a server. Specialized tools could be used to lock the floppy drive, prevent changes to the Registry, and prevent users from installing new software. Additional tools could back up configurations and keep a database of such configurations. Under Windows 98, many of these options are included in the operating system and its Resource Kit. Standalone options such as SMS still remain separate products.

Microsoft is also promising future tools, such as the Microsoft Management Console that will be a part of Windows NT 5.0. This tool will work via the new Active Directory service to enable administrators to control these activities on workstations.

In working with Windows 98 now and planning to implement a Zero Administration strategy, you are primarily working with Registry settings that you can make using the System Policy Editor. You are also working with Registry backup tools such as CFGBACK.EXE and ERU.EXE, both included on the CD in the \TOOLS\MISC directory and the \TOOLS\RESKIT\REGISTRY directory. You must also consider a means of installing software over the network, such as the System Management Server.

For more on these tools, see Chapter 20, "Protecting Data." I show you how to deal with networked workstations in Chapter 2. To see how to use the System Policy Editor, see Chapter 18.

When you install a single workstation, you want to have a plan to limit the cost of its administration. A simple plan looks like this:

1. Purchase a roll of duct tape and some plastic bags.
2. Make an Emergency Startup Disk when you install the workstation, or copy one.
3. Fill the 385,024 bytes available on the Emergency Startup Disk with (a) CFGBACK.EXE; (b) a backup done with CFGBACK.EXE; and (c) critical system files such as CONFIG.SYS, AUTOEXEC.BAK, and MSDOS.SYS.

4. Run ERU.EXE against the system and make an Emergency Recovery Disk for the system. Note that this disk is not an Emergency Startup Disk. It works only with the Emergency Recovery Utility to restore a system from an ERU backup directory.

5. Insert the two disks in a plastic bag and use the duct tape to tape these two disks to the system case somewhere the user is likely not to see them. (Underneath the case is a good choice.)

6. Edit the Registry with the System Policy Editor to set up any restrictions on what the user may do. Good suggestions are to disable Registry editing, limit access to the Control Panel, allow only certain Windows applications to run, and disable the MS-DOS prompt. You may also wish to disable certain TCP/IP services, such as FTP.

Why go to this trouble? Because you want to make certain that users cannot behave irresponsibly with their systems. Such behavior costs support time while you repair the damage. And because if the system goes down, you need the tools to repair it right at hand, not tossed into a box of hundreds of disks all with similar labels back in the computer lab. You need to know where those disks are, and you need them at the location where the problem exists.

Planning for Multiple Boot

Multiple-boot computers host two operating systems. You might have an engineer who must run UNIX–only software or Windows NT–only software, but who must also do work under the standard corporate Windows 98 desktop. You may want to have a machine that will boot into Windows 98 for client administration and into Windows NT for Windows NT administration. (The tools for administering Windows NT from Windows 9x workstations are not as complete as those for administering Windows NT from a Windows NT workstation.)

You have three choices for creating a multiple-boot machine. First, you can create a separate partition for each operating system and run FDISK from a floppy to change the active partition when you want to change operating systems. This method has the advantage that it works with any operating system. Its disadvantage is that FDISK is risky software to place in users' hands.

The second option is to use a third-party tool—such as OS/2 Boot Manager, System Commander, or Partition Magic—to set up both partitions for the operating systems and a menuing system that enables you to choose operating systems. The advantages here are that the menu drives the user choice of the operating system, and such tools work with almost any operating system. The disadvantage is that more administrative work is required when the system is installed.

The third choice applies to a dual boot between Windows 98 and Windows NT. You need only install Windows 98 first, and then Windows NT. Windows NT will automatically install dual boot capability, along with a menuing system. The advantage is ease of use and installation. The disadvantage is that this option works only for Microsoft operating systems.

Getting Back Your Former Configuration

If you want to be able to return to your former Windows 95 configuration, you must make a decision to save your former configuration at setup time. Windows 98 Setup selects this option by default, and creates two files in the root directory of the boot drive: `WINUNDO.DAT` and `WINUNDO.INI`. To retreat back into Windows 95, you follow these steps:

1. Open the Control Panel.
2. Open the Add/Remove Programs icon.
3. In the list box on the Install/Uninstall tab, select the Uninstall Windows 98 option.
4. Click on the Add/Remove button, and follow all onscreen directions. Windows 98 will use the two files it saved to restore your former configuration.

Installing from Scratch

So far I have talked about installing Windows 98 as an upgrade to Windows 95. What if you are not upgrading? Then you need to work with a bootable disk that can access your CD-ROM drive. The next two sections show you how.

Installing on a Formatted Hard Disk

Technical Note: If you have chosen to install Windows 98 on a freshly formatted hard disk, as when a disk has gone bad and you have had to replace it, you need the equivalent of the Emergency Startup Disk. You need a floppy that is system-formatted and contains both `FDISK.EXE` and `FORMAT.COM`. In addition, you will need to copy the real-mode drivers for the CD-ROM drive in your computer, the drivers for any necessary SCSI card, and `MSCDEX.EXE` onto the floppy. You need to set up `CONFIG.SYS` and `AUTOEXEC.BAT` files on the floppy that install the drivers for your CD-ROM drive and activate `MSCDEX.EXE`.

Now the procedure is as follows:

1. Boot from your floppy.
2. Use FDISK to partition the drive, if necessary.
3. Format the drive using the `/s` parameter (`FORMAT C: /S`, for example).

4. Optionally, you can copy the CONFIG.SYS, AUTOEXEC.BAT, and CD driver files over to the newly formatted drive and reboot. You can also just undertake the next step booted from the floppy.

5. Run SETUP.EXE from the Windows 98 CD in the CD-ROM drive.

Setup will run normally and install Windows 98 on your drive.

Installing on a Blank Hard Disk

Technical Note: Setting up on a completely blank hard disk is called an OEM setup, because it is the way Original Equipment Manufacturers set up systems with Windows 98 preinstalled. Usually, you must have an OEM license to be able to undertake this type of setup. However, OEM licenses have sometimes been distributed as a part of the Microsoft Developer Network subscription, so you may have access to one.

To undertake OEM installation, you need a different type of floppy. Give this floppy a system format as described in the preceding section, and then copy the following files from the Windows 98 CD—and *only* the Windows 98 CD—to the floppy:

```
AUTOEXEC.CD

COMMAND.COM

CONFIG.CD

DRVCOPY.INF

FDISK.EXE

FORMAT.COM

HIMEM.SYS

IO.SYS

MSCDEX.EXE

MSDOS.SYS
```

Typically, these files will be gathered together into a BOOTFLOP directory somewhere on the CD. If not, you may have to expand these files from the CD. The command for extracting files from the cabinet files is as follows:

```
extract /A /L DestinationDirectory precopy1.cab FileToExtract.xxx
```

The required MSDOS.SYS file contains only the following line:

```
;SYS
```

Therefore, it is easier to create it yourself than to extract in most cases.

You must then undertake these steps:

1. Run the command ATTRIB -R *.* to make certain all the files are not read-only.

2. Copy AUTOEXEC.CD to AUTOEXEC.BAT.

3. Copy CONFIG.CD to CONFIG.SYS.

4. Copy your real-mode CD and adapter card drivers for the CD to the floppy disk.

5. Boot from the floppy. OEMSETUP automatically starts, partitions, and formats the drive if necessary, and starts to copy files.

6. After the file copy operation begins, remove the floppy from the drive; otherwise first boot restarts OEMSETUP.

Installing New Hardware

Adding new hardware under Windows 98 is just like adding new hardware under Windows 95. If you set the system up and then have to add hardware, you use the Add New Hardware Wizard. This wizard automatically starts during the boot after you installed the hardware, but you can start it from the Control Panel at any time. The wizard searches for Plug and Play devices and presents a list of those found. If you are configuring a legacy device, you tell the wizard that the device is not on the list, and proceed with either legacy hardware detection or selecting the device from the device list. After you have selected either the Plug and Play device or the legacy device from one of the lists, Windows 98 copies the driver from the CD or enables you to use the Have Disk button to copy a manufacturer's driver into place.

Installing New Software

After completion of Setup, if you need to install software, you have the same three options you always had. If the CD for the software includes an AutoRun program, you can always just click the button that is labeled to start the setup routine.

You can also use the Add/Remove Programs icon. Follow these steps:

1. Open the Start menu, choose the Settings option, and then select Control Panel from the cascading menu that appears.

2. Double-click on the Add/Remove Programs icon.

3. Place the CD or first floppy in the drive.

4. In the Install/Uninstall tab, click on the Install button, and follow the directions.

You can also use the Run dialog box, following these steps:

1. Open the Start menu and choose the Run option.
2. In the Run dialog box, enter D:\Setup, where D: is the drive letter designation of the CD-ROM drive or the floppy drive containing the setup disk. Keep in mind that some vendors do not use the standard setup program name, so you may want to browse to find the setup program.
3. Click on OK, and Setup runs.

Summary

Well, you have been on the guided tour of Windows 98 single-system setup. We have reviewed the entire process. You have learned what user interaction there is, and how to build systems when you are not upgrading. The following chapter focuses on how to alter the setup process so that you can upgrade your entire installation efficiently.

On Your Own

It's time to try Setup yourself. Try setting up a single computer. Then try adding a board to see how the Add New Hardware Wizard works. Then install a program. Be sure that you practice creating an Emergency Startup Disk. Try running ERU against a drive to prepare for this method of emergency recovery.

Next, you should practice making a bootable floppy that will enable you to format a drive and install Windows 98 on the freshly formatted drive from the CD. If you can spare the time, it is wise to practice this skill. Chances are you will need it early in the rollout.

2

Preparing for a Rollout

Peter Norton®

The first chapter showed you how to install Windows 98 on a single machine. It made several assumptions. First, it assumed that you needed to get a single system up quickly. Second, it assumed that you were upgrading a Windows 95 computer. Finally, it showed you how to install either on a freshly formatted drive or on a completely clean drive.

What you may have noticed in Chapter 1, "Reviewing Basic Installation," are the following facts:

- Microsoft sees Windows 98 as an upgrade to Windows 95 and as an operating system that can be installed on new systems.

- There is an upgrade path from MS-DOS and from DOS/Windows; however, you should probably install Windows 98 into a separate directory and remove DOS and/or Windows manually. The upgrade path from Windows 3.x was an afterthought, originally intended to be released months after Windows 98 was released.

- The upgrade path from Windows NT 4.0 is the same as it was for Windows 95—that is to say, nonexistent.

Tip: Windows 98, like its cousins Windows 95 OSR1 and OSR2, apparently disables the capability to boot back to MS-DOS. However, if you use the FAT16 file system, you will find that the TweakUI add-on for Control Panel enables you to re-enable booting to the former operating system.

These facts have considerable implications if you want to install Windows 98 on a variety of systems throughout an enterprise. This chapter is designed to help you plan for these implications in such a way that you reduce the amount of administration that you have for these systems. As the number of PCs that you must maintain rises, the costs of maintaining them also rise. Microsoft's two initiatives, integrated into Windows 98, to deal with this cost issue are known as Total Cost of Ownership (TCO) and Zero Administration.

This chapter covers the following topics:

- Developing a rollout plan, the means for installing large numbers of Windows 98 systems in your organization

- Executing a rollout plan

- Using a variety of tools to install Windows 98 in accordance with the rollout plan

Developing a Rollout Plan

Rollout planning is absolutely essential. You must determine at least what computing resources you have and how you will install Windows 98 on those resources. Each element of the plan will have a cost associated with it, and you will of course want to minimize the cost. You will also want to minimize the cost of post-rollout administration of the systems and training of the users.

Peter's Principle: Plan to Minimize Total Cost of Ownership

Total Cost of Ownership (TCO) is an important planning guideline. Recently *ComputerWorld* reported that IS managers and CEOs believe that there are realistic returns from implementing computing technology on the desktop. However, their statisticians cannot yet provide any sound evidence to support this belief. Nevertheless, a practical assumption is that you want to minimize the cost of ownership so that you can devote more of your budget to production and selling services rather than to owning computers. If nothing else, because return on investment is so difficult to calculate, taking practical steps to minimize the investment makes good sense. As a result, the rollout guidelines provided here focus on reducing the TCO associated with your computing efforts.

Planning for Zero Administration

If the goal of the rollout is to introduce a new operating system (and possibly related user software) while reducing the overall cost of computing, you need to break the TCO issue into at least three practical goals: determining the hardware platform, reducing the overhead of installation, and reducing the overhead of post-installation administration. Microsoft's TCO initiative depends on a mixture of such elements as network PCs, software included in the BackOffice suite, and modifications included in Windows 98 itself to achieve these three goals.

For you to reach your own TCO initiative requires that you evaluate how you want to implement these three sorts of solutions. The network PC, a processor with only the minimal hardware necessary to serve as a network client on a network where all software would be run from a server, is a classic example of how you will have to arrange your plans relating to TCO. Recently, this thin client PC was hailed as the way to go, reducing the amount of hardware and software maintained on the desktop and focusing attention on network-delivered software and resources, thereby reducing the cost of hardware, licensing, and maintenance on the network. However, because many corporations, including Microsoft, jumped on the network PC bandwagon, the standard has fallen on misfortune. Different approaches and different concepts have produced rifts in the groups promulgating the network PC. As a result, you must make a decision about what hardware you want to maintain and which of the current bandwagons you wish to ride. You could rush to the network PC only to find that the rift among the standards promoters has rendered the network PC an obsolete concept, and you will have to invest again in a different hardware platform.

Note: *Thin client* in the context of TCO discussions has usually meant a minimal hardware platform for a workstation connected to a network. The client is "thin" because it does not require hardware for disk storage. Network servers meet all storage needs.

Peter's Principle: My Preference Is for Thick Clients

I must confess that my preference is to stay with the typical PC on the desktop, the so-called thick client. My reason is that, given the software tools now available for centralized maintenance and the diffidence surrounding the network PC standard, there is no reason to rush to a thin client. What you would save on hardware by implementing network PCs can be offset by reductions in maintenance costs when you work with thick clients and centralized maintenance software. In addition, some software is not well-suited to network delivery, and some offices need to continue some level of work even in the face of network failure. At best, you should use a mixture of thin and thick clients to protect your options for fault tolerance and efficient software delivery.

The software option to improve network management in Microsoft's BackOffice suite is the System Management Server, Microsoft's centralized network management tool. This tool will maintain a hardware inventory, facilitate the delivery of software and updates to any type of client, and assist your help desk in reducing total cost. SMS Server enables you to automate tasks from a central server that formerly required you to send a person with disks to visit a computer. You save the cost of travel time and you save greatly on the cost of installation time, and will probably find yourself reassigning personnel away from troubleshooting to other, more useful tasks. SMS is not the only such solution on the market. IBM, Intel, HP, and others offer centralized network management products. Such solutions, however, merit careful consideration because the one that suits your needs will save you money.

For more information about solutions like SMS Server, see Chapter 6, "Understanding the LAN Connection."

An example of changes to Windows 98 is the Windows Update. This tool connects to a Web site to download updates to the operating system and its drivers. Although this may seem like a great idea—IS never has to update systems again—it could equally turn out to be a nightmare. Users may not all update their systems on the same schedule. As a result, your help desk people may have difficulty knowing what configuration they are facing while troubleshooting. Users who update may introduce viruses to your network. And, because of the virus risk, you may wish to limit who has the right to download software—any type of software—from the Internet.

Obviously TCO and the related Zero Administration effort are thorny issues to consider. As we go through the sections on rollout planning, I will try to give you hints about how to evaluate the various issues. Even if you disagree with what I recommend, you are closer to defining the needs for your implementation. So feel free to disagree, but do define the issues for yourself.

Choosing the Team

The first step in planning the rollout is to appoint leadership. The rollout manager has to have some special qualities. I look for these:

- An overall understanding of the organization's use of technology
- An acquaintance with each of the technologies employed
- Familiarity with both the hardware and software in use
- An eye for detail
- Ability to delegate to team members
- Ability to manage a budget
- Ability to listen to and evaluate alternatives

If you choose to outsource your rollout planning and/or rollout installation, you should be interested in working with a lead consultant who shows these qualities. The team the manager assembles to plan the rollout will need several specialists. Some are obvious, others are not. You should have a team with at least these members:

- An advocate for the users of the systems
- An advocate for the perspective of senior management
- A hardware specialist
- Software specialists who are intimate with the software you intend to run on the Windows 98 platform
- A Windows 98 specialist who has received training in the operating system and who has had an adequate opportunity to test the operating system
- A security specialist familiar with the details of the enterprise-wide security scheme in place
- An advocate for the installation team
- An advocate for the support team

Some of these roles may be combined, but those representing certain advocacies should remember the importance of their role. Advocates inject the point of view of their constituencies, and thereby help to bring about compromises that will improve usability and efficiency of the systems while keeping offsetting costs as low as possible. Essential characteristics for the team members are the ability to speak freely and diplomatically. Good plans are never the result of team members deferring to one another for reasons of respect, position, or politics. An essential quality of the group process is respect for open expression of ideas and differing points of view. Compromise is what will produce the plan. The rollout manager, however, must have the authority to resolve disputes and settle questions.

Planning the Configuration

After you have the team assembled, planning the configuration requires that the team undertake two steps. First, you must determine what hardware and software you have. Second, you must determine what hardware and software you want to support after the change in the operating system. As a part of this second step, you determine what you have to abandon and how to replace it, because some of what you have may not work properly with the new operating system.

Determining What You Have

Inventorying hardware and software is quite difficult. Users often do not know what cards are in their machines. Records of machine modifications may not be accurate or may be difficult to trace. Users may not have kept their manuals, original disks, or other software documentation. Departments may not have preserved purchasing records accurately, or may have moved computers and peripherals in haphazard manner.

If you have not invested in the equivalent of Microsoft's SMS Server, consider doing so now, if for nothing else than the automated inventory capability. The $15,000+ initial investment may in fact repay itself several times in saved inventory labor. The SMS Client can be configured to return a hardware and software inventory to the server for storage in a central database on each boot. If changes are made, the changes are automatically recorded so that you can track the history of any given machine.

Without automated inventory, you need to assemble a group of individuals who will open each system, list its components and peripherals, identify its software, locate the software licenses, and record all of these facts on durable medium. This activity is a labor-intensive task, and it may take you more time than you really want to invest. Imagine having to inventory a toy store the day after the Christmas rush subsides, with no automated tracking of goods sold at the cash register. No one knows what is left on the shelves, so you have to make order out of the mess left by frantic shoppers, count all items, and calculate their value. This is a slow, relatively expensive task. Using barcoded tags to log inventory sold at the register drastically reduces the cost of this activity. Without automated inventory, you are like a toy store without barcoded tags.

Determining What You Want

To determine what configuration you want, you need to answer the following questions:

- What hardware do we have that will not work with Windows 98? You need to make a list and determine the reasons. Is it too little memory? Outdated and in need of replacement? Upgradable? Translate your answers into a list of hardware purchase requirements.
- What software do we have that will not work with Windows 98? You need to translate your answers into a list of upgrade purchases, new software purchases, or reprogramming plans.

- What features of Windows 98 do we wish to implement? Translate your answers into a set of scripting requirements for the machines you plan to install. You might plan to install Windows Update, for example, but not the TV Viewer. If you are automating installations using installation scripts, you need to know what options to include in the script.

- What network clients, addressing, and protocols do we need? Begin with the servers you intend to support and work backward to the client configuration for the workstations that must attach to those servers.

- How will users interact over the network? Will you be supporting electronic mail, file transfers, external access, or Internet access? Translate these answers into the configuration settings necessary for each Windows 98 client on the network.

- How will users interact with their desktops and machine configurations? Translate these answers into sets of system policies to employ.

- How shall we enforce security on this configuration? Pay particular attention to the questions of who will be sharing resources, how resources will be shared in general, how network access will be granted, and how keyboard access will be granted.

- What documents and resources do we need to review in order to determine implementation options and costs? Resource kits, third-party books, and independent reports from groups such as the Gartner Group or Giga Information Group can help with these discussions. Studying the Zero Administration Kit for Windows 98 may help you to plan system policies and configurations.

Note: You can download the Zero Administration Kit and a training course for it from www.microsoft.com. Search the site for "zero administration" to find the link. This kit gives you sample system policies for machines of particular types. You can implement the policies out of the box, or implement them with the modifications you choose. The kit was intended to reduce the amount of administration related to implementing Windows by providing the policies you might wish to implement as preconfigured options. However, most commentators on the Zero Administration Kit say that it will not reduce your administrative effort to zero. The kit may give you some good ideas, but it will not significantly reduce your costs. In addition, the kit is designed for a test network only. You need to carefully test your implementation of the kit before you take it to your production network, a step that incurs cost.

- How many dollars do we wish to invest in the rollout? Begin with no restrictions, determine an initial number, and then scale into reality. Be sure to phrase the final budget plan in terms of the benefits for the cost.

- How do we wish to deliver the rollout? You can install all by hand, or you can automate the installation in various ways. You can perform the rollout with internal personnel, or you can outsource the job. Compare the costs carefully.

Tip: Tools such as the SMS Server can automate your delivery of software and upgrades as well as take inventory of your equipment and software.

After you have answered these questions, you should be able to construct a map of your network and fill in notes on the configurations necessary at each node. You can characterize groups of machines by hardware similarity. From there, you can begin constructing a test bed to verify that your planned configurations will work.

Testing the Configuration

Ideally, you need a test lab with the following characteristics:

- One machine that represents roughly each hardware configuration you intend to use
- Ability to participate on the network and interact with all types of servers that client configurations must interact with
- Ability to interact with other clients on the network in roughly the same way that clients will interact after the rollout

You need to install Windows 98 on each test client to determine that client's viability to run the operating system. You need to install each software configuration to determine its fitness to run with Windows 98. If possible, use a software testing program to generate scripts that represent typical activities users undertake, and run the scripts against the installation. Don't run the scripts just once. Run them repeatedly, preferably under a variety of scenarios. You will want at least short-term runs of varied test scripts in sequence to simulate a typical day's activities. You will also want a long-term—at least 36-hour—stress run of your scripts as well. What you are trying to determine is what errors you are likely to see during ordinary work, as well as what happens when a Windows 98 system runs continuously. Sometimes desktop environments slow down as the system runs continuously without rebooting.

Running a Pilot

The last thing you want to do is to move from testing individual systems straight to a rollout. Instead, go through at least two preparatory stages. First, implement your planned delivery method on your test systems. Install the same way that you plan to during the rollout, and verify that your scripts work as planned, your delivery method works on each hardware platform, and that you can install all software the way you had planned. At this stage, back up and correct any problems. Re-verify the methodology until it works. Use the repeated installations to train the rollout personnel.

After you know that a limited test of the delivery method works, take a small segment of your network and do a pilot rollout. Something will go wrong, so critique the event carefully. You are looking for the weaknesses in the plan that might interfere with orderly work or with business processes. Build contingency plans for dealing with known issues, and imagine at least three disaster scenarios. One might be that installation causes one third of your nodes to lose connection with the network for a day. Another might be that Windows 98 clients somehow cause a critical server to crash because of badly implemented client/server software. Yet another might be that rollout falls behind and causes serious delay in completion of an urgent project. Build plans for dealing with your disaster scenarios as well. These are your fallback plans. Use the pilot rollout as final training for your rollout personnel, and make sure they all participate in the review sessions. Everybody needs to know what is likely to come when the main event takes place.

> **Note:** After rollout, you should expect two immediate issues to crop up. One of these is training for your staff. Ideally, you should begin training prior to the rollout so that users have a sense of what is coming when it arrives. Support will be critical immediately after rollout. As a result, you need to prepare your help desk staff in advance, plan additional staff hours so that you can cover the increased load, and prepare quick reference materials for users to refresh their training.

Executing the Rollout

Conceive of your rollout as a series of stages, with goals and metrics that will tell you how you are doing. Daily and weekly intervals make excellent timing points and evaluation points. You should know about how much you want to accomplish in a given day. Testing should help you to determine average timing for installing a system, and this information will help you to predict the timing for your rollout.

At each timing point, evaluate how you are doing. Be prepared to make "go" and "no go" decisions for the next stage. If things are going wrong, better to fix the problems in the rollout scenario than to waste money fixing problems with the system after the rollout. Unexpected events will occur, and no amount of planning and testing will reveal all potential problems. As long as a delay does not cost in terms of lost business, better for someone to be on Windows 95 one more day than to expend funds on setup problems. Remember that dates can be self-fulfilling prophecies in the minds of many managers. Proceeding when you are not ready is costly. If a "no go" decision makes the best sense, stop and fix the problems. You will waste less time than if you meet your date prophecy with an ill-prepared rollout.

When you finish the rollout, take time to do a critique with an eye cast forward toward the next ones. What have you learned? What tools are in place to simplify the next set of upgrades? What tools might you consider acquiring now to make the next rollout run smoother?

Attending to Practical Issues

The most practical issue to which you must attend in planning is the exact method for installing Windows 98. Ideally, you would like to make a wish and have the rollout finished, correctly, in one quick move. However, software installation usually requires human intervention, and typically a lot of it. One choice is to send out an army of technicians with CDs and to plan on them spending at least 75 minutes on the average installation. However, you can cut down at least the personnel cost in several ways. Some options enable you to install Windows 98 without much human intervention at all. The next few sections discuss these options.

Using BATCH.EXE

The easiest way to automate setup is to use a utility called BATCH.EXE, included in the \TOOLS\ RESKIT\DEPLOY\BATCH and \TOOLS\RESKIT\BATCH directories on the CD. The difference between the two directories is that the second contains all the system files that need to be updated to support the utility, and a Setup program that copies them to your system. You should use the second directory and its Setup program to build batch scripts on a Windows 95 workstation.

BATCH.EXE enables you to build a setup script, which you store in a file ending with the extension .INF. Scripts enable you to answer questions posed by the Setup program so that a human operator does not have to. Using such scripts, you can create hands-off installations of Windows 98.

After you have built a script, you use it by passing it as a parameter to the Setup program. The command line to enter at a DOS prompt or in the Run dialog box is as follows:

```
Setup myfile.inf
```

The Windows 98 installation files can be copied to a shared directory on the network. The script files can also be stored in such a shared directory. As a result, you can run batch installations over the network.

> **Tip:** If you perform installations over a network, be sure to copy the Windows 98 installation files to a server drive. If you share the CD, your setups will run slowly due to the access speed of the CD drive.

The Batch program is very straightforward. When you run it, you see the initial screen presented in Figure 2.1.

In the initial screen, the most interesting improvement over previous versions of this program is the Gather now button. Clicking it causes Batch to pull the current Registry settings into the script options. As a result, you need not fill in all the machine-specific settings again. You can retrieve them from the machine, and then blank out those that you need to change for each machine or machine type.

Figure 2.1.
The initial Batch screen enables you to import Registry settings.

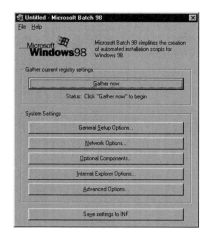

The next button, General Setup Options, presents the dialog box shown in Figure 2.2. This dialog box is new to the Batch program. It provides access to a host of settings that formerly could not be included in scripts.

Figure 2.2.
The General Setup Options dialog box enables you to specify settings about desktop and user issues.

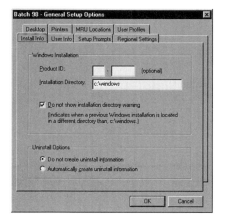

This dialog box and its tabs enable you to enter the product ID and installation directory name. You can also enter the user's name and information, as well as the NetBIOS name for the computer, the workgroup name, and a description. You can also determine which setup prompts may appear, regional settings, the desktop icons that will be installed, whether the first run dialog boxes such as the Windows Tour will appear, which printers to install, where to store most recently used lists, and whether user profiles are enabled.

The General Setup Options dialog box enables you to customize the setup responses and settings for the particular machine. The Network Options button presents the dialog box shown in Figure 2.3.

Figure 2.3.
*The Network Options
dialog box enables
you to customize
setup on the network.*

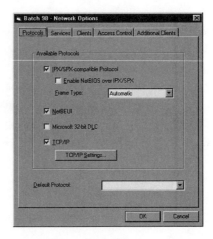

Using this dialog box and its tabs, you enter your network settings. You describe the protocols to install, the clients to install, how to handle detection of adapter cards, whether to activate the personal Web server and file and printer sharing, and the type of security you wish to use.

The Optional Components button presents the dialog box shown in Figure 2.4.

Figure 2.4.
*The Optional
Components dialog
box enables you to
define the type of
installation.*

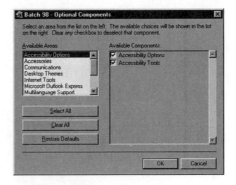

In previous versions of Windows, you would be asked which general type of installation—compact, typical, portable, or custom—you would like to run. You now have complete choice of all the components without having to choose one of the four general setup categories. Here is where you would, when performing a custom installation, select whether to include the TV Viewer application in the installation.

The Internet Explorer Options button, whose related dialog box is shown in Figure 2.5, enables you to control Internet options. In a sense, this might be the hedge Microsoft uses with the Department of Justice to allow you a non-IE version of Windows 98. You can control whether the Active Desktop is enabled, what appears on the Quick Launch toolbar, and all the settings for the browser. In conjunction with the General Setup Options dialog box, where you can turn off the IE icon on the desktop, you can create a version of Windows 98 that does not automatically enable Internet Explorer features. Or you can configure IE as you want it to be a part of your installation.

Figure 2.5.
The Internet Explorer Options dialog box enables you to choose which components are part of the Internet Explorer installation.

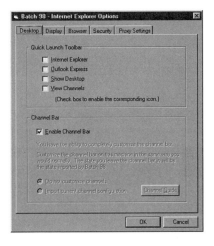

The Advanced Options button, which opens the dialog box shown in Figure 2.6, enables you to specially configure the Registry. If you have REG files you would like to include, you can specify them on the Additional Files tab. You can therefore merge custom Registry settings for options that the INF file for setup scripting cannot cover. You can also specify the location of policy files. In addition, you can choose to disable the Windows Update feature, which many administrators may indeed prefer to do.

Figure 2.6.
The Advanced Options dialog box enables you to choose to make advanced Registry modifications at setup time.

After you have filled in all the information, you are ready to click the Save settings to INF button and save your script. This action presents a standard Save dialog box that prompts you for a filename.

Automating Installations

Setup scripts enable you to automate much of installation. However, they will not automate everything in the setup process. Setting up applications, for example, is not supported. Nor is skipping past some of the setup process. To completely automate Windows 98 Setup, you need to use conventional automation support, or you need to turn to server-based tools to carry out setup.

Conventional Automation

Conventional automation involves the use of setup switches to bypass items that script files cannot automate and the use of logon scripts to initiate Windows 98 Setup. The switch settings for SETUP.EXE are the following:

- /T:tmpdir   Points to the directory where Setup copies temporary files. The directory is created if necessary. If there are files in the directory already, they are destroyed.
- /im   Prevents the memory check.
- /id   Overrides the disk-space check.
- /ie   Prevents creation of an Emergency Repair Disk.
- /ih   Prevents the Registry check.
- /is   Prevents the routine system check.
- /iq   Prevents the check for cross-linked files.
- /iv   Stops display of billboards during setup.
- /iw   Prevents display of the license notice.
- /p c-   Forces a search for all CD drives, sound cards, and network interface cards.

Using these switches on the Setup command line, you can control which portions of the Setup program run, and therefore what responses are necessary from operators. You can also tell Windows 98 where to store temporary files, so you can overcome a problem of limited space on the desired installation partition.

The simplest way to force automation of Windows 98 installation is to place a setup command in a user's logon script. Actually, you must place at least two commands in the script, one to map a drive to the Windows 98 source files and the second to initiate setup. The exact mapping commands depend on the network server that stores the logon scripts. On a Windows NT server, the commands look like this:

```
Net use DRIVELETTER \\NTSERVERNAME\SHAREDDIRECTORY
DRIVELETTER:\setup DRIVELETTER:\PATHTOSCRIPT\script.inf
```

On a NetWare server, the commands look like this:

```
Map DRIVELETTER:servername/share
DRIVELETTER:setup DRIVELETTER:script.inf
```

Of course, switches can be added to the Setup command line as necessary, and all paths can be modified to reflect the actual location of the relevant files. In addition, it is useful to add some conditional logic to make certain that you do not rerun Setup every time the user logs on. The setup commands could be placed in a batch file, for example. The first line could abort the batch file if a particular file exists. The last line of the batch file—after the setup commands—would create the file the first line checks for. Such a block would look like this:

```
If exist filename exit
Net use DRIVELETTER: \\NTSERVERNAME\SHAREDDIRECTORY
DRIVELETTER:\setup DRIVELETTER:\PATHTOSCRIPT\script.inf
Echo "file" > filename
```

Most managers face two critical problems in running such scripts against multiple systems: NetBIOS names and IP addresses. You must have a unique one of each for each machine. Batch 98 provides you with a means of building a file that contains these settings so that your script can correctly assign NetBIOS names and IP addresses to each machine. Follow these steps:

1. Using Notepad, create a file that has lines containing the machine name followed by the IP address, like this: MyNetBIOSName 144.19.74.200.

2. Open the File menu in Batch 98 and select Multiple Machine-Name Save.

3. Click the Machine Name File button (see Figure 2.7) and specify the text file that will hold machine names using a standard Open dialog box.

Figure 2.7.

Multiple machine-name save enables you to designate machine names and IP addresses.

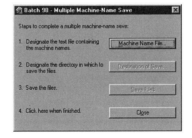

4. Batch 98 reads and processes the names and addresses. Click Destination of Save and specify the folder where the multiple INF files you are creating will be saved.

5. Click the Save Files button. Batch 98 saves one file per machine using the filename `Bstp0001.inf` for the first machine. Each filename contains an incremented number, with the maximum value being `Bstp9999.inf`. Your only task is to remember which file goes with which machine name, and to use that script to drive Setup for that machine.

6. Click the Close button when you are finished building the multiple setup scripts.

Tip: Use a standard naming convention for your machines, and make the uniqueness of the computer name be a number from 1 to 9999, as in MyNetBIOSNa0001. You will have an easy time determining which script to run on each machine.

Tool-Based Automation

Conventional automation can get you through most Windows 98 installations. When you want to automate more than setup of Windows 98, however, setup scripts have many weaknesses. You need to know precise Registry settings for the software you want to install. The software must have a valid Windows 98 INF file provided with it. And you have to include the INF file in the correct location, register it, add several lines to your script file by hand, and then pray that it all works. To say the least, this option is haphazard and not recommended.

If you need to automate the installation of Windows 98 and additional software, I strongly recommend that you turn to system management tools. You have two general types of options.

System Management Options

One option is to use a network management tool such as Microsoft's System Management Server. Several on the market include software delivery as a part of the package, including Tivoli and Norton Administrator. In general, these tools enable you to set up shared network directories that contain the installation files for the software you wish to deliver. Then they provide a means for a network client to initiate the installation. They record the progress of the installation, and provide certainty that, if interrupted, the installation will be restarted again. In addition, they keep track of what was done, which options were installed, and when the upgrade took place. If you want to know the status of any system at any time, you just query the management tool's database.

This option, of course, requires an investment in the tool and the hardware to run it. It is most appropriate only to networked situations. You will normally find that the investment will be returned to you in cost savings after you have gotten through your first rollout. If you have anything other than a small network to manage, you should carefully consider this option.

Sector Copy Options

A different option is provided by sector copiers such as Ghost. This line of products makes an exact duplicate image of a drive. You install the system and all the software as you desire it to be in the final configuration. The tool then makes an exact image of the installation on the drive and copies it exactly to another machine.

This technique proves useful when you are setting up identical, new machines for delivery to desktops. It is appropriate to both networked and non-networked situations. However, with Windows 98 there is a limitation. After the clone installation is completed, Windows 98, on its first boot, inevitably finds some new device to add. Someone—you or some operator—needs to be ready with the appropriate CD or disks to supply appropriate drivers and files as required. The cloned installation will only rarely avoid this problem.

Summary

This chapter has shown you your rollout options. We have looked at how to conduct rollout planning. We've considered team membership and agenda options for the team. We have focused on the planning options the team needs to review, and on the critical evaluation process the team needs to review. We've reviewed the issues you need to examine and how they turn into action plans for implementing installation scripts. We have also seen some techniques for doing a mass rollout.

On Your Own

Try creating a setup script file using BATCH.EXE. Try out the Multiple Machine-Name Save option in Batch 98. Build a script file and run a batch installation. Try automating an installation using a logon script. If you have network management software, build an installation package using its provided tool set.

3

Reviewing Basic User Interaction

Peter Norton®

On the one hand, Windows 98 has not significantly changed the user interface. On the other hand, Windows 98 has significantly changed the user interface. These two opinions launched into the trade press as soon as alpha previews of Windows 98 were available. The truth is that if you are used to working with Windows 95 with Plus! and a Web browser, you have experienced most of the Windows 98 user interface. A few things are different—very different and interesting. But an average user in an average corporate setting may never notice the difference.

This chapter reviews the user interface. It is not intended as a comprehensive guide. Instead, I'm shooting for what is critical for the system administrator who has had Windows 98 mandated on his or her network. You need to know this information, because you need to be ready to prepare users for your planned implementation. Users, after all, call the help desk. This is the quick tour of the most important new elements. This chapter covers the following topics:

- Fundamental changes in the shell
- Changes in the way you interact with folders, files, objects
- Changes in how you work with printers
- Changes in the Control Panel
- The new broadcast architecture
- New access to online services
- New uses for ActiveX technology

Working with the Shell

The Windows 98 shell program is still the Explorer—the interface to the features of the operating system. Explorer has all of its same quirks. Plus signs appear next to items in the Tree view that cannot be expanded. The two panes can still get out of synchronization. Mysteriously, Explorer opens with a view only of your C: drive, until you expand My Computer to show your other five drives.

Many of the items that you probably wish Microsoft would fix in the next major revision will still annoy you. But woven into this mix of advantages and disadvantages is a host of new features.

Living with New Features

The new side of the shell is indeed helpful. Features that you needed to purchase as add-ons, for example, have been incorporated into the operating system. A lot of helpful features have been integrated as well. In general, we can group these features as follows:

- New look and feel
- Graphics effects formerly found in Windows 95 (Plus!) features
- Web features
- New mouse hardware

Experiencing the New Look and Feel

Look and feel changes originated from two sources: Microsoft's usability lab, and Microsoft's desire to unify several of the programming elements in the Win32 Software Development Kit, the set of C language functions that enables you to create Windows programs. When right-clicking was introduced in Windows 95, the new feature was created because the usability lab discovered that the mass average of world citizens are double-click–challenged. Several of the features briefly explored in this chapter reflect similar concerns. On the programming side, Microsoft unified menus and toolbars in Office 95 so that users could modify both using a single, consistent set of procedures and dialog boxes. The unification of these two elements is now complete and a part of the operating system. As a result, toolbars have acquired features once only associated with menus, and vice versa.

The following list summarizes the look and feel changes:

- Additional ToolTips are a part of the operating system. They were introduced to help make Windows 98 more self-interpreting. Rest your mouse over the Minimize button and a ToolTip appears to explain its function. You may feel that this feature should be extended to include ToolTips for even more interface elements, but it helps computer-intimidated users to understand what many of the operating system controls do, without asking either you or a contract trainer.

- Operating system menus are now animated. They slide from the mouse click point out to the opposing diagonal corner.

- You can choose to allow a single-click to run programs. This feature makes Windows 98 even more accessible to the mouse-challenged, which includes most of us.

- You can toggle between two versions of the desktop—what is now known as the Classic Desktop and the Active Desktop, shown in Figure 3.1—via a menu choice. You must set a default, and then you may choose to view the desktop, if you have chosen the Active Desktop as default, or the desktop as a Web page, if you have chosen the Classic Desktop as default.

- Toolbars are context sensitive, like menus. As a result, when you change the task, the toolbar can adjust to offer you the appropriate tools for the task now at hand.

- The taskbar may contain multiple toolbars, known as desk bands. By default, you see at least two. One band displays the buttons for your other programs. The other, known as Quick Launch, directly launches applications whose shortcuts you have dragged and dropped on the band. You can right-click on the taskbar and use the Toolbars option on the context menu to choose from among four predefined toolbar options, or to create toolbars of your own. (Several icons appear by default in the QuickLaunch band: IE4, TV Viewer, Show Desktop, and View Channels.)

- The connection icon that appears in the System Tray when you dial out has changed. You now see two monitors, which flash to indicate traffic incoming or outgoing. A ToolTip provides you with the connection speed and number of bytes transferred over the connection.

- Your Web browser Favorites list appears as an item on the Start menu and many context menus. You can easily launch a connection to your favorite Web sites by using this feature.

- New accessibility features, described in Chapter 15, "Configuring for Ease of Use," have been added to make Windows 98 easier to use for the physically challenged. Actually, many of them are useful for the less than challenged. Do not view these options as for the minority of users.

- A time zone editor has been included in the Windows 98 Resource Kit Sampler, included on your Windows 98 CD. If you need to create settings for a time zone Microsoft had not heard of, you can do so using this editor.

Figure 3.1.
The Active Desktop is the new, Web-enabled version of the desktop.

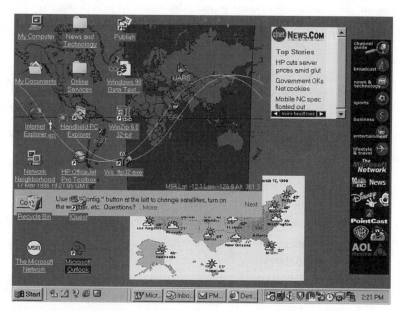

Note: The Indiana Legislature recently proposed that the state, which does not observe daylight savings time except in the regions near Chicago, IL, and Louisville, KY, resolve the difference between the opposing factions that supported and did not support the adoption of daylight savings time uniformly across the state by adjusting clocks one half hour during the summer. Happily, this proposal failed. If it is ever successful, system administrators in Indiana will need the time zone editor.

Using the Effects Features

If you read the pre-release articles on Windows 98, you heard about the Icons! Features of Windows 98. These features have been renamed mainly as Effects because they appear mostly on the Effects tab of the Display properties sheet. These features were formerly included in the Plus! Pack for Windows 95. Now that Windows 98 abandons 386 support, as noted in Chapter 1, they are included in the operating system proper. (The Plus! Pack was originally created to comprise the features for Windows 95 that required an 80486 microprocessor.) They include the following:

- Full window drag, so the contents of windows remain visible as you drag them.
- Font smoothing, to rid your screen of jagged edges when fonts display.

> **Note:** Unless your system is reasonably fast, especially with graphics operations, disabling font smoothing and full window drag might be wise. You can use the Solitaire game to evaluate the effects of full window drag on the system. Use WordPad to check the effects of font smoothing. Enable the features and time routine operations, however roughly you do it. Then disable the features, and repeat the tests. If you perceive slower performance with these features enabled, disable them, and let the user live with outline dragging and jaggy fonts.

- Wallpaper stretching, so even small graphics can be displayed as one large picture covering the desktop background.
- Large icons, so you can choose to make icons easier to see on your screen at high resolutions.
- A desktop icon changer (see Figure 3.2), so altering your My Computer icon to something more pleasing can be done without editing the Registry.
- The taskbar animates its hiding feature and behaves like any other toolbar, so its behavior is more predictable for users.

Figure 3.2.
You can easily substitute new icons for default desktop items by using the icon changer.

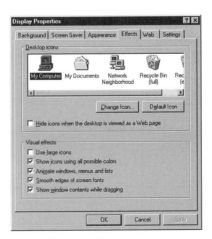

Web-Enabling the Shell

As a part of its Internet strategy, Microsoft integrated the Internet Explorer into the operating system. As a result, you can display a Web toolbar in any window, and use the standard backward, forward, and URL controls to navigate either the Web or your own file system. To facilitate such navigation, you can choose to display either the entire interface or only selected windows as Web pages. You can display any of the Internet Explorer toolbars wherever toolbars can be displayed in applications or Explorer windows. The taskbar can display the Links toolbar, for example, and any element of the operating system that can display as a Web page can hold ActiveX controls, including the taskbar. You can subscribe to special sites that use a structure called Web Channels, which allows information to be sent automatically to your desktop when you are connected to the Web. You also get a stripped-down version of FrontPage, called FrontPage Express, to help you build and publish Web pages.

Note: As you plan your desktop configuration, you should test your desktop software on each configuration that you plan to support. During the beta cycles of Windows 98, incompatibilities between some applications and certain desktop configurations were noted by some testers. How well these will be resolved in the release product, of course, remains for those implementing the release version to find out. Testing your planned configuration is always the wisest path.

Wheeling Your Mouse (and Other Details)

Windows 98 includes a driver for the Microsoft IntelliMouse, which has a wheel between the two buttons that you can define for different actions. If you roll the wheel, for example, you scroll a set number of lines. Tapping the wheel scrolls you a page. Holding the wheel down and dragging gives you a rapid scroll, just like dragging a scroll box on a scrollbar. The time-honored Microsoft mouse now has a new hardware feature that your users will either love or hate. Personally, I have not found the wheel to be very useful, but that is just my working style.

Working with Folders, Files, and Other Objects

Folders and files remain the same in the way that you interact with them. To find out what you can do with any object that you can view in the Explorer, right-click it. A context menu appears that describes what you can do with that object. The context menus will not be the same on everyone's system. What appears depends on what you have installed on your machine, both in terms of hardware and software. Novell's IntranetWare 32-bit network client, for example, adds four specialized items to the context menu that appear when you right-click on the Network Neighborhood. Any programmer can extend the shell to include new options. The Explore From Here utility included in the Powertoys, for example, adds an item to context menus that enables you to open the two-paned Explorer with the current folder as the root showing in the Tree view.

Shell extensions are not the preoccupation of third parties alone, however. Microsoft has added some shell extensions itself, which you might find very useful. Microsoft Office applications, for example, support an extension included in the Windows 98 API and, therefore, is available to any vendor. The properties sheet and context menu for a Word document, for example, contain a great deal of detail about the document not previously available under Windows 95. Resting the mouse cursor above an Office document enables you to see summary information in an extended ToolTip that makes identifying the document easy.

Using the New My Documents Folder

Microsoft has moved the My Documents folder and created a shell extension that places the buried folder on the desktop, just like it was before. The folder is now buried in `\Windows\Profiles\NameOfProfile\Desktop`. When you think about it, this is a rather inconvenient location to browse to. However, the folder appears on the desktop for the user, and it appears in the Explorer Tree view equal in rank with My Computer, and at the top of the Documents submenu on the Start menu. The folder is therefore readily accessible, yet it remains personal to the user as a part of the user's profile. Each user who logs on to a system sees her own My Documents folder, which provides a namespace that abbreviates the path to the actual location of the files.

Technical Note: This shell extension seems to have a further purpose that is only partially realized at present. At the 1998 Professional Developer's Conference, Microsoft indicated that, under Windows NT 5.0, the My Documents folder would be replicated to the server as a part of the server-based roving user profile, a profile made available to a user no matter which workstation the user logged on to. User data would therefore always be backed up as soon as the user logged off, and doubly backed up as you run backup tapes of your servers. The shell extension in Windows 98 aims at cooperating with this strategy; the data in My Documents replicates to a Windows NT 4.0 server. The replication algorithm copies only the changes in the folder so that you do not copy every file at every logon and logoff.

You may see potential problems with this strategy. Under Windows 95, elements of a user's profile were stored in the user's home directory on a Windows NT Server or a user's mail directory on a NetWare server. They were also stored on the local machine as a locally cached profile. If the server were unavailable, the local version of the profile, if present, would be loaded. If users logged on to several machines, they would have a local profile on

continues

each computer to which they logged on. Now that My Documents is a part of the Desktop folder in the profile, 500MB (or more) of documents might be replicated to several machines for a given user in the locally cached profile. This replication would waste disk space, slow logons, and network bandwidth.

Fortunately, you can limit the locations to which files in the profile will copy by adding a value stored under HKEY_LOCAL_MACHINE\Network\Logon in the Registry. Add a new DWORD value to this key named UseHomeDirectory. You do not need to specify anything other than the default, blank value. The presence of this value alters the default behavior of copying the profile to a local cache; thus, if the server containing the user's home directory is unavailable, the user will still have a profile to work with. Adding this value causes the files to be replicated only to the user's home directory, not to each machine to which the user logs on.

Finding New Things

The Find function that first appeared in Windows 95 has been extended under Windows 98 in the following ways:

- You can search for files and folders quickly by using the services of Fast Find, which indexes your drive's contents (in the background as you work) to make searching more efficient.

Technical Note: The version of Find Fast distributed with Microsoft Office, versions 95 and 97, had known memory leaks that limited system performance. A memory leak occurs when an application marks memory as "in use" and then never frees it. This area of memory is therefore permanently marked as in use, and becomes unavailable to any application or to the operating system. If you experience system slowdowns with Windows 98, see what happens when you disable Find Fast by removing it from the StartUp folder. You may find that some of the memory leaks have not been plugged. An easy way to test for this problem is to run Windows 98 continuously with Find Fast enabled and no applications performing work. Check to see whether the system slows down. Opening the Start menu is a simple enough test. If you get a slowdown, repeat the test with Find Fast disabled. If you experience no slowdown, or the slowdown takes much longer before it is noticeable, you know that Find Fast is leaking memory on your systems.

- You can search for computers on the network.
- You can search for items by using the services of Microsoft Outlook, which allows you to search Microsoft Office files for contents and other parameters.

- You can search the Internet for sites directly from the Start menu.
- You can search for people whose information is stored in an address book maintained on the system.
- You can save your searches for reuse in the future, as well as save the contents revealed by a search for later use.

Exploring the Network

Exploring the network happens the same way it did under Windows 95, the Network Neighborhood. As before, you can specify the contents of the Network Neighborhood by setting a policy. You need to drag and drop the items you want in the Network Neighborhood from the Network Neighborhood in the Explorer to another folder in the Explorer. Then you use the User icon in your policies file to set up a custom Network Neighborhood, which points to the folder you just created to obtain the contents of the Network Neighborhood. The policy option for this setting is located under Windows 98 System | Shell | Custom Folders | Custom Network Neighborhood, as shown in Figure 3.3. Windows 98 uses custom folders by default when you set up user profiles. Setting up custom folders of your own enables you to provide a standard desktop interface for the users on your network.

Figure 3.3.
You can set a policy to restrict the icons that appear in the Network Neighborhood.

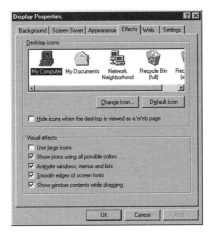

Exploring the Web

The Explorer has also been extended to function as a Web browser. The Internet Explorer is an icon in the Tree view equal in rank to My Computer. When you select this icon, the right pane of the Explorer effectively becomes your browser, and the left pane gives you a Tree view of your favorite URLs (see Figure 3.4). Wherever you are in Windows 98, you can get to the Internet easily.

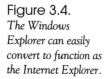

Figure 3.4.
*The Windows
Explorer can easily
convert to function as
the Internet Explorer.*

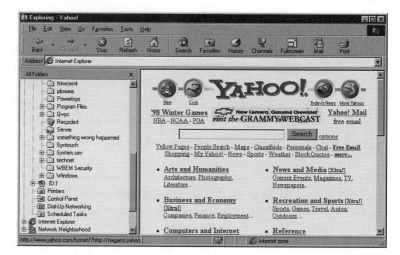

Working with Printers

Working with printers is easier under Windows 98. The Printers folder is your one-stop-shopping place for attaching to printers, be they local or remote. You use the Add Printer Wizard to add whatever kind of printer you want to add.

Installing Printers

Installing printers is a matter of opening the Add Printer icon. This action starts the wizard. The wizard guides you through the process of setting up the printer. If it is a local printer, you need only to know the name of the printer and select an appropriate driver. If it is a remote printer, you need only a valid protocol path to the printer to be able to install it. If you are installing a remote printer, you do not need to install a local copy of the driver. The driver needs to be installed on the printer server. When you attach to the printer to undertake the installation process, the system copies the driver from the printer server to the local machine. (If no appropriate driver is present, the system prompts you to provide a valid path to the appropriate driver, which means you can pull the driver from a Windows 98 CD or an alternative path where the driver has been stored. You can even search the Windows Update Web site for an updated driver if you wish.)

Microsoft includes protocols and software for managing JetAdmin printers, remote procedure call interaction with UNIX printers, services for interacting with NetWare printer queues, and facilities for interacting with DEC PrintServers. All you need to do is to install the appropriate protocols and clients for the printers. The Add Printer Wizard steps you through the process of connecting to such printers.

Using Image Color Matching

Image Color Matching (ICM) is a technology introduced to Windows in Windows 95 that allows disparate scanners, printers, and displays to map their unique, hardware-determined colors to a consistent color reference standard. The idea is that the colors you see on your display should be the colors that you scan and should also be the colors that you print. ICM, implemented as a part of the operating system, adjusts the colors so that each device sees the same color.

How do you interact with ICM? You can load an ICM file that matches your particular display, printer, or scanner. The ICM file contains the color mappings to adjust the colors to match across all your hardware. Each device will have a Color Management tab in its properties. Windows 98 includes several ICM files to load. But chances are you will need to get the ICM file for your device from its manufacturer.

Using Imaging by Eastman Kodak

Microsoft has included an imaging program provided by Eastman Kodak in Windows 98. You open it by using Start | Programs | Accessories | Imaging. This program, shown in Figure 3.5, gives you basic photo editing capabilities. With it you can scan, apply color matching, annotate, and manipulate images. If you need special effects, image enhancement, and similar capabilities, you will want a more sophisticated editor. For basic business documents, however, you can do a lot with this imaging system.

Figure 3.5.

Kodak's imaging program enables you to scan and manipulate pictures for documents.

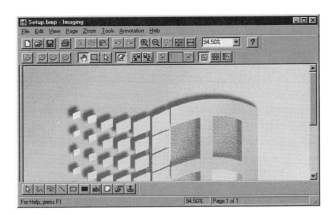

Working with Microsoft Fax and Exchange

Because the Exchange client has been divorced from Windows 98, faxing capabilities have been divorced from the Inbox, which has been converted into Outlook Express. Faxing options are not actually a part of Windows 98 any longer, and now appear on the Accessories menu when the faxing add-in for Microsoft Office has been installed. You can compose faxes, edit cover pages, and receive (or request, as the menu item says) faxes. The Fax Editor is now a wizard (see Figure 3.6). It steps you through the process of building a recipients list, creating the message, and attaching files. The Fax Requester is also a wizard that steps you through the process of calling a fax information service to retrieve a fax. You can still receive faxes directly. Use the Mail and Fax icon in the Control Panel, the Dialing tab, to configure the modem to answer the phone after a certain number of rings.

Figure 3.6.
Wizards have taken over the process of faxing under Windows 98.

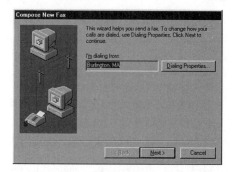

Working with the Control Panel

The Control Panel under Windows 98 is much the same as Windows 95. You have all the same icons, with some new ones, to control the Registry settings for the operating system. Some new capabilities have been added. The following sections describe these additions.

Using TweakUI to Control the Interface

One tool included in the Powertoys for Windows 95 is included in the Resource Kit Sampler for Windows 98: a Control Panel for Windows 98, TweakUI, shown in Figure 3.7. (It is in \Reskit\Powertoys on the Windows 98 CD.) This applet contains 12 tabs that give you safe access to Registry settings that everyone learned in Windows 95 by reading the trade press and hacking away at the Registry.

TweakUI can do the following things for you:

- **Mouse tab.** Adjust settings for menu speed, sensitivity, and wheel use (for the Intellimouse).

- **General tab.** Turn on and off animation effects in the user interface, set the location of special system folders, and select the search engine you wish to use in the Internet Explorer.

- **Explorer tab.** Adjusts the appearance of shortcuts and the way Windows 98 handles 8.3 filenames.

- **IE4 tab.** Adjusts many characteristics, visual and otherwise, of Internet Explorer 4.0.

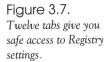

Figure 3.7.

*Twelve tabs give you
safe access to Registry
settings.*

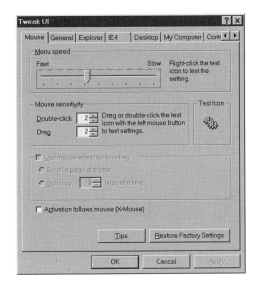

- **Add/Remove tab.** Adds or removes entries in the Add/Remove Programs applet. You are most likely to use it to remove entries for programs that you removed, but that remain in the list anyway.

- **Boot tab.** Adjusts the boot characteristics of the machine, such as whether function keys are available, whether the Boot menu can be displayed, and whether F4 will boot you to another operating system.

- **Repair tab.** Enables you to repair various aspects of the Windows 98 interface such as inaccurate URL lists, icons that no longer match, and file associations that have become inaccurate.

- **Paranoia tab.** Enables you to set various lists to be cleared after each logoff. That way no one can tell what seamy sites you have visited on the Internet, whose files you might have opened, and so forth, just by looking at your history lists. This tab also enables you to define the autorun characteristics of both audio and program CDs.

- **Desktop tab.** Enables you to determine which icons appear on the desktop, and to create such icons as files so that they can be placed in any folder whatsoever.

- **My Computer tab.** Enables you to specify which drive letters will appear in the My Computer window. You can hide any drive from user access that you would like.

- **Control Panel tab.** Permits you to determine which applets appear in the Control Panel. Unlike system policies, you can select on an applet-by-applet basis.

- **Network tab.** Sets up an automatic logon for a given user. The logon dialog box will not appear on startup, and the user is logged on as a part of the startup process.

- **New tab.** Controls which items appear on the New submenu that appears on context menus.

Using QuickRes

The QuickRes application is a part of the Windows 98 Resource Kit, rather than a part of the Powertoys. When you choose to use it, an icon appears on your System Tray. Right-clicking on the icon enables you to open a menu of the possible resolution and color depth settings for your machine. You can change to these resolutions on-the-fly, unless you have required that the machine be shut down when resolution settings change in the Display properties. (Many display adapters, such as those from Diamond and ATI, come with their own utilities for controlling such features—including specialized features—of the card.)

Adjusting the Refresh Rate

The Display properties now include the capability to adjust the screen refresh rate. Choose the Settings tab and click the Advanced button. In the set of tabs that appear in the dialog box, you will find the ability to set the refresh rate for the display. Please be aware that changing this rate can damage your monitor, so check your hardware documentation carefully before adjusting this setting away from the default.

Using Hardware Panning

Also hiding behind the Advanced button in the Display properties will be, if your display adapter supports it, the settings for hardware panning. Hardware panning enables you to set your screen resolution to a value higher than you can actually display. Moving the mouse around the screen or using defined panning keys enables you to scroll your view of the screen to see the hidden portions that cannot be displayed. Sometimes the capability is available without settings being provided. On my laptop, for example, I have automatic hardware panning as the cursor moves to the edge of the screen when I use 1024×768 resolution. The screen can display only 800×600. The display scrolls to reveal the hidden pixels.

Using the Multiple Display Settings

If you use PCI video cards, plugging in more than one enables you to use multiple displays for your desktop. Windows 98 automatically adjusts to take advantage of the additional screen real estate. To take advantage of additional monitors, open your display properties. Each monitor will have a tab for setting its characteristics. Each monitor can have different characteristics, including display resolutions. To allow the monitor to participate in desktop display, check Extend my Windows desktop onto this monitor.

Watching TV

Yes, every manager's productivity dream has come true: Lucy and Andy Griffith can appear on your desktop. You need to install the Web TV Viewer application, and you need a video card with television capabilities. High among these on the hardware compatibility list is the ATI All-in-Wonder. Connecting an antenna, satellite receiver, or cable system enables you to watch TV signals on your TV monitor. You can also receive IP packets sandwiched into the broadcast signal. As a result, you can obtain TV listings from your local PBS affiliate's signal. This capability points to Windows 98 as being a home entertainment-oriented system. Using closed circuit systems, however, you could also deliver video training directly to desktop monitors.

Accessing Online Services

Signing up for online services couldn't be easier under Windows 98. In a desktop folder called Internet and On-line Services, you find icons for CompuServe, AOL, AT&T Worldnet, Prodigy, and the Microsoft Network. Opening the icon causes installation of the software. You need only choose the one(s) you want, install them, and dial up the service to open an account.

Working with ActiveX

The entire Windows 98 operating system is ActiveX enabled. Under Windows 95, you had scraps—selections of data that you dragged from the application and dropped on the desktop. These items were copied to a special file format and stored on the desktop. You could open the scrap to see what was in it, or drag and drop it into any application to copy the scrap into a new location. Scraps were great for boilerplate text and frequently used objects. They in fact were OLE containers, and could accept any type of OLE object. This was the first integration of OLE capabilities, now called ActiveX, into the operating system.

ActiveX began life in Windows 2.x as Dynamic Data Exchange (DDE), a way for applications to establish conversations and exchange data. However, DDE was notoriously unreliable. You could not guarantee delivery of the data, and DDE over a network was just impossible. As a result, DDE evolved into Object Linking and Embedding 1.0 (OLE). OLE was a way to describe containers in compound documents. You could place Excel data inside a Word document. Double-clicking on the Excel data would activate it for editing within the Word document. Excel's menu would replace Word's, and Excel's spreadsheet would overlay the Word document while you edited the spreadsheet data.

OLE grew into OLE 2.0, which added robustness and extended the feature set. OLE 2.0 was still not very compatible with networking objects, and so the model once again evolved into the Common Object Model (COM). COM had evolved into DCOM, the Distributed Common Object Model that Microsoft is now implementing. Along the way in this evolution, the canned objects that you could embed in applications, known as OLE Controls and distinguished by the file extension .ocx, came to have a poor reputation. As a result, Microsoft renamed them ActiveX objects, and introduced a few improvements. *Active* has become the generic prefix in Microsoft technology that means new. ActiveX has spread to refer to the entire object model. The term, like Microsoft network, seems to mean whatever anyone wants it to mean now. DCOM is a term that appears only when Microsoft wants to discuss its Distributed Network Architecture for Windows NT 5.0, which seems to be the new incarnation of DCOM.

Windows 98 enables you to place ActiveX controls just about anywhere. In each coming chapter, you will experience the effects of ActiveX integration in Windows 98. You will be able to exploit the functionality that ActiveX controls offer on your desktop and in your documents. In essence, you can use these program parts to reprogram the operating system.

Summary

This chapter has focused on what is new in the user interface. We have looked at changes in the operating system shell. We've looked at improvements in interacting with printers. We have seen new Control Panel capabilities, the TV capabilities, and the ActiveX capabilities.

On Your Own

Open Windows 98 and try out the new features. Play with your video settings. Change resolutions by using the Quick Change feature. Shift between Web views of Windows and classic views. Try hardware panning, if your device supports it. Install the TV Viewer and see how TV plays on your monitor. Work with TweakUI and try out a printer installation. Drop ActiveX controls onto the desktop. Connect to the Desktop Gallery to see what new controls are available.

4

Choosing the Active or Classic Desktop

Peter Norton®

One of the biggest issues in administering Windows 98 on your network will be the choice of desk-top. Microsoft has created a new type of desktop, called the Active Desktop, for Windows 98. The Active Desktop treats the desktop like a Web page. All titles for icons are underlined, for example, so they look like hyperlinks to other Web pages. Even the Explorer has the look and feel of the Web browser.

Microsoft's goal, of course, is to give all the resources on a computer a single interface, the interface that originated with the Internet. Now your applications, your operating system, your file manage-ment tools, and your network access will all look and feel the same. You need not be concerned where a resource is because all resources are now as identical as they possibly can be. You need to be concerned only whether a particular resource is available for you to use.

Part of the reasoning behind this goal is the availability of Internet channels, which can help those whose work depends on access to Internet sites stay up-to-date easily. Push technology brings you information from your chosen channels straight to your desktop without your even having to make the request. This type of information delivery can be a great convenience. But there is a darker side to the Active Desktop, and this side is related to training costs and security.

To help you decide which desktop to deploy, this chapter reviews the critical issues you need to consider. This chapter covers the following topics:

- What the issues are in choosing a desktop
- Choosing the Active Desktop or the classic desktop
- Building the Active Desktop
- Understanding the dangers of the Active Desktop
- Understanding the advantages of the Active Desktop
- Working with zones to control security

Choosing the Better Desktop

Windows 98, in a clean typical install to a new drive, defaults to the Active Desktop, shown in Fig-ure 4.1. You have to accept this desktop at least long enough to find out how to get your old desktop back. In upgrade installations, Windows 98 retains your original desktop, but adds the Channel Bar you see in the Active Desktop.

As a result, you will start out, unless you do a default clean installation, with the desktop you had. You need to choose what you want to deploy rather than accepting the defaults. You may prefer the Active Desktop because of the features it provides, or you may prefer to stay with the classic desk-top. One thing you definitely need to decide, because it affects your support costs, is whether users will be allowed to select their preference. If users can decide, you have to train your support staff on both desktops.

Figure 4.1.
The Active Desktop has a unique look and feel, and may be confusing the first time you see it.

Selecting Classic or Active

In choosing the desktop you plan to support, you need to realize that many of the features that comprise the new interface are also available under the classic desktop. You can use Web channels, for example, under either desktop. The Internet Explorer toolbar can be displayed in any window. The Explorer can access the Internet as well.

The Active Desktop consists of the following elements:

- The capability to place Web content on the desktop. Anything you can create in HTML can be displayed on the desktop.

- The capability to display Web content in folders. If a folder contains HTML content, the HTML code will be interpreted and displayed as a part of the background.

- The capability to single-click to open icons. For those who have never mastered the double-click—and Microsoft's usability studies indicate that a lot of us fall into this category—you can provide a solution.

- The capability to display icons as Web links, with the caption underlined. The underline can be on all the time, or only when the icon has the focus.

You control these features from the General tab of the Folder Options property sheet, which you choose from the View menu of any system window. As Figure 4.2 shows, you can choose the Web style, Classic style, or Custom options. The Web style option turns on all features of the Active Desktop. The Classic style turns off all the features of the Active Desktop and leaves you with the

Windows 95 desktop. The Custom option enables you to pick and choose features, permitting you to build a custom Active Desktop.

Tip: If you have lost the view of your desktop icons, the setting that controls their display is well hidden. In the View tab of the Folder Options dialog box, third from the bottom of the list, is a check box that hides the icons in the Web page view of the desktop. Use View | Folder Options from any Explorer window to reach this dialog box.

Figure 4.2.
The Folder Options dialog box enables you to enable or disable the Active Desktop.

In reality, choosing to use the Active Desktop is not an all-or-nothing proposition. Each of the options has advantages and disadvantages for users. Table 4.1 summarizes their strengths and weaknesses.

Table 4.1. Advantages and disadvantages of Active Desktop elements.

Element	Advantages	Disadvantages
Web content on desktop	Permits custom design of the desktop	May confuse users who use multiple machines unless standardized
Web Content in Folders	Allows folders to have a browser look and feel	Blurs the distinction between local and Web resources
Single-click	Eases use of the interface	Causes problems to open for users who accidentally open items with stray mouse clicks
Icons displayed as Web links	Gives consistent interface to local resources	Blurs the distinction between operating system and Web browser

As the table shows, for users (and for administrators managing users), the critical issues are ease of use, consistent interface, and distinction between the local and the remote. Each of these issues has no easy resolution. If you allow users to select their own Web content for the desktop, for example, you may never have a consistent user interface for any given system again. If you allow this choice, however, you have probably made that machine easier to use for its primary user.

If you mandate a consistent Active Desktop for your organization, you reduce training costs and maintenance costs. When users travel, however, they may have difficulty using a machine at a different location. If you make every resource look like a Web page, you may risk users not being able to tell whether information is proprietary or public, because all the resources look the same. Proprietary information could be accidentally released. In addition, because users can modify the Web page by adding ActiveX controls and channels, the updates they force thereby have an impact on network bandwidth.

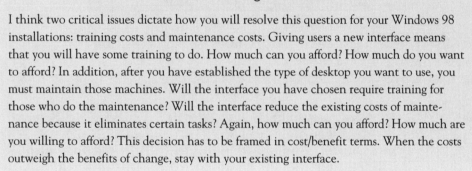

Peter's Principle: Active or Classic? When to Stay with Your Existing Interface

I think two critical issues dictate how you will resolve this question for your Windows 98 installations: training costs and maintenance costs. Giving users a new interface means that you will have some training to do. How much can you afford? How much do you want to afford? In addition, after you have established the type of desktop you want to use, you must maintain those machines. Will the interface you have chosen require training for those who do the maintenance? Will the interface reduce the existing costs of maintenance because it eliminates certain tasks? Again, how much can you afford? How much are you willing to afford? This decision has to be framed in cost/benefit terms. When the costs outweigh the benefits of change, stay with your existing interface.

Building the Active Desktop

You have several methods for building an Active Desktop. If you want to take the all-or-nothing approach, you need to take two actions. First, go to the Folder Options property sheet and select the Web style option in the General tab. Second, right-click on the desktop and select Properties from the context menu. In the Display Properties dialog box, check the View My Active Desktop as a Web Page check box. You now have an Active Desktop with all the default options that apply, as shown in Figure 4.1 earlier in the chapter.

You can customize your Active Desktop in three ways. First, in the Display Properties, you can select what HTML content to include on the desktop (see Figure 4.3). Just click the New button and enter the URL for the resource in the dialog box, and then click OK. Before you see the dialog box, Microsoft offers you the chance to link to their gallery of desktop elements, from which you can choose items to include on your desktop.

Figure 4.3.
*The Display
Properties enable you
to add Web elements
to your desktop.*

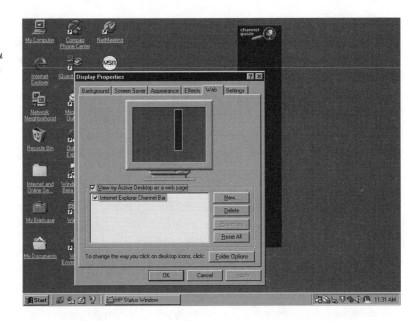

Second, you can use the Background tab in the display properties to place any HTML page on the desktop as a wallpaper. Just use the Browse button to browse for the file, locate the HTML file you want to use, and click OK or Apply (see Figure 4.4 for the end result).

Figure 4.4.
*HTML files can be
used as wallpapers
under Windows 98.*

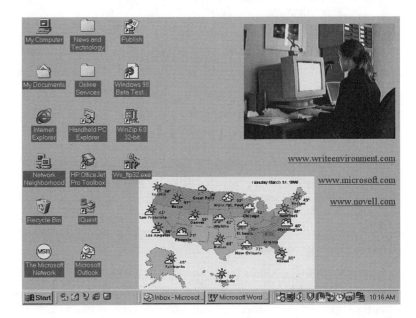

Third, you can select View | Folder Options from any system window menu bar. On the General tab, select Custom, based on the settings you choose, and then click Settings (see Figure 4.5). Use the resulting dialog box to select the settings you want, which was discussed in the preceding section.

Figure 4.5.
You can select custom settings to personalize your Active Desktop.

> **Tip:** If you are in IE and are browsing the Web, you just right-click on a Web object and select Set as Wallpaper. This causes the object to appear as the Internet Temporary WallPaper in the `Windows` directory.

The real power of the Active Desktop comes from the capability to place HTML content on the desktop. This capability gives you the power of customizing the desktop behavior, because any HTML code that Internet Explorer can interpret is legal, including scripts. Do you need a policy dialog box to appear each time a user logs on that is more extensive than system policies can provide? Do you want to display a set of links to resources on the background of the desktop? Do you want special graphics that identify your organization or department? All these are available through Web elements that you can include either on the desktop or as an HTML wallpaper.

Understanding the Security Risks of the Active Desktop

The Active Desktop can be a dangerous place from the network administrator's point of view. Consider Web channels, for example. They are great from the user's point of view. Content from Web pages automatically comes down to you. You stay up on the latest business news, stock quotes, or Disney movies. Because the information flow has become automated, it seems to make work easier.

Administrators must, however, think about security. Packets streaming down from the Internet automatically means that you now have a stream of packets that can deliver viruses or what have you. You need to be concerned about virus scanning and integrity checking—in short, protecting your network from all the sorts of dangers familiar to Internet access. More importantly, you have a user management and a traffic management issue. What if a poorly designed channel starts to stream a lot of packets to 35 desktops all at once. What will that traffic do to performance on your network?

If you allow Active Desktops with user-defined HTML pages, keep in mind that FrontPage Express, included with Windows 98, contains enough possibilities for HTML coding without really knowing HTML to cause you headaches. Users can run Java programs from out there on the Internet by linking to them. Again, these programs might generate traffic, introduce unfriendly code, and cause both traffic and security concerns.

In addition, if the user sees items on the desktop that are really from the Web, he may mistakenly trust the items and content as much as the content of a company file server. They may actually consider it on the same level as corporate sponsored white papers or approved programs for installation. More than just a virus issue, this is an issue of inadvertently supplying information to unknown outside agencies in an uninformed manner. In other words, trojan horse programs may be downloading from these Web-based resources, proving more dangerous than any simple virus, because they can represent an organized attack on proprietary information. I know users who will never allow Microsoft to place a cookie or control in their browser because they fear Microsoft is spying on their computer configuration. Probably the greatest computer urban myth in history, this paranoia is not necessarily misplaced. Push technology could be reversed to pull data down from a drive, and jealous competitors could create Web sites that would attract your users just to exploit this option.

Another question is how your firewall will react to the user-chosen HTML links, or to items such as stock tickers streaming data in from Internet sources. The security architecture of your network may have to be adjusted to allow you the kind of Internet access you want for critical features of the Active Desktops you have chosen to implement.

The critical issue for implementing Active Desktop on a corporate network is planning. What freedom will users have? What limits must administrators set? The defining criterion for determining answers to these questions does not relate to cost. Instead, for these issues, the question is what functionality do you desire to have attached to the desktop. After you have specified functionality, trace and test what you think will happen if you implement the functionality along two dimensions, traffic and security. Then consider the costs associated with implementing both Active Desktop and the related traffic and security management. Only then will you have a sense of whether Active Desktop is worth implementing in your situation.

Understanding the Advantages of Active Desktop

Despite all the warnings I have issued, the Active Desktop can be a very powerful business tool. Consider the needs of a financial analyst. Her desktop can manage a great deal of information for her. Her desktop can activate channels to connect with *Forbes*, the *Wall Street Journal*, and PointCast Business Services. She can also hook into CNN Online to get custom news services tailored to her clients' needs. For each channel she chooses to activate, she receives updated information so long as she is connected to the Internet. The information is pushed onto her desktop, where it becomes available when she chooses to access it.

Note: To activate a Web channel, select the Channels icon (the satellite dish icon) in the Internet Explorer, and select the channel in the channels pane that appears. You will be transported to the Web site, where you will find an Active Desktop button. Select that button to activate the channel on your desktop. (Chapters 3, "Reviewing Basic User Interaction," and 5, "Looking at the Core of the Operating System," contain more information about channels.)

In addition, in the Microsoft Active Desktop Gallery, there is a stock quote control that can be placed on the desktop. Throughout the trading day, our analyst can get the most recent price information on the markets. In addition, any programmer with Visual Basic 5.0 can build her custom ActiveX controls that deliver custom information from the company database or from online services to support decisions she must make throughout the day.

When Bill Gates talks about information at your fingertips, he means it with Active Desktop. In addition to Web channels and ActiveX controls that pull information from external sources, Visual Basic—the common macro language of Microsoft applications—supports the automation of applications. The financial analyst we have been using as an example can build client portfolios as a set of related databases and documents that read the content coming in from the Internet and continuously update themselves. A set of hot buy prospects, for example, can be identified by a Visual Basic program that scans a database looking for records that match specified criteria. Relevant information in the records can be pulled out via the ODBC connector and fed into spreadsheets, a local Access database, or Word documents. Printing a mailer for clients about what the best buy options are for the coming two weeks could be as simple as printing a document that is automatically updated via these means.

Obviously, an Active Desktop can be a simple or a complex affair. Much of its potential relies on the willingness of a company to do custom development. Its potential, however, may in fact make resolving the security concerns surrounding its use very worthwhile. And Microsoft has provided you with a means for addressing such security issues in the design of the Internet Explorer.

Working with Internet Explorer Zones

Microsoft provides a security model for the Internet and intranets. It depends on the use of digital certificates. The provider of a site creates the certificate and registers it with a registration service. When a site sends you an ActiveX control object, for example, it presents your browser with a copy of the digital certificate for the object. This certificate usually links back to the registration service, so you can verify the integrity of the control by checking the credentials of the company providing the control. If the link does not hook back to the security service, check the links available, and consider carefully whether to accept the certificate.

This security model is very unlike that of a firewall, which typically applies several ways of separating the internal network from the external network and of filtering packets considered to be potentially dangerous. Often, information does not travel to the internal network unless it has been checked for viruses and other potential problems. Digital certificates depend on trusting a third party to vouch for the integrity of the party providing the certificate. No active filtering or checking of the elements is provided for download. As a result, most security managers prefer to use both the certificates and some form of a firewall to protect their networks. You need to remember that you have to trust the verifier of the digital certificate. Reports have circulated about some verifiers who were failing to do background checks before issuing certificates. Certificates remain, as a result, a situation of "buyer beware."

Microsoft's Internet Explorer divides the universe into four zones for applying security. You configure these zones by accessing the Security tab of the Internet properties sheet, which can be accessed from either its icon in the Control Panel or the View menu of the Internet Explorer. Microsoft names the zones as shown in Table 4.2, and provides the security options shown in the table as well.

Table 4.2. The Security Zones of the Internet Explorer.

	Restricted Internet Sites	*Trusted Intranet Sites*	*General Sites*
Definition	Sites you do not trust	Sites on Internet you trust	Sites on your completely internal network
Security Options	High, Medium, Low, Custom, ability to add sites	High, Medium, Low, Custom, ability to add sites	High, Medium, Low, Custom ability to add sites

Microsoft provides each of these zones with three default security settings, and the option of your defining your own security properties (see Figure 4.6). The Restricted Sites should have high set for security, preventing any kind of interaction with the site that could damage a computer. Of course, this level of security may prevent users from interacting with the site as the designers intended. These sites are ones that you need to access, but you would prefer to guard against. The best security information is often available at hacker sites, for example. You may need access to this information, but you may not want to allow that site the option of hacking away at your computer in return. For this zone, you need to click Add Sites and enter the URLs of the sites you want in this category.

Figure 4.6.
You have great control over the security settings associated with any zone.

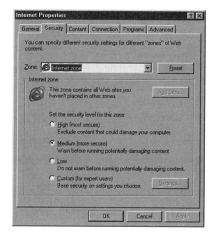

The Internet zone consists of any Internet site not on the list of Restricted Sites or Trusted Sites. By default, security is set to medium for these sites. Internet Explorer will warn the user before a potentially damaging interaction. The user is warned, for example, when a site attempts to download an ActiveX control. However, the user may agree to allow the action to take place. The responsibility for the consequences in this zone resides with the user.

The Trusted Sites by default receive low security. These are sites whose creators you trust completely. You allow them to download controls to your machines without challenge. You accept their certificates as valid by default. You should add very few sites to this list, and you should make certain that you can trust these sites completely. Even Microsoft has been known to distribute viruses by accident.

The intranet sites are local to your network. You can place sites in this zone by adding their URLs individually; however, the Add Sites button for this zone reveals three general categories that you can include. You must click on the Advance button in the Add Sites dialog box to add individual URLs. By default, all sites not listed in other zones are intranet sites, as are all sites that do not go through a proxy server. You can also include all UNC names used to access resources on the network. By default, these sites are assigned medium security. Microsoft's assumption is that even though these sites are local, your local network can contain damaging material. Consider a shared directory used by programmers to store work in progress. Some of these programs may contain code that could corrupt data. As a result, you need some level of warning even on your internal network.

Microsoft makes it possible for you to customize security setting by assigning custom security to any zone. When you click on the Settings button, you see the dialog box shown in Figure 4.8. This dialog box presents the Internet/intranet security options you can invoke. You can, for example, decide to allow ActiveX technology to run in a zone, but not Java technology. You can allow controls to run from the server side, but not the network side. When Microsoft says that custom settings are for expert users only, they mean that each choice has security implications. Mis-setting any security option could result in allowing unwanted access, in permitting a virus to be introduced, or in data being corrupted. You need to consider the implications of each of these settings carefully within each zone if you choose to set up custom security. You need not only to be an expert user, but also well versed in recent hacks that you need to protect against.

Wondering how to manage all these Internet settings remotely? See Chapter 15, "Configuring for Ease of Use," to see how to set up for remote administration.

Figure 4.7.

*Custom security
enables you to select
from many different
options.*

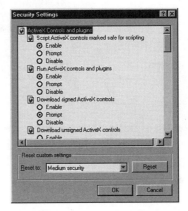

Summary

This chapter has focused on how you would deploy the Active Desktop. Issues covered in this chapter include choosing between the classic desktop and the Active Desktop, designing an Active Desktop for your firm, and considering security risks you incur with the Active Desktop, as well as what advantages you have with the Active Desktop. Finally, you have seen the security scheme that Microsoft employs with its Active Desktop technology.

On Your Own

Set up both a classic desktop and an Active Desktop. Try customizing the Active Desktop options by changing the click style, folder view, and icon display. Set up security zones for your desktop, and then try to violate the security constraints you have defined to see whether you can break through with an HTML page and cause a Web form to write data on the local drive.

II

Understanding the Windows 98 Architecture

5

Looking at the Core of the Operating System

Peter Norton®

When Windows 95 appeared, Microsoft introduced an entirely new core design for Windows. Instead of DOS down below and Windows the operating environment up above, Microsoft claimed to marry the two together. In his *Unauthorized Windows 95* (ISBN 1-56884-305-4), which came out before Windows 95 did, Andrew Schulman made a serious argument that Windows 95 really was DOS plus Windows, and that there had been no fundamental changes, except the recompiling of some components using a 32-bit compiler and the reallocation of memory into a 32-bit heap. Despite this argument, I think that Windows 95 represented a seriously different architecture, even if it was a DOS plus Windows architecture.

Windows 98 does not offer as radical a shift in operating system design. Instead, it represents an extension of the original concept, offering greater robustness and additional features. Many of the core elements remain the same. If you insist, you can still find a DOS/Windows dividing line. You still have the same basic features introduced in Windows 95. Windows 98 continues the use of virtual machines to isolate program address spaces from one another, helping to prevent one program from interfering with another. Windows 98 also does not rely on limited resource heaps, so you will not see Out of Memory errors when you know your machine has megabytes free. Windows 98 uses installable file systems to allow the operating system the option of reading file systems that we have not yet heard of. A driver for that new file system just installs like any other driver. You see compatibility with the 16-bit world, a primary feature for backward compatibility inherent in the design of Windows 95. In addition, you find that more of the core of the operating system, especially device drivers, relies on 32-bit protected mode operation.

Technical Note: By the year 2000, according to Microsoft, there will be only one version of Windows—Windows NT. As a result, most of the changes you see in Windows 98 are related to the process of merging the code base for Windows 95 with that of Windows NT. Various sources have described the future of Windows as being an operating system with several flavors: a personal version, a business desktop version, a small business server version, an enterprise server version, and so forth. All these versions will be built using the same APIs, and programs for them will be written using the same APIs. The central differences between the versions will be security and scalability.

This chapter aims to make you familiar with some of the subtle changes taking place in the design of Windows 98 operating system. Understanding these changes arms you to troubleshoot the operating system, as well as to plan the types of hardware and software you would prefer to use with it. This chapter covers the following topics:

- The design of the core services
- New hardware support
- New software support

Presenting the Core Services

To diagram the basic structures of Windows 98, you just copy the structural diagram of Windows 95. Basic structures are all the same (see Figure 5.1). The system relies on codes running at two privileged levels on the Intel processor, Ring 0 and Ring 3. Ring 0 code has complete access to the hardware. For Ring 3 code, the processor provides protection services, keeping processes separate from one another. At Ring 3, code must use Ring 0 services to interact with hardware and is limited as to where it might read and write in memory.

Technical Note: If you examine the Intel documentation for its processors, you will find a Ring 1 and a Ring 2 that represent varying balances between complete access to hardware and complete restriction from access to hardware. However, Windows 98 does not use Ring 1 or Ring 2, nor does Windows NT. The reason is that transitioning between ring states is a costly operation, requiring several CPU cycles. Such transitions would slow the system. The Microsoft designers decided to use only the ring states necessary to prevent unwanted performance penalties.

Figure 5.1.
Windows 98 has the same core architecture as Windows 95.

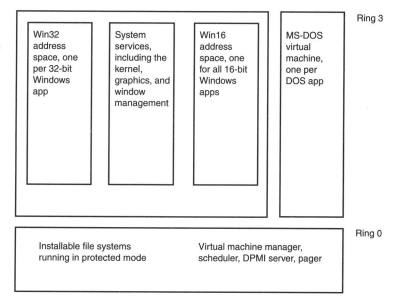

At Ring 0, you find the following kinds of system services, which make up the Windows 98 kernel:

- The Virtual Machine Manager (VMM), which builds and manages the virtual DOS machines where code runs at Ring 3

- The Pager, which swaps 4KB pages between memory and disk
- The Scheduler, which determines what thread to schedule next on the processor
- The DOS Protected Mode Interface server, which manages the use of extended memory by programs running under protected mode on the processor
- The file systems and Installable File System Manager (IFSM)

At Ring 3, code runs in Virtual DOS Machines (VDM), a service provided by the Intel processor since the 80386. A VDM really has little to do with DOS anymore; Windows NT makes use of this architecture as well, and it is as far from DOS as you can get in the Microsoft world. VDMs are processor-assisted entities. They virtualize the processor and memory services, convincing each application that it has its own computer to run on. They also identify barriers across which applications cannot cross, and they protect those barriers by conducting processor-level asserts. An *assert* tries out a memory operation to see whether a violation occurs. If the violation takes place, the operation is prevented from continuing. In this way, Windows 98 protects applications from one another when they run in separate VDMs.

Most applications, however, do not run in separate VDMs. In fact, if you run only Windows programs, you run only a single virtual machine, called the System Virtual Machine. Only when you run MS-DOS applications do you start a second virtual machine. The reasons should not surprise you. The System VM, using 32-bit device drivers, can virtualize the hardware for Windows programs; DOS programs, which cannot recognize 32-bit device drivers, need their own VDM in order to see the virtualized hardware services. In addition, to maintain compatibility with Windows 3.*x*, interprocess communication (IPC) mechanisms such as Dynamic Data Exchange (DDE), Windows applications—even Windows 98 applications—cannot cross the VDM barrier. If Windows applications ran in separate virtual machines, which they could, you could not conduct DDE conversations between applications, and your objects might not link and embed. By contrast, Windows NT implements these interprocess communication strategies across VDMs for 32-bit applications, which contributes to its robustness. However, even Windows NT cannot maintain such communication across the VDM barrier.

As a result, to protect Windows applications from one another, Microsoft relies on the system kernel, which provides services to intercept general protection faults, renamed by Microsoft as "illegal operations." Windows 98 also maintains memory padding between applications in the System VM so that they are less likely to trample on one another.

Each 32-bit Windows application is assigned its own address space. All 16-bit Windows applications share an address space. The memory padding between applications separates these address spaces so that they cannot conflict. The use of separate address spaces makes less likely events in which one application damages another and in which one 16-bit application damages other applications and the system.

Also in the System Virtual Machine are the major system services, formerly divided into three files—`user.exe`, `gdi.exe`, and `kernel.exe`—but now distributed among at least six files with similar names.

The user component represents routines that handle user interaction with the system using the keyboard, mouse, or other input devices. The GDI component represents the graphics device interface, which draws all the graphics elements on the screen. The kernel comprises high-level file system and network interactions, such as writing a file to a remote drive or reading a file from a CD. If you are wondering what the APIs so often mentioned are, these files represent the Win32 APIs that programs are built on. Other APIs call these functions to perform most of their work, and extend the functionality offered by these APIs to give programs additional features. When you pop up a context menu, you call a function in the user component that provides the context menu and its items. Knowing which components perform which actions can help you to diagnose what kinds of system-level file corruption you may be facing, for example.

Windows 98 does contain DOS-like components. To handle startup in real mode (the starting mode for all Intel processors), for example, you need some real-mode code to initiate the system load. However, after the system loads, real mode is left behind. The 16-bit services needed by 16-bit applications are provided in virtual 8086 mode, not real mode. As a result, Windows 98 avoids costly transitions to real mode when servicing real-mode programs and device drivers, improving system performance. Windows 95, because of its support of the 80386 processor, could not rely on virtual 8086 operating mode. As a result, to service real mode programs and device drivers, Windows 95 needed to execute a costly transition to real mode. The use of virtual 8086 mode under Windows 98 improves the operating system's speed.

The command prompt/graphical user interface dividing line is still present in Windows 98. However, the command prompt is your interface to the system kernel, not to DOS. Microsoft has not supported all debugging options under the graphical shell. If you need to exclude memory ranges from Windows 98's use, for example, you do so using switches on the command line that runs the graphical shell. (Type win /? at a command prompt to get a list of the switches.) This arrangement enables you to work with the kernel sans interference from the shell for really low-level troubleshooting. And you are dealing with an entirely 32-bit kernel. The only way to introduce 16-bit code into the kernel is to install a 16-bit device driver.

To get to the command prompt in Windows 98, you have four options. You can run the MS-DOS Prompt from Start | Programs, in which case you interact with the kernel through the windowing services of the graphical shell. If you want to boot to the command prompt, you can do so by pressing F8 immediately after the boot process begins (or hold down the Control key during the system test) and choosing Command Prompt Only from the menu that appears. In addition, in the TweakUI Control Panel applet, select the Boot tab and uncheck Start GUI automatically. Finally, you can edit the MSDOS.SYS file and change the BootGUI setting to equal 0.

When you are at the command prompt only without the GUI loaded, you can start the GUI by typing the command WIN. This action causes the graphical shell to load. The critical difference between Windows 98 and Windows NT is that Windows NT must load the graphical shell. You are not allowed an interface for direct communication with the kernel unless you set up for kernel debugging, in which case a separate computer hooks into the kernel and gives you command-line interaction with the remote kernel over a serial cable. Anyone who has attempted this type of inter-action with Windows NT would appreciate the direct command-line interface you have with Windows 98.

Microsoft insists that Windows 98 is more stable and robust than Windows 95. Most of the robust-ness claim involves the conversion of much 16-bit code to 32-bit code. The division between 16-bit and 32-bit code in the kernel is now limited to maintaining compatibility with 16-bit programs, for example. The 16-bit kernel is just a set of thunks that invoke 32-bit routines. All critical functions in the GDI have been written in 32-bit code. Only the graphics routines that must write into the client areas of 16-bit programs are retained as 16-bit code. Much of the user component has remained 16-bit, but these routines mainly service input devices, and remain as 16-bit code for compatibility with earlier Windows and DOS programs. Most of these routines are running in virtual 8086 mode so that they can be loaded into high memory and to avoid the transition to real mode to run them.

Technical Note: *Thunk* is a horrible sounding term with a curious history. Thunks have been in Windows since at least Windows 2.11. Because the Windows operating system optimizes memory usage by moving blocks of filled memory to maximize the size of free memory areas, a program cannot ever be quite sure where its code is. Under Windows 2.11, Windows maintained a table of code and data entry points, called the Burgermaster after a hamburger restaurant just down the street from the Microsoft campus. Windows always knew where in memory the Burgermaster was located. If an application needed to call code stored in memory, it did not actually call the code. Instead, it called a routine named a thunk (and I wish I knew the reason for the name) that called the Burgermaster. The Burgermaster would supply the address of the code and forward the call to that address to be completed.

In Windows 95, thunks were created to translate between 16-bit and 32-bit addresses. Older programs do not know how to understand 32-bit addresses. As a result, calling a memory address from a 16-bit program means having to translate between the 16-bit and 32-bit addressing schemes. In Windows 98, Windows NT, and almost any Microsoft program these days, thunks are address-translation routines of some kind.

Examining New Hardware Support

One of Microsoft's reasons for claiming greater robustness is a wide variety of support for new hard-ware. Rather than using software workarounds to implement functionality, newer computers will be using direct hardware support. With the hardware supporting the operating system more directly, operations are less likely to fail. One of the more important new options supported is large disk support.

Choosing the FAT32 File System

As you know, disk storage capacity has rapidly outstripped an operating system's capability to manage large storage capacities. For DOS to support a 1GB volume size, it must use a 32KB cluster size. Because a cluster is the minimum amount of storage allocated to write even a single byte file, the large cluster size inevitably leads to wasted space on hard drives. To deal with this issue, Microsoft created the FAT32 file system. It is one hardware option you definitely want to consider.

Looking at the Case For

Unfortunately, there is a case for and a case against using FAT32. Speed is simply not an issue. In most cases, you will not notice a speed difference. The real issues in favor of using FAT32 are the following:

- **Partition size.** FAT32 supports single disk partitions larger than 2GB in size. The actual upper limit is now irrelevant for your purposes—measured in terms of terabytes, petabytes, and exabytes—volumes so large that we don't have disks to support them yet.

- **Cluster size.** FAT16 reached a cluster size of 16KB with a volume size of 512MB. FAT32 does not reach a 16KB cluster size until you reach a volume size of 16GB. The 32KB cluster size does not become operative until the disk volume is greater than 32GB in size. For most average desktop disk installations, FAT32 uses a 4–8KB cluster size.

> **Warning:** If you are partitioning a new drive, fdisk makes default FAT32 disks of partitions over 512MB. It asks you whether you want to enable large volume support, not whether you want to use FAT32.

Looking at the Case Against

The case against using FAT32 may be formidable if you need to attend to these issues:

- Third-party disk management software might make a disk hang or pause for a long period of time during boot.

- No disk compression is available. Microsoft seems to have assumed that the reduction in cluster size was efficiency enough.

- Windows NT will not support FAT32 until version 5, which means dual-boot machines should stay with FAT16 for the boot partition. Other partitions may be formatted to FAT32, but these partitions will be as invisible to Windows NT 4.0 as NTFS volumes are to Windows 98.

- Generally, you lose the option to dual boot among a variety of operating systems if you want your entire boot drive to use FAT32. Linux, OS/2, and MS-DOS will not be able to understand the FAT32 partition.

- On laptops and power-efficient desktops, hibernation mode may cause you to lose data under FAT32. Microsoft warns you not to proceed unless you are absolutely sure your power management options will not interfere with FAT32. The test procedure is to enter hibernation mode, wake up the machine, and determine whether you can still read the FAT32 partition.

- You may lose the capability to run some 16-bit software. If you depend heavily on a business database programmed under a DOS RDBMS, you may be wise to stay with FAT16. To use FAT32, you must plan to be migrating to the latest versions of the programs you use.

After reviewing this list, if you have made the decision to convert, run Start | Programs | Accessories | System Tools | Drive Converter. A wizard steps you through the process. Remember, there is no converter to take you back to FAT16. Just so you know, all my Windows 98 machines are capable of hibernation, so I have not converted. The warning about data loss bothers me too much. Data loss has a way of appearing when you least expect it and when you least need it.

Tip: You can, of course, disable hibernation on the computer and then use FAT32 with relative safety. You need to be aware, however, that a moment's incaution relating to your configuration could cause a costly accident.

Supporting Multimedia

Multimedia support has become more important to Microsoft because of the emerging Internet and PC-based entertainment industry. Most of the improvements in Windows 98 multimedia support are deeply under the hood. Graphics functions in the SDK have been rewritten to take advantage of new technologies. From your point of view, if you have the hardware support on your chip sets, you have the new capability. Other features were available as enhancements for Windows 95, and with Windows 98 are installed automatically. The following are the key multimedia improvements Windows 98 supports:

- **MMX support.** Intel's MMX Pentium chips provide 57 new processor instructions that support multimedia sound, video, and graphics. In addition, processor data handling has been optimized to speed multimedia operations. To take advantage of this technology, make sure your Pentium has MMX support.

- **DirectShow and DirectX.** DirectX is a family of video functions that Microsoft created to attract game developers and multimedia developers to Windows. Originally, the concept was to provide for direct video writes to speed graphics-intensive applications. DirectShow, a part of DirectX, is a streaming video technology that supports playback of standard video-graphics files. DirectShow was formerly known as ActiveMovie; however, the ActiveMovie control, using DirectShow technology, still appears on the Entertainment submenu of the Accessories menu. Using this control, you can demonstrate DirectX technologies by playing any file format supported by DirectShow.

- **Accelerated graphics port.** This new type of video port, which promises improved graphics acceleration, has begun to appear on Pentium II and comparable clone PCs now. Most of us will not be using this technology for a year or more, given our PC purchasing plans. However, when we upgrade, we can use this new device to full advantage. The advanced graphics port is now available in its second generation; so as we upgrade machines, we can expect considerable performance improvement in our graphics displays.

Using the New Driver Model

With Windows 98, Microsoft introduced the Win32 Driver Model (WDM). Actually, what Microsoft did was merge the Windows NT Driver Model and the Windows 95 Driver Model in Windows 98. The goal of this model is for Windows, whatever flavor, to provide a uniform interface to devices, and for drivers to translate that interface for the particular device. Drivers written for one version automatically work in the other version. Many analysts feel this was a move to increase the pool of Windows NT drivers available. For the Windows 98 community, the new driver model means that device drivers are easier to create and debug. We can expect better device support from all vendors.

The drivers now follow the universal/mini driver model. Because of the standard interface to all such devices provided by the universal driver, the Windows Driver Model improves stability of applications using the device. The universal driver also virtualizes, convincing each application that it has full control of the device, improving the capability to share the driver among multiple applications. In Windows 98, the implementation of this model maintains compatibility with earlier drivers, and the default action is not to update drivers during installation unless the changes are so significant as to require the update. Significance, in this case, is a matter of Microsoft's opinion. During the beta cycle, I have had to update drivers for CD-ROMs, display adapters, and SCSI cards over those left in place by Microsoft. As a result, a clean install may give you much different characteristics than an upgrade install.

Here are some of the new technologies to which these drivers provide access:

- **Universal Serial Bus devices.** The advantage of the new Universal Serial Bus (USB) is that it gets around the problems associated with interrupt requests in the current Intel architecture. Adding serial devices becomes a bit like adding SCSI devices. You add one onto the bus and it configures. The bus can accept up to 127 devices, and it operates at speeds well beyond what traditional serial ports can handle. Not many such devices are available yet. USB monitors, hubs, speakers, and sound systems are available. The bus has cameras, both still and full motion, as well as input devices available.

- **Human Input Devices (HID).** Surprisingly, Human Input Devices are just keyboards, mice, and alternatives to keyboards and mice. They attach, however, to your computer using different connectors and are built according to the Human Input Device standard, providing improved support for multiple devices on a single machine, because they attach through the USB.

- **IEEE 1394 Bus (Firewire) devices.** The IEEE 1394 bus provides support for 200Mbps communication between host and peripheral. If you have one of these adapters, you are supporting high-speed streaming input. The only devices currently available are video cameras and digital cameras, but additional devices will appear.

- **Digital Video Discs and the UDF File System.** Digital Video Discs (DVD) promise to bring incredible densities to the standard 5.25-inch CD. Entire movies fit on the smaller form factor. These devices offer realistic streaming video playback, as well as quality (AC3 Dolby Digital) sound. The Universal Disk File System (UDF) is the read-only file system used for DVD disks. Windows 98 includes an installable file-system driver for it.

Working with PCMCIA Cards

Support for the PCMCIA card, also known as the PC Card, has improved in Windows 98. The following are the critical enhancements:

- **PC Card32 support.** The PC Card32 bus allows 32-bit drivers to support this small form factor. The principal advantage is the capability to deliver high-speed networking through a PC Card adapter.

- **3.3 volt support.** PC Cards can now function on as little as 3.3 volts of power, offering manufacturers the chance to improve battery life by reducing power demands for laptop peripherals.

- **Multifunction card support.** Multifunction cards have been available for some time, but Windows 98 allows the different functions (for example, LAN and modem) to be configured separately. The separate functionalities can also be enabled and disabled independently.

Using Infrared Data Association

Windows 98 includes support for the Infrared Data Association (IrDA) standard version 2.0. Included are device drivers for both Fast Infrared (FIR) and Serial Infrared (SIR) devices. In addition, the Fast Infrared Protocol is included, supporting infrared communication with devices connected to a LAN and serving as a LAN adapter. Windows 98 users with infrared devices on their laptops or handhelds can easily connect with other infrared devices, such as printers and LAN adapters. Information-transfer options using IrDA devices are wider with the Windows 98 operating system.

(IrDA was included with the OEM2 version of Windows 95, and it is available as a download from Microsoft for current Windows 95 users.)

Implementing Power Management

Three new power management features have also been included in Windows 98. The most important is support for the Advanced Configuration and Power Interface version 1.2. Under this standard, applications can respond to the power state of their devices. One example of what applications might do if the system is powering down is prompt users to save. Applications could shift processing of disk-intensive data to a RAM disk, for example, when battery power is engaged, and return to hard disk processing when line power is available.

In addition, the battery metering capabilities are more accurate, and two batteries can be monitored simultaneously. A Suspend option can be displayed on the Start menu, giving users easy access to sending their systems into hibernation. PC Card modems can be completely powered down when not in use, and resume power either when accessed by the user or when the phone line rings. Because even wake on ring is supported while the machine is suspended, for example, only enough of the machine must be powered up to receive a fax.

Examining New Software Support

New software support in Windows 98 is also very behind the scenes. The operating system is capable of executing faster shutdowns because the shutdown functions have been optimized for speed, as have the Registry-access functions. Because Registry access is faster, applications also spend less time loading and configuring on-the-fly. Fewer clock ticks are spent on finding out how applications are configured, changing configuration settings, identifying ActiveX components to load, and determining the configuration of ActiveX components.

Furthermore, the graphics library has been optimized for speed, so the GDI can draw to the screen and to the printer more efficiently. The 32-bit spooler now also optimizes its throughput, placing less of a drag on background processing.

One problem that Windows has had historically is the liberal use of the Reset or Power buttons. Under Windows 3.x, improperly powering down could cause some problems. Under Windows 95, those problems magnified into nightmares. Files are open, the Registry is open, and corruption of the file system can easily happen without a proper shutdown. Windows 98 attacks this strategy by setting a flag that must be unset during proper shutdown. The operating system can tell whether it is recovering from an improper shutdown, and runs nongraphical ScanDisk automatically on boot to repair possible errors during the boot sequence. (This feature was introduced in the OEM2 version of Windows 95.)

Scheduling and scripting were also problems in previous versions of Windows. Without the Plus! Pack in Windows 95, you had no scheduler. Scheduling is integrated into Windows 98 as a part of the system. It works identically to Windows 95, except you cannot schedule the backup application. If you properly set up the user environment, however, you have less need to be concerned about losing data. So long as your users keep their data in the My Documents folder on their desktops, their data is automatically backed up to the server, so long as the user logs on to a Windows NT domain account or to a NetWare server or directory tree. When users use server accounts to log on, their profile is saved on exit to the server. In a Windows NT domain, the profile appears in the user's home directory. On a NetWare server, the profile goes in the user's mail directory.

Warning: Although the automated backup of user data might make you feel comfortable, it is not an excuse for not backing systems up. Data loss always occurs when we do not rely on multiply redundant backup strategies. The only good solution is to back up data in multiple ways so that you don't lose data.

Note: The Windows 98 and Windows NT user profiles can never be mistaken. The Windows 98 profile is stored in the user's home directory. The Windows NT profile is stored in the user's Windows NT profile path. Both can be set using the User Manager for Domains on a Windows NT server.

Scripting has become simpler under Windows 98. First, on the CD in the Tools folder are some command-line tools that resolve problematic issues. WinSet, for example, sets profile strings on the local computer when run from the server. TimeThis determines the length of time it takes to execute a command or batch file. WaitFor enables you to wait for user input or a result before continuing the execution of the script. However, you can use the Windows Scripting Host to use any standard scripting language to create scripts. With VBScript, JavaScript, or Perl, you can script just about anything you would like.

The Windows Scripting Host is described in Chapter 15, "Configuring for Ease of Use."

Summary

Windows 98 has much new functionality and much that is the same as Windows 95. This chapter has described the architecture underlying Windows 98, what is new and what is not. It has also covered the new hardware devices supported, as well as new software support.

On Your Own

Review the industry press to determine the release status of the latest hardware devices. Review your needs to determine how you might take advantage of these devices. Locate a demo machine with a USB interface, and try out the components that are available. Compare the Windows 98 architecture with the Windows NT Workstation architecture (see *Peter Norton's Complete Guide to Windows NT 4 Workstation*) to determine which is better for your desktop environment.

6

Understanding the LAN Connection

Peter Norton®

One of the major reasons that Windows 3.0 finally attracted business users was its "LAN awareness." The previous version of Windows, version 2.11, could be networked, but was genuinely unaware of the network communication going on beneath the GUI. That was the responsibility of the underlying operating system, DOS, and DOS had never been designed with networking in mind. Network managers ran into frequent problems getting Windows, as an operating environment, to communicate with DOS-based network clients.

Windows 3.0 resolved many of these difficulties by providing network awareness in the API functions that comprise Windows. Windows 3.1, and finally 3.11, enhanced the awareness, finally making the Redirector, which connects the client computer to the server, a component of Windows. Windows 95 further increased this awareness, making the entire network client a 32-bit component of Windows. Windows 98 consolidates and expands the integration of the client by providing additional services for communication with the latest network protocols.

Understanding how Windows 98 communicates with a network helps you to approach installation and troubleshooting of networked software with confidence. You can conceptually isolate different components, and devise strategies for telling whether you have an application problem, a network problem, or a Windows 98 problem. To explain the Windows 98 architecture, this chapter covers the following topics:

- Basic network architecture
- Available network clients
- Network management tools

Understanding the Basic Network Architecture

 A network is two or more computers connected together by using a cable so that they may send signals to one another across the cable. At each end of the cable is a transceiver, so that each computer can transmit and receive. These machines could use any code to communicate; ever since the first cables for a network were laid at the Xerox Palo Alto Research Center, however, standards have evolved to describe how computers communicate across a network.

One of these standards is Ethernet, created by Bob Metcalf at Xerox, who later founded 3Com. Another is Token Ring, developed by IBM. The standards associated with these technologies were created by the Institute of Electrical and Electronic Engineers (IEEE) through a committee that first met in February 1980. This was therefore named the 802 committee. The standard description of Ethernet is known as standard 802.3, and the standard for Token Ring is standard 802.5.

The concept of networked data communications is described by a model known as the Open Systems Interconnect (OSI) model. It was a standard developed by the International Standardization

Organization (ISO) and advanced by several standards-making bodies. However, the most popular networking software does not actually implement the OSI model. As a result, it is known as the OSI Reference Model, because it is the standard against which all other standards were defined.

The OSI Model

The OSI model is diagrammed in Figure 6.1. It presents a layered approach to designing network operating systems, describing how communication takes place between applications and the physical apparatus of the network. Each layer carries out a specific function, and provides a well-defined interface to the layer above and to the layer below. In addition, each layer defines an interface to the equivalent layer running on another machine. Although communication with that equivalent layer may require the services of other layers, the layer interfacing with its equivalent is not aware of those additional services. They are encapsulated in the interfaces defined, so you have a virtual circuit from layer to equivalent layer on any two machines engaging in networked communication.

Figure 6.1.
The OSI Reference Model describes the fundamental processes of network data communication.

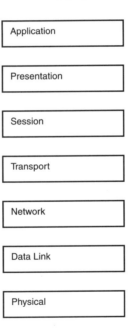

As a result, network designers can substitute in any component at any layer, so long as the interfaces are maintained consistently. The internals of the component can change, but it must communicate vertically and horizontally among the layers just like any other component does. This feature of the model was intended to make it extensible and adaptable. You can extend any layer to accommodate new hardware or software by adding components that handle the particular hardware or software. You can adapt a network to changing conditions by rewriting the internals of any component.

The layers of the OSI model, and their specific functionality, are the following:

- **Application.** Although its name implies so, this layer does not represent applications. It represents services that applications can use to communicate with the network. Functions for sending email, accessing databases, communicating with the server or client portion of a program, and similar activities reside in this layer. Typically, these components represent the APIs for building network awareness into a program. On receipt of information from the Presentation layer, the Application layer passes the information to an appropriate application.

- **Presentation.** This layer focuses on data representation. If translation between one standard code used by the application maintaining the data and another standard code used by the network for communication must take place, that translation occurs at this layer. Data encryption, if it is in use, also occurs at this layer. The Presentation layer, on receipt of information from the Session layer, reverses the encryption and code translation process.

- **Session.** Session layer components focus on establishing, maintaining, and closing connections between two computers. To carry out a communication session with a server, for example, a client must first request a session. Once granted a session, the two communicate using the session's services. Finally, one of the computers must initiate the close of the session. Functions to carry out these activities are included in this layer. On receipt of information from the Transport layer, the Session layer passes it up to the Presentation layer.

- **Transport.** The Transport layer focuses on error recognition and recovery. It calculates checksums and attaches them to the data. On receipt of a packet, it recalculates the checksum and compares the new calculation to the attached checksum. If the two don't match, the Transport layer requests retransmission of the packet. The Transport layer also initiates breaking the data up into transmittable units that can be reassembled into the message at the other end. On receipt of a packet from the Network layer, the Transport layer checks for errors and sequences the data as a part of the incoming message. The message is then handed to the Session layer.

- **Network.** At the Network layer, the primary issue is addressing, routing, and relaying information. Source and destination addresses are placed on the packet, and any routing information necessary is included. On receipt of a packet from the Data Link layer, the Network layer strips addressing information and hands the packet to the Transport layer.

- **Data Link.** The Data Link layer packs frames, the formal name for the transmittable packet. It adds the final wrapper for a chunk of data and hands that chunk off to the Physical layer for transmission. On receipt of a frame from the Physical layer, the Data Link layer strips the wrapper off and hands the packet off to the Network layer.

- **Physical.** This layer constitutes the physical equipment associated with networked communication—the cards, cables, routers, repeaters, connectors, and so forth. This layer attends to the transmission and receipt of bits of information.

Note: In creating its standards, the IEEE decided that the Data Link layer encompassed too much. As a result, it split the layer into the Logical Link Control layer (LLC) and the Media Access Control layer (MAC).

The Windows 98 Version of OSI

Microsoft, like most network operating system developers, has not implemented the full OSI model in any of its operating systems. In fact, before Windows 98, each Microsoft operating system had a different network architecture. With the advent of this version of Windows, the networking architecture for the current releases of Microsoft products is the same. Windows NT 5.0 has even been called a superset of Windows 98.

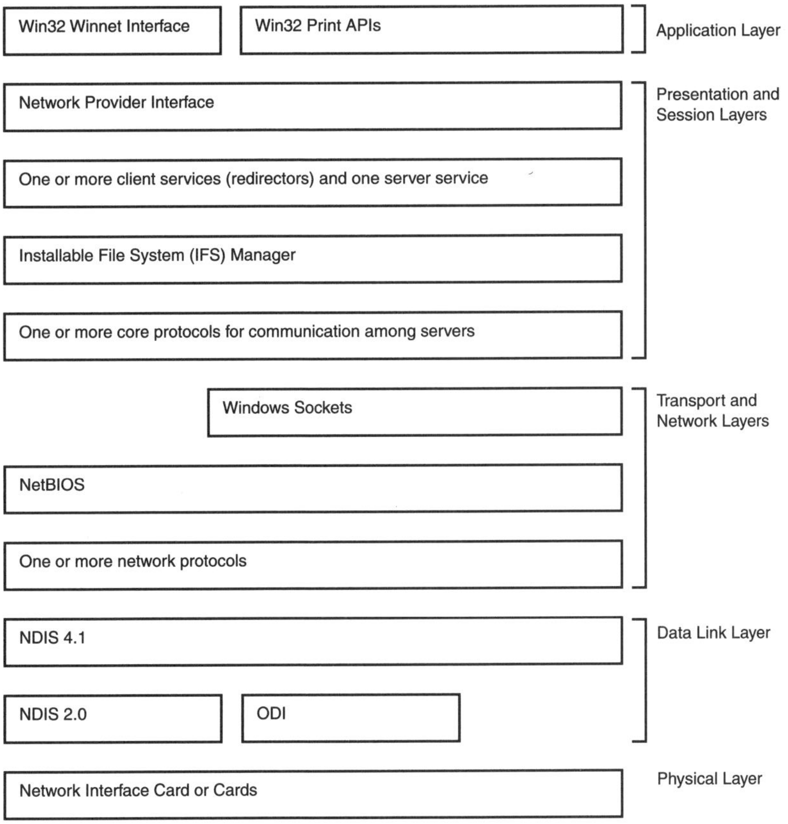

Figure 6.2.
Microsoft has used a modification of the OSI model in designing Windows 98 networking.

Win32 Winnet Interface	Win32 Print APIs

Application Layer

Network Provider Interface

Presentation and Session Layers

One or more client services (redirectors) and one server service

Installable File System (IFS) Manager

One or more core protocols for communication among servers

Windows Sockets

Transport and Network Layers

NetBIOS

One or more network protocols

NDIS 4.1

Data Link Layer

NDIS 2.0	ODI

Network Interface Card or Cards

Physical Layer

The layers in the Windows 98 network architecture, diagrammed in Figure 6.2 with their OSI/IEEE equivalents listed, are the following:

- **API Layer.** The Application, Presentation, and Session layers are combined into a single layer in Windows 98. At this layer, the client service(s), the server service, and the application interfaces reside. You may have more than one client installed. So long as they are 32-bit clients, Windows 98 can multiplex them effectively (or make certain that communication from layers above is matched with the correct client). You may have one server service, called File and Printer Sharing in Windows 98, installed. And you may have any number of application interfaces installed. Typical ones are the Messaging API, Telephony API, and Winnet API. The network APIs allow applications to communicate with various services provided by the network—sending email, for example. These APIs communicate with the Network Provider Interface, which provides a uniform interface to the client services and server service you have elected to install. This interface translates from its uniform interface to the vendor-specific interface of each client or server service.

- **Protocol Layer.** At the top of the Protocol Layer is a component called the Installable File System Manager (IFSM). Its job is to provide a uniform interface to transport protocols. As a result, applications do not need to be written to use the unique interface of each protocol you have installed. They communicate with IFSM, and IFSM translates and hands off the communication to the appropriate protocol, enabling you to install multiple protocols. The protocols reside below IFSM, and they communicate with a uniform interface to the network cards provided by the Network Device Interface Standard (NDIS). Microsoft uses two services to communicate from the protocols to the NDIS interface: NetBIOS and Windows Sockets. NetBIOS is the set of functions defined by the NetBEUI protocol, and Sockets is a TCP/IP stack that provides a means of connectivity across the network. For Sockets to communicate with Microsoft Server services, which use NetBEUI services for their basic communication, the Sockets stack must use some of the services provided by NetBEUI.

- **NDIS Layer.** The NDIS Layer provides a unit of software called the NDIS wrapper, which provides a uniform interface to the network cards for the layer above, and also provides a uniform interface to card drivers supplied by manufacturers. As a result, the drivers that manufacturers must write are smaller and more efficient.

- **Physical Layer.** The network interface cards represent the Physical Layer to the Windows 98 network. The cards communicate with the OS software via their drivers, and the NDIS Layer immediately above can multiplex communication with multiple cards. Windows 98 computers can therefore be connected to several physical networks via multiple interface cards.

Note: If you want your computer to function as a router, you must install the Routing Information Protocol (RIP), provided on the CD. You should be clear in your intentions if you enable routing on a Windows 98 computer. Enabling routing has implications for general network architecture, and will affect how you configure Windows NT hosts, UNIX hosts, NetWare hosts, and dedicated routers on your network.

In the Windows 98 network architecture, the key elements are the clients and the transport protocols. Clients provide the capability to access remote resources, and the capability to redirect file system and other function calls out to the appropriate share resource destinations on the network. As a result, clients are often called redirectors. Microsoft and other vendors supply enough 32-bit, protected-mode clients that you should not have to resort to 16-bit, real-mode clients to access any network. Microsoft provides a client for Microsoft networks and a client for Novell networks. If you do need real-mode networking, however, the architecture still enables you to install a single 16-bit client, just as real-mode device drivers are still supported. If you have DOS applications that cannot communicate with a network except via a 16-bit client, you have this fallback.

Protocols are just agreed-upon methods of communicating across a network. They describe how to format packets, how to address packets, and how to assemble packets into messages, as well as provide services for error correction. Windows 98 provides the following four protocols:

- **NetBIOS Extended User Interface (NetBEUI)**, which has been Microsoft's traditional protocol for networking. Unfortunately this protocol is broadcast oriented, so it consumes network bandwidth unreasonably as your network grows larger. If you can avoid this protocol on large networks, you avoid the traffic problem it creates. NetBEUI cannot be used with routers because it is not a routable protocol. You need to realize that NetBEUI is a protocol for managing network communication, and NetBIOS is the API for communicating between application and NetBEUI. If you have a protocol—any protocol—that is NetBIOS enabled, you can avoid installing NetBEUI. You can enable NetBIOS over both IPX/SPX and TCP/IP if you wish.

Tip: NetBEUI is no longer required if you wish to use the Network Neighborhood for browsing. Microsoft has included the NetBIOS over TCP/IP component in Windows 98. Dropping NetBEUI from the protocols you have installed reduces broadcast traffic to a certain extent and reduces the overhead tied up in network communication.

- **Internet Packet Exchange/Sequenced Packet Exchange (IPX/SPX)**, originally created by Novell, but written in this 32-bit, Novell-compatible version by Microsoft (known as NWLink). This protocol provides connectivity with Novell servers and clients on your network. Because it is largely self-configuring, it is easy to set up and configure. It is also reasonably efficient, avoiding broadcasts for most purposes. You can avoid using this protocol, however, if your Novell servers are running TCP/IP. NWLink can be used with routers.

- **Transmission Control Protocol/Internet Protocol (TCP/IP)**, which forms the backbone of the Internet and is used on most networks these days. TCP/IP provides a logical addressing scheme that you can manipulate to control traffic on your network. It also provides a host of utilities for file transfer, Web communication, and diagnostics. It is a complicated protocol to set up; however, it provides excellent communication on both WANs and LANs. It is well worth the trouble, and it routes. If you are concerned about setting up IP addresses on a small, private network, don't be. Windows 98 supports automatic private addressing. Set your clients to obtain IP addresses from a DHCP (Dynamic Host Configuration Protocol) server. If no server is present, they will assign themselves addresses from the 10 network, which is a class A IP address that cannot be routed over the Internet and is always available for private addressing. For more information, see *Teach Yourself TCP/IP in 14 Days*, *TCP/IP Blueprints*, or *TCP/IP Unleashed*, all from Sams Publishing. From an administrator perspective on the Windows platform, you may particularly want to look at *Networking with Microsoft TCP/IP* from New Riders.

- **Data Link Control (DLC)**, which governs communication with IBM mainframe computers and older network printers. Microsoft has provided a 32-bit version and a 16-bit version of this protocol. When possible, use the 32-bit version if your connectivity software allows it. Fewer and fewer devices require the protocol. As a result, you can probably avoid implementing this protocol.

Using Windows Sockets

Everyone talks about sockets, but nobody ever explains sockets. Under the TCP/IP protocol, TCP provides 65,532 possible session connection points to any connecting computer. These connection points are called ports. Some of these ports have well-defined, agreed-upon uses, and are called well-defined ports. If you connect to an FTP server, for example, by convention you connect to port 21 on the server computer. The port number identifies both the session to the server computer and a writable address for the client computer. The FTP software on the server monitors port 21 for incoming information. The FTP software on the client computer writes information to port 21 on the server computer.

Knowing the port number, however, does you little good if you are a client that wants to write a file to the FTP server. You need a channel that uniquely identifies both the server computer and the session on the computer that you wish to write to. To uniquely identify the destination computer and the port to write to, you bind the IP address of the server and the port number into a unit called a socket. When your FTP program writes to the socket, the information it writes goes to the correct IP address and port number. Having an IP address is like knowing a telephone number to a large corporate switchboard. Having a port number is like knowing the extension of the telephone you need to reach after you hit the main switchboard. Binding the two into a socket is like having advanced speed dial that can go straight through a switchboard to an extension in one quick move.

The Windows Sockets interface has been updated for Windows 98. It supports a wider range of third-party utilities that rely on the Sockets interface, such as proprietary online service software and third-party Web browsers. You may remember the accusations that flew in the early days of the Windows 95 release regarding the Sockets stack. The Sockets interface, originally created for the Berkeley Standard Distribution of UNIX, was never fully standardized. As a result, the sockets stacks built by different parties were never quite the same. The Windows 95 Sockets stack seemed to conflict with everyone else's sockets application, or so the claims went.

Windows 98 Sockets resolve these issues. The `Winsock.dll` file provides a widely supported means of implementing the Sockets interface. Microsoft, especially since its push toward the Internet, has embraced this standard.

Using NDIS and ATM

NDIS, as implemented in Windows 98, still provides a protocol interface and a driver interface. In version 4.1, however, it adds a few new features. First, it supports Plug and Play more effectively. Second, it provides support for Asynchronous Transfer Mode (ATM) network adapters. Finally, it provides a new driver model. The network drivers for Windows 98 are binary compatible with those for Windows NT. As a result, with the release of Windows 98, Microsoft will drastically increase the number of drivers available for Windows NT.

Implementing the Distributed Common Object Model

In the past, we would tout the OLE option of Windows. After that, we touted Network OLE, and then the Common Object Model (COM), and now, with Windows 98, the Distributed Common Object Model. From your point of view, there is little to know or care about in relation to DCOM. It is buried in the operating system internals, and its actual architecture is relevant only to software developers.

What is relevant to you is that DCOM so suffuses the Windows 98 architecture that you can use its most visible form, ActiveX controls, anywhere you want to extend the functionality of Windows 98. These controls can serve either as containers for data or as containers for applications. They can manage links from data sources anywhere on your network, or they can manage the embedding of data without links in any document. These controls can go on the desktop, on HTML pages, and in system-browsing windows. You can script your interaction with these controls and automate their behavior using the Windows Scripting Host. The presence of DCOM means, quite simply, that the ability to extend Windows functionality is in your hands. You can make this operating system do what you want it to.

Controlling Networked Configurations

Microsoft has included two types of network control information in the Registry for Windows 98. First, the Registry supports the Internet Engineering Task Force's Management Information Block (MIB). Actually, it supports MIB-II, the latest generation of the standard. In addition, the Registry supports the Desktop Management Interface (DMI), created by the Desktop Management Task Force. Both of these standards allow client computers to communicate information about their configuration to servers on the network. As a result, network control software such as Microsoft Systems Management Server (SMS), Intel LanDesk, HP OpenView, IBM Tivoli, and others can interact with Windows 98 to report information back to the network control interface. You can monitor the condition of your network systems from the network control software.

To use either of these capabilities, you must use the agent that communicates with the central network manager. The DMI agent is included with Windows 98. The Simple Network Management Protocol (SNMP) agent is included in the Windows 98 Resource Kit Sampler. To install this agent, double-click on its INF file. The default action when you open an INF file is to initiate installation.

Summary

This chapter has focused on basic network architecture. You have reviewed the OSI model and seen how Windows 98 implements features of this overarching model of network communications. You have also reviewed the available network clients provided by Windows 98, as well as the network management tool support included with the operating system.

On Your Own

Scan the properties for the Network Neighborhood to get a sense of what networking components you are using and how they relate to the network architecture presented in this chapter. Review which clients you have used in the past, and see which ones can be upgraded to 32-bit, protected-mode clients. Try installing the SNMP agent. If you have a network management software package, use it to connect to a Windows 98 computer to see what support the DMI and SNMP agents provide you. Try removing a client or protocol from the list of installed options to see what you can still access over the network.

7

Working with the WAN Connection

Peter Norton®

Wide area networking (WAN) is an important topic to more world citizens than ever before. With the popularity of the Internet, individual households engage in WAN links without even realizing it. We all just think about it as dialing out with a modem. In reality, we connect to a vast WAN infrastructure that few of us understand well, if at all.

WANs are important to the smallest of businesses because WANs are how business is done today. Launching a product? You need a Web page. Selling services? You need a Web page. Fewer fingers walk through the Yellow Pages because more fingers are surfing the Internet to find the same information. How easily, for example, could you locate in a library up-to-date Business to Business Yellow Pages for the five top cities in your marketing region? The answer in my area is that you can't. You would be lucky to find directories that were only three years old.

Your organization needs a WAN, even if a simple one. To understand how Windows 98 interacts with WANs, this chapter covers the following topics:

- Basic WAN architecture
- The Windows 98 WAN architecture
- Windows 98 WAN technologies

Reviewing Basic WAN Architecture

The simplest, most practical definition of a WAN that I know is data communication between widely separate locations using the available means of cabling and exceeding lengths supported by traditional LAN cabling methods. At the sending end, you need some sort of connector to the cable system. At the receiving end, you need some sort of connector to the cabling system. The connector can be as simple as a modem using a plain old telephone system (POTS) line, or, with the advent of Direct PC, it can be as complicated as a satellite earth station. For cabling we must accept a very loose definition. We could be using microwave transmission.

A very common WAN architecture is diagrammed in Figure 7.1. The outward connection is through a router, as is the inbound connection. Communication takes place over some sort of telephone line. This could be a 56Kbps line, an ISDN line, a T1 line, or a T3 line. The cabling is supplied by some sort of a service provider, as often is the connection point at either end. Data communication takes place via routable network protocols.

Figure 7.1.
*A very common
WAN architecture.*

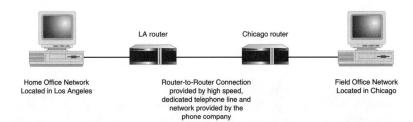

Home Office Network
Located in Los Angeles

LA router

Router-to-Router Connection
provided by high speed,
dedicated telephone line and
network provided by the
phone company

Chicago router

Field Office Network
Located in Chicago

Examining the Windows 98 WAN Architecture

The actual network architecture for wide area networking in Windows 98 does not change from that provided in Windows 95. The basic stack of components is the same from top to bottom. Where the differences come are three specific places: above the Application layer, where you run different software components to manage WAN connections; at the Physical layer, you may or may not run additional hardware to support your WAN links; and at the Protocol layer, depending on the type of WAN link you are using, you may run additional protocols. We will start our look at these issues with hardware, and then move on to protocols, and end with the software that handles WAN connections.

The most common WAN connection scenario for Windows 98 involves using Dial-Up Networking in some form to connect to the Internet. When you use Dial-Up Networking, you are generally creating a WAN situation because you are dialing outward over some sort of telephone network to connect to a remote host. When you click on your Web browser to connect to `www.microsoft.com`, you are telling Windows 98 to cross the WAN and get some information for you. Windows 98 translates this action into invoking Dial-Up Networking to access the external network. Either Dial-Up Networking dials out over the modem and creates the link, or detects that an Internet connection is already available, either through the LAN or through a previously dialed but not disconnected link, and makes the connection to the Web site.

Looking at WAN Hardware

To run a WAN connection, you may not need additional hardware. You may connect using a standard modem and a POTS line. Or you may connect to the WAN via a router, so all a workstation needs to link to the WAN is a standard network interface card. WAN connections that link an entire LAN usually require a router, and a firewall or proxy server to protect the LAN from intrusion. To connect an individual computer directly to a WAN line, you need appropriate hardware at that computer. If you intend to use an ISDN line, you need an ISDN adapter for the computer. From Windows 98's point of view, the only change is that you have an additional piece of hardware at the hardware layer and an additional driver at the NDIS layer. The remainder of the protocol stack can use the WAN connection as long as these two additions are made.

Choosing Your WAN Protocols

To communicate over a LAN, you need to use a routable protocol. That is, the protocol needs definite, unique addresses for the computers on your network and the devices that connect to the WAN. These addresses can be collected into a table that maps the route from the communicating device to the next link in the communication chain. Specifying the default gateway when you set up TCP/IP on a computer is an example of providing primitive routing information. The default gateway address is where the computer sends packets that need to travel to an address that can only be identified as not being on the local segment. The computer knows that it cannot locate the address, but that the default gateway (a router, actually) will be able to at least send the packet to the next router in the communication chain, and eventually some router will be able to deliver the packet to an appropriate network segment.

The routable protocols included with Windows 98 are TCP/IP and IPX/SPX (remember NWLink, as Microsoft has applied it). Either one can function over a WAN, but TCP/IP and its related protocols are preferred, mainly because they are the protocol the Internet is based on. In my experience, TCP/IP is the most robust routable protocol available. Even Novell, which created IPX/SPX, has shifted to supporting TCP/IP on its servers.

Additional protocols can be important to WANs. One is the Data Link Control protocol (DLC), which is used to communicate with IBM mainframes. For Windows 98, Microsoft wrote a 32-bit, protected-mode version of this protocol. Its advantages are greater reliability and greater speed. You have no transition to real mode when the protocol is active. This version can handle both 16-bit and 32-bit DLC terminal emulation programs. It conforms to the NDIS 3.1 standard. You might also use this protocol to connect to network printers that require it.

Point-to-Point Protocol (PPP) and Serial Line Internet Protocol (SLIP) may be important to your WAN operation. Both of these are used to negotiate dial-up connections. SLIP is the older, slower protocol with less device support. However, some of your clients may have to use SLIP because they do not support PPP. PPP is the faster, more robust protocol. As a result, it is preferred for negotiating dial-up connections. If you can avoid using SLIP, do. PPP provides you better connectivity in dial-up situations.

The other protocol you may choose to use is Point-to-Point Tunneling Protocol (PPTP). PPTP enables you to create virtual private networks. Imagine having your own private tunnel from one point on the Internet to another. Through that tunnel, you can send any packet you want. Other users on the Internet can intercept your packets, but they have to decrypt them to read their contents, a less-than-likely event. But at the other end of your tunnel, the packets unload onto another LAN in your organization, where they can be used normally for LAN communication.

Essentially, a virtual private network with PPTP builds such a tunnel between two LANs. You ship packets back and forth enclosed in a PPTP wrapper with the ferried packet encrypted inside. One computer at the sending end is responsible for wrapping the packets, and one at the other end is responsible for unwrapping the packets. You borrow the Internet infrastructure rather than purchase a high-speed phone line at $1,000 per month to service your private connection needs.

To support virtual private networks, Windows 98 includes a dial-up adapter called the Microsoft Virtual Private Network adapter. It installs just like the dial-up adapter and has similar properties. But rather than setting a dial-up connection to use a modem, you select the VPN adapter in the modem drop-down list instead. You configure the properties to point to the IP address of the computer on your distant LAN that is to receive the packets. (You can use WINS, DNS, LMHosts files, or Hosts files to resolve a domain name to the address.) You can then dial your ISP and connect to the Internet. Your tunneled packets will be directed to their gateway and be addressed for the Virtual Private Network adapter on the other machine.

Exploiting a WAN Connection

After you have established your WAN connection, you can begin to make use of it. If you are directly connected via a firewall to the Internet or to a telephone connection that links your networks directly, you have immediate access through your WAN networking protocol, usually TCP/IP. You open your browser or your Network Neighborhood, and you should have access to the resources provided by the WAN link. Often, however, you use dial-up connections to establish remote WAN sessions. Windows 98 makes using Dial-Up Networking easier.

Using Dial-Up Networks

No matter how you want to dial into a WAN, Windows 98 provides support for doing so. The basic software for managing such connections is the Dial-Up Networking connection. To create any type of dial-up connection, select Start | Programs | Accessories | Communication | Dial-Up Networking. You open a folder that contains the Make New Connection icon and your existing connections. To create a connection, open the New Connection icon. The Make New Connection Wizard, shown in Figure 7.2, guides you through the process of creating the connection.

Figure 7.2.
The Make New Connection Wizard guides you through setting phone numbers and dialing options for a connection.

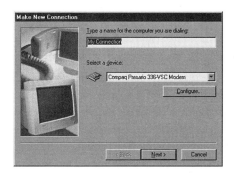

After you have filled in the name of the connection, the name of the modem to use, and used the Configure button to set the phone number to dial, an icon for the connection appears in the Dial-Up Networking folder. Unless you specifically choose to configure your modem by clicking on the Configure button, the wizard accepts your default modem configuration. To use the connection, double-click it.

Using the Internet Connection Wizard

Dialing up or directly connecting to the Internet can require extra configuration. Microsoft helps you to manage this configuration by providing the Internet Connection Wizard (see Figure 7.3). This wizard steps you through the three possible scenarios announced on its second page by running any configuration program necessary to set up the type of connection you want. The wizard can even connect you to a referral service that helps you to locate an Internet service provider. What seems like a complicated and overwhelming process to many Windows 98 users is greatly simplified by this wizard. If you run it, you wind up with the kind of Internet connection you want with a minimum of effort. You find this wizard on the Start | Programs | Internet Explorer menu. (In many cases, of course, your company will have established a relationship with an ISP and you will be connecting to the Internet through a LAN connection.)

Figure 7.3.
The Internet Connection Wizard steps you through the process of locating an ISP and establishing a connection.

Supporting Dial-Up Scripting

Windows Dial-Up Networking has supported scripting capabilities in the past, but they have been somewhat buried out of the sight of most users. In Windows 98, scripting is supported via a tab in the Connection Properties sheet. Right-click on any connection, choose Properties from the context menu, and select the Script tab (see Figure 7.4). You can now specify any SCP file as the script to manage the connection. If you press the Browse button, you will find the sample scripts provided by Microsoft to give you a sense of how to script a connection. The basic procedure is to define what you need the connection to do. If you supply a script, the script controls and automates the connection process. Commonly you apply scripts to manage connections where users would have to engage in several complex actions to complete the connections. Applying a script improves the reliability of making the connection and reduces the need for users to call the Help Desk.

Table 7.1 shows the common scripting verbs and what they do. You build a script by specifying the appropriate verbs and arguments. You can set port characteristics, transmit characters (including Ctrl+M for a carriage return), and respond to input. Using these verbs, and relying on the sample script files provided with Windows 98, you should be able to script any connection.

Table 7.1. The common verbs used in scripting connections.

Verb	Meaning
proc	Marks the beginning of a script procedure. Followed by the procedure name.
endproc	Marks the end of a procedure.
waitfor	Receives input from the host. The input to wait for follows in quotes.
set	Causes a setting for a device to take a particular value.
transmit	Transmits text to the host. The text to transmit follows in quotation marks.
label:	Establishes a label to which you can jump.
goto	Executes a jump to a label.
while	Indicates to perform a set of commands until a value is reached.
if...then...endif	Creates a condition (following *if*) that must be satisfied for the command following *then* to execute. endif marks the end of the conditional.
integer	Instantiates an integer variable.
boolean	Instantiates a boolean variable.
string	Instantiates a string variable.
delay	Causes the script to pause execution for a given number of seconds.

The following script and its comments illustrate the use of many of these commands for establishing a text-based terminal connection to CompuServe. For further examples, consult the sample scripts in the Dial-Up Networking folder.

```
proc main

    ; CompuServe has long used nonstandard databit and parity settings
    ; Set the port properties to support these nonstandard settings

    set port databits 7
    set port parity even

    ; Fire off a carriage return to get CompuServe's attention
    transmit "^M"

    ; Wait for the CompuServe host to respond with a request for a
    ; host name.  When the prompt appears, respond by sending "CIS,"
    ; the name of the host, followed by a carriage return.

    waitfor "Host Name:"
    transmit "CIS^M"

    ; Wait for CompuServe to prompt for a user ID.  When it does, pull
    ; it out of the properties for this connection using an
```

```
; environment variable and transmit it.  Transmit it as raw data
; so that CompuServe will not translate it.

waitfor "User ID:"
transmit $USERID, raw

; Transmit the CompuServe GO command for the type of connection
; you want.
transmit "/go:pppconnect^M"

; Wait for the password prompt.  When it comes, pull the password
; out of the properties for the connection and transmit it raw to
; CompuServe followed by the carriage return required to start
; password validation.

waitfor "Password: "
transmit $PASSWORD, raw
transmit "^M"

; Wait for CompuServe's response to starting password validation.

waitfor "One moment please..."

; Return the port settings to standard so that PPP can properly
; negotiate the port settings required for connection.

set port databits 8
set port parity none

endproc
```

The need for such scripts has greatly diminished since online services began to provide their own connection software. Most Internet service providers require no script as well. Still, you may encounter the need to script connections to various hosts on your network or in your organization. Use the samples to help you sort out how.

Supporting Multilink Channel Aggregation

You can use multiple telephone channels to service a connection under Windows 98. Typically you use two modems to double the bandwidth of the connection. This channel doubling does require a special setup. Most ISPs, for example, do not support this type of connection. For your internal dial-up connections, you can easily support this configuration. Doing so would help you to optimize file transfers over standard POTS (plain old telephone system) lines, especially when telecommuters need to engage in NetMeeting sessions that must include voice and data transmissions.

You need two dial-up entrance ways to your dial-up server. You need to physically install two modems on your Windows 98 computer. Then you need to use the Modems Control Panel applet to configure both modems. You then configure your Dial-Up Server to accept calls using Connections | Dial-Up Server on the Dial-Up Networking window's menu.

Next, go to the Multilink tab in the connection's properties sheet, shown in Figure 7.4. Use the Add button to add the additional modem, and specify a phone number for it to dial. In your primary configuration, you will already have specified one of the two numbers for the other modem to dial. Here you specify the second number. Then you make the connection in the normal way.

Figure 7.4.
Multilink settings establish additional modems and the phone numbers they should dial for multilink communications.

Using the ISDN Configuration Wizard

Integrated Services Digital Network (ISDN) is a type of phone service that gives you two 64Kbps lines in one service connection. You can use one of them for voice transmission and one for data transmission simultaneously. Or you can combine the two lines to create a 128Kbps data transmission line. ISDN gives reasonable access for small businesses or campus-to-campus links at a reasonable cost. You need an ISDN device adapter for your computer, and a service provider that can supply you with an ISDN line. Costs for adapters vary. In my area, ISDN lines run $300 per month. In more populous areas, however, the price is significantly lower.

After you have all the components, open Start | Programs | Accessories | Communications | ISDN Configuration Wizard to set up your service. The wizard will not run unless you have an ISDN device installed.

Using Remote Access Services Provided by Dial-Up Networking

If you need to grant a mobile user remote access to a Windows 98 system, you can do so as long as you have installed the Dial-Up Networking component. If it is not installed, use the Add/Remove Programs icon in the Control Panel, the Windows Setup tab, to add the component to the system. Dial-Up Networking is listed under Communications.

After you have installed the component, the Connections menu on the Dial-Up Networking window's menu gives you access to the Dial-Up Server. Selecting this menu option presents the dialog box shown in Figure 7.5. Select Allow Caller Access, and click the Server Type button to select the server type. Normally this setting reads Default, but you can set it to match the dialing-in operating system if you so desire. Doing so speeds up the connecting process because the connection does not have to negotiate server type with the dialing-in computer. If you will accept calls from any type of Windows remote access software, however, you should leave the setting at Default.

Figure 7.5.
You can easily set the
Dial-Up Server to
answer calls.

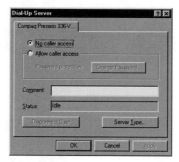

Security on the dial-up connection depends on the type of access control you have granted. If you choose share-level, you can set a password on the connection, as shown in Figure 7.5. If you choose user-level, you can select which users will have access; the security provider on the network, either a Windows NT Domain or a NetWare server, will authenticate the users for access.

Using Broadcast Services

Windows 98 provides a broadcast architecture so that you can transmit video content over your network. Although one of the more interesting tools which demonstrates this technology is the TV Viewer, the broadcast architecture has another component that probably is more useful for businesses: NetShow. NetShow leverages ActiveX technology to deliver broadcast video and audio over a network.

NetShow supports all industry standards for delivery of audio and video. It compresses the signals in real-time for delivery over the limited bandwidth of your network. It automatically adjusts to the bandwidth available, from a 28.8 modem connection to the higher bandwidths of the high-speed telephone networking systems.

To use NetShow, you need to set up a Windows NT Server to deliver the content. The server component either receives the broadcast signal for transmission on the network or generates the broadcast signal from audio or video files. The NetShow server sets up video streams that deliver content to the network. Microsoft claims that an individual Windows NT Server can handle 1,000 streams of video over 28.8Kbps connections. NetShow servers, therefore, represent reasonable scalability, capable of handling large numbers of streams and large numbers of connections. They can deliver broadcasts to your local network or to a WAN.

Because the NetShow client is an ActiveX control, it can appear as a part of the NetShow applet provided with Windows 98, which you can install from the Add/Remove Programs Control Panel applet, from the Multimedia group of applications. You could also place it on a Web page, designing your own means of viewing video within the Internet Explorer or another browser, or even placing the viewer as the wallpaper on the desktop.

Supporting Mobile Computing

Laptop users have been the traditional mobile computers. However, now you have a new sort of dial-in user to consider. The advent of Windows CE on handheld information appliances creates a new breed of mobile computers. A typical Windows CE 1.0 computer has 2–4MB of RAM in which both programs and data must be stored. Windows CE 2.0 can boost the amount of RAM to 6MB. The RAM is entirely volatile, but supported by two independent battery systems for safety. But because programs and data can be more easily lost from volatile storage than from physical storage, you have a new breed of user whose data is at greater risk than the traditional laptop user.

Figuring out how to support these users leads you to a good general support policy for mobile computing. Although a laptop can just be the user's computer, a handheld cannot be a substitute for a desktop system. A handheld needs to be synchronized with another computer and backed up to another computer periodically to guarantee the usefulness of its data. Unfortunately, the user must be the primary person to undertake this synchronization, which usually takes place via a serial cable. As a result, user education has to be one of your primary goals in any mobile computing policy.

For traditional laptop users, the best strategy is to make the laptop their primary CPU. Connect them to the network when they are in the office, and write a logon script that runs from a server that backs up critical data. Because you have VBScript and JavaScript available, you can be quite sophisticated in what you ask your script to do.

Encourage traditional laptop users to make use of the Windows 98 Briefcase to check out files from the server for use on the road. The Briefcase, shown in Figure 7.6, helps with file synchronization when multiple users may have checked out and changed the same data. Checking out files is a matter of dragging and dropping files onto the Briefcase. The user then opens the files from the Briefcase to work on them. Once connected to the network again, the user uses one of the update options on the Briefcase menu to synchronize the files with the server.

Figure 7.6.

The Briefcase helps traditional laptop users to keep server files organized.

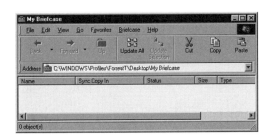

For handheld users, strategies are more difficult to apply. The Handheld PC Explorer, which is the software that manages the host side of the communication, automatically synchronizes data between the two computers. The user must periodically make the connection, however, and no user is going to make the connection often enough to completely protect the data. For these users, use a scripting language to write a script that runs on a schedule. This program should insist that the user connect the handheld and synchronize. Of course, the user still has to heed the reminder. But this is a method to help protect the volatile data on these small appliances.

Working with an Integrated Internet Shell

As we have all heard, Microsoft integrated Internet Explorer into Windows 98. The Web toolbar is available in every window. Reaching out to the Web across WAN links is now easier than ever. To help users achieve seamless wide area networking, Internet Explorer 4.0 supports the following standards:

- **A Java Virtual Machine.** This allows the Internet Explorer to run Java applications and JavaScript. Although Microsoft has not produced exactly a standard Java Virtual Machine, it does get the job done.

- **Support for Dynamic HTML.** Dynamic HTML is an object-oriented HTML. The new capabilities include precise 2D positioning of controls, support for ToolTip-style windows, and support for several layers of information on a single page.

- **Support for Webcasting.** This technology enables a user to subscribe to a Web site, and then for the Web site to deliver changes to the user's computer whenever the user connects to the Internet.

- **Support for channels.** A channel is a client placed on the user's desktop that facilitates the delivery of information from a Web site subscription. Via channels, users can set up highly personalized information delivery, using the options provided by the channel designer.

Examining the Tools Suite

In addition to integrating the browser into the operating system, Microsoft has provided a tools suite that extends the Internet capability of the browser. Included in this suite are the following:

- **Outlook Express.** An e-mail and news client. This program supports URL insertion in messages, spell checking, digital signatures, mail encryption, Lightweight Directory Access Protocol for interaction with directory services, rules-based filtering of messages, and multiple email and news accounts.

- **NetMeeting.** A network collaboration program. NetMeeting supports chat, video conferencing, voice conferencing, application sharing, and multiple user collaboration in creating documents.

- **Personal Web server.** You can set up a small Web server using Windows 98 as the host and wizards to create the initial pages for the Web site.

- **NetShow.** A video delivery system. NetShow supports video conferencing and delivery of quality video to the computer desktop.

Using WBEM

Web-based Enterprise Management (WBEM) is Microsoft's effort to make management of systems possible from the Web. The idea is that, using HTML pages and a Web browser, you should be able to do remote administration of both servers and clients from a Web browser, whether you are located on a LAN, WAN, intranet, or the Internet. Windows 98 includes a WBEM service, which you can install using Add/Remove programs, that facilitates access to your system from a browser. The tool provides a manager, shown in Figure 7.7, that enables you to grant access to a Web-based manager. You set a password under share-level security, and you set specific users and groups for access under user-level security. After you have set up access, your Web-based management strategy can include attaching to Windows 98 clients and undertaking remote administration.

Figure 7.7.
You can grant access to a Web-based system manager.

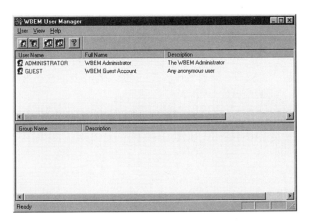

WBEM is not a strategy you implement from Windows 98 alone. You must implement the strategy across all your servers and clients by installing a package of Web-based management software. As this initiative is currently evolving, this is a feature of Windows 98 that looks more toward the future.

Summary

This chapter has examined Windows 98 in relation to your WAN. You have reviewed WAN architecture and how Windows 98 supports that architecture. You have seen some of the WAN services provided by Windows 98. You also have seen the tools Microsoft provides for interacting with WANs.

On Your Own

Create a dial-up connection to access work from your home. Create a dial-up connection for an Internet service provider. Try out the Internet capabilities by subscribing to a Web channel. Try building personalized access to MSNBC and CNN. Investigate Outlook Express, NetMeeting, and NetShow as tools for sending and receiving information.

III

Peter Norton®

Configuring Windows 98 Clients

8

Setting Up a Microsoft Client

Peter Norton®

In Chapters 6 and 7, you took a look at the networking architecture associated with Windows 98. You also examined the types of connectivity that you can create using the various networking options you have. Now it's time to see how you cause a Windows 98 client computer to communicate with servers on the network.

Technical Note: First, however, we need to clarify two terms, *Microsoft network* and *Microsoft networking*. The reason that we need to clarify these terms is that Windows 98 includes a Client for Microsoft Networks. Over the years, Microsoft has meant a number of things by both terms. Those used to a Novell or UNIX network might feel uncomfortable with the imprecision associated with these terms. In fact, at times, the two terms mean the same thing.

If you intend to connect to such a network, you might as well know what you are connecting to. In general, a Microsoft network has a server operating system manufactured by Microsoft running on it. Microsoft networking refers generally to the process of running Microsoft operating systems on a network, virtually any type of network. These definitions are clouded by the fact that Windows for Workgroups includes a Server service and can function as a server on a network. Windows 95, Windows 98, and Windows NT Workstation also have a Server service. As a result, you could describe a small network with Windows clients and a single Novell server as a Microsoft network, if you so desired, especially if you shared data using the Windows Server service. Those used to UNIX and Novell networks certainly would prefer not to call such a network a Microsoft network, and probably would say that Microsoft networking can only be applied because the clients use client software built by Microsoft. Nevertheless, Microsoft uses the terms fairly interchangeably, and does apply them to such limited contexts.

Understanding Microsoft Networks

Microsoft networking refers to connecting computers using Microsoft network operating systems.

Technical Note: Originally, a Microsoft network was based on DOS client software and LAN Manager as the network operating system. Later, such networks were based on Windows for Workgroups and LAN Manager or Windows NT. With the advent of Windows 95, yet one more operating system fell under the aegis of Microsoft networking.

Microsoft networks, however, are not based solely on Microsoft operating systems. In the literature describing such networks, you may notice that they include Novell servers, UNIX servers, connections to mainframes of varying sorts, and all types of non-Microsoft operating systems and hardware.

Sometimes you would swear that a Microsoft network is a network that somewhere somehow has a Microsoft operating system connected to it, and you can even find passages of documentation that support this theory. Generally, however, you expect to find a preponderance of Microsoft operating systems in a central role on a Microsoft network. A typical Microsoft network is diagrammed in Figure 8.1.

Figure 8.1.
A Microsoft network can include several types of computers.

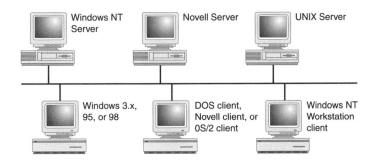

When you log on to a Microsoft network, you do not log on to a server. Sometimes, depending on the operating systems in use, it is difficult to tell what you are logging on to. In general, you are logging on to a network made up of a set of computers. If Windows NT is the server operating system on the network, you may be logging on to a domain, an organizational unit that defines secure communications among a set of Windows NT computers.

In general, your username and password for a Microsoft network grants you access to the total set of resources shared on the Microsoft network. These resources might be shared from Windows for Workgroups computers, from Windows 95 computers, from Windows 98 computers, or from Windows NT computers. The mechanism for granting this access is to collect a username and password and to hold these items for future use when user validation is required. The type of validation required and the exact mechanism for validation depends on the operating system sharing the files to the network.

Windows NT, for example, uses a component called the Local Security Authority to look up the username and password in its Security Account Manager database. If the username and password match those stored in the secure database, the user is granted access to the resources. If not, the user is excluded from using the resources. This form of security is called *user-level security*.

Windows for Workgroups, at the other extreme, uses only a password—the same password for every user on the network—to grant access to a shared resource. Each user attempting to connect to a shared resource is queried for a password. The type of access, read-only or full, depends on the password the user supplies. Windows for Workgroups can manage up to two passwords, therefore, per shared resource. This type of security is called *share-level security*, because the password is associated with a shared resource rather than a user.

Windows 95 and Windows 98 can use both of these security schemes. You can choose the type you wish to use by using the Access Control tab of the Control Panel's Network applet. After you make the choice, however, you stay with that security scheme for all shared resources. If you choose user-level security, you must have a Windows NT server or a Novell server on the network whose user list can be borrowed. Windows 95 and Windows 98 do not maintain their own database of users.

Because so many different operating systems on a Microsoft network can share resources with other computers, the traditional definition of a server becomes less applicable. Microsoft networks are not server-centric—where there is a single server or a group of servers where all the shared resources are located—as on typical Novell or UNIX networks. On Microsoft networks, almost any computer can share resources. As a result, any computer that has a server service activated appears as a server in the Network Neighborhood. For Windows NT computers, the service called the server has to be running. For Windows 98, Windows 95, and Windows for Workgroups computers, file and printer sharing must be activated. File and printer sharing constitutes the server service on these operating systems.

You will see how to activate file and printer sharing in Chapter 19, "Securing Shared Resources."

Tip: Windows 98 and Windows 95 computers do not appear in the Network Neighborhood unless file and printer sharing has been activated.

Installing the Client for Microsoft Networks

To connect a Windows 98 computer to a Microsoft network, you must have client software, often called a *redirector*, installed. The purpose of the client is to recognize, when the user accesses the file system or a peripheral device, whether the user has accessed a local resource or a remote resource. Local resources are of course installed on the Windows 98 computer. Remote resources are attached either directly to the network or to other computers that function as servers on a network. If the resource is local, the client allows the Windows 98 operating system on the local computer to handle the request. If the resource is remote, the client redirects the request to the address on the network where the resource is located. The function of a redirector is diagrammed in Figure 8.2.

To allow connection to remote resources, the Microsoft client must collect a username, just in case user-level security is in force at the remote server, and a password. These it collects in a Logon dialog box that appears when the client initializes during startup or when a user logs off. However, the client by default just collects the username and password as filled in by the user. This dialog box has no code behind it to support validation of the username and password. It stores these two items for later use should validation be necessary. As a result, filling in the dialog box and clicking OK does not mean that a user has logged on to anything. No processing of the username or password occurs, and no user validation occurs. I will show you in the following section how to force a server to validate a user logging on via the Microsoft Client.

Figure 8.2.

A redirector, or client, sends requests to use shared resources to a server.

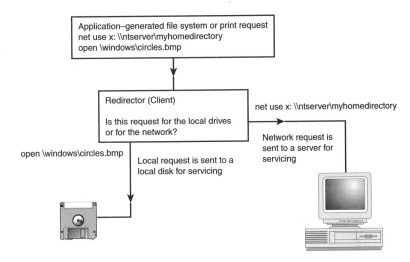

To use the Microsoft Client, you must first install it. If Windows 98 did not install the Client for Microsoft Networks during setup, follow these steps:

1. Open the Network Control Panel applet. You can right-click on the Network Neighborhood and select Properties from the context menu or open the Start menu, choose Settings, select Control Panel, and double-click on the Network icon.

2. In the Configuration tab, click on the Add button.

3. In the Select Network Component Type dialog box, select Client and click on the Add button (see Figure 8.3).

4. In the Select Network Client dialog box, select Microsoft in the Manufacturers list and Client for Microsoft Networks in the Network Clients list. Then click on the OK button, as shown in Figure 8.4.

5. If you are prompted to insert the Windows 98 CD, do so. Windows 98 will copy the files for the client in place. Sometimes, however, the files are present on the drive from a previous installation, so Windows 98 just reuses them.

6. When you are prompted to restart your system, do so. Network clients cannot initialize except during the boot operation.

Figure 8.3.
*Select Client as the
component type to see
a list of available
clients.*

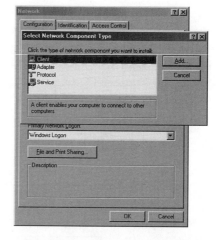

Figure 8.4.
*Select the Microsoft
Client for Microsoft
Networks and click
OK.*

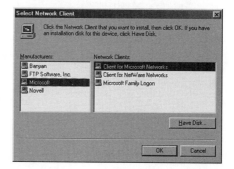

Configuring the Client for Microsoft Networks

The Client for Microsoft Networks has very few configuration settings. To see the configuration options, open the Network Control Panel applet by using one of the procedures described in the preceding section. Select the Client for Microsoft Networks in the list box and click on the Properties button. Figure 8.5 shows the Properties sheet.

You have three possible settings, one of which is optional, two of which make up a required choice. The option is to log on to a Windows NT domain. If your network is served by Windows NT servers that comprise a domain, you probably want this client to participate in the domain. As a result, you would check the check box and enter the name of the domain in the text box.

The required choice is a choice of when to connect to persistent drive mappings and network connections. Selecting the Quick Logon option button allows the client to log you on to the network rapidly. Persistent connections are not restored until you actually use them. Selecting the Logon and restore network connections option button forces the client to restore all connections when you log on. This operation may take some time, depending on the number of connections that must be restored and activity on the network. As a result, this option can cause delays that may agonize users if they log off and on frequently. When you opt for Quick Logon, the delay is parceled out to each attempted network connection the user tries to make. If she needs to access files on drive Q:, the mapping for drive Q: is not reestablished until she actually attempts to access the files. Under this scenario, the delay would be shorter than the delay at logon if 20 drive mappings had to be reestablished. And, of course, the delay never occurs if the user never accesses the resources.

Figure 8.5.
Use the Properties sheet to set configuration options for the Microsoft Client.

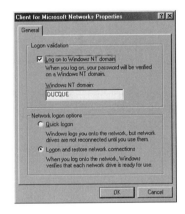

The Client for Microsoft Networks has no inherent logon script processing. However, the domain controller that processes the logon can run a script. If you use logon scripts, you can include batch commands that will set up the environment of the client computer. A domain-based logon script always runs on the client computer logging on.

If you need to set environment variables under Windows 98 in a domain logon script, you cannot use the SET command. SET in a domain logon script creates environment variables in the Windows NT environment only. In the \tools\ResKit\NetAdmin\Scrpting folder on the Windows 98 CD, Microsoft provides a command called WINSET that you can use in a domain logon script to set Windows 98 environment variables. These variables are set in the global Windows 98 environment.

The Client for Microsoft Networks can function with any of the three protocols supplied with Windows 98: NetBEUI, IPX/SPX, or TCP/IP. It will work with other special-purpose protocols as well. However, it will not grant access to other types of network operating systems besides those manufactured by Microsoft. If you wish to connect to a Novell server, for example, you must also have a Novell client installed. For a general discussion of network protocols, refer back to Chapter 6, "Understanding the LAN Connection," and Chapter 7, "Working with the WAN Connection."

You can force Windows NT (or NetWare, for that matter) to validate a user before Windows 98 will grant access to the computer. The easiest way to do so is to set the policy Require Validation By Network for Windows Access using the System Policy Editor. You can set this policy either by editing the local Registry with the System Policy Editor or by setting the policy generally on your network. When you do and you are using the Client for Microsoft Networks, the client must log on to a Windows NT domain. A successful log on to the domain must occur. If the log on fails, Windows 98 redisplays the Microsoft Networking logon dialog box. If the Windows NT domain is down for some reason, the user cannot log on. Windows 98 will not let the user past the Microsoft Networking dialog box. Pressing Esc does not grant access.

For more information on system policies and the System Policy Editor, see Chapter 17, "Securing the Desktop."

Using Microsoft Family Logon

A Windows 98 computer can be configured to support a single user or to support multiple users. This configuration is entirely separate from the configuration of the Client for Microsoft Networks. The purpose of supporting multiple users is usually to allow each user to have independent desktop settings. One user could stay with the classic desktop, for example, and another go with the Active Desktop. Because such users must identify themselves with a username and password when they prepare to use the computer, Windows 98 knows which settings to load.

When you configure for multiple users under Windows 98, Windows 98 displays a Logon dialog box, shown in Figure 8.6, to collect the username and password that identify which desktop settings to load. This dialog box is entirely independent of any other Logon dialog box displayed by a network client. As a result, on a typical networked system, users must satisfy two logons to gain access to the system: the Windows 98 logon, and the logon for their network client.

Figure 8.6.
Windows 98 can display its own dialog box.

What happens when a user fills in the Windows 98 Logon dialog box and clicks on OK? First, Windows 98 uses the username to locate that user's profile in the Profiles folder, which is stored in the Windows folder. Second, Windows 98 uses the password as the key to open the user's password cache, or password list (.PWL) file. Any time a user logs on to a resource after the password cache is open, the username for that resource and the password for it are stored in the password list file. As long as the cache is open, the next time the user connects to the resource, the username and password are pulled from the cache and used to satisfy the required logon. For the user, this creates the illusion that he has only one username and password to remember, the pairing that identifies him to Windows 98.

In addition, to help preserve this illusion, the Logon dialog boxes that appear under Windows 98 pass the username and password entered on to the next Logon dialog box in the logon sequence. If the username and password match the requirements for that dialog box, the dialog box does not actually appear onscreen. It is just satisfied, and the user is logged on the resource. Windows 98 can therefore give the illusion that it has only one dialog box.

Logon dialog box sequences can function in two ways. When the Windows 98 Logon dialog box appears before the network client Logon dialog box, as just discussed, the Windows 98 Logon dialog box passes the username and password on to the network client dialog box. If the username and password supplied are valid for the network client, the network client performs the required logon processing in the background and never appears.

But what if the user has a different username and/or password for the network client? In the case just discussed, the username and password sent forward would not satisfy the network client dialog box, and the dialog box would appear. The user would have to enter the appropriate username and password and click OK. However, if the password cache is open and the appropriate username and password are in the password cache, these elements will be pulled from the password cache and used to satisfy the dialog box. The client dialog box will not appear under these circumstances. The password cache is opened only after the Windows Logon dialog box is satisfied. The only prerequisites for pulling a logon username and password from the password cache, therefore, are that the Windows logon has been satisfied, the user has logged in once using that dialog box while the password cache is open, and use of the password cache has not been disabled through the use of system policies.

Tip: The Network Control Panel applet enables you to select the first, or primary, Logon dialog box from the Primary Network Logon drop-down list on the Configuration tab. You get to decide which one appears first.

Under Windows 95, you configured Windows to support multiple users by opening the Passwords Control Panel applet, selecting the User Profiles tab, selecting the Single User Profile or Multiple User Profile option, and clicking on the OK button. Windows 98 enables you this option still. When you carry this procedure out, the Windows Logon dialog box appears and you create a user by entering a username and password, and clicking OK. Windows 98 asks you whether you would like to maintain your settings, creates a profile folder for you, and creates a password cache.

Windows 98 provides another option for creating users called the Microsoft Family Logon. This component is a service that installs when you set up Windows 98. The service provides a wizard for creating users.

Tip: If you would prefer that users not be able to create other users on their systems, remove the Microsoft Family Logon Service by using the Network Control Panel applet. If you do not have the Control Panel icon, install the service by using the Network Control Panel applet.

To use the Microsoft Family Logon, follow these steps:

1. Open the Start menu, choose Settings, and then select Control Panel.

2. Double-click on the Users icon.

3. On the Enable Multi-User Settings page (see Figure 8.7), click on the Next button.

Figure 8.7.
A wizard helps you to enable multiple users under the Microsoft Family Logon option.

4. On the Add User page (see Figure 8.8), enter the username and click on Next.

Figure 8.8.
The Add Users page allows you to define a unique username.

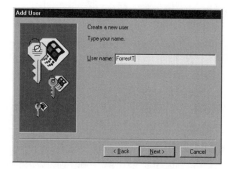

5. On the Enter New Password page (see Figure 8.9), enter and confirm a password, and then click Next.

Figure 8.9.
You are required to create a password, even if it is a blank password.

6. Choose which items you want included in the user's profile by using the Personalized Items Settings page (see Figure 8.10). The user can customize any of the items you check and keep these settings as a part of her profile. You can create copies of the items as they appear in the current profile, or you can create new items based on default settings.

Figure 8.10.
*You can use
Personalized Item
Settings to determine
which elements
appear in a user's
profile.*

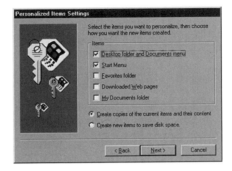

7. On the final page of the wizard, click the Finish button.

Tip: After you create your first user, the Users icon in the Control Panel presents a single properties page that enables you to change passwords or settings for selected users, or to add new users. This page also shows you the list of users on the system.

Using Older Clients to Access Microsoft Networks

Microsoft networks have been around since the early days of networking. As a result, there are systems out there that use LAN Manager clients to access a network—in particular, MS-DOS computers. If these computers are running Windows 3.1 (not the Workgroups version), they must use the LAN Manager DOS client to access the network. This client will allow such a computer to access shared resources provided by a Windows 98 computer.

When you upgrade a computer running this client to Windows 98, you should of course use the Windows 98 Client for Microsoft Networks. However, you might actually use the old LAN Manager client to perform the upgrade. Included with Windows NT is a tool called the Network Client Administrator. This tool can build a disk, originally designed to launch the Windows 95 Setup program, that enables you to boot a computer under DOS, connect to the network using the DOS client, and initiate the Setup program from a shared network drive. You can use this client to initiate the Windows 98 Setup program as well.

Communicating with the Apple World

If you want a Windows 98 computer to communicate with a Macintosh computer, the Windows 98 computer does so through the Microsoft Client. However, you must have a Windows NT Server configured to run the Services for Macintosh. On this server, a shared disk volume will be available that both Macintosh and Windows 98 can read and write to. As a result, the two platforms can share files using this intermediary. Windows 98, however, does not include the AppleTalk protocol, so greater connectivity requires a third-party solution.

Summary

This chapter has shown you how to install and configure the Client for Microsoft Networks, and has taken a look at what a Microsoft network is. You have also seen how to use the Microsoft Family Logon to create new users. You have seen how different Logon dialog boxes can interact, and how the password cache functions. These basic features enable users to log on to their own systems *and* to a Microsoft network.

On Your Own

Try installing and configuring the Microsoft Client for your network. Then add a user or two. When you add the users, make sure that their Windows 98 password does not match their Microsoft networking password. This mismatch will force both of the dialog boxes to appear. Then use the Passwords Control Panel applet to make the passwords the same. Only one dialog box will appear.

9

Setting Up a
NetWare
Client

Peter Norton®

In Chapter 8, you saw how to create a client for a Microsoft network. Many of you will not be interfacing with a Microsoft network, however. Instead, you will be interfacing with Novell servers, and you need to see how to make Windows 98 a Novell NetWare client.

Installing Novell client software is as easy as installing Microsoft client software. You have several choices for client software, and each of these choices is discussed as this chapter covers the following topics:

- Choosing the best client for Novell
- Installing the Microsoft NetWare Client
- Using Microsoft's Service for NetWare Directory Services
- Configuring the Microsoft NetWare Client
- Installing the Novell NetWare Client
- Configuring the Novell NetWare Client

Installing the Microsoft NetWare Client

Unlike Microsoft networks, Novell networks have a very defined structure. They are server-centric in the sense that you log in to your server and it handles most of your file and printer sharing services. You may attach to other servers, but these servers are not responsible for your primary validation as a user on the network. The server to which you log in is known as your preferred server.

Novell NetWare version 4.0 and later provides a different way to organize your network. This version of NetWare introduced NetWare Directory Services (NDS). Within NDS, you organize users and servers into a hierarchical tree that reflects your business organization. Management users and management servers are collected together under the same node of the tree (the same with floor workers and their servers). Users log in to the tree, not to a particular server that maintains a user list. The NDS tree structure prevents you from having to maintain separate but identical user lists on multiple NetWare servers. A login to the tree validates the user for access to all servers and resources for which the user has access permissions. You have a single, central store of users and resources that you manage as a single entity, no matter how large your network or how many servers you use.

Windows 98 can work with either form of Novell network organization. Microsoft provides a client for NetWare that handles the server-centric type of login, and an add-on service that permits login to an NDS tree. The following section reviews the advantages and disadvantages of the types of clients available to you. Then the discussion turns to show you how to install the client and service, and how to set up logins under each.

Choosing the Best Client for Novell

You have several choices for clients that support Novell networking. You can still use a 16-bit client, so long as it is the only such client you run on the machine. Other network clients must be 32-bit protected-mode clients. You can use the Microsoft client and services provided with Windows 98, or you can use the Novell Client 32 package, available for download from www.novell.com. Table 9.1 summarizes the issues involved in selecting a client.

Table 9.1. Features of the various NetWare clients.

Feature	Microsoft Client	Novell Client 16	Novell Client 32
Support for NDS	Yes	No	Yes
Support for Bindery mode	Yes	Yes	Yes
Use graphical	No	No	Yes
Management tools	Yes	Yes	No
Support for 3.x servers	Yes	Yes	Yes
Support for 4.x servers	Yes	Yes	Yes
Support for 32-bit protocols	Yes	No	Yes
Requires latest version of client	Yes	No	Yes
Provides access to many client properties at login	No	No	Yes
Possible incompatibility with Windows 98	No	Yes	Yes
Possible limited support for Novell	Yes	Yes	No

As you can see, the case for choosing a particular client is not clear cut. If you want the best support for Novell features—if support for older NetWare management utilities does not matter, and possible incompatibilities with Windows 98 do not matter—choose the Novell client. If you want the best compatibility with Windows 98 and limited support for Novell features does not matter, choose the Microsoft client. The best piece of advice I can give you about 16-bit clients is a single word: *don't*. You limit performance on 32-bit computers by making this choice, and you have no reason to accept this choice now that both Microsoft and Novell manufacture 32-bit client software. The 16-bit clients belong on 16-bit machines, and nowhere else.

Peter's Principle: Use Novell Clients for Novell Servers and Microsoft
Clients for Mixed Server Environments

The main piece of advice I can give about choosing clients is this: If you use Novell servers exclusively, use the Novell client software; if you work in a mixed server environment, you may prefer the Microsoft client. In general, the Novell client is faster than the Microsoft client. It is more feature-rich than the Microsoft client. It is more attuned to Novell features than the Microsoft client.

I have experienced slight problems, however, forcing the Novell Client 32 version 2.2 to coexist with other clients. Loading the client was not a problem, as was configuring the client. Removing the client was a significant problem. Actually, the only solution I found for successfully removing this client was `fdisk`. You should not experience such problems, however, because the Novell client should go through a revision for use with Windows 98 that should resolve these issues. But you should carefully test compatibility with Microsoft-supplied clients before you settle on the Novell client. Check to see what happens when you try to uninstall the Novell client and return to a former configuration.

When you are mixing more than Microsoft and Novell servers, testing of clients for coexistence is extremely important. Clients and their bindings can cause conflicts. Remember that under Windows 98 you cannot select the exact order in which bindings are used in accessing the network, as you can under Windows NT. You have no guarantee that the manufacturer of the client has tested it for compatibility with other clients. You need to test for speed, feature use, and cross-client interference.

Using the Client for NetWare

The Microsoft Client for NetWare Networks grants you access to server-centric Novell networks. The possible relationships are diagrammed in Figure 9.1. As noted earlier, these are typically networks that run versions of NetWare prior to version 4.0. However, version 4.0 and higher servers can run in a mode called Bindery Emulation. The bindery is the central database of user accounts used in earlier versions of NetWare. Rather than present a true NDS tree database, servers running in Bindery Emulation mode simulate a bindery database. Microsoft's client gives you access to such servers running in Bindery Emulation mode.

Tip: When you run 4.x servers in Bindery Emulation mode, be sure to enable user logins in Bindery Emulation mode. If you don't, the server will never locate the user account for validation.

Figure 9.1.
The Microsoft Client for NetWare permits access to NetWare servers using bindery databases.

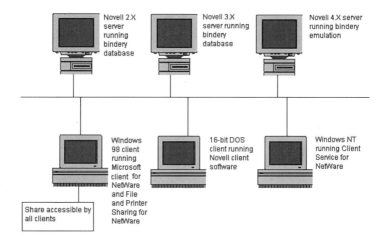

Why would you resort to Bindery Emulation with 4.x Novell servers when you have the services of NDS available to you? In general, you wouldn't unless you were trying to maintain compatibility with a large number of 3.x servers that have yet to migrate to version 4.x NetWare. I mention this restriction in passing mainly because Microsoft's strategy for building its client software is to provide bindery support in the client and to add NDS support using a service. If you install only the client, you must use bindery support; otherwise the client will not supply the desired access to Novell servers. If you select this client and want to use NDS, you must also install Microsoft's Service for Novell Directory Services.

Technical Note: As you may be aware, Microsoft provides both File and Printer Sharing for Microsoft networks and File and Printer Sharing for NetWare networks. Only one of these may be installed at a time. You should use File and Printer Sharing for NetWare Networks only when you will share information from the Windows 98 computer to NetWare clients. This version of the Server service is tuned to servicing Novell clients only, and will not grant access to other types of clients. It will grant access, however, to 16-bit NetWare clients that may be running on your network, and to Windows NT computers running a NetWare client, as shown in Figure 9.1.

To install the Client for NetWare networks, follow these steps:

1. Open the Network Control Panel applet.
2. In the Configuration tab, click the Add button.
3. In the Select Network Component Type dialog box, select Client and click the Add button.

4. In the Select Network Client dialog box, shown in Figure 9.2, select Microsoft in the Manufacturers list and Client for NetWare Networks in the Network Clients list (choose the latest client if more than one appears). Click the OK button.

Figure 9.2.
Install the latest version of the Microsoft Client for NetWare if several appear on your list.

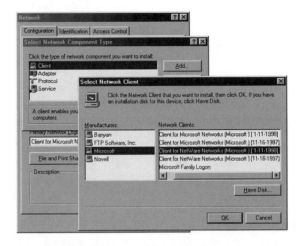

Technical Note: When you install network clients, you may not see exactly what is represented in the figures included with this chapter. Windows 98 is exceptionally good at analyzing your configuration and presenting different installation options based on what hardware and software you have running on your network.

5. Click OK in the Network dialog box. Windows 98 copies files from the installation medium and prompts you to restart your system. Restart the system to activate the client.

The Microsoft NetWare Client presents a Logon dialog box similar to that presented by the Microsoft Client for Microsoft Networks, as shown in Figure 9.3. The user must enter a username, password, and server name. On clicking OK, the client contacts the server so named and requests validation of the user. In addition, the client adds a command to the context menu associated with the Network Neighborhood. You can run the NetWare WhoAmI command from this menu. Your login information is reported back in a dialog box for the servers to which you are attached.

Warning: Do not assume that the Microsoft Client for NetWare will permit login to a server not running bindery emulation. If you are also running the Client for Microsoft Networks, and the Client for Microsoft Networks is the Primary Network Logon, you will not see the NetWare Login dialog box and you might readily assume that the login was successful. If the NetWare server is running NDS, the login actually fails and the user is not warned. To log in to an NDS server, you must have the NDS service in place.

Figure 9.3.
The Microsoft NetWare Client presents a Logon dialog box that appears in addition to the Windows Logon dialog box.

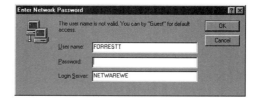

To configure the Microsoft Client for NetWare Networks, follow these steps:

1. Open the Network Control Panel applet and select the client in the Configuration tab. Click on the Properties button.

2. The Properties sheet presents two tabs. On the General tab, shown in Figure 9.4, you can select the preferred server and the first drive letter to use for mapped drives using two drop-down lists.

Figure 9.4.
The General tab enables you to configure the main login options.

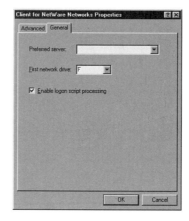

3. If you want to run login scripts from the NetWare server, you must check Enable login script processing on this tab.

Tip: If login scripts are not running, the first place to check is the General tab or the Client for NetWare Networks Properties sheet. Failing to check Enable login script processing is a common configuration error.

4. On the Advanced tab, you can determine whether you want case to be preserved in filenames (see Figure 9.5).

Figure 9.5.
*The Advanced tab
enables you to
preserve the case of
folder names and
filenames stored on
the server.*

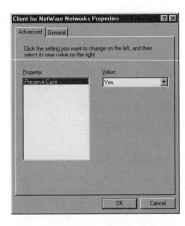

Tip: If you want to use long filenames on your NetWare servers, an administrator must execute the command `load namespace long` when you configure the server. On older versions of NetWare, the namespace may be called OS/2 rather than long. An administrator must load this namespace to store profiles on a NetWare server.

Using Microsoft's Service for NetWare Directory Services

In order to log in to an NDS tree, you must install the Service for NetWare Directory Services, or install Novell's client for Windows 98. To install and configure the Microsoft service, follow these steps:

1. Open the Network Control Panel applet, and click the Add button on the Configuration tab.

2. In the Select Network Component Type dialog box, select Service and click Add.

3. In the Select Network Service dialog box, select Microsoft in the Manufacturers list and Service for NetWare Directory Services in the Network Services list (see Figure 9.6). Click OK.

4. In the Network dialog box, scroll down the list in the Services tab and select Service for NetWare Directory Services. Click Properties.

5. In the Service for NetWare Directory Services Properties sheet, enter the name of the preferred tree (the one on which the user's account is defined for login) and the context within the tree (the level in the tree where the user's primary resources are defined) where the workstation user is defined (see Figure 9.7). Click OK, and then click OK in the Network dialog box.

Figure 9.6.
*Select the Service for
NDS in order to
allow login to an
NDS tree.*

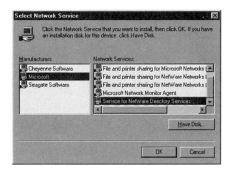

Figure 9.7.
*Enter the name of the
tree and the context
for the user and
workstation.*

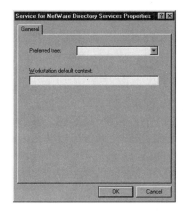

6. Windows 98 copies files into place and then prompts you to restart the computer. Restart to activate the service.

After the service is in place and configured, the user logs in to the NDS tree rather than a preferred server running in Bindery mode. When you run WhoAmI, you see that you are logged in to the tree rather than as a user on a server (see Figure 9.8).

Figure 9.8.
*With the Service for
NDS installed, you
log in to your default
context in the tree.*

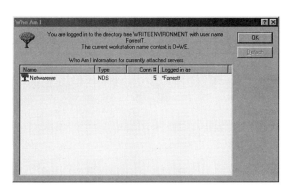

Installing the Novell NetWare Client

Novell provides its own client for use with Windows 95 and Windows 98. If you are running Windows 98 on either a Novell-only network or a mixed network, you may in fact prefer the Novell client. It provides many features that you may prefer over the combination of the Microsoft Client for NetWare and the Services for NDS. To install this client, follow these steps:

1. Download the client files from www.novell.com. The download can be done either as six 1.7MB files, or you can download a single zipped file. You need at least version 2.2 of the client.

2. Unzip the six executable files and locate them in a temporary directory.

3. Run each executable file to extract the compressed files stored inside.

4. Run the program SETUP.EXE to install the client. For most installations, this process is simple. You click Yes to accept the license, accept a Typical installation by clicking the Install button, and the client copies itself into place.

5. Reboot your computer to activate your client.

> **Peter's Principle:** Use Novell Clients for NetWare and Microsoft Clients for Mixed Networking
>
> In general, I have found that you should use the Novell client when you are working with an exclusively Novell server setting. You should use the Microsoft clients when you are working in a mixed server setting. Novell's client provides excellent connectivity with NetWare servers, and greater access to the features of Novell networking. However, I have run into difficulties getting the Microsoft clients and Novell client to coexist. You don't need the struggle of forcing them to get along. Choose your clients for overall compatibility, but remember that each company tends to take care of its own product line.

Configuring the Novell NetWare Client

Novell's Client 32 has many more settings available than the Microsoft client. Configuring it requires more extensive decision making. Your first choice is just how much control you wish to grant users at login. By default, the client presents the simple Login dialog box shown in Figure 9.9.

However, the client can also present the dialog box shown in Figure 9.10. The first tab is the standard Login tab. The second tab enables you to define the connections you want to make. The third tab controls execution of your login script. The final tab enables you to pass variable values to the login script. The Client Configuration Settings control not only which of these tabs appear, but also any other setting for NetWare that you could imagine wanting access to.

Figure 9.9.
Novell's Client 32 can present this simple dialog box.

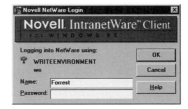

Figure 9.10.
Novell's client can also display additional tabs in the Login dialog box.

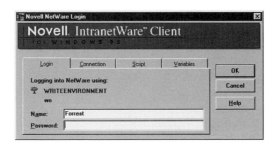

You access the settings for the Novell client just as you do those for any other client. Open the Network Control Panel applet, select the client in the list on the Configuration tab, and click Properties. After you do this, you see the property sheet shown in Figure 9.11. The IntranetWare Client tab enables you to set preferred servers, preferred tree, context within the preferred tree, and first network drive letter.

Figure 9.11.
The first tab on the property sheet gives you access to the standard server and tree settings.

The Login tab, shown in Figure 9.12, enables you to control the appearance of the Login dialog box. Check boxes determine which of the additional tabs appear. You can determine whether the login is to a bindery server or to an NDS tree, and whether existing connections should be cleared. This last setting is necessary because you can display the Login dialog box at any time by right-clicking on the Network Neighborhood and selecting the Intranetware Login option from the context menu.

Figure 9.12.
The second tab controls the appearance and behavior of the Login dialog box.

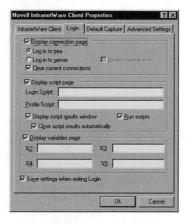

The script options enable you to set up a login and a profile script. You can also choose whether to show the script results window, whether scripts will in fact run, and whether to close the script results window after it displays. The Variables section enables you to determine default values for up to four variables to pass to your login scripts. You can also choose whether changes the user enters into the Login dialog box will be saved.

The Default Capture tab, shown in Figure 9.13, displays default settings for any port captured by a printer. You can specify banners, timeouts, whether to hold and keep jobs, and whether to use form feeds. These are settings you would normally pass as parameters to a capture command placed in a login script.

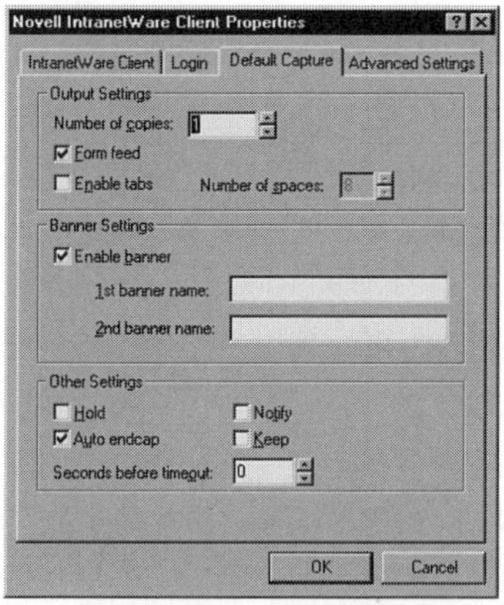

Figure 9.13.
The Default Capture tab enables you to set capture settings.

The Advanced Settings tab (see Figure 9.14) gives you access to a host of NetWare settings. Some, such as whether to sound alert beeps, you could set at the server or the client by issuing commands. Others relate to details of the client and server-side interaction. Use this tab to define exactly how you want the client to interact with the chosen server connections. In general, you won't need to adjust these settings as an end user. As administrator, you may need to adjust some settings to provide an appropriate context for the user's workstation.

Figure 9.14.
The Advanced tab enables you to set a host of NetWare settings.

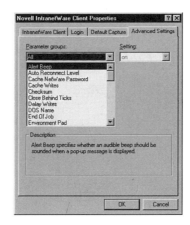

A typical setting you might need to adjust is the caching of the network password. Some administrators would prefer not to use the password cache, or password list file, because it can easily be compromised by a user deleting, copying, or moving it. Others would like the file to be present, but not to keep the server or NDS password in it. Turning off the caching of the network password prevents placement of the server or NDS password in the password cache.

Using Older NetWare Clients

Windows 95 documented extensive methods for loading and using 16-bit real-mode network clients. You could load one 16-bit client and any number of 32-bit clients. Although this compatibility for real-mode drivers is still supported, you have absolutely no reason to continue using 16-bit drivers under Windows 98. The Microsoft-provided drivers are at least acceptable, and most vendors have 32-bit drivers available. The protected-mode drivers are more robust and faster than their older counterparts.

If you want an example of the performance hit you can take, go into the Control Panel and open the System icon. Select the Performance tab, click on the File System button, and turn off all the protected-mode features. Then restart your system. You won't like the result any more than you will using 16-bit network clients.

Summary

This chapter has shown you how to install the Microsoft NetWare Client and how to use Microsoft's Service for NetWare Directory Services. In addition, it has shown you how to install Novell's Client 32 for NetWare. You have also learned how to configure each of these components. This discussion has also provided enough information to help you choose the client that you would prefer to use.

On Your Own

Try installing each of the clients and services discussed to see which ones best meet your needs. Visit the Novell Web site to review the latest information on the Novell client. Check for any patches or updates that might be available. Install each client that you are considering, and use System Monitor and its counters to review the impact on your system. Adjust each setting for each client to see how your adjustments affect network performance. Remember that you may encounter problems removing the Novell client from your system. Be sure that you have the latest version of the Novell client before you attempt the installation.

10

Dealing with Multiple-Client Hosts

Peter Norton®

Chapter 8, "Setting Up a Microsoft Client," and Chapter 9, "Setting Up a NetWare Client," treated setting up network clients as though you will connect to one—and only one—type of server operating system. Chapter 8 assumed that you would be connecting only to Microsoft server platforms and Server services, principally servers running Windows NT or desktop systems sharing resources via the Windows 98 Server service. However, I often run into questions like this one: "We're running both Windows NT Servers and NetWare. What's the best way to get Windows 98 to communicate with both servers?" I always answer that the best way depends on what you want to make the best. Does best mean lowest cost? Does it mean lowest network overhead? Does it mean best performance? Does it mean with minimal hardware investment? The reason I ask these questions is that they identify the requirements for choosing an appropriate solution. The answers define the solutions I could recommend.

Peter's Principle: You Have Many Options for Connecting to Diverse Servers

My preference for multiple clients is an opinion, with which you should feel free to disagree. As an action item, check out the Microsoft and Novell Web sites at www.microsoft.com and www.novell.com for additional connectivity options. You do have multiple options for providing connectivity between clients and diverse types of servers. For example, visit http://samba.anu.edu.au/samba/, where SAMBA and other UNIX connectivity options are available.

SAMBA is a tool that you can set up on your NetWare servers and UNIX servers that allows them to communicate using server message blocks (SMBs), the format Microsoft uses for packets that communicate among its servers. Your client for Microsoft Networks should be able to see your NetWare server and to communicate directly with shared NetWare resources provided by these servers. Your client should also see the UNIX servers and their resources.

This solution is cheap, but SAMBA sometimes does not cause NetWare servers to become visible immediately to Microsoft clients, causing some serious troubleshooting that requires the rebooting of the Novell servers, sometimes several times. In addition, I have not experienced the kind of reliability that I would like from SAMBA. Like most UNIX utilities, however, SAMBA undergoes continual renovation. Check the Web for the latest versions.

You could also set up the Gateway for NetWare Networks on a Windows NT Server. This package enables you to display the contents of NetWare servers as though they were managed by the Windows NT Server running the gateway. Users see a set of shared resources on the Windows NT Server. They do not even need to know that they are accessing a NetWare machine. In addition, Microsoft and Novell have a host of connectivity packages—most more or less successful—to hook the two kinds of servers together in a variety of ways. Microsoft offers, for example, the File and Printer Services for NetWare, commonly called FPNW, which allows Windows NT to share printers to NetWare clients. Novell offers similar packages for Windows NT, most recently NetWare Directory Services for Windows NT.

The gateway provided by Windows NT is reliable and can display resources from multiple NetWare servers. It is also free, in the sense that it is included with Windows NT Server. However, several of my customers have had problems accessing NetWare printer queues from clients while the gateway is in place. File and Printer Services for NetWare and NDS for Windows NT require licensing. Both suffer from lack of support by the opposing vendor, making minor glitches in functionality a common problem among those who have chosen these options.

Because of the limitations associated with these add-ons and services that make servers visible to many types of clients, I have found that the most elegant solution is to use multiple clients on each host to allow connections with servers. The client software components usually provide more functionality and greater reliability than the specialized add-ons and services for the servers.

My favorite way, however, to handle connectivity to multiple types of servers is to run multiple clients on the client workstation. The reason this method is my favorite is that I don't have to resolve issues relating to conflicting security systems, conflicting network service models, and conflicting client models. Until we have an overarching cross-platform directory service supported by all vendors—and Microsoft recently announced it will not support Windows NT Servers on which NDS for Windows NT has been installed—I would prefer to choose one network operating system as the basic security provider, synchronize passwords or create the single logon by enabling password caching, and use multiple clients to grant access to networks of different types.

This chapter focuses, therefore, on the multiple client solution; it is also the Windows 98 solution to the problem. I will justify it as a choice and try to clarify when you might choose other solutions as I explain this option. Use my opinion and explanations as a touchstone for evaluating what you think your best solution would be. This chapter covers the following topics:

- Why you would choose multiple clients
- How to bind protocols to multiple clients
- What your network architecture becomes when you have multiple clients
- How to order the clients for best security
- How to configure the clients to cooperate with one another

Choosing to Use Multiple Clients

When you build connectivity between networks or servers of varying types, you must decide where you want to add the overhead. My preference for adding overhead as additional clients arises from the following issues:

- Additional services added to a server affect multiple clients as well as the performance of other software on the server. A performance problem with a connectivity service is likely to affect multiple computers, not just the computer on which it is installed.

- Troubleshooting services that involve client/server transactions over the network are more difficult than troubleshooting the interaction of a local client with the network. Most connectivity services involve some sort of client/server interaction.

- Performance of a client can be more readily and directly tuned in Windows 98 than interaction of a client and a network service on a server.

- You usually have more options among clients and vendors of clients than among connectivity services.

As a result, I usually choose to use multiple clients on mixed networks under Windows 98. If I have to support older client operating systems such as MS-DOS NetWare clients, I find that the multiple-client approach gives me more options for connectivity among the clients of diverse types and Windows 98 as well.

Dealing with Overhead

The overhead associated with additional clients is minimal. The System Information utility reveals that the Microsoft Client for NetWare Networks is 178,694 bytes (about 175KB) in size, and the Microsoft Client for Microsoft Networks is 161,341 bytes (about 158KB) in size. Clients from other vendors may be larger in memory footprint, but memory footprint is only of concern on machines that are trying to run Windows 98 in less than 16MB of RAM and are supporting a great deal of multitasking. My preference clearly is to optimize network performance by adding memory and clients at the client workstation rather than by introducing services on network servers. Where memory is at a premium, however, you should seek server-based solutions to promote network operating system connectivity and compatibility.

Dealing with Performance

Aside from having enough memory to handle your client overhead, you have an additional performance factor to consider. Windows 98 does not have an exceptional algorithm for matching a particular network request to the client/protocol/adapter binding path that can service the request. Windows 98 tries one out, waits for the request to time out, and then tries the next, and so on.

Windows 98 can usually tell what client is involved, because each client is associated with a server, directory tree, or domain uniquely. The operating system, however, must just try the binding paths from that client in sequence until one works.

On single-protocol networks, network bindings to additional clients create very little in the way of performance penalties. On multiple-protocol networks, however, the protocol accessed most frequently should be marked as the default protocol. Windows 98 will try it first, and because most work is accomplished using that protocol binding, most work will be accomplished with no performance penalty. To set the default protocol, open the Network Control Panel, select the protocol binding in the list, and click on Properties. Select the Advanced tab in the properties sheet, and check Set this protocol to be the default protocol (see Figure 10.1). On networks that have a clearly favored protocol, adding additional clients usually creates few performance penalties.

Figure 10.1.
Check the box to set this protocol binding as the default protocol.

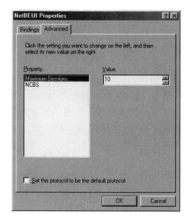

Technical Note: In Windows 98, when you set a default protocol you also set a default network interface card. Setting TCP/IP bound to the Dial-Up Adapter as the default protocol places it first in the search order. This setting means that you will always attempt to access the Dial-Up Adapter first, and your permanent LAN connections second. Each attempt to access the main LAN connection will have to wait for the dial-up binding to time out. This performance penalty could cause lengthy delays for the user, because the Dial-Up Adapter will prompt the user to dial out at each attempted network access. As you can see, you want your most frequent network connection *and* the most frequently used protocol set as your default.

On workstations where you have three clients installed—one accessing a domain, one accessing a NetWare server, and one accessing a UNIX server—you could encounter performance issues if the workload is balanced among the three network clients. In this case, you would have difficulty running a single protocol, and you may choose to run three. In any case, one of the protocols will be ordered ahead of the others in the bindings. The one that is last in line will be slower than the others. In this situation, you may prefer to use other connectivity products and methods so that you can avoid running multiple protocols and clients on the client workstation. By installing the Windows NT Gateway Service for NetWare, for example, you could make the resources of NetWare servers available via a Windows NT Server, avoiding the need to run the NetWare client and the NWLink protocol. You could run only TCP/IP and connect to all your resources through the Microsoft client. You would have a single binding path, eliminating any waits for bindings to time out.

Choosing and Binding Protocols

When you are configuring a multiple-client computer, you need to choose protocols wisely. An easy choice is to run one protocol per client: NetBEUI to communicate with Windows NT, NWLink (the IPX/SPX compatible protocol from Microsoft) to communicate with NetWare, and TCP/IP to communicate with UNIX. However, running additional protocols adds to the overall load of network traffic, so you want to be careful in your choices so that you can optimize network traffic.

To evaluate whether your client and protocol choices are working optimally, use the System Monitor and a network monitor to evaluate performance. See Chapter 12, "Learning to Use the System Monitor," Chapter 13, "Monitoring System Performance," and Chapter 14, "Monitoring Network Performance," for additional information.

Protocols are just agreements by which networked computers communicate. They are often called protocol stacks because they consist of a number of software layers. How many protocols you need to use depends on the requirements of your clients, the requirements of your servers, and the requirements of the connectivity options you choose.

One protocol you will always use when you work with Microsoft operating systems is NetBEUI. NetBEUI is a simple protocol, often called "light and fast" by Microsoft. It has few requirements other than that you assign each computer a name. It uses server message blocks (SMBs) as the packet format for communicating command and control information between clients and servers. Under Windows 98, you must have some means of communicating SMBs between your client and its Microsoft servers. Usually this means running NetBEUI. If you choose not to run NetBEUI, you must run a NetBIOS add-on atop your alternate protocol to enable the use of SMBs. As shown in Figure 10.2, the properties sheet for a protocol includes a check box for enabling the hosting of NetBIOS atop the protocol.

Why do you need NetBIOS or NetBEUI in place? To permit browsing in the Network Neighborhood. For better or worse, Microsoft designed the browser service and the Network Neighborhood using NetBIOS and NetBEUI. Without some form of the protocol in place, the Network Neighborhood remains blank. It cannot populate itself with a list of servers.

No matter which protocol you use, you do not always need multiple clients. You need to raise the question of what role the server is playing to determine whether you need a client for the protocol that forms its network. If your Novell server functions only to host a client/server application, you can run NWLink, the protocol necessary to allow your client and the server application to communicate, but you do not need a NetWare client in place. You need a NetWare client only when you need to communicate using NetWare Core Protocol (NCP) so that you can browse the server's file system.

Figure 10.2.
NWLink allows you to enable NetBIOS as an add-on to permit handling of SMBs.

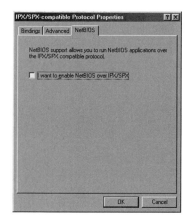

As noted in Chapter 8, the Client for Microsoft Networks can communicate using any of the three basic protocols included with Windows 98. What it cannot do except over NetBEUI is browse a server file system. Two critical question, therefore, in choosing clients and protocols are the following:

- What servers do you need to communicate with?
- What file systems do you need to browse?

You need to choose the protocols necessary for allowing your applications to communicate with servers. You need to install clients for the protocols that communicate with the servers whose file systems you need to browse. Or you need to install connectivity packages that enable you to extend a client to browse an alien server.

After you have selected your clients and protocols, you must choose how to bind them to the clients. *Binding* describes the communication paths from entities such as client services and server services through a protocol to a network interface card. Binding a client to a protocol means that the client can communicate using the protocol. By default, Windows 98 binds all clients to all protocols. You may choose to change these bindings because you want to limit the protocol to communication with a given client only.

To control protocol bindings, each protocol property sheet includes a tab that describes possible bindings (see Figure 10.3). For each protocol, you can see what clients can be bound. As Figure 10.3 shows, you can also see what server services (for example, File and Printer Sharing for Microsoft Networks) can be bound to the protocol. You activate a binding by checking the box, and deactivate a binding by unchecking the box. Clicking OK on the property sheet causes the binding to be set up. You need to restart your computer to completely activate the binding.

Note: To open a protocol property sheet, select a protocol binding to a network adapter in the Network Control Panel's Configuration tab. Then click Properties.

Figure 10.3.
*Checking boxes on
the Bindings tab
activates particular
bindings.*

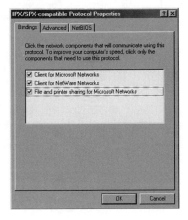

Having extra bindings active normally does not cause any damage. Only one communication path will be followed for any given network transmission. Having a lot of bindings active, however, means that the search process for the appropriate network path of communication is longer, having more possible steps. You can gain some optimization, therefore, by using only the bindings that you need.

If you use IPX/SPX as the primary protocol on your network and use a dial-up connection only for Internet access, for example, you have little reason to bind IPX/SPX to your Dial-up Adapter. In fact, limiting the binding of TCP/IP to the Dial-Up Adapter and IPX/SPX to your NetWare client makes good sense. You can communicate with the Internet. If someone on the Internet tries to connect to your computer, however, he or she has no valid protocol path for communicating with the rest of the internal network on which your computer resides. Typically in this setting you would want to disable the binding between TCP/IP and file and printer sharing. If you leave that binding in place for the Dial-Up Adapter, folders that you have shared are available to Internet users if they know (or can discover) the IP address of your computer.

To clear a set of bindings for a protocol/adapter path, select that path in the Network Control Panel's Configuration tab. Open its property sheet, select the Bindings tab, and clear all the check boxes. In our example, you would select IPX/SPX-compatible Protocol | Dial-Up Adapter and click Properties. Select the Bindings tab and clear all the check boxes. After you click OK and restart, the NWLink protocol is no longer bound to the Dial-Up Adapter.

To unbind TCP/IP from the file and printer sharing service, select TCP/IP | Dial-Up Adapter and click Properties. Clear the check box for file and printer sharing, and then click OK. After you have restarted, your file and printer sharing service cannot communicate with the TCP/IP protocol.

Often you do not wish to use a particular protocol to communicate throughout the entire network. Often you isolate protocols for security purposes. Microsoft's Proxy Server, which functions as a firewall and Internet connection point, uses protocol isolation to protect your internal network from the external network. The Proxy Server runs both TCP/IP and IPX/SPX. It uses TCP/IP to communicate with the Internet. It uses IPX/SPX to communicate with your internal network. Your internal network needs to run only IPX/SPX, and can use the services of the Proxy Server to access the Internet.

> **Warning:** As you adjust your bindings, make certain that you have one valid protocol path for communication between the Windows 98 computer you are using and any remote host it must communicate with. A common problem when adjusting bindings is disconnecting a binding on which communication depends.

Understanding Your Multiple Client Architecture

Windows 98 supports multiple clients using a flexible architecture. Figure 10.4 diagrams the architecture when it is configured for accessing three types of servers, correlated with the OSI reference model. Understanding the architecture helps you to understand how communication takes place on the network, especially which components and which protocols are involved. If you engage in network monitoring, as described in Chapter 14, knowing these components will help you to understand what you see in the monitor. You will have a sense of how network packets correlate to the software components that send and assemble them. This tour begins at the highest level of the stack and continues to the lowest level.

At the highest level are the application interface components, the Win32 Winnet interface and the Win32 Print APIs. These two components contain functions that application programs can call to request either network or printing services. Because of these two components, applications see a standard set of functions for addressing the network, not a set for IPX/SPX, a set for NetBEUI, and a set for TCP/IP. The application does not need to be concerned about the protocol stacks or other network interfaces that may be involved in the communication. The application communicates with the network using these API calls. The rest is handled by other components.

Below the application interface lies the Network Provider Interface (NPI). The NPI allows the standard application-layer components to communicate with a variety of different network types. The NPI provides a standard interface that the Win32 Winnet and Print API functions call. Below the

NPI is a layer of components provided by different network vendors. Each of these components translates the standard NPI calls into network-specific calls. The Winnet 16 component, for example, translates the network request for 16-bit Windows for Workgroups networking; the NetWare component translates the calls for the NetWare Network Provider and Print Provider. The component for 32-bit Windows and UNIX networks (Network File System) are also shown in the diagram.

Figure 10.4.
Windows 98 uses a layered network architecture to accommodate multiple providers.

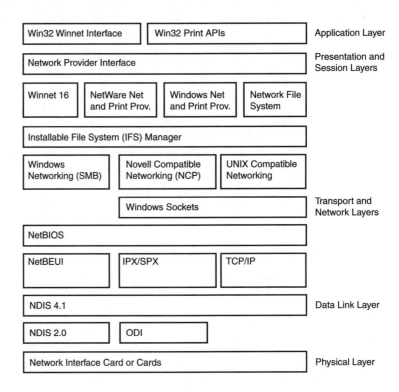

Each of these network provider components communicates with a redirector, or client, via the Installable File System (IFS) Manager. Windows 98 treats networks in the same manner as file systems. As a result, the redirector is a virtual device driver that knows how to verify whether the request is for the local file system or a network file system. If the request is for the network of the type the redirector supports, the redirector redirects the request to the network file system. It calls an appropriate transport API, which it identifies from its bindings, to carry out the communication over the network.

Technical Note: Two more general APIs overarch the transport protocols. One is Windows Sockets, which was based on Berkeley Sockets, a networking API first distributed with the Berkeley Standard Distribution of UNIX. Classically, a socket is the union of a network port and an IP address. Under UNIX, connections over the network are made by attaching to numbered ports exposed by the operating system. Particular connections are assigned particular port numbers by convention. The FTP port, for example, is usually 21. To connect a session to a remote FTP server, you must connect to port 21 at its IP address. This combination of port and IP address is therefore your socket for carrying out the file transfer. You read data from and write data to the socket to carry out your communication. The Windows Sockets API provides functions that will carry out such communications over TCP/IP, the original protocol for which sockets was designed, and over IPX/SPX, to which sockets has been extended.

Each transport protocol represents such a transport API. Microsoft also provides a NetBIOS API that can communicate with other protocols. This API is essential because the browser software has been programmed to it. In addition, it is the API that handles SMBs. NetBIOS communicates natively with NetBEUI, its original protocol partner. Microsoft has extended it to speak natively to both IPX/SPX and TCP/IP. As a result, you are no longer required to run NetBEUI as a protocol to support the Network Neighborhood.

Below API layers provided by Windows Sockets and NetBIOS are the protocol stacks themselves. Each is implemented as a 32-bit driver. These drivers can be loaded and unloaded dynamically. When a laptop user inserts a PC Card network adapter, the appropriate transport protocols and other network drivers are loaded. They can be unloaded at undocking time. (Sixteen-bit drivers do not share this capability.) The transport protocols manage breaking the network communication into transmittable chunks known as packets or frames. They handle establishing connections and sessions between the relevant computers, placing addressing information on the packets, and then hand the packets over to the NDIS drivers for transmission.

Each protocol stack sees a single drive below. Microsoft has implemented the Network Device Interface Specification (NDIS), version 4.1, layer to provide a standard interface to all card drivers. The manufacturers of network interface cards supply a small driver that links the NDIS 4.1 interface to the electronics of their card. The NDIS 4.1 layer can also link to 16-bit NDIS 2.0 and ODI-compliant drivers that you may still be using on some clients.

The net effect of this architecture is to allow smooth, efficient communication with a variety of networks. Any provider can provide a component for the NPI layer and a redirector, which will allow communication with its network. Additional protocols can be inserted into the mix as well. This architecture enables you to set up the type of network you want to have—mixing and matching resources, both new and legacy, as you need to.

Ordering the Clients for Best Security

One implication of having the possibility of multiple network providers installed is that users have to log on to multiple networks. (See Chapters 8 and 9 for a discussion of the dialog boxes provided by the Microsoft and NetWare clients.) To provide a single logon solution for Windows 98, Microsoft used a combination of tools. First, if all your logon names and passwords are the same, you have a single logon. Successive Logon dialog boxes, one for Windows 98 (see Figure 10.5) and one for each redirector, appear in sequence. Each dialog box passes the username and password it received on to the next. If you had three Logon dialog boxes to satisfy—one for Windows 98, one for a domain, and one for a NetWare server—you actually see only one Logon dialog box, the first in the sequence. Because each subsequent dialog box is fulfilled by information provided by the preceding one, Windows 98 does not waste time displaying it.

Figure 10.5.
*The Windows 98
Logon dialog box
gives you access to
your password cache.*

Having a single username and password may not meet the security policies in your organization, however. To cover this contingency, Microsoft created the password cache. This cache is a file that stores your list of connections and passwords, a list called the Password List. The passwords are encrypted, and the key to decrypting them is the logon you provide to the Windows 98 Logon dialog box. Until you have satisfied this dialog box, your password cache is not available to you.

Ordering of network logons is important if you rely on the password cache. If you place your Windows 98 logon first, you always have access to the password cache. You can satisfy any subsequent logon with a password from the cache. If you place another logon first, say the Microsoft Network logon shown in Figure 10.6, and the password is not the same as for Windows 98 logon, you will have to fill in the Windows 98 Logon dialog box manually. If you cancel this Logon dialog box, you will gain access to your machine. However, you will not have access to the passwords stored in the Password List file, because you never satisfied the logon that unlocks the file. You will wonder why you are having to type passwords to reattach to all the network resources you normally attach to.

Figure 10.6.
*The Microsoft
Network Logon
dialog box admits
you to Microsoft
networking.*

Note: The Microsoft Networking dialog box has two variants. The one shown in Figure 10.6 undertakes no validation. It collects a username and password to use later when you attempt to attach to network resources. The other variant appears when you configure the Client for Microsoft Networks to logon to a domain. This version causes you to be validated as a user in the domain (see Figure 10.7).

You can affect the order of the Logon dialog boxes in only one way. On the Configuration tab in the Network Control Panel, you can select your Primary Network Logon using a drop-down list box that contains the available clients. If you set this value to Windows Logon, the Windows 98 dialog box appears first and you always open the password cache. You always have access to your stored passwords.

Now you face a security issue, however. Canceling the first Logon dialog box cancels all subsequent ones. Windows 98 admits you to the system and gives you the default user profile. In the preceding scenario, you would cancel your domain and NetWare logins. You would not be connected to network resources, but you could always attach by giving your password and username when prompted during the attachment process. Anyone can gain access to the local machine in this fashion, and anyone could then attempt to maneuver around the network to examine resources. The solution to this problem is to place a server logon in primary position and set the system policy to require validation by a server for Windows access.

Server and domain dialog boxes, such as the one for Microsoft Networking, shown in Figure 10.7, and the one for the Client for NetWare Networks shown in Figure 10.8, have a different function. They always seek the services of a server to validate the user's credentials against a user database. As a result, they require the naming of the server or domain that provides the security. They use a process called pass-through authentication to send the username and encrypted password to the server and to get back the results of the validation.

Figure 10.7.
The Microsoft Networking Logon dialog box can be set to use validation.

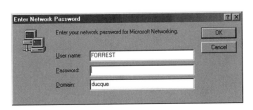

Figure 10.8.
The NetWare Client Login dialog box always engages in validation.

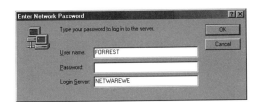

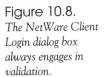

Peter's Principle: Security with Convenience—The Best Way to Configure Multiple Logons

The best way to configure logons is to make a server or domain logon primary and force validation by a server for Windows access. This configuration guarantees that some

continues

network security provider has validated the user. You won't have to worry that someone has pressed Esc and gotten control of the machine or that the Microsoft Client has permitted access with no validation.

You can simplify the complex logon for users by making the Windows logon username and password identical to the server logon. The server logon will validate the user, and the Windows logon will open the password cache in the background. Subsequent attachments can have any password or user ID that you would like. Users will have to log on only one time, and then the password cache will satisfy all additional logons. You can use the Passwords icon to make passwords for a domain and Windows 98 identical.

Summary

This chapter has focused on how to configure computers that must communicate using more than one network client. It has introduced the multiple-client architecture that Windows 98 allows and has shown how to install and configure multiple clients. In addition, it has mentioned alternatives to using multiple clients and made suggestions about how to tell when multiple clients are an appropriate solution.

On Your Own

Set up a computer to communicate using both the Client for Microsoft Networks and one other client. Practice adding and deleting bindings, and plan how you might lay out the bindings appropriately for your network. Finally, determine what protocols and clients you need to run on your network. Experiment with the order of your network clients to see what implications the order has for your network.

IV

Tuning
Windows 98

Peter Norton®

11

Implementing Basic Performance Tips

Peter Norton®

Everybody wants his computer to run fast. When you consider what we thought was blinding speed just five years ago, it causes some wonder. A 386/20 seems terribly slow now, however, and our main push in computing seems to be to avoid waiting that extra second for something to happen.

If you compare the capabilities the machines give us to the perceived lack of speed, you have a hard time understanding why that extra second matters. As a writer, I am probably 40 times more productive than I could be with a typewriter. Word processing has profound productivity enhancements for me. What does it matter if I have to wait a few hours for a printout rather than half an hour? The recent television commercial bemoaning the fact that we all were once 28.8 users gives similar pause.

Nevertheless, Windows 98 places new demands on systems, and we as users expect more of our hardware because of Windows 98. The need for speed does not arise alone from the desire to do streaming video over the Internet. We want information on demand, at our fingertips, as Bill Gates used to say. Windows 98 enables us to take advantage of many more strategies for using that information, and we always face the increasing pace of our business lives. We also have new technologies arriving, including continuous speech recognition. Such systems demand fast processors and a lot of memory. They usually demand a lot of disk space as well. The future of computing technologies literally depends on our willingness to buy more hardware that is faster and better suited to the tasks.

In addition, Windows 98 is arriving on a hardware scene where serious changes are coming to PCs. The old Intel architecture, based on a limited number of interrupt request lines, will be giving way to more flexible architectures. The PCI bus, currently the preferred bus, already enables devices to share interrupt lines. Some of the new options will enable us to free up even more of the existing lines.

Planning for performance is therefore essential. You need to plan for it as you think about the following issues:

- Purchasing new hardware
- Maintaining existing hardware
- Maintaining the operating system
- Maintaining applications

This chapter also covers the following issues and technologies:

- The Universal Serial Bus (USB)
- Firewire (IEEE 1394)
- Multimedia display options
- Broadcast architecture
- Smart Cards
- 16-bit versus 32-bit options
- Windows 98 tune-up options

Planning Hardware Acquisitions

Windows 98 is very much the operating system for current and soon-to-be-released hardware. A number of new hardware types and standards are supported, including chips sets that won't generally be available until the second quarter of 1998. As a result, in planning hardware purchases, you need to consider these technologies and their impact for your organization. You may want to limp along on the hardware you have for a few months while you wait for machines that offer you stronger capabilities. Or you may wish to modify your hardware choices based on capabilities that are ready now for your use. Here is a list, arranged in descending order of importance, of the hardware devices you should be considering as you plan new acquisitions:

- **The Universal Serial Bus.** This bus architecture enables you to attach a serial hub to the machine, through which you can link multiple (up to 127) serial devices. Data communication speeds are considerably higher over this serial bus. Microsoft demonstrated that such devices can be hot swapped using Plug and Play technology at its Professional Developer's Conference in October 1997. In addition, USB will support a variety of alternative Human Interface Devices to improve accessibility to computing resources. Windows 98 will even support multiple pointing devices; therefore, an accessibility device and an ordinary mouse can be attached to the system simultaneously.

- **ISDN access and multilink for modems.** These two technologies fall together as connectivity options. Integrated Services Digital Network line charges are falling, making this technology an attractive alternative to analog phone lines for dialing in to the corporate network. Shifting to ISDN modems rather than Plain Old Telephone System (POTS) lines may make good sense, especially for telecommuters. If ISDN is not attractive, using multilink to combine two modems and two POTS lines to improve the speed of remote access may be an appropriate alternative. If you select the multilink option, USB makes very good sense, because it provides for faster throughput without interrupt conflicts. Additional communication technologies, such as ADSL and cable modems, are on the immediate horizon, and they may affect your choices. Scan the Internet and watch the trade press to stay abreast of these issues.

- **Sound cards, video cameras, video capture, and microphones.** Why are these four elements so important to future computing on networks? The answer is one word: NetMeeting. Increasingly, conferencing is likely to take place over PC terminals using NetMeeting. The cost is considerably lower than flying everyone to a central location, and the productivity is considerably higher than a conference call. Participants can hear each other, see each other, share data, and share applications. They have all the appliances of a meeting room on their PC. You will probably want to support this technology in any large organization.

- **Infrared Data Association (IrDA).** This technology enables you to transfer files between a handheld PC or a notebook PC and the desktop. In the future, IrDA will probably become a popular interface to just about everything. Some printers offer the option now, for example. Handheld PCs from Casio, Compaq, Phillips, HP, and others also offer the option. My suspicion is that the handheld PC with Windows CE will become increasingly popular as an alternative to the notebook form factor. You can get an amazing amount of work done on one. With this option encroaching on mobile computing, users will be demanding IrDA ports. Many IrDA connections can self-configure when a device comes in range, so you do not have to explicitly initiate the conversation between devices. Some of them, however, depend on straight-line communications.

- **IEEE 1394 (Firewire).** This new bus architecture supports certain types of devices, including video cameras and digital video (DVD). Watch the market to stay abreast of what devices are available so that you can make an informed decision about whether to seek this bus in the machines you purchase. My advice is that if IEEE 1394 is available as a reasonable cost option, buy it. You will find a use for it later on.

- **Multiple displays and hardware panning.** Both these technologies are designed to improve the viewing real estate per dollar cost on the monitor. With two multiple PCI video cards in place, you can spread the desktop over multiple reasonably priced monitors. For many, this is a good alternative to a 21-inch monitor. Usually, desktop publishing is advanced as the arena for this technology. However, any job function where multiple views of data are required can make profitable use of dual monitors, such as programmers who want a view of code on one screen and a view of the debugger on another. Hardware panning allows the video display adapter to maintain a larger desktop than the monitor can display. Keyboard controls are provided to allow scrolling, or "panning" in camera operator's terminology, to view the hidden portions. Users who work with graphics-intensive applications may find this technology useful; they can focus on a part of the graphic in an exploded view and move easily to view other areas.

- **Multimedia Extensions (MMX), Advanced Graphics Port (AGP), Digital Video Drives Discs (DVD).** These devices are all designed to improve multimedia on the desktop and notebook computer. Multimedia in a business setting has always been questioned, except in training situations. The reason, of course, is that users would rather play Doom than work. You will probably find, however, that you cannot avoid MMX and AGP, as they will probably start coming as a part of the computing package. DVD may have many applications within your business, especially in training. But the watchword I have received from many in the industry is to wait for the second generation of drives if at all possible. The price will drop, and the standard will be implemented better. In addition, DVD-RAM, a use of this technology for storage, is on the immediate horizon.

- **Smart Cards.** The Smart Cards that have gotten a lot of press lately are all VISA cards. They are credit-card–type devices with a microchip onboard, and they allow information and applications to be embedded within the microchip. Replenishable debit cards—where you carry a certain amount of "cash" in the card and each use decrements your store of cash—are one application. Security devices are another application. Windows 98 supports

Smart Card readers that are currently available. In point-of-sale applications, e-commerce applications, and user-recognition scenarios, you may find very productive uses for these devices. These devices are already well accepted in Europe. Many anxiously await their debut in the U.S. market.

- **Broadcast services.** Broadcast services allow unused portions of the television bandwidth to transmit additional information, such as Web pages. This technology is very new, and it is difficult to tell how the marketplace will respond to it. It has tremendous potential, allowing both video and data to travel the same input line. Exactly how businesses will use the option remains to be seen. My advice is to keep an open mind and think creatively about applications. I would try to get a test machine set up to explore possibilities. Already, Microsoft TV sponsors video training. Imagine having the video training signal and supporting class documents arriving over the same feed.

- **TV access.** Just what every manager wants, a television on every desktop! Now you don't have to miss Lucy and Andy Griffith reruns while you work. Although TV tuning capabilities may seem to be a home issue only, installing a video card with a tuner may have solid uses in business. Video training could be beamed to every desktop via internal channels, for example, maximizing the training dollar. Combined with NetMeeting discussion groups, a great deal of training and work could be done over several sites separated by miles. With that type of access to video resources, you may wish to install the device but not connect each PC to the local cable company.

Peter's Principle: Bottom Line for Hardware Planning

After you review the list, you may wonder what the bottom line is. My recommendation is this: On new machines, you want USB, ISDN or multilink capability, an IrDA port, and video and sound appropriate to supporting conferencing. Those are directions in which I think both Windows 98 and business strategies are pushing us.

The IEEE 1394 bus support is still untried, and without a lot of device support at the moment. It will, however, be a coming arena in networking and device attachment. Watch this arena, and implement it when it is appropriate.

I think you will find specialized uses for dual monitors, multimedia devices, broadcast services, Smart Cards, and TV viewing. You acquire support for many of these devices on Pentium II machines, regardless of whether you ask for them. When you think about CDs, remember that DVD, at approximately $150 more per unit, provides a 20X CD-ROM as well. I doubt, however, that you need to implement all of these technologies on the average desktop. Which of these devices you need may be difficult to justify in your current environment. Within two years, however, hardware acquisitions done with foresight may indeed lead you to solutions you cannot imagine now.

In addition to these recommendations, you need to follow these basic tips:

- Whenever possible, match the bus width of adapter cards to the bus width of the system. You will get better performance out of 32-bit network cards on a PCI machine than out of legacy 8-bit ISA cards.

- Get decent hardware-accelerated video (remember, AGP with Pentium II machines) with as much memory as you can afford. Video performance always becomes an issue as the system ages. The better it is to start, the easier it is to upgrade later.

- Focus yourself on the latest generation of processor technologies. Although Pentium 200 chips are great, why buy those when you can protect your investment over the long haul by purchasing Pentium IIs? Consider alternatives to the Intel world as well. AMD's K6 chip is reported to be exceptionally fast. Remember, however, that heading toward less-than-standard technology often leaves you with limited upgrade paths.

- Buy enough memory. My recommendation at this point is at least 32MB of the fastest RAM available. Microsoft still says that Windows 98 will run on a 164MB 4386—and it will. No one wants to use it, though; everyone would prefer at least 32MB of RAM for performance. My suspicion is that, as the next generation of office software appears, 64MB will look very attractive.

- Purchase enough disk space to keep at least 100MB free, above any other storage requirements, including swapping. Preferably keep this free space on the same drive as the system partition, because that is where temporary file space gets allocated. Windows 98 is faster with that amount of free space, and you will need plenty of free space if you need to reinstall. One installation I undertook during the beta consumed 384MB of free disk space.

Keeping Your Hardware in Shape

Hardware is always trouble. Unlike software, you can't just reload it when it has problems. And it does wear out. Chips can develop shorts or overheat. Drive surfaces decay. You need to pay attention to your hardware, because eventually it will let you down.

Keeping your hardware in shape starts with installing your hardware. Check carefully when you put any device into the machine. Is the card truly square, or does the bracket lean ever so slightly away from the mounting screw? If it does, consider a slight field modification with a pair of pliers, bending the bracket so that the card seats without any tension pulling against it from the tied-down bracket. That tension will eventually unseat the card, causing mysterious hardware failure.

Are all the screws and nuts tight, especially those for the tie-down fittings for cables? If not, use some Lock Tight, a compound that hardens in the screw threads, to prevent the threads from turning at unwanted times. The noise of a loose nut falling inside the case as you unscrew a cable tie down can be most annoying.

Check all cabling to make sure the cables run free without binding and tension. I have had devices whose cable had to run over and around fittings and that would work only when the screws for the case were tightened just so and the monitor sat atop the case only in a certain position. Tension on a cable can also cause it to loosen over time. Any cable that can be tied down needs to be tied down.

In addition, any time the case happens to be open, clear the dust that inevitably creeps in. Check for loose chips, broken connections, and loose wires. I have opened cases to find that CPU chips have spontaneously jumped out of locked zero-insertion-force sockets, nonessential cables have decided to escape their fittings, and CPU fans have decided to slide off the CPU and swing free on their wires. Gremlins do live inside computers, and they can accomplish the most amazing feats when we think the machines are safely closed up and beyond damage.

Outside the case, when you connect cables, tie them down. Make certain that external peripherals are placed in secure locations where they cannot be subjected to accidental physical damage. Keep cables away from areas where they can be kicked, and make sure they are not binding on surfaces as they snake their way to their destinations. And make certain you have adequate ventilation, especially for convection-cooled devices. Occasionally DeGauss your monitors, clean your floppy drives, and clean your CD-ROM drives.

The main piece of equipment that needs periodic maintenance is, of course, the fixed disk. I still believe in running the hard drive all the time so that it does not cycle from the operating temperature of the powered-on state to the temperature of the powered-off state very often. The idea is that avoiding this temperature cycle is easier on the chips and devices, making them last longer. In addition, the power surge of starting up, no matter how small, is hard on the device. The dictates of power management, however, now thwart my intention. Drives automatically spin down and power down to conserve power. I still believe in leaving the computer powered on all the time.

To protect the disk and all other electronic components, I use surge suppressors and power line conditioners. Usually, I put each piece of equipment on a UPS to implement these strategies. That way, with good software, I can implement an elegant shutdown of the machine to avoid file system damage in the event of a power outage. You may be surprised to learn how dirty your line power is. I have had to shut off the audible alarms on the UPS equipment. Late at night my home office sometimes screams of impending power loss, only to quiet down when the anticipated voltage loss never takes place. As your organization gets larger, you may go to building-level surge suppression with backup generators that kick in before power is lost. You will want to choose a power schema that makes sense for the scale of your situation. One factor, however, is that local power backup sitting next to the machine is probably more reliable than a centralized power backup. You may find the expense of both to be appealing, depending on your need for 24×7 reliability. Redundancy always leads to reliability, but it has a cost. You also need to consider overall budget as a critical factor.

One other piece of equipment needs protection—your phone line. Especially if your lines are aboveground, you need to be concerned about surges generated by lightning. If you are in this situation, you need to install a lightning arrestor between the phone line and your modem. You should consider surge suppression for any phone line, buried or above-ground. The reason is that surges can be induced in the line for many reasons, lightning-induced ground currents among them. Not only can you lose a modem, but the surge can be transmitted back through your modem to the motherboard, causing very serious damage.

Physical wear and tear on your drive can be a major menace to your data. Sectors do go bad, and files become fragmented. Without periodic maintenance, you run the risk of losing data. Windows 98 provides the following options to keep your disk in top shape:

- Control over what programs start automatically to give you the quickest Windows 98 startup time.

- Conversion to the FAT32 file system, for more efficient management of hard disk space allocation. (Remember, however, that if your computer slumbers, you may lose data under FAT32.)

- Disk defragmentation, including storing programs so that the most frequently used will run the fastest. Files are placed on the disk in the order they start, contiguously.

- Hard disk error correction using ScanDisk.

- Deletion of unnecessary files.

Each of these options is conveniently managed by the Windows Tune-Up Wizard. To set up optimization of your hard disk, start the wizard by selecting Start | Programs | Accessories | System Tools | Windows Maintenance Wizard Tune-Up. Then follow these steps to configure your system for regularly scheduled tune-ups:

1. Read the first wizard screen. Select Express or Custom setup, and then click on Next to continue. The text on this screen outlines what the wizard does. Choose Custom for this exercise so that you can see all the options.

2. On the second page, select or deselect which programs you want to run at startup by checking the appropriate boxes. Choose a maintenance schedule (see Figure 11.1). The number of programs that run at startup governs how quickly Windows 98 boots and presents the user interface. If you don't like the ones offered, choose one anyway and customize it later using the Scheduled Tasks icon in the System Tray. To continue, click on Next.

3. On the third screen of the wizard, you have three choices. You can select which programs will run at startup, as shown in Figure 11.2. You can choose to optimize your hard drive—to schedule the optimization at a later time, or not to optimize. These programs appear because they appear on your StartUp menu or on the load or run lines in Win.ini. Unchecking a program causes it not to start automatically, making Windows 98 startup faster. Click Next to continue.

Figure 11.1.
Select the programs you want to run at startup to adjust the speed of the Windows 98 boot maintenance schedule you prefer.

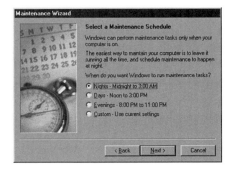

Figure 11.2.
You can choose to convert your drive to FAT32—to schedule the conversion or to not convert which programs to run at startup.

4. The next screen describes the optimization process. Windows 98 will convert the drive to FAT32, which means that you cannot then uninstall Windows 98 or compress the drive. The FAT32 file system uses smaller cluster sizes than FAT16, however, approximately the same size you would use if you compress the drive. This enables you to schedule defragmentation regularly (see Figure 11.3). As a part of these settings, you can have your applications arranged on the drive with their files in contiguous blocks in the order the files load. This arrangement speeds up the load and response time of the program. The Settings button opens a dialog box that enables you to select the drive to defragment, whether to arrange application files for fastest loading, and what the percentage of fragmentation must be to undertake the defragmentation process. Click Next to continue.

Note: You should be aware that defragmentation can be a lengthy process. If the drive has not been defragmented in awhile, or if you have upgraded to FAT32 and gotten a new cluster size, expect defragmentation to take an hour or more. If you are using DriveSpace compression, defragmentation may halt in the middle of the process for no apparent reason, just as if you had canceled the defragmentation operation.

Note: For the pros and cons of converting to FAT32, see Chapter 5, "Looking at the Core of the Operating System."

Figure 11.3.
You can schedule the defragmentation operation, including intelligent defragmentation, which speeds your applications.

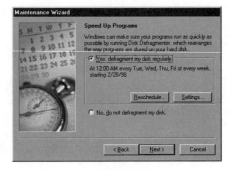

5. The wizard now scans your drive for programs that will not work with FAT32. If it finds such programs, you can choose not to convert or not to use the program. Click Next to continue.

6. The next screen enables you to schedule defragmentation of your drive (see Figure 11.3). As a part of these settings, you can have your applications arranged on the drive with their files in contiguous blocks in the order the files load. This arrangement speeds up the load and response time of the program. The Settings button opens a dialog box that enables you to select the drive to defragment, whether to arrange application files for fastest loading, and what the percentage of fragmentation must be to undertake the defragmentation process. Click Next to continue.

7. The next screen enables you to schedule ScanDisk to check your drive for errors. By default, this is a standard check, and it does not automatically fix errors. Click Next to continue.

8. The next wizard page enables you to select which files to delete on a regularly scheduled basis. Clicking the Settings button reveals that you can schedule for deletion Temporary Internet Files, Downloaded Program Files, Temporary Setup Files, files in the Recycle Bin, Old ScanDisk files in the root folder, Temporary files, and Windows Setup temporary files. Choosing all options keeps the maximum free space on your disk.

9. The final page of the wizard, as seen in Figure 11.4, reviews the operations you have selected and offers you the chance to perform each of these actions by clicking the Finish button. After making your choices, click Finish to complete the wizard.

If you do not choose to use FAT32, you have one other option for reducing the cluster size on a large drive to conserve drive space. You can compress the drive. This option does not optimize speed. Because the compressed drive uses an 8KB cluster size, however, it enables you to store more on your drive. DriveSpace 3.0 is included as a part of Windows 98 (see Figure 11.5). Select the drive to compress, select File | Compress, and click on the Start button in the Compress a Drive dialog box. The process could not be easier.

Figure 11.4.
*Verify your options,
and then click Finish
to apply your choices.*

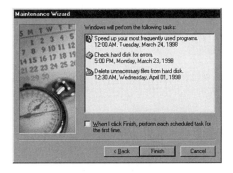

Figure 11.5.
*Compressing a drive
is a fairly automated
process in DriveSpace
3.0.*

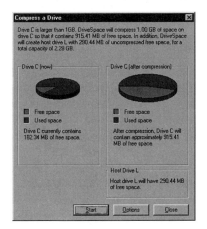

I avoid compressing drives whenever possible. The performance penalty is not high, but it depends on the level of compression you use. However, the technology leaves you and your data at a certain risk. If a single sector of the compressed volume file where the data is stored goes bad, you may lose all the data in the compressed volume file. In addition, horror stories relating to corrupted compressed volume files abound. Personally, I have not had a compressed drive that survived daily use for more than six months. If you choose this option, you should back up your data frequently and carefully. If you compress your C: drive under Windows 95, you will have to uncompress the drive to install Windows 98, because you must unmount your Compressed Volume File to upgrade to Windows 98.

Keeping Your Operating System in Shape

Operating systems age just like people do. Windows 95 came out in the "gold" edition, then as OSRWindows 95 with Service Pack 1, and then as OSR-2. Office 97 updated many system DLLs, as did Visual Basic 4, Visual Basic 5, and a host of other Microsoft products. One thing that updated

DLLs bring you is DLL conflicts. Something that ordinary use brings you is the possibility of system file corruption. Recognizing these issues, Microsoft has provided two tools in Windows 98 to help deal with the problem.

To help deal with system updates that cause problems, Microsoft has provided the Update Information tool. You launch this tool by clicking Run on your Start menu, typing qfecheck into a dialog box, and pressing Enter so as to call up the executable from your Windows folder. (If qfecheck.exe is missing on your system, you might need to download it from the Microsoft Web site first.) Once launched, the Update Information tool displays the Properties dialog box, shown in Figure 11.6, which helps you to track system changes. The Registered Updates tab shows you a list of system file updates stored in the Registry. When a setup program installs an updated system file, it can register the update with the system. All such registrations are shown in the Registered Updates tab.

Tip: In my experience, the easiest way to resolve the DLL conflict has been just to take the copy of the DLL that an application needs and put it in the same directory as the main executable for the application. This is the default search path for every application.

Figure 11.6.
You can find out which files have been registered as updated by setup programs.

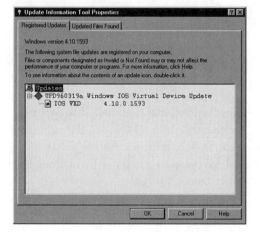

On the Registered Updates tab, certain kinds of DLL problems can surface. If a file is marked as Invalid, the version information registered for the update does not match the version information stored in the file itself. This conflict would point to some application or user having copied an older version of the file into place, either during setup or by manually overwriting the file. If you are experiencing system problems, a solution might be restoring the correct version of the updated file.

If a file is marked as Not Found, it is no longer at the location specified for it in the Registry. The problem you experience with the system is related to a missing or moved file. You can restore the file to its proper location by rerunning setup for the application or for the operating system, or you can search for the file to see whether it has been moved on the system. To search, select the Updated File Found tab and use the Search dialog, shown in Figure 11.7, to search the Windows folder or any path you choose—with or without subdirectories included—for the missing file.

Figure 11.7.
You can search anywhere on your system for missing system files.

The search result shows you all files that have been updated, no matter how they were installed on the system (see Figure 11.8). Finding a lot of files on this list implies strongly that you have been placing updates on the system without using the setup programs provided. If you find a missing file somewhere on the system, you can always return it to its proper location. You can also use the search results to record additional updated files so that you are aware of their existence.

Figure 11.8.
The search result reveals all updated files in the search path.

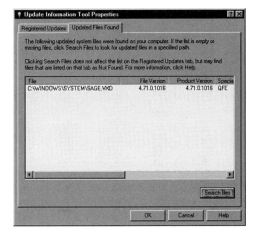

Note: Although the Update Information tool helps with DLL conflicts, it does not provide for complete DLL management. You may prefer to use a third-party product, such as DLLigator, to track, back up, and restore system file changes. Sometimes newer DLLs cause problems for some software and devices that expect an older version to be in place. Perfect DLL management would track all these issues and automatically make the correct DLL available 100 percent of the time. I do not think we have reached Nirvana yet, but many tools currently available can help with the problem.

To deal with the file-corruption problem, use the System File Checker, which is accessible from the Tools menu of the Microsoft System Information Utility. Open System Information from Start | Programs | Accessories | System Tools | System Information. You can also start System File checker easily from the Run dialog box by typing sfc and pressing Enter. This tool presents a window that gives you two options, scanning files for errors or extracting a compressed file from the installation medium (see Figure 11.9). This tool greatly simplifies the process of protecting the system from accidental change.

Figure 11.9.
The System File Checker offers you two options to help protect system integrity.

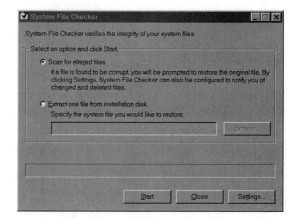

To understand what the System File Checker actually does, click on the Settings button. You see a property sheet containing three tabs, the first of which is Settings (see Figure 11.10). This tab enables you to choose what the System File Checker will do if it encounters a file that must be restored from the installation medium. You can choose whether and where the existing version of the file will be backed up. You can choose whether to log actions and whether to overwrite or append to the log. You can also select the actions the System File Checker undertakes. It can check for files that have changed either attributes or checksums, as well as files that have been deleted.

Figure 11.10.
The Settings tab enables you to control backup, logging, and checking behavior.

The Search Criteria tab enables you to select the types of files you want to check and the folders in which to check for them (see Figure 11.11). By default, only files that represent system code are checked. Only the subfolders in the Windows folder that contain such code are checked. This setup makes for an efficient search of critical files—those that could cause system misbehavior. You may wish to search for other files as well to track their integrity—for example, those that make up your basic applications suite.

Figure 11.11.
The Search Criteria tab enables you to determine which folders and files are examined.

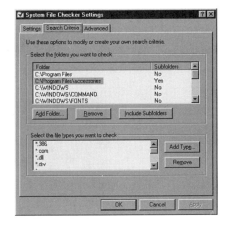

The Advanced tab, shown in Figure 11.12, enables you to create or specify an alternative System File Checker database. If you create a database, it is used only for the current session with the System File Checker. If you wish to return to the default database at any time, just click Restore Defaults. Creating a database is just a matter of clicking on Create and providing a filename and location using a standard Save dialog box. Once it's created, you can reuse the database any time you wish. Such a database can track files that you wish to be tracked (such as updates downloaded using the Windows Update utility), while the default database can remain to track the Windows files that came on your original CD only.

Figure 11.12.
The Advanced tab enables you to create the database that tracks file information.

Clicking on Start while Scan files for errors is selected (in the main dialog box shown in Figure 11.9) initiates the scanning process. The progress bar announces the progress of the operation. When a suspect file is found, you see the dialog box shown in Figure 11.13. You have the following options for dealing with the file:

- **Update the information in the database.** Choose this option if you know that the file has been upgraded intentionally before the system check.

- **Restore the file.** Choose this option if you suspect corruption or an incorrect version.

- **Ignore the message and continue.** Choose this option if you are uncertain what to do.

- **Update information for all files.** Select this option if you have just done a major upgrade and would rather not answer a dialog box for each changed file.

Figure 11.13.
The File Changed dialog box enables you to decide what to do about suspect files.

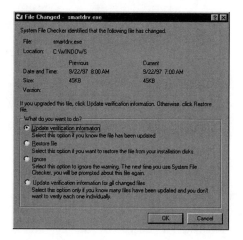

The File Changed dialog box presents the date and time stamp for the previous and current versions, the size of each version, and the version number for each version. Keep in mind that sometimes an upgrade file might be older or of a lower version number. Sometimes upgrades do not work out and you have to revert to an earlier version of the file. You may need this information if you call a vendor's help line for help with troubleshooting.

Sometimes you know a file is damaged or missing, and you just want to restore it without doing a complete system check. The Extract one file from installation disk option enables you to name the file you need to extract and restore it (refer to Figure 11.9). You can enter the name of the file or you can browse to the current version on the system. Clicking on Start causes the installation medium to be searched for the filename. Windows 98 scans CAB files and compressed files alike, locates the appropriate file, and extracts it from its compressed version. The installation medium location is kept by the system for future use. As long as you place the medium in the same location before initiating the extraction process, you will not need to specify a changed location. This feature greatly assists in automating this process if you install from shared network drives or folders.

Keeping Your Applications in Shape

Keeping applications running well is more an art than a science. Much of what works gets discovered by trial and error. Some of your options will be true voodoo and curiosity. Much will relate to particular hardware platforms. Here is my list of suggestions:

- Buy enough memory. To evaluate how much memory you actually need to minimize swapping to disk, monitor the Memory Manager counter Swapfile in Use. This tells you in megabytes how much of the swapfile is actually in use. Theoretically, if you add this amount of memory to the system, you will provide enough memory for applications without swapping. You must monitor during a period of typical system activity for this counter to predict accurately. (See Chapters 12, 13, and 14 for more information about monitoring.)

- Keep enough free disk space. My experience with the Windows 98 beta versions indicates that about 100MB of free disk space is absolutely essential, over and beyond any other disk requirements imposed by Windows 98.

- Use System File Checker to build a database of application files. Use this database to check whether application files have changed from what they should be.

- When you install software, pay attention to the Version Conflict Manager messages. Do not knowingly overwrite a newer version of a file with an older version. Some applications do not check what they are doing and therefore do not provide a warning. Keeping an up-to-date System File Checker database can be very helpful in tracking such problems.

- Occasionally reboot your systems. Windows 98 ages poorly. After running continuously for more than about 15 hours, it can slow down. Applications more often than not assist this aging by leaking memory—that is, allocating memory and never freeing it. Even Microsoft products have been known to leak memory. Although Windows 98 can clean up such resource losses better than any preceding version of Windows, the leaking process has to stop before the clean-up can occur.

- Use the Tune-Up Wizard to schedule deletion of temporary files. Often temporary files orphaned in a system crash can prevent an application from running correctly.

- Schedule both ScanDisk and the Disk Defragmenter to run on a regular basis to prevent file system corruption and fragmentation of files. Both can damage application performance.

- Encourage users to migrate old data to tape or CD storage so that a large backlog of data does not consume valuable disk space. If users store archival data, encourage them to use compression software to manage their archives.

Summary

This chapter has shown you how to plan for the coming technologies that Windows 98 supports. It has also shown you how to keep your hardware in top shape and how to care for the Windows 98 operating system. You have also seen how to protect application performance.

On Your Own

Make a list of the technologies that you have to support on every workstation, and those that you need to support only on special-purpose workstations. Use the Windows 98 Tune-Up Wizard to optimize one of your systems. Run the System File Checker and Update Information utility on a system. Calculate the amount of memory that one of your typical systems ought to have to avoid swapping to disk.

12

Learning to Use the System Monitor

Peter Norton®

As Chapter 11, "Implementing Basic Performance Tips," showed, you can perform a variety of standard maintenance tasks on any Windows 98 computer to protect its operating efficiency. However, problems with performance can arise even if you keep up your maintenance routine. For example, suppose that small workgroup that you set up in a department whose research and development work you want to keep isolated from your domain reports that its Windows 98 print server is very slow. You had set aside an older workstation, attached two printers to it, and shared them to the rest of the workgroup. Your strategy was to prevent performance hits on a user's workstation because of other users attaching to a shared printer. A check of your maintenance records reveals that everything is in top shape, yet the users are still complaining. What can you do to diagnose this situation, especially if, as part of your zero administration effort, you would like to diagnose the machine over the network wire?

Note: Many organizations use workgroups to isolate organizational units whose work could interfere with ordinary business if they participated in the domain. Often these are groups such as the in-house programming staff, who need complete control of their computer configurations and cannot effectively participate in the policies governing the domain because they reconfigure their workstations and test beds frequently. A workgroup provides a simple administrative organization that can be entirely separate from the domain, even when connected on the same physical wire to the network.

Fortunately, Microsoft provides a System Monitor for Windows 98. This tool is not automatically installed if you perform a Typical installation. As a result, many have failed to notice this tool. It can provide you with direct evidence of what is happening inside the system. System Monitor may not always tag the problem exactly, but it does provide key evidence for identifying the problem.

This chapter focuses on how to use the System Monitor. The next chapter focuses on using the System Monitor to manage both small and large networks. This chapter discusses the following issues related to the System Monitor:

- How the System Monitor works
- How to install the System Monitor
- How to conduct a monitoring session
- Which counters you should routinely monitor

Explaining the System Monitor

The System Monitor acts as a window onto a section of the Registry that is kept in RAM and continuously updated by the operating system as the computer runs. This portion of the Registry contains counters that record different types of activity within system components. The group of counters active on any given machine depends on the components that you have installed. Third-party components can add their own sets of counters. The dialog box shown in Figure 12.1 gives you a sense of the kinds of counters available.

Figure 12.1.

The System Monitor provides a variety of counters to track the performance of system components.

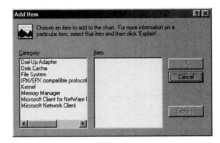

Notice that the components listed in the Category list may not reflect all the components you might wish it to include. What counters are available depends on the counters provided by the vendors whose software is installed on the Windows 98 system, including Microsoft. The system from which this information was taken has three networking protocols installed: NetBEUI, IPX/SPX, and TCP/IP. Note, however, that only IPX/SPX shows in the list of components available for monitoring. As a result, for problems related to these protocols—or for really complex problems—you may have to turn to other tools.

One such tool is Microsoft's Network Monitor, included with the System Management Server and, in a stripped-down version, with Windows NT Server 4.0. You learn how to use this tool in Chapter 14, "Monitoring Network Performance."

To diagnose the print server situation mentioned in the introduction, you would monitor the activity of the system components that seem relevant and reason backward from what you see to possible causes for the problem. Because this process is not an exact science, you must often engage in "what-if" scenarios, trying a change in the system configuration to see whether System Monitor reports an acceptable change in counter activity.

System Monitor reports on two kinds of counters: raw and rate. Raw counters report the number of events that have happened. The Windows 98 kernel, for example, keeps a count of the number of threads active. Each time a thread is started, the count increases; each time a thread is killed, the count decreases. This is a raw counter, just reporting the number of threads in use.

Rate counters express a count in terms of another count or a possible count. The default counter displayed on the System Monitor when you start it is Processor Usage. This counter is expressed as a percentage of the available processor time. As a result, you can tell that your system is maxed out when Processor Usage approaches 100%. Your system has processing capacity available when Processor Usage is below 100%.

Both types of counters are useful to you. Often you need to know how many programs are running, or whether any hidden processes are active on the machine. You can use the thread count to investigate these issues. At other times, you need an estimate of how much of a resource is used up. Rate counters such as Processor Usage are useful for this purpose.

Installing the System Monitor

Although the System Monitor is not automatically installed by default, it is a part of the Windows 98 Accessories. Installation is therefore handled using the Add/Remove Programs icon in the Control Panel. Follow these steps:

1. Open the Start menu and choose the Settings option.

2. Select the Control Panel option from the cascading menu.

3. Double-click the Add/Remove Programs icon.

4. In the Add/Remove Programs Properties dialog box, click on the Windows Setup tab (see Figure 12.2).

Figure 12.2.
You install the System Monitor from the Windows Setup tab.

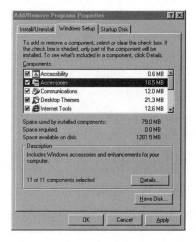

5. In the Components list, select Accessories and click Details.

6. In the Components list, scroll down and select System Monitor. Make sure the check box next to the text is checked (see Figure 12.3).

7. Click on OK to close the two dialog boxes. Windows 98 then copies the System Monitor files from the CD to your system drive and adds its shortcut to the System Tools submenu of the Accessories menu.

Figure 12.3.
*Check the check
box next to the
System Monitor
and click OK.*

Conducting a Monitoring Session

Using the System Monitor is actually quite easy. By default, the System Monitor shows you the Processor Usage (%) counter, giving you a quick assessment of how busy your system is. (As you alter both the view and the number of counters displayed, however, System Monitor will return you to the last configuration you had when you closed the application.) You can add other counters to the chart to investigate other aspects of system performance at will. You view the response of the counters in real time on a line chart that is approximately 100 data points wide. You can also view the same data as a bar chart or a numeric chart.

The Windows 98 System Monitor does have its problematic side. Although you can save the data you see on the chart for future reference, you cannot view the logged data in the System Monitor. A usual monitoring strategy is to take a snapshot of system performance when the system is running under nominal conditions, as well as a snapshot of the system when it is performing under a normal load. You may be wondering how you would view your logged data, and you may have noticed that the Help file does not provide much information about logging.

You can work around these limitations, however, as is pointed out as you work through a sample monitoring session. In fact, begin that session now. Follow these steps:

1. Use the Start menu to open the System Monitor (Start | Accessories | System Tools | System Monitor). When it appears onscreen, the System Monitor should look like Figure 12.4.

2. Open the File menu and choose the Connect option. In the dialog box shown in Figure 12.5, enter the NetBIOS name of the system you want to monitor, and then click on OK. (This name is the one that appears in the Identification tab of the Network Properties dialog box.) To monitor another machine, you must have been granted access, either by a share-level password or a user-level permissions assignment, to perform remote administration on that machine.

Figure 12.4.

The System Monitor
always opens with this
default configuration.

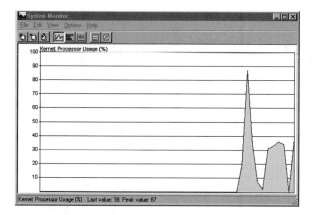

Tip: If you are running only TCP/IP as your network protocol, you need to have some method of name resolution in place to be able to monitor systems on another subnet. NetBEUI, the source of NetBIOS names, will not route. Name query requests, broadcasts that NetBIOS- and NetBEUI-compliant programs use to resolve names, typically do not route either. If you have set up a WINS server, a host file, or a DNS server, however, you provide the name resolution necessary.

Figure 12.5.

Use the Connect
dialog box to attach to
remote systems.

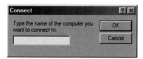

3. By default, you see only Processor Usage (%) on the chart. Open the Edit menu and choose Add Item to add additional counters to the chart. You will see the dialog box shown in Figure 12.6.

Figure 12.6.

Use the Add Item
dialog box to add
counters to the chart.

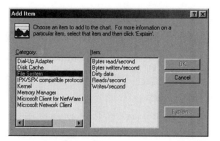

4. Take the time to select each item in the Category list to see what counters appear in the Item list. To add an item to a chart, select it in the Item list and click on OK. Add the

remaining two Kernel counters (Threads and Virtual Machines) to the chart. You can use the Ctrl and Shift keys to make multiple selections. Your System Monitor should now look like Figure 12.7.

Figure 12.7.
The System Monitor can be used to monitor several counters simultaneously.

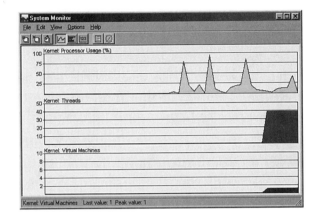

5. You can now verify that only the system virtual machine is running with a certain number of threads. (The number you see depends on what software is running on your system.) You have verified one architectural principle of Windows 98—that all 32-bit Windows programs run in the system virtual machine.

6. Choose the Remove Item option from the Edit menu. You will see the dialog box shown in Figure 12.8. Select the item you want to remove and click on OK. In this case, select the Threads item and delete it.

Figure 12.8.
Use the Remove Item dialog box to delete items from the System Monitor.

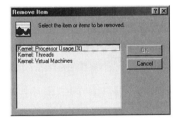

7. Choose the Edit Item option from the Edit menu. The Edit Item dialog box, which looks exactly like the Remove Item dialog box, appears. Select the item you want to edit and click on OK. You will see the dialog box shown in Figure 12.9, which enables you to change the color and scale of the chart for the item.

Tip: The Edit Item dialog box does not change its characteristics as you shift among views of the chart.

Figure 12.9.
You can alter the color and scale of any item on the chart.

8. Open the View menu and choose in sequence the Line Charts, Bar Charts, and Numeric Charts items. You can use these three views to help you to understand the system's performance. Bar charts show you both the immediate activity and the peak activity in one convenient format. Numeric charts display the most recent activity in a numeric report format. For record-keeping purposes, you might wish to keep screen captures of the Bar Chart view (see Figure 12.10). Although this view loses a sense of the volatility of certain data, it does record the peak value and give you a sense of what a current value happens to be. You can use the peak values as a benchmark to help determine whether a system with problems is performing differently from when it was first set up.

Figure 12.10.
The Bar Chart view is best for seeing the difference between peak and current activity.

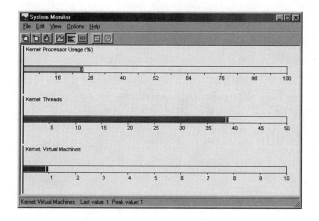

9. To see the last configuration option you have for the System Monitor, select the Options menu and choose Chart, the only item. You will see the dialog box shown in Figure 12.11, which enables you to adjust the number of seconds between updates of figures on the chart. With the Windows 98 System Monitor, this is the only way you have to adjust the amount of information you can keep on record about your system in a screen capture, especially if you are capturing the Line Chart view. Remember, however, that the greater the time interval between data points, the less information you have about volatile system counters. You will miss some of the wild swings that occur.

Figure 12.11.
You can adjust the time interval between counter updates.

This sample session with System Monitor was designed to show you your options in working with the tool. Now that you have mastered these basics, the question is what to monitor on a routine basis. The following section makes some recommendations.

Deciding What to Monitor

Monitoring a system enables you to keep track of its relative health. With perhaps seven items per category, however, you can monitor a great deal of activity. In fact, you could monitor so much that you could easily create a fog through which you would have a great deal of difficulty finding a problem with system performance. A central question is what is critical to monitor. Here are some practical recommendations.

First, you need to be aware when the Windows 98 kernel has become overloaded. A processor can execute only a certain number of instructions per second. When the processor reaches that limit, you have no choice but to make changes in the configuration of the machine; otherwise, your computer functions ever more slowly, and you get less work done. A good counter for assessing the activity of the kernel is Processor Usage (%). It is a rate counter that tells you the ratio between how much of the time the processor could be executing instructions as opposed to actually executing instructions. As a result, an increasing percentage means the processor is approaching its capacity to execute instructions. As this value reaches a consistent 100%, you need to take action to alleviate the processor bottleneck.

Second, virtual memory activity is important to monitor. As physical RAM becomes scarce, your system swaps pages to disk. As this activity increases, your system can become so busy swapping—creating the sound affectionately known as thrashing as the head swings back and forth—that little other work gets done. A good counter for assessing virtual memory activity is Page-outs in the Memory Manager category. This tells you the number of pages swapped to disk per second. As this value increases, your disk becomes a bottleneck. You need to take action to improve throughput to the swapfile or to reduce the need to swap pages from memory.

Finally, you need a sense of how long the wait is to write to disk. If you constantly have a long queue of disk jobs waiting to be finished, your disk has become incredibly inefficient. This inefficiency slows reads and writes conducted both by applications and the virtual memory manager. A good counter to monitor for gauging this problem is the raw counter Dirty Data in the File System category. It tells you the number of bytes waiting to be written to disk. This number can be misleading if you look just at the total. If you save a large file, the value will increase dramatically. As a result, peaks are not as important as a consistently high average over time.

You also need to monitor network usage to make certain that your network connection has not become a bottleneck. Unfortunately, Windows 98 does not provide a good counter for this purpose. You will, however, learn how to do this in Chapter 14.

Let's return to the printer server problem. If you connect to the server over the network and monitor these three counters, you could diagnose the problem. In this case, Dirty Data and Page-outs seem irrelevant. They are consistently low values. You note, however, that Processor Usage (%) consistently spikes up to 100%. In fact, it stays at that value approximately 50% of the time. You wonder what could be causing this problem.

Because it is not a long walk to the system, you decide to take a look. You discover that someone has installed a graphics-intensive screen saver on the system. You remove the screen saver and then check Processor Usage (%). It has dropped to a much more acceptable value, and the users stop complaining about slow printing.

Summary

This chapter has shown you how to use the System Monitor tool. You have looked at what the tool does, and I have made suggestions for counters to routinely monitor to keep track of the health of a system. We have also explored a scenario that gives you a sense of what you can diagnose about a system by using the System Monitor. We have avoided the question of how high a counter value is too high, especially for Page-outs and Dirty Data. To make decisions about such issues, you need to have a monitoring strategy, and that is the subject of the next chapter.

On Your Own

Open the System Monitor and add some counters to the display. Try changing views to get a sense of how you can best use the different data displays. Connect to a system with a screen saver running. Try several different screen savers, and note how Processor Usage (%) is affected. Connect to a system whose disk is spinning fairly frequently. Check to see what the culprit is. Is it related to swapping? Is it related to a disk-intensive application? Is there some aspect of the file system that is overloading the disk?

13

Monitoring System Performance

Peter Norton®

Monitoring systems individually enables you to keep track of how the system is performing. The data, however, can be confusing. If you have 15 counters showing contradictory trends, you may not know which trend to accept as real. A good, focused monitoring plan helps to resolve this confusion.

> **Peter's Principle:** Your Monitoring Plan Enables You to Interpret Your Data
>
> When you plan monitoring, you need to remember that your plan is what will help you to make sense of the data you collect. You need to adhere to your plan strictly in order to be in possession of the data you need to make decisions. The central reason for this admonition is that you must make decisions based on sets of data points. If you lack some of the data sets, your decisions will be less accurate.
>
> Your plan will be driven by several factors, chief among them the cost of each data item you collect. You need to remember that monitoring costs money, in terms of person hours at least. You need to determine how much you can afford in your budget to collect data, and then plan to collect the amount of data that you can afford and that will give you the best view of your systems. You are buying the data on which you will make the decisions.
>
> In choosing your strategy, the issue is purchasing enough data to give you a basis for making good decisions. Your plan, including this cost assessment, is what enables you to interpret the data you collect. The best strategy is to collect the most data that you can for the cost you can afford. If you automate monitoring, remember, you cut the costs.

Take a simple example that every system administrator has experienced. A user comes to you and says, "Gosh, Windows 98 is really running slowly these days. Can you come and speed it up for me?" Running slowly, unfortunately, is not a technical term, nor is speed it up. To understand how to diagnose the problem, you need more information. Certainly, you can run the System Monitor and look for problems. But how do you know a problem when you see one? To what will you compare the System Monitor charts? If you had some charts on record, you would have an easier time.

Building a monitoring plan really assists in troubleshooting and maintenance of systems. This chapter discusses the following topics to help you build a monitoring plan:

- The components of a monitoring plan
- Special considerations for monitoring on a small LAN
- Special considerations for monitoring on a large LAN
- Special considerations for monitoring on a WAN

Building a Monitoring Plan

Consider this scenario. You manage a 40-station LAN at your main office site and a 20-station LAN at a remote site. The remote site is linked to the main site via a 56Kbps WAN line. Periodically, you hear complaints from both sides of the WAN line that Windows 98 systems are slowing down—and sometimes crashing—really interfering with getting work done. Management has gone ballistic because of the lost revenue. They want you to find the problem and fix it—preferably overnight— so that everyone can get back to business as soon as possible. They also would like a complete report about what went wrong, so that (a) they know that it is fixed, and (b) they know what it is and that it will never happen again.

Now consider your solution. What is your plan of attack? You work on a primarily Microsoft net- work, with Windows NT Servers and just a few NetWare servers. You know the WAN link is not the problem, because the only traffic it handles is the occasional e-mail or file transfer, as well as the synchronization of the domain controllers on each side of the line. Because your account database does not change often, you know that synchronization happens only occasionally, maybe once or twice a month. Your servers are all monsters with more RAM than necessary and light-duty loads, by design. Management was willing to throw money at the servers, so you bought extra capacity. The problem has to be with the Windows 98 systems.

If you have been routinely monitoring your systems, you have some place to go to begin looking for a solution. Are you cramped for disk space or memory? If you pull your monitoring logs from soon after you installed the systems and compare them to current readings, you should be able to tell. My main point is that you have to have the records. If you don't, your troubleshooting problem magni- fies in size two- or threefold. If you are like many businesses I have worked with, your initial starting point is that you are clueless. You have no records, you have no organized knowledge about your systems and how they perform, and you probably cannot fix the problem soon enough to satisfy management. To build the indispensable records, you need a monitoring plan.

To build a monitoring plan, you have to figure out how to work around the limitations imposed by System Monitor. The major problem is the lack of an Open option on the File menu. You can save the information displayed in the monitor for future use. However, you cannot open a log in the System Monitor. A second problem is the inability to include more than 50 data points on a chart. A third is that all charts must fit within the client area of the System Monitor window.

If you carefully establish a baseline and a routine, however, you can overcome these limitations. First, although you cannot open a log in the System Monitor, you can in any spreadsheet. Unlike its cousin, the Performance Monitor in Windows NT, System Monitor saves its logs as comma- separated-value text files. You can import such files into any spreadsheet and build both reports and charts of your data for future use. In addition, using statistical procedures on the data you collect can help you to make planning decisions about supporting your systems. And most spreadsheets make performing complex statistical analyses wizard-guided operations.

Note: To create a log, select File | Start logging by using the menu. Fill in the name of the log file in the Save dialog box, and save the file. Stop logging by selecting the Stop Logging menu option. You can start and stop logging more easily by using the Start and Stop buttons, the last two on the right of the System Monitor toolbar.

Establishing a Baseline

The first record you need is a baseline for each system. A baseline is a snapshot of system performance that you use as a reference point. To understand a system's performance, you must know how it operated when it was healthy. To know whether a busy system is in fact experiencing problems, you need to know what a healthy system looks like when it is busy. You therefore need two reference points: one for the system under nominal conditions, and one for the system under working conditions.

Each system will have its own performance characteristics. As a result, you need a baseline of data for each system. Ideally, the baseline would include about 30 minutes of data sampled roughly every five seconds. When you run the System Monitor, set up an appropriate interval and log data for the specified period of time. You can use the Scheduled Tasks icon in the System Tray to schedule the monitoring session if you like.

Warning: You must be careful when using very long sampling intervals. The more time between the updates, the more data points you skip in the presentation. These lost data points may contain critical information about your system's performance.

One unfortunate fact relating to the System Monitor is that, although you can start it using the Scheduler, you must manually initiate logging and end logging. Although scripting has been added to Windows 98 via the scripting host, an application like the System Monitor must display objects to the scripting language to allow control of the application. No object model has been documented for the System Monitor. As a result, if you wish to completely script the logging session, you need to map out the keystrokes necessary to initiate the logging session. After you have the keystrokes mapped, you can use a tool such as WinBatch, a scripting language for Windows, to control the logging session. If you are comfortable with VBScript, you can use the SendKeys statement to play the keystrokes to the System Monitor. Those who prefer JavaScript, or another scripting language supported via third-party extensions to the scripting host, would use the equivalent statement in those languages.

To record a baseline, you need to save logs of the monitoring sessions previously described. If you have many different types of hardware in use under a lot of different conditions, you need at least to monitor each type of hardware under both nominal conditions and representative system loads. To ease this workload, you should work to establish a standard desktop, which includes both a standard hardware set and a standard software load. You can then build baselines for representative systems, rather than for each system. You choose your representative systems based on two factors: the hardware involved and the kind of work intended for the workstation. A graphics workstation for the desktop publishing unit obviously will look quite different from an administrative assistant's desktop, both in the hardware and the software loaded. The type of work places demands on different resources on each machine. If you have a set of standardized systems in your organization, you can keep a set of standardized baselines for each type.

In creating baselines, you want to make your life as easy as possible. The more you standardize software, hardware, and operating system configurations, the easier a time you have with maintenance of your systems. This truism applies not only to keeping baselines for reference relating to system performance, but also to troubleshooting hardware and software problems. The fewer products you have to support, the greater the knowledge base you can build about those products. Baselines are one part of that knowledge base. Another critical part is the personality of your chosen configuration. Each combination of software and hardware will have its own set of quirks, special workarounds, and problem resolutions. The more you can know from experience with the machines you use, the easier your job supporting them.

When you think of recording information about a system for the baseline, you should follow these guidelines:

- As soon as possible after installation, collect the baseline.
- Collect two baselines—one with minimal software running and no user working, and one with the normal working software running and a user working.
- Create a log of data sampled every second for 30 minutes. With this amount of data, you can easily evaluate how the system performs under nominal conditions. If you need different views of the data, you can create a sample from your log. To see performance at a granularity of five seconds, select every fifth entry in the data log.
- Import the log into a spreadsheet and build a chart of the system performance.
- Archive the screen shots for future reference, both on disk and paper.

And now for the question I have been begging throughout this session. *What should you monitor?* You need a restricted set of counters that you monitor uniformly on your systems in order to watch for bottlenecks that steal performance. Any system has four very likely performance bottlenecks: the processor, memory, network connection, and disk drive. Of these, Windows 98 provides counters for monitoring three: processor, memory, and disk drive. Good counters for monitoring these three bottlenecks were mentioned in the preceding chapter. As a refresher, they are the following:

- **For the processor, Processor Usage (%).** This counter is an estimate of how much useful work the processor can do. If it is at or near 100% for extended periods, the system is processor bound. Corrective action for this item is to upgrade the processor, stop running as many applications simultaneously, or to schedule certain tasks during periods of system inactivity (such as overnight).

- **For memory, Page-outs**. This value tells you how many pages of memory were swapped to disk per second. When this value exceeds 50, you are becoming disk bound. Corrective action for this item is to reduce the number of applications running simultaneously, to add more memory to allow for a larger disk cache, or to get a faster disk to speed up paging. You can try adjusting the role of the system in the System Control Panel applet (desktop, mobile, or server) to alter system parameters, but this solution is not guaranteed. My experience indicates that maintaining at least 100MB of free disk space also helps to ease the pressure on paging.

- **For the disk, Dirty Data mentioned in the preceding chapter, and Maximum Cache Pages**. If Dirty Data is consistently larger than the Maximum Cache Pages, your system may be disk bound. The cache is filling more rapidly than the disk can accept writes, so data is queuing waiting to be written. Corrective action includes moving to disk technology with wider bandwidth (that is, from IDE to Ultrawide SCSI), installing a faster disk, running fewer applications that routinely save data, and offloading disk storage to network servers.

Establishing a Routine

To monitor systems effectively, you have to establish a baseline. The initial logs for a system will tell you where the system started. The next question, however, is what do you want to learn from monitoring? Are you just concerned about performance? Do you want to plan for the future growth of your network? Or do you want to predict system loads and traffic?

You also need to consider the basic architecture of your network and your business plan to determine what and when to monitor. The monitoring effort to manage a workgroup or a single server LAN will be quite different from that for a multiserver LAN (or WAN) for a large organization. If you are involved in a client/server environment, the performance of your servers is probably more important to your business mission than the performance of workstations. The routine you follow needs to be appropriate to the type of work you are doing and the type of network you have.

To monitor for performance issues on a workgroup or small LAN, you need a baseline and you need comparable readings at regular intervals to check whether the machine has deviated from its baseline. The intervals can be quite some time apart. I would recommend sampling performance every three months. Repeat the process of taking a baseline, compare the figures, check for bottlenecks present or impending, and take corrective action.

Tip: For serious system management, you want to consider augmenting your efforts with a tool such as SMS (System Management Server). Such tools collect a range of additional statistics, such as free disk space, that help you to forecast needs.

Monitoring to plan for future growth on a small LAN requires more frequent sampling. You need to be able to predict trends; as a result, you need data that has some immediacy, because any computing resource will reach capacity much sooner than you plan for it to. I recommend monthly monitoring. If resources are disappearing rapidly, monitor every two weeks so that you can stay ahead of the trends and request appropriate budgets.

For larger networks, you need to decide first which systems are most critical to the work being done. If you are heavily engaged in client/server work, the performance of your servers is critical to your mission. If they suffer performance degradation, everyone working on the network suffers. As a result, you should continuously monitor your servers with software appropriate to their operating systems. You should review their logs daily. You want them at peak performance.

For workstations on large LANs and in client/server environments, routine monitoring may prove entirely counterproductive. You may not have the staff to keep up with 1,000 workstations even on a monthly basis. In this setting, having standardized desktops with baselines established for each standard platform is very helpful. You can respond to reported problems by monitoring the problem system and using the baseline for comparison, planning your troubleshooting strategy from the comparison of the problem log to the baseline. In this way, you cut the cost of monitoring by collecting only the critical information, but also give yourself the information necessary to resolve problems when they occur.

When you find yourself somewhere between the extremes of a workgroup and a client/server enterprise LAN, choose your routine based on the systems most critical to the operation. If your focus is desktop publishing, the servers that support the effort and the DTP workstations are most critical—although other machines may be peripheral—to your effort. If you do a lot of statistical analyses, the servers that store the data and the CPUs that do the number crunching are the critical machines. If you are supporting a telemarketing or customer-service call center, the database servers supporting the call center and the workstations used by the operators are critical, much more so than the receptionist's workstation. You want to monitor strategically to support your critical functions, and work with the baseline/problem log comparison for other machines.

> **Tip:** When you are trying to predict trends, you need to enter your data into a spreadsheet so that you can apply statistical techniques to forecast trends.

To predict system loads and traffic, you need to monitor representative systems weekly. For this type of information, you need to get used to your business cycle. You want to know when the systems are most stressed, or whether there are annual swings in the demand for disk resources. If February is your busiest month, you would like to plan your maintenance activities so that (a) your systems are in good shape for the crunch, and (b) maintenance does not subtract from performance during the busy time. Just to emphasize the point, representative systems will enable you to see the business cycle. Choose systems in each area of the business that seem to carry the typical workload in each unit. Choose two or three workstations and servers of each type, depending on your network size, and monitor these systems as the index machines for determining the business cycle.

The simplest way to monitor to learn cycles is to monitor weekly as long as necessary to learn the business cycle, and then to shift to monthly monitoring. With this sort of plan, you can meet all three of the different goals of monitoring. You learn the activity cycle, and then you have enough data to predict trends and plan for future growth. You also have a reasonable record of system performance. After you have a strong sense of your business cycle, you can rotate monitoring so that occasionally you monitor each system on the network over a one- to two-year cycle. On large networks, you may never be able to monitor every system in a timely fashion. When you reach the point where you can rotate the systems monitored, however, you have better records when problems occur, and you can apply statistical procedures as you see fit to check the evolving performance of the systems on your network.

Many IT professionals feel that they are not business analysts. Someone else in the organization ought to be responsible for understanding the business cycle. In a sense, I agree with this point of view. But I also think that IT professionals need to understand the impact of business cycles on the machines they maintain. If you do not have a rudimentary sense of how business cycles impact your machines, your machines are likely to fail when unexpected stresses hit. At times like that, the excuse "Who would have figured?" doesn't carry much weight. Forewarned of problems is prepared to meet problems. You need to keep yourself forewarned.

Consider our scenario one more time. Had you built a plan that started out with weekly monitoring, and then shifted to monthly monitoring, you could pull your records and look for trends. Has disk space been decreasing on the systems? Have the processors become inadequate to the task? Are you low on memory? Is it time to run the Disk Cleanup application to get rid of unused files? Should you visit the Paranoia tab in TweakUI to cause some items to be deleted when users log off? Are you just in the peak of your order cycle and some slowness will have to be suffered? Monitoring records can indeed give you an answer.

Applying Statistics

To stay ahead of problems, you can forecast trends. To forecast trends in the usage of your network, you need to apply a statistical tool called *regression analysis*. You have no need to fear the math. Most spreadsheets automate the process of using this tool so much that doing the analysis is a matter of pointing and clicking.

To conduct such an analysis, you need to enter your data into a spreadsheet. Fortunately, your logs are comma-separated-value files. Just opening the file in a spreadsheet invokes a conversion filter. You may need to specify, as you do in Excel, that the comma is used as a delimiter (but most conversions are automatic or wizard driven). Figure 13.1 shows such a spreadsheet opened in Excel.

> **Note:** Remember that to do statistics with Excel, you must have installed the Analysis Toolpack. Use the Tools | Add-Ins menu option to install the toolpack.

Figure 13.1.
You can load your log easily into a spreadsheet.

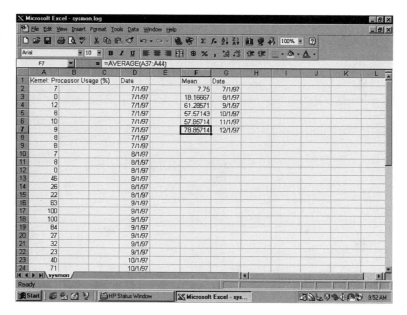

To include logs from several monitoring sessions, you must create separate log files and merge them separately into a single spreadsheet to create a view of a system over successive logging events. In addition, you need to supply a date field for each monitor record in the spreadsheet if you want to forecast trends over time, shown already inserted in Figure 13.1. In addition, if you want averages of raw counters or rate counters, you must create those averages yourself in the spreadsheet for any given monitoring session. Although you may have to massage your data a bit, the end result is quite worth it.

To create a forecast, build a chart out of the data. For forecasts, you need to insert date information. You may also want to create selected averages so that you can view, for example, average processor load in a series of months rather than in a series of seconds. Then select the data columns appropriate for your chart, open the Chart Wizard (Insert | Chart), and build a line chart. After you have the chart built, you can insert a trendline on the chart (Chart | Add Trendline). Figure 13.2 shows the Add Trendline dialog box.

Adding a trendline is a simple way of performing complex regression analysis on your data. The type of analysis is governed by which type of trendline you choose. Normally, you want to select the Linear type. Most performance data will describe linear trends. However, some data describes curvilinear trends. You can usually tell by inspection of the plot on the line chart. If the general shape of the data points is bowed in any way, try fitting one of the curves to it. You should easily be able to tell after the line is on the chart whether the line seems to fit the data. If your data is all over the chart or seems to fit the general form of a wave, try the Polynomial line. If you are using the workaround method described earlier, try the Moving Averages method. It adjusts for the possible overestimate of the trend.

Figure 13.2.
The trendline Type tab enables you to select the type of trendline you want to use.

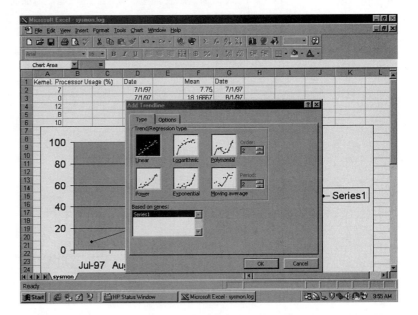

The Options tab, shown in Figure 13.3, enables you to select the forecast period. Use the Forward spin button to select the number of periods. You want to forecast forward until the resource zeroes out or hits 100 percent for most trends. For polynomial trends, however, you just want to see where it goes, because such a trend may not maximize or minimize. You may have to use trial and error to reach an appropriate maximum or minimum. The point at which maximum or minimum is reached, however, tells you when you have to plan to add resources to the system.

Figure 13.3.
The Options tab enables you to select your forecast period.

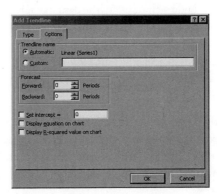

Figure 13.4 shows a chart of processor usage plotting data for six months. A forecast for the next nine months shows that in January this user is likely to hit 100 percent processor usage on her current system. As a result, you know that you have about four months to plan for how to adjust this system to accommodate this user's needs. You could order a processor upgrade, order a new system, or monitor the system to see what other changes might reduce the load on the processor.

Figure 13.4.
This chart of processor usage predicts when a user will need an upgrade.

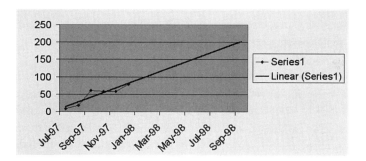

You want to forecast trends at least every three months so that you can plan for the capacity your systems will need to meet the demands of your users.

Monitoring an Individual System

When you monitor an individual system, you can take the readings for nominal conditions while you are seated at its keyboard. To take readings from a busy computer, however, you need to attach to it over the network. You want to schedule the monitoring session with the user when you know that the user will be engaged in normal activity on the system. Use the Connect option on the File menu to attach to the system, and set up the counters that you want to use. Then start your log. When the log is finished, open it in a spreadsheet, add a date column to the data, and save the spreadsheet as the archived form of your log.

Tip: Remember to set any system up for remote administration that you want to monitor over the network. See Chapter 15, "Configuring for Ease of Use."

Monitoring a Small LAN

The easiest way to monitor a small LAN is to monitor all the systems. In this fashion, you collect a complete picture of system and network health. As the number of systems grows beyond about 20, however, you may want to sample the LAN rather than monitor every system every period. You should monitor systems critical to your business function every period. For user workstations, however, you can easily use either a random or a systematic sample to gain a sense of average performance.

You could use a sampling method to select a sample size that would yield an average of performance within a given bound on the error of estimation. If you want to do that, I suggest you study any reference book on sampling methods and apply the techniques. What I recommend is that you reduce the monitoring load, especially because of the limitations of the System Monitor, by using a systematic sample. In a systematic sample, you select every ith computer on your network, where i is a number of convenient size. By convenient size, I mean a number that will enable you to monitor each system on your network at least every six months, assuming that you will repeat the sample using different systems during each monitoring session. If you monitor 600 systems monthly, i must be six to monitor each system once every six months. In addition, on your list of systems, you begin your selection at system 1 in month 1, system 2 in month 2, and so forth, to select your systematic sample, monitoring every sixth system after the starting position in the list each month.

This sampling technique accomplishes three goals. First, it reduces monitoring to a manageable load. Second, it gives you on average a monthly view of how your systems are doing. Third, it gives you a periodic sample of each system to compare against its baseline. You can respond to problems developing on individual systems as they appear in the individual system record. You can respond to problems on the network, or predict when to take a close look at individual systems, from the more general sample each month.

Remember that monitoring strategies, as indicated earlier, depend on what goals you have in mind, how much you can spend on system maintenance, what resources you have available (human and computer) to conduct monitoring, and how important maintaining peak performance is to the business plan. Your strategy will inevitably be a compromise among these factors. Ideal recommendations (like many of mine in this chapter) can be seen only as best-case scenarios. You will have to determine your own best case, choose which machines to monitor to protect the critical features of your business effort, and do your best to stay ahead on system maintenance by examining the data you collect.

Monitoring a Large LAN

When your LAN becomes large and has several subnetworks, you have two choices. First, you can plan your monitoring load so that you get enough information from the System Monitor for planning and maintenance, while reducing the monitoring load so that the monitoring task can be accomplished. Remember, to monitor with System Monitor, you must monitor by hand. You cannot save except through screen captures. This is an inexpensive and workable solution, but you will find that you lose data in such a scheme. Keeping up with the monitoring load consumes time and resources, and you will probably find that an acceptable workload does not give you a perfect picture of your systems.

The alternative is to use system-management software to replace the System Monitor. As your LAN increases in size, this is the preferred method of managing your systems. You will find a trade-off with this choice as well. A package such as SMS or Tivoli will not track the same counters as the System Monitor. However, such tools provide automation, great flexibility, and scheduling. On large LANs for routine monitoring tasks, you need to use such a tool.

Monitoring on a WAN

Monitoring systems attached to a WAN usually means setting up monitoring within each segment connected by the WAN lines separately. You do not need to limit the performance of your WAN links, however high, by consuming bandwidth with monitoring activity. Approach monitoring as you would controlling broadcast traffic. Strategically locate your monitoring tools so that monitoring traffic remains within the LAN segment and the WAN link's bandwidth is protected.

Summary

This chapter has shown you how to use the System Monitor to take a snapshot of system performance. I have introduced the concepts of counters and categories, and we have looked at counters that are good for tracking the health of your systems. I have also recommended some strategies for monitoring the Windows 98 workstations on your network.

On Your Own

Try installing the System Monitor on your system, and then practice with it to review your own system's performance. Then link to a system over the network. Practice setting your monitoring interval, and practice taking the three types of system snapshots discussed in this chapter.

14

Monitoring Network Performance

Peter Norton®

Microsoft has bet heavily on the client/server paradigm for networks and software utilization. The clients are, of course, Windows 95, Windows 98, and NT Workstation loaded with all sorts of software such as Office, Outlook, and Domino (Notes). The servers are NT Servers, at least in Microsoft's eyes. These provide the Back Office applications, SQL databases, connectivity with mainframes, Remote Access Service, and configuration management software. It goes without saying that the clients and the servers need to communicate constantly on a Microsoft network. As I indicated in Chapter 12, "Learning to Use the System Monitor," you need to monitor the health of your network to manage your Windows 98 clients effectively. Because the servers are considered the controllers of the network, they contain most of the tools to monitor network activity.

Windows NT Servers provide a set of counters that you can monitor using the Performance Monitor, the counterpart of the System Monitor, to check the basic health of your network. You can use these counters, related to the protocols you have installed and the network monitoring agent, to gather basic performance statistics. One counter is percentage of bandwidth consumed, for example, a counter that you can easily watch to tell when your network traffic is exceeding capacity, or heading close to the problem level.

Unfortunately, the Windows 98 System Monitor includes no category of counters that enable you to easily assess network traffic. Fortunately, your servers, especially your Windows NT Servers, can provide you with appropriate monitoring tools. Microsoft has provided a miniversion of its Network Monitor with Windows NT Server. It resides on the Windows NT Server CD in a subfolder of the i386 folder.

If you don't have a Windows NT Server with its Network Monitor to leverage, you can purchase other network monitoring tools from third parties, some of which, of course, require you to buy the Windows NT Server anyway. They come as part of software products such as SMS Server and Tivoli. They are also available as standalone software. You can also purchase hardware products with which you can monitor your network and conduct a variety of other network tests.

No matter what monitor you use, my intent in this chapter is to show you what to watch for. This chapter covers the following topics:

- How to choose a network monitor
- How to install the Microsoft Network Monitor
- How to use the Microsoft Network Monitor
- How to monitor a network for problems

Choosing a Network Monitor

Why should you be concerned about monitoring network traffic? What does it have to do with managing Windows 98 workstations? As always, the answers to these questions is "it depends." If you are working on a large network, network monitoring may not fall within the scope of your job. Although monitoring may remain somebody else's problem, however, what somebody else discovers by monitoring has impact on the configurations you have to manage. The teams I have worked with who manage networks of 200 or so nodes have been small enough that everyone on the team had to know a little about all the job functions, because they all had to back up each other's job functions. If you are in this situation, you should know at least the basics of monitoring. If you manage a small network, you probably have to undertake everything. Although monitoring the network may seem less important than other tasks, as soon as you connect one office to another via a phone line or a 56Kbps line, you may need to turn to monitoring to resolve problems.

What are your typical goals in monitoring your network? On large networks, you need to check the integrity of routers and subnets, check to see whether your subnetting scheme has been effective, make decisions about whether to stay with hubs, whether to move to switching hubs, and so on. Most of these decisions will not be the concern of the Windows 98 administrator. However, as mentioned earlier, the discoveries others make impact on your configurations.

To illustrate the implications for administering Windows 98, I keep coming back to a team that managed a 200-node secure network that I once worked with. This was the group who had to share job functions to keep their network functional. As a team, they had to choose a design for the physical layer of their network. They knew that their existing single server network was overloaded, because users were waiting far too long to save files to the server, open applications, and carry out routine housekeeping tasks on the network. Yet they had no clue about why the network was so slow. A consulting firm provided them with their new architecture, and fortunately, they had the budget to purchase the equipment. The consultant's design (and it wasn't me) was definite overkill. This network could expand from its current 200 nodes to 10,000 or more nodes without difficulty. I feel strongly that this group could have made a better purchasing decision if they only had known what traffic was consuming the bandwidth, and they could have purchased hardware more suited to their needs and purposes. Most of the network load was invested in word processing and simple spreadsheets. However, they were configured to handle intense client/server database work well into the future.

As the scale of the network becomes smaller, the goals for monitoring become much more focused on the hardware near at hand. If our small network is approaching the limits of its bandwidth, the central question is why. We can speculate and guess, try one thing or another to improve the situation, but there is no substitute for finding out what traffic is traveling down the network wire. If a lawyer's office with 30 nodes is experiencing network trouble, they are experiencing it for a reason. You can wander from machine to machine tweaking, but the best way to solve the problem is to locate the culprit. To find the problem, you need to know who is sending packets to whom. A network monitor will tell you.

Perhaps the best network monitors are the hardware units, also known as *protocol analyzers*. You can connect them into your network cable and sniff packets directly. You do not need to use a workstation or a server to do the monitoring. You also have little impact on the network when you use such a monitor. You have no impact on any of the workstations and their users. On the up side, you can probably get more information from a hardware monitor than from a software monitor, but the extra information comes at a high price. The cheapest one that I have seen runs about $7,000 street price. That's a bit rich even for my sophisticated and demanding taste, and it is usually more than the owner of the average LAN wants to pay. For large LANs, however, such an investment can be very wise. When you have to manage multiple segments, when you have to investigate routed protocols, and when you frequently have to verify the integrity of cables, the expense is entirely justified. On large networks, you may also want to invest in cable testing hardware, and possibly a tool called a time domain reflectometer, which helps to verify the integrity of cables and connections. You can easily gauge when you need such tools. Calculate the person hours invested in tracking problems without them. I would invest in these tools when the cost of labor tracking such problems equals the cost of the equipment in a single year.

Software monitors come in a variety of packages. If you buy a tool like the Microsoft Network Monitor as a standalone tool, you can expect to invest about half the cost of a hardware monitor. Licensing for such tools often depends on the number of nodes on your network, and pricing often makes up for the fact that you might carry a single copy to several machines, installing and then uninstalling, to work around the constraints of nonconcurrent licenses. A standalone software monitor is probably the cheapest way to approach network monitoring. For all but the smallest of networks, and for any, no matter how small, that must connect two offices over a telephone line, I recommend acquiring a software monitor. For small networks, the cheapest way is to install one Windows NT Server on your network.

Such monitors also come as part of system management packages, however. SMS Server, for example, includes the Microsoft Network Monitor, which is actually the Intel Network Monitor, licensed by Microsoft for use in the product. Tivoli includes a network monitor, as do other comprehensive network monitoring packages. The cost associated with these is the cost of implementing the management package on your network. A minimum practical cost, given the servers and licensing requirements, is $15,000; in fact, this figure quite simply increases as the size of the LAN increases because of the licenses required, and possible backup servers. The advantage of such management suites is that they provide you with a wealth of information well beyond what you would get from the network monitor software alone. On large LANs this increase in capability more than justifies the cost, because you end up saving dollars in other categories. The labor associated with rollouts of new software, for example, can be drastically reduced. You can also use the information generated by such tools to improve capacity planning as well as to analyze and predict the network traffic that you view directly with the monitor. Your basic approach is to rely on the higher level, more summative information provided by other components in the package to identify and predict problems, and then analyze the problems directly with the network monitor component.

Peter's Principle: The Best Approach to Network Management

The best approach to network troubleshooting and capacity planning is to use an integrated management suite. Companies that offer such packages include McAfee, Intel, Tivoli Systems, Microsoft, Cisco, and Bay Networks, among others. Some of the packages, of course, are related to particular routers or other network hardware components. Some suites favor certain operating systems, or offer limited feature sets as opposed to others. The reason I make this recommendation is that, in return for your investment, you will derive more information about your operation from such a software suite. You will be better suited to predict problems and required capacity than if you follow another approach.

Each of these products automatically builds a database of your hardware inventory, and keeps track of hardware settings and statistics. They can also monitor software licensing and use. The statistics kept depend, of course, on the capabilities of the management suite; however, you can query the database of statistics and build reports that enable you to make informed decisions about how to improve your network and protect its performance.

Software monitors also come as separate packages. You can buy Microsoft Network Monitor separately from the SMS package. Novell has offered its LANalyzer separately from any package for some time. With a software monitor alone, you are limiting yourself to examining protocol traffic, packet by packet. From this point of view, you have difficulty making predictions about bottlenecks or similar problems because of the overwhelming detail you receive. As a result, if you purchase only the monitor, you will want to use the System Monitor, or some other monitoring facility, to get less granular views of what is happening on your network. A software monitor alone is the cheapest route to go, but you need to rely on other tools for identification and prediction.

If you are moving into distributed objects or extensive client/server applications, you may want to consider a specialized network monitor designed to analyze the traffic between objects or client/server components. Optimal Networks, for example, offers Application Expert, which sniffs packets, analyzes their purpose, and predicts application performance over WAN links. Network Associates offers Sniffer, and Compuware offers EcoScope, both similar in purpose, but with fewer predictive features. Although the feature sets of these sniffers differ, their basic purpose is to identify the traffic generated by your application, and where the traffic is directed on the network. Their goal is to help you avoid bottlenecks by helping to see current traffic and to predict future traffic. Licensing for these products can be hefty. Application Expert runs approximately $15,000.

The cheapest way to get a network monitor is to buy Windows NT Server. You get a limited copy of the Network Monitor on the CD with the operating system. It is relatively easy to install, gives you some basic capabilities, but has some serious weaknesses. It must run on the server, for example. You can monitor traffic only to and from the server where Network Monitor is installed. You cannot edit packets. You may not see why these factors are limitations if you have not worked with a monitor before, but they do in fact limit what you could use the monitor to accomplish. We will use this version of the Microsoft Network Monitor to demonstrate some of what you can accomplish, however, mainly because it is available to anyone using Windows NT Server.

Installing the Microsoft Network Monitor

To get a sense of how to use the Network Monitor, you have to install it. It does not come onboard in the default load of Windows NT. Installation is easy and straightforward. Follow this procedure:

1. Right-click on the Network Neighborhood on the Windows NT Server, and choose Properties from the context menu.

2. In the Network Properties dialog box, select the Services tab, shown in Figure 14.1.

Figure 14.1.
Use the Services tab to install the Network Monitor.

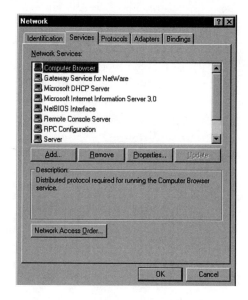

3. Click on the Add button.

4. In the Select Network Service dialog box, select Network Monitor Tools and Agent, as shown in Figure 14.2.

5. Click OK. Windows NT copies the appropriate files into place and prompts you to restart the system. After you have restarted, you are ready to undertake network monitoring from the server.

Figure 14.2.
*The Network
Monitor Tools and
Agent service
comprises the
Network Monitor and
the Network Monitor
Agent.*

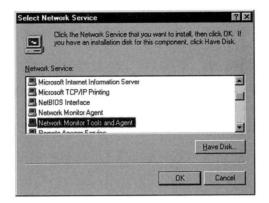

Using the Microsoft Network Monitor

A session with the Microsoft Network Monitor breaks down into three phases: capturing the data, filtering the data, and analyzing the data. Although you can capture and filter at the same time, I always recommend capturing all the traffic without filtering if you are analyzing a problem. You capture all the packets. Although you run the risk of having to sort through a lot of irrelevant detail, you do not run the risk of having failed to capture the packets that represent the problem. When you have to explore a problem, capture everything to make sure you capture the symptoms of the problem.

To conduct a basic session with the monitor, follow these steps:

1. Use Start | Programs | Administrative Tools (Common) | Network Monitor to start the Network Monitor. You now see the Capture window (see Figure 14.3). The upper-left pane shows you quick summary statistics, including percentage of network utilization. The pane below it lists the active sessions, either broadcast or computer-to-computer connections, on the network. The bottom pane lists the statistics for each type of packet tracked. The right pane offers summary statistics for the capture session.

2. Use Capture | Start to initiate the capture session. The panes of the Capture window become active, as shown in Figure 14.4. Note that percentage of network utilization is very low. There is a broadcast session on the network, and the broadcasts are emanating from the computer named Alfred.

3. Use Capture | Stop and View to end the capture session and open the View window (see Figure 14.5). You now have a view of the actual packets captured, including the source and destination addresses, the protocol generating the packet, and a general description of its purpose.

4. Double-click on any packet to reveal a description of its contents, as shown in Figure 14.6. You see a general description of each section of the packet, and its actual data in both hex and ASCII in the pane below.

Figure 14.3.
*The Capture window
provides information
about network traffic
during the capture
process.*

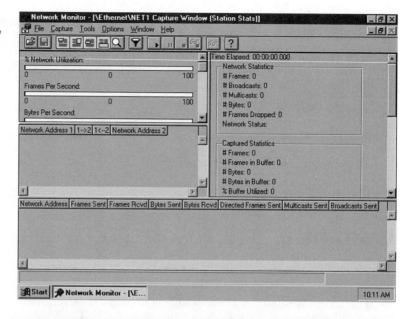

Figure 14.4.
*The top-left two
panes reveal the most
important information
for assessing network
traffic during a
capture.*

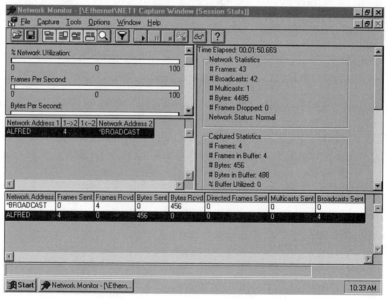

Figure 14.5.
*The View window
provides summary
details about
individual packets.*

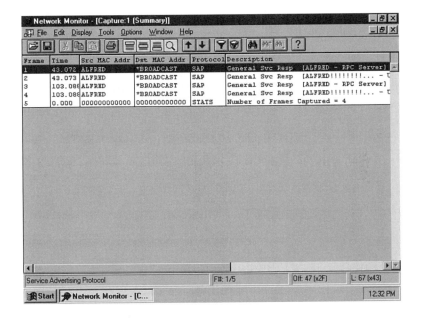

Figure 14.6.
*Double-clicking on a
packet reveals its
details.*

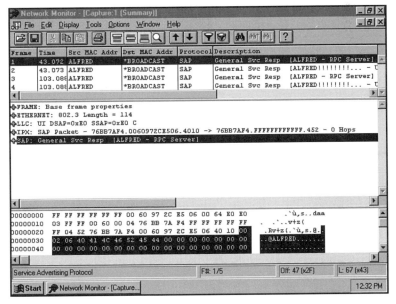

5. Click on the plus sign to reveal the individual fields of a packet section and their contents (see Figure 14.7). Note that the actual field is highlighted in the hex/ASCII data pane. The file you select and the selection in the data pane always stay in synchronization.

Figure 14.7.
Select a field and view its actual contents in the data pane.

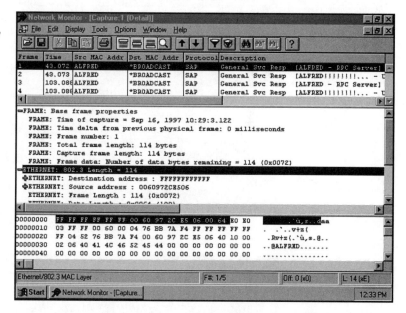

6. Select Display | Filter to select a possible filter for the packets. The dialog box shown in Figure 14.8 appears. The cryptic tree means that you are currently displaying packets from any protocols and packets traveling to and from any computer on the network.

Figure 14.8.
The Display Filter dialog box reveals the display filter currently in use.

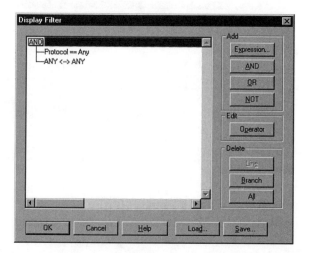

7. Double-click on any line below the conjunction to reveal the Expression dialog box, as shown in Figure 14.9. The expression defines what packets you display. You can display packets traveling from an address to another address, you can display packets generated by a particular protocol, and you can display packets with certain properties.

Figure 14.9.
The Expression dialog box enables you to define the filter for displaying packets.

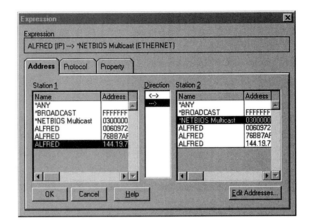

8. Select the Protocols tab to define a protocol filter, the one you will use most frequently, as shown in Figure 14.10. Click the Disable All button to clear all the protocols out of the filter, select the ones you want to see, and then click Enable.

Figure 14.10.
You must first disable all the protocols, and then enable the ones you want to view.

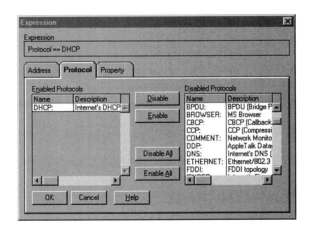

9. After you practice for a while with filters, you can build very complex ones. Figure 14.11 shows a filter that displays all packets except those whose Backup Browser field contains the text 'Alfred.' This is an example of a filter that uses properties to select or exclude packets.

Figure 14.11.
Filters can become quite complex, both including and excluding packets on a variety of criteria.

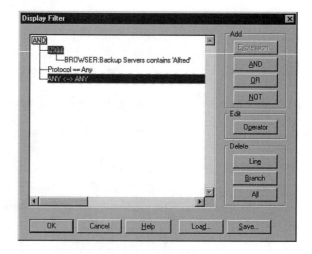

This ends the cook's tour of the Network Monitor. Critical points to notice are that you can get an assessment of the percentage of bandwidth consumed from the monitor. You can also identify traffic by computer, protocol, or contents (also known as properties). You can identify which computers are sending packets of certain types, so you can identify the culprits responsible for certain traffic.

If you install the SMS version of the Network Monitor, you can remotely monitor from any system on your network. Windows 98 includes a service called the NMAGENT, which provides the connection point for remote monitoring. You install it just like any other network service, using the Add button on the Default tab of the Network Control Panel applet. This agent provides a Control Panel applet for configuring password security on the remote monitoring connection point (see Figure 14.12). You can set a capture password and a display password. You need to set a capture password. Those who possess the password can capture packets by connecting to the remote network card across the network. Those who possess the display password can only display packets previously captured by someone in possession of the capture password.

> **Tip:** Remote monitoring enables you to assess traffic on different segments without actually visiting the remote segment. Because each packet, once captured, has to be sent back to the monitor over the network, however, you double network traffic during the remote monitoring session. To avoid this kind of impact, you could use a hardware monitor on the remote segment or set up a software monitor on a workstation in that segment.

Even if you plan to do no remote network monitoring, you should install the NMAGENT on each Windows 98 workstation where you intend to use the System Monitor. The reason is that NMAGENT adds several counters to the System Monitor that are available from no other source (see Figure 14.13). These counters are especially useful for analyzing Ethernet or token-ring traffic via the System Monitor. Unfortunately, none of these counters give the percentage of bandwidth consumed. Under Windows 98, you need to rely on the Network Monitor or the Windows NT Performance Monitor for that information.

Figure 14.12.
You can set password security on the remote monitoring agent.

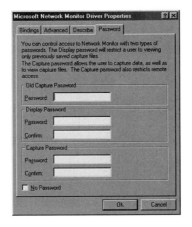

Figure 14.13.
NMAGENT adds several counters to the System Monitor that are available from no other source.

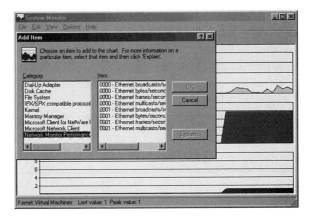

Network Monitoring Strategies

How, you may inquire, would I examine network traffic? What are the circumstances that would lead me to investigate the traffic? What would I do if I identified what I thought was a problem? These are legitimate questions. To answer them, you often have to combine the resources of several operating systems, as noted before. You may have to fire up the Performance Monitor on one of your Windows NT Servers to gauge the percentage of bandwidth consumed. You may have to use the System Monitor to track the rough amounts of traffic generated by the protocols you use on your Windows 98 systems. And you may need the Network Monitor to identify traffic patterns on the network. In any case, you need to develop some strategies for investigating network problems.

Tip: Although the Performance Monitor provides a different user interface from the System Monitor, the Performance Monitor works in substantially the same way, using the same Edit menu to add items for tracking.

To answer these questions under Windows 98, you need to rely on all the resources mentioned, including the services of other software and operating systems. If you have Windows NT Servers on your network, you should use their Performance Monitors to track the consumption of network bandwidth, monitoring the value %Network utilization. You would want to schedule this monitoring periodically, and at each interval, you would look for these danger signals:

- On 10Mbps Ethernet, turn to the Network Monitor when bandwidth is consistently 35–40 percent consumed. Beyond this level, the collision lights on your hubs should be lit consistently, and much of the remaining bandwidth is being consumed by collision noise.

- On 16Mbps token ring, turn to the Network Monitor when bandwidth is consistently 70–75 percent consumed. Beyond this level, network performance degrades as traffic progressively consumes the remaining bandwidth.

If you do not monitor bandwidth consumption with the Windows NT Performance Monitor, you can monitor it from the Microsoft Network Monitor. Again, you need to schedule this monitoring to occur periodically, and you need to take action when you see the preceding critical values exceeded.

If you are not monitoring either of these ways, you need to watch for these symptoms:

- Sluggish performance for any task that requires network access
- Slow logon performance, with delays of more than 20 seconds to initiate logon script processing
- Timeouts for accessing servers through the Network Neighborhood
- Messages that a network connection has been dropped after it has been established
- Difficulty connecting to systems over the network to perform routine administration
- Little improvement in user-perceived network performance after normal working hours

Be aware that once you have experienced these symptoms, you already have a problem. The only way to proactively prevent problems is to monitor from your Windows NT Servers or from the Network Monitor.

Now that you know how to recognize the circumstances that would cause you to investigate network traffic, the question then becomes what to do to correct those circumstances. When you get a warning that trouble is coming, or once trouble has arrived, you need to recognize the source of the problem. Network problems occur because you and your users are placing more traffic on the wire than the wire can sustain. You must therefore adjust the network so that you avoid these circumstances.

You have these general options:

- Acquire more bandwidth. Under the conditions of Internet access, this just may be a matter of adjusting your proxy server or firewall to allow access to more bandwidth. Or it could mean calling your ISP and upgrading your connection to a higher bandwidth. Both of these are reasonably inexpensive alternatives. Within the LAN, however, it means new network interface cards, hubs, routers, connectors, perhaps switches, and possibly new cables. Depending on how your connection was established, the upgrade of the telephone connection alone could require complete rewiring. Usually, these alternatives are seriously expensive.

- Reduce broadcast traffic, especially that tied to *name resolution*, the process of matching a computer's name to either its MAC or its IP address. Network broadcasts tie up resources because each client must process them. The fewer the broadcasts, the better.

- Segment the network using routers, and configure the routers to filter traffic that you don't want to cross segment boundaries. You might choose to filter SAP packets sent out once per minute by NetWare servers, for example, or to allow only every *x* SAP packet to pass.

- Reschedule server-based software so that it runs after normal use hours.

- Distribute software to servers local to the segment. If everyone runs Office from a server, have an application server for this purpose on each segment, and carefully configure filters to prevent this traffic from crossing routers.

- Keep user home directories on a server local to the segment. User data access traffic will therefore not cross the router unless users reach out to servers across the router.

- Restructure your network so that server-to-server traffic and administrative traffic can be removed from the user segments. You can find several such schemas discussed on Microsoft's Web site or any network hardware vendor's Web site. The current buzz word is the *three-tier client/server architecture.*

The only solution that you can implement under Windows 98 to limit broadcasts used for name resolution is to use hosts or lmhosts files for name resolution. Under NetBEUI, if a computer needs to access another computer by NetBIOS name on the network, the NetBIOS name must be paired with a network address of some kind before any communication can take place over the network. This network address can be an IP address or a MAC address, depending on the protocol you use to carry network traffic. Windows 98's default method of name resolution is not very efficient. NetBEUI conducts a name query request. That is, it broadcasts a packet to every client that asks whether the client recognizes the name. The client that recognizes the name responds by sending back the appropriate network address.

Hosts and lmhosts files are used on TCP/IP networks to avoid such broadcasts. Each computer maintains such a file in the Windows folder. It contains lines that have two items separated by white space (tabs or spaces). The first item is an IP address, the second a NetBIOS name or a domain name for the system. When the need for name resolution arises, Windows 98 will not issue a name query request unless the hosts or lmhosts files do not contain an entry for the name under question. (Of course, if you have disabled NetBEUI, no name resolution can take place unless these files contain entries for each system you might access.) According to Microsoft, the hosts file is for systems on the local segment, and the lmhosts file is for remote servers. Sample files with complete documentation for how to build them appear in the Windows folder. Remember that these files must be saved without extensions.

Other solutions that you can apply are the following:

- Assign each machine an IP address manually, rather than using the Dynamic Host Configuration Protocol to assign IP addresses. You avoid the network traffic associated with DHCP. DHCP under most circumstances, however, does not significantly impact network performance, because it generates only about eight packets at the beginning and half-life of a lease.

- Do not enable BootP traffic on your routers. If you do, all Bootstrap Protocol traffic will cross your routers, including that for remote boot systems and DHCP. This traffic can be enough to saturate a 56K WAN line at certain points during a working day.

- Use WINS Servers running under Windows NT for name resolution, or implement DNS servers on your network for name resolution. When Windows NT 5.0 brings Dynamic DNS, use it for name resolution.

- Implement a transaction server and a message queue server system, either Microsoft's or someone else's, to guarantee delivery of Windows messages and client/server transactions across the network, even if there are delays due to slow cables or downed equipment.

- Distribute backup domain controllers around the network to process logons without requiring logon traffic to cross routers or WAN links. When Windows NT 5.0 comes, the distinction between backup and primary domain controllers will disappear, but you will still need enough domain controllers to prevent logon traffic from causing bottlenecks.

- Distribute preferred NetWare servers around your network so that logon traffic need not cross routers.

These are all general-purpose solutions. By using the Network Monitor to examine traffic, you can determine the following:

- **Which machines generate the most traffic.** After you have located the highest bandwidth consumers, determine which protocols are generating the traffic. Try to determine whether this is a hardware problem in which bad hardware is constantly broadcasting (beaconing), or a software problem. To identify the biggest traffic generators, sort the packets captured by machine name.

- **Which protocols generate the most traffic.** Specifically, is this a user problem indicated by a lot of SMB traffic? If so, move from a Network Neighborhood to premapped drives for granting access to resources. Is it TCP/IP traffic? Track down how much of it is related to

Internet access, either HTTP or FTP. Consider applying new Internet use policies. To identify the protocol source of the packets, sort the packets by protocol.

- **Which users seem to generate the most traffic.** You can track user names through the SMBs that process logons, and you can filter packets for contents by using the user name as the string to search for. Perhaps you need to focus on user discipline.

- **Which applications are generating the traffic.** Are people playing Doom on the network? Search for common executable names by filtering for contents.

Using these strategies, you can resolve most network traffic problems.

Controlling User Behavior: An Example of Managing Network Traffic

Some of my clients had a serious problem on their network. They were running 10Mbps Ethernet in a simple star configuration. They used one NetWare server (version 3.11), from which they ran all their applications and on which they stored all their data. They had 200 workstations on the network, which was only minimally secure, even though the client had a highly secured facility that required at least secret clearance for entry. Their network was slow, not painfully, but slow enough that they realized they could not add workstations, which they needed to do. This client desired a near-term and a long-term solution.

For the near-term, we implemented network monitoring using LanAlyzer, which they had purchased from Novell but never used. The first thing we did was a capture of data during the slowest periods, and then we sorted the packets several ways. A sort by workstation name revealed no particularly heavy users. A sort on application names revealed some unapproved software, mainly games, both Doom and flight simulators among them. A check of bandwidth consumption revealed they were congested, hitting above 50% most of the time.

The near-term solution was relatively inexpensive. First, we established a use policy that outlawed gaming, and we used network monitoring to enforce the policy. Second, we divided users into those who needed to run software from the server, because they could not handle local control of their software, and those who could handle local installation of software. We shifted some of their most frequently used software to local installations on about 50 percent of their workstations. Both of these solutions provided enough relief from the traffic problem to keep their network going.

The long-term solution required redesign of their network. First, they acquired several new servers, some running Windows NT and some running NetWare. These servers implemented user management, primary domain control, firewall services, data repositories, and system management using SMS Server, and they communicated with one another on a private 100Mbps Ethernet connection. They communicated with workstations via a 10Mbps Ethernet connection, which meant that the workstations needed no upgrade in terms of network adapters and cabling. The workstations were placed on four subnets, overkill for the near term, but appropriate for the client's expansion plans. Each subnetwork had a backup domain controller that served as the department server. Users ran their applications from these servers and stored most of their data on these servers.

The goal of this long-term plan was to isolate network traffic into subnetworks. By placing the workstations on subnets, each user shared a cable with 50 users rather than 200 users. Traffic generated by loading applications and storing data was limited to the subnetwork, as was the traffic associated with normal network housekeeping. Although the overall bandwidth was technically not upgraded for the users, much more of it was available to them. By placing most of the servers on a private high-speed network, most administrative traffic and backup traffic took place on the private network. It never fell over to the 10 Mbps user network, again freeing bandwidth for the users.

We still kept the ban on playing games in force.

For more information about network solutions, see Chapter 29, "Troubleshooting Network Connections."

Summary

This chapter has reviewed the types of network monitors available and the reasons for choosing a network-particular monitor. You have seen how to install the free version of the Microsoft Network Monitor. You have stepped through a typical session with the monitor, and you have seen common strategies for attacking network problems.

On Your Own

Install the Network Monitor on one of your Windows NT Servers. Try capturing packets, and then try examining and analyzing the packets. Apply filters to reduce the detail and to focus on particular types of packets. Examine typical logons, logoffs, startups, and shutdowns for your systems.

15

Configuring for Ease of Use

Peter Norton®

Computers now come with warning labels that read, "Ordinary use of this equipment may be hazardous to your health." As a writer, I have become intimately acquainted with the joys of repetitive strain injuries. Forearm tendinitis, my particular problem, is very painful and does not get as much press as carpal tunnel syndrome. In fact, the majority of the repetitive strain injuries are not related to the carpal tunnel. They can affect the eyes, the arms, the shoulders, the back, and the legs. All of them are equally debilitating and can prevent people from being able to do their chosen work.

Accessibility to equipment is an equally important issue in the workplace. As PCs become a standard desktop appliance, we can lock out large numbers of potential users by making the equipment inaccessible as effectively as if we changed all the passwords. If I can't perform my job because the screen presents characters too small for me to read, my eyesight prevents me from performing many jobs that I could perform before PCs entered the workplace. If I cannot use Ctrl+B to format text because I do not have full use of my hands, I can make a reasonable case that Ctrl+B ought to be replaced with a keyboard action that I can perform. The graphical user interface need not be limiting. One of the brightest Windows gurus I have met has been sightless since birth.

Even less obvious are the limitations that configuration can impose on productivity. I don't know how many times I have seen individuals manually performing tasks that a computer could do more efficiently because the company has always done that task by hand. The State of Indiana, for example, keeps all corporate records on paper. To find all corporate filings relating to Eli Lilly in the past 10 years means that someone must manually search through several feet of rotating file cabinets by hand. The job takes, on average, four hours to complete. The state is in the process of scanning these documents into an indexed database. When the project is complete, those four person hours will be reduced to person minutes.

All administrators need to be aware of the potential for injury and discrimination relating to the use of computer equipment. We need to be even more concerned, however, about the potential loss of productivity. We need to know how to configure equipment to reduce the potential for these problems. This chapter addresses these issues, focusing on the following topics:

- Windows 98 features that assist in reducing injury and potential discrimination, and improving productivity
- Configuring to improve accessibility
- Configuring to reduce injury
- Configuring to improve productivity

Using the New Features

Microsoft has built in a number of features to make Windows 98 more accessible, less likely to cause injury, and more likely to improve productivity. These features are separate from the hype about the new interface, faster program launches, and so on. You really can think in terms of improving the usability of your systems by turning features on or off. Some of these features are new in Windows

98; others have been around for some time. Here's a quick overview, and then the discussion focuses on how to configure machines using these features.

Being Accessible

Those with disabilities, however major or minor, know the frustration that working with computers can present. Normally simple actions are difficult, and even devices intended to improve accessibility can be frustrating. Dictation software, for example, until very recently required you to pause briefly between each word. Speaking in this manner allowed you to dictate to your computer and to use voice commands, but writing a simple letter could be an excruciatingly slow process. To ease the arm pain, I bought a copy of Kurzweil Voice. Unfortunately, the style of speaking required interrupted my normal thinking process so much that I went back to typing.

Tip: Both IBM's ViaVoice and Dragon Systems' NaturallySpeaking offer continuous speech recognition, which does not require pauses between words. Kurzweil is likely to have a product soon. NaturallySpeaking is probably the superior product, having won several awards. Kurzweil Systems' president, however, believes that truly useful dictation software is still five years away.

Windows 98 offers some truly useful features to help those with disabilities to use the system. They can be invoked on a per-user basis, and you can set them to turn off after a preset period of time. As a result, users who become temperamental with the features can invoke them on an as-needed basis. You can choose from among the following items:

- Microsoft Magnifier, which explodes the view of the screen area near the mouse in a window at the top of the screen.
- Large titles and windows, so you can read title bars and manipulate window elements more easily.
- Capability to change the font size without changing the window size, to increase readability without changing the onscreen look.
- Capability to change the screen resolution, to affect the total size of all elements.
- Capability to set scrollbar and window border size, to make these elements easier to manipulate.
- Capability to set the icon size to improve visibility.
- Special color schemes that improve screen visibility.
- Capability to display visual warnings when the system plays warning sounds so that poor hearing does not prevent communication of system warnings.
- Capability to display captions for sounds—if the application supports this option—so those with limited hearing can be aware that a nonwarning sound has played. (Warning sounds

are accompanied by dialog boxes, so long as programmers are following appropriate Windows 98 design guidelines.)

- StickyKeys, so Control key sequences can be pressed without holding the keys down simultaneously, making Ctrl+Alt+Del available to those who have difficulty using the keyboard.

- BounceKeys (also called FilterKeys), to filter out repeated keystrokes caused by shaking hands.

- ToggleKeys, so that a sound is played when keys such as Caps Lock are pressed.

- Extra keyboard help, which displays ToolTips explaining how to do mouse actions from the keyboard when the mouse cursor rests over an object on which you would normally click.

- MouseKeys, which turn the keys on the numeric keypad into mouse navigation, clicking, and double-clicking keys.

- Special mouse cursors that improve visibility of the mouse cursor itself.

- Capability to swap the actions assigned to mouse buttons, to support left-handed users.

- Capability to adjust mouse speed and double-click speed to match user abilities.

- Mouse trails, which improve your ability to spot the moving cursor onscreen.

- Capability to set default accessibility settings and to save settings to a REG file so they can be merged into another machine.

- Support for SerialKey augmentative communication devices, which enable users who cannot manage conventional keyboards to enter information.

Microsoft provides a wizard to help you set up these features.

Using Multiple Displays

One option for improving both accessibility and productivity is multidisplay support. On systems with a PCI bus and for display adapters that have at least a Windows 95 driver, you can install multiple video cards in PCI slots, attach a monitor to each, and extend the desktop to display on all monitors. At first glance, this capability may seem to be only for the limited few. However, it has greater application than you might think.

Consider these scenarios:

- You have a user who must use large titles and windows to see the screen well. This user does not have enough screen real estate, however, to multitask applications. A second monitor can provide the needed real estate.

- Your desktop publishing shop wants to view multiple pages simultaneously and be able to read them as well. They need more screen real estate than they have to be able to shift out of a compressed view of the pages.

- A programmer wants to have multiple views of development software so that she can see the debugger window on one screen and the application run on another.

- You would like to use two screen projectors to present a PowerPoint presentation, and you would rather not use two PCs to deliver the presentation.

- A financial analyst wants to have several applications open simultaneously, but not have them stacked one on top of another. Expanding the desktop to an additional screen would allow fewer applications to stack up and would enable the analyst to separate incoming stock quotes from spreadsheets visually.

Microsoft maintains that you can have as many graphics cards and monitors installed as you would like, but the practical limit for the average PC with a standard configuration is two. Typical motherboards have three or four PCI slots, one of which should be devoted to the network card and one of which should hold the SCSI controller, if one is present. You can shift other peripherals to ISA slots without loss of performance, but you really should keep the main I/O devices on the PCI bus.

One display adapter functions as the primary adapter, and the others function in a secondary role. Windows 98 supports multiple displays automatically, because the underlying screen and graphics APIs have been modified to support multiple monitors. The modifications support all the popular graphics chip sets currently in use. As a result, you do not have to follow a special installation routine. Windows 98 is designed to recognize the multiple displays during setup. Your display properties will show a Monitors tab, and you need only check the check box labeled Use This Device as Part of the Desktop.

Be aware of the two limitations to multiple monitor support. First, if you have a display adapter built into your motherboard, you need to install Windows 98 with only that display adapter installed. Then you should shut down and install the additional adapters. On booting Windows 98, allow the Plug and Play routines to detect the additional cards and install drivers for them. You should then find the Monitors tab in the display properties.

Second, multiple monitor recognition is under the control of your system BIOS chip, not Windows 98 and not you. The BIOS has to contain basic hardware-level support for the possibility of multiple video cards. Very likely, your CMOS setup will have no settings to adjust for multiple monitors. If multiple monitors do not work on a particular machine, chances are the machine just cannot support multiple monitors. The only solution is to seek a BIOS upgrade and hope that the upgrade resolves the incompatibility.

One objection to the use of multiple monitors is that you incur additional expense to deliver what might seem frivolous or unnecessary advantages to users. Users could, after all, just learn to multitask on a single monitor more effectively. When you consider the cost of large monitors for applications that require a readable and large viewing space, however, the cost of multiple monitors becomes quite reasonable. Because Windows 98 can support different monitor types, resolutions, and sync rates on each display adapter, secondary monitors need not always be the most exceptional items.

When additional screen viewing space is required for whatever reason, multiple monitors may in fact be the cheaper solution—especially if you can pull VGA monitors off old machines no longer in use, such as an aged 486 that no longer is up to your desktop requirements.

Accessing the Internet

Internet access may not strike you as an element of improving productivity. All of us know how to waste an amazing amount of time surfing the Web. However, items on the Web *can* improve productivity. We probably need to think, as a result, about appropriate Internet access to support productivity.

Web-enabling the desktop, one option under Windows 98, can help you to build appropriate access and help you to exclude inappropriate access. Active Channels, for example, have the capability to push information onto the desktop without user intervention. If you need stock quotes, if you need news from particular topic areas, if you need updates from a supplier's online catalog, setting up a channel can deliver this information directly to you so that you always have the latest information at your fingertips. If you want to limit creation of Active Channels, use the TweakUI Control Panel applet to prevent changes to the Active Desktop. This setting is found on the IE4 tab (see Figure 15.1).

Figure 15.1.
TweakUI gives you the opportunity to prevent changes in the Active Desktop.

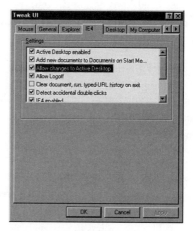

Configuring for Accessibility

You have two methods for configuring computers for accessibility. One is to use three or four icons (Accessibility Options, Display, TweakUI, and possibly Keyboard and Mouse) in the Control Panel to set up accessibility features. The other is to use the Accessibility Wizard to perform the configuration (see Figure 15.2).

Figure 15.2.
The Accessibility Wizard organizes the configuration of a computer.

The Accessibility Wizard offers great convenience. It organizes the settings around commonly known disabilities. You select the type of disability you need to adjust for, as shown in Figure 15.3, and the wizard assembles the settings you need to consider. Subsequent wizard pages offer you the opportunity to set the system characteristics you would like to use. As a result, there is no single path through this wizard. If you do not check off all the disabilities when offered the chance, the wizard limits the options presented to those you have selected.

Figure 15.3.
You select the disability you want to compensate for from a list.

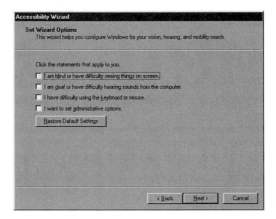

In addition to providing organization of disability settings, the Accessibility Wizard enables you to save these settings into a file that can be merged into the Registry of another computer, as shown in Figure 15.4. (The file is a text file with the .REG extension. The default action for such a file when double-clicked is to merge with the Registry.) This option is not available from the Control Panel. The wizard also enables you to decide whether the features you install can be turned on with shortcut keys, or whether they run as the default options. In the Control Panel, you must make this decision on a feature-by-feature basis.

Figure 15.4.
The Accessibility Wizard enables you to save a configuration for reuse.

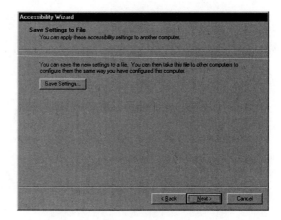

Configuring to Avoid Injury

Windows 98 does not provide a specific group of settings to help prevent repetitive strain injuries. As you set up systems, however, you can apply certain principles to prevent injuries. First, you need to be certain that the working surface is approximately 28 inches high, so forearms are level as the user is working. You need appropriate chairs so that the users' thighs are parallel to the floor. The monitor needs to be at eye level, or slightly below. Chair arms should not interfere with arm movements as users type at the keyboard.

Next, you need to consider an ergonomic keyboard. The Microsoft keyboard and its imitators provide a couple of features that do help prevent injury. First, it can be elevated from the rear, so the user types downhill. Second, the keys are split at an angle that keeps the hands and wrists in a more natural position. A decent wrist rest projects from the back edge of the keyboard, so users can rest their hands between typing activities, taking some strain off shoulder muscles.

Note: Other ergonomic keyboards do exist, but they tend to be expensive and to focus on solving particular types of injury conditions.

After you have an appropriate physical environment, you can consider system configuration issues. Repetitive strain causes injuries by creating tiny tears in the muscle and nerve fibers. Two kinds of events that you want to avoid are hyperextension and sustained repeated motion. In other words, you don't want to force users to extend muscles beyond their normal working reach, and you don't want users to cycle through the same motions without breaks for periods longer than 30–45 minutes. As you configure software, keep these two factors in mind.

When designing document templates, for example, try to group keyboard shortcuts toward the center of the keyboard and under the control of the index, middle, and ring fingers. One painful injury occurs when users reach to the outside of the keyboard with the little finger. When assigning function keys, start from the center of the keyboard and work outward. Keep the most common functions toward the center of the keyboard. Remember that the hands approach the keyboard from an angle. The most comfortable position for the hands is in a straight line with the arms. Reaching to the outside of this angle usually causes hyperextension.

Encouraging breaks and changes in the action can be done obviously or subtly. You could place a VBScript on the Active Desktop that starts a timer and reminds the user to take a break periodically. (You can recognize someone in the early stages of injury by the kitchen timer or alarm clock sitting near his or her workstation.) You can also design the activity of using your software to vary the tasks intentionally. Placing macros on a toolbar or menu, for example, encourages use of the mouse to carry out common actions. You interrupt the cycle of the hands at the keyboard momentarily, causing variety of movement and the easing of the strain on muscles involved in repetitive motion. If you can, sequence actions in your software so that different types of movements necessarily occur in the sequence of performing the work. Interrupting periods of data entry at the keyboard with a series of macros that require mousing through dialog boxes can help to prevent injury.

Building an Interface for Productivity

Productivity has become a major element of the Windows 98 marketing hype. You can do everything more easily, faster, *whatever*. The plain truth is that, as a system administrator, you can capitalize on some features to make the work of your users much more productive. One of the key elements in boosting productivity is your ability to program the interface to meet your needs and your users' needs. Because so much of Windows 98 can be based on HTML, and because you have a simple tool for building HTML pages in FrontPage Express, you have the complete power to program the interface that you and your users want to have.

Planning for Productivity

To be able to create an interface that improves productivity, you need to consider these issues:

- What is the work that your users do routinely?
- How can the desktop be designed to simplify this work?
- How can you automate the majority of this work?

Designing for productivity means building a background for the desktop that matches your users' working habits. Imagine dividing the desktop in half, reserving one side for traditional shortcuts and the other for hyperlinks to the resources your users most often need. You can create a Web page to serve as background for half the desktop. You can build this page in FrontPage Express. It can hold all the hyperlinks, channel links, and ActiveX controls that your users need. The traditional side of the Windows 98 desktop can be available in the other half of the screen.

Building the Interface

This half-and-half strategy is a thinking tool to help you imagine design possibilities. In fact, you can cover the entire desktop with an HTML page, completely hiding the shortcut icons. Users can toggle between the HTML desktop and the classic desktop by selecting or deselecting the View as Web Page option from the Active Desktop submenu of the desktop context menu. You can use only an HTML page for your interface. You can place VBScripts or JavaScripts on the page to automate whatever features you want.

Later chapters cover working with FrontPage Express, JavaScript, VBScript, and HTML in general. The main thing emphasized here is that you can literally build whatever you want to happen into the Windows 98 desktop. The desktop can contain any ActiveX control that you desire. Would you like an array of command buttons to launch applications? Perhaps a tab control to present several pages of options, each keyed to separate tasks that the user must undertake? Would you like your user to make choices of activities from a list box? Would you like to change the desktop layout based on the choice of tasks from a drop-down list box? All these are now possible. As long as you can work with an HTML editor, you, too, can build these options.

See Chapter 16 and Chapters 21 through 23 to learn how to work with HTML to produce such effects.

Configuring for Ease of Administration

Although you ought to focus on making the user's job easier, you also need to focus on making your job easier. You need to prepare your systems for remote administration. You have a simple choice. You can walk to each machine to perform administrative tasks; you can also attach over the network to perform such tasks.

To perform remote administration, you need to enable the possibility in the Control Panel, and you need to install a service. In the Control Panel, you need to open the Passwords icon, select the Remote Administration tab, and enable remote administration by checking the check box (see Figure 15.5). If you are using share-level security, you can set a password to control who may perform remote administration. If you are using user-level security, you can select which users from the user list may perform remote administration. After you have made these choices, a user may connect over the network and manage files and printers. The connecting user must provide the appropriate password or possess the appropriate user identity, depending on the type of security you have chosen to use.

In addition to enabling remote file and printer management, you need to enable remote Registry management. To do so, you must install the Remote Registry Service. This service enables you to connect to another computer's Registry over the network. You must install the service on both your workstation and the remote workstation. Follow this procedure:

1. Open the Add/Remove Programs icon in the Control Panel.

2. Select the Windows Setup tab.

3. Click on the Have Disk button.

4. Use the Browse button to navigate to `\Tools\ResKit\netadmin\remotereg`.

5. Select the `RegServ.inf` file and click OK.

6. Click on OK in the Install from Disk dialog box.

7. Click on Install to initiate the setup process. Windows 98 copies the appropriate files into place.

8. Reboot your computer to make the Remote Registry Service active.

Figure 15.5.

Use the Control Panel's Passwords icon to enable remote administration.

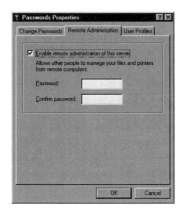

Having activated the Remote Registry Service on both machines, you can use the Connect Network Registry option on the Registry menu of the Registry Editor to attach to and edit a remote Registry. (See Chapter 30, "Investigating the Registry," for more information about editing the Registry.)

Summary

This chapter has focused on Windows 98 features that assist in reducing injury, preventing potential discrimination, and improving productivity. We have looked at configuring systems to improve accessibility by providing keyboard access, visual access, and sound reinforcement for those with special needs. This chapter has discussed how to configure systems to reduce injury by planning the type of interface devices and their placement in relation to the user. You have seen a bit about configuring systems to improve productivity by trying to automate work. Later chapters show you specific tools for implementing some of these strategies.

On Your Own

Try implementing each of the accessibility features to see how they work. Try them out with people who might not ordinarily think of using them to see which ones might be implemented generally. Set up one system configured to reduce injury. Interview some of your staff to see whether any of them see benefits personally from the new configuration. Try your hand at designing an HTML interface to your desktops. You might want to jump ahead to Chapters 16, 21, 22, and 23 for some hints. Prepare checklists that you want to use for setting up systems for people with disabilities in your organizations. Be sure to include the visually impaired, the hearing impaired, and those who have lost the use of at least one hand.

16

Using the
Scripting
Host

Peter Norton®

Scripting is just a method of telling the operating system or an application to do something.

"I want you to copy this file over here every day."

"I want to reset the time of day when the user logs on to make sure that it matches the file server's time of day."

These are simple tasks we often assign to scripts, or batch files as we called them in the DOS world, and still call them in the Windows world. One of the biggest problems historically for Windows, however, was the lack of a macro language capable of taking advantage of the graphical nature of the new operating system. When Windows sat atop DOS (which many claim it still does), you had a graphical interface but no way to perform graphical operations automatically. You can still run DOS batch files, but DOS contains no commands for scripting window events. Just try to tell a DOS batch file to "click on the OK button" or "Start Excel and build a graph based on the parameters in a file." How about something actually useful, like creating an icon for a new group of network applications on a server, or adjusting Registry settings to fix those little problems that can't be resolved any other way?

This chapter explores how scripting has changed for Windows 98 and for Microsoft's operating systems in general. You will see how to begin to leverage this powerful new feature called the Windows Scripting Host (WSH) to improve your ability as an administrator to configure, control, and maintain your flocks of user machines and servers. In general, this chapter covers the following topics:

- How to choose when to script
- What the Windows Scripting Host is and how it works
- How to run a script
- How to choose your scripting language
- How to create scripts

Before continuing, you must understand that scripting is essentially programming in a basic form. You will not need any interface other than Notepad. You will, however, need to understand the concepts involved in putting together a simple program. WSH and the languages it supports (VBScript and JavaScript) are very powerful. The more you learn, the more features you can leverage to achieve your scripting goals. We will be focusing on VBScript because of the popularity and simplicity of Visual Basic (and Visual Basic for Applications, [VBA]). There are several excellent books on the subject of VBA programming. If you visit the Microsoft Web site (or get Technet) and search for "VBScript," you will find well over 300 technical papers with examples for programming everything from connecting network drives to complex integration with Microsoft Office applications. The first rule of programming is always "Never create what you can copy from a competent source." Of course, pay attention to appropriate copyrights if applicable.

Choosing Your Scripting Opportunities

We delve further into the world of scripting by exploring its general uses. Consider these possibilities:

- You can create elaborate logon scripts for users, mapping drives, setting up environment variables, altering Registry entries, running programs, building desktop shortcuts, altering the Start menu, and much more.

- You can build one shortcut script that launches entire projects. Assume that projects always consist of a database, two documents, and a spreadsheet. Your script could collect information from the user about how to define and name these files, create them, initialize them, and create a shortcut for launching the project.

- You can create scripts that automate common tasks such as the building of monthly reports from data stored on a server. You can use Access or Excel to pull the data table down, chart the information, and present standard blocks of text in a document depending on the data values presented.

- You can create scripts that, at shutdown of an application, clean up and back up data.

- You can create scripts that you schedule to carry out common administrative housekeeping tasks such as checking for disk space used in the user's home directory and reporting both to you and the user whether the user has exceeded practical limits. This type of script would be especially useful on Windows NT, which does not currently enforce disk quotas.

- You can build scripts that carry out personal tasks that you repeat often, so you don't have to run the risk of forgetting a step.

This chapter explores the methods and the tools needed to achieve these goals after explaining how the scripting process works.

The New World of Windows Scripting

A first attempt at a graphical scripting method appeared in Windows 3.x. The Windows Recorder was a program that would record mouse and keyboard actions and play them back to Windows. The Recorder made it possible to create macros for programs that did not have macro languages. You recorded your input, and you could play it back. The Windows Recorder made it possible to do just about anything you wanted to in a Windows macro. However, it was plagued with problems relating to the windowing environment's fluid nature. Mouse input created problems, because the mouse input was always played back to grid coordinates of some type, relative to either the desktop or a window. The window locations were often not predictable, causing missed "click" operations.

Because information was recorded based on grid coordinates, if the windows weren't in the right spot, the macro produced unpredictable results, if not a flat-out error. The environment itself could be different. Screen settings (800×600 or 640×480?) would change the display of the windows, resulting again in macro recorder failure if played on a machine with a different screen resolution. The flexibility of program installation and configurations meant that the applications might not look and behave the same on everyone's machines. Again, the macro recorded on one machine may not play the same on another because of the difference in the application settings. These problems still exist. Without a common language for operating within the environment and interaction with applications in the environment despite configuration differences, any "macro recorder" is doomed to limited success. Therefore Microsoft had to take a different approach. In general, they had to try to solve the following problems:

- Independence from screen settings
- Integration with the Windows environment
- Cross-platform usage
- Flexibility to adjust to a variety of scripting languages

Clearly, we have already demonstrated the need to fulfill the first two points. Cross-platform usage and flexibility are in response to the scripting method to be able to maintain its popularity. If the scripting mechanism cannot adjust to changing times, much as the DOS batch file cannot, it will have limited use.

Windows Scripting—although presented here with a distinct focus on Windows 98—is common to Windows 95 and Windows NT 3.51+ and is integrated into Windows NT 5.0. On Windows 95 and Windows NT, you will need to go to the Microsoft Web site to download the Windows Scripting Host and install it on the machines that you will want to execute your scripts on. All the information in this chapter applies to any of these environments as well as to Windows 98.

Windows 98 does not depend on recording keyboard and mouse input and then replaying it. Instead, Windows 98 has been built with a scripting engine integrated within the operating system. An *engine* in this case refers to a common component of the operating system that performs a service on behalf of other applications. The *scripting engine* accepts requests from scripting interfaces and reacts to (or services) those requests in a consistent manner. To gain and maintain popularity, a characteristic lacking in macro recorders, the engine has been given extensibility. This means that it can be changed by an experienced programmer to accept input from new and varying interfaces or can generally be altered to deal with situations the Microsoft developers never anticipated. The interfaces are programming languages in this case. Currently, Microsoft Windows Scripting Host supports two programming languages, VBScript and JavaScript. Microsoft has also created the possibility of using additional scripting languages, such as Perl and REXX, if third parties create the module that relates the particulars of these languages to an object called the Windows Scripting Host. You should be able to port scripts from non-Windows platforms to Windows platforms.

The Windows Scripting Host (WSH) is a feature that makes Windows 98 an exceptionally flexible operating system. The host enables you to run scripts from both the command line and from the graphical interface. In addition, WSH is common among all of Microsoft's 32-bit environments, making it an excellent tool for NT or Windows. Next, you will learn how to launch scripts and how WSH executes scripts.

Running Scripts

WSH is a language-independent Scripting Host implemented as an ActiveX object. You can download this host for Windows 95 and Windows NT 4.0 from the Microsoft Web site, and it will be integrated as a part of the Windows 98 and Windows NT 5.0 operating systems. As an ActiveX component, the host makes itself available to a scripting language as a set of objects. The basic procedure for using the host is to instantiate the host objects and then use their properties and methods to perform the scripting tasks you need to undertake.

A script, therefore, is a set of statements in a language designed to carry out appropriate actions. Because the scripting engines support programming languages with rich feature sets, you will probably find that you cannot fail to accomplish what you want to undertake in a script. Running a script is a process of launching the Scripting Host and loading the script. Under the graphical interface, the Scripting Host has default actions registered for file extensions. Double-clicking on a VBS file, for example, causes the host to load and execute the VBScript in the file. At the command line, a command with arguments can launch the script.

The capability to work either from the GUI or from the command prompt implies that the Scripting Host comes in two versions. In fact, it does. The graphical program is WSCRIPT.EXE, and the command-line version is CSCRIPT.EXE. You have three ways to run a script using WSCRIPT.EXE:

- Double-click on a script file, or right-click on it and select Open from the context menu.
- Select the Run command from the Start menu, enter the name of the script file, and click OK.
- Run WSCRIPT.EXE with the filename of the script as a parameter.

Tip: If you run WSCRIPT.EXE without any parameters, you gain access to the Windows Scripting Host Properties page, just as if you had right-clicked on a script file and selected Properties from the context menu.

Using the graphical version of the Scripting Host, you have the ability to set two options. When you right-click on a script file and select Properties, you see the Windows Scripting Host Properties page, shown in Figure 16.1. This dialog box enables you to control how long scripts run by enabling you to stop them after a specified number of seconds. This helps to avoid those errant scripts from sticking around and using computer resources forever. The properties options enable you to control whether a logo appears when the scripts execute in the command prompt window. If you are running the scripts as part of some other process, such as part of the logon process, you may not want to bother the user with the logo information. Also, if the script might be running on a server when no one is logged on, having an interactive screen trying to pop up could cause problems. Setting these properties affects the execution of all scripts.

Figure 16.1.
The Windows Scripting Host enables you to set two properties in Graphical mode.

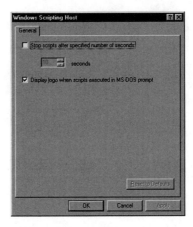

CSCRIPT.EXE provides you more options in running scripts, and thus is the more powerful method for launching scripts. Its command-line syntax is the following:

```
cscript [//OptionsForHost] [MyScriptFileName] [/OptionsForScript]
```

Typing the command at a command prompt and pressing Enter causes the Scripting Host to display a list of host options and its command syntax. Table 16.1 defines the host options.

Table 16.1. Host options for the Windows Scripting Host.

Option	Meaning
//B	Suppresses all output except that to the command prompt
//H:cscript	Sets the Scripting Host file to CSCRIPT.EXE
//H:wscript	Sets the Scripting Host file to WSCRIPT.EXE
//I	Allows input requests and output to be displayed under the GUI (opposite of //B)
//Logo	Displays logo banner
//NoLogo	Prevents display of logo banner
//S	Saves command-line options for this user
//T:seconds	Sets the number of seconds before the script is stopped by the Scripting Host

As you can see, the command-line script option allows more flexibility in running scripts. You can enter Batch mode, save command-line options, control display of the banner, and set a timeout on the script. Note that these are all host options. They affect the running of the script on the host.

The options for the script that appear on the command line are defined by the script. These options are just parameters that would be passed to the script. All script options begin with a single slash (/), as opposed to the double slash (//) that begins the host options. An example of a script option would be a script that connects to a network drive based on the user's name. The user's name would be passed to the script as a parameter (or script option), as follows:

```
Cscript //Nologo mapnet.vbs /pnorton
```

In our mythical script here, the logo display is prevented by the script host option and the /pnorton is the user's name passed to the actual script MAPNET.VBS that maps our network drives based on the user's name. Script options may affect either the host or a client.

The division between host and client processing is quite relevant when you consider scripts running on the Internet Information Server (IIS). If a script runs on the Web server, it may need to carry out certain actions, such as retrieving items from a database, on the server. The database used to display information on a Web page typically does not exist on the Web client. However, it may need to carry out actions on the client as well, such as copying cookie files or initiating the download of a file.

This division is also relevant to running logon scripts. Some processing in the script, such as mapping drives, primarily affects the client. Other actions, such as updating log files, may affect the server only. As you work with scripts, therefore, you need to keep clear both whether the code affects the client or server and whether the switches affect the script or the host. Confusing the two leads to common bugs in scripting. If you experience such difficulties, check to make sure this division has been clearly maintained.

The final method for running the script and controlling the options is to utilize a WSH file. This file is a standard text file that controls the options for the script. It also indicates the script to be run. For example:

```
[ScriptFile]
Path=C:\Windows\MyScripts\netmap.vbs
[Options]
Timeout=0
DisplayLogo=0
BatchMode=0
```

This appears much like the familiar INI files that you might be used to from Windows for Workgroups days. The [ScriptFile] section enables you to indicate the script to be run. In this case, it is a VBScript called NETMAP.VBS found in the C:\Windows\MyScripts directory. The [Options] section enables you to set the host options for running the scripts. When you double-click on the WSH file, it will run the script indicated with the options specified. The options displayed in the sample file here are all the ones currently available. You may also generate this file automatically from the Explorer interface by following these steps:

1. Right-click the script file in Windows Explorer.
2. On the context menu that appears, select Properties.
3. On the Properties page, choose the settings you want to take effect when the script runs.
4. Click OK or Apply.

The WSH files are useful when you want to be able to apply different options from the defaults for running scripts in Windows 98.

The CSCRIPT.EXE method is by far the most flexible and the most useful, although a combination of any of these methods can offer flexible choices to achieve just about anything.

Figure 16.2 shows the processing model used by the Windows Scripting Host. After you run a script file, the operating system launches the Scripting Host. The host identifies the type of file passed to it via its file extension, looking up relevant details about that file type and its mapping in the Registry. Next, the host parses the script based on the type of programming language it has detected. Finally, the scripting engine runs the script, communicating with the underlying operating system, using the services of the Scripting Host as necessary.

Figure 16.2.
The Windows Scripting Host follows a specific processing model.

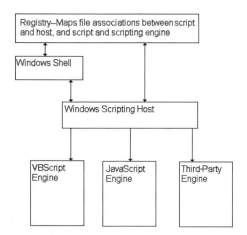

Selecting a Scripting Language

Now that you know how to run scripts, you might want to begin creating scripts. Unfortunately, you really have to learn a scripting language to build scripts. As a result, you will want to figure out which scripting language suits you better. You can accomplish just about anything in either Java or VBScript. Which one you use probably should reflect your background with computer languages.

Java is very like C++ in form and structure. If you are used to C programming or C++ class libraries, you will probably find Java very easy to pick up. Java is generally considered to be a cross-platform language. In an environment where you have UNIX as well as NT/Windows, you may want a language that ports easily.

Visual Basic is related to the BASIC language that was needed to program an Apple II-series computer. Personally, I think Visual Basic's syntax is easier to master than that of Java, but I know plenty of programmers who disagree. Visual Basic also has the advantage of being tightly integrated in the Microsoft Office suite of products. Visual Basic for Applications (VBA) is used in applications such as Word and Excel to automate many operations. Therefore, if you plan to write scripts that leverage Office integration, VBScript may be the one for you.

Microsoft supplies samples of both on its Web sites and on the Windows 98 CD. Both are powerful and also have a Web orientation, making them suitable for standard scripting as well as HTML page coding (see Chapter 23, "Using VBScript and JavaScript," for more details on Web development). Both languages can have scripts generated from a simple text editor such as Notepad, or you can purchase graphical-development environments with a rich set of tools to develop professional and complex code quickly and efficiently. This discussion focuses on VBScript. I will compare and contrast it with Java, especially in Chapter 23. Essentially, I made this choice because the focus of this book is Windows 98 administration, including the applications that may be running on the operating system. This commonly includes at least some portion of Microsoft Office. In addition, the scope of this book does not allow much in the way of UNIX coexistence and integration.

Select your language and press on to begin learning how to code for the WSH.

Mastering Some Preliminary Concepts

Because the purpose of this chapter cannot be to teach you all there is to know about programming scripts, I will focus on some common concepts that you have to master to work with scripts. These concepts are common to both VBScript and JavaScript. The scripts that we build will implement only a few of the instances of each of these concepts, but they will give you a sense of how these concepts play out in the scripts. What you will notice, of course, is that JavaScript and VBScript name their implementations of these concepts differently. They also use different syntax, different reserved words, and different operator symbols. At the conceptual level, however, these languages do work in the same way. After you master these concepts, you will have an easier time working with scripts.

Sample Scripts

Through the course of investigating these concepts, we will be referring to sample files that Microsoft has provided to get you started with scripting. You will find in your \Windows\Samples\Wsh folder a set of sample scripts written in both VBScript and JavaScript (see Figure 16.3). If you double-click on these scripts, they run; they are very instructive about what you need to do to use the Windows Scripting Host productively. They show the presentation of charts, the ActiveX automation of Office applications, retrieval of environment variables, and reading and writing to the Registry.

Figure 16.3.
The sample scripts.

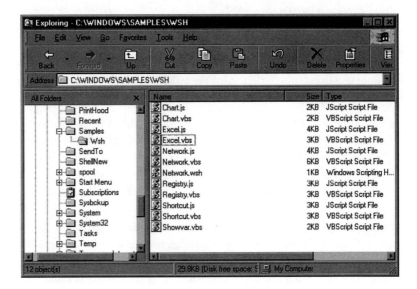

Objects

Objects, formally, are segments of code that perform a process. They consist of a *type*, which specifies the functionality of the object, the kind of data it manages, and its interface. The type is an abstract specification, and it is nothing without an *instance*, which is an instantiation of the type under a particular name. Each object specifies its interface, or how either users or other objects may interact with it. They may or may not present a graphical interface to the user.

Both Java and VBScript use objects. Typically, the objects involve a graphical interface displayed to the user, such as a button, and they are intended primarily for user interaction. Objects can also be defined that have other purposes. In VBScript, a timer is an object that presents no graphical interface to the user and just serves to report when a certain amount of time has passed. We will use objects created by both JavaScript and VBScript as we build our dialog boxes. Let's examine a section of the SHORTCUT.VBS script:

```
' Create a shortcut object on the desktop
Set MyShortcut = WSHShell.CreateShortcut(DesktopPath & "\Shortcut to notepad.lnk")
' Set shortcut object properties and save it
MyShortcut.TargetPath = WSHShell.ExpandEnvironmentStrings("%windir%\notepad.exe")
MyShortcut.WorkingDirectory = WSHShell.ExpandEnvironmentStrings("%windir%")
MyShortcut.WindowStyle = 4
MyShortcut.IconLocation = WSHShell.ExpandEnvironmentStrings("%windir%\notepad.exe, 0")
MyShortcut.Save
```

In this case, we are creating an object called a shortcut on the user's desktop. The object is assigned to a temporary variable called MyShortCut. We can then perform actions on an object or set properties. In the preceding sample code, we adjust the properties of the shortcut object in the four lines below the Set shortcut object properties and save it comment. We then perform an action on the object called Save—MyShortcut.Save as it appears in the code. This finalizes the creation of the shortcut on the desktop and saves the associated properties.

Events

After you have an object sitting on the desktop or a Web page, users can interact with it. Their interaction produces *events*. When a user clicks on a button, the system code generates an event called a *click event*. You can respond to the click event within the script. When a button is clicked, usually something changes within the interface. Code runs, a dialog box opens or closes, a screen is refreshed, or something similar happens.

An action produces the event that the code or script can respond to or ignore. The actual process is one of generating a message. A message is actually a number, nothing more. Usually, there is a text string associated with the message that you use to describe both the message and the event. Moving the mouse cursor over an object typically generates a mouse move event and message, for example. When the code receives the message, it can respond or not respond. The response might be something like highlighting the object. Turn your attention to the SHORTCUT.VBS again. When you run the SHORTCUT.VBS, by double-clicking on it, you are first presented with the dialog box shown in Figure 16.4.

Figure 16.4.
The message dialog box from the welcome routine.

When you click on the Cancel button, you generate a mouse-click event for that particular object. The code then reacts to this event by exiting the program.

```
'Start of Program
L_Welcome_MsgBox_Message_Text    = "This script will create a shortcut to Notepad on your
➥desktop."
L_Welcome_MsgBox_Title_Text      = "Windows Scripting Host Sample"
Call Welcome()
'The Welcome Subroutine.
Sub Welcome()
    Dim intDoIt
    intDoIt =  MsgBox(L_Welcome_MsgBox_Message_Text,_
                      vbOKCancel + vbInformation,_
                      L_Welcome_MsgBox_Title_Text )
    If intDoIt = vbCancel Then
        WScript.Quit
    End If
End Sub
```

In the `'Start of Program` section, a couple of variables are set to produce the text for the message box. In the `Welcome` subroutine, the message box is displayed using the `MsgBox` function with the appropriate parameters. The variables with `vb` in front of them are system variables that are always present in VBScript. The `MsgBox` function returns a parameter. The condition statement checks to see whether you have cancelled the execution of the code, `intDoit = vbCancel`. Then the program terminates. Notice the use of the underscore at the end of a couple of lines in the code. This is used in Visual Basic to indicate that the command continues on the next line. This is useful when you want to be able to see the lines of code onscreen; otherwise, the line of code could stretch past the right edge of the screen, making it difficult to view.

Methods

Methods are your means of causing an object to take action. If you want an object to receive the focus, you can stare at it intensely and wish, or you can respond to an event by executing the object's `SetFocus` method. Focus refers to an object being the center of attention for the program. When you highlight a file in Explorer that you want to copy, it will have focus. When you place the mouse over a link on a Web page, that link has the focus. After an object has focus, the actions you take, such as clicking the mouse, are understood to be intended for that object. Other methods include being able to save, delete, or alter an object in any number of ways. Remember in the shortcut example when the script executed `MyShortcut.Save`? The `save` is a method for the `MyShortcut` object, indicating that an action—namely, saving the object and parameters—should be executed.

Whoever programs the object creates its methods and exposes them to users and programmers through an interface. Each object, therefore, can have any number of methods. The typical interface for executing a method is to use a line of code that adheres to this syntax:

```
ObjectName.MethodName
```

This so-called dot notation is familiar to both Visual Basic and Java programmers.

There is always a default object, typically the one that has the focus at the moment. You can take action on a default object with lines of code that look like this:

```
MethodName
```

We will use methods related to objects created by both JavaScript and VBScript as we build our dialog boxes.

Subroutines and Functions

Methods enable you to cause objects to take actions. What do you do when you need a routine that will cause three objects to all take the same action? You write a subroutine or function containing the three statements that invokes the appropriate methods. You name your subroutine, and its name can be used in code to invoke those same three actions at any time. Look again at our now-familiar shortcut example. The subroutine `Welcome` is used to generate a message box describing what the script will do. We define a couple of parameters and call the subroutine that generates the message box. If you take a look at the other sample Microsoft scripts, you will find the exact same `Welcome` subroutine in all them. Instead of rewriting code, they use the same code and pass a couple of parameters to it to make it look different for each script. Finding common operations like this message box and writing a generic piece of code like the `Welcome` subroutine helps reduce the amount of time and effort it takes when you need a new script. Just reuse the old parts of other scripts that performed similar actions.

Java and VBScript differ in the use of the word *function*. Java uses this word to describe units of code that VBScript calls subroutines and functions. In VBScript, what I described in the preceding paragraph would be called a subroutine. Subroutines are typically written by the programmer for a particular script. A specialized bit of code that performs a specific activity—such as calculating the length of a string—supplied by Microsoft with VBScript would be called a function.

> **Technical Note:** In technical terms, BASIC originally defined a subroutine as a block of code that performs an action and does not return a value. A function is a block of code that performs an action and returns a value. In VBScript, you will find that functions typically return values, and subroutines don't. In the literature surrounding Visual Basic, however, this distinction sometimes blurs. Subroutines typically respond to events, but functions tend not to. Subroutines often change values stored in variables, but functions typically return a value through a variable that also serves as the function name. As you begin working with methods, you may find yourself hard-pressed to fit methods into a clear separation between functions and subroutines. Remember, however, that methods are typically subroutines associated with an object.

Flow Control

When your script executes, you need to control its order of execution. If you need to repeat an action three times, you can use a set of code lines called a *loop* to accomplish the repetition. If you need to set up alternatives, as when telling the difference between the user clicking OK and the user clicking Cancel, you can use code that implements if-then logic. If you need to repeat an action until a user provides input, you can create a loop that runs a block of code until the user provides the required input, called a `While` loop. Each language provides such structures, but JavaScript and VBScript use different keywords and formalizations to implement them.

Variables

A *variable* is an area of memory set aside to store information for your script. To identify this location, you give it a name. Whenever you write a statement that contains the variable name followed by an assignment operator followed by some information, you have placed (or assigned) that information to the memory location you have so named. Typically, the assignment operator is an equal sign (=).

Variables may be typed—that is, they can contain only a certain type of information, such as an integer or a floating-point number. Variables may also be untyped, meaning that they can contain any type of data. In most of your scripts, you will probably work with untyped variables for simplicity's sake. We will use variables to hold the messages to be presented in our dialog boxes.

Operators

To cause mathematical, logical, and similar hardware-level operations to take place, you need a special set of symbols called *operators*. If you look at a keyboard numeric keypad, you can easily find the operators for addition, multiplication, subtraction, and division. Each scripting language provides a set of operators for these, as well as logical comparisons and assignment to variables. For a complete list of operators, you can consult any reference on JavaScript or VBScript.

Now that you understand some of the concepts, take a look at a beginner's sample of the objects, methods, and properties available when you're creating scripts. Figure 16.5 shows the object model associated with the Scripting Host. The Scripting Host uses seven objects, only three of which are exposed to programmers directly. The other four are container objects; programmers have access to them via properties that you can set and clear.

Figure 16.5.
The Windows Scripting Host provides programmers an object model that allows interaction with Windows 98. The double-boxed objects are exposed to programmers.

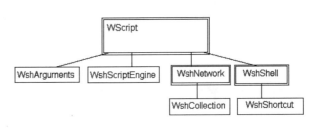

What can you do with these objects? The next few sections give you a sense of the properties and methods available to you. As elsewhere in this book, I can't provide a complete command reference. These are only the highlights. You can download the complete documentation from the Microsoft Web site.

WScript

WScript is the scripting engine itself, from your point of view. You create an object that references this engine, and then you use its properties and methods to interact with the operating system and your applications. WScript offers an `Application` property.

This property points to the script file itself. You can use it to identify which script is running. WScript also offers an `Arguments` property. This property points to the list of arguments (or options) passed to the script file. You can use this collection to identify what arguments you need to respond to in your script, if you allow the passing of arguments. Essentially, this will create an array for you that will contain a listing of the script command-line options that have been sent to the script. Take a look at a piece of code from EXCEL.VBS in the Windows 98 samples:

```
'
' Show command-line arguments.
'
Dim colArgs
Set colArgs = WScript.Arguments
Call Show("Arguments.Count", colArgs.Count, "Number of command line arguments")
For i = 0 to colArgs.Count - 1
    objXL.Cells(intIndex, 1).Value = "Arguments(" & i & ")"
    objXL.Cells(intIndex, 2).Value = colArgs(i)
    intIndex = intIndex + 1
    objXL.Cells(intIndex, 1).Select
Next
```

We will look at the whole program shortly, so don't worry too much about the `Show` subroutine or the `objXL.Cells` variable. We focus on the use of `WScript.Arguments` to assign the command line's arguments to a variable that becomes essentially an array of the items on the command line. Therefore, if we were to execute the script like this:

```
Wscript c:\Windows\samples\wsh\excel.vbs arg1 arg2
```

The result would be that an array called `colArgs` would have two items in it:

```
colArgs(1) = "arg1"
colArgs(2) = "arg2"
```

Passing parameters to your scripts is very powerful. It enables you to write a script that can react to situations or the environment. For example, assume that you have a set of shortcuts that point to applications installed on servers that you want to place on a user's desktop. But the icons depend on what the job duties of the user are and what the closest server is. A secretary might need Word running off server A, whereas a manager might need MS Project running off server B. You could pass a script some parameters like this:

```
Cscript C:\Setshrts sec A or
Cscript C:\Setshrts mgr B
```

This script would then react to these arguments and create the appropriate shortcuts pointing to the correct servers.

In addition to these properties, WScript includes a `FullName` property. It contains the fully qualified pathname to the executable file on the host computer. This property reveals whether WSCRIPT.EXE or CSCRIPT.EXE is executing your script. In addition, you have an `Interactive` property. This property reveals whether the script is running in Batch mode, in which the only output allowed is directed to the command line, or in Interactive mode, in which users may interact with the script.

The `Name` property contains the "friendly name" of the Scripting Host. You can expect it to contain `"Windows Scripting Host"` or a similar string.

Similarly, the `Path` property identifies the folder path to the Scripting Host executable file, WSCRIPT.EXE or CSCRIPT.EXE.

ScriptFullName Property

This property gives the full path and filename of your script file.

The `ScriptName` property provides the filename of your script, stripped of the path information.

Similarly, the `Version` property contains a text string that identifies the version number of the Windows Scripting Host executable you are using.

WScript offers you a method for creating objects, called `CreateObject`. It takes one parameter in parentheses, the string name of the file for the program that becomes the object. Technically, you instantiate this file as an object.

> **Tip:** Remember to place text strings inside double quotation marks ("like this") when using them as parameters for these methods.

Stop for a moment and take a closer look at the EXCEL.VBS sample script:

```
' Windows Script Host Sample Script
'
' --------------------------------------------------------------------
'               Copyright (C) 1996 Microsoft Corporation
'
' You have a royalty-free right to use, modify, reproduce and distribute
' the Sample Application Files (and/or any modified version) in any way
' you find useful, provided that you agree that Microsoft has no warranty,
' obligations or liability for any Sample Application Files.
' --------------------------------------------------------------------

' This sample will display Windows Scripting Host properties in Excel.

L_Welcome_MsgBox_Message_Text    = "This script will display Windows Scripting Host
➥properties in Excel."
```

```
L_Welcome_MsgBox_Title_Text      = "Windows Scripting Host Sample"
Call Welcome()

' ******************************************************************************
' *
' * Excel Sample
' *
Dim objXL
Set objXL = WScript.CreateObject("Excel.Application")
objXL.Visible = TRUE
objXL.WorkBooks.Add

objXL.Columns(1).ColumnWidth = 20
objXL.Columns(2).ColumnWidth = 30
objXL.Columns(3).ColumnWidth = 40

objXL.Cells(1, 1).Value = "Property Name"
objXL.Cells(1, 2).Value = "Value"
objXL.Cells(1, 3).Value = "Description"

objXL.Range("A1:C1").Select
objXL.Selection.Font.Bold = True
objXL.Selection.Interior.ColorIndex = 1
objXL.Selection.Interior.Pattern = 1 'xlSolid
objXL.Selection.Font.ColorIndex = 2

objXL.Columns("B:B").Select
objXL.Selection.HorizontalAlignment = &hFFFFEFDD ' xlLeft

Dim intIndex
intIndex = 2

Sub Show(strName, strValue, strDesc)
    objXL.Cells(intIndex, 1).Value = strName
    objXL.Cells(intIndex, 2).Value = strValue
    objXL.Cells(intIndex, 3).Value = strDesc
    intIndex = intIndex + 1
    objXL.Cells(intIndex, 1).Select
End Sub

'
' Show WScript properties
'
Call Show("Name",            WScript.Name,           "Application Friendly Name")
Call Show("Version",         WScript.Version,        "Application Version")
Call Show("FullName",        WScript.FullName,       "Application Context: Fully Qualified
➥Name")
Call Show("Path",            WScript.Path,           "Application Context: Path Only")
Call Show("Interactive",     WScript.Interactive,    "State of Interactive Mode")

'
' Show command-line arguments.
'
Dim colArgs
Set colArgs = WScript.Arguments
Call Show("Arguments.Count", colArgs.Count, "Number of command line arguments")
```

```
For i = 0 to colArgs.Count - 1
    objXL.Cells(intIndex, 1).Value = "Arguments(" & i & ")"
    objXL.Cells(intIndex, 2).Value = colArgs(i)
    intIndex = intIndex + 1
    objXL.Cells(intIndex, 1).Select
Next

' ****************************************************************************
' *
' * Welcome
' *
Sub Welcome()
    Dim intDoIt

    intDoIt =  MsgBox(L_Welcome_MsgBox_Message_Text, _
                    vbOKCancel + vbInformation,      _
                    L_Welcome_MsgBox_Title_Text )
    If intDoIt = vbCancel Then
        WScript.Quit
    End If
End Sub
```

Many interesting and useful scripting techniques are going on here. First, we see that we are calling the standard `Welcome()` subroutine that displays a message box enabling the user to accept or cancel execution. Next we use the `CreateObject` method:

```
Set objXL = WScript.CreateObject("Excel.Application")
```

The "creation" of the object actually causes the registered application (Excel) to launch. So we know how to launch an application from within our scripts now. The next few lines first make the application "visible"—it's no fun if you can't see it, right? The next lines then operate within Excel, adjusting column widths and preparing the Excel spreadsheet to be populated with data. Notice that we are referring to `objXL` and not "Excel" with our functions. When we assigned the `Excel.Application` to the variable `objXL`, we told the WSH that we would be referring to `Excel.Application` as `objXL` for short. You will see a subroutine call `Show` next. `Show()` populates the Excel spreadsheet shells with data. We get some of the data by using various properties of the `WSCRIPT` object, such as `wscript.name` and `wscript.path`. To get the command-line arguments, we use a `For` loop to cycle though the array generated through the `wscript.arguments` method that we have already discussed. This script generally has shown the following tasks:

- How to open an application like Excel from a script
- How to address the opened application and alter it
- How to get the command-line arguments and display them
- How to use `For` loops and subroutines
- How to use WScript properties to acquire information

Not bad for one little script.

Additional methods available include the `GetObject` method. This method retrieves an existing object or objects. Its parameter is a comma-separated list of the string names or the full pathnames for the objects you want to use. After you have created an Excel object, for example, you can assign it to a variable using this method. After the object is assigned to an object variable, you can access its properties and methods. This is often done using the `CreateObject` method that we used before. But sometimes the application is already running and you only need to assign it to a variable, like `objXL` in our example, to be able to send the application instructions.

The `Echo` method performs a familiar action common in DOS batch files. Like the `echo` command in DOS, this method places a string of text in a dialog box and displays it, or displays such a string on the command line. The text string follows the method and is not enclosed in parentheses.

The `GetScriptEngine` method gives you a script-engine object for a script engine present on your system. You will use this only if you create a scripting engine and need to create a registration routine for it. The argument in parentheses is the string name of the script engine. After you have an object reference, you can use the script engine's `Register` and `Unregister` methods to undertake registration or removal from the Registry.

Finally, you have a `Quit` method. This method ends the execution of the script. If you place an error code in parentheses, the method returns it to the command line or in a dialog box.

`WScript.Shell` Object

The `Shell` object gives you access to the Explorer interface to Windows 98, or the operating system shell, as it is often called. You are likely to interact with this object extensively as you write scripts. It contains methods only, but they are very useful methods.

A fine example appears in our old friend, the SHORTCUT.VBS script:

```
Dim WSHShell
Set WSHShell = WScript.CreateObject("WScript.Shell")
```

Notice that before we can utilize any of the methods, we must first assign the shell to an object variable, much as we did with the Excel application in the preceding example.

`CreateShortcut` Method

The methods for the `Shell` object include the `CreateShortcut` method. This method, obviously, creates a shortcut in the current folder. It takes the string path to the file object as a parameter in parentheses.

`DeleteEnvironmentVariable` Method

The `DeleteEnvironmentVariable` method enables you to delete a single environment variable. In parentheses, it requires one object, the name of the environment variable. Optionally, you can place a second argument following a comma, the location of the environment variable. Possible locations are System, User, Volatile, and Process. System refers to system-level variables. User refers to variables particular to the active user's environment. Volatile refers to variables currently in memory without affecting the permanent settings. Process refers to variables created by the current process.

Normally, you won't worry about where it is. On occasion, however, you may wish to temporarily adjust a parameter such as Path to be different while your script executes, but you want it to return to the user's default settings. For a quick list of system and user-environment variables, open a command prompt, type SET, and press Enter.

The GetEnvironmentVariable method retrieves the value of an environment variable. It takes the same arguments as the DeleteEnvironmentVariable method.

The Popup method displays a message box. It may take four arguments, separated by commas and enclosed in parentheses. The first is required, and it is the text to display as the message. The second is the number of seconds to display the message box. If nonzero, the box disappears after the number of seconds you indicate. If zero, the box requires user interaction to be dismissed. The third argument is the title to display in the message box. If left out, the title is "Windows Scripting Host". The final argument, if present, is a number that governs which buttons and icons appear. It must be one of the numbers shown in Table 16.2, or a sum of several of the numbers.

Table 16.2. Values that determine the style of a pop-up message box.

Value	Meaning
0	OK button
1	OK and Cancel buttons
2	Abort, Retry, and Ignore buttons
3	Yes, No, and Cancel buttons
4	Yes and No buttons
5	Retry and Cancel buttons
16	Stop Mark icon
32	Question Mark icon
48	Exclamation Mark icon
64	Information Mark icon

In addition, this method returns a value that indicates which button the user clicked to dismiss the dialog box. You can use this value to determine what action to take when the dialog box has been dismissed. Table 16.3 shows the possible return values.

Table 16.3. Return values for a pop-up message box.

Value	Corresponding Button
1	OK
2	Cancel
3	Abort
4	Retry
5	Ignore
6	Yes
7	No
8	Close
9	Help

Here is an example of using the popup method:

```
Dim wshshell
Set WSHShell = WScript.CreateObject("WScript.Shell")
'Popup with 2 buttons and no timeout
Dim respnse
respnse = WSHShell.popup("May I connect your network drives for you?","0","Little Network
➥Helper","1")
If respnse = vbCancel then
  Wscript.quit
end if
' code to setup users network drives
'completed message with 3 second timeout
response=wshshell.popup("Done",3,"Little Network Helper",0)
```

We start, of course, by setting up our object WSHShell with the CreateObject method. Then we present the user with a message box asking whether we should connect their network drives for them. This first message box prompts the user and will not close unless the user selects an option. The options available are OK and Cancel; the last parameter is 1. After the user responds OK, some action is taken to connect the drives. Another popup is displayed, indicating the operation finished. This second popup waits three seconds and disappears. The only button displayed is the OK button.

An alternative to the popup method is the MsgBox function that is commonly used in Visual Basic. This function is used in the Microsoft sample files and is well documented in the Visual Basic Help files.

Tip: You may have noticed the use of the SET command in front of CreateObject statement in the example:

```
Set WSHShell=Wscript.CreateObject("Wscript.Shell")
```

continues

You should also note the absence of the SET command in front of the response variable:

```
response=wshshell.popup("Done",3,"Little Network Helper",0)
```

Generally, use SET when you are setting or creating an object as opposed to a regular text or numeric variable-like response. Otherwise, WSH will think that you intend the variable to be an object that usually creates errors.

The next few methods have to do with retrieving and modifying Registry entries. Of course, the standard warnings apply! Make sure that if you write scripts that modify the Registry, you test them thoroughly on a machine that you really don't care about. Messing up the Registry is the fastest way to make a machine inoperative.

In addition, you have some methods to permit interaction with the Registry. The RegDelete method deletes a key from the Registry. Place the keyname as a text string following the method, but not in parentheses.

Tip: You can use the following abbreviations for Registry keys to simplify using these Registry methods: HKCU for HKEY_CURRENT_USER, HKLM for HKEY_LOCAL_MACHINE, and HKCR for HKEY_CLASSES_ROOT.

The RegRead method fetches the value stored in a value name. Place the value name as a text string following the method in parentheses.

The RegWrite method creates a key or a value or sets the value associated with a value name. Two parameters follow the method, and parentheses are not used to contain the parameters. The first is the name of the key or value to set; the second is the value to enter. Optionally, you can specify the data type of the value to set, if you wish. The method automatically converts the value to the data type of the value if you omit the data-type parameter.

The REGISTRY.VBS shows a very straightforward application that adds and removes entries from the Registry. Notice that the creation and deletion of the keys and the values is the same process. One word of extreme caution: Windows 98 and Windows NT operate differently in regard to the deletion of Registry keys. In Windows NT, if you ask to delete a Registry key that contains subkeys, such as HKLM\Software, NT will generate an error. In Windows 98, it will happily delete HKLM\Software and all the subkeys below it. This, of course, would be devastating to the operation of Windows. Again, testing is important!

Another method, the Run method, runs a program—the path to which you specify as the first parameter, no parentheses. You can include up to three comma-separated parameters. The path to the program is required. The second is an integer that indicates the window style—0 for hidden, 1 for normal, 2 for minimized, and 3 for maximized. The final parameter indicates whether to return to the script or to wait for the program to terminate before continuing to run the script. Not specified or FALSE returns control to the script immediately. TRUE causes Windows 98 to wait until the program terminates before returning to run the script.

Finally, you have the SetEnvironmentVariable method. This method sets an environment variable. It takes three parameters, not enclosed in parentheses. The first is the name of the variable; the second is the value of the variable. The final parameter is optional, and indicates the location of the variable. This parameter takes the same parameters as described for the other environment variable options.

WScript.Network

This object gives you access to network information relating to the current session. Use this object to find out what settings are in force and to carry out common networking functions. Much like the Wscript.Shell object, you will need to use the Wscript.CreateObject("wscript.network") to create a reference object.

The Network object offers several properties. ComputerName contains the NetBIOS name of the local computer. Use it to identify the computer engaged in the session. The UserDomain property contains the name of the domain the user has logged on to. Use it to identify the home domain for the session. And the UserName property contains the username of the logged-on user. Use it to find out who is logged on for this session.

Among the methods offered by the Network object is the AddPrinterConnection method. This method creates a remote printer connection. It may take five parameters, the first two of which are required, and none of which are placed in parentheses. The first is the text string that will represent the name of the local printer. The second is the text string that designates the UNC name of the printer to connect to. The third takes the value of TRUE or FALSE and indicates whether to store this connection in the user's profile so that it can be accessed again when the user logs on next time. TRUE indicates to store the connection; FALSE or missing indicates not to store it. The last two optional parameters are text strings that represent the username and password for attaching to the remote printer.

This is one of my favorites! In general, it is a real administrative issue trying to get users connected to the appropriate printer. Now you can use this method in a logon script to get them pointed to the right device. Here is the basic code:

```
Dim WSHNetwork
Set WSHNetwork = wscript.createobject("Wscript.Network")
WSHNetwork.Addprinterconnection "My Laser", "\\ServerA\HPLaser",TRUE
```

This example just attaches to a printer on ServerA being shared as HPLaser. The printer in Settings | Printers on my desktop will appear as My Laser. Lastly, the printer will be saved to my profile and automatically connected whenever I log on.

Using the other methods and properties previously illustrated, you can determine the user's domain, name, or machine name and select a printer from a list if you like. You can also check to see which printers the user is connected to and disconnect if the printer is no longer appropriate.

In addition, you have the `EnumNetworkDrives` method. This method fetches the current network drive mappings and places them in an object variable, which you have previously created. You can then retrieve the mappings by examining *objectvariable.Item(ZeroBasedIndex)*, where each item in the collection contains a drive mapping.

Similarly, the `EnumPrinterConnections` method fetches the current network printer connections and places them in an object variable, which you have previously created. You can then retrieve the mappings by examining *objectvariable.Item(ZeroBasedIndex)*, where each item in the collection contains a printer connection.

The `MapNetworkDrive` method creates a network drive mapping. It may take five parameters, the first two of which are required, and none of which are placed in parentheses. The first is the text string that will represent the name of the local drive letter. The second is the text string that designates the UNC name of the share to connect to. The third takes the value of TRUE or FALSE and indicates whether to store this mapping in the user's profile so that it can be accessed again when the user logs on next time. TRUE indicates to store the mapping; FALSE or missing indicates not to store it. The last two optional parameters are text strings that represent the username and password for attaching to the remote share.

Conversely, the `RemoveNetworkDrive` method removes a drive mapping. It may take three parameters, the first of which is required, and none of which are placed in parentheses. The first is the text string that represents the name of the local drive. The second takes the value of TRUE or FALSE and indicates whether to force removal even if the resource connection is currently not in force. TRUE indicates to remove the connection; FALSE or missing indicates not to force removal. The last parameter also is Boolean in nature, indicating whether to update the user's profile. TRUE means the mapping should be removed from the profile, and FALSE or missing means to leave the mapping in the profile.

Similarly, the `RemovePrinterConnection` method removes a printer connection. It may take three parameters, the first of which is required, and none of which are placed in parentheses. The first is the text string that represents the name of the local printer. The second takes the value of TRUE or FALSE and indicates whether to force removal even if the resource connection is currently not in force. TRUE indicates to remove the connection; FALSE or missing indicates not to force removal. The last parameter also is Boolean in nature, indicating whether to update the user's profile. TRUE means the connection should be removed from the profile, and FALSE or missing means to leave the connection in the profile. Our final example is the NETWORK.VBS from Windows samples. Not only does this particular sample display the method and objects illustrated here, but it also utilizes some other programming techniques—namely, `Function` and `InputBox`. Let's start with `Function`:

```
Function TryMapDrive(intDrive, strShare)
    Dim strDrive
    strDrive = Chr(intDrive + 64) & ":"
```

```
      On Error Resume Next
      WSHNetwork.MapNetworkDrive strDrive, strShare
      TryMapDrive = Err.Number = 0
End Function
```

Up to this point, we have been using subroutines. We pass parameters, and the subroutine does something for us. The function is the same, except that it returns a value. We would typically check the value to see whether the operation succeeded or failed. In the preceding example, the `TryMapDrive` function attempts to map the drive. If it fails, it returns a zero. If it succeeds, a nonzero number is returned. To return the value, we just set the function name to the value we want to return:

```
TryMapDrive = Err.Number = 0
```

This particular example is a tricky little piece of logic that you may have to look at for a while to convince yourself that it works, but it does. If `ErrNumber` is `0`, success; then the expression `ErrNumber=0` evaluates to `TRUE`.

The `InputBox` function, like the `MsgBox` function, is particular to Visual Basic and enables you to get input from the user:

```
strShare = InputBox("Enter network share you want to connect to ")
```

The user types in the share name, and the value is stored to the variable `strShare`.

Scripting in Visual Basic

Now let's review some of the basic rules for scripting in Visual Basic that this chapter has demonstrated. When you are scripting in Visual Basic, the first thing you must do is gain access to the Windows Scripting Host object. First you must dimension an object variable, and then you must use the Scripting Host's `CreateObject` method to give you a pointer to the object. The following lines of code accomplish this task:

```
Dim wshShellObject
Set wshShellObject = WScript.CreateObject("WScript.Shell")
```

> **Tip:** If you need to gain access to an application like Excel, you use the same syntax, going through the Scripting Host object to open the Excel object, using this line of code:
> ```
> Set objExcel = WScript.CreateObject("Excel.Application")
> ```

To work with the Scripting Host object, you apply its properties and methods. You can use the `SpecialFolders` method to return the path to any system folder by name. You can use the `CreateShortcut` method to create a shortcut in any path you choose. The `ExpandEnvironmentStrings` method enables you to use environment variables maintained by the system when setting properties for the shortcut. The following code shows the use of these methods and sets three properties, including `WindowStyle`, for the shortcut:

```
Dim shctPMA, strStrDesktopPath

strStrDesktopPath = wshShellObject.SpecialFolders("Desktop")

Set shctPMA = wshShellObject.CreateShortcut(strStrDesktopPath & "\Shortcut to
➥notepad.lnk")

ShctPMA.TargetPath = WshShellObject.ExpandEnvironmentStrings("%windir%\notepad.exe")
ShctPMA.WorkingDirectory = WshShellObject.ExpandEnvironmentStrings("%windir%")
ShctPMA.WindowStyle = 4
ShctPMA.IconLocation = WshShellObject.ExpandEnvironmentStrings("%windir%\notepad.exe, 0")
ShctPMA.Save
```

You can use the Echo method of the Scripting Host to either place text in a dialog box or display text at the command prompt. The following line of code shows the simple syntax for doing so:

```
WScript.Echo "A shortcut to Notepad is on the Desktop."
```

The Popup method accomplishes the same goal. However, the Popup method will not work when you are not in Interactive mode. The Echo method is therefore a general-purpose messaging method, but the Popup method is best used only for the graphical environment. The Popup method also enables you to set a time limit on the display of the dialog box. The following line of code demonstrates the use of the method:

```
WshShellObject.Popup "Create key HKCU\PMARegTopKey with value 'Top key'"
```

Using the Registry methods of the Scripting Host, you can create, write, and delete keys and values. You can specify the data types for values if you wish. Remember that if you do not specify data types, automatic type conversions occur for existing values. The following lines illustrate the various options you have: creating a high-level key, creating a subkey of the high-level key, writing some values, and deleting keys:

```
WshShellObject.RegWrite "HKCU\PMARegTopKey\", "Top key"
WshShellObject.RegWrite "HKCU\PMARegTopKey\PMAReg2ndKey\", "2nd key"
WshShellObject.RegWrite "HKCU\PMARegTopKey\IntegerValue", 1
WshShellObject.RegWrite "HKCU\PMARegTopKey\PMAReg2ndKey", 2, "REG_DWORD"
WshShellObject.RegWrite "HKCU\PMARegTopKey\PMAReg2ndKey\BinaryValue", 3, "REG_BINARY"
WshShellObject.RegDelete "HKCU\PMARegTopKey\PMAReg2ndKey\BinaryValue"
WshShellObject.RegDelete "HKCU\PMARegTopKey\PMAReg2ndKey\"
WshShellObject.RegDelete "HKCU\PMARegTopKey\"
```

As noted in the description of the methods, you can make use of constants, predefined integer values, to determine what appears in a dialog box, as well as to set window styles. In the shortcut code, we showed you how to set a window style using an integer value. The following example shows you an alternative method for using constants. You will also learn how to use any VBScript statement in your code and how the Quit method works. Note the use of constant names, such as vbOKCancel and vbInformation. These are predefined names in Visual Basic that are associated with dialog box styles. VbOKCancel is equivalent to 1; vbInformation is equivalent to 64. Adding these two together as the second argument of the MsgBox function sets the style of the dialog box to display the Information icon and to provide both OK and Cancel buttons. Other constants enable you to check return codes, as shown by the use of vbCancel in the If statement. The If statement demonstrates the appropriate use of the Quit method:

```
Sub TwoButtonMessageBox()
    Dim intReturnValue

    intReturnValue =  MsgBox(strMsgBoxText,       _
                      vbOKCancel + vbInformation,      _
                      strMsgBoxTitle )
    If intReturnValue = vbCancel Then
        WScript.Quit
    End If
End Sub
```

Although you have not seen an exhaustive VBScript reference, you do have some good basic lines of code that work to get you started. Check out the samples that Microsoft provides to gain additional insights, especially into how to handle errors when working with the Network object. Unfortunately, networks are chancy places—where things work most of the time, but not all the time. The file NETWORK.VBS shows you some good error-handling techniques. In addition, you should remember that all good Windows programmers steal working code wherever they can find it. Copying and pasting, and then revising to suit your needs, can save you from a lot of bugs later on.

Scripting in Java

Scripting in Java works very much the same way as scripting in Visual Basic, except that Java requires C syntax and some different keywords. After you have access to the Shell object, you work in the same way. Examine the following lines, and compare them to the VB code that performs the task of creating a shortcut:

```
var WshShellObject = WScript.CreateObject("WScript.Shell");

var StrDesktopPath = WshShellObject.SpecialFolders("Desktop");
var ShctPMA = WshShellObject.CreateShortcut(StrDesktopPath + "\\Shortcut to
➥notepad.lnk");

ShctPMA.TargetPath = WshShellObject.ExpandEnvironmentStrings("%windir%\\notepad.exe");
ShctPMA.WorkingDirectory = WshShellObject.ExpandEnvironmentStrings("%windir%");
ShctPMA.WindowStyle = 4;
ShctPMA.IconLocation = WshShellObject.ExpandEnvironmentStrings("%windir%\\notepad.exe,
➥0");
ShctPMA.Save();

WScript.Echo("A shortcut to Notepad is on the Desktop.");
```

Note that you need to use var rather than Dim to create a variable. All statements must end with a semicolon. All methods use parentheses to surround parameters; VB, on the other hand, allows some statements to function without the parentheses. Comments begin with double slashes (//) rather than single quotation marks ('). Those are the basic differences. Of course, as you move into using Java statements, you will find additional differences. Consult a good Java reference for the particulars of the Java language, and a good VB reference for the particulars of the Visual Basic language.

Summary

This chapter has outlined the use of the Windows Scripting Host. You have reviewed its object model, seen basic methods for using the Scripting Host, and examined some sample scripts. In addition, you have looked at some common scenarios when scripts of this type might be employed.

On Your Own

Try running the sample scripts Microsoft provides, using both WSCRIPT.EXE and CSCRIPT.EXE. Experiment with the command-line options for CSCRIPT. Try taking the NETWORK.VBS sample and modifying it so that it works with printers instead. Alter the questions to try to get the appropriate information to locate and connect to the proper printer. Use the various properties and methods to collect information about the user, network drives, and printers. Then store the information in an Excel spreadsheet or a Word document. This is handy when you are troubleshooting later and want to see what these settings and variables might have been before problems started.

V

Securing
Windows 98

17

Securing
the Desktop

Peter Norton®

No matter whether you have selected the Active Desktop, the classic desktop, or some hybrid in between, in any organization the security of the desktop is at issue. When Microsoft brought out Windows 3.0 and businesses started the flock to Windows, desktop security was a major complaint. I was managing a public access, networked computer lab at the time. Almost daily I had to reset colors, rebuild program groups, or repair Control Panel settings. Sometimes I had to rebuild the Windows directory—all because individual users saw a shared system as their own to do with as they pleased.

Some organizations give users complete control over their desktops. However, giving complete control can lead to help desk calls; and help desk calls, especially for trivial reasons, lead to expense. I have never seen a formal estimate, but I know that 50 percent of my time in managing that public access network went into repairing, albeit mostly well-meant, user adjustments to systems.

The cry for desktop security after the appearance of Windows 3.0 led to the debut of Program Manager edit levels in Windows 3.1. With that, administrators could provide a setting in the WIN.INI file that could limit or prevent users from changing the Program Manager settings and program groups. This scheme had a fatal flaw: Any user could edit the file and change the settings. And any user who bought the *Windows 3.1 Resource Kit* knew the settings.

As a result, Microsoft provided a stronger desktop security scheme in Windows 95 called system policies. That scheme was later imported into Windows NT 4.0, and it continues in Windows 98. This chapter examines this scheme, as well as makes a variety of recommendations about managing the desktop. This chapter covers these topics:

- Permitting users to control the desktop
- Editing the Registry to control the desktop
- Using system policies to control the desktop

Permitting the Wide Open Desktop

Users like choice, much to the dismay of system administrators. With the Windows 98 desktop, you are going to be facing a greater demand for choice. Some users will want the Active Desktop. Some will want the classic desktop. Some will only want certain features associated with each desktop type. Supporting such choice could be a nightmare.

The easiest way to support this new demand is to allow users to set their desktop features themselves. You focus on providing training and self-help materials to cut the support costs, and just live with the support calls about dekstops.

Opting for user choice of desktops is appropriate to the following sorts of user environments:

- You have highly motivated users who can be trusted to take care of their systems.
- You support a group of users who must often reconfigure their systems to evaluate or test either software or configurations.

- You have a strong training program that teaches users the basics of their operating system.
- Your users are independently motivated to learn about their computing environment.
- You have users who can be trusted to solve their own computing problems.
- Your organization does not view the desktop as a corporate resource to be allocated and controlled.
- You aggressively train in desktop problem-solving, especially focusing on the Undo options and the limitations of the Undo levels.

If you do not work in such an environment, allowing open choice of the desktop is asking to increase support costs. The increase will come in direct proportion to the inexperience of your users.

Obviously, open choice might be appropriate to some groups of users within your organization. It might not be appropriate to others. You have a range of other choices, which the following two sections examine.

Securing the Desktop by Editing the Registry

As you might expect, the Registry is the key to controlling the desktop in Windows 98. If you need to control an individual system, the easiest way is to edit the Registry. You can use the Registry Editor, but this tool is extremely inefficient for this purpose. You would have to remember a list of all the values and all the keys they reside within. You would need to remember the appropriate range of settings for each value. And you would have to set them for each system that you wanted to control.

Microsoft has provided the System Policy Editor to simplify this task. This editor provides you with a comfortable interface for finding and setting the appropriate values. It also enforces type checking on the values you enter. You cannot enter an inappropriate value that would prevent proper operation of the system.

Warning: You can, however, enter an inappropriate text string. For text values, the system usually displays whatever you enter. The System Policy Editor cannot prevent you from entering an inappropriate text string.

The System Policy Editor does not install automatically as a part of the Windows 98 standard load. As a result, to use the editor, you must install it. Follow these steps:

1. Open the Control Panel, double-click the Add/Remove Programs icon, and select the Windows Setup tab.
2. Click the Have Disk button.

3. In the Install From Disk dialog box, click Browse.

4. In the Open dialog box, navigate to `D:\TOOLS\RESKIT\NETADMIN\POLEDIT`, where D: is the drive letter of your CD-ROM drive. Accept the default selection of the INF file and click OK.

5. Click OK in the Install From Disk dialog box.

6. Select the System Policy Editor check box in the Have Disk dialog box. Select Group Policies if you want to install support for group policies as well. Click Install. (Group policies are covered later in the chapter.)

7. Windows 98 copies the appropriate files into place. It then updates the system settings. You can close the Add/Remove Programs dialog box and the Control Panel when you are ready. You do not need to restart the system to use the System Policy Editor.

The System Policy Editor is added to the System Tools menu. Figure 17.1 shows the System Policy Editor in its startup configuration. Obviously, you must take some action before you are ready to set policies. On an individual system, that action is opening the Registry. Open the File menu and choose Open Registry.

Figure 17.1.
The System Policy Editor is blank when it opens.

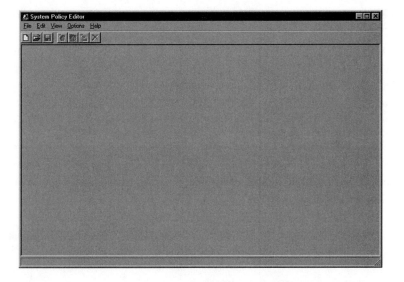

After you have opened the Registry, you are presented with two icons in the client area of the System Policy Editor (see Figure 17.2). These two icons open on double-clicking to reveal two dialog boxes that enable you to control system settings. Local Computer gives access to the Registry settings that control the default environment of the computer. Local User gives you access to Registry settings that control the environment for the logged on user.

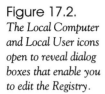

Figure 17.2.
The Local Computer and Local User icons open to reveal dialog boxes that enable you to edit the Registry.

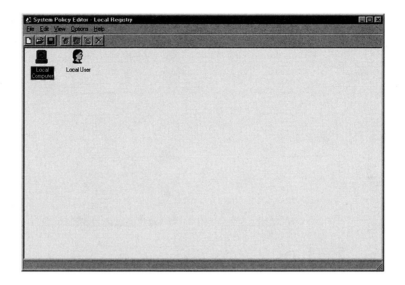

When you open one of these dialog boxes, you see a familiar tree interface. As you open the books in the tree, you see particular groups of settings controlled by check boxes (see Figure 17.3). Selecting an item in the tree often causes controls for adjusting the setting to appear in the user interaction pane near the bottom of the dialog box. You use these controls to set the parameters of the value, and these controls do check the type of the value you enter for appropriateness.

When you work with the System Policy Editor, you must remember that when you save policies you save a setting for each item marked by a check box, regardless of whether a check appears in the box. That is, each setting has an on value (checked) and an off value (unchecked). When you save policies, you save a value—on or off—for each setting available in the System Policy Editor. You may in fact save the wrong value without thinking. (This is a less disastrous error than you might make with the Registry Editor. This editor makes changes instantaneously, and it has no Undo feature or type checking associated with it. You can easily enter a value in the wrong key, or enter a value that is inappropriate and causes the system to fail.)

Warning: You can unintentionally save values using the System Policy Editor. If system behavior changes unexpectedly, check for unintentional policies.

You can control many system and user settings by using the System Policy Editor. When you think about desktop control, however, you are primarily looking at settings described as restrictions. The open books shown in Figure 17.3 show a set of restrictions you could set. There are several, all related to the Local User, and these are examined here by group to give you a sense of how you can control desktops. Keep in mind that you can set each restriction independently of the others. You can take very tight control, or you can take very selective control.

Figure 17.3.
*The System Policy
Editor offers a check
box interface to
control Registry
settings.*

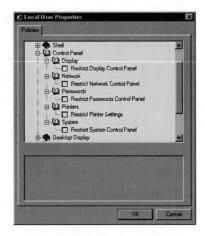

Control Panel Restrictions

There is one location for setting Control Panel restrictions, a book labeled Control Panel under the Local User I Windows 98 System book. The following list explains each setting:

- **Control Panel I Display I Restrict Display Control Panel** provides a set of check boxes that permits you to control which tabs appear in the Display Control Panel applet. You can prevent access to the entire Display applet, or you can hide the following individual tabs: Background, Settings, Screen Saver, and Appearance. Using these settings, you can control what about the display settings a user can change.

- **Control Panel I Network I Restrict Network Control Panel** enables you to hide the Network Control Panel applet or to limit access to the Identification and Access Control tabs. You can therefore prevent users from adjusting all network settings, or prevent changes only to identification and access control.

- **Control Panel I Passwords I Restrict Passwords Control Panel** enables you to prevent users from accessing the Passwords applet entirely, or enables you to hide specific tabs. You can hide the Change Passwords tab, keeping users from altering passwords. You can also hide the Remote Administration and Profiles tabs, keeping these settings under the control of system administrators.

- **Control Panel I Printers I Restrict Printer Settings** can prevent complete access to the Printer folder, or you can prevent access to the printer settings on the General and Details tabs, keeping users from altering settings for a particular printer. You can also prevent deletion of printers or addition of new printers.

- **Control Panel I System I Restrict System Control Panel** enables you to grant selective access to the System applet. You can selectively hide the four tabs presented. Each tab you hide limits what users can do to the system. Hiding the Device Manager keeps users from altering drivers. Hiding the Hardware Profiles tab keeps users from creating or modifying hardware profiles. Hiding the File System and Virtual Memory tabs reserves alteration of these settings to administrators.

Peter's Principle: Restrict Access to the Control Panel

On a network of any size, I recommend restricting the following to limit support costs. Prevent access to the Network Control Panel. Few users need access to these settings, and accidental changes can have far-reaching consequences.

As for printers, limit the ability to delete printers. Most users don't need to delete printers. Often when they do delete them, they can't replace them properly, requiring administrator intervention. If you prevent the adjustment of printer settings by hiding the General and Details tabs provided by the printer driver, you must accept the burden to create a printer on each system for each printer setup users may need. If you prevent the creation of printers, however, you prevent productive use of point-and-print technology. You must then create printers on each system for each user by visiting the computer, increasing the administrative burden.

I think you should allow users to change their passwords, but would restrict access to the other Passwords tabs. I would hide the System applet altogether for most users so that unintended device changes do not harm system performance.

Shell Restrictions

The Shell book offers you 11 different restrictions. The following list explains each of them, which are found under the Shell | Restrictions book:

- *Remove Run command from Start menu* prevents users from using *Run* to start software. This setting helps prevent installation of and use of unauthorized software or unlicensed software. A workaround is to run software from the MS-DOS prompt.

- *Remove folders from Settings on Start menu* removes the Control Panel and Printers folders from the Settings menu, the Explorer, and the My Computer icon. This limits access to these items from the Start menu.

- *Remove Taskbar from Settings on Start menu* removes the Taskbar entry from the Settings menu, limiting a user's ability to alter taskbar settings.

- *Remove Find command removes the Find* command from the Start menu and disables the option on the Tools menu in the Explorer. This action prevents users from going on searches around the network to discover resources you would rather they not access.

- *Hide drives in My Computer* hides all the drives in My Computer and all drives but the system drive in the Explorer. This action prevents users from accessing removable media drives, helping to prevent running of unauthorized software and unauthorized copying of information. However, all drives remain accessible through the MS-DOS prompt.

- *Hide Network Neighborhood* prevents access to the Network Neighborhood, preventing browsing of network resources. If you implement this option, you need to provide an alternative means, such as drive mappings, to allow users access to network resources they need.

- *No Entire Network in Network Neighborhood* enables you to hide everything but the user's own workgroup or domain in the Network Neighborhood, the list of servers that appears by default. The Entire Network item is not available, and so only the resources of the home domain or workgroup can be explored.

- *No workgroup contents in Network Neighborhood* prevents display of workgroup servers in the Network Neighborhood. You could use this setting to prevent use of workgroup computers for sharing files while allowing access to domain servers for that same purpose.

- *Hide all items on desktop* hides the standard icons that appear on the desktop, such as the Internet Explorer icon. This option forces the use of the Start menu to access these items, and you can, of course, control what appears on the Start menu.

- *Disable Shut Down* command prevents users from shutting down the system except by using the power switch. Use this option to prevent users from shutting down when you need systems up 24 hours per day for particular reasons.

- *Don't Save Settings On Exit* keeps users from saving changes to their Windows 98 system when they log off. If users alter settings during a session, by default the system saves the changes as a part of the logoff sequence. By restricting this system default behavior, you force users to retain a consistent desktop from session to session. What appeared at logon last time is what appears at logon next time, no matter what changes the user tries to introduce.

I can't offer you general principles about whether to implement the preceding restrictions. They are, in a sense, matters of taste and network style. One thing you should do, however, is to limit access to the MS-DOS prompt by using a policy discussed in the next section, if you intend to limit access to drives or the Run command. I once broke into a network and made administrative changes when I was demonstrating our product by opening a DOS prompt on a set of Windows 95 machines. And the administrator of that network was sure he had locked down his systems so that no one had unauthorized access to system settings or network resources.

System Restrictions

System restrictions are found under one book, Windows 98 System | Restrictions. The restrictions found here enable you to control a great deal about what users can and cannot do with their systems. The following list amplifies these restrictions:

- *Windows 98 System | Restrictions | Disable Registry editing tools* enables you to prevent users from running Regedit. It does not prevent users from running the System Policy Editor to edit the Registry. This option prevents users without access to a Windows 95 CD from editing the Registry. (If they have CD access, they can get the System Policies Editor.) I think it is wise to enable this option.

- *Windows 98 System | Restrictions | Only run allowed Windows applications* limits users to running only the applications you specify on the list associated with this entry. If it is not on this list, it will not run. If you need to prevent access to the System Policy Editor, limit users to running only specific applications. You can also use this option to prevent running of unauthorized applications.

- *Windows98 System | Restrictions | Disable MS-DOS prompt* prevents users from accessing the MS-DOS prompt. You should set this option when you want to make certain that users cannot use the MS-DOS prompt workaround to overcome your security restrictions. This option also prevents users from accessing DOS applications from the command prompt, as well as Windows 98 commands. To completely prevent access to DOS programs, you need also to disable the Run command.

- *Windows 98 System | Restrictions | Disable single-mode MS-DOS applications* prevents users from running DOS applications that require use of MS-DOS mode, in which Windows 98 swaps out of memory except for a stub that allows reloading Windows 98 when the application exits. Essentially, this option prevents entry of MS-DOS mode from the GUI. You should set this option to prevent users from running DOS applications of only limited compatibility with Windows 98.

Again, these options are more a matter of taste and style in managing your network, except two. Unless you plan for users to run DOS applications, you should disable the MS-DOS prompt. You prevent a number of possible security workarounds if you do. In addition, if you are in a tight security environment, you should limit the applications users run to a list of approved Windows applications. You prevent the maximum number of security workarounds if you use this option. You should also disable access to Registry editing tools.

Warning: Never, ever set the option to run a limited list of applications and fail to put applications on the list. You will not like the result, nor will your users. I invite you to try this once.

Additional Policy Editor Settings

As you may have noticed, the System Policy Editor contains options that permit you to control other aspects of systems. These options do not relate directly to desktop control, but touch tangentially on this topic. The following two sections outline these additional control options.

Remaining Local User Settings

The remaining Local User settings enable you to set up corporate options for the desktop. The Desktop Display book, for example, enables you to set the Wallpaper and Color Scheme, allowing you to create a uniform desktop for sets of users. This could be a uniform desktop for the entire organization, or for particular subsets of users.

The Shell book contains the Custom Folders book. Within this book are settings that enable you to specify the paths to folders to be used for the Network Neighborhood, Programs menu, Startup menu, and Start menu. In addition, you can opt to hide Start menu subfolders so that only the top-level options on the menu are available. You can use this option to provide some users access to the subfolders, while others may have no access to the subfolders.

Warning: Custom folders are used to specify the folders for any given user's profile. If you have implemented user profiles, do not uncheck any of the options that begin with the word *Custom*. If you do, the user will receive the default profile for the system. You can restore the user's profile by rechecking these items and manually re-entering the path to the appropriate folders in the user's profile folder. This operation can consume some time, so you are wiser never to uncheck these items.

To implement varying options for different users, you must implement system policy files, as described later in this chapter in the section titled "Securing the Desktop with System Policies."

The Local System Settings

Within the Local Computer icon, you can find several books of settings. The first, Windows 98 Network, contains multiple subbooks. The following list identifies their function:

- *Access Control* enables you to choose whether to use user-level access control (by checking the box) or share-level access control.
- *Logon* enables you to set up a logon banner, to choose whether the last entered username will appear in the Logon dialog box by default, and whether a user must be validated by a network server for logon. Logon banners typically announce system use policies. Never make your banner "Welcome to my computer," because courts have interpreted such a banner as an invitation to hack. Hiding the last entered username and forcing validation by a server are both wise in any secure environment, minimally secure or maximally secure.

See Chapter 10, "Dealing with Multiple Client Hosts," for more information on using forced server validation for improving security.

- *Passwords* permits you to determine whether a typed password will be hidden by asterisks. It also enables you to set minimum password length, to require both letters and numbers in the password, and to turn off the use of password list files, also known as password caching. In secure environments, you want passwords to be masked by asterisks. You also want a minimum password length to limit a hacker's ability to guess a password using brute force algorithms. Requiring both letters and numbers makes passwords harder to guess, but may also decrease a user's ability to remember the password. In highly secure environments, you want to turn off password caching. Whoever can copy the Password List file—and anyone can from the keyboard side of the machine—can easily crack or misuse the passwords inside.

- Following *Passwords*, you see one book for each network client service that you have installed. These books enable you to control the same settings as the Properties sheets for your network clients. As a result, you can force consistent configuration of clients across your network, or make allowances for individual machines, as necessary, using system policies.

- Following network settings, you have two books that enable you to adjust settings for File and Printer Sharing for NetWare Networks and File and Printer Sharing for Microsoft Networks. You may have only one of these services installed on a given machine at any one time. For the NetWare service, you can turn the Server Advertising Protocol (SAP) on or off. This service normally broadcasts a server's presence every 60 seconds, creating extra network traffic that is routable. For the Microsoft service, you can turn either the sharing of files or printers on and off.

- The *Dial-Up Networking* book enables you to determine whether dial-up options are enabled or disabled. As a result, only certain machines on your network can be granted the privilege to dial out or to receive calls. You can prevent users from attaching a modem and receiving calls, possibly exposing sensitive network resources to compromise.

- The *Update* book directs Windows 98 where to look for a system policy file, either the default or automatic location or the one that you have defined. This option also includes a check box that determines whether policy error messages are processed, and whether the system makes an effort to balance policy updates among all the logon servers.

The automatic update locations are described in the following section.

The next book, *Windows 98 System*, contains four subbooks. The first, *User Profiles*, contains one setting that allows you to enable or disable the use of profiles. The second, *Network Paths*, enables you to conserve resources on your network by specifying a path to the Windows 98 setup files and to the Windows 98 tour. You can place the setup and tour files in a single location and point several machines to use these shared directories, conserving drive space on the local machines and enabling network setups of these machines if the operating system ever needs to be refreshed.

The third book, *SNMP*, enables you to define communities, traps, and permitted managers, and Internet Management Information Block files (MIBs) if you are using Simple Network Management Protocol to manage your network.

The fourth, *Programs to Run*, specifies a list of programs to run on startup. You can choose to run the program at each startup using the first check box. You can choose to run the program one time at startup and then disable its run using the second check box. (This option is used for setup routines that must manage final configuration of the machine, for example.) You can also choose to run a service at startup. A *service* is a background program that manages some optional function within the operating system. Downloading TV channels for the TV viewer on a daily basis, for example, runs as a service.

Securing the Desktop with System Policies

So far, this chapter has examined only the use of the System Policy Editor to edit the Registry. The System Policy Editor, however, has another purpose: You can save the settings not to a Registry, but to a file. If you locate the file in the proper place on the network, these computers settings are automatically merged into the Registry when the machine boots, and these user settings are automatically merged into the Registry when a user logs on.

To create a policy file, follow these steps:

1. Open the System Policy Editor.

2. From the File menu, choose New Policy. If you have already created a file, you can open it using File | Open Policy.

3. The System Policy Editor now has the look shown in Figure 17.4. You see a Default Computer and a Default User. These icons open dialog boxes like those you have already seen, except these are the policies that apply to a computer or user if no other policies are named for that computer or user. Edit the policies using these icons as you want.

4. To create policies for a specific computer, select Edit | Add Computer. Enter the NetBIOS name of the computer in the dialog box that appears and click OK. An icon named after that computer appears in the editor. Double-click on the icon to set policies for that computer.

Note: Check boxes when you are editing a policy file have three possible states. A check means that the on value of the policy will be applied to all systems and users to which the icon applies. A cleared check box means that the off value of the policy will be applied to all systems and users to which the icon applies. A grayed check box means that whatever is currently in the Registry for a system or user will remain as is.

5. To create policies for a specific user, select Edit | Add User. Enter the username in the dialog box that appears and click OK. An icon named after that user appears in the editor. Double-click on the icon to set policies for that user.

Figure 17.4.
The System Policy Editor can create default policies for systems and users.

6. If you have groups of users for which you want to set policies, select Edit I Add Group. Enter the name of the group in the dialog box that appears and click OK. An icon named after that group appears in the editor. Double-click this icon to set policies for the group.

7. If you have set policies for more than one group, you need to select the order in which these policies will be applied. Open Options I Group Priority. The dialog box shown in Figure 17.5 appears. Sort the names of the groups up and down using the buttons provided. The policies at the top of the list are the ones applied last. If a setting for one group conflicts with a setting for another group, the last applied group policies take force. If I am a member of Users and a member of Managers and Users is below Managers on the list, the last applied policies are those of the Managers. If the Users are not allowed dial-up access and Managers are, I will have dial-up access. If a new administrator is working with the policies and re-sorts the list so that Users is above Managers, I would lose dial-up privileges at my next logon.

8. Save the policy file by using the File I Save option on the menu.

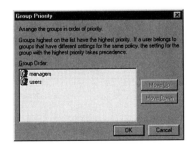
Figure 17.5.
You can sort group policies to determine the order in which they apply.

Note a couple of things about policy files. If a policy file is placed in a default location, it is applied whenever a system boots or a user logs on. On Windows NT Servers, this location is the Netlogon share (\WINNT\SYSTEM32\REPL\IMPORT\SCRIPTS). On NetWare servers, this is the PUBLIC directory. You should make certain that policy files are replicated to all domain controllers and logon servers. The policy file is applied from the server that answers the logon request.

You can use the setting Remote Update (Computer | Windows 98 Network | Update | Remote Update) in the computer policies to set an alternative path for locating the policy file. If you take this option, you can use several different policy files to control systems, but each system must know where to look for its policy file. If that location ever becomes unavailable, the policies will not be applied. Unless someone directly edits the Registry, missing policies are not a major problem. When they are available again, the policies will be applied again.

When policies are available, a user can't do anything to circumvent their application.

Summary

This chapter has discussed the issues surrounding securing the Windows 98 desktop. You have seen that desktop security can be handled in one of three ways: not applying security, editing the Registry to implement a variety of settings, and implementing system policies to enforce security. In addition, you have seen the various settings for controlling both systems and users available in the System Policy Editor.

On Your Own

First, install the System Policy Editor. Then back up your Registry. Then back it up again. You are now safe to try editing your own Registry with the System Policy Editor. Next, connect to a remote system and edit the Registry, but only after backing up that Registry. Finally, create a policy file and use it to implement policies on your network. When you create the file, however, create one that reverses the settings you have created. If you need to step back to the prior state of policies, you will need a policy file to do so. Trying to create a clean-up file later is very difficult.

18

Securing
the System

Peter Norton®

The preceding chapter focused on securing the desktop, mainly from accidental or intentional changes made by the user. Securing the desktop may leave you with the sense that you have somehow secured the system. However, nothing could be further from the truth.

Under Windows 98, whoever sits at the keyboard using the computer has complete control over the resources of that computer. No file system security prevents deletion of all the Windows 98 system files. There is no way on a system shared by multiple users to keep a file completely private. Whatever resides on the local drive is accessible to whoever is logged on at the keyboard.

If such security is required, you do have some options. One of Microsoft's options is to choose a different operating system, Windows NT Workstation. But you may have reasons for not choosing to use Windows NT. You may have hardware incompatibilities, for example. You may not wish to invest in the memory required. You may be supporting legacy applications that will not run under Windows NT. Under these circumstances, you may in fact have to choose Windows 98.

A critical question, therefore, is how to make Windows 98 machines as secure as possible given that the operating system is not terribly helpful. This chapter covers the following topics:

- Locking resources to prevent physical access
- Disabling resources
- Protecting against viruses
- Protecting against unwanted network sessions
- Ordering network clients
- Forcing validation by a server
- Placing storage on servers
- Using encryption

Keeping Physical Security

Whoever possesses the physical device on which the data is stored has complete control of the data. That possession gives such control is a sad fact of computer security. If I steal your hard drive, even though you may have encrypted everything on it, I can read it with a sector editor and attempt to assemble and decrypt your files. Given infinite time and computer resources, I will be successful. In the meantime, if I have your data and you don't, you could be out of business.

Given logon and file system security associated with Windows 98, therefore, you need to make every effort to keep the physical computer apparatus under control. For tight security, you need to control who has access to removable storage devices, especially boot devices such as the floppy drive or a removable hard drive. You need to control who has access to the case of the machine. And you need control over removal of any form of nonvolatile storage from the premises.

Peter's Principle: Living in the World of Tight Security

I have had the opportunity to work as a contractor in two secured government facilities. Tight physical security is extremely important and requires extreme measures. At both facilities, for example, I was required to be under escort 100 percent of the time. At one, I was not allowed to bring in anything that could be used to record data, including a cellular phone and pager. At the same facility, whenever I was present, a flashing red "lubber light" (the Navy term for it) had to be turned on to warn of the presence of someone without a security clearance.

If you need to protect data as trade secrets, you need to take at least the following measures. You need to have ironclad sign-in and sign-out policies so that you know who has been on the premises. You need an escort policy for visitors. You need visitor badges to identify outsiders. You also need a policy governing what happens to old storage devices. If you throw out a hard drive, competitors may thank you for not wiping it clean first.

In addition, you may need policies governing what types of recording devices may be brought onto the premises. You may need exit search or detection policies. You may need metal or magnetic detectors to alert you when storage devices are leaving the building. Although some of these requirements may seem extreme, in highly competitive environments, data about competitors can lead to a serious advantage in the marketplace.

Locking Resources

One way to secure physical resources is to lock them up or bolt them down. It is very hard to remove a system when it has a large table permanently attached to it. Someone is bound to notice the thief. A variety of security resources are available to you.

You can purchase special bolts that secure a system case to a table or desk. You can purchase special eyes that attach to the surface of the case or the monitor with adhesive. Then you pass a cable through all the attachment eyes you have glued down and secure the cable with a locking device that links to an object considered immovable. You can also purchase locking screws for cases or cases with locks already attached. There are locks for floppy drives as well that prevent their use while the lock is in place. For removable drives, you can use mounting racks that include locks to prevent removal of the drive from the system.

Tip: Many of the keys to the locks produced by certain manufacturers are identical. This fact is either a convenience or a nightmare, depending on your point of view.

You can also secure systems with alarms. Usually, this arrangement requires that you use a cable security device, and the cable is attached to a motion-sensing device. Motion along the cable trips the alarm, attracting attention to the computer that has been disturbed.

Oddly enough, in the secured facilities where I have worked, physical locking devices were rarely used. Although these devices are available, you see them more often securing systems at trade shows. The focus within a secure building seems to be on preventing removal by guarding access points to the building. The technicians who care for the systems and the network rarely want to have to unlock or unbolt a system just to perform routine maintenance. The critical exception I have seen is case locks on servers. Usually you want only people who are authorized to access the server cases. A usual way of authorizing these people is to grant them the key or the special tool that opens the server case.

Disabling Resources

One way to prevent anyone from gaining unauthorized access to data is to prevent him or her from being able to copy the data off the system. As a result, in secure facilities, you need to limit access to removable media (writable drives). The easiest way to do so is to disable the drive itself. Just disconnecting it and then locking the case is one strategy. Not installing removable-cartridge hard drives is another.

You may feel that disconnecting the drive would be an inconvenience in performing maintenance tasks. Under some circumstances, you may need to boot the system from an alternative drive to undertake maintenance. You may also need to move large files from one system to another, or from one site to another, on physical media. Obviously, the working patterns within your secured facility will determine the wisdom of pursuing this course of action.

One alternative to handling this issue is to install bootable CD-ROM drives. You can then dispense with the floppy and boot from a CD-ROM that you burn with the contents of the Emergency Repair Disk when you need to undertake serious maintenance. The system is left without writable, removable media, and you can still boot from an alternative device.

Tip: If you need an alternative way of booting into the New Technology File System on Windows NT machines, especially your Windows NT Servers, a bootable CD-ROM with either the contents of the Windows NT Emergency Repair Disk and the three boot floppies or a mirror image of the Windows NT installation can be extremely useful.

In the secure facilities that I have seen, however, Windows 98 machines are usually secured in a different way. Usually the CPU is locked in an enclosure, so the computing device itself does not need any disabling. It can have all the normal devices, but they are just locked away from the user.

The user input devices are accessible, as is the screen. Technicians performing maintenance need keys to the cabinets and no other special tools.

Vaccinating Against Viruses

Would that the world had never seen computer viruses. All of us in information technology management would be much happier. However, viruses are a fact of computing life, and good management practices demand that we take reasonable precautions against them. Viruses can be considered either a software security issue or a hardware security issue. I have chosen to address them as a hardware security issue because viruses typically attack via a hardware device. Software virus protection is entirely a post-infection solution. The trick is to secure the usual hardware entry points for infection and to apply software virus protection vigorously in case a virus slips through.

Reasonable precautions begin at the attachment points where viruses may enter a network of computers. Several good antivirus products exist, with offerings from McAfee, Symantec/Norton, Computer Associates, and others. In general, you need to think of your antivirus strategy as having layers. You need to deploy the right kind of security at each layer.

At the network layer, we normally think of firewalls—computers (a hardware solution) that manage the attachment point to the external network, usually the Internet. A firewall can prevent hackers from breaking in using known methods and can monitor for unknown methods by watching for suspicious activity, including the activity associated with virus attacks. They can also filter network packets to prevent certain types of unauthorized traffic from reaching the internal network. One type of traffic that can bring in viruses is FTP. Whenever you transfer files, using FTP or any other network protocol, you transfer whatever happens to be in them, including infecting viruses. As a result, you need to plan what firewall features to implement, and especially what types of traffic to control.

One approach to managing virus attacks at the network layer is to filter all packets that could possibly cause infection. Usually this strategy has undesirable side effects. Administrators cannot download files using File Transfer Protocol, and administrators usually need to do this. If you want to engage in Web-based management strategies, you have to open your firewall to those packets.

As a result, you usually want to implement one of the software packages that can reside on the firewall and scan files for viruses before they are passed back to the internal network. Using such a package enables you to open up options for file downloads and receipt of electronic mail containing attachments without exposing your organization to a serious virus threat.

Note: To see how you can employ Web-based management and remain secure, see the discussion of WBEM security in Chapter 7, "Working with the WAN Connection."

Your second line of defense against viruses is at the operating system level. On an individual machine, you need system-level software that checks for viruses. These checks occur in two ways. One is a system service, typically appearing as an icon in the System Tray, that monitors for virus activity. You can usually select the types of activity to monitor for. In addition, these services also scan files of certain types, such as executables and dynamic link libraries, on-the-fly. You can usually select the types of files you want to scan.

The second type of virus check is an active scan of all the files on the system. Such programs accompany the system-level services, but they are only as good as the frequency with which they are applied. As a result, you should schedule active scans of your system on a regular basis—at least weekly, but I prefer daily. Why give a virus the chance to propagate?

The key to protecting against viruses at the operating system level is using up-to-date virus signature files. These files describe the patterns to search for in the files scanned. You want to download and distribute a new copy of this file monthly, roughly the frequency with which most virus software manufacturers update them. The easiest way to distribute such files is to use a system management tool such as SMS Server.

The final layer of virus protection is at the hardware level. Most motherboards offer BIOS-level protection. You should turn this protection on. Some system administrators, however, argue a case for leaving it turned off. Unless you can remotely manage CMOS settings, turning on BIOS-level virus protection can interrupt your remote administrative activities. Imagine your roll-out of Windows 98 being interrupted by system boards refusing to allow writes to protected areas of the physical disk. So much for your intended update to FAT32. You may find justification for not enabling hardware-level protection on your networked machines, unless you want to return to the days of visiting each machine to undertake certain administrative tasks.

Securing Against Errant Network Sessions

In a secure facility, you may need to prevent unknown individuals from attaching over the network to your systems. In general, to prevent such attachments, you need to pay attention to three issues: securing cables, securing remote access, and securing network access.

Securing cables is just a matter of making certain that cables cannot be accessed by someone who can cut the cable, insert a connection, and join the network. In general, you need to avoid running cables over the carpet in a secure facility. Instead, place them in conduits. You need wall plates to which computers make connections. You need appropriate locks on your wiring cabinets. You need to map each of the attachment points and make certain that none are available beyond those you know about.

You are essentially making certain that if someone wants to sneak a node onto your network, he will have to work very, very hard at it. It should not be a matter of clip, crimp, and hook up (or slip into the wiring closet with a handheld PC and plug in a wire). You want him to have to go to a great effort. If you are concerned about someone monitoring transmissions off your network cable, you should consider using fiber optic cable.

In opening up your system for dial-in access, you need to be certain that you have appropriate authentication in place. The Windows 98 remote dial-in feature provides limited, password-based security. You can leverage a user list from a server if you have implemented user-level security. You probably want to opt for a more robust third-party dial-up server, one that will provide the hardware, manage its own security, and enable you to monitor usage in greater detail than the Windows 98 Dial-Up Server enables. If you want a software solution, consider using a Windows NT machine for your dial-up server. The security associated with the Remote Access Service in Windows NT is greater than that associated with the similar service in Windows 98.

Securing network access means making certain that only authorized users may connect from one system to another over the network. For your servers, this issue is not so much a problem. Server operating systems are designed to support user connections, and they supply the user authentication and security features that go along with such designs. Windows 98, on the other hand, was modeled after the peer-to-peer model, which assumes that everyone using the network is trusted.

To secure network access under Windows 98, consider the following options:

- Disable file and printer sharing on your Windows 98 machines. This prevents them from accepting network attachments, because they do not have a server service running. Place all shared resources on servers that run network operating systems with appropriate security.
- Do not enable TCP/IP services such as FTP or TCP/IP client services such as Telnet on Windows 98 machines. If you do not provide TCP/IP server services or client services, no one can attach successfully using these services to machines on the network.
- If you do enable TCP/IP connectivity services, edit the Services file in the Windows directory to change the port numbers associated with the services. To change the FTP port from the well-defined port 21 to another port, for example, reset its setting to any value greater than 1023 and less than 65532. The line you modify reads `ftp 21/tcp`. Just change the number `21` to the desired port number. For users to connect, after reaching the FTP prompt, they must use an open command that reads `open IPAddress PortNumber`—for example, `open 127.0.0.1 5432`.
- Do not enable any more protocols or bindings than you need to. You may accidentally enable connection strategies that you did not anticipate.
- Use user-level security so that you can protect resources with Access Control Lists.
- Disable the binding between TCP/IP and file and printer sharing if you directly access the Internet from your computers. With this binding enabled, anyone who knows the IP address of the computer can reach its shared files and printers directly from the Internet.

Promoting System Security

So far, this discussion has focused on physical security issues. How do you prevent outside access to the data on the system? The next topic, preventing unwanted network connections, concerns the software side. Now it is important to look at the issue of securing the system against the logged-on user and preventing unauthorized access from the keyboard side of the computer. How can you make certain that only authorized users log on? How do you keep data safe from an authorized user who is not supposed to see all the data placed on the machine by other authorized users?

Ordering Your Network Clients

One option you have is to order your network clients so that logon to a server or domain is first in the sequence. You accomplish this feat by setting the Primary Network Logon in the Configuration tab of the Network Control Panel. By placing a server or domain logon first, you require that the user actually be validated before gaining access to the system. Remember that the Microsoft client itself, unless domain logon is configured, does not validate the user. The Windows logon just makes the password cache available.

Forcing Validation by a Server

You can also require that a server validate the user before logon to the system can be completed. Use the System Policy Editor to edit the Registry or to set the policy Require validation by network for Windows access under the Logon subbook of the Windows 98 Network book under Default Computer or Local Computer. Combining this setting with placing the server or domain logon first in the client order prevents logon unless the user is validated by the server. Canceling the logon prompt will not give the user access to the system. The only way for a user to gain access would be to boot from a floppy. If you limit access to the floppy drive, only authorized users will be allowed access to the system.

Placing Storage on Servers

One way to limit access to data is to keep the data on servers whose operating system provides file-level security. Access Control Lists then limit access appropriately for users. The difficulty is that granting access to appropriate users means that they could make local copies of the data, where Access Control Lists would no longer be valid. The only solution to this problem is to use diskless workstations that remote boot from a server and make use only of server storage.

Using Encryption

If data is completely sensitive, it should be encrypted. Most utility packages for Windows 98 include an encryption program. These are typical single-key encryption programs that ask the user to provide a text string to serve as the encryption key. The bit pattern in the key is used to transform the bit patterns in the data so that they are not recognizable as the data. To decrypt the file, the same bit pattern that encrypted the file is used to reverse the transformation. Such encryption is useful for the private purposes of a user. To share encrypted files, however, you must share the key, compromising the security provided by the encryption with each sharing.

To share encrypted data, you should use public key encryption. In this schema, two keys are required. One key is kept private by the user. The only use for this key is decryption. As a result, this key is never shared with anyone. The other key is distributed publicly. Its only purpose is encryption of the data. If you wish to send me an encrypted file, you encrypt it with my public key. I freely distribute my public key to anyone who needs to send me data. Only I can decrypt the file, because I am the only one who knows the private key.

The essential feature of public-key encryption is the use of one-way keys. The public key has one and only one purpose, creating a hash of the data that only the private key can undo. The private key has an equivalent purpose, decrypting the hash created using the public key. If you imagine public-key encryption schemes as creating a secure pipeline for communication, the schema becomes a bit easier to understand.

Imagine that I have a red liquid that I need to send to you by pouring it down a pipe, but I don't want anyone to know that it is red. I need to keep the color of the liquid a secret, but there are any number of taps into the pipe where interlopers could open a spigot to check the color of the liquid. What I do is place a dye in the liquid, the public key, which changes the color of the liquid. The dye is freely available to anyone and does a great job of masking the color of any liquid. When you receive the liquid, you apply a secret dye neutralizer, the private key, to restore the actual color of the liquid. This neutralizer is a closely guarded secret, not freely available on the market. Only you have it, so we can communicate secretly with great ease.

The weakness of public-key encryption is that you must use one key pair per user, and that can be a lot of keys to manage. Several software packages from vendors such as Pretty Good Privacy and Xerox, however, enable you to undertake such a project.

Summary

This chapter has shown you that Windows 98 computers cannot be secured very well. However, you can physically secure the system and its removable storage devices. You can run virus checkers. You can relocate your connection ports. You can order your network clients and force validation.

And you can encrypt data. The operating system cannot secure the data stored on the computer, however. Microsoft did not design it that way.

On Your Own

Try securing a networked Windows 98 computer from unauthorized keyboard access. Design a physical enclosure for the system. Review and choose virus software. Try relocating the FTP port, placing the server client first, and forcing server validation of the logon. If you are really adventurous, download encryption software from the Web and encrypt some files.

19

Securing
Shared
Resources

Peter Norton®

Sharing is what networks are about, be they networks of colleagues or networks of computers. The reason for running the wires among the machines is that we grew tired of working in isolation and carrying data physically from machine to machine. Network operating systems originally provided a way for us to link terminals to a central computer, which provided data processing power to remote locations. The processor we used when I was in college was located in Cincinnati, while we were up in Oxford, OH, entering our data and program instructions via punch cards.

With the advent of personal computers, networking was not initially perceived as necessary. The whole point of a personal computer was that it was yours, to do with as you pleased. As the Homebrew Computer Club at Stanford began to find uses for the technology, and Wozniak and Jobs created the Apple, arguably the first useful personal computer, we began to see a reason for networking. When Dan Bricklin wrote VisiCalc, we had a definite reason for linking machines together. We needed to get the data for the spreadsheet from where it was to our Apple so that we could run the numbers in the spreadsheet. Novell obliged by creating a network operating system.

Novell's approach was that the server was like a mainframe. It provided shared file and printer services, and you logged on to the server just like you would logon to a mainframe. Your node on the network functioned very much like a remote terminal did, and all shared resources were centralized at the server. Your workstation shared nothing except via the services of the server.

Microsoft's approach with Windows has been to avoid the server-centric approach, which explains why you see the security models you see in Windows for Workgroups, Windows 95, Windows 98, and Windows NT. Instead of a centralized server, Microsoft assumed that any node on the network could be a server. As a result, any user could use the server service provided by the Windows operating system to share resources. Networks could become very democratic places where anyone who chose to could independently share files and printers. The peer-to-peer network was born, and the notion of share security entered the scheme.

With Windows NT, the same rules apply. Any node on the network can function as a server. You also have machines that specialize in being servers, which are the ones that run Windows NT Server as opposed to Windows NT Workstation. The organizational unit of Windows NT is a domain, however, and a domain does not consist of servers. When you log on to a domain, you log on to the aggregate of the network resources managed in the domain. You are not attached to a single server— or even a group of servers—and using the resources of the server. You are attached to the entire domain and the full set of resources it provides. Certain machines maintain logon accounts for the domain, and they are known as the domain controllers. They provide centralized logon services to a group effort at networking.

As a result, you see two types of security models in the Windows 98 operating system for resources shared and accessed over the network. One is based on democratic and open sharing. The other leverages the centralized logon accounts provided by the domain. Fortunately or unfortunately, depending on your view as administrator, these two security models can be freely mixed on your network. In addition, Windows 98 provides software to help manage both the share-level and the user-level servers on your network. This chapter explains how to use both of them on your network, focusing on the following topics:

- How to choose a security scheme
- How to use share-level security
- How to use user-level security
- How to manage shared resources and servers

How to Select a Security Scheme

The central question in choosing your security scheme is just how open and democratic you want the sharing of information to be. Table 19.1 summarizes the characteristics associated with each security model. If you see your networked operation as having the share-level characteristics, share-level security is what you want to implement.

Table 19.1. Characteristics of share-level and user-level networks.

Share-level	User-level
Your users each carry out independent job functions.	Your users work as teams and are interdependent in their job functions.
Each job function is responsible for maintaining its own pool of data.	Job functions are dependent on central stores of shared data.
Users performing different jobs need only limited access to data maintained by coworkers.	Users performing different jobs need widely varied access to the data stored in central pools.
Users within the organization have a high degree of trust for one another.	You cannot assume the level of trust necessary to allow users to carry out administrative functions on their own machines.
The pool of users is fairly small.	The pool of users is fairly large.
Different users do not need highly differing access to the information.	The organization maintains large pools of sensitive or confidential data.
Users can be trusted to perform administrative tasks on their workstations.	The sensitive data on the network must be accessed by a variety of users, each of whom may need to have limited access to some data but complete control over other data items.
The organization does not maintain large pools of sensitive or confidential data.	The sensitive data on the network is under the control of a limited number of users who can be trusted not to share it.

Share-level security assumes that each user will function in an administrative capacity of at least a minor sort. Most specifically, individual users will determine what data to share from their workstation and whether to share their printer. They will control the type of access to the shared resources, either complete access or access governed by passwords. Because these users are the ones who create the data and maintain it on their workstations, they are the ones who need to determine what is shared with coworkers.

Warning: Do not expect security to apply to the user at the keyboard accessing the local drives. Windows 98 enforces security only when resources are accessed over the network. The security models discussed in this chapter apply only to access initiated through the Network Neighborhood, via the net commands, or through drive mappings.

Obviously this schema breaks down as the size of the network increases. First, it becomes harder to tell where the data that you need is. Second, the security scheme of passwords becomes very confusing. Each shared resource has a different password. As shared resources multiply, it becomes harder and harder to keep track of the number of passwords—over which there is no central control—that you must use to access shared resources.

As the network grows in size, the characteristics of user access have to change. Sharing of information must at least become more organized. It makes no sense to search through 200 machines in the Network Neighborhood looking for the new location of the contact list. If your networked operation has the user-level characteristics listed in Table 19.1, you should choose user-level security for your network.

User-level security depends on Access Control Lists. These lists are attached to resources such as folders and printers as attributes of the object. They are made up of entries that contain the unique identifier for a user or group and the access permissions that the user or group has. Before allowing access to the resource, Windows 98 checks the Access Control List to see whether the user attempting access has the required permissions, either granted to her user account or to a group she belongs to. Passwords are not necessary. By virtue of your user identification, Windows 98 can tell whether to grant you access.

Tip: Groups are named collections of user accounts. They can be added to Access Control Lists just like a single user account can be.

Windows 98 does not maintain a database of user accounts on its own. As a result, it must borrow such a database from one of your servers. Windows 98 can borrow this list from either a Windows NT Server or a NetWare server. Users from this database are then assigned entries in the Access Control List as the user of the computer desires. An Access Control List contains only the entries added. It does not contain the entire list of users unless the entire list gets added.

The whole purpose of groups in user database administration is to reduce the length of Access Control Lists. If all users belong to a single group, you can set security for all users by making an entry on the Access Control List for the group. If you create other groups wisely, you need only to set permissions for a limited number of groups rather than for the entire list of users. In addition, as group membership changes, you do not need to change security on 500 resources. Group access remains the same even though the group membership has changed. On any network, therefore, using groups to control access to resources makes eminent sense.

The presence of groups means that there must be an inheritance relationship between group and user accounts. Whatever permissions have been assigned to the group accumulate to users who are members of the group. Members of multiple groups inherit all the permissions of the groups to which they belong. One exception to this rule applies under Windows 98, which makes the user-level security model quite different from the equivalent model under Windows NT. If a user account appears on an Access Control List, the permissions assigned to that account override inheritance from groups. If you name an account individually on the list, the permissions you assign to it are the permissions that account has. Under Windows NT, permissions assigned to an individual account just accumulate as a part of the total group of permissions assigned. The only way to override permission assignments is to grant no access.

Peter's Principle: Use User-level Security Whenever Possible

I favor using user-level security over share-level security in every circumstance where I have a server that can supply the user list. My reason is that user-level security always provides greater control over who may access resources. If necessary, each individual user can be granted different access. If you must have security, you want this level of control.

Share-level security creates a situation where abandoning passwords or using one password for all shares is encouraged. Users have one password per share to remember. As new shares appear, more passwords proliferate. This overwhelming load of passwords causes users to want to simplify the system. They will either abandon using passwords as they share resources, which they may do, or they will all begin to use the same password. Either situation weakens network security by making it easier to guess the access password.

You can use either of these security models on your network. You can mix and match them to suit your needs. Because Windows 98 is the operating system that implements the security model, each Windows 98 node on the network may use a different one. It is wise, however, to use a consistent security model. You need to remember that the user of the system can change the security model under Windows 98. As a result, you may wish to use one of the Registry management tools, such as Full Armor from Micah Software, to prevent users from making changes to the Registry. Or you may wish to implement system policies that set the security model each time the computer boots.

Using Share-Level Security

By default, Windows 98 comes set up for share-level security. However, sharing is not activated by default. Because sharing is not activated, a Windows 98 computer does not appear in the Network Neighborhood by default. To participate in sharing resources over the network, therefore, you must activate the sharing features.

Many system administrators prefer not to have users in control of sharing resources on the network. Unfortunately, Windows 98 is an operating system under the user's control. If you would prefer to control who shares resources, set a system policy that either enables or disables file and printer sharing. This policy is a part of the computer policies. If you would prefer that users not be able to re-enable sharing, you must set policies that take away the Control Panel tabs that enable them to make the changes.

To enable sharing of resources, follow these steps:

1. Open the Network Control Panel.
2. Click File and Print Sharing.
3. Check the check boxes as appropriate to share either files and/or printers (see Figure 19.1).

Figure 19.1.
Check the appropriate boxes to share files or printers.

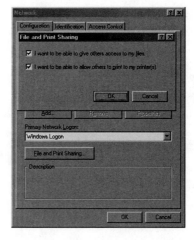

4. Click on OK in the File and Print Sharing dialog box and the Network Control Panel applet.
5. Restart your computer when prompted to do so.

Now that you have enabled sharing, you can share three types of objects: folders, drives, and printers. To share one of these objects, follow these steps:

1. Right-click on the object and choose Sharing from the context menu.

2. In the Sharing tab of the Properties dialog box, click on the Shared As button (see Figure 19.2).

Figure 19.2.
Name the share and
set its access type and
password.

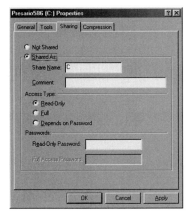

3. Enter a Share Name and Comment. The share name is required, and has some rules associated with it. It should not contain spaces or illegal DOS characters. If MS-DOS network clients will access the shared resource, the name should conform to 8.3 naming conventions. The comment is a text string that appears next to the share's icon in the Network Neighborhood in Details view.

Technical Note: Microsoft documents that names for shares are supposed to be limited to 15 characters, but actually can be longer. I gave up when I hit 120 characters. If they contain spaces, you must treat them as long filenames and enclose them in quotation marks when you use them in shortcut properties, in the Run dialog box, and at the command prompt.

4. Use the option buttons to set the access type. If you select Depends on Password, you must enter and confirm both a read-only and a full-access password. If you select one of the other two options, passwords are optional. All users use the password you set to access the share. You cannot assign a password to each user.

Technical Note: For printers, the only options are to set a share name, comment, and password (see Figure 19.3).

5. Click on OK to share the resource.

Figure 19.3.
Printer sharing
provides fewer
properties to set.

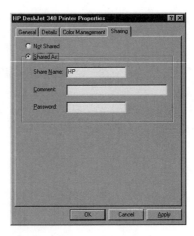

Having shared the resource, the next time the browser updates, the share will appear listed in the Network Neighborhood when a user double-clicks on your computer. The user will be prompted for a password if you set them. If you set privileges depending on the password, the Password dialog box contains two text boxes, one for the read-only password and one for the full-access password. Only one will work.

Technical Note: The browser is a service that runs under all versions of Windows. Its purpose is to maintain a list of servers on the network. Any operating system running a server service, including Windows 98, is tracked by the browser. The browser service starts automatically when the operating system boots. Its first task is to locate a computer that is acting as master browser. This computer is maintaining the list of servers on the network and a list of computers, called backup browsers, that hold backup copies of the list. To locate the master browser, the browser service broadcasts in search of it. The master browser responds to the broadcast by entering the booting server in the list of servers and sending back a list of the backup browsers. When you open the Network Neighborhood, you need the list of servers to display. The browser service on your computer contacts a browser, usually the nearest one by proximity, and asks for the list. The browser returns the list to your computer so that the Network Neighborhood can display the list of servers you can contact. Servers re-announce themselves every 12 minutes. However, the master browser does not delete a server from the list until it misses three announcements, at least 36 minutes from the time the server became unavailable. The master browser replicates its list to the backup browsers every 15 minutes. As a result, unavailable servers can persist in the Network Neighborhood up to 51 minutes before they are completely deleted, assuming that your computer gets its list from the backup browser.

Peter's Principle: Adding Some User-Level Control to a Share-Level Server

The privileges you grant on a share-level server are those that you have chosen for all objects in the shared resource. All files and folders on a drive, and all files and subfolders in a folder, are assigned either read-only or full access. You can share the same resource with multiple names and different permissions and passwords. In this way, you can grant multiple sets of users a means of accessing your files using descriptive share names and appropriate permissions. The accountants at one client office could attach to the accounting share and the managers attach to the management share. Accountants might have read-only access with no password, and managers might have full access with a password. The different groups know that they can attach to the share named after their job function and receive the privileges they need. In such cases, always make sure that the users with read-only access have no password, while the users with greater access have the password. In this way, you prevent granting more privileges than you intend by mistake.

Notice that share passwords will be rather well-known commodities. Everyone who accesses a share knows the same password for it. As a result, the passwords are not entirely secure. Windows 98 helps to protect their confidentiality by caching the passwords for shares in the user's password list (PWL) file. After using the password one time, the user does not need to enter it again. Windows 98 uses the password stored in the password list file for the share that it is paired with, until the password is no longer valid. Password list files are encrypted. However, any user at the keyboard of the system can copy them. The only key you need to open the password list file is the username and password for the user who caches passwords in the file. Yes, you can copy a PWL file to another system and log on as that user—and gain access to all of that user's shares on the network. Do not allow blank passwords, as a result. Set the system policy on each computer to require a minimum password length or to require alphanumeric passwords.

Using User-Level Security

User-level security works in much the same way as share-level security, except for how you specify access to a shared object. You are still limited to sharing drives, folders, or printers. Users, however, do not use passwords to attach to them. They present their user account information to your copy of Windows 98, which checks the information against the Access Control List to determine which type of access to grant. To validate whether the user is allowed to access the share, Windows 98 queries the server from which it gets the list of user accounts. Windows 98 relies on the server that serves as security provider for all validations.

To employ user-level security, you must inform Windows 98 that you wish to use it. You must also have enabled file and printer sharing as described in the preceding section. To activate user-level security, follow these steps:

1. Open the Network Control Panel.

2. Select the Access Control tab.

3. Select User-level access control and fill in the name of the domain, Windows NT Server, or the NetWare server that will act as security provider (see Figure 19.4).

Figure 19.4.
Identify the security provider from which to get the list of users.

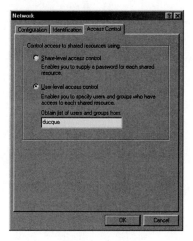

4. Click on OK to close the Network Control Panel applet. You will see a warning that all objects shared will no longer be shared. Because you have changed your access control method, you must reshare all objects that you want available on the network from this computer. Click Yes to continue past the Warning dialog box.

5. Restart your computer when prompted to do so.

Sharing an object works in exactly the same way, except now you must specify the Access Control List for the object you have chosen to share. The Sharing tab in the object's properties looks like that shown in Figure 19.5. Click on Add to populate the Access Control List.

The Add Users dialog box, shown in Figure 19.6, enables you to select users to add to the Access Control List. Multiple selections are allowed. Select the users or groups to add to the list, and add them using one of the three buttons in the center of the dialog box. Read Only grants read permission only; Full Access grants full control; and Custom enables you to select what you want. Click OK to add the users.

When you select the custom option for any user or group, you see the dialog box shown in Figure 19.7. This Change Access Rights dialog box appears for each user and group that you granted custom access to in sequence. It enables you to select from seven individual permissions to grant to the user or group. The permissions are self-explanatory, but some notes are essential. Read also means execute a program file. List means show the list of files in a folder in dialog boxes such as Open and Save As, but not the Windows 98 Explorer. You will see the list of files in the Explorer, but be limited in your access rights.

Figure 19.5.
The Sharing tab enables you to enter an Access Control List for the resource.

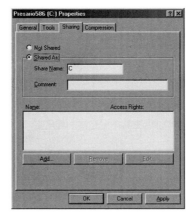

Figure 19.6.
The Add Users dialog box enables you to control the access that users and groups have.

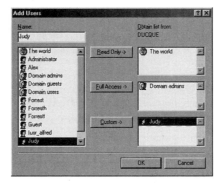

Figure 19.7.
For custom access, you can choose from among seven permissions.

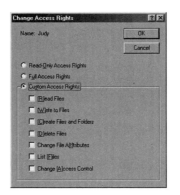

After you have created your Access Control List, you will see it displayed on the Sharing tab. You can remove any entry by selecting it and clicking the Remove button. Clicking on Edit opens the Change Access Rights dialog box for the selected user. After you have set your Access Control List (see the one shown in Figure 19.8), click on Apply to make it active. Click on OK to make it active and close the Properties dialog box. If you are just establishing the share, the object will become available in the Network Neighborhood and users can attach to it. If you are editing the Access Control List, attached users will have their former permissions until their sessions end. When they re-attach, they will have their new permissions.

Figure 19.8.
Click on Apply to make the Access Control List active.

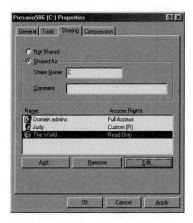

You may be surprised to learn that connections are not easy to end under Windows 98. Even when users disconnect a drive mapping, the connection exists at the server until it times out. The time out process can take between 10 and 15 minutes. It is important, therefore, to become aware of the methods you have for managing shared resources.

Managing Shared Resources and Servers

To manage shared resources, you need to manage browsing, what is shared, who is connected to what is shared, and what they have opened for use. To manage browsing, you control the properties of file and printer sharing. First, you need some background about determining what to set as you manage the properties.

Managing the Browser

The browser was originally built on the NetBEUI protocol, which is broadcast-related and hence fairly chatty. The logical address for any computer under NetBEUI is the string name that you assign to the computer. As a result, this protocol will not route, because there is not enough information included in the logical addressing scheme to build routing tables. NetBEUI undertakes almost any action on the network by including a broadcast in the operation. As a result, it can hog bandwidth considerably.

The browser also focuses on broadcasts. To find the master browser, for example, the booting server broadcasts. To determine which computer will be master browser, a considerable number of broadcasts are required to hold an election—the process by which a new master browser is selected. Each server on the network must be made aware of the election, requiring a broadcast.

Then a packet must be passed among all the computers with server services running. Each server examines the packet for an election weighting. It calculates its own election weighting based on a number of criteria and, if its election weighting exceeds the one stored in the packet, inserts its name and election weighting into the packet in place of the packet's original contents. The packet is then passed on to another server. To locate the next server, name resolution is required. The server's string name must be equated to a Media Access Control address associated with that server's network interface card. But NetBEUI keeps no table of this information. Instead, it broadcasts to find the server identified by the string name.

Electing a new master browser is a fairly noisy process. In general, you want to avoid elections. You want a master browser that is a stable presence on the network; you want stable backup browsers; and you want no booting server to call an election, which it does when it cannot find a master browser. When you resegment your network, an election has to take place on the new subnet. Because NetBEUI will not route, a master browser will not be present on the new subnet, and an election will be held.

Technical Note: Because NetBEUI does not route, you cannot browse across subnets unless you configure your primary domain controller (PDC) to serve as domain master browser. This configuration happens automatically if you use the Windows Internet Name Service (WINS) provided with the Windows NT Server operating system. If you do not run WINS, you must use an LMHOSTS file for name resolution. You must preload the name of the PDC into the name cache using the #PRE directive, and you must identify the PDC's name as the primary domain controller by using the #DOM directive. A sample LMHOSTS file is stored as LMHOSTS.SAM in the Windows directory. You can edit it to add the lines you need and save it as LMHOSTS, no extension.

You have two settings that you can use to control the browser, LM Announce and BrowseMaster, which you control from the properties for file and printer sharing. Open the Network Control Panel, select File and Printer Sharing for Microsoft Networks, and click Properties (see Figure 19.9). You change the values by using the Value drop-down list.

You want to set LM Announce to No, its default value, and leave it there unless you have clients on your network that absolutely require you to use the Yes setting. (If you have such clients, you should strongly consider replacing them.) Setting this value to Yes causes even more broadcasts on your network. Your server service operates under the old LAN Manager rules for announcing servers, which are for each client to broadcast a request for server identification and for each server to broadcast back to announce its presence.

Figure 19.9.
Properties for File and Printer Sharing control the browser.

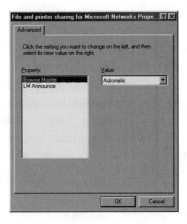

BrowseMaster has three potential settings. Automatic, the default, allows this server service to participate in elections. This computer could therefore become the master browser. It could also become a backup browser. Disabled means that this computer cannot participate in elections. Enabled increases the election weighting of this computer in an election to attempt to cause it to become master browser.

Note: Windows establishes roughly one backup browser for every 32 computers on the subnet.

To control browsing, you want to decide which machines will participate in browser elections. You want to set BrowseMaster to Enabled or Automatic on these machines. You will need one computer set this way for every 32 computers on the network, and you will need one additional one per subnet for a master browser. You do not need to worry about the domain master browser. This role is always fulfilled by the PDC.

You should set BrowseMaster to Disabled on the other computers, especially any mobile computers you may have on the network. You can have election wars on your network if a set of laptops capture the role of master browser and then unplug to head out to the field during the day. Every time the master browser unplugs, you will have another election.

Under Windows 95, you control the browser exactly as you do under Windows 98. Under Windows NT and Windows 3.x, you use a setting called MaintainServerList. It takes the values of Auto, Yes, and No, corresponding to Automatic, Enabled, and Disabled. You set this value in the

HKEY_LOCAL_MACHINE\System\CurrentControlSet\Services\Browser\Parameters key in the Windows
NT Registry, and in the SYSTEM.INI file, [Network] section, under Windows 3.x. If you are using File
and Printer Sharing for NetWare Networks, you use the value Workgroup Advertising in the properties for this service to control browsing. Your options are May Be Master, Preferred Master, and
Will Not Be Master. You can also control whether Windows 98 advertises using the SAP protocol
by setting the value SAP Advertising to Enabled or Disabled. SAP advertising is enabled by default.

Managing Shares and Users

To manage users, shares, and open files, you use a tool called Net Watcher. To run this tool, use the
menu path Programs | Accessories | System Tools | Net Watcher. However, Net Watcher is not in-
stalled by default. You must use Add/Remove Programs from the Control Panel to add Net Watcher.
You will find its check box in the Accessories group.

When you start Net Watcher, you see the view shown in Figure 19.10. When you first open Net
Watcher, you see a view of the local computer. You can select any Windows 98 server on your network, however, using the Administer menu's Select Server option. You of course need remote administration privileges for the remote server.

Tip: The server you wish to manage must be configured for the same type of access control
as the machine on which you run Net Watcher. Net Watcher will mistake a NetWare
server for a Windows 98 server, but it cannot manage a NetWare server.

Figure 19.10.
*Net Watcher enables
you to manage
connections, shares,
and open files.*

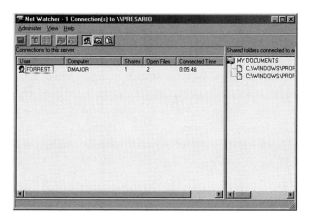

The default view of the server shows you the users who are connected, the computers they are logged
on to, the number of shares connected, the number of open files, the connect time, and the idle

time for each user. For the selected user, you see a Tree view of the shares and open documents in the right pane. The only other action you can take in this view is to select a user and use Administer | Disconnect User to end the connection. You receive a warning that data in open files may be lost, but you can click Yes to end the connection anyway. This is the only way to explicitly end a connection to your computer without waiting for the session to time out.

> **Tip:** On any workgroup computer that will share resources, make Net Watcher available so that the owner of that computer can manage connections.

Using the View menu, you can change the view in the client area of the window to display shared folders or open files. The Shared Folder view appears in Figure 19.11. In the left pane, you see the path to the folder, its share name, the type of access, and the comment that has been entered as a share property. In the right pane, you see a Tree view of connected computers and open files for the selected shared folder.

Figure 19.11.
The Shared Folder view displays information about connections for each shared folder.

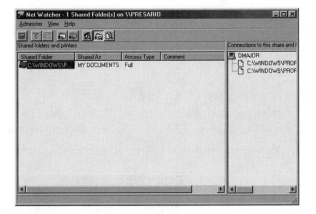

The Open File view of Net Watcher appears in Figure 19.12. This view is the only location in Windows 98 where you can explicitly close a shared file. To do so, use the Close File option on the Administer menu. After you exercise this option, the file is closed. The user's connection to the file has ended, but not the user's connection to the shared folder. Use this option when you need to end access to a file so that you can perform a maintenance task on the file that you cannot perform while it is opened by another user.

> **Warning:** Most of the actions you take with Net Watcher that terminate connections or access qualify as catastrophic events. You could cause data loss by taking them. You will be warned and allowed to opt out of the action. Be wary of taking these actions unless they are absolutely necessary.

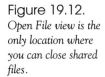

Figure 19.12.
Open File view is the only location where you can close shared files.

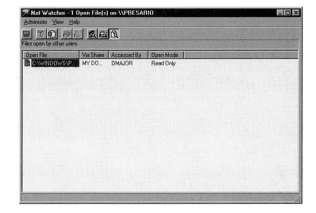

Summary

This chapter has covered the two security models available in Windows 98: share-level and user-level. You reviewed reasons for choosing one model or the other, and you reviewed how to set up and use each method of securing shared resources from network access. You also saw how to manage sharing issues, including the browser service. Finally, this chapter covered using Net Watcher as a management tool.

On Your Own

First, set up a machine for share-level security. Create a shared folder and printer. Then try attaching to them from another computer. Convert to user-level security and repeat the process. Then use Net Watcher to manage the shared folder's properties.

20

Protecting Data

Peter Norton®

As the saying goes, there are only two types of users: those who have lost data, and those who will. An unfortunate truth of computing is that hardware and media wear out. I have never kept a disk drive up and running longer than three years. And I have had some unfortunate accidents. Although everyone's experience is going to be different, the main point is that eventually you will have to rely on backups of your data to protect your mission-critical computers from data loss. You want to make certain that your backups are going to protect you when hardware failure comes.

The last time I had to depend on an analog tape (whose manufacturer shall remain nameless) for a backup under emergency conditions, I experienced great misfortune. After replacing the primary drive in the system and starting the restore, I was feeling confident that all would be well. Halfway through the restore, however, a dialog box appeared announcing that the backup program was "experiencing media defects." This dialog box suggested that I reformat the tape and try the operation again.

"No problem," I smugly thought, "I'll just finish running the tape and hope for the best." When I clicked on OK to dismiss the dialog box, however, *the backup program stopped executing.* I was not a happy user at that moment.

To keep you from experiencing such joy, this chapter covers ways of protecting your data from loss, including the following topics:

- Defining a backup strategy
- Backing up your system
- Using ERU, LFNBACK, and CFGBACK
- Restoring your system

Defining a General Strategy

Losing data is eminently easy. Despite your best engineered efforts, users find a way. As a result, any strategy for protecting data must demonstrate two practical features: automation and redundancy. You need automation because users will not, repeat, will not remember to do what they need to do to protect their own data. You need redundancy so that ordinary handling of backups does not cause data loss, and so that catastrophe cannot result in data loss. The insurance industry is quick to point out that most businesses who lose their data to a fire do not recover. You need automation and redundancy.

Microsoft has provided your first line of defense against data loss for you. Windows 98 automates ScanDisk whenever the system has failed to shut down properly. Windows 98 tracks a flag that indicates whether shutdown occurred. If the flag is still set on startup, Windows 98 engages the command line version of ScanDisk to check the drive. You see a message that ScanDisk will run because of improper shutdown. Touching any key initiates the scan.

Although not as robust as the transaction logging used in the NT File System (NTFS), automatic ScanDisk does protect the structure of the file system against corruption of the sort that can occur during improper power off. You need to supplement this procedure with backup strategies, and you need to automate your backups using Scheduled Tasks. After you have scheduled backups, however, you need to remember that the scheduled events are only as good as the users remembering to leave their systems powered on. These backups also depend on human operators remembering to change the backup media.

I prefer to have three levels of redundancy in my backup strategy. You may prefer more. At the first level, my office systems back up critical files related to the user of the system to a backup server once per day. This server is a NetWare 4.1 server whose only purpose is to keep these files safe on its disk. I chose NetWare because of its advantages for providing file services to the network. The backup job is defined under McAfee's QuickBackup and scheduled to take place after hours. My company has a policy of leaving computers powered up continuously, and we set the backup software to overwrite existing files. Even if the user forgets to change the media, a fresh backup should go onto the backup server once per day.

At the second level, most of the files a user creates are stored in home folders on servers. We defined the My Documents folder as a part of the desktop kept in the user's profile. Because we log on to a Windows NT domain, Windows 98 automatically stores the profile—including the contents of the My Documents folder—on the server in home directories at log off. At the third level, we use digital audio tapes (DAT) to back up the servers nightly, again overwriting the tape so that even if we skip a media change the backup is written. Theoretically, even if a file is damaged, we should have two independent copies. Once a week we rotate a tape into a fire safe and a safe deposit box as safeguards against catastrophe.

As a final check against disaster, we also have a policy that is our weakest link in the strategy (because users forget). We require that users keep critical projects in two locations, preferably on separate physical devices, and to set software to make automatic backup copies. Although weak as a strategy, this policy has saved more than one file from oblivion.

Warning: If you recall the Windows 95 Plus! Pack, you remember that the scheduling agent would schedule Windows 95 Backup to run at intervals you defined. Windows 98 Backup does not retain this capability. Even worse—and we learned this the hard way during the beta program—the Task Scheduler seems to schedule the operation. You will not easily see that the backup operation is failing unless you check the media or the logs. You could go a long time without realizing your backups are failing if you just upgrade Windows 95 machines on which the backup has already been scheduled.

This simple but redundant backup strategy is appropriate to a small office like mine. It would not be appropriate for a large network, where servers of different hardware types and operating system types may be present. Servers could be using RAID storage devices, for example, to reduce the danger of data loss from damage to a single physical disk. On larger networks, this RAID strategy is well worth the implementation. In the next few sections, I will try to give you a sense of the options you have. You will want to choose from these options to define your own data protection strategy.

Defining a Backup Strategy

Backing up means keeping copies on a separate physical device. You have your choice of devices, and you have several strategies that you can apply. In general, you want a strategy that provides you with the greatest protection for the dollar investment. In addition, you need to factor in the risk factor if a backup should fail. If the greatest risk is having to retype a letter or contract, you can easily rely on cheaper backup strategies and devices. If the risk is the loss of three hours worth of customer orders over an active Web server, however, you probably want to invest more in your backup technology.

Using Disk Drives

Among the disk devices you can use for backup are the venerable floppy disk, removable fixed disks, and hard drives. Floppy drives are useful only to a limited extent. They do not have the capacity to back up many files, and they are easily damaged. They are also highly portable, allowing sensitive data to be carried where you would rather it not go. For users with critical data, however, they can be a useful protection tool.

On networks or moderately sized systems, removable fixed disks or additional hard drives are a better bet. Removable fixed disks come in a variety of capacities, from 100MB to 1GB. They are reliable, and reasonably durable. In addition, they are quiet and fast. They can be as easily archived as tapes, and they are often portable; therefore a roving backup team could use them on multiple user systems without placing undo traffic on the network. However, 1GB cartridges are relatively expensive.

> **Warning:** Keep removable fixed disks inside their protective cases at all times when they are not in the drive. If you drop these disks, they can shatter, rendering the backed up data useless.

Using disks on servers, you can employ redundant arrays of independent disks (RAID) to provide a level of protection. Both Windows NT and Novell NetWare can support such arrays. Generally, you purchase a hardware controller that builds and manages the array. Windows NT Server, however, includes a fault-tolerant disk driver that enables you to create arrays of disks using only software.

Technical Note: You have two varieties of RAID protection that you can employ easily, mirrors (RAID 1) and stripe sets with parity (RAID 5). In disk mirroring, two drives maintain exact copies of the same data. When a disk write takes place, it is written to both drives in the array. When a read takes place, data is read from the primary drive in the array. If you have a read failure on one drive, the data is automatically read from the other drive. A write failure usually causes the array to break apart, with the good disk continuing to support the system. If you are concerned that a controller card may damage both disks, place the two disks on separate controllers, in which case the array is called a disk duplex.

Stripe sets with parity use a different data protection strategy. Instead of maintaining copies of the data, stripe sets focus on reconstructing missing data. Such an array requires at least three physical disks. Data is written in stripes, or sets of sectors, on each disk. A stripe for a given file is roughly the same size on each disk. As a result, only part of the file is written in a stripe.

In a three-disk array, in fact, the file is split in half, with half of the information written to two stripes. The third stripe consists of the results of an XOR operation performed on the other two stripes. The resulting data is called parity information.

Now that the three stripes have been written, the file in question is protected as follows. If the disk containing the parity stripe goes down, you still have all the data in the other two stripes. You have no need to recover the file, because it is in fact present. If a drive containing a data stripe goes down, the missing stripe can be reconstructed. The system reverses the XOR operation using the parity stripe and the remaining data stripe. The result is the stripe containing the missing data.

Peter's Principle: Use Hardware Controllers for RAID Devices

I prefer to use hardware controllers for RAID devices rather than software tools like those provided with Windows NT Server. Hardware controllers are more robust, and they usually enable you to change a single disk without powering down. They manage the mirroring or striping completely, including rebuilding a replaced disk on-the-fly. RAID controllers and cabinets are well worth the hardware dollar you spend for them.

By contrast, Windows NT Server's fault-tolerant disk driver stores information about the array in the Registry, which is of course stored on disk. If you lose the disk containing the array information, or if that portion of the Registry becomes corrupt, you must rebuild the array information manually using a tool called FTEdit (Fault-Tolerant Disk Editor) included with the Windows NT Resource Kit. There is much less to fail in a hardware RAID solution.

The best disk option for backup depends on your purposes. Floppy disks are limited to personal backups for users. Removable fixed disks are excellent for backups under 2–3GB in size, because a 1GB Jaz cartridge can hold that amount of data with compression. Hard drives and RAID arrays can be scaled to most needs, but are limited in respect to archiving. It is harder to archive a 4GB SCSI drive than a Jaz cartridge. For large-scale backups, tapes are still the preferred tool.

> **Warning:** If you implement RAID, do not fall into a false sense of security. You do need to back up your RAID array. Multiple points of failure have been known to occur.

One other disk option does exist, and that is writeable CD. You can acquire such a drive for under $600, and each CD will store up to 660MB of data. Most of these devices do not allow the rewriting of media. One special type of rewriteable CD is available, but it has a limited lifetime of about 20 overwrites. Writeable CDs are useful for archiving files that you want protected in backup for a considerable time. Retrieval is easier than from tape, and the CD is the most durable backup medium presently available. CDs are also easy to archive. Keep in mind, however, that CDs do not provide permanent storage unless you get special media that does not degrade over time. Ordinary recordable CDs are relatively cheap. The more durable version is more expensive and difficult to find.

> **Warning:** When you are working with any medium, but especially when you are working with CDs, you should attempt a restore at regular intervals to verify that the medium can be restored from. CDs have some quirks associated with their file systems, and they may not restore your data with the correct filenames at times. In addition, CD writes are prone to buffer underrun errors that destroy the entire CD. You need to check your media carefully. You need to verify your backups. You also need to attempt restores to make certain that everything about your backup strategy has worked perfectly and that you are capable of restoring your data.

Using Tapes

Tape drives have been consistently favored for backups over other drive and media combinations. The reason is simple: A single tape can hold a great deal of data. Originally tapes came on large spools of the type you see on a reel-to-reel tape recorder. They could hold a tremendous amount of data. As tape drives came to personal systems, tape cartridges were employed in about the size of the drive you might wish to back up. As time has marched on, tape drives and tape cartridges have increased in capacity. The latest DAT drives and cartridges measure capacity in gigabytes, not megabytes, of storage.

The disadvantage of tape is that tapes are difficult to search for a single file. Although they can be random access devices, reaching the file that needs to be accessed can mean streaming through hundreds of feet of tape. As a result, limited restore operations from a complete backup can take some time. In addition, tapes can be damaged easily, about as easily as floppy disks. They need careful storage to protect from dust, and if they come near magnetic fields they can lose data.

Tapes are the medium of choice when you have a lot of data to back up. Their capacity cannot be topped by any other medium. The cost per megabyte stored is the lowest of any medium. Your main choice is whether to go with an analog tape device or a digital tape device. Analog tapes record data as a continuous modulation of an electrical signal on the tape. Digital tapes convert the data to numbers and store the numbers on the tape. I prefer digital tapes over analog for critical backups because I believe that digital tapes are less vulnerable to errors that occur because the tape has stretched.

Technical Note: When you work with tapes, you normally work with a rotation schedule. You also typically work with different types of backups. A *complete backup* copies all the files on the drive to tape. A *differential backup* copies all the files that have changed since the last complete backup. An *incremental backup* copies all the files that have changed since the last complete backup on the first incremental, and then since the last incremental backup thereafter.

Typically you run differential or incremental backups daily, and periodically run a complete backup. You should verify each backup to make certain that the files have copied correctly, even though the verify operation roughly doubles the time necessary to complete the backup. When you have to restore a system from backup tapes in an emergency, you will greatly appreciate having run the verification.

You can easily build a backup schedule, with as few as 15 tapes, that protects files for up to six months. The rotation starts on Friday, when you do a complete backup of the system with tape 1. Monday through Thursday you run incremental or differential backups using tapes 2, 3, and 4. On the second Friday, you run a complete backup on tape 5, and move tape 1 to offsite storage. Repeat the second week of daily backups with tapes 2, 3, and 4. Do not overwrite files on these tapes until you absolutely have to.

The cycle continues on the second Friday with a complete backup on tape 6. You take this tape to offsite storage and retrieve tape 1. You continue with the weekly cycle, allowing tapes 7 and 8 to serve as weekly complete tapes. At the end of one month, however, you keep the weekly tape, in this case tape 8, as a monthly backup in offsite storage. Such tapes are not retrieved until the six month cycle is complete.

You continue the weekly cycle, now storing a weekly tape and the monthly tapes in offsite storage. At the end of six months, you recycle the oldest monthly tape back into the pool of tapes to use.

Following this plan, you should be able to retrieve any file from backups from versions as far back as six months old. You should also have daily protection of the file versions.

> **Tip:** I prefer differential to incremental backups because of the restore sequence. To restore from differentials, you restore two tapes, the last complete and the last differential. To restore from incrementals, you restore the last complete and every incremental in sequence until you are current.

You can place a tape drive on each server and desktop, but often it is easier to centralize backup. Place tape drives on the systems that you will use for backups, and then map drives to the administrative shares on the systems you need to back up. Define the backup jobs and schedule them. Make sure users and administrators are educated to leave the systems on for backups.

If you are backing up large quantities of data, consider using a tape library. Companies such as StorageTek have been making these devices for mainframe computers. Now they are beginning to appear for smaller computers. A library stores a set of tapes and contains a set of drives. It can load tapes into drives and automate the backup jobs according to the schedule you define. The tapes stay in a controlled environment, so they are not likely to be damaged. Tape libraries represent a substantial investment. For large networks, however, they may indeed be a worthwhile investment.

Backing Up to the Internet

The Web being all the rage, it is not surprising that McAfee and other companies are offering Internet-based backup. Such schemes enable you to use someone else's disks and tapes to store your data, with the guarantee that they will take very good care of your data. Typically such a service would run a large RAID 5 array which they back up methodically. For a fee, they grant you the right to use, say, 30MB of their array to store your critical files. You transfer your files using a Web-based tool, complete with compression and the other features associated with other backup tools.

Internet storage has positive and negative attributes. The main worry is security. You are handing over your data to a third party. They literally could attack your encryption and compromise trade secrets and sensitive records. They probably won't, but your security now depends on your trust of that third party.

The advantage is that you do not have to maintain as much protection locally. You are renting someone else's RAID device and tape library. Even if you need a lot of storage space, the annual rental may be less than maintaining the equipment yourself. In addition, this storage is offsite, so catastrophe is less likely to affect you.

Using Internet storage is not an excuse for failing to protect your data locally. You will still want to do local backups, for redundancy if nothing else. You may find, however, that renting protected storage alleviates the need to invest in RAID and storage devices to a certain extent. You have to factor in what keeps the corporate mind at peace in your situation, and allow the corporate mind to spend its dollars in the way that keeps it peaceful.

Backing Up to an Intranet

If other companies can use the Internet to sell backup storage, you could set the same sort of scheme up on your own network. You could make a server with a RAID array available to users and grant them a certain amount of storage for critical files. You could help them to plan folders for storing such files locally, show them how to attach to the backup server with the backup program, show them how to define and save a job, and show them how to schedule that job. Or you could set these items up when you install the system and tell users which folders to use for files they want backed up.

The advantage of pursuing this strategy is that your backup server now backs up a central drive array rather than a lot of individual systems. The disadvantage is the network traffic created, hence the need to schedule the jobs so that you balance the traffic load appropriately. Even the simple Windows 98 Backup program enables you to carry out this strategy.

Backing Up Your System

You have your choice of products for backing up systems. Windows 98 Backup comes with the system, and it is a fairly functional program. You also have agents for the two leading network backup programs, ARCServe and Backup Exec. In addition, you have some third-party options that offer unique capabilities. The following sections examine each of these options in turn.

Using Windows Backup

Windows 98 Backup offers you a practical, basic backup program. It gives you the options necessary to back up your system efficiently. It supports both tape drives and removable cartridge disk drives. It also provides a wizard interface to help you define a backup job. To back up your system, follow these steps:

1. Open the Backup program from the Start menu (Start | Programs | Accessories | System Tools | Backup). The wizard shown in Figure 20.1 greets you.
2. Accept the default option in the wizard (Create a new backup job) and click on OK.
3. Next the wizard prompts you to select either a complete backup or a backup of selected files. For this example, choose Back up My Computer, and then click Next.
4. Now the wizard asks whether you want to back up all selected files or only new and changed files. Select All selected files, and then click Next.

Figure 20.1.
Microsoft Backup
provides a wizard to
guide you through
creating a backup job.

5. The next wizard panel, shown in Figure 20.2, enables you to specify a backup destination. For this example, accept the defaults and click Next. Note that by clicking the button next to the destination path you can select any drive location on your network for the backup.

Figure 20.2.
The wizard enables
you to select the
format and destina-
tion for your backup.

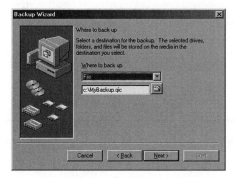

6. The next panel enables you to determine whether to verify the backup against the original files and whether to compress the backup. I recommend that you select both options. Click Next to continue.

7. The final panel of the wizard enables you to name your backup job, as shown in Figure 20.3. Enter a name and click Start. The backup job then initiates.

Warning: The Backup Wizard does *not* have you set a couple of options that are important to a good backup strategy. First, by default, Windows 98 Backup does not back up the Registry. Second, the Backup default is to append the new file to the backup media, not overwrite the existing files. Finally, no password is set on the backup for security. You may wish to modify these factors before pursuing the backup job, and especially before saving it for reuse later.

Figure 20.3.
The wizard asks you to name the backup job so that you can reuse it.

To modify these options, cancel the backup operation, and then click the Options button in the Backup tab of the main window for the program. Use the dialog box shown in Figure 20.4 to adjust the properties of the backup to your liking. Registry backup is set on the Advanced tab. Overwriting the preceding backup file is set on the General tab and passwords are set on the Password tab.

Figure 20.4.
Use the Backup Job Options dialog box to set advanced properties for your backup job.

When you exit the backup program, you are prompted to save the job for reuse later. You can also save the job by using the Save option on the Job menu.

Using Alternative Backup Software

Microsoft's Windows 98 Backup gets the basic job done, but it does not enable you to back up a remote node over the network. You can store your backup on a remote node, but attaching to another system to back it up is not supported.

To implement remote backups, you would need to use third-party backup software. Windows 98 includes remote agents for two popular network backup programs. You install these as network services, using the Network Control Panel applet.

Technical Note: You may also have noticed that Windows 98 Backup depends on the GUI. It has no command-line version. As a result, to restore a system, you must first reinstall Windows 98. You may not care for this option, and third-party programs do enable you to restore from a bootable floppy disk. The moral of this discussion is that you may wish to consider third-party backup seriously.

Choosing the Seagate and Cheyenne Clients

To opt for the remote backup options available, you need to first purchase and implement either Cheyenne Software's ARCServe or Seagate Software's Backup Exec. You can then install the agent for your chosen software on the Windows 98 workstations on your network. To install the agent, follow these steps:

1. Open the Network Control Panel applet.
2. In the Configuration tab, click on Add.
3. In the Select Network Component Type dialog box, select Service and then click Add.
4. Select the software company that built your backup solution, and select its agent (see Figure 20.5). Then click OK.

Figure 20.5.
Select the appropriate agent for your software and click OK.

5. If necessary, provide the path to the Windows source files and click OK. Windows 98 copies the agent into place.

6. Close the Network applet by clicking OK. Windows 98 copies more files and then prompts you to restart.

To configure your agent, select it in the Configuration tab of the Network Control Panel applet and click on Properties. The agent provides a dialog box like the one shown in Figure 20.6. You can set up passwords to allow secure backups. You can also exclude files and disable backups.

Figure 20.6.
Backup agents provide a dialog box that enables appropriate configuration.

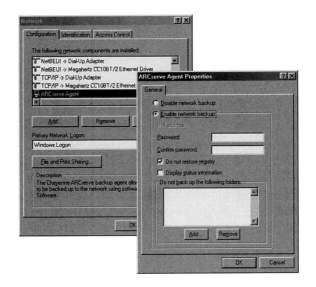

Choosing Other Third-Party Options

You do have other software options for backing up files. One example is McAfee's backup product, which offers two features not found in other personal backup solutions. The first is a command-line version of the restore program that can be booted from a floppy disk. It can load the drivers for your backup media and restore a drive without first having to load Windows 98. The second is the possibility of renting Web storage for critical files.

> **Tip:** A personal backup program is designed to enable a user to back up files on a workstation. It is not designed to support remote backups.

Although most additional third-party options tend toward personal backup programs, you do have options in network management tools for backup of critical files. In the SMS Server, for example, you can designate that copies of critical files be maintained in the SMS database. After a file is so tagged, when it changes, a new copy is placed in the database. You can track system changes and restore to previous states easily.

Using CFGBACK, ERU, and LFNBACK

Three other backup utilities are included on the CD-ROM with Windows 98. They are stored in various subfolders of the Tools folder. The first, the Emergency Recovery Utility, backs up critical files and provides a utility that restores your system. The second, Microsoft Configuration Backup, keeps Registry backups. The third, LFNBACK, protects long filename information. You should investigate these tools to see how you might benefit from their use.

Running CFGBACK

Microsoft Configuration Backup, whose initial screen is shown in Figure 20.7, keeps backups of the Registry files. You find it in the Tools\ResKit\Registry folder on the Resource Kit CD. The utility is referenced in the documentation as a part of the Resource Kit Sampler, but is not actually present. (The full Resource Kit is available as a separate product.) These files are stored in your Windows folder in files with the extension .RBK, for Registry Backup. Configuration Backup can manage multiple backups. As a result, you should be able to return to previous states or alternative configurations of your system with ease.

Figure 20.7.
Configuration Backup enables you to make multiple backups of the Registry.

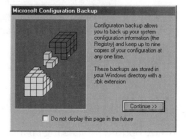

Using Configuration Backup is easy because of the wizard-like interface. Follow these steps:

1. On the initial screen, click the Continue button.
2. Read the second screen, which explains the backup process. Then click on Continue. Do the same with the third screen, which explains the restore process.
3. Enter a name for the backup and click Backup, as shown in Figure 20.8.

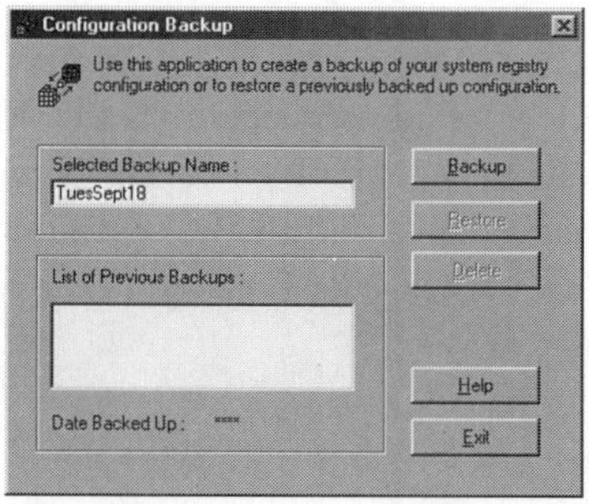

Figure 20.8.
You must name the backup file and click Backup to initiate the save process.

4. Click Yes when the dialog box appears asking whether you want to back up the current configuration. The program saves your Registry to a file and compresses it. You may copy this file to any location, but you can restore it only from your Windows folder.

Peter's Principle: Keeping Multiple Backups of the Registry

I believe in keeping multiple backups of the Registry, using multiple tools. When I do a tape backup, I always back up the Registry. I like keeping copies of changing system configurations with Configuration Backup. I like backing up the configuration to a network location using ERU. It always seems that when you need a Registry backup it is not available.

Restoring one of these copies is as simple as selecting the copy in the list of previous backups and clicking Restore (see Figure 20.9). Windows 98 decompresses the file and uses the Registry `Replace` function to undertake the restoration.

Warning: Configuration Backup has been known to fail, reporting an internal error, on occasion. Although it is a useful program, do not depend on it as your sole source for Registry backups.

Tip: A more reliable way to back up your Registry is to open Regedit and use the Registry | Export menu option to save the entire Registry as a REG file. These files are text files. Their default action when double-clicked—the action associated with the file extension `.REG` by Windows 98—is to merge the settings contained within into the Registry.

Figure 20.9.
Use the Restore button to restore the Registry from a backup.

Running ERU

The Emergency Recovery Utility saves critical system files to floppy disk or to a network drive. You find it in the Tools\Misc folder on the full Resource Kit CD. ERU is not included as a part of the Resource Kit Sampler on your Windows 98 CD. As seen in Figure 20.10, the utility provides a wizard-style interface. To save your system files, follow these steps:

1. In the opening panel, click Next.

2. Select the destination, either drive A: or a directory, in the second panel and click Next.

3. If you selected a directory, confirm the location in the third panel and click Next.

4. The next panel (see Figure 20.11) shows you the files that will be saved. To alter the list, click Custom and use a check box interface to select the files that you want to save. When you are ready to save, click Next.

5. ERU copies the files and displays a dialog box explaining the restoration process. Click OK to dismiss this dialog box, and the utility exits.

Figure 20.10.
ERU also provides a wizard-style interface for system backup.

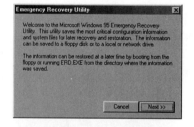

Figure 20.11.
ERU shows you the files it will copy and enables you to customize the list.

Using LFNBACK

LFNBACK is a utility that you find in the \Tools\Reskit\file\lfnback folder on the Windows 98 CD. LFNBACK is a command-line utility that backs up long filenames. The only reason to use this utility is when you must use an older, DOS-based utility to perform maintenance on a drive. Microsoft mentions the following utilities specifically as requiring the use of this tool:

• Norton Utilities by Peter Norton Computing

• PC Tools by Central Point Software, Inc.

- Microsoft Defragmenter for MS-DOS version 6.0, 6.2, 6.21, or 6.22
- Stacker 4.0 by STAC Electronics

LFNBACK is not a tool that you might use often. You may have to support drives that use Stacker 4.0, but by and large these are tools that you might resort to in a crisis setting. A drive is failing, for example, and you have to resolve the source of the problem with these tools because Windows 98 tools are not providing the resolution you need. Before you use these tools, you must back up your long filename information because these tools will permanently sever the long from the short filenames on your drive.

To back up long filenames, first go to the Control Panel's System icon, select the Performance tab, click on the File System button, and check Disable long name preservation for old programs. Then execute the following command line:

```
lfnback /b DriveLetter:
```

You can now restart your computer and perform whatever maintenance you desire to undertake with the old utilities. After you are finished, execute this command line:

```
lfnback /r DriveLetter:
```

Next, uncheck Disable long name preservation for old programs. Restart your computer, and hope that the old utilities solved the problem.

Restoring Your System

Restoring is perhaps even more important a process than backing up. It occurs usually under distressing conditions, it has to work, and if it fails serious losses take place. It is best to practice restores occasionally so that you are ready for the event when it must occur. The next three sections step you through basic restoration steps.

Restoring from Windows Backup

To restore using Windows 98 Backup, start the Restore Wizard (Tools | Restore Wizard), and follow these steps:

1. Confirm the filename from which to restore in the first page of the wizard (see Figure 20.12), and then click Next.
2. Select the backup set stored within the file and click OK in the Select Backup Sets dialog box.
3. Select the files and folders to restore (see Figure 20.13), and then click Next.
4. Select the destination for the restore (original or alternative location) and click Next. If you select an alternative location, you must provide that location in the next wizard page.

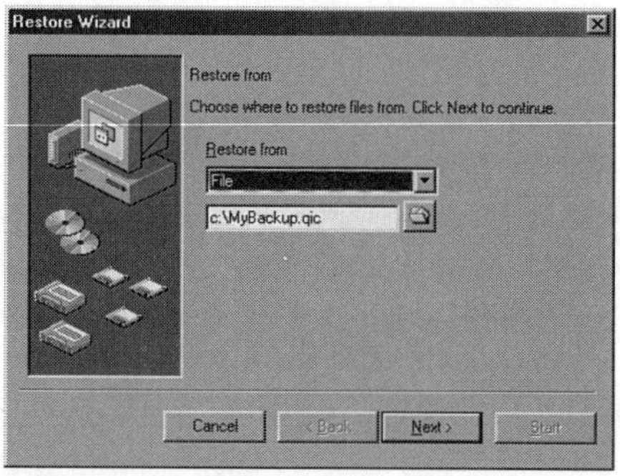

Figure 20.12.
Select the media type and filename from which to restore.

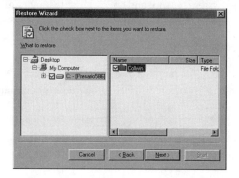

Figure 20.13.
Use the tree and check boxes to select the files and folders to restore.

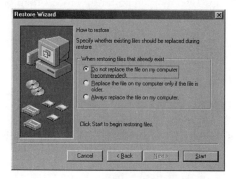

5. Select the location from the option buttons that are available when you must replace a file that already exists (see Figure 20.14). Then click Start.

Figure 20.14.
The Restore Wizard enables you to select what happens when a duplicate file exists.

6. Confirm the media required in the Media Required dialog box and click OK. The name of the media required will be the name of the backup set stored in the file or on the tape when you created the backup. This name will not be the name of the file as you see it on the disk. The name of the file is the name you gave the backup file in the first page of the Backup Wizard. The name of the backup set is stored in the file. Windows 98 Backup restores the files.

Restoring from Alternative Backup Software

Restoring from the Cheyenne, Seagate, McAfee, or other backup product is substantially similar in process to restoring from Windows 98 Backup. With the remote products, however, you need to remember the password used to attach to the system to which you wish to restore. If you are restoring from a floppy disk, you must first make certain that the drive to restore is ready for restoration. It needs to be partitioned and formatted to be ready to accept restored files. You also need to make sure that you have the appropriate drivers installed on the disk you use for restoration, so that you have access to all the devices necessary during the restoration process.

Running ERD

If you have used ERU to back up critical files, you can restore these files with a utility called ERD that is located on the media to which you backed up the files. You will find `ERD.EXE` on the disk or in the folder to which you directed these files.

You cannot run ERD from within the Windows 98 graphical shell. You must run it from a command prompt in MS-DOS mode. Either boot from a disk, or shutdown and boot in MS-DOS mode. After you are at the command prompt, change to the directory where ERD is located, and run the file.

The following line appears onscreen:

```
Emergency Recovery Utility. Press'Y' to recover, or any other key to exit
```

Actually, you must press "Y" and then press Enter. The following message then appears onscreen:

```
Please wait…recovering files
```

After the utility has completed restoring the files, you see the following lines onscreen:

```
Recovery Completed Successfully!
The configuration files have been restored.  The
Computer will need to be rebooted for the changes
to take effect.

To undo the recovery type:  ERD.EXE /UNDO
Press Any Key To Continue
```

Reboot the computer using Ctrl+Alt+Del to return to using the Windows 98 graphical shell with the restored settings.

Summary

This chapter reviewed how to protect data under Windows 98. Topics included backup strategies, the several options for backup software, and backup and restore operations. In addition, several more specialized tools for configuration backup were presented, with basic procedures and warnings about their use.

On Your Own

You should first devise a backup plan for your systems. What do you need to keep copies of, where will they be stored, and how will you collect the backups? Then practice with your chosen backup software. Back up a non-essential folder, and then restore and verify it. You want to make sure the software and hardware are producing error-free copies. Then try out the more specialized tools, and verify whether they suit your needs.

VI

Participating on Intranets and Internets

21

Creating a
Web Server

Peter Norton®

Web pages are all the rage. If you don't have your own personal page, you must be square. For businesses, a Web page is absolutely essential. For the first time in history, we have an information conduit that anyone can exploit without high cost. The Web is like having the library at Alexandria flowing into your computer, only our world has thousands of times the knowledge that the ancient Egyptians had before their library burned, one of the great tragedies in the history of ideas. With the endless replication of electronic information, such a tragedy is much less likely with the Web. Of course, some of the sites on the Web might be considered similar tragedies, as you know if you have surfed around.

Your Web page informs your clients and customers about you. It may enable them to order your goods. It may enable them to register your products. It may enable them to answer surveys, provide timely feedback, or provide whatever information you need to collect. You can provide technical support and much of your customer-service effort from your page. In addition, your Web page establishes your image with clients and customers. It says a lot about who you are. Having the right tools to build a Web page is therefore essential.

Whether you want to place your page on the Internet or on an intranet, you need an operating system to host the page, you need a Web server to display the page, and you need to build HTML code to create the page. Windows 98 can host a Web page. It includes the Personal Web Server that will display the page, and it provides FrontPage Express to help you build the page.

This chapter focuses on using the Personal Web Server and FrontPage Express to build your Web page, focusing on these issues:

- How to choose the right Web server for your project
- How to set up a Web page using the Personal Web Server
- How to set up a Web page on other types of servers

Choosing a Web Server

Windows 98 does indeed provide a Web server that runs on any computer that supports Windows 98. However, you should not let this fact mislead you. Your Web project may have requirements that exceed those that the Personal Web Server provided with Windows 98 can deliver. When you consider setting up Web pages, you need to carefully consider the capabilities of the servers available. You need a Web server that delivers the capabilities you need and matches your skills as a Web developer.

Table 21.1 summarizes the features of the major types of Web servers available. The following sections elaborate.

Table 21.1. Feature comparison of major categories of Web servers.

Server	Personal Web	Peer Web	IIS	NetWare	UNIX
Connections	10	10	Unlimited	Unlimited	Unlimited
	WWW only	WWW, FTP, Gopher	WWW, FTP, Gopher	WWW, FTP, Gopher	WWW, FTP, Gopher
Security	Limited	NT	NT	NetWare	UNIX
TCP/IP	Limited	Robust	Robust	Robust	Robust

Using the Personal Web Server

The Personal Web Server provided with Windows 98 enables you to deliver a Web page from nearly any system running on your network. It installs easily, manages connections and security according to the security model you have chosen, and runs in the background with only minimal impact on foreground activity. As a result, you can easily use a workstation as a Web server without dedicating the workstation to that function.

Note: The Personal Web Server includes several components to manage traffic and to assist in the development of Web pages using other Microsoft tools. The Microsoft Message Queue Server, for example, is a way of delivering messages to message-driven applications so that delivery is guaranteed. Applications that work with this server may be offline for awhile, but receive their messages from the queue server when they come back online. Processing, although it may be interrupted, is guaranteed to complete. Visual InterDev is a graphics development environment for Web development. It relies on Visual Basic Script to build Web pages with exceptional functionality. The Microsoft Transaction Server enables you to organize events that may transpire on your Web page such as database updates, to function as a transaction or a single unit. If users enter an order using a credit card number, for example, you would not want to record the order without charging the credit card account. You want both these events to take place, or to be able to roll back the transaction to its pre-starting state. You would rather not fill the order, if the Web page went down midstream, if you are not getting paid for it. The Data Access Components enable you to access databases from your Web page using the services of the Microsoft Data Connector. You can install all these options with the Personal Web Server.

The Personal Web Server has the following drawbacks, however:

• Only 10 network connections are allowed simultaneously, and Windows 98 is not good at timing out unused connections.

- Only World Wide Web services are supported. If you need file transfer using FTP or Gopher, you need to choose another Web server.

- Security is limited by the Windows 98 security model. Whoever sits at the keyboard of the Web server has full control of the files on the server. Security is enforced only on network connections to the Web server.

- TCP/IP under Windows 98 has some features that make the Personal Web Server a poor host for Web files on the Internet. Bindings for TCP/IP can be adjusted by any user of the system, unless you enforce system policies. Even then, anyone who can boot the system from a floppy disk can alter the bindings. If TCP/IP is bound to File and Printer Sharing and the computer is connected to the Internet, anyone who knows the IP address of the computer so set up can gain access to its drive and files over the Internet.

Because of these limitations, the Personal Web Server works best for workgroups or other small networks where you intend to set up an intranet. As the number of users attaching to the Web server exceeds 10, and as trust of users declines, and when the Web page must be available on the Internet, the Personal Web Server is not a wise choice.

Using the Peer Web Server on a Windows NT Workstation

Another choice for a Web server is Windows NT Workstation. With this operating system, you receive the Peer Web Server. It is similar to the Personal Web Server in scale, but overcomes two limitations that the Personal Web Server imposes. Compare these features to see whether the Personal Web Server meets your needs:

- As with the Personal Web Server, only 10 network connections are allowed simultaneously. Windows NT Workstation, however, is better at timing out unused connections than Windows 98.

- World Wide Web services, FTP, and Gopher are all supported.

When you install a Web server that includes security capabilities, you need to be aware of certain issues. The server, by default, may not encrypt passwords. FTP access can be granted anonymously, which means you need to be careful about how you secure your FTP directories. Anonymous and nonanonymous users need read and write access, but should not accidentally gain control over other folders on the machine. You need to know the capabilities of the server you have chosen, and you need to review each setting to make certain you are not opening security holes in your Web site. For a concise review of Web security issues, surf to http://luna.bearnet.com/www-security-faq.html. Another good resource is the Internet guide included as a part of the Windows NT 4.0 Server Resource Kit, although it does not cover some of the issues identified at this Web site. Checking www.infoworld.com for recent articles on security issues is a good idea when you are investigating Web servers for projects, because the complexities of Internet and intranet security change rapidly.

- Security matches the Windows NT security model. If you use the FAT file system on the workstation, security is equivalent to that provided by Windows 98. If you use the NTFS file system, you have user-level security imposed on both users sitting at the keyboard and users connecting over the network.
- TCP/IP under Windows NT Workstation is more robust in its implementation than under Windows 98. You use group membership, system rights, and system abilities to control who can change network protocol bindings. You have much less risk of malicious intrusion from the Internet with this Web server.

Despite the advantages the Peer Web Server offers, because of its limit on numbers of connections, it is best suited to small networks and workgroups where security is of concern and an intranet needs to be implemented.

Using IIS on an NT Server

If you need an Internet Web page or a Web page that will support a lot of connections, Microsoft's solution is the Internet Information Server (IIS) running under Windows NT Server. Obviously, you need a hardware platform capable of supporting Windows NT Server as an operating system, as well as sufficient RAM to support the connections and transfers you expect. At minimum, you should plan 64MB of RAM, and you should monitor the server frequently to see whether its resources are being outstripped. Microsoft has optimized IIS to work on older hardware platforms. They offer the 80486 as an appropriate platform for intranet servers.

IIS compares to Microsoft's other offerings in the following ways:

- No artificial limit has been imposed on the number of network connections.
- World Wide Web services, FTP, and Gopher are all supported.
- Security matches the Windows NT security model. If you use the FAT file system on the server, security is equivalent to that provided by Windows 98. If you use the NTFS file system, you have user-level security imposed on both users sitting at the keyboard and users connecting over the network.
- TCP/IP under Windows NT Server is robust in its implementation. You use group membership, system rights, and system abilities to control who can change network protocol bindings. You have much less risk of malicious intrusion from the Internet with this Web server. Windows NT Server can be coupled with firewall software to provide even greater security.

For these reasons, IIS is well suited for use as a general Web server, for use on the Internet and on intranets. You should be aware, however, that many system administrators complain about scalability in relation to both Windows NT Server and IIS. It is the preferred choice, however, if you want to use Active Server Pages to present your Web site.

Using NetWare

Novell offers a product called IntraNetWare, often called after its code name Green River. This product is associated with version 4.11 of the NetWare network operating system. IntraNetWare allows the hosting of Web pages on a Novell server.

By and large, this is a robust intranet Web-hosting system. The main constraint you face is that Novell does not yet use virtual memory; as a result, you must have sufficient RAM on your system to handle the number of hits you expect on the server. On the other hand, this focus on physical memory has kept NetWare fast and efficient for file and printer services. Although some claim that Windows NT has caught up on this score, many reports show NetWare is 20 percent faster for these services. Web hosting is, of course, a file service.

IntraNetWare compares to Microsoft's Web hosting options in the following ways:

- No artificial limit has been imposed on the number of network connections.
- World Wide Web services, FTP, and Gopher are all supported.
- Security is enforced by the Novell server, and many prefer the Novell security model to the Windows NT security model. On a Novell server, all users are network users. There is no such thing as a local user of the system. In fact, only a limited amount of administration can be done at the console of the server.
- TCP/IP under NetWare is in its infancy. Novell has relied on its proprietary IPX/SPX protocol, and the company is just switching to TCP/IP. As a result, you may prefer an operating system that has been more focused on supporting TCP/IP for a connection to the Internet, if only because security issues are better known.

Novell's Web server is a good choice for running a large intranet. You may even choose it for Internet support. Much of this choice will probably depend on your existing familiarity and comfort with previous Novell offerings.

Using UNIX

UNIX is the operating system you both love and hate. To listen to the gurus, UNIX can do anything, or can be made to do anything. Much of the software you need, including Web-hosting software, is free. To listen to the detractors, UNIX is a complex operating system with many cryptic commands. The manual is, to say the least, daunting. UNIX is the operating system that has supported TCP/IP the longest, however, and so it has the most mature implementation of the protocol that runs the Internet. UNIX is probably still the best and most flexible system for hosting Web pages. As a result, for Internet Web pages, it is probably the operating system of choice.

It compares to other offerings in the following ways:

- No artificial limit has been imposed on the number of network connections.

- World Wide Web services, FTP, and Gopher are all supported.

- Security has improved over the long history of the operating system's evolution. Although some say there is no security under UNIX, the major security problems and hacks are well known and well discussed. The UNIX community is active in finding and plugging security holes. Security is applied to both local and network users. Files can as easily be protected from local users as under the NTFS file system.

- TCP/IP under UNIX is robust in its implementation. Firewalls were originally implemented under UNIX, and so the technology is as mature as it gets for this operating system.

If you are implementing a large intranet or a high-volume Internet Web server, you probably should choose the UNIX operating system. It is the most scalable Web solution. The only disadvantage is that support for Microsoft's Active Server Page technology may not be the best. Through Java and Common Gateway Interface (CGI) scripts, however, UNIX makes up for this limitation.

However, additional factors may play into your decision. UNIX security and administration may not be the forte of your staff. You may prefer to use Active Server Pages. You may want a set-it-and-forget-it style of administration, which UNIX is less likely to provide. An excellent source of reviews of varying servers appears in Yahoo! at Top:Computers and Internet:Software: Reviews:Titles:Web Servers. These reviews can point you to product options and help you evaluate your choices. Be sure to examine Lotus Domino 5.0, as well as offerings from O'Reilly Associates. O'Reilly, for example, offers a server that does not limit connections and runs on a Windows NT Workstation.

Setting Up an Intranet Page with Personal Web Server

Having reviewed the possible choices of Web servers and operating systems, we will proceed with two sample scenarios. First, I will describe how to set up a Web server under Windows 98 using the Personal Web Server. Second, I will show you how to set up a Web page for hosting under either the Personal Web Server or another Web server using the tools supplied by Windows 98. In this way, we will review the kinds of options you have for building both intranet and Internet solutions.

Installing the Personal Web Server

Installing the Personal Web Server so that you can host a Web page under Windows 98 requires running a separate installation program. Follow these steps:

1. You have two methods for installing the Personal Web Server. One is to open the Start menu and choose Run. Navigate by using the Browse button to the \add-ons\pws folder on

the Windows 98 CD, and run the Setup program in this folder. The other method is to use Control Panel | Add/Remove Programs | Windows Setup Tab | Internet Tools. The Personal Web Server and FrontPage Express are options in this category.

2. The Setup program announces that it is initializing, and then the Personal Web Server Setup splash screen appears, as shown in Figure 21.1. Click on the Next button to start the setup process.

Figure 21.1.
The Personal Web Server provides a wizard to guide you through setup.

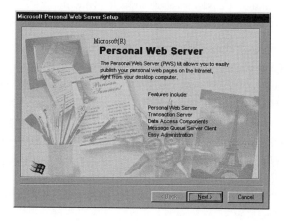

3. Click on the Accept button to agree to the license. As with all Microsoft products, unless you agree to the license, you cannot continue with setup.

4. Now select the type of installation you want. The Typical installation works for most Web sites (see Figure 21.2). You get enough documentation to guide you through the process of building and maintaining your site. The Custom installation gives you the option of installing support for the Microsoft Message Queue Server, Visual InterDev development and remote deployment, and additional data access components.

Figure 21.2.
Typical installation works for most sites.

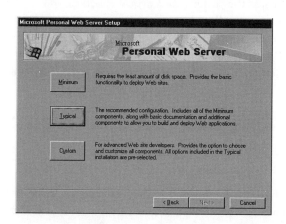

5. Select the location for your wwwroot folder by typing a directory path in the text box. In most cases, the default works well.

> **Note:** Although the installation dialog boxes provide the option to install FTP and applications, note that you cannot make the FTP option or the Application Installation Point options go active. They are not supported in this version of the Personal Web Server.

6. The Setup program now copies files into place. When it is finished, click on Finish to exit. Then restart your computer.

Creating the Index Page

Now that the Web server is installed and running, you need to create an index page, the Web page that users connect to when they connect to the site by its name. This page is also known as a default page, and other Web servers may have different required names for the page. The Personal Web Server uses *Default* and a file extension, .asp for an Active Server Page or .htm for an HTML page.

To create your index page, follow these steps:

1. Double-click on the Personal Web Server icon in the System Tray.
2. Double-click on the Web Site icon in the left pane of the Personal Web Manager window. The first time you click on this icon, you start the Home Page Wizard (see Figure 21.3). Click on the wizard's image (or the Home Page Wizard button) to start building your page.

Figure 21.3.
The Home Page Wizard guides you through building the first page for your Web site.

3. Select a theme for your page, and then click the >> button.
4. Choose whether to have a guest book by selecting Yes or No, and then click the >> button.

5. Choose whether to have a drop box by selecting Yes or No, and then click the >> button.

6. Click >> to customize your page with your own information.

7. On the Customize page, shown in Figure 21.4, you can alter your selections so far by altering the controls, and you can add information to the text boxes to place certain kinds of text on the page. You can use the Add New Links controls to create links to other pages on your site, if they are ready at this time.

Figure 21.4.
The Personalize page enables you to enter text on your Web page.

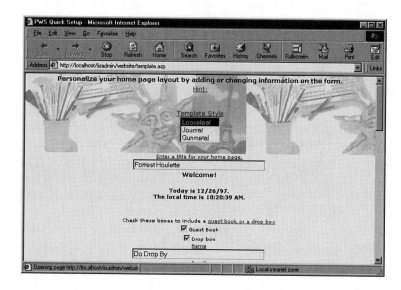

8. Click the Enter New Changes button (midway down the page) to move on to the preview of the page (see Figure 21.5). You can use the browser's Back button to back up to make alterations. When you are finished, exit the Internet Explorer. You have created your index page.

Building Links to Other Pages

To add links to other pages on your site, follow these steps:

1. Return to the Personal Web Page Manager and select the Web Site icon. The Home Page Wizard appears. Select Edit your home page (see Figure 21.6).

2. The Customize page appears. Scroll to the bottom and enter the link information in the Add New Links area. Use the appropriate URL (Universal Resource Locator) string to identify the page, and then click Add Link (see Figure 21.7).

3. Click Enter New Changes to complete editing the page.

Figure 21.5.
Here is the final page that the wizard builds for you.

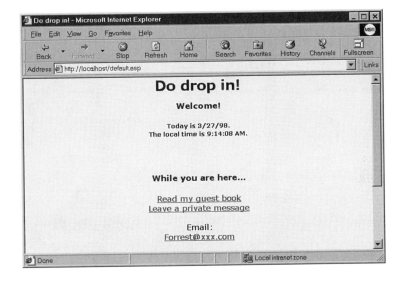

Figure 21.6.
The Home Page Wizard enables you to edit your existing page at any time.

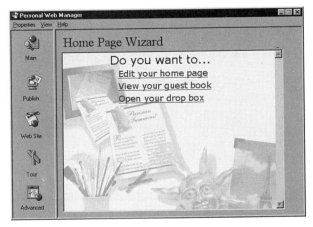

Tip: The Personal Web Server names your site after the host name specified in your TCP/IP settings for your network interface cards. If one of these cards is configured to use name resolution, the host name entered will be used.

You can use Microsoft's FrontPage Express, included with Windows 98, to create additional pages. I will show you how to do this when the discussion turns to hosting your page on another type of Web server.

Figure 21.7.
*Enter the URL string
to build the link,
including site name
and filename.*

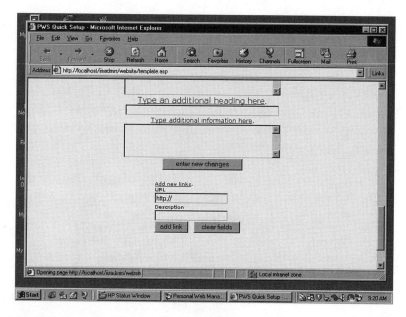

Using a Web Browser as a Client

To connect to your site, you must know the host name of the computer that hosts the Web page. What your host name happens to be depends on the way you resolve names on your network. Names for computers are paired with IP addresses using one of several methods, as indicated in the following list, which presents the options in their system search order:

- **Domain Name System (DNS).** If you set up a Domain Name System on your network, you have a Domain Name System server that you specify as a part of the TCP/IP settings. When a name appears in a command, TCP/IP asks the DNS server for the address corresponding to the name. If this method applies on your network, the host name of your Web server is the name entered in the DNS server's tables that corresponds to the Web server's IP address.

- **Windows Internet Name System (WINS).** Microsoft created WINS as an automated way to do DNS. You have a WINS server that registers NetBIOS name/IP address pairs sent to it by WINS clients when they boot. A WINS client is a computer that has a WINS server specified in its TCP/IP settings. If this method applies on your network, the host name of your Web server is the name entered in the Identification tab in the Network Control Panel applet.

- **Hosts or LMHosts files.** Under TCP/IP, if no other method of name resolution is specified, the TCP/IP protocols check a file named Hosts (no extension) or LMHosts (no extension) for the name specified in a command. Paired with the name in this file is the corresponding IP address. If this method applies on your network, the host name of your Web server is the name entered in the Hosts file or the LMHosts file that corresponds to the Web server's IP address.

- **NetBIOS name resolution.** If you have no other method of resolving names, NetBIOS broadcasts a request to each computer on the local segment asking each computer to identify whether it has that name. This broadcast is called a name query request. If this method applies on your network, the host name of your Web server is the name entered in the Identification tab in the Network Control Panel applet, the NetBIOS name of the computer.

After you know the host name of the Web server, you connect to it by using an URL of the following type in your Internet browser:

```
http://HostName/PageFileName
```

Keep in mind that, unless you specified otherwise, the Personal Web Server named your index page Default.asp.

> **Warning:** If you cannot connect to your Web server, make sure you have the right host name, and check your browser settings. If your browser is configured to connect to the Internet via a modem, you may not find your Web server on your LAN. Your browser will attempt to dial out, and will only search the LAN after you cancel the dial-out effort. Finding your server on your LAN is not reliable after you cancel a dial-out connection.

Setting Up Your Page on Another Server

Having seen how to set up a home page using the Personal Web Server, you need to be aware that you cannot just transfer this page to another Web server and expect it to work. The Personal Web Server builds an Active Server Page. Such a page is built using Visual Basic Script. In addition, the page has the capability to use an Internet database connector (a Microsoft product) to allow real-time updates of data on the page, as well as storage of information entered on the page directly to a database. As a result, the page you just created needs to be hosted on a Web server that supports Active Server Pages. Microsoft's IIS, not surprisingly, supports this technology, as does the Peer Web Server. Other Web servers may not fully support such pages.

You need to be aware of the requirements of alternative Web servers for other reasons. The Internet service provider (ISP) that I most frequently deal with, for example, hosts Web pages on UNIX. They require the file for your index page to be named index.html (as most ISPs do). Lowercase is required. If Windows 98 has placed a capital letter in the first position, as it likes to do by default, your page will not be found by the Web server. The filename `index.htm`, used by many systems that support 8.3 naming conventions, is not the same as `index.html`, and will not run as the index page on this ISP's servers. This ISP supports long filenames, but not long filenames with spaces in them. As far as I know, they do not yet support Active Server Pages, and all scripts that you use must not access special directories on the server.

Although the Personal Web Manager is not appropriate for creating Web pages for this ISP, FrontPage Express, an optional component of Windows 98, is quite suitable. You install FrontPage Express by checking its check box on the Windows Setup tab of the Add/Remove Programs icon in the Control Panel. Select Internet Tools in the main list of components, and then click Details, to find the entry for FrontPage Express. You can use this tool to create an index page and to create additional pages for your Web site.

Creating the Index Page with FrontPage Express

Creating an index page is as simple as writing a file of HTML code and naming that file after the default filename convention for your Web server. If you have ever looked at HTML code, however, you probably would prefer not to have to look at it. If you remember using word processors with dot commands, you have a sense of working with HTML. Creating a page with Notepad and HTML, although perfectly possible, is not easy.

FrontPage Express enables you to create pages visually, as do many other HTML editors. FrontPage Express creates the code for you; you just provide relevant information to dialog boxes. In this section, I am going to step you through creating a fairly complex index page to show you how easy it is to create pages in FrontPage Express. In preparation for building these pages, I have prepared two files. One is `Alex5.gif`, a picture of a young girl working at a computer. I created this picture using a Casio digital camera and downloading it from the camera using Microsoft Photoeditor. The other is `Logo.jpg`, a representation of two special characters in a company's logo. I created this file using Paint. It serves to show the characters correctly even on computers that do not have the special Wingdings font that contains the characters.

To try out FrontPage Express, follow these steps:

1. Open FrontPage Expresss (Start | Programs | Internet Explorer | FrontPage Express) and work with the default new page presented. We are going to build an index page for a small company called Write Environment, Inc., to give you a sense of how to work with FrontPage and some tips about Web page design.

2. Select Format | Background from the menu. Because the `Logo.jpg` file that I created does not take a white background color very well—it looks smudged—select silver as the page background color to match the logo file. Because we want to control the look of text against the background color, select black for the text color (see Figure 21.8).

Figure 21.8.

Select silver as the background color and black as the text color for the page.

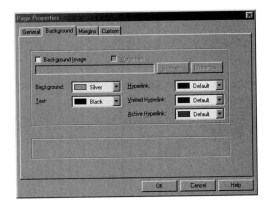

3. Next, insert a table. Open Table | Insert Table, and create a two-column table with six rows. Set Border Size to 1 and both Cell Padding and Cell Spacing to 0 to give the table a very narrow border. Check Specify Width and select 640 pixels, as shown in Figure 21.9. With this width, your table will appear in any browser running minimum VGA resolution. It will also serve to format graphics on the page without difficulties.

Figure 21.9.

Build a table to format both text and graphics on the page.

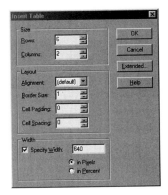

4. With the cursor in the upper-left sell, select Insert | Image, and use the Browse button to locate `Alex5.gif`. Click the Open button to insert the image. Repeat this process to insert `Logo.jpg` in the cell directly to the right.

5. Right-click on each cell containing a graphic and choose Cell Properties from the menu. Set Vertical alignment to Top and Specify Width to 320 pixels (see Figure 21.10).

6. Enter the text for the company information shown in Figure 21.11. Adjust the size of `Logo.jpg` so that it is centered in comparison to the company name. Click on the graphic and use the sizing handles to make the adjustment. To enter a line break without the attendant spacing before and after the line, use Insert | Break. Use a Normal line break to achieve the effect. Also, use Insert | Horizontal Line to add the line using default values. Use the indentation buttons on the toolbar to indent the text as necessary.

Figure 21.10.
*Change the format-
ting of the cells so that
the graphics align
better.*

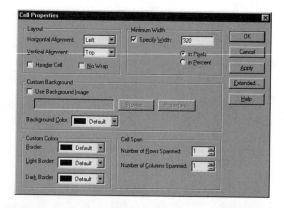

Figure 21.11.
*Enter text to identify
the company.*

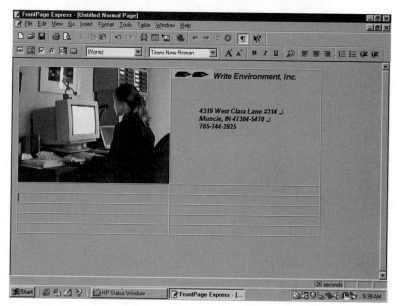

7. Select each row and use Table | Merge Cells to make each row one cell wide. Into these
   cells, we will insert code of two types that links to other pages. Also, use Table | Insert
   Rows or Columns to insert a row above row 1. Place your cursor in row 1, select the menu
   option, and specify to add the row above the current selection. Merge the cells in this row
   as well. In addition, add a bulleted list of information about the company in row 3, placing
   all the bullets in row 3. Use the Bulleted List button on the toolbar to achieve the effect.
   Your Web page should now look like the one shown in Figure 21.12.

You have now completed building the basic Web page. Next, we will use two different methods to
add some links to other pages.

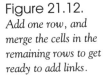

Figure 21.12.
*Add one row, and
merge the cells in the
remaining rows to get
ready to add links.*

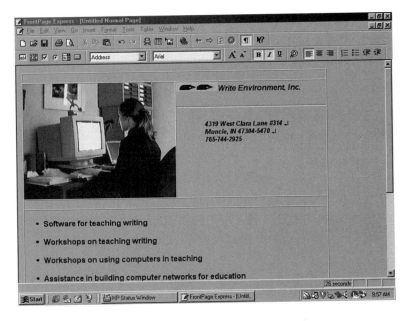

Building Links to Other Pages

You may have noticed that we have added no links from page to page. My reason for not including links on this page is that I want to be able to include one set of links on each page of the site. As a result, I will create a separate page containing a table of links, and then use a WebBot to merge that table with the index page just created.

> **Tip:** WebBots are bits of code that carry out a function such as including elements on your page, inserting HTML code on your page, and so forth. FrontPage Express includes a limited number of WebBots. The full FrontPage product contains many more.

In addition, to improve the visibility of the site, I need to add links to banner exchanges—services that display graphical banners that advertise members' Web sites. This client is an educational software consultant, and seeks to gain visibility by placing a graphics banner on other sites that are also members of the banner exchange. To participate in such exchanges, Web sites add code to their sites that links to the banner-exchange site and downloads the applet that displays a member banner. Another WebBot enables you to build this link.

Follow these steps to achieve these goals:

1. Create a new page with a table like that shown in Figure 21.12. This is a three-column, six-row table. In each cell, enter the text that will be used to create the hyperlink. Select the text, and click on the Hyperlink button on the toolbar. Enter the URL for the page to link

to. In this case, these are additional pages that I created, and they are all stored on the client's Web site, www.writeenvironment.com.

Figure 21.13.
Build a page containing a table of hyperlinks to other pages.

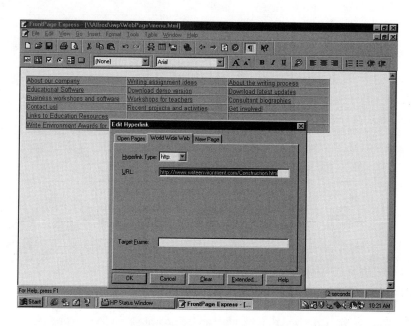

Tip: I have used the full URL to the site page rather than file links on the local machine. I have had difficulty keeping the links active when the page is transferred to the ISP's server when I have used file links.

2. Place your cursor in the cell below the bulleted list. Select Insert | WebBot Component. From the list in the dialog box, choose Include. Then click on OK. Enter the URL to your menu page in the next dialog box, and click OK. Your menu will be fetched by the bot and placed on your current page.

Warning: WebBots do not always update a page dynamically. If you change your menu, you need to open each page on which it is included and allow it to update before saving each page.

3. To insert the HTML code provided by banner exchanges, insert another WebBot in one of the remaining cells. Select Insert | HTML Markup from the menu. Paste the code provided by the banner-exchange site into the dialog box shown in Figure 21.14, and click OK. The site is now linked to the banner exchange.

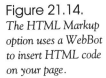

Figure 21.14.
The HTML Markup option uses a WebBot to insert HTML code on your page.

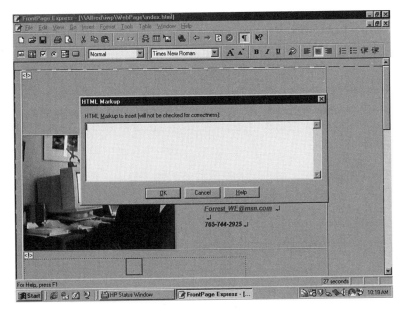

You have now created links of two types to other pages. To present this site on the Internet, I connect to the ISP's server using FTP and copy the pages into place. The ISP's server takes care of the rest.

Hosting Your Pages on the Personal Web Server

Just because these pages are not Active Server Pages does not mean that you cannot host these pages on the Personal Web Server. You cannot do so by default, but you can modify one of the advanced properties of the Personal Web Server to enable you to host or test pages that you are planning to host on another Web server. Follow these steps to modify the default properties of the Personal Web Server:

1. Open the Personal Web Manager by double-clicking on the Personal Web Server icon in the System Tray.
2. Select the Advanced icon in the left pane.
3. Enter the name of your index document on the Default Document(s) line, and then exit the Personal Web Manager. Your documents need to be stored in the wwwroot folder for your Personal Web Server so that they can display.

Summary

This chapter has reviewed how to choose the right Web server for displaying a Web page, whether you intend for that display to be on an intranet or the Internet. You have also seen how to use the Personal Web Server provided with Windows 98 to create a Web page. I also gave you a guided tour of creating pages in general using FrontPage Express. Overall, the goal has been to build your awareness of how to use HTTP, HTML, and related tools to display useful information to your staff and customers.

On Your Own

Install both the Personal Web Server and FrontPage Express. Create a default Web page using the Personal Web Manager, and create some pages to link to it using FrontPage Express. Reset the advanced properties of the Personal Web Server so that you can display an index page other than the default home page you created. Review the Web link suggested on security and verify that your site has the security you need.

22

Creating Web Pages and Extended Desktops

Peter Norton®

As you saw in Chapter 21, "Creating a Web Server," you have several options in choosing a Web server and in using Windows 98 tools to build Web pages. You have seen how to build a personal home page using the wizard associated with the Personal Web Server, and you have seen how to build a simple index page.

In this chapter, I want to focus on Web pages as desktops. Windows 98 enables you to display Web content on the desktop. As a result, you can display anything you can write in HTML as the background or the foreground of the desktop. Because of this capability, you can design the desktop you would like, using the same tools you use to design Web pages. As you will see in the next chapter, you can use JavaScript and VBScript to enhance this desktop. In addition, you can modify the way that system windows are displayed by rewriting the HTML code that creates their display. Especially if you are adventurous, you can take advantage of some undocumented built-in controls to create the displays. If you prefer to work with documented controls, you can work with the wide variety of available ActiveX controls.

This chapter focuses on the following issues while reviewing desktop design, but also discusses some additional techniques that you can use to display information on Web pages:

- Elements of a desktop concept
- Various HTML controls that you can use to display information
- Links that access files from the desktop
- Built-in files that control the Web view of folders

Building the Desktop Concept

Technical Note: Although desktops and Web pages now have much in common, desktops are slightly different from Web pages. Unless you intend for each user to have Internet access 100% of the time, for example, you probably will not choose to place links to Web pages on the desktop. If you do place links to the Internet on the desktop, you will probably select them very carefully for content related to the user's job function. As noted in Chapter 15, "Configuring for Ease of Use," the capability to place Web content on the desktop places you in a situation of conflict. On the one hand, you don't want to reduce productivity by placing distractions on the desktop. On the other hand, you can increase productivity by leveraging ActiveX technology.

One solution is to avoid creating links to the Internet entirely. You can set up a server that will automatically receive the desired information from the Internet, and then users can link to the information on this server via your intranet. You need to keep in mind that creating desktop links can lead to the blurring of the distinction between internal and external information. What looks to be an internal resource might turn out to be an external resource, and vice versa. Such confusion could lead to the accidental release of private or proprietary information, and you want to be careful to avoid such confusion as you design your desktop.

We will try to wend a middle path through this conflict as we design a corporate desktop using HTML. Our example will reflect a common concern among companies: that the desktop be relatively uniform across computers. The purpose of the HTML page placed on the desktop will be to implement such uniformity and to help in the enforcement of uniform policies related to computing. As a result, we will use the page to establish the following:

- A corporate identity
- Appropriate use warnings
- Access to appropriate policy files

Creating the Basic Page

Our corporate desktop example begins, of course, in FrontPage Express. Open FrontPage Express (Start | Programs | Internet Explorer | FrontPage Express), and then follow these steps to add a corporate identity to the page:

1. Open Word and open a document that bears the company letterhead.
2. Select the company logo and copy it to the clipboard.
3. Paste this logo into the Web page.
4. Adjust the background colors and foreground colors to suit the logo by right-clicking and choosing Page Properties from the context menu. Figure 22.1 shows what your page should look like at this time.

Next, you want to draw attention to the computer-use policies that apply to this computer. Because this Web page will eventually fade into the background, you want this reminder to call attention to itself. As a result, you will make it a scrolling marquee. To build the marquee, follow these steps:

1. Open the Insert menu and choose Marquee.
2. Enter **Computer use policies apply to this computer. For more information, select Use Policies below** into the Text box.
3. Accept the default settings for the scrolling and click OK.
4. Click on the marquee and size the marquee box to fit the message. Figure 22.2 shows what your page should look like at this time. (Note that the marquee cannot scroll in a static picture. As a result, the partial sentence you see in the figure is actually the scrolling marquee caught midstream during the scroll.)

Figure 22.1.
*A desktop HTML
page with the
corporate identity
established.*

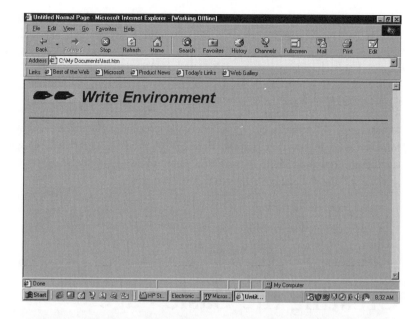

Figure 22.2.
*Use a scrolling
marquee to draw
attention to the use
policies that apply.*

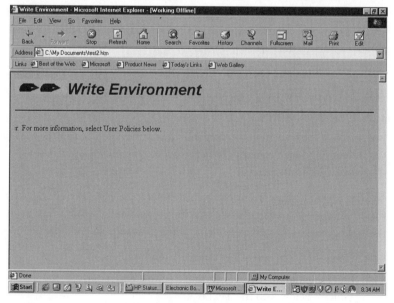

To add access to appropriate documents, add hyperlinks below the scrolling marquee. Press Enter with your cursor at the end of the marquee and type **User Policies**. Select this text, click on the Hyperlink button, and fill in the path to the policies document. This document can reside on the local computer, on a server on the network, or on the Internet somewhere. These links are active even after you set the page to be the desktop background. Figure 22.3 shows the page so far, with the policies hyperlink in place.

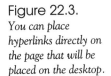

Figure 22.3.
*You can place
hyperlinks directly on
the page that will be
placed on the desktop.*

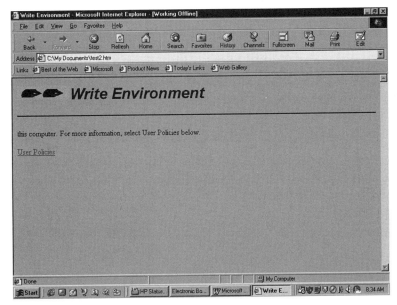

Elaborating Your Page

At this point, you have created a rather standard Web page. It differs from the index page you created in the preceding chapter, primarily in that you did not use a table to format the page. This section shows you how functional you can make your desktop. Microsoft provides a Web Gallery to help you add functionality to your desktop. To find a link to it, turn on the Internet Explorer's Links toolbar (View | Toolbars | Links). In Microsoft's Web Gallery, you can find all sorts of means to elaborate the functionality of a desktop page. Specifically, you will find the following:

- **Scriptlets.** Short VB scripts and Java scripts that perform specific functions, such as providing a calculator or a tabbed dialog box
- **ActiveX controls.** Some from Microsoft, but others at links to sites that review, evaluate, sell, and provide access to freeware controls
- **Graphics.** Backgrounds, pictures, clip art, lines, bullets, and other graphics objects to enhance your pages
- **Templates.** For use with FrontPage and Visual Interdev to help you build specific types of pages

To elaborate the page you are designing, this example uses three ActiveX controls and some VBScript. Assume that while examining the requirements for this company, you found several needs to be paramount. Users need frequent access to the Windows Explorer to manipulate files. In addition, users frequently need to look up date information on a calendar. Specifically, you want to add the following functionality to the desktop itself so that these functions will be available any time the user can see the desktop:

- A Tree view of the drives and folders available on both the local computer and the network

- A List view of the files and subfolders available in the resources pointed to by the Tree view

- A calendar to provide date information readily for the user

By adding this functionality to the desktop, you simplify using Windows 98 for the users. To gain access to frequently needed information, users must minimize applications and work with the desktop.

Tip: As you design your desktop, don't overlook the Quick Launch desktop band. It provides instant access to applications or controls, and such items do not clutter the desktop. In addition, if you use the Active Desktop and hide desktop icons behind an HTML page or wallpaper, the Quick Launch band gives instant access to applications without your having to show the desktop.

To provide this functionality, you will use two ActiveX controls. The first is called Explorer, and it is a free control available from the Web Gallery. It provides a Tree View and a List View panel, and these can easily be linked using three lines of VBScript code. In addition, you will use a `calendar` control provided with Visual Basic Enterprise Edition. It needs no code to provide date information. You just need to place it on the page.

Note: Visual Basic comes in three editions: Standard, Professional, and Enterprise. Each includes different controls and features. The `Calendar` control comes with the Enterprise Edition. A similar control comes with Microsoft Access.

To insert the controls on the page, use the Insert | Other Components | ActiveX Controls in FrontPage Express. Select the control by name using the Pick a Control drop-down list box. Enter a name for the control in the Name text box, and then click on OK. The control is added to the page at the current cursor position. You can size the control by selecting it with the mouse and dragging the sizing handles that appear.

Because the `Tree View` and `List View` controls are related, I have placed them next to one another to simulate the Windows 98 Explorer. I placed the `Calendar` control below the simulated Explorer. On an 800×600 screen, all the controls will be available if the taskbar is in Auto Hide mode. Figure 22.4 shows the layout of the Web page.

Figure 22.4.
The final layout of the page that will function as the desktop background.

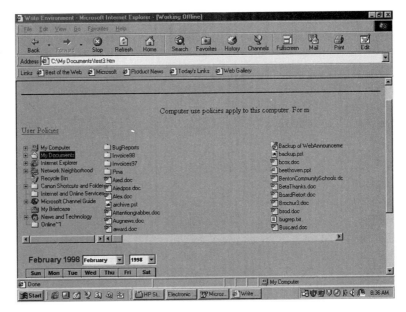

All that remains for elaborating this page is to install the script that links the Tree view and the List view. To do so, you need to respond to one event fired by the controls. Windows communicates with its component parts by sending messages from one component to another. In the case of the control ExplorerTree1, every time the Tree-view data changes, ExplorerTree1 sends out a TreeDataChanged message. When you fill in this code, you are responding to that message—or event as messages are often called in VBScript—by linking the list data to the tree data. When the two are set equal, a change in one control causes the update of the data in the other control. Open Insert | Script and enter the following code into the text box:

```
Private Sub ExplorerTree1_TreeDataChanged()
ExplorerList1.TreeDatas = ExplorerTree1.TreeDatas
End Sub
```

You must make certain that the names of the controls are entered correctly as you named them. With this line in place, whenever the tree data changes, the list data also changes to reflect the current tree data. When you click on a folder, for instance, in the tree, the List view updates to show the contents of the folder.

Placing the Page on the Desktop

Placing the page on the desktop is easy. Open the Display Properties, either from the Control Panel or by right-clicking on the desktop. Select the Background tab. Select the background you want to use from the Select an HTML Document or a picture list box. If your document does not appear in the list box, use the Browse button to locate it.

After you have selected the desktop background, you need to decide how icons will display. This setting is on the Effects tab of the Display Properties dialog box. To place your HTML background on top of the desktop and its icons, check Hide icons when the Desktop is viewed as a Web page. When this box is checked, icons will not appear over the HTML document unless you click on the Show Desktop button in the Quick Launch toolbar. When this box is unchecked, the icons float over the HTML document just as if it were a picture wallpaper. Figure 22.5 shows the HTML document you just created as the primary layer of the desktop.

Figure 22.5.
An HTML document on the desktop with the Hide Icons option enabled.

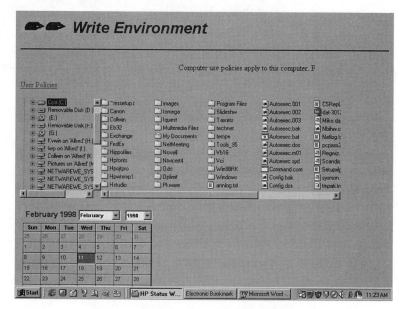

Building Excellent Desktops and Web Pages

You don't need to know a great deal of HTML code to build a Web page anymore. The graphics tools do the coding for you, and the Java and Visual Basic add-in components do more to make your Web pages functional than HTML will.

If you want fancy Web pages, you need to be using ActiveX controls, Java applets, VBScript, and JavaScript to achieve them. Therefore, unless you plan to learn all the details about programming in one of these languages, you need to have a good library of controls and components. You need to choose whether you want to use Java or Visual Basic. The choice here is largely what you are comfortable with. But you do need to locate the kinds of controls and applications that will assist you.

Microsoft's Web Gallery is one location to look. There are others. ZDNet, sponsored by Ziff-Davis Publishing, is a good source of useful information about these technologies and an excellent source of freeware and shareware controls. Searching the Internet for either Java or ActiveX reveals a variety of sites that provide controls. You have many resources out there. You need to acquire the controls you need and go to work.

Warning: One word of caution, however: Just because someone publishes an ActiveX control does not mean that it is worth acquiring. Be sure to seek out reviews where possible. The first spelling checker that I bought for an application I built using Visual Basic was an excellent spelling checker—as long as you wanted to check the spelling of text in a Microsoft Text Box control. This spelling checker was of limited usefulness with our word processing control. Unfortunately, you usually cannot get enough detail about the technical details of the control to know whether it will work for you in advance. If at all possible, try to get a return-if-not-satisfied guarantee. In addition, *InforWorld* has reported that some controls are actually Trojan horse programs. Once installed and used, they transmit information to a Web location without notifying the user that the transmission is taking place.

On a brighter note, on several Web pages (including ZDNet), you will find a complete set of controls for building Web pages on a try-before- buying basis. You can create menus, frames, fancy graphics, all the details that Web pages exploit well. The sets I have seen look quite good. Happy hunting for the tools that meet your needs. But do try to have some taste about how you lay out your pages. Too much gingerbread does not necessarily make a Web page attractive.

Modifying the Built-in Files That Control the Web View of Folders

Having seen how to modify the desktop, you should also know that you can modify the Web view of your folders. If you select to view your folders as Web pages, HTML code draws the background for the folders, and ActiveX controls display the files and folders, or the other objects that are appropriate to the window. You can easily modify this HTML code to suit your needs. To make the modification, select View | Customize this Folder in the Windows Explorer. (You must be in the application labeled the Windows Explorer on the Start menu. Other Explorer windows do not have this menu option.) A wizard, shown in Figure 22.6, guides you through the process of modifying the HTML code that provides the folder background.

You have two options for customizing your folders: You can choose a background picture, in which case the wizard shows you a file list box of available pictures for you to choose from; or, you can navigate to any folder using a standard browse button, and you can set the text and background color for the text (see Figure 22.7). After this screen, you see a page that tells you what file you have selected. Clicking on the Finish button sets the picture.

Figure 22.6.
A wizard helps you to customize folder backgrounds.

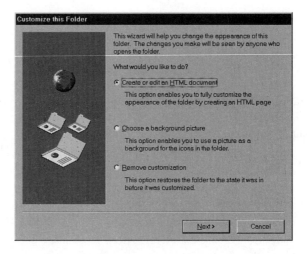

What value do background pictures provide you in designing a desktop? First, they add interest for the user. Second, they can be an important strategy in identifying the function of the desktop. If you have secure areas and nonsecure areas in your building, for example, you could use different backgrounds for windows on those desktops. Users get immediate reinforcement not only of the computing behavior required in the secure area, but also the general behavior required.

Note: I once taught a training course at the National Security Agency. Because I do not have a security clearance, whenever I was present in a room, the staff was required to turn on a rotating red light mounted in the ceiling. This light notified all present that classified information should not be discussed in the presence of unknown individuals or in easily overheard ways, because someone who was not cleared to receive that information might be present and within earshot. Your background image can serve as visual reinforcement on computer screens of the kinds of behavior required, just like that rotating ceiling light.

You can also edit the HTML code directly, as shown in Figure 22.8. When you select this option and click Next, you see a page that explains the overall editing process. Clicking on Next opens the editor, enabling you to make and save modifications to the code.

If you select to edit the HTML code, you are in for some surprises. First, the editor is Notepad, not FrontPage Express, so you are creating code at the lowest level possible when creating Web pages. You have none of the support provided by the FrontPage Editor. Second, Microsoft did not use Visual Basic as the scripting language in the code that displays the generic Web view of folders. If you want to work with the controls provided to display folder contents, you must modify the JavaScript code. Finally, Windows 98 includes some deeply embedded ActiveX controls that Microsoft uses to display folder contents. You can tell because they are called using a Class ID number, not a control name. As a result, the use of these controls is undocumented, even in Microsoft's Windows 98

Resource Kit. You can experiment with modifying the code that scripts these ActiveX controls, but you must do so carefully. You must be prepared for your fair share of failures.

Figure 22.7.
You can use the controls provided to select any picture as your folder background.

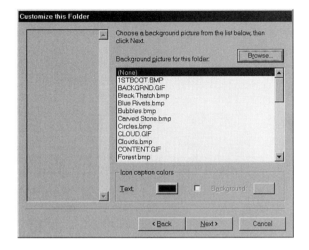

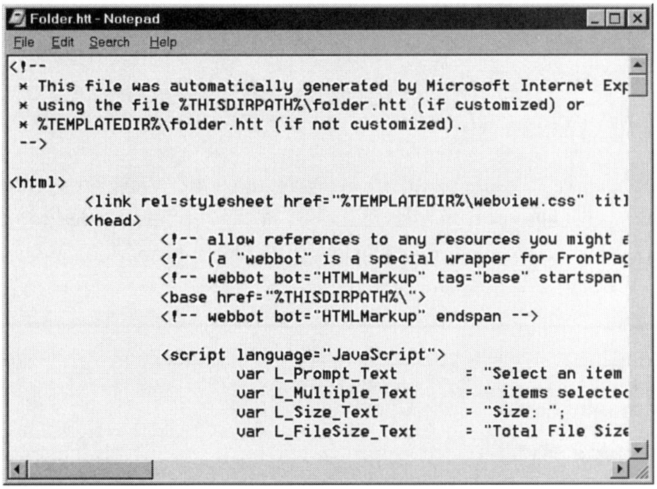

Figure 22.8.
You can use Notepad to modify the HTML code that creates the folder display.

You have an automatic protection feature if you choose to attempt modifying HTML code. The third option on the wizard is to remove your customization. If you or any user seriously screws up the folder display, this option regenerates the generic code that creates the generic Windows 98 folder display.

After you have created a custom folder, you can propagate that look across all folders. Open any View menu from any Explorer window. Choose Folder Options, and then select the View tab. Click on the Like Current Folder button to make all folders match the current one (see Figure 22.9). Use

Reset All Folders to reverse this option. In the Advanced Settings list, you can adjust the behavior of various folder elements as well.

Figure 22.9.
You can easily propagate your customizations across folders.

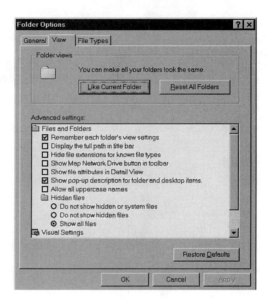

Summary

This chapter has focused on additional ways to create Web pages, especially those you intend to use as desktop backgrounds. We have looked at how to build a desktop concept, and at some of the controls you can place on HTML pages to display information. We have also shown how links can be made functional from the desktop.

On Your Own

Develop your own desktop concept, and design a page to fulfill it. Search the Web for the types of controls and applets that will satisfy your needs. Try working with several different free controls to see what their weaknesses are. Develop a desktop that you could use for administering of systems, and one that you would like to use for troubleshooting. Try creating a desktop that contains links to these two desktops, so that you create a desktop menu of desktops. Try adjusting your Web view of folders by editing the built-in HTML files.

23

Using
VBScript
and
JavaScript

Peter Norton®

In Chapter 16, "Using the Scripting Host," you read about scripting for the Windows Scripting Host in some detail. Scripting was not developed only for the Windows Scripting Host, however. In fact, it wasn't developed for it at all. Scripting was written initially to allow Web pages to become more interactive with users. Scripting enables one to collect information from Web users and react to input from them. The Microsoft hosts (or scripting engines to follow the Chapter 16 terminology) that permit scripting are as follows:

- Server services such as IIS or Personal Web Server
- Internet Explorer
- Windows Scripting Host (covered in Chapter 16)

Okay. "So what!" you might be thinking at this point. "I want to administer Windows 98, not create a Web site," you say. Fair enough. Consider then what you have already learned from this text: Web pages are becoming more and more a part of the operating system. Windows 98 as well as Windows NT with IE 4.01 loaded allow the normal Explorer interface to be replaced with a Web-style interface. This Web-style interface is viewed using Internet Explorer, which naturally can run the scripting. Thus, controlling the user interface and functions can be done using a common language for all Microsoft 32-bit platforms. In addition, regardless of the operating systems (or the Web browser) that you are using, your users can almost always get to a Web page and click buttons on the Web page. If you can write a few scripts, you can ease your administrative burden a little. You can write simple pages with scripts that perform duties such as the following:

- Downloading hardware drivers for users on demand
- Downloading and installing anti-virus updates on demand or automatically
- Allowing the user to place a help-desk service call
- Allowing the user to check on the status of his service request
- Providing online help or frequently asked question (FAQ) responses

With a little proactive work, therefore, you can develop simple yet functional Web pages using tools that have applicability in general administration (see Chapter 16).

This chapter discusses some ways to incorporate the scripting techniques utilized in Chapter 16 into Web-page development. Of course, to do this, you will have to learn a little more about HTML code along the way. You have already been introduced the FrontPage Express earlier in this text. As most of the separate topics are reviewed, you can think of this as sort of a pulling-it-all-together chapter. This chapter covers the following topics:

- How to determine when to use a Web page
- How to incorporate scripts in HTML
- How to build more elaborate scripts by exploiting the features of the scripting languages

Where to Begin

The first thing to, of course, is to have something to do! Think of tasks that you routinely perform at users' requests. Notice that I mention "user request." Certainly, if you have maintenance operations that happen at regular intervals, whether the user requests it or not, a general scripting solution is more appropriate. In these cases the user input is typically neither required nor desired. In this new situation, you are trying to anticipate user needs. You want to provide immediate response to user questions and requests through Web pages with scripted solutions supporting them. You are giving the users the power to improve or resolve their issues faster than they ever could by calling.

Consider your own needs for a moment. As administrative support, you are the knight in shining armor roaming the countryside, rescuing people in distress. It would be poor form to not have a battle-axe when you need one. Perhaps writing a Web page with scripts that run your favorite utilities for troubleshooting might be in order. Then, the knight is never without his sword. And how about summoning the great knight? If your users have a Web page on the intranet in which they may log trouble calls, you can give them the impression of always being prepared to receive their requests.

Also consider the many tasks that administratively are simple in the sense that they have predictable operations involved—installing a virus update, for example. Without proper guidance, however, the users may not be able to complete the task effectively. Again, items such as driver updates, virus updates, handy tools, and updates to software can all be scripted and put on an intranet, ready for the users to just click a button.

Now that you have some ideas, it is time to review the scripting languages available and see how scripting might be implemented.

Using VBScript and JavaScript

Scripting languages enable you to improve your Web sites by causing events to take place or responding to events that take place. Originally scripting was a matter of writing statements defined by the Common Gateway Interface (CGI). The term *CGI scripts* has grown in scope to mean roughly the scripting language supporting the active components of a Web page. This, of course, includes languages such as Java and Visual Basic among others. As you have seen, Java and VB are standalone programming languages that have the capability to act as scripting languages for the purpose of WSH or Web pages.

Tip: Although Java and VB are both very complete and very powerful languages, the scripting forms of these languages do not always include all the functions of the fully developed environment. Unfortunately, there is no definitive resource at this time for what is and is not implemented. If you don't know for sure, try it!

The purpose of the scripts is to cause the Web browser to respond with an action. A script attached to a button or hypertext link, for example, could cause another copy of the browser to start. Or it could display a dialog box to collect input from the user. It could also cause information entered in a form to be written to a file.

Scripts can, in fact, become quite elaborate. They can download and run Java or VB code on the client computer, for example. They can also run entirely on the server, carrying out functions appropriate to the server side of the interaction. When utilizing server-side scripting, you typically use Active Server Pages (ASP). ASPs are supported by the following:

- Windows NT running Internet Information Services (IIS) 3.0
- Windows NT Workstation 4.0 running Peer Web Services
- Windows 95/98 Personal Web Server

Tip: If you want to use ASP with either the Windows 95 Personal Web Server or Windows NT Workstation's Peer Web Services, you must install the Active Server Pages components after installing your server software. These were not originally distributed with the Setup programs for Personal Web Server or Peer Web Services. Go to the Microsoft Web site in the IIS product section to download the components.

As discussed in Chapter 16, selecting the scripting language is always a matter of personal preference. The discussion in this chapter, however, focuses on VBScript and points out some Java script when appropriate. One major difference between Web scripting and WSH scripting is that you are permitted to mix the scripts in HTML code. Therefore if you know them both or see a cool piece of coding in Java in a magazine and you would like to use it on your Web page that is mostly VB scripted, go right ahead!

Creating a Simple Script

To implement a script, you first need a Web page. You can develop a Web page by using a tool such as FrontPage Express (see Chapter 22, "Creating Web Pages and Extended Desktops").

Take a little look at creating a Web page for help-desk requests. You will just ask the user what he would like to do and then let him know that you have carried out his request. You start by opening FrontPage Express and putting some basic text and buttons on the page, as shown in Figure 23.1. The page is simple—no animation, no fancy backgrounds. You can dress it up later. Right now you just want to get the basics down.

Now that you have your simple Web page, you need to write some script to go with it. The script will be used to react to the users' selection after they have clicked on the Submit button. To respond to this event, you can place the script anywhere on the HTML page. It has to be enclosed between `<SCRIPT>` and `</SCRIPT>` HTML tags. The following block of code frames the script you are creating:

```
<script language="VBScript"><!--
'Option Explicit
Dim strMsgBoxTitle
Sub Window_Onload
strMsgBoxTitle="Thank you!"
End Sub

Sub cmdSubmit_OnClick
   For cnt=0 to 2
       If frmCall.r1(cnt).checked then
            Select Case cnt
              Case 0
              MsgBox "Service Call Submitted", 0, strMsgBoxTitle
                 TODO:  Actually send the order.
              Case 1
         ' TODO : Code to allow user input
         MsgBox "Service Call In Queue", 0 , strMsgBoxTitle
              Case 2
         'TODO : Service Call Cancelled
         Msgbox "Service Call Cancelled per user request",0,strMsgBoxtitle
              Case Else
         Msgbox "Invalid Entry",0,"Warning"
         End Select
       End if
   Next
End Sub

--></script>
```

Figure 23.1.
Example of a simple user input page.

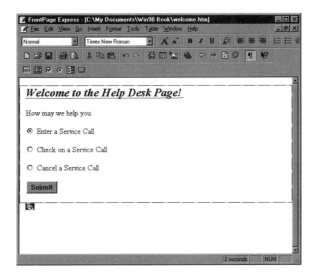

Tip: Any text that appears after a single quotation mark (') in VBScript is treated as a comment and is not executed as code.

FrontPage provides a convenient method for including the code into a Web page. Inserting a script in FrontPage Express is easy. Locate your cursor where you would like the script to appear on the page, and then choose Insert | Script from the menu. Enter your script in the dialog box that appears (see Figure 23.2). Do not worry about adding the <SCRIPT> tags. The WebBot that manages the script will add them for you. Select the VBScript button, and leave the Run Script on Server check box unchecked. Click the OK button. You have added the script to your page!

Figure 23.2.
Adding script to a
Web document.

You should now examine this little script more closely. There is a default subroutine that should be included just for good practice, the Window_OnLoad. This routine is run when the page loads. Notice the position of the Dim statement. The Dim statement is used to predefine variables. In Web scripting, VB variables are understood to be variants. This means they are free to take on any value type that suites the value assigned to them. This typically defaults to a string type.

Tip: The variant type can be a mixed blessing. You need to be careful if you are trying to do other operations than basic string manipulation. VB will happily add a string to a numeric. A="Paul" and B=2, for example. A+B="Paul2" and B+A=2. Because A was a string and it was first, VB assumes a string manipulation. In the second one, B is a numeric and "Paul" translates to 0 in numeric, so 2+0=2.

Traveling down the code, you encounter the next subroutine:

```
Sub cmdSubmit_OnClick
```

The `cmdSubmit` is actually the name that I assigned the button I created on the Web page with FrontPage Express. I could easily call this button whatever I want, but `cmdSubmit` will do. The `OnClick` is an event description that tells VB when to execute this particular subroutine. Thus when the `cmdSubmit` button is clicked, VB reacts by running the subroutine.

At this point, I will assume that you understand `For` loops and `If-Then-Else` logic. We did cover it a little in Chapter 16, and you can find all sorts of material and examples on program flow.

Examine the following line:

```
If frmCall.r1(cnt).checked Then
```

The `frmCall` is an object that represents the Web page. I named the Web page (or form, in VB-speak) `frmCall` in FrontPage Express. The `r1` is an object within the form called a *radio button*. The radio button is a little circle that the user selects to pick a choice. The `r1` actually is a group of three buttons. The state of the buttons is recorded in array-type format. `Checked` is a property. If `Checked` for the object is `true`, then I know that the radio button was selected at that time.

Table 24.1. Initial value of radio buttons.

Button	State on Form	frmCall.r1(cnt).checked
Create Service call	Selected	true
Check Service call	Not selected	false
Cancel Service call	Not selected	false

In this way, you can determine which selection was made when the Submit button on our form was pressed.

> **Tip:** To see or set the properties of any form or object in FrontPage Express, right-click on the object and select Form-Properties or Properties. These choices will appear at the bottom of the context menu.

After I have determined which of the options was selected by the user, I can perform some action. In the example here, all we do is display a message box indicating the type of action that was intended to take place.

```
MsgBox "Service Call Submitted", 0, strMsgBoxTitle
```

The `msgbox` function is a common function used in VB to display messages to the screen. It is quite handy and flexible. Any of the VB documentation will list the options available for it. In this case, we are doing the basics. We display the message `Service Call Submitted` (see Figure 23.3). We use the standard OK button, second parameter of `0`. The message box has a title determined by the value of `strMsgBoxTitle`. Note that the value of this variable was set in the `Window_Onload` subroutine. I did that just to demonstrate that I could use a variable if I so desired.

Figure 23.3.
The `MsgBox` *function displays a message to a user.*

`MsgBox` can take up to five parameters, which govern its appearance. We used three of these parameters: `Prompt`, `Buttons`, and `Title`. The remaining two are for help-file–type parameters that we will not be using here. The `Prompt` is the text string displayed in the dialog box, and the `Title` is the string that appears in the title bar of the dialog box. As another example, the following script provides a simple What's New dialog box for a Web page:

```
<SCRIPT LANGUAGE="VBScript"> 'Marks the beginning of the script and identifies the
script language

Sub Window_OnLoad 'Marks the beginning of the OnLoad event handler
MsgBox("What's New!", , "We've added a new set of links to our site.")
End Sub   'Indicates the end of the OnLoad event handler
</SCRIPT> 'Marks the end of the script
```

> **Tip:** In VBScript, when you leave out parameters at the end of a statement, you just omit them. If you leave out a parameter between two other parameters, you must insert a blank space between commas. Leaving out a parameter invokes default behavior for the object or function.

The only difficulty with this script is that to edit the dialog box you must edit the actual parameters in the `MsgBox` statement. Changing the message can be awkward under these circumstances. If you use two variables to hold the strings, however, you can easily change the contents of the variables as you want the text in the dialog box to change. Occasionally you may want to use a third variable to receive the return code that MsgBox provides. After MsgBox runs, it places a code to tell you what happened in this variable. To create variables, first you dimension—or set aside memory space for them—and then you assign values to them. The following code does so:

```
<SCRIPT LANGUAGE="VBScript"> 'Marks the beginning of the script and identifies the script language

Sub Window_OnLoad 'Marks the beginning of the OnLoad event handler

Dim strTitle
Dim strMessage
Dim retValue

strTitle="What's New!"
strMessage="We've added a new set of links to our site."

RetValue=MsgBox(strMessage,1, strTitle)

End Sub  'Indicates the end of the OnLoad event handler
</SCRIPT> 'Indicates the end of the script
```

Notice that the syntax of the Msgbox command changes slightly. The parameters now are enclosed in parenthesis and a variable, RetValue, appears with the '=' in front of the command. This syntax change tells MsgBox to return a value that indicates the button that was pressed to close the box. This is handy when you want to ask the user something simple, like OK/Cancel, as we did here.

Note: You can also use Public and Private in place of Dim to create variables, a process also called declaring variables. Public makes them available to all scripts on the page. Private makes them available only within the script where the variable appears. Dim can act like either Private or Public. If Dim appears outside a function, the variable is equivalent to Public. If it appears inside a function, the variable is Private to that function.

Tip: Normally you run scripts on the client. Some scripts must run on the server, however, especially scripts that store form data on the server. Remember, server-side scripts run as Active Server Pages (ASP). Therefore, when you save your document, save it as an .asp type rather than .htm/.html.

Before leaving this subject and taking a look at some of the difference with Java scripting, take a look here at the finished HTML code. Recall that I created most of this with a graphical interface. The coding took a little typing, but not much:

```html
<html>

<head>
<meta http-equiv="Content-Type"
content="text/html; charset=iso-8859-1">
<meta name="GENERATOR" content="Microsoft FrontPage Express 2.0">
<title>Welcome to the Help Desk Page!</title>
</head>

<body bgcolor="#FFFFFF">

<form method="POST" name="frmCall">
    <p><font size="5"><em><strong><u>Welcome to the Help Desk
    Page!</u></strong></em></font><u> </u></p>
    <p>How may we help you: </p>
    <p><input type="radio" checked name="R1" value="1">Enter a
    Service Call</p>
    <p><input type="radio" name="R1" value="2">Check on a Service
    Call </p>
    <p><input type="radio" name="R1" value="3">Cancel a Service
    Call</p>
    <p><input type="submit" name="cmdSubmit" value="Submit"></p>
</form>
<script language="VBScript"><!--
'Option Explicit

Dim strMsgBoxTitle

Sub Window_Onload
    strMsgBoxTitle="Thank you!"
End Sub

Sub cmdSubmit_OnClick
   For cnt=0 to 2
       If frmCall.r1(cnt).checked then
           Select Case cnt
               Case 0
                   MsgBox "Service Call Submitted", 0, strMsgBoxTitle
               ' TODO:  Actually send the order.
               Case 1
                   ' TODO : Code to allow user input
                   MsgBox "Service Call In Queue", 0 , strMsgBoxTitle
               Case 2
                   'TODO : Service Call Cancelled
                   Msgbox "Service Call Cancelled per user
request",0,strMsgBoxtitle
               Case Else
                   Msgbox "Invalid Entry",0,"Warning"
           End Select
       End if
   next
End Sub
--></script>
</body>
</html>
```

Tip: To edit HTML code directly in FrontPage Express, choose View | HTML from the menu. It is an excellent learning tool!

Working in Java

JavaScript has many shared features with VBScript. The same sort of frame surrounds the script code, and basically the same types of statements appear. The means of attaching script code to an event, however, is more complex.

If you merely want a dialog box to appear before the Web page draws, you can use the following script:

```
<SCRIPT LANGUAGE="JavaScript"> //Marks the beginning of the script and identifies
the script language

//Presents the dialog box with the message
alert("We've added some new links to the web site");

</SCRIPT> //Indicates the end of the script
```

Placed anywhere on the page, this script runs and presents a dialog box similar to the one created before. You have no control over the title of the dialog box, however, only the message. Note that the command that creates the dialog box is called `alert` rather than `MsgBox`. It takes only one parameter—the text to display. Note also that comments in JavaScript begin with double slashes (//) rather than single quotation marks. Note also that JavaScript statements end in a semicolon.

If you want the page to load before the dialog box displays, you use the `onLoad` event related to the document object that JavaScript uses. Unlike VBScript, however, where you write an event handler that has a specific subroutine name, you must define an event handler in your HTML code and then write a JavaScript handler for the function you define.

To define a function handler for the `onLoad` event of the document object, you must find the `<BODY>` tag of your HTML code for the page, and add the following text to it before the final bracket:

```
OnLoad="loadfunc()"
```

The `<BODY>` tag may have many qualifiers in it, but its basic form with this code added is the following:

```
<BODY onLoad="loadfunc()">
```

Next, you create a JavaScript function in your script. The function has the following form:

```
<script language="JavaScript"><!--
function loadfunc() {

alert("We've put some stupid links on the link page");

}
// --></script>
```

The `function` keyword indicates that you are defining a function. `loadfunc` is the name for the function, and the parentheses following, like the curly braces, are just required by the language. You use the same line of JavaScript code to invoke the dialog box.

You can create a variable to hold the message in JavaScript as well. The form of the statement that does so is the following:

```
var variablename=value;
```

Adding the following line before the `alert` statement in the function and substituting the variable name for the quoted string in the `alert` function makes this script the exact equivalent of the VBScript we wrote in the last section:

```
var strMessage="We've put some stupid links on the link page";
```

The dialog box that this script draws appears in Figure 23.4. Note that it has a slightly different appearance from what the similar VBScript produced in the preceding example.

Figure 23.4.
The JavaScript dialog box has a slightly different appearance.

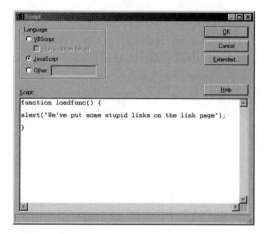

Elaborating Your Scripts

So far we have created rather simple scripts. In this section, I want to show you how you can create more elaborate scripts. First, I will show you how to implement greater functionality by adding flow control to your scripts. Then I will discuss the primary technologies associated with building greater functionality in both scripting languages.

Elaborating in VB by Adding Flow Control

To add flow control to the VB script you created, you need to modify the dialog box so that users have a choice of input they give you. `MsgBox` enables you to use the second parameter to specify which buttons appear in the dialog box. The reference page for `MsgBox` indicates that a value of `4` for this parameter places Yes and No buttons in the dialog box. If you select this option, you can ask the users in the final part of the message whether they would like to go to the new content directly. The return value that we already collect will tell us what button the user clicked. A value of 7 indicates the Yes button.

After the user sees the dialog box, we can check the value of retValue to see whether it equals 7. If it does, we can send the user to the URL of the page with the new content. If it does not, we just exit the function and let the browser continue to respond to user input. Here is the modified code to carry out these actions:

```
<SCRIPT LANGUAGE="VBScript"> 'Marks the beginning of the script and identifies the
script language

Sub Window_OnLoad 'Marks the beginning of the OnLoad event handler

Dim strTitle
Dim strMessage
Dim retValue

strTitle="What's New!"

'Note the question has been added to the message.
strMessage="We've added a new set of links to our site. Would you like to go to the
new material now?"

'Note that the second parameter is in use.
retValue=MsgBox(strMessage, 4, strTitle)

'Here is the If block that makes the decision
If retValue=7 Then

'The location object controls the current page location.
'Modifying this object sends you to the new location.
Location.href="http://www.writeenvironment.com/linksto.html"

End If

End Sub  'Indicates the end of the OnLoad event handler
</SCRIPT> 'Indicates the end of the script
```

Figure 23.5 shows the dialog box that you have created.

Using ActiveX Controls to Elaborate a Page

The main way of adding functionality to VBScript pages is to add ActiveX controls to the page. To use ActiveX controls, you either build or purchase objects designed to meet the ActiveX standard. You can then use those objects, called controls because they typically control information flow or user interaction, on your Web pages. Under FrontPage Express, choose Insert | Other Components | ActiveX Control from the menu. In the ActiveX Control dialog box (see Figure 23.6), select the control (Banner, in this case), assign a name to the control, describe its position on the page, and click OK. The control is now available on your Web page.

Figure 23.5.
The revised dialog box now enables users to make a decision about where to start viewing the site.

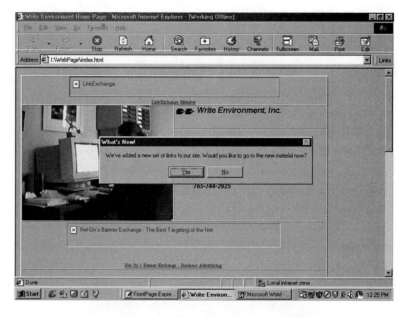

Figure 23.6.
You select ActiveX controls from a list box and describe their dimensions and position on the page.

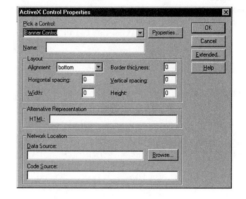

After the control is on the page, you use VBScript to set its properties, respond to its events, and invoke its methods. You use statements of these types to accomplish these tasks:

```
MyControl.Property=value 'assigns a property value
MyControl.Method  'invokes a method that takes an action
Sub MyControl_Event  'begins an event handler
'Code to handle the event
End Sub 'ends an event handler
```

Obviously, to work with a control, you must have documentation for it, or at least some means of discovering the properties, events, and methods for the control. Windows 98 itself does not provide such a means, nor does FrontPage Express. And documentation is a bit thin. Microsoft does provide products that give you better documentation and an object browser, a tool that examines the control and reports back the properties, methods, and events associated with it. FrontPage (the full product), Visual Interdev, and Visual Basic all provide these capabilities. In addition, in these products, you can right-click a control and get a list of its properties and their values. Setting initial properties is a matter of entering or choosing new values in the dialog box. In addition, in Visual Basic 5.0 you can create your own ActiveX controls.

Why use such controls on your page? Because they can make your page look good and give you a lot of functions that are available in no other way. Figure 23.7 shows a sampling of available controls. You can display calendars, multimedia controls, and full-motion video. You can play music, create spreadsheet grids, link to data, and perform a host of other activities. Thousands of controls are available. All you need to build an exciting interface with a lot of fancy features is the right controls, the documentation, and the willingness to write VBScript.

Figure 23.7.

These are a few of the useful ActiveX controls that you can use on a Web site.

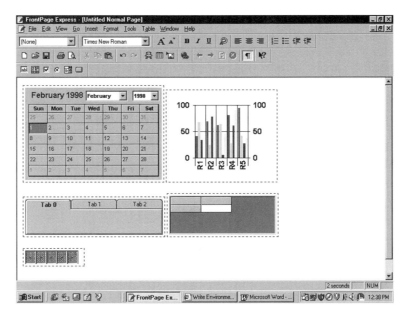

Elaborating in Java by Adding Flow Control

To add flow control to your Java script, you need to modify the dialog box to allow user choice; you need to add a variable to collect a return code; and you need to add flow control statements to process the user's response to the dialog box. To modify the dialog box, change the function used to invoke the dialog box to confirm, a function that gives you OK and Cancel buttons in the dialog box. confirm returns a value of true if the OK button is clicked. We use a var statement to create a variable, and we use the familiar IF statement to process the user's response. The function now looks like this:

```
<script language="JavaScript"><!--
function loadfunc() {

var retval;  //dimensions the variable

//the following displays the dialog box and collects the result
retval=confirm("We've put some stupid links on the link page. Click OK to go see them.");

//the following tests to see if retval is true, changing location if so
if (retval) {

location.href="http://www.writeenvironment.com/linksto.html";
}
// --></script>
```

Things to note in this script are that the test following the `if` keyword does not require and equation, because `retval` contains the value for either `true` or `false`. The `location` object is what controls the page the browser loads. The `href` property is the property that holds the current URL. Figure 23.8 shows the dialog box this script creates.

Figure 23.8.
JavaScript can also respond to user input using this dialog box.

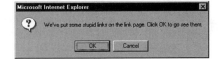

Using Java Applications to Elaborate a Page

Java is the main way to elaborate a page with custom objects if you are working with JavaScript. Java is a programming language very like C++. It organizes objects into units of code known as classes. The `Date` class, therefore, represents the `Date` object. After you write the code, you compile the code, and then reference it on your Web page using the `<APPLET>` tag.

You can accomplish very extraordinary effects with Java applets on Web pages, as many extraordinary effects as you can create with ActiveX controls. Applets are often available free of charge, and the market in components that you can add to Web pages is growing. You may not have to program your own applet to get the functionality you desire.

Java applets function, therefore, like insertable objects on a Web page. In fact, to insert one in FrontPage Express, use Insert | Other Components | Java Applet. You see the dialog box shown in Figure 23.9. Enter the information necessary to identify the object, click OK, and you have embedded a Java object on your page. With Java applets, you depend on documentation to identify properties, methods, and events. You respond to events with event handler functions like the one we have already created. Using methods and setting properties uses the same dot notation syntax as VBScript.

Figure 23.9.
You can easily add
Java objects to your
Web pages.

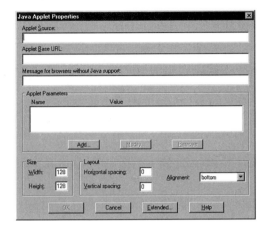

Summary

This chapter started with a discussion of leveraging the Web components of the Microsoft operating systems including Windows 98. The discussion then focused on showing you how to add to your Web pages by working with scripting languages. You have seen how to write a simple VB script, how to write a simple Java script, and how to build more elaborate scripts by using additional features of each scripting language. You have received a basic introduction to both scripting languages and the elements they employ.

On Your Own

You may have noticed in the Service Call example that there were several lines commented with 'TODO'. This is left for you "to do"! Start by trying to duplicate the Web pages in these examples. The HTML and the VBScript were provided in this text for just that reason. See whether you can make it work and then enhance the Service Call Web page to save information to a text file or a database if you are brave. Database connectivity is a powerful feature of HTML coding, but a topic more suitable for a real developer's manual. Do you recall the examples of good uses for Web scripting presented at the beginning of this chapter? Take a look and see whether one might serve you and your users. See whether you can develop the pages and scripting for one or more of those suggestions. This chapter has outlined all the techniques you need!

24

Imple-menting Special Web Security

Peter Norton®

Now that you have had a chance to see the options you have for setting up Web pages to service your Windows 98 clients, it is time to think about security. Web pages are great ways to share information. They can create a wonderful forum for teams to communicate with each other, communicate with managers, and communicate with other teams. However, this is a public forum, and you can expect all the kinds of behavior that take place in public forums to take place on your Web. Windows 98, as an operating system, cannot enforce good behavior.

We have all heard of Web-page hacks on the Internet, the CIA and the FBI not being immune to having their pages rearranged by an individual with some strong opinions. If you allow personal pages, a major focus of the Windows 98 Personal Web Server, you may find that information one individual wants to share is not information others wish to see. If you allow pages at all, you must make certain that only nonsensitive information appears on them. Although such events will probably not be common in your working setting, they can be offensive, can damage communication among the individuals for whom you were trying to facilitate communication, and can be extremely frustrating for all the individuals involved. A single event is more than you want to deal with. As a result, you have to think about how you should secure the information content of Web pages.

Tip: Any Web server option that you choose to implement, including Windows 98's Personal Web Server, will enable you to set access permissions on the shared files that make up the Web page. Use these permissions to govern who may make changes to Web pages while viewing them in a Web browser.

In addition, the Web server you have set up can be attacked in other ways. Such a server opens up an access point to your network and to your information. You could get simple denial of service attacks launched by disgruntled employees. You could also get more insidious attacks launched by individuals who know the TCP/IP protocol suite very well. They may seek an entry point that would allow them to slip past your security to find sensitive data or to acquire more privileges than you desire them to have on your network.

Warning: Remember that someone well versed in TCP/IP and in possession of a tool such as Microsoft's Network Monitor can send packets on your network. Carefully crafted IP packets are one favorite method used by hackers to gain access to systems. Be sure to limit access to such tools to individuals who need to use them, and monitor the activity of these individuals using the facilities of your network operating system.

The whole point behind Windows 98 is to open up Web-based access to information. Using the basic tool of HTML, users can customize their own desktops, link to an intranet easily to retrieve information stored in central repositories, hook to an extranet to make use of another company's resources, and link to the Internet with ease directly from their desktops.

With such openness and freedom comes responsibility. The goal of this chapter is to describe the kinds of responsibility you must exercise on a Windows 98 network when choosing to share information from a Web server, and the kinds of responsibilities you must expect users of that network to exercise when they access this information.

> **Warning:** Remember, if you want anyone to exercise responsibility on your network, you need written policies describing your expectations. Courts have determined that without written policies, you do not have recourse against misuse of a network.

Six possible methods for arranging your security and policies appropriate to a Windows 98 network are described here. I'm sure there are others including hybrids, but these six will help you to see the possibilities. I am presenting them in order, from the least secure to the most secure. Refer to Table 24.1 for a bird's-eye comparison of their respective strengths and weaknesses while studying the details of each scenario in the following sections:

- Trusting the universe
- Using protocol isolation
- Replicating from Web server to LAN server
- Using a firewall
- Transferring information via sneakernet
- Isolating a Web server

Table 24.1. Comparison of the possible security schemes.

Security Scheme	Advantages	Disadvantages	Access to Internet
Trust the universe	Useful in small offices, small workgroups, and setting where trust in and integrity of individuals using the network is high. Provides complete and easy access to Web resources.	Virtually no security.	Complete, through a network connection.
Use protocol isolation	Provides security for network resources that you do not wish exposed to the Internet. Relatively easy to implement.	Can become confusing to administer. Vulnerable to hacker attacks. Can be compromised by anyone who can add protocols in the Network Control Panel.	As permitted either by dial-up access or through the network, depending on the protocols installed at the client.

continues

Table 24.1. continued

Security Scheme	Advantages	Disadvantages	Access to Internet
Replicate from Web server to LAN server	Provides greater security than protocol isolation. Provides virus protection and protects your network against many hacks based on sending packets to your Web server.	Vulnerable to viruses and Trojan horses that can be concealed inside a file. Does not provide protection against attacks introduced from internal sources.	Via dial-up by using a modem, or via the network by using a separate connection through a router.
Use a firewall	Provides greater security than replication, including protection of ports. Can filter packets of different types to prevent both unwanted traffic and dangerous traffic from entering your network. Provides virus protection and other protective features, depending on the firewall implemented. Can proxy requests, thus protecting your allocated IP address pool.	Can limit access to the Internet. Can be difficult to administer. Usually comes with default settings that you must change to achieve the level of protection you desire.	As permitted by the firewall through a network connection.
Transfer information via sneakernet	Provides greatest protection against attacks on your Web server while still allowing information delivered to the server to be available on your network.	Completely vulnerable to human error. Dependent on someone physically transferring the data from the Web server to a removable medium and then transferring the data to a network drive.	Via dial-up by using a modem, or via the network by using a separate connection through a router.
Isolate a Web server	Provides complete protection against an attack on your network initiated through connection to your Web server.	Does not allow information to be available on your local network.	Via dial-up by using a modem, or via the network by using a separate connection through a router.

Trusting the Universe

One method of allowing access to Web-based information is to trust everyone who accesses your Web server to behave responsibly. In other words, you do not worry about security. You assume that each user who has access both to the machine that runs the Web server and to the pages that make up the site will leave the Web server and its site alone. If users can gain access to the machine, they will not make any changes. If they can gain access to the page files over the network, they will not alter them. Generally, this security scheme allows users full access to all files. The most likely restriction would be to limit network access to read-only. The assumption under this model is that anyone with a system could put up his own personal Web page.

This approach works well under the following circumstances:

- When all the people working in the setting trust one another.
- When any prank that coworkers play on one another is nondestructive.
- When the information on the Web server does not need to have limited access, as when some members of the team should see one page but not another.
- When all the information placed on the Web server can be labeled "For Public Consumption."
- If the server is connected to the Internet, it makes no difference who in the world might view the information.
- When accidental loss of information from the server will not be traumatic.

Under these circumstances, you can use any of the Web servers discussed in Chapter 21, "Creating a Web Server." Your connections to the Web server can be diagrammed as shown in Figure 24.1.

Although setting up a Web server using this scheme is quick and easy, and although the group using the Web server may trust one another completely, you must take two precautions. First, secure the Web pages by setting access permissions on them. Even if you opt to use Windows 98's Personal Web Server, you need to limit how users can interact with the files that represent the pages. Users should be allowed write access only to files that they are allowed to update, for example.

Second, you need to secure the computer on which the Web server is installed. Under Windows 98, you have no security on the file system for any user who has access to the keyboard. As a result, you might want to turn the key in the system lock, if the computer provides such a locking feature, so accidental changes cannot happen. And accidents do happen. Backups have saved me from losing critical data any number of times. You also need to methodically run antiviral software against this server.

This complete trust model is useful in small offices where no sensitive information is kept, in workgroups of 5 to 10 individuals who want to share notes by saving HTML pages out of their word processors or spreadsheets, and in environments where an investment in personal responsibility and integrity is high. Do not use it under any other circumstances. And no matter what anyone says about wanting to provide easy access over the Internet to a Web page he wants to run with minimal administration, do not use it when connecting the Web page to the Internet.

Figure 24.1.
The complete trust model of setting up a Web server provides open connections to any host on the network.

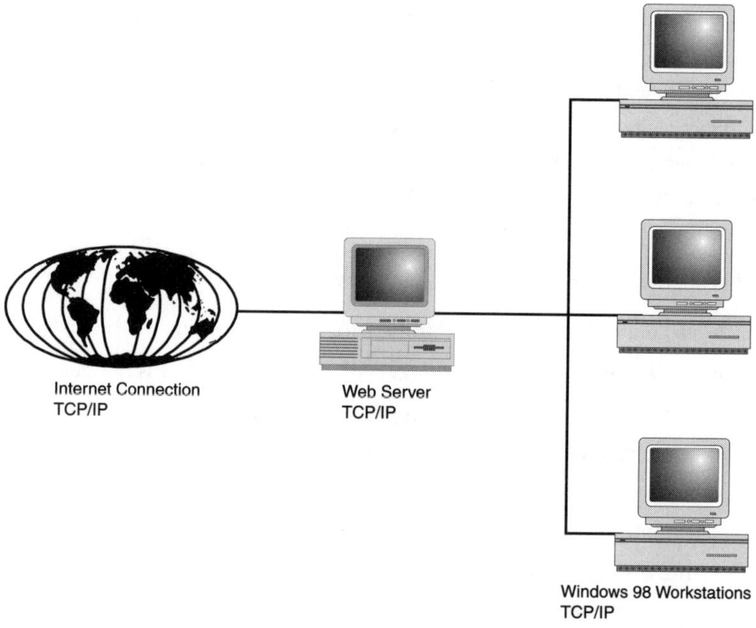

Internet Connection
TCP/IP

Web Server
TCP/IP

Windows 98 Workstations
TCP/IP

Peter's Principle: Why You Cannot Trust "The Complete Trust Approach" to Web Security

In general, I don't like the complete trust approach. I have two stories that illustrate the problem. During the Chicago (aka Windows 95) beta, a midwestern publisher (which shall remain nameless) served as a beta site. This publisher had a Novell network that served several imprints. As a result, when one of the editors installed Chicago, his Network Neighborhood immediately populated with views of all the NetWare servers that serviced each of the imprints. Being curious, this editor double-clicked on a server icon just to see what would happen. When a logon dialog box greeted him, he entered the name *supervisor* and the name of the imprint as the password. He thought that no one would be foolish enough to use such an obvious password for the account with all rights on the server. He was wrong.

Not so long ago, I received a call from an individual who wanted to break into consulting. He wanted to put up a Web page using anonymous, and decided he would offer dial-in access to one of his office computers and host the Web page on Windows 95. He wanted to run TCP/IP as the single protocol on his network. Because he would give the access number only to trusted clients, he could see no problem. Actually, he would have been exposing his office network to anyone who could connect.

Passwords and access numbers never remain good secrets for long. The longer they exist, the greater the chance that they have been compromised. I have been burned too often by complete trust models, and prefer to take stronger security precautions even when I trust the parties involved completely.

I don't like the complete trust model because it relies too much on everyone who uses the network behaving responsibly. Far too often, users of a network slip up in exercising responsibility, and network security is compromised.

Using Protocol Isolation

You can select from among a number of security schemes other than complete trust, each of which has its advantages and disadvantages. A simple, easy-to-implement scheme is called protocol isolation. Under this scheme, you divide your network access between local (that is, a computer connected to the LAN) and external (that is, a computer connecting from outside your organization). The local computers use one network protocol to access shared resources; the external computers use another protocol. This arrangement is diagrammed in Figure 24.2.

Figure 24.2.
Protocol isolation provides good connections to any host on the network, while enabling you to block access to some hosts.

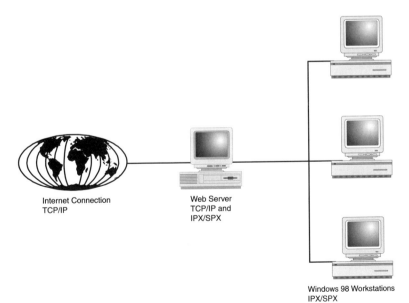

Internet Connection
TCP/IP

Web Server
TCP/IP and
IPX/SPX

Windows 98 Workstations
IPX/SPX

Protocol isolation is based on the assumption that network packets cannot hop from one protocol stack to another. Therefore, if I dial up using TCP/IP and the rest of the network runs IPX/SPX, the packets from my TCP/IP-based conversation with the dial-up server cannot communicate with the computers running only IPX/SPX. As a result, whoever dials in can communicate only with other computers running TCP/IP on the LAN, and with TCP/IP bound to their network adapters.

Warning: Protocol isolation can be broken by clever hackers. Don't rely on it in high-security situations.

To clarify how this scheme works, look at a situation that does not involve a Web server. Suppose you have a traveling employee who needs dial-up access to his computer while he is on the road. You agree to allow him to dial in to retrieve and to update critical files in a shared folder so that others can access the updated versions while he is away. You grant him remote access to his Windows 98 workstation.

When you set up remote access, you install a Dial-Up Adapter, which has protocol bindings. Whatever protocol (or protocols) is bound to that adapter will allow the dialed-in user to view the network. As a result, if you allow the Dial-Up Adapter to communicate using only IPX/SPX, the dialed-in user can see shared resources on other computers on the LAN if and only if they also have IPX/SPX bound to their network adapters. If not, the resources are invisible.

Note: You set the bindings on an adapter by opening the properties for the adapter in the Network Control Panel applet. Double-click on the Network icon in the Control Panel, select the adapter in the Configuration tab's list box, and click on the Properties button.

To use protocol isolation to protect a Web server, that server must run TCP/IP. It must also run IPX/SPX. TCP/IP must be bound to the adapter that communicates with external computers, no matter whether that is a Dial-Up Adapter or a regular network interface card. IPX/SPX must be bound to the standard network interface card that allows the server to communicate with the LAN.

Warning: Do not use NetBEUI for protocol isolation. Imagine a setting where the Web server is attached to a segmented network. The only machines that could see the Web server would be the ones on the same segment as the Web server. NetBEUI does not route. If the Web server is across the router, you could not access it.

The clients on this network have IPX/SPX bound to the network interface card that communicates with the LAN. They have TCP/IP bound only to their Dial-Up Adapters, if they have it installed at all. IPX/SPX is the protocol that allows communication on the LAN. TCP/IP is used only to communicate to the Web server under dial-up conditions. In other words, the only way to get to the Web server is via modem or via the Internet (accessed through a modem). There is no direct connection to the Web server via the local area network, because the LAN clients have no protocol in common with the Web server over their LAN connections.

Now when a remote Web user dials in to access the Web server, the Dial-Up Server answers the phone and negotiates the connection using the PPP protocol or the SLIP protocol, whichever you have selected in the Dial-Up Server's configuration. After that, the Dial-Up Server allows access to the LAN via TCP/IP. The Web user can see the Web server, but she cannot see the other computers on the LAN. The reason is that none of these computers share the TCP/IP protocol with the Web server via their LAN connections.

If the Web server is connected to the Internet via a non–dial-up connection, Internet users still cannot see the other resources on the LAN. They connect to the Web server over the Internet via TCP/IP. However, the Web server shares no other protocol with the remainder of the network. No communication is possible.

The local users on the network may also access the Web server. However, they must do so through their Dial-Up Adapters using a modem. When they access the Web server, they will not have access to IPX/SPX through the dial-up connection because the Dial-Up Adapter is not bound to IPX/SPX.

Sound confusing? Definitely, and such confusion is probably the number one reason to avoid the use of protocol isolation in this setting. But if you are good at picking nits and testing your configurations carefully, you can make it work. You will want to run some robust antiviral software on all your computers if you select this configuration.

Note: As you increase security, you necessarily limit visibility of users on your intranet to the Internet. Such visibility and security are in an inverse relationship.

Peter's Principle: To Use Protocol Isolation for Security, Use Windows NT as the Operating System That Supports the Web Server

If you wish to use protocol isolation, you should use Windows NT as the operating system that supports the Web server. There is a very simple reason: Windows NT enables you to designate the network protocol to be used for remote access connections. In addition, Windows NT gives you more explicit control over bindings. Windows 98 uses check boxes in Properties pages to control bindings. As a result, you never see the complete set of bindings in a single view. Windows NT allows this single view in the Bindings tab of its Network Control Panel applet.

Replicating from Web Server to LAN Server

If protocol isolation sounds either too confusing or not secure enough for your situation, you have another option. One of the main issues relating to security on a network with a Web server, especially one that collects data, is what potential bombs lie in the content on the Web server. The hack into Lawrence Livermore labs described in *The Cuckoo's Nest* relied on leaving a file behind that could execute and create an administrator's account for the hacker, for example. As a result, you want to protect your Windows 98 clients from whatever might be left behind at the Web server. Protocol isolation prevents communication from the server to the clients through a shared protocol. It does not, however, isolate information in any way.

Imagine a hacker slipping something onto your server. You want to gain some time between the delivery of the problem and its reaching some point on the network where it could do damage. This time allows you to detect the problem and address it before damage can be done. Isolating the information on the Web server from the rest of the network allows you to gain such time, because you have to check the data and then transfer it to a point where it is accessible to the network. Without such a check, the information, and any potential problems, never reach the network. One way to isolate the content on the Web server is to use a replication scheme. Such a scheme is diagrammed in Figure 24.3.

Figure 24.3.
A replication scheme isolates the content of the Web server, so you can check for problems before releasing information to your network.

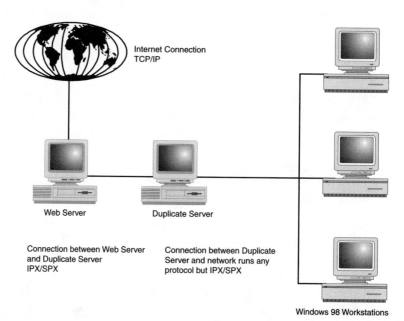

Internet Connection
TCP/IP

Web Server

Duplicate Server

Connection between Web Server
and Duplicate Server
IPX/SPX

Connection between Duplicate
Server and network runs any
protocol but IPX/SPX

Windows 98 Workstations

The key components of this scheme are two servers—one that holds the Web page and one that receives the data from the Web server after the data has been checked. Ideally, these servers will be multi-homed hosts—that is, each will have two network interface cards. On the Web server, one NIC is bound to TCP/IP and communicates with the Internet, intranet, or extranet to which the Web server is attached. The other is bound to another protocol, most likely IPX/SPX, and connects directly to a similar network card on the duplicate server. The second NIC in the duplicate server is bound to the protocol that the rest of the network runs, and this is not the protocol used for the private communication between the two servers. The Web server has no other connection to the LAN except by this private cable.

The only network traffic that travels over the private cable is replication of information from the Web server to its duplicate. This replication occurs only after the data has been appropriately checked, using virus software and visual inspection of the directory structure and files.

When I order 200 widgets through the Web page, that order is stored in a database on the Web server. The order remains on the Web server, unavailable to the staff who must process it, until a scheduled scan of the data takes place. After the data is approved for release to the network, it is copied down to the duplicate server, from which the order-processing staff can process my order and send me my 200 widgets.

Good virus software automates the scans, and an operating system that supports replication can automate the copying of the data. As a result, you can pretty much automate everything but periodic visual scans of the data. These requirements, of course, pretty much rule out using Windows 98 and the Personal Web Server under this scheme. Windows NT Server 4.0 running the Internet Information Server makes a much better choice. UNIX is also a possibility.

Replication provides significant advantages over other schemes in terms of security. You can scan information for problems before you release the information to your network. However, it carries penalties in terms of cost and labor. You need an additional server and you need an administrator with time to manage the replication scheme. The cost of replication, however, is significantly lower than the cost of a firewall.

Tip: Windows NT Server has a replication feature that can automate this copying, but you must install Service Pack 3 under version 4.0 for replication to work properly.

Using a Firewall

Firewalls elevate the level of security surrounding your Web connection one more level. Firewalls are computers that actively screen against known methods of attack, check for viruses, and allow you to screen packet types before those packets go zinging out to your network. Figure 24.4 shows a typical firewall scheme.

Figure 24.4.
A firewall adds active screening to your security plan.

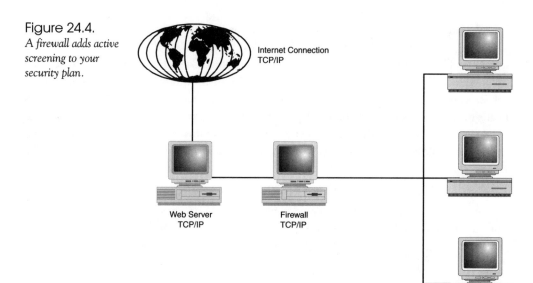

Internet Connection
TCP/IP

Web Server
TCP/IP

Firewall
TCP/IP

Windows 98 Workstations
TCP/IP

Firewalls can be quite extensive in the ways they block interaction from the great beyond with your network. They can hide the actual IP addresses of your Windows 98 clients from the Internet itself, for example. Whenever one of your client computers needs to interact with the Internet, it borrows an IP address from the portion of the firewall known as the proxy server, and the proxy server stands in (as a proxy for the actual computer) to route traffic out to the Internet and then back to the actual IP address of the computer.

Firewalls can also actively filter packets. Want to block someone from attaching to a particular TCP port on a Windows 98 client? Filter such packets and don't let them back to your network.

> **Note:** A number of good firewalls are on the market. Microsoft's offering is its Proxy Server, a part of the BackOffice suite. Offerings from IBM, Raptor Systems, and others are also available, some tightly tailored to a particular purpose and others more general in their focus. A search of Yahoo!, using the keyword "firewalls" reveals some 60 different options, each of which is supported by a Web page that describes the firewall products and services offered by these companies.

Very obviously, the operating systems involved on the servers that enforce the firewall would have to be Windows NT or UNIX. Very typically, you would choose the same operating system for all systems you locate outside the firewall with connections outward.

Transferring Information via Sneakernet

One way to improve protection against unwanted intrusion on your network is to avoid the firewall altogether and just break the line with your LAN. This scheme is diagrammed in Figure 24.5.

Figure 24.5.
You can break the link between your servers and transfer files by floppy disk.

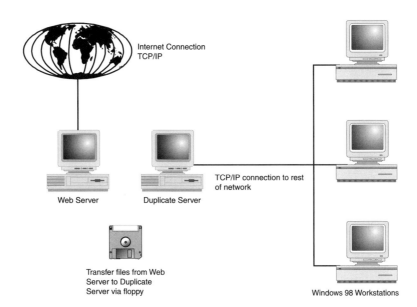

You have the same setup that you have for replication of information, except you do not use multi-homed hosts and you do not have a private cable linking between the Web server and the server that distributes information to your network. However, you still maintain the relationship between the Web server and the distribution server. Windows 98 clients on the network access information only from the distribution server. Information arrives only at the Web server. The link between the two is a human being who carries floppy disks, tape cartridges, or disk cartridges between the two servers, manually copying the information.

Although this scheme provides for excellent isolation of the Web server content, it requires quite a bit of maintenance. Like any high-maintenance system, it is prone to human error. Someone could forget to transfer the data in a timely fashion, skip the virus check because he or she is pressed for time, and so forth. Relying on a certain level of automation using replication and a firewall might actually be the more secure option because of the risk of human error in this schema.

Peter's Principle: Beware of the Human-Error Factor

Human error is the most likely cause of errors in network administration. Everyone has a network horror story related to human error. My favorite personal experience relates to the first network I ran. The tape backup unit had a separate power switch, which one of our technicians turned off at night because she did not think we were using that peripheral after hours. However, she religiously changed the tapes before powering down the unused equipment each evening. It never occurred to her that without power the tapes never ran, and the backups were never made. We were lucky. We lost no data. We did lose a technician. All sorts of other errors occur when such a process is not automated. You can copy files the wrong way; you can copy to a disk and delete the file, only to discover the disk is bad. So watch vigilantly for the human-error factor as you manage your Windows 98 network.

Isolating a Web Server

The most secure Web server is one connected to the Internet but not to your network. For the highest level of security, you do not transfer information back to the network. When you need to work with the information on the Web server, you go to the keyboard of the Web server to do it. This scheme is diagrammed in Figure 24.6.

Figure 24.6.
*The most secure Web
server is one that is
completely isolated.*

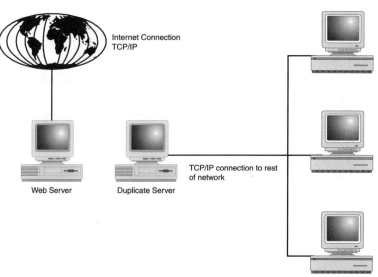

Internet Connection
TCP/IP

TCP/IP connection to rest
of network

Web Server   Duplicate Server

Windows 98 Workstations

Under this scheme, the only way to connect to the Web server is via the Internet, the intranet, or the extranet on which it is located. There are no other connections. Your LAN is entirely separate; the two do not mix. Although highly secure, this arrangement can be extremely inconvenient, and so it is typically not used. It is appropriate, however, for information kiosk kinds of operations, where you are providing content outward and need to receive nothing in return. Updating the content of such a server means attaching to it over the Internet, intranet, or extranet, and manually copying files. You would be wise to activate an FTP server on such a machine. Under these circumstances, almost any operating system will do; but you typically choose one, such as Windows NT or UNIX, that allows you to set security on individual files and audit actions taken within the file system. In this way, you can keep track of what happened and who was responsible in the event problems occur.

Summary

In this chapter, you have explored the ways in which you can protect the Web pages you have set up to serve your Windows 98 network from accidental damage and intrusive hacking. Choosing and implementing such a security scheme is especially important if you have invested in scripted enhancements to the pages. A good Web site can represent a significant investment of effort, as well as an important conduit of information for your organization. You want to avoid having to redo your work as much as you want to avoid contamination of the Web-based information you collect.

On Your Own

Sketch out the security requirements for the Web servers you need to set up. Can you live with complete trust in your organization? Can you rely on protocol isolation? Is replication your best solution? Or, do you need to invest in a firewall? Which operating systems should you use? Remember to refer to Table 24.1 for a summary of the security schemes.

Brainstorm your reactions to each of these questions. You should begin to see a pattern that fits the types of Web servers you are going to need to set up. Department Web pages, for example, may be able to fit the complete trust model, but protocol isolation is more likely the best route. Windows 98 should work fine as the operating system. However, any page that will need to support more hits or that will connect outward will need both a more robust operating system and greater security.

VII

Troubleshooting Windows 98

Peter Norton®

25

General Trouble- shooting Strategies

Peter Norton®

Troubleshooting Windows 98 is a very simple process: Shut down, power down, and restart. If this action does not resolve the problem, reinstall the operating system. If reinstallation doesn't work, buy more hardware, especially memory. These strategies have been the best methods for trouble-shooting operating systems since operating systems were invented. They are the least-convenient methods of troubleshooting, however, especially if the problem is frequent and can cause data loss. Although restarting can be convenient when the problem is isolated and limited, you would prob-ably prefer to discover why you had to shut down and reload the operating system. Definitely you would like to prevent the possible data loss that surrounds having to shut down, rebuild, and restart. And you would like to avoid the loss of shared resources that accompanies these troubleshooting strategies.

To resolve computing problems efficiently and effectively, you need to be aware of a set of general tools and strategies available to you. Being aware of these tools—and actually using them—will make your work easier to perform and will make troubleshooting less frustrating. Many computing profes-sionals I have met get trapped in self-defeating strategies when they are confronted with problems. They rely too much on their own memories, they rely too little on the experience and perspectives of others, and they rely too much on brute-force strategies. For example, I have seen system manag-ers reboot a machine several times when it clearly will not boot, hoping that just once they will hit the magic path past a corrupt operating system file. I have also seen people reinstall repeatedly when installation is obviously failing, hoping that some voodoo will cause Windows to finally recognize or activate problem hardware. Falling into these traps places you in the same position as a mechanic who solves the problem of a part that does not quite fit by getting a bigger hammer to force the part into place. The part may go in and it may actually work, but down the line the force involved in making the fit will revisit you by causing subtle damage.

Effective troubleshooting means relying on some general methods. This chapter covers the follow-ing tools and general strategies:

- Working through questions from users
- Working with the troubleshooters
- Working with the Knowledge Base
- Searching other resources
- Building a database of solutions

Working Through Questions from Users

Help-desk questions usually begin with "Why can't I...?" or "How do I...?" Usually at the other end of the question is a user who is deeply frustrated and upset because the system isn't working the way he thinks it should. To get to the root of the issue, you need to filter through all that frustration. You have to find out exactly what the user is doing or not doing and determine whether the user wants to simplify what he is doing so much that he is combining a lot of small steps into gigantic ones. When you need to know what he clicked, in sequence, to try to open a file, he wants to tell you that he tried to open a file and it didn't happen. The user has described the general process, not the exact sequence of actions he actually took.

User-management skills are critical to getting to the root of application problems. You need to both calm the user down and refocus his attention, often not very easy tasks. I always try to redirect his frustration to some other target—Microsoft comes to mind—and sympathize with his plight. Such a maneuver usually puts the user in the frame of mind to provide the information that I need. I always remind users not to try to rush troubleshooting, and that they need to do stupid things when they are troubleshooting. We all know how it is supposed to work, but we need to step through a bunch of tiny steps to see how it really is working.

The most critical factor in understanding application problems is to isolate the exact actions that the user *and* the software are undertaking. The user probably did not create the problem. The software has been his able partner in the endeavor. If you have good technical information on what the software does, that helps. Often, however, you have to search for that information. As a result, you have to treat most applications as a black box when you troubleshoot them.

For "why" questions, have the user rehearse every single action with you up to the point where the problem occurs. If you have remote viewing capability, set it up so that you can watch the user create the problem. Or go visit the site and watch the user create the problem. Have him go through his story one time just to acquaint yourself with it, and then step him back through under your able, questioning control.

Start with the question of what he clicked to initiate the action. Did he right-click or left-click? Does he have a center button or wheel on his mouse? What appeared when he clicked? What did he do when it appeared? Be reassuring during this process, and focus on all the little details. If you have a user problem, this process will reveal it. Remember, you are friend, therapist, confessor, and interrogator when going through this process. Don't forget any of these roles.

> **Note:** The leading user problem that I have experienced with Windows 95 and Windows 98 is the double-click while rolling the mouse. Users navigating the Explorer double-click to open a folder. If the mouse moves at all between clicks, however, Windows 98 interprets the action as a drag and drop. The default action for drag and drop with a folder is typically to move the folder. The folder will disappear into the one above or below it in the directory tree. Remind users that the Explorer has an Undo button, but it is effective only if used immediately. It does not provide multilevel undo.

For "how" questions, the most important factor is to keep the user from feeling stupid. Often the answers to these questions are readily apparent, even to the user himself. However, the user just has not explored far enough or has blocked himself from seeing the obvious. If the user does feel stupid, I usually share a similar story about myself.

Most help-desk questions relating to Windows 98 will take the following form if you are migrating from Windows 95, because users are expecting the Windows 95 behavior and getting Windows 98 behavior:

- Why isn't it doing *x?*
- Why is it doing *y?*
- Why is *z* giving me an illegal operation?
- Why is it hung?

The last two questions relate to file corruption, memory corruption, and bugs, so I won't discuss them now. The first two are the kinds of issues you can expect to occur because users have adjusted settings in the Control Panel and gotten unexpected results. To be ready to resolve these issues, you need to have a healthy sense, first of all, of how the system was supposed to be set up, and, second, what the symptoms tell you about what has changed. You need to remember that users may be comparing their home systems with their business systems and wondering why they do not have the same system behavior they expect from their home systems.

> **Tip:** If you are migrating from Windows 3.*x* to Windows 98, you can expect many questions of the type "Where is the functionality in Program Manager or File Manager in Windows 98?" In training system managers, I have found many of them running 16-bit File Manager under Windows 98 and wondering why they have difficulty recognizing files with long filenames. Old habits die hard. You will need to support a long learning curve for this migration from Windows 3.*x*. Focus especially on showing users the Help files, especially pressing F1 for context-sensitive help. If users are working with Office 97, focus on the Office Assistant. Users will either love or hate the animated assistant, but it does provide good, tightly focused help.

An example of a question you might expect is "Why doesn't my system appear in the Network Neighborhood?" The user will insist that it ought to because it does on his home system. In resolving this problem, you need to tactfully ask the user about his expectation. You need to clarify why he has that expectation. Often, it will be the assumption that all Windows systems should act the same, except for user-defined issues such as color schemes. This assumption was reasonable under both Windows 3.*x* and DOS clients interacting with Novell networks. The Windows world, however, has evolved away from this assumption. You need only clarify that local systems on your network are not allowed to share files or printers, and for that reason they do not advertise themselves to the Network Neighborhood. You might also want to explain the reasons your organization has chosen not to allow local systems to share files. One important point that easily ingratiates you is to point out that, on a 1,000-node network, the user might prefer to have a Network Neighborhood that is not cluttered with systems that are not actually functioning as servers.

Many user questions will be based on assumptions built on Windows 98's behavior. Something will have stopped taking place. The question will focus on something that was happening yesterday or last week and is not happening now. Resolving these questions depends on your ability to lead the user through a detailed exposition of the problem. "I can't print anymore" needs to be elaborated into "I can't print to the shared printer named Clarissa." You can then begin to track the network path between Clarissa and the user's computer and begin to reason about what might be wrong.

Asking the user to attempt some simple actions can bolster your reasoning. If this printer is a TCP/IP printer, ask him to ping the printer's IP address. You need to read the command to him over the phone and make him read it back character by character, including blank spaces. Or, if you are using some other type of printer connection, have him attempt a net use connection to the printer. Often under Windows 98 the connection can be made, but not through the expected channel. If you can narrow down the problem by eliminating the channels that do work, you can usually resolve the problem. Unfortunately, the appropriate answer to many such questions is shut down, power off, and restart. Why? Because a DLL has probably gone corrupt in memory, and the only way to clear the corrupted code and reload it at the system level is to reinitialize the operating system.

Sometimes problems can be resolved by closing a component and reopening it. If a system application such as Explorer is misbehaving, closing the application might resolve the problem, because the appropriate DLL will reinitialize when you reopen the application. Whether this strategy works depends entirely on which DLL has gone awry. It usually works for the TV Viewer and related drivers, for example.

Other problems will arise when a user encounters misbehavior from hardware. The mouse pointer can disappear, for example. When such events happen, you need to ask users to try to carry out the behavior associated with the hardware device. Right-clicking, for example, might display a context menu. Even though the pointer is not present, the mouse might still be functioning. Typical solutions are to turn on mouse trails or to change the mouse pointer. You can also change the hardware to a mouse that does not present the problem. (Hint: Almost any version of Windows works well with a Microsoft mouse. Surprise, surprise, surprise.) These actions are usually sufficient to force the mouse cursor to appear.

Dealing with user questions always places you in a difficult position. You are the most available focus for blame, and the blame may have nothing to do with the system problem at hand. "Screamers" on the help-desk line often have had a bad day for other reasons. You need to remember that fact, and you need to try to focus their attention away from problems and toward solutions. One of the most effective policies for maintaining the sanity of help-desk workers is a mandatory 15-minute break following a "screamer" call. One of the most effective strategies for dealing with users is to sympathize with their plight but keep reminding them that there is a solution. The trick, of course, is to make certain that you can always deliver a solution.

Working with the Troubleshooter

Windows 98 provides tools to help in troubleshooting hardware. As Figure 25.1 shows, opening Hel and examining the Troubleshooting book reveals troubleshooters for network connections, modems printers, memory, video displays, sound, hardware conflicts, direct cable connections, and PC Cards You will want to find *The Best Printer Manual Ever* on the TechNet CD, which provides settings an configuration information for most printers that you might have installed. All these are valuabl tools related to hardware problems

Figure 25.1.
Windows 98 provides a set of troubleshooters to help with hardware and software problems.

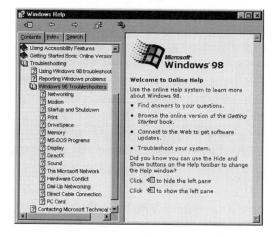

To use a troubleshooter, you double-click on it in the Help file. You are then stepped through a series of structured questions. Buttons take you directly to the property sheets and dialog boxes that control the devices you are troubleshooting. The real value of the troubleshooters is that they force you to think in structured ways. You need to think in very structured ways. You need to reason from symptoms to possible causes along a binary path. You need to attempt solutions by changing one item at a time and then waiting to see whether the problem is resolved. As a result, you can very quickly screen the problem. You will not leave out steps because you are rushing to solve the problem and get the system back online, and you will not overlook key evidence.

Windows 98 provides troubleshooters for almost every component of the operating system (see Figure 25.2). Each of these Help files presents a sort of wizard that steps you through the reasoning process. You select a symptom, click Next, and answer questions. You see buttons that, when clicked, open the relevant configuration property sheets to enable you to make changes. Very often, a troubleshooter will get you to an answer quickly and efficiently. They are miniature expert systems that remember all the things you might forget under the pressure of the moment. I strongly recommend using them and even building similar ones for yourself for problems that you have solved. To build a wizard, you need to use Visual Basic or a similar Windows programming environment.

Figure 25.2.
The MS-DOS program trouble-shooter is an example of an application troubleshooter.

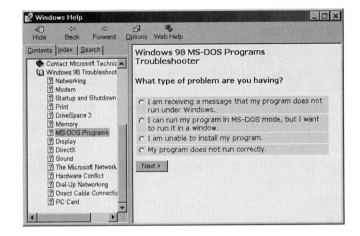

Tip: You can get expert system add-ons for Visual Basic that enable you to encode the kind of reasoning required by troubleshooting.

If you are troubleshooting applications, be sure to check the application Help system to see whether it provides a troubleshooter. If it does, work through the troubleshooter to see what results you get. Application Help files may also contain descriptions of known error states. Be sure to build the Find list and search by keyword, using all the keywords in the Help file.

The last stage of any troubleshooter, however, is this: `You have encountered a problem that this troubleshooter cannot resolve.` This comment is as useful to you as `Please call your system administrator for assistance.` When you hit this point, you know why they pay you the big bucks for being an administrator.

The question, of course, is what to do when the troubleshooter fails you. You have probably stepped through all the reasonable troubleshooting steps that you would have applied independently. You are probably facing a bug in the program, a driver problem, a DLL conflict, or a hardware conflict. If you have a hardware conflict, it will probably show up in the Device Manager, although I have seen some that don't. If the problem is causing the system or an application to crash, you want to immediately set up Dr. Watson so that you can capture the state of the system as it goes down. (See Chapter 28, "Troubleshooting Hardware," for more information.) You may wind up with a lot of information that you don't know how to interpret, but you will have a lot of information to share with the vendor when you try to get help.

The reasoning process for these more mysterious errors is the same, careful, binary approach. However, you need to arm yourself with technical information to make it work. You need to know what devices and files this application interacts with, because the problem probably lies in between one of these interactions.

Working with the Knowledge Base

One of the key places to look for information about systems running on Windows of any flavor is the Knowledge Base. The Knowledge Base is a database of problems and solutions relating to Microsoft products. You can search it for keywords using a variety of Boolean operators, as well as an operator called near that finds its two arguments within eight words of one another.

You gain access to the Knowledge Base either through Microsoft's Web site, www.microsoft.com; through TechNet, a CD subscription service offered by Microsoft; or through the Microsoft Developers Network (MSDN), another subscription service offered by Microsoft. Online searches always bring up the latest articles. Having the Knowledge Base on CD, however, gives you access to the information even when you can't be online. If you receive either TechNet or MSDN, you also receive a host of other technical backgrounders and product documentation.

Figure 25.3 shows searching the TechNet CD, which includes the Knowledge Base, to give you a sense of the power you have with this tool. As this figure shows, the TechNet viewer enables you to see a table of contents as well as any given article. The Search Results dialog box enables you to sort the items returned by number, title, or source book. You can do very focused searches if you want. I find that sometimes the best troubleshooting strategy is to allow a broad search and then check the titles returned to see whether they fit the problem. Scanning 400 titles may seem like a waste of time. But if the 20 minutes or so that it takes solves the problem, the scan is worth the time. It also forearms you for working with related problems. With many application problems, you will find either the fix or a description of how to work around it.

Figure 25.3.
Searching TechNet is often a fast way to find solutions.

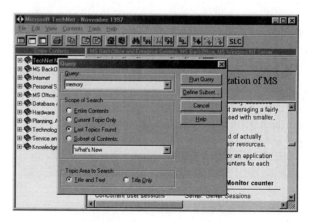

In using the Knowledge Base, you need to keep the following strategies in mind:

- Use the near keyword when searching for terms that co-occur. This keyword finds matches within eight words of each other, and you can use the Settings options to set the number of words in the span if you wish. This strategy tends to pull out more appropriate matches for problems than straight phrase searches.

- Place quotation marks around words separated by spaces that you want to be treated as a single word in the search. This strategy cuts down the number of articles returned by forcing the search for the words separated by a space as a string that must occur together rather than widely spaced throughout the article.

- Search broadly, and scan the article titles. Reviewing a lot of titles might create associations that help you resolve the problem.

- Read articles about related operating systems. Something that happens in Windows NT 4.0 or Windows for Workgroups may shed light on the current problem.

- Read articles that are not identical to your problem but sound similar. Again, associations may arise that help you to reason through to a solution.

The Knowledge Base is helpful, but it won't answer all questions. The most frightening line that can appear is `We are researching this problem`. Usually this means you are stuck with the problem for a while. Under these circumstances, you need to turn to other strategies and tools.

Searching Other Resources

Another strategy is to search the Web using keywords to see what you can extract. Given the size of the Web, however, you may have trouble focusing your search. It is great for everyone to have his or her own Web page. It is really frustrating when my poodle's picture shows up in your troubleshooting search. One of the areas for which I write software routinely turns up 46,000 matches in a Yahoo! search. I have experimented with different search strategies, and I can narrow it down to a mere 2,200 sites. The Web search will either lead you to someone who knows how to solve the problem or lose you in a sea of information.

A better strategy is to go to the Web site for the software vendor that produces the offending application. More often than not, I have found fixes already posted. If not, you can at least communicate with the experts who are part of the problem and should be able to solve it.

Additional sources of information are the magazines that cover the software industry. You may not relish the thought of searching through stacks of back issues. You may wish to use a tool such as Computer Select, which gives you 12 months of the text of over 1,000 resources on a CD—a little out of date, but eminently more searchable than a stack of back issues. Other such services have appeared with more specific focus, so watch for the emerging resources that make your job easier. In addition, check the Usenet newsgroups. You might find `msnews.microsoft.com` especially useful.

Building a Database of Solutions

After you have found a solution, you need to record it in searchable form. You can buy a third-party help-desk system. Or you can create a database yourself using a tool such as Microsoft Access. If you create your own, you can have it track exactly what you want it to track. If you use Microsoft Access, you can use the Service Call Management Database that you can build with the Database Wizard as a starter template.

You need at least a free-form text field where you can enter the solution to the problem. You may want separate fields for symptoms so that you can search for symptoms more readily. You can even set the database up on a server so that your staff can access it during service calls, entering the information directly rather than waiting until later.

As you review this database—which you should do periodically—you need to watch for common patterns. Does a particular type of computer interact in the same strange way with a single network card, for instance? Think in terms of mining this data the same way that data warehouse managers can to discover that men buy beer and diapers on Thursday evening at grocery stores. You want to see the patterns; they can help you evaluate the fitness of equipment for your particular purposes.

> **Tip:** Tools such as SMS Server that provide inventory and help-desk features can also be very helpful in tracking problems. You can cross-reference inventory against your database of problems, for example.

Summary

This chapter has shown you some of the general strategies necessary for effectively troubleshooting Windows 98. We have looked at how to handle help-desk questions. We have shown you the troubleshooters, the Knowledge Base, and some Web-based tools that are useful to you. We have also focused on building your own database of solutions to save you time.

On Your Own

If you don't work on a help desk and have never worked in such a capacity, visit your help desk and shadow one of the team. You need to have your eyes opened to the kinds of situations that they face. Open the Help system and try out a troubleshooter to work on one of the problems you encounter at the help desk or in your own work. Visit the Knowledge Base and search for solutions to the problem you used the troubleshooter for. Search the Web in general, and attach to a vendor's Web site to see what problem-solving materials might be available. The next time you encounter a problem, write out the steps you use to solve it. Try to build your own troubleshooter from these steps by creating the questions to ask users. Be sure that they have the same types of yes/no answers that a Help file troubleshooter has.

26

Trouble-shooting the Operating System

Peter Norton®

In this chapter, I mean by the "operating system" the files that execute as a part of Windows 98 from the time it loads and through the time that you interact with the system using the Explorer up to the time that you shut down. This chapter focuses on troubleshooting problems that occur with these files as you work with Windows 98 or run applications atop Windows 98. The focus is on problems caused by the software components that are part of the Windows 98 operating system. Chapter 27, "Troubleshooting Applications," focuses on troubleshooting problems based in files associated with applications that you purchase and install after you have installed Windows 98. Chapter 28, "Troubleshooting Hardware," focuses on problems based in the hardware itself. Chapter 29, "Troubleshooting Network Connections," describes solving problems that relate to your network.

True operating system problems can be a great mystery. For some that I have worked on, no answer was ever found. A new version came out, or we replaced the hardware, and the problem went away. Knowing the likely sources of problems helps you to plan ways to avoid them, and I will share those sources with you in this chapter. For Windows 98, keeping problems to a minimum has proven to be about 80 percent proactive maintenance and about 20 percent reactive problem solving.

You need to have the right mind-set to understand the kinds of problems you are seeing. You also need to have a strong awareness of the system architecture, as explained in Chapter 5, "Looking at the Core of the Operating System." In this chapter, we aim to help you develop that mind-set by covering the following topics:

- Dealing with the most common problems
- Keeping the system up to date
- Performing general troubleshooting
- Using troubleshooting tools
- Thinking through typical operating system problems

Dealing with the Most Common Problems

You know you are facing an operating system problem when you have applied the general strategies recommended in the preceding chapter and you still have a user calling you with a problem that occurs even when no applications are loaded. Sometimes applications will be loaded, but the problem relates to printing, networking, communicating through a modem, and similar problems where the operating system must be involved. The setup for the application is correct, but the problem still occurs.

Your user will be saying, "I tried what you recommended and it still does not work." Or the user will say that the fix worked for awhile, but now the problem is back. Often the hardware involved seems to have adopted extremely erratic behavior or seems to have stopped functioning. Under these circumstances, probably some component of the operating system software, somewhere between the hardware and the user interface, is the likely culprit.

Deciding what to try to resolve the problem means focusing on system architecture. To what kind of operating system component does the problem seem most related? Study the architectural layout of Windows 98. Make your best guess as to the layer of the operating system that seems involved. You don't have to be right, but you need a focus from which to start reasoning.

In general, the strategies for answering help-desk questions boil down to these:

- Prompt the user to elaborate on the nature of the problem. Ask leading, informed questions aimed at forcing the user to release details.
- Separate the channels causing the problem from those not causing the problem.
- Try shutting down the component involved and restarting.
- Try updating or replacing the driver. You may have a bug or a corrupt file.
- Try removing the device using the Device Manager and rebooting. If Windows 98 does not automatically reinstall the component, reinstall it manually. Then reboot to see whether the problem is resolved.
- Try booting from the powered-off state.

If the problem seems as though a device has been damaged, for example, you need to consider two issues: first, whether the hardware is actually broken (see Chapter 28 for more information), and second, whether the low-level operating system software that communicates with the device has failed. In either case, at the operating system level you are dealing with the driver layer, and you should focus on the universal driver components and the related minidriver. Under these circumstances, try updating the driver through the System icon in the Control Panel. The properties for any device displayed in the Device Manager include an Update Driver button, as shown in Figure 26.1. Using this button forces files to be recopied if a newer driver is available either from a CD or disk, or from the Microsoft driver update Web site. If this option fails, delete the hardware device and reboot. If Windows 98 does not recognize it through Plug and Play during the boot process, run the Add New Hardware Wizard from the Control Panel to identify and install the new hardware.

For other layers of the operating system, you need to examine other issues. If the problem is related to networking, for example, you need to focus on the networking components. If the problem is related to mail, you need to work with the messaging components. The Control Panel conveniently breaks the configuration options for different components into convenient categories. Use these icons to check the configuration. If the configuration is correct, remove the component, reboot, and re-install the component. Remember that some components can be removed and installed from the icon related to their function in the Control Panel; others must be so managed from the Add/Remove Programs icon.

Some operating system problems do not relate to specific components, and therefore do not present easy solutions. One of the most frustrating factors for me throughout the Windows 98 beta cycle was the 15-hour run life of Windows 98. On my systems, I had to reboot after about 15 hours of continuous execution. The operating system and its processes seem to age to the point where the system slows down appreciably. I have not been able to tie the slow-down to memory or any particular set of drivers. But the phenomenon is real. One practical suggestion is to reboot the system every morning.

Figure 26.1.

The Update Driver button can often solve problems with a corrupt or buggy driver.

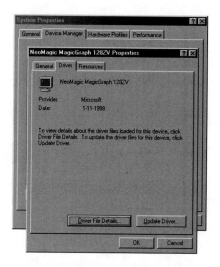

Keeping the System Up to Date

One of the best ways to avoid general problems such as the 15-hour run life is to focus on preventive maintenance. If illegal operations are appearing frequently from multiple sources or the system is hanging on a regular basis, you have these potential sources for the problem:

- A software bug, within either the operating system files, driver files, or application files
- A DLL conflict, probably within the system files
- A hardware problem, such as a minor incompatibility or a failing chip or electrical connection
- Disk corruption, caused by either an electrical event or a marginal disk or drive controller
- Firmware (the system BIOS) that is older than the operating system expects
- Transient electrical events caused by something outside the computer system

Each of these sources requires proactive preventive maintenance. Waiting for a failure to occur means that you risk losing data, you will have nonproductive downtime, and you will be performing maintenance at the worst possible time. To prevent the latter kind of problem, you need to plan your system's electrical system carefully, both inside the box and outside the box. If you are building servers that have to be up 24 hours a day, seven days a week, you would of course put in redundant power supplies and uninterruptible power supplies (UPSs). If your office kitchen space is running on the same circuit as your server room, however, something as simple as making coffee in the morning could cause an overload on the electrical system. When you are upgrading to new software, examine whether BIOS upgrades are available. If they are, upgrade the BIOS and the software together.

Whenever I describe electrical-system failures that damage systems, listeners and readers often reply by saying, "How could anyone be so stupid?" The answer to this question is that it is easy to be that stupid, and situations like this happen daily. The weakest links in our network planning are those that do not fall within the scope of the planner's interest. As you plan your systems, every time a line in the plan leads to another system, check the delivery capabilities of that system as it relates to your computing needs. Important lines to consider are electrical-power connections, telephone links, and interfaces to noncomputing equipment. At least one Internet service provider in central Indiana has been known to outstrip the capability of the telephone system when delivering calls to its modem bank. I personally have heard the telephone company error message "All circuits are busy. Please try your call again later."

Windows 98 provides facilities to help with the other four sources of error mentioned in the preceding bulleted list, notably ScanDisk, the defragmenter, and the troubleshooters. As Microsoft evolves its Windows strategy into Windows 98 and Windows NT 5.0, they promise a possible solution to DLL conflicts. The problem relates, of course, to there being a single, central repository of DLLs, the \Windows\System folder. As upgrades and new software change the contents of this directory, you often find that you have an operating system and software that require different versions of the same file. One workaround solution is to place DLLs in a directory owned by the application involved, and to place such locations in the search path. Installation programs do not always cooperate with this strategy, however, and you may have manual copying to do.

One factor you need to consider in working with any of the Windows 98 facilities about to be discussed is that you must factor proactive planning into the mix. Drives in my systems seem to last about three years, for example. If I assume that protecting my data is more important than squeezing the last ounce of life out of a drive, I will replace at the three-year point before it crashes. You need to keep track of your failure cycles and plan to perform maintenance when you have good backups and before the potential of losing data arises.

Using Windows Update

To resolve many problems with system maintenance, Microsoft has created the Windows Update option, which appears on the Start menu. The purpose of this option is to connect you to a Web site that provides all the appropriate updates for your system, including drivers from various vendors (see Figure 26.2). In addition, you can search the Technical Support databases for information about problems you experience. You can also file trouble reports at this site.

Figure 26.2.
The Windows Update Web site contains the files necessary to keep your system up to date with the latest fixes and tools.

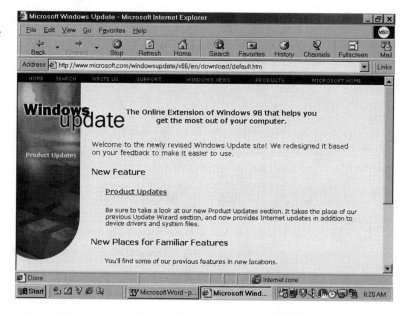

To connect, choose Windows Update from the Start menu. Windows 98 automatically kicks off your Internet connection and attaches you to the site. At the site, you select either the Update Wizard or Technical Support hyperlinks, depending on which activity you want to undertake. The Update Wizard guides you through the process of finding updated files and drivers for your system.

You should run the wizard against your systems on a regular basis to keep them refreshed with the latest versions of system files and drivers. Theoretically this process prevents problems from occurring. However, you should run the update against a test system to see whether it introduces new problems. Microsoft has not always been the perfect vendor at fixing its systems. On occasion, they have been known to introduce problems rather than solutions.

The Windows Update option is a good defense against possible DLL conflicts and software bugs. It is a much better solution than searching the Web for a vendor who might have updated a driver. Of course, its success depends on both vendor and user support. As a result, you need to consider it as an experiment until its track record is proven. Occasionally search the Web for alternative update solutions from vendors, just in case they choose not to participate.

Using the System File Checker

To help fight the corruption of system files, Microsoft has introduced the System File Checker. The System File Checker, which you launch from the Tools menu of the System Information tool, described in detail later in this chapter, serves two purposes. It can extract a single file from the installation disks and place it within the appropriate Windows or System folder, and it can scan all system files for corruption and replace those that seem to have been damaged, as shown in Figure 26.3. You would extract a single file when a particular file causes illegal operations or seems to be related for other reasons to system problems.

Figure 26.3.
The System File Checker offers you two options for repairing file corruption.

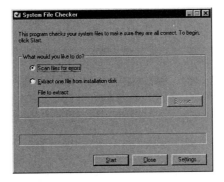

To replace an individual file, just enter the filename, without path information, in the text box. You can browse for the filename if you wish. Clicking the Start button initiates a scan for the file on the installation medium. Windows 98 maintains a record of its installation path and begins its search for the file along that path. It also maintains a record of the target directory for the file and uses this path as the initial destination for the copy operation. The System File Checker tells you these locations in a dialog box before it undertakes the copy. You can then enter alternative paths, or browse for the correct path, if you are not satisfied with the paths on record. If you have installed from a network drive, you may have to redirect the System File Checker to a local CD. If you do not have a local CD, you will need to make certain the files are available on the network.

For less precise problems—crashes that involve several files reporting illegal operations, for example—you would choose the other option provided by the System File Checker. The System File Checker monitors the file attributes, including date and version number, as well as checksums. It reports to you that the file has changed at least one of these attributes, and gives you the option of updating the file's record, replacing the file, ignoring the warning, or updating the file records for all files found to have changed (see Figure 26.4). The System File Checker maintains records of file attributes in a file called Default.sfc, which represents the installation state of your system. When you choose to update records for a file, the information about the file is stored in Default.sfc. Obviously you want to update file records only when you are absolutely certain that the change was caused by your having installed a newer copy of the file. If you are not certain, don't update the record until you are.

The Settings button in the System File Checker opens a dialog box that enables you to control the behavior of the System File Checker. The most important tab is the Settings tab (see Figure 26.5). Here you control whether you are prompted before changes are made, whether and where the replaced files are backed up before the copy operation, whether a log of the operation is kept, and whether you are checking only existing files or also checking for files crucial to normal system operation that have been inadvertently deleted. The Search Criteria tab enables you to adjust which file extensions participate in the search. In general, you would not need to increase the scope of the search, because the default settings search for all files involved in the execution of Windows 98. The Advanced tab enables you to create a new SFC file for storing file attributes. You would create a new file when you suspect that the original has become corrupt, or when you want to maintain copies that represent the system status on a certain date. With these additional copies, you could take the system files back to their status after installation (using Default.sfc), or on any date on which you created a new SFC file.

Figure 26.4.
The System File Checker offers you four options for dealing with file changes.

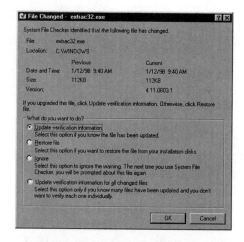

Figure 26.5.
The Settings dialog box enables you to control the behavior of the System File Checker.

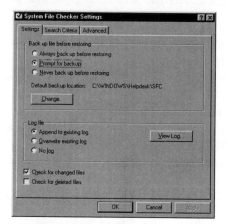

Using Windows Maintenance

To help you solve problems related to poor system maintenance, Microsoft has provided the Windows Maintenance, accessible from Start | Programs | Accessories | System Tools. The Windows

Maintenance is a wizard that steps you through the process of scheduling common maintenance tasks, which every user should run on his or her system. It schedules deletion of unnecessary files, speeding up programs by running Disk Defragmenter, and checking drives for errors with ScanDisk. You can run Windows Maintenance in two modes, either Express or Custom (see Figure 26.6). If you choose Express mode, you see two more pages. The first asks you to choose a three-hour block of time when the Maintenance process will run. The second informs you of the options that have been scheduled.

Figure 26.6.
You can run Windows Mainte-nance in Express or Custom mode.

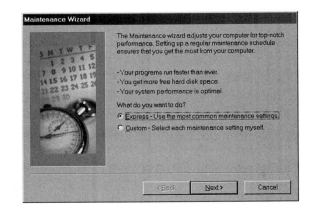

When you run in Custom mode, you see the page that asks you to choose a three-hour block of time. You see another that enables you to choose which of the programs on your Start menu you want to speed up. You also see one page like that shown in Figure 26.7 for each disk operation being sched-uled. These pages enable you to reschedule the chosen time and days for the operation using the Reschedule button. You can also choose the settings for the program to be run from the Settings button. Custom mode gives you full control over when each operation is performed.

Figure 26.7.
Custom mode presents pages that give you access to all settings for the applications you schedule.

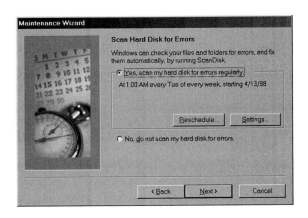

You should run the Maintenance Wizard on each system that you set up. Even if the user interrupts these operations, after they are scheduled, they will run at least occasionally. (You need to make certain that the system is on so that scheduled maintenance can take place.) As a result, you are one step ahead with deleting clutter from drives, maintaining the format of drives, and reducing drive fragmentation.

Using the Performance Tab

Microsoft provides an additional tool for adjusting the performance of Windows 98—the Performance tab in the Control Panel's System applet. Figure 26.8 shows this tab. It lists several statistics that relate to your system's performance. You see the amount of RAM, the percentage of free system resources, and whether the file system and virtual memory are using 32-bit drivers. Under most circumstances, this tab will announce that your system is fully optimized for best performance.

Figure 26.8.
The System icon's Performance tab monitors various factors that can affect total system performance.

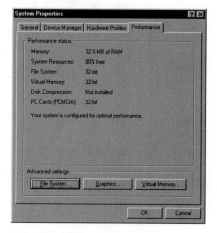

Although being perfectly optimized might be great news, the news is of no value when the system is running slower than you know it should. Within the Performance tab, you can adjust some settings to improve performance. One factor that you can adjust, for instance, is the role of the computer and the size of read-ahead buffers, as shown in Figure 26.9. To reach this dialog box, click the File System button on the Performance tab.

The desktop role adjusts the optimization of the Server service to reflect the number of connections likely to take place. On a desktop system, you would expect relatively few connections, because the average desktop is not likely to share resources for the network. As a result, the Server service does not need as much memory allocated to it. By contrast, a server (a machine whose primary role is to share resources) would need more memory allocated to the Server service to improve its capability to service the relatively large number of connections it would need to service. Mobile systems can allocate resources away from networking most of the time, because they are likely to be networked only on an occasional basis.

Figure 26.9.
You can adjust the desktop role and read-ahead optimization.

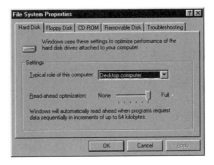

You can set read-ahead buffers for both hard drives and CD drives that you are using. In general, you want them to be as large as possible, because reading ahead on the disk usually improves performance. The data you are most likely to need next from the disk is the data that immediately follows what you have already read into memory. If you read extra data in with each read, you reduce the total number of disk accesses, because you access the data directly from memory at speeds much higher than you can read it from the disk. You can adjust the size of the buffer for hard drive access from the Hard Disk tab. You can set the access speed and buffer size for CDs from the CD-ROM tab.

Another factor that affects performance is caching of write operations. Write-behind caching is enabled for your hard drives. Data is written to a buffer, where it is held until disk activity drops below a certain threshold. When the disk is relatively quiet, the write operations take place. Using this caching scheme allows the system to favor reading data over writing data; thus, your work, which relies more on reading data than writing data, proceeds apace. Write-behind caching is typically disabled for removable drives, on the theory that you could remove the disk prior to the cache being flushed to disk. If you use removable-cartridge hard drives, however, you may wish to enable write-behind caching for removable media drives, which you can do using the Removable Disk tab (see Figure 26.10). This action should speed up access to the removable disk drives, a particularly good decision if you are booting from an IOmega Jaz drive (a 1GB removable cartridge drive), for example. You need to educate users, however, as to the possibility of data loss.

Figure 26.10.
You can improve the performance of removable media drives by enabling write-behind caching.

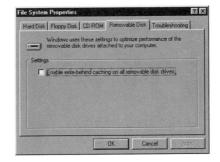

The Graphics button enables you to adjust the hardware acceleration of your display adapter using a slider control like that controlling disk buffer size. Clicking the button reveals a dialog box with this single setting. In general, you will find that acceleration is boosted to full by default. The Virtual Memory button displays a dialog box that enables you to relocate your swap file. The settings are Let Windows Manage My Virtual Memory Settings and Let Me Specify My Own Virtual Memory Settings, as shown in Figure 26.11. In general, you should let Windows manage virtual memory. If you want to protect performance, never exercise the option to disable virtual memory. There are two circumstances where you want to choose the location of virtual memory, thus changing the default. First, you will want to specify the location of the fastest hard drive installed on the computer. Placing the swap file on this drive will improve performance. Second, you want the swap file on a drive that can maintain at least 100MB of free space. My testing has shown that you need this amount free, in addition to the swap file, for Windows 98 to remain a happy operating system.

Figure 26.11.
You can adjust the virtual memory settings to a certain extent.

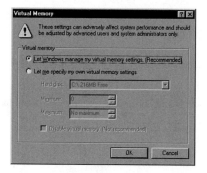

Technical Note: Although Windows 98 says that you can manage virtual memory, in reality, all you can specify is where the swap file will be. After you adjust the settings on your own, you will eventually reboot the computer. After a reboot, re-examine the virtual memory settings. You will find that Windows is back in control, but using the location that you specified for the swap file.

You will find a Troubleshooting tab in the File System dialog box. In general, no settings on this tab will enhance performance if you select them. All these settings turn off critical performance features of the file system. These settings are useful if you are experiencing apparent hardware problems with the file system. You can switch back to real-mode file system drivers, for example, to see whether your controller card or drive electronics are incompatible with the 32-bit protected-mode drivers. In general, if you make this discovery, to protect performance you would replace the hardware.

You need to know that the Performance tab is available to you. In general, however, you want to make sure that everything is set to match the role of the computer, to match the speed of the CD drive, and to provide the largest buffers possible. These settings are usually autodetected and provided by default. When you are troubleshooting, you want to review this tab and make sure these settings have not changed. You may wish to disable parts of the file system to troubleshoot Windows 98 and its relationship with the drive electronics. The solution, however, is to buy new hardware rather than permanently disable performance features of the file system.

Doing General Troubleshooting

If you are not in a situation where you are answering typical help-desk questions or updating system files, you are doing the more difficult type of troubleshooting that I call "general troubleshooting." The operating system is working well enough, but it has lost some functionality or is misbehaving in some other way. Usually these issues do not cause data loss. They are more likely to cause intermittent loss of features. Loss of a mouse pointer is a typical example. Or loss of input to a particular application, so that the application is labeled as "not responding" in the Close Program dialog box. These problems are caused by Registry conflicts, bad drivers, corrupted drivers, or similar software bugs. You have several strategies for dealing with these possible problems. The next several sections review these strategies.

Dealing with Registry Conflicts

Registry conflicts occur when the vision of the system as represented by the Registry does not match the actual state of the system. The reasons for these deviations from system reality are not entirely clear. Sometimes they are related to Plug and Play identifying devices that are not present or misidentifying devices that are present. Sometimes they seem related to improper Registry updates from applications or system components. Sometimes they are just genuinely mysterious. The types of problems you are likely to encounter are the following:

- Devices present that are not in fact present on the system. Unknown monitors and TV hardware are popular items in this category on the systems I use.

- Installed devices being marked as not present or with incorrect drivers. Mice and other pointing devices are popular items in this category on my systems.

- Installed devices installed with incorrect drivers, or otherwise misidentified. My Synaptics touch pad, for example, is routinely identified as an IBM PS/2 mouse.

- Software that has incorrect Registry settings, leading to erratic behavior. The example of troubleshooting Outlook in the Registry chapter is an excellent example of this type of problem.

- Software that initializes with incorrect or unexpected values. Network user profiles have sometimes developed erratic habits on my systems.

You have four approaches for dealing with these problems. On the hardware side, visit the Device Manager in the Control Panel's System applet. If you open the properties for any device, one of the tabs in the property sheet, usually the Driver tab, will have an Update Driver button. Clicking this button enables you to search for a new driver on your installation medium, on other media, and on the Web. Try this button first for misbehaving hardware.

If updating the driver does not work, follow this sequence:

1. Open the Device Manager.

2. Select the offending device, and click the Remove button.

3. Confirm the removal.

4. Shut down the system. (Do not restart the system.)

5. Power the system off.

6. Power the system on and let it boot. Allow the Plug and Play resources to identify the hardware and reinstall it.

This procedure usually works. If it does not, try a manual setup of the card using the card's software-configuration utility or jumpers. Sometimes this strategy works. Also, reseat any card not integrated on the motherboard. Clean contacts often resolve the problem. Clean the inside of the system. Ionized dust particles settling on electronic devices can cause problematic behavior. Also check to see whether the motherboard or the adapter has firmware upgrades available. A new BIOS can do wonders. If all these strategies fail, consider replacing the hardware. Very likely you are facing a situation in which the hardware will continue to be troublesome, sometimes working and sometimes not working. Keep in mind that if the device is a peripheral, the problem could be the peripheral or its connection to the system. If you have a lot of problems with repeating peripheral problems, consider replacing the motherboard or the ports that connect the peripherals. And, of course, if the Registry persistently causes problems, you can always reinstall the operating system and all the applications.

Using CD-Based Tools

On your Windows 98 CD, you will find two tools to help with troubleshooting. Both resolve specific problems. The following two sections introduce these tools.

Pwledit

If you have users who complain that they have to type passwords for resources unexpectedly, you can pretty much guess that something is awry with their password list file. The Password List Editor (in \Tools\Reskit\Netadmin\Pwledit on your CD) enables you to view a list of resources, but not the passwords associated with them (see Figure 26.12). You undertake only one action with this editor. You remove the password causing the problem by selecting the resource associated with it and clicking Remove. When the user logs on again, she will have to enter the password one more time. This time the entry in the password list will be reconstituted, however, and it should work correctly thereafter. Notice, however, that the user must be logged on to the system where the Password List Editor is running. Only the active user's PWL file can be loaded.

Figure 26.12.
The Password List Editor enables you to remove damaged passwords from a PWL file.

Lfnback

Lfnback is in the \Tools\Reskit\Files\lfnback folder. It is a command-line utility that backs up long filenames. Its intended use is to back up long filenames in case you intend to use an older utilities package to do maintenance on a Windows 98 disk. You need to know this utility exists, because you may find some occasion on which you need to run pre–Windows 95 disk utilities against a hard drive. I have a hard time imagining, however, why you would have to undertake an operation of that sort at this time. Most tools have been updated to work with Windows 95 and later, and many of them already support FAT32. If you ever feel you need to back up long filenames so that they can be restored at a later time, however, read the lfnback.txt file and carefully run the utility from the command line.

Using the Troubleshooting Tools

Microsoft also provides some troubleshooting tools to help with both specific and general troubleshooting. Some are focused specifically on software problems, some are more focused on hardware issues, and some touch only tangentially on resolving operating system issues. Each of these, however, has its purpose in troubleshooting Windows 98.

Using the System Logs

As it installs, starts, and runs, Windows 98 maintains several logs. You can use these logs (open them in Notepad or WordPad) to seek out operating-system–level problems and find possible solutions. You will find them in the root directory of your boot drive. The following list describes each log and its role:

- Bootlog.txt describes the last logged boot. This will be your first system boot after installation, or any subsequent boot that you initiated by pressing F8 during startup and selecting to boot with logging from the menu. This log announces the attempted initialization and successful initialization of each component. If something goes wrong, a line containing the word *FAIL* is written in the log. If you are having problems, log a boot and search Bootlog.txt for the word *FAIL*. You will at least discover what component is possibly causing the problem.

- Detlog.txt logs the hardware detection process. It contains a list of the devices detected and includes lines that describe the resources reserved for a device. When you scan this log, you are looking for devices that should be present that are not present, devices that report errors, and devices that get settings reserved that you know are incorrect. Each of these events could reveal a problem.

- Netlog.txt records the events that lead up to the initialization of the network clients, protocols, and Server service. A number of these lines may mean nothing, but you at least can see names of familiar components that you expect to be present. As you scan this log, you are looking for missing components, any line that looks like an obvious warning, or components that you did not think were installed. Each of these events could reveal a problem.

- Setuplog.txt records events related to setup. You will discover what components were installed, which files were copied where, and what settings were initialized. In scanning this log, you are looking for things missing or present, for something that is happening that should not, or for something that is not happening that should. If this log is too large to load in Notepad, it will load in WordPad.

- Scandisk.log reports errors found and fixed by ScanDisk. In scanning this log, you are looking for patterns of error that may indicate impending disk failure. If ScanDisk routinely finds directory or cluster problems, the disk may be aging. You may want to refresh its format or consider replacing it.

- Modemdet.txt records where modems were or were not found. In reviewing this log, you are looking for out-of-the-normal events, a modem not being found, or one being found on the wrong port.

- Ndislog.txt records events related to the NDIS-compliant network drivers on your system. In this file, you are looking for entries. No entries is very good news.

Using the Automatic Skip Driver Agent

Microsoft created the Automatic Skip Driver Agent to resolve the problem of drivers that prevent the operating system from booting. When a driver causes the boot process to crash, that driver is the last recorded in the bootlogging process. When the operating system attempts to restart, safe recovery routines cause the offending driver to be skipped. After you have booted, you can get information about the Automatic Skip Driver event from the System Information utility. You will find the option on the utility's Tools menu.

Using System Information and Dr. Watson

The System Information utility is available from Start | Programs | Accessories | System Tools. This utility provides you with information about the hardware and software on your system. On its Tools menu is the Dr. Watson utility, which provides you with information about system crashes. Both these utilities are more focused toward hardware troubleshooting. However, they can reveal two facts that can help with operating system troubleshooting. First, System Information provides a report of both the 16-bit and 32-bit system components that are loaded. Second, Dr. Watson logs the name of any file that initiates a page fault. You can find out what components are potential suspects and which caused disastrous errors. Keep in mind, however, that some page faults are misreported as to the source. Be aware that Dr. Watson can create red herrings for you to investigate.

The System Information utility and Dr. Watson are discussed in more detail in Chapter 28.

Using Remote Administration Tools to Troubleshoot Windows

After you have established that you have an operating system problem that resolves to Registry settings, you can use remote administration utilities to change settings over the network. Primarily, you can use two tools to help resolve operating-system–level issues, the Registry Editor, described in Chapter 25, "General Troubleshooting Strategies," and the System Policy Editor, described in Chapter 17, "Securing the Desktop." Both these tools can connect to a Registry over the network and change settings in a remote Registry as necessary. To make such changes, your systems must be configured as described in Chapter 15, "Configuring for Ease of Use."

Working Through the Thinking Process

To successfully troubleshoot Windows 98, you need to learn to think like the Microsoft developers. Quite frankly, I have spent 10 years trying to discover how to do just this, and I am still honing my skills. To pull forth some general principles to help you out is in a sense a mind-boggling task. Nevertheless, here is what I can offer to help you approach troubleshooting the operating system:

- Use the troubleshooters. They are free, and they help you see how the designers thought about the problem.

- As soon as you have exhausted the troubleshooters, head for the Knowledge Base. The answer might be there. If it is, your time to solution is good.

- Think associatively, especially as you review the Knowledge Base. Many times problems can be solved in similar manners.

- Constantly think about what happened just before and what was supposed to happen just after. Sometimes the troubleshooting tools misreport the source of the problem. Try to reproduce the problem under slightly differing and increasingly controlled conditions so as to narrow down the list of possible culprits.

- Isolate the general source of the problem. Try to rule out NetBEUI and IPX/SPX as sources of the problem if you are struggling with network protocol issues. Then you can at least focus on TCP/IP as the problem candidate.

- After you have ruled in an area of the operating system, try to divide it into sub-areas for testing. If you know you are dealing with the mouse, try to determine whether you are facing a settings problem or a driver problem.

- Keep records of what you have tried. You avoid needlessly repeating steps, and you may discover interactions of components in your notes.

- Remember that multimedia devices and their drivers can interact strangely with the operating system. If the system hangs right before you hear the shutdown sound, one possibility is the sound driver (or the multimedia drivers more generally).

- Remember that hardware may not always be as compatible as advertised. Sometimes the solution is just getting better hardware.

- Remember that the processes of an operating system do age, and sometimes periodic rebooting is the best answer. Windows 98 seems to be particularly susceptible to such aging, at least in the early stages of its evolution as a product.

- Remember to power down as well as shut down when troubleshooting. Sometimes hardware devices need to power down to fully reset.

- Finally, if shutdown, power-down, restarting, reloading Windows 98 from scratch, and similar strategies don't work, it is time to replace the hardware.

Summary

In this chapter, I have sketched out strategies for troubleshooting the operating system. The discussion has focused on resolving typical help-desk issues, keeping the system up to date, performing general troubleshooting, and using troubleshooting tools. Most importantly, I have tried to help you develop a troubleshooting mind-set. As you develop experience troubleshooting Windows 98, remember to reason associatively from your experience. You should be able to resolve most problems using this type of reasoning.

On Your Own

Find every tool mentioned here and at least have a look at it. The time to try and find the right tool is not when you are in an emergency situation. Of all of them, pick a couple that seem particularly useful to you and investigate them further. Compare a couple of systems. If possible, look at the way a laptop is configured and compare it to a desktop machine. On a test machine, delete a system component or purposefully configure an IRQ conflict. Looking at known situations ahead of time will make it easier to identify the mysterious ones later.

27

Trouble-shooting Applications

Peter Norton®

Operating systems would run much better if we never installed applications and never allowed users to touch their computers. However, users wanting to use applications is usually the reason we acquired the computing equipment in the first place. We have to resign ourselves to dealing with users and supporting the applications they want to run.

Application problems can be maddening. With the trend toward less documentation in print and more documentation online, often all you get with an application is just enough to be mystified when it doesn't work the way it says it will. With most support now on a pay-per-call basis, you would rather spend time and money puzzling out a solution yourself than talking to someone on the phone who may know little more than you do.

My goal in this chapter is to give you some help with the puzzling through. This chapter focuses on the following strategies:

- Using all the available resources to work through questions
- Isolating critical problems
- Fighting DLL conflicts
- Using third-party tools

Using the Available Resources

The first stage of any application troubleshooting is to work through the general strategies described in Chapter 25, "General Troubleshooting Strategies." If your searches and research do not produce an answer, however, how do you proceed? After you know something about the interactions of the application with the operating system and other applications, you can begin thinking about which of those interactions were involved in the problem. You can then investigate and experiment to see whether altering the context of the problem will resolve the problem. Can you revert to an earlier version of a DLL? Is there a later version available that you could try? Check the Version Conflict Manager (found on the Tools menu of the System Information application) to see whether any upgrades have occurred on the system. You may be able to restore the older version by clicking one button (see Figure 27.1).

A very productive line of inquiry is whether any changes have been made to the system at all. Check with the user, and ask about stupid things to help jog her memory. Did you change your screen resolution or colors? Did you go to the Control Panel for any reason recently? If so, what was the reason? Questions like these help jog the user's memory and may help you get the information you need.

Be sure to check for new hardware, new software, upgrades to products other than the one that is causing the problem, and just about anything else you can think of. The problem may not be the application's fault. I always say that you have to be sneaky and devious when you are troubleshooting these sorts of problems.

Figure 27.1.
The Version Conflict Manager can help you restore older versions of system files.

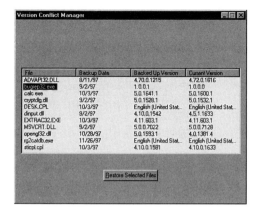

Using NetMeeting for Troubleshooting Applications

I mentioned the possibility of setting up for remote viewing of a user's screen. You can purchase tools that enable you to do this. SMS Server, for example, has this feature in an integrated network-management package. PC Remote provides only the remote control feature. pcANYWHERE is a popular package that enables you to connect via modem or network, perform remote control diagnosis and repair, and share a voice channel with the user. Windows 98 provides NetMeeting as a part of the Internet Explorer 4.0 package; you can do a limited amount of remote viewing using NetMeeting, as well as have a voice and video channel for communication with the user.

NetMeeting, shown in Figure 27.2, is simple to use. The only requirement is that NetMeeting be running on both systems. You need not worry about whether you have sound and video. Although they are helpful, they are not required. Using NetMeeting, you can ask a user to share the application and then watch what he does with the application that causes the problem. You also have a chat window that you can share with the user, as well as a whiteboard to facilitate communication.

NetMeeting installs as a part of the Internet Explorer. If you do not have it installed by default, use the Add/Remove Programs icon in the Control Panel to update your installation. You have three methods for opening NetMeeting. One is to use Start | Programs | Microsoft NetMeeting. If you set up NetMeeting prior to having installed Windows 98, this item will appear on your menu. Another method is to choose Internet Call from the Go menu of Internet Explorer 4.0. The third method is to use Start | Programs | Internet Explorer | Microsoft NetMeeting. Windows 98 builds this menu path when it installs Internet Explorer. After you open NetMeeting, you will work through a wizard that configures the playback sound and microphone volume level. After you work through the wizard once, you do not have to do so again. After the wizard, NetMeeting displays the window shown in Figure 27.3.

Figure 27.2.
NetMeeting enables you to communicate with a user over the network to help solve problems.

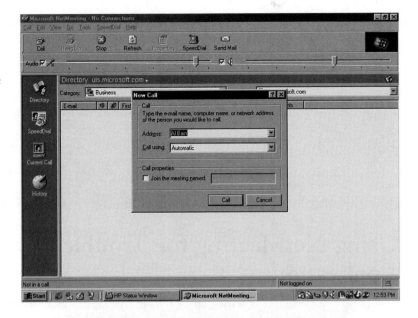

Figure 27.3.
NetMeeting enables you to place calls over your LAN, over a modem line, or over the Internet.

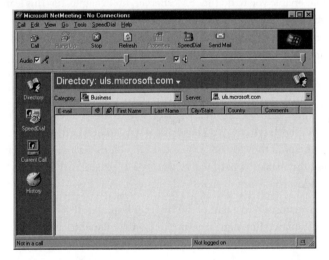

To place a call, click on the Call button on the toolbar. Enter the name of the computer on your network, an e-mail address, or a person's name in the dialog box shown in Figure 27.4. Select the method for making the call as well. Your options include Network (TCP/IP), Directory Server, and Automatic. If you see an existing call listed in the client area of NetMeeting, you can enter its name in the text box to join that call. Then click on OK.

Network TCP/IP uses the TCP/IP protocol to place a call to a computer on a network. If you use a dial-up connection, placing the call will automatically invoke the dialing sequence if you are not already connected. If you explicitly choose Network TCP/IP, you must be dialing a valid network address. Usually you specify the NetBIOS name of the computer, but IP addresses or resolvable domain names work as well. If you use a Directory Server, you need first to have one set up or know the address of one on the Internet. You can select from among the servers known to NetMeeting by using the Server drop-down list just above the NetMeeting client area. Such servers—Microsoft maintains a couple of them—enable you to find individuals by name or e-mail address.

Figure 27.4.
*You have several
methods available for
placing a call.*

After you have placed the call, sit back and wait. The call negotiation process can take some time. After the receiving computer has been located, if NetMeeting is running, the call is accepted. The computer produces a ringing sound and presents an Answer dialog box, as shown in Figure 27.5. The user on that computer clicks Accept to answer the call.

Figure 27.5.
*The receiving user has
the option to accept or
reject the call.*

After the receiver accepts the call, entries for both users appear in the list box in NetMeeting's client area. Other users will see an entry for the call in the same location when they click on the Directory icon on the left side of the window. As a result, additional computers can attempt to participate in the call. They must, of course, be accepted or rejected by the user who placed, and therefore owns, the call. In addition, if you have video cameras, you will see your call partner's image in the video window on the right side. If you have microphones, you can converse with one another. In the absence of these accessories, you can open a chat window and a whiteboard for communication from the Tools menu.

Of greatest value for troubleshooting, however, is the capability to share an application window. After the application is open, the user with the problem can share the application by clicking on the Share button on the toolbar. You then see the application on your screen, and you can watch the user's actions that lead to the problem you are trying to solve. If the user clicks the Collaborate button on the toolbar, you can take control of the application, as shown in Figure 27.6, and show the user the proper way to avoid the problem. All mouse movements and results of keystrokes are seen on both computers in the call. Although you do not have complete remote control, you do have the option to see remotely what the user is doing with the application.

Figure 27.6.
NetMeeting offers you remote control over a single application to help you diagnose application problems.

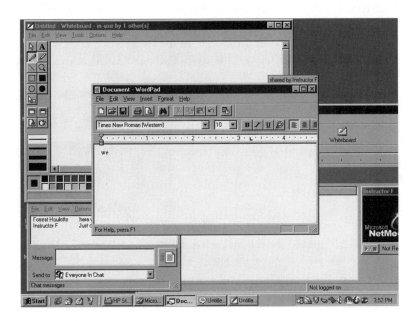

Tip: Products such as SMS Server give you complete remote control capabilities.

Isolating Critical Problems

Every troubleshooting procedure I have ever reviewed insists that you must isolate the critical problem. Just what is the critical problem? It seems to be something you discover only after suffering several critical "Aha!" reactions in troubleshooting situations. The best example I know, although not strictly an application problem, illustrates the kind of reaction required by troubleshooting. If you dual boot between Windows NT and Windows 98, you could encounter a system that no longer boots to Windows NT. Knowing that the BOOT.INI file will reveal the exact source of the problem means that you must have seen both scenarios. Knowing that in one scenario the BOOT.INI reveals the source of the problem is to know that you can check the file to learn which problem you have. You can use the file to pin down exactly which problem you have—if you pull all the facts together in the correct way at the correct time.

Note: Psychologists recognize a set of problems as requiring "Aha!" reactions. That is, you cannot solve the problem without perceiving it and the solution as a Gestalt whole. There is no step-by-step solution that can be documented, or any kind of discrete cognitive process involved. You must engage in a complex suite of cognitive processes, possibly unique to the individual. You either see the entire solution or you don't, and there is no partial solution or middle ground in solving the problem. A lot of party games and word puzzles rely on them. Here's an example:

Glass
———
Pheasant

This translates to "pheasant under glass."

To isolate this issue, you have to pull together several facts. One is that any user can set the default operating system and timeout for the Boot menu under Windows NT. If the user chooses Windows 98 and sets the timeout to zero, the system boots to Windows 98, and you never see a Boot menu. In this case, the BOOT.INI file will label Windows 98 as the default operating system and will contain a 0 value on the timeout= line. The solution is to reset the timeout in the BOOT.INI file. You can then boot into Windows NT and reselect the default operating system. (You could also edit the BOOT.INI file to place Windows NT on the default= line.)

In addition, you have to know that the only other way to boot to a single operating system is to have altered the boot sector. The Master Boot Record, stored in MBR.EXE, can be located at boot because it is always in the same place on the drive—first. It executes, describes the drive to the system, and then seeks the boot sector at a given location on the drive. Whatever boot sector is there is the one that executes. If the Windows 98 boot sector is there, Windows 98 starts. If the Windows NT boot sector is there, Windows NT boots. In the case where the boot sector has changed, BOOT.INI will look normal. This file is in fact not being used. As a result, you never see a Boot menu in this scenario. The solution is to replace the boot sector, which you can do by using the Windows NT emergency repair procedure.

Isolating critical problems takes experience, and the only road to experience is making any number of mistakes that lead you to say "Aha! Now I see the problem." The examples I have for troubleshooting applications are all slightly out of date or apply only to in-house applications that you will never see. A classic occurred in Word 6.0, prior to version A, when Windows 3.11 or Windows 95 crashed on you. Because the operating system seized, all of Word's temporary files were orphaned in your TEMP directory. Word, on starting, checked to see whether any temporary files were available. If you reopened the file you last worked on and then attempted to save it, Word told you that someone else had the file open, and you could not save your changes. Word mistook the orphaned temporary file for another open copy of the file.

Of course, as you finally see the problem, you probably feel pretty foolish for not having seen it before. In this Word example, you could search for hours to find a solution. But this is a case where you just needed to know something about temporary files. Applications typically sign them so that they are recognizably owned by that application. One thing that could fool Word into thinking a second copy of the file was open would be to see a signed temporary file in the right place. Deleting the temporary file solved the problem. But you had to pull together widely diverging tiny bits of information and relate them in a unique way, a way that almost defies logic. That is all a part of the process. That feeling makes you remember the solution the next time you see the problem.

You can use some guidelines, however, to isolate the critical problem. Use these concepts as rules of thumb, or heuristics, to guide your thinking:

- Isolate what the problem is *not*. Decide which components could not be a part of the problem so that you can focus on the components that are likely candidates.
- Watch for driver interactions among components that are part of the process. Many software problems can be traced to attempts to use drivers that conflict with one another.
- Watch for bizarre interactions. Components that have only minor roles in the process can in fact be the culprit.
- Draw pictures of the problem. Flow charts and block diagrams force you to translate the problem from one medium to another. The translation process can help you see the problem in a different light.
- Talk through the problem with someone. The activity of talking about the problem will help you reconceive it.
- Whenever possible, identify the DLLs loaded at the time and their role. Microsoft System Information (see Chapter 28, "Troubleshooting Hardware") can tell you what is loaded, and resources such as TechNet can help to identify their roles, as can the file header that you read using the file's properties.
- Reconceive the problem by backing up and starting the troubleshooting process over. Look actively for things you ruled out earlier.
- When you are really stumped, back away and let your thoughts incubate. Do something else and come back to the problem. You will often gain perspective and new ideas through this process.

These rules will help where you have little experience. They will help you gain the critical experience that makes troubleshooting easier. Remember that with any new software, we all begin at ground zero with troubleshooting.

Fighting DLL Conflicts

Dynamic link libraries have been causing problems for Windows users since the inception of the software. They simplify development by providing separate components of the software that can be upgraded individually without providing new copies of every part of the software. As parts get updated, however, other parts may not be able to cooperate with the update. This problem often occurs when a piece of software updates a DLL that other programs use, such as the OLE DLLs or the common dialog DLLs.

Very often you have no control over the updates. You install the latest version of your office suite and it updates the files that it needs to update. It may not even tell you what files it has changed, and it may install older versions than you already have. To make matters worse, you have no guarantee that newer versions of a DLL are backwardly compatible with older versions and the software that uses the older versions.

What can you do to protect your systems under these awkward circumstances? You should take at least these steps:

- Whenever you knowingly replace a DLL, you should record the fact. You should also try to keep a backup of the DLL. Windows 98 has facilities that keep backups, but some programs can fool these facilities. You can pull a copy off a system that has not been upgraded yet if necessary.

- When offered the opportunity to copy an older file over a newer version, decline the option. With the Microsoft Version Manager, this action means clicking the Yes button.

- Keep the installation media for at least one version back for each software package that you use. If you discover that you need an older DLL version, chances are it will appear on those disks.

- Practice extracting single files using the System File Checker. This skill is essential for replacing DLLs.

- Seek to use a set of DLLs that all your software can coexist with. Experiment with older DLLs to see whether your new software can still use them.

- If you have software that needs a special version of a DLL, launch it from a batch file that copies the appropriate version into place and restores the newer version after the program exits. Warn users that while this software is loaded, they may experience problems with other programs.

Using Third-Party Tools

My general experience with troubleshooting tools is that you can probably do what they do on your own with the resources provided by the operating system. Troubleshooting tools often provide greater convenience, however. They automate tasks, and they often provide a friendly or in-your-face interface to help you get the job done.

Three kinds of tools are useful. One group is the general utilities packages, the best known of which is Norton Utilities from Symantec. They provide a wide range of tools to help you deal with a number of problem situations. You may never need the tools at all, but they are a real security blanket.

When you have a problem that demands, for example, a sector editor to rebuild some disk files or a Master Boot Record, having the utilities is absolutely essential. General utilities packages usually emphasize data protection and recovery.

The second group falls into the uninstaller and tune-up category. Products such as CleanSweep and WinTune represent this category. They offer automation for removal of unused files, uninstallation of software, and setting system parameters for improved performance. Often these tools do some performance monitoring dynamically, and they emphasize improving performance and minimizing consumption of precious disk real estate. They can indeed help improve and maintain system performance with less attention from you and the user.

The final type of useful tool is the DLL management system, best exemplified by DLLaGator. These tools monitor the replacement of DLLs and keep the records of upgrades for you. They keep backup copies of the replaced files, and they enable you to restore missing or problem DLLs from backup. For managing large networks, my opinion is that such tools are more important than even a general utilities package. DLL conflicts have been traced as the major source of the general protection faults (now called illegal operations) thrown by software packages. You need to strongly consider investing in such a system.

Working Through an Application Problem

To give you a sense of what it is like to support applications under Windows 98, we will work through a scenario based on a Knowledge Base article. Suppose you get a call from a user who says, "I'm trying to save my Word 97 document to a floppy disk. I just got an illegal operation. What's going on? It worked yesterday." You respond with several questions—for example: "Can you save the file to your hard drive? Can you save the file to your home drive on the network?" The user answers yes to both questions. In fact, she had saved the file first to the hard drive and then to the network for a backup. She needs the floppy disk to take to the Cincinnati office tomorrow for a sales meeting. You now know that the problem is not with the save logic in Word 97. The software can clearly save files, at least under some circumstances.

Obviously, the problem is not that the user cannot save a Word document. Clearly, Word can save, just not to a floppy disk at the moment. Now you need to focus on your user-interviewing skills. Step the user through the process of the save as precisely as possible. Have her remove the floppy disk from the drive and inspect it physically. Is it write-protected? Does there appear to be any physical damage to the disk? The user answers no to both questions. You have successfully established some of what the problem is not.

So far you can be certain that this is not a hard disk problem. You can be certain that it is probably not a bug in the save logic. Such logic in a program rarely cares what the medium is. You must further narrow down the problem. Have the user get a brand new disk. Even if you buy formatted disks, step the user through the process of formatting the disk. Now you are certain that you have ruled out formatting problems, bad sectors, and a host of other issues relating to the medium.

Ask the user to try saving the file. Was she successful? She says yes. She is pleased. It must have been a bad disk. To confirm, have the user try to save the file again to the original disk. Indeed, the answer comes back that the error has reappeared. An easy assumption would be that this is a media problem. However, you are slightly suspicious. Error messages are always created by program designers. She could save the file on the floppy disk yesterday, and she cannot today. Either the floppy disk has come in contact with a magnet, or something else is going on.

Ask the user to show the properties of the A: drive in the Explorer with the floppy disk in the drive. Ask her to describe the properties of the floppy disk. She says that it looks fine. It has 100KB free and all the directory listings appear normal in her Explorer. Ask her how large her file is. She answers that it is 98KB in size. She says it should fit on the floppy disk.

In theory she is right. In fact, she is wrong. You tell her to use the fresh disk, and you will get back to her. You have a suspicion, so you connect to the Knowledge Base via the Web. You search for articles on Word for Windows related to floppy disks, and an interesting article appears. It reports that you can get illegal operations when saving to a floppy disk with tight disk space. Your guess is that 2KB is not enough overhead on a floppy to avoid this problem. Although there is no way to confirm it exactly, you are probably right. Word is actually misreporting the source of the error. No GPF has actually occurred. However, an error condition has occurred that Word has no other way to handle. As a result, it crashes. Inelegant, but that happens.

When your user returns from Cincinnati, you e-mail her the solution. Don't let your floppy disks get too full. Make sure that you have available at least 10KB more on the floppy disk than the file you are trying to save. Although this is not the most elegant solution, it works. It will work well enough until the application designers provide a better resolution to this error condition.

The inability to save to a floppy disk could be just due to a hardware failure, or rather an operating system problem, or could even be the result of faulty interaction between Word 97 and Windows 98. Through a systematic process of elimination, you identified it as an application-specific shortcoming that has nothing to do with either the hardware or the operating system. It was an error condition that could be fixed with an application-specific patch.

You will face application problems like this frequently. The secret is adhering to the basics of interviewing users, discovering what the problem is not, focusing on conceiving the problem in different ways, and being open to solutions other than the apparent one. If you can develop all these habits of mind, you will be able to resolve application problems easily.

Working Through the Thinking Process

Troubleshooting applications can be easy, but it can also be difficult. Inevitably, the users you interview misreport what they are doing with the application. They leave out critical details. Opening `excel.xls`, which they created two years ago with an earlier version of Excel, becomes "I opened a file." You have to ferret out the critical details. Successful interviewing skills include the following:

- Active listening, the ability to pay attention to what the user is saying while responding with queries that focus what the user is saying. Often, generic responses such as "Tell me what you did next" work fine. Sometimes, however, you need to base your questions on the last thing the user said, refocusing or summarizing what he said in the question or prompt that you use.

- Understanding the possible actions that users can undertake with the application. In other words, you need to know the application well yourself.

- Understanding the ways that users commonly shorthand actions that they have undertaken. Be sure you know how to translate statements such as "I copied some text" into specific, discrete steps required to undertake the action.

- Using focused questions to elicit more information from users. Because you know the possible actions, you can help users deconstruct the problem into the exact actions they took that led to the appearance of the problem. This questioning technique involves the raising of alternatives—for example, "Did you use Ctrl+C to copy the text, or did you right-click on the text and select Copy from the menu?"

- Asking users to demonstrate what they attempted. If you can get a demonstration, either in person or by remote control, watch carefully what the user does. Note all the actions. Sometimes you have to be present because the problem is being caused by extraneous behavior on the part of the user. The reason the user drops off the network periodically could be that his chair occasionally runs over the network cable, causing a short in the wire.

- Exhibiting patience with all user problems. You will only offend users if you are not patient.

- Maintaining the attitude that the user is not really insane, inane, or computationally impaired. Be very careful about the attitude you exhibit. Do not convey superiority. Users will not accept that attitude.

In addition, use these tips to help you identify actual causes:

- The leading cause of application errors with Windows 98 is a DLL conflict. Watch for which DLLs have been updated because of software installations. Be sure to find out whether the user has installed anything lately.

- If you don't have a missing or corrupted file, chances are you have a Registry setting that has become mis-set. You can try to edit the settings, but reinstallation is usually the best way to refresh Registry settings.

> **Tip:** If you reinstall an application, be sure to uninstall it using the uninstallation option for the program. Sometimes uninstalling is necessary to prevent the installation routine from preserving bad settings in the Registry.

- If the error leads to dialog boxes that do not announce a general protection fault or illegal operation, you probably have some problem in the options that you can set for the application. Review your options and customization dialog boxes to see whether you can resolve the problem.

- If the error is unexpected behavior, you have two options to investigate. The most likely is unexpected user behavior. The next most likely is incorrect option settings for the application.

- Be sure to check application documentation for hidden settings and switches that may resolve the problem. Often changing a startup switch in the shortcut command line is the answer to seemingly frustrating problems.

Summary

This chapter has tried to attune you to the issues necessary to troubleshoot applications running under Windows 98. You have seen the kind of focus you need to deal with application issues. You have seen what you can do with NetMeeting to simplify remote troubleshooting. You have worked through a case study of not being able to save a file to a disk to apply the basic troubleshooting principles. You have also reviewed the kinds of reasoning steps, hints, and practical rules you need to know to troubleshoot applications.

On Your Own

Alas, I can't very well say "Go find an application in trouble and solve it." You could go weeks or months without being able to apply that advice. You can, however, get ready to deal with the problem efficiently. Learn your application's basic functionality. Learn where you control its settings. Practice making calls with NetMeeting. Use the Version Conflict Manager to track DLL changes. Set up a system with Windows 98, and then check the Version Conflict Manager. Install Office 97, and check the Version Conflict Manager again. Do you see any changes? Install Office 6.0, and record the changes you find in the Version Conflict Manager. Install an in-house application. Do you see changes in the Version Conflict Manager? Sometimes you will, and sometimes you won't. Were you warned during installation about these changes? Sometimes you are warned, and sometimes you are not. Review the hints and questions until they are second nature. Practice your user-support attitude daily.

28

Trouble-shooting Hardware

Peter Norton®

If there is one thing I hate in computing, it is troubleshooting hardware. Hardware is rarely smart enough to be able to communicate to you what is wrong. If you really want to debug hardware problems, you need a good symbolic debugger that can run on a remote machine and an intimate knowledge of the source code for the operating system. Because most of us fall outside these two categories, we are left to divine as best we can what has gone wrong. Through trial and error we reconstruct the conditions that led to the failure. Let me emphasize this point clearly. The trial-and-error process is often slow and frustrating.

The hardware problems that are easy to troubleshoot are the ones where you plug a new card in and nothing works. You take the card out, and everything works. You know what the problem is, at least in gross terms. Your operating system does not like the new device.

The hardware problems that are difficult to solve are the insidious, intermittent ones that show no trademark set of trigger conditions. Chasing these can be a long and slow process. Back in the days of Windows 3.1, for example, a friend of mine upgraded his motherboard to the latest 486-based option. He had new speed and great video, but his machine just stopped every once in awhile. He tried replacing all his peripherals. He tried replacing all the cables. He called Microsoft—back in the days when support calls were free—and Microsoft worked on the problem. They even suggested changing the case, just on the outside chance that the new motherboard was binding in some curious way on the mounts.

Absolutely none of these efforts solved the problem. Everyone had assumed that a new motherboard would be flawless. This one, it turned out, had one broken connection. Everything worked fine as long as electricity did not have to travel that path. When it did, the machine froze. Every technician who worked on the problem overlooked the obvious issue. We changed the motherboard and things stopped working. We should have suspected that the change in motherboard was the problem. Instead, we assumed that new boards always work. When troubleshooting hardware, never assume, and never overlook the obvious. Often, the obvious is the answer.

This chapter focuses on building some of the reasoning skills that help you not to overlook the obvious. We cover the following issues:

- Understanding how Plug and Play might fool you
- Understanding how legacy hardware might fool you
- Using Windows 98 tools for troubleshooting
- Using third-party tools for troubleshooting
- Working through case studies to reinforce these reasoning skills

Working with Plug and Play

Plug and Play was formally introduced by Microsoft, Intel, and Compaq in March of 1993. Its intention was to give PCs something the Macintosh had had since the beginning—dynamically configurable hardware. Press releases claimed that you would have no more jumpers to set, no more software-configuration programs to run from the DOS prompt, and no more long hours tracing device conflicts. You would just plug the new device in and power everything up, and the operating system would configure the new device.

> **Tip:** When troubleshooting hardware, especially Plug and Play hardware, reset the machine by powering off, performing a cold boot. Always wait about 20 seconds after powering down. A power-on reset using the Reset button, also called a warm boot, sometimes does not reset all the cards you have installed.

Plug and Play quickly earned the nickname "Plug and Pray." It worked fairly well when it appeared as a part of Windows 95, but it never worked quite well enough. Often you would have to manually reconfigure legacy devices so that Plug and Play could configure the rest. With Windows 98, the good news is that Plug and Play is considerably more robust. The bad news is that it still can misconfigure a device.

To take a simple example, I installed an ATI All In Wonder video adapter so that I would be able to demonstrate the TV Viewer in Windows 98 to clients. Windows 98 did not recognize the card as an All In Wonder. Instead, it recognized the three separate components on the card—a TV tuner, video capture port, and Rage II/II+ display adapter—and installed separate drivers for those devices, all of which failed to function. When I install either the All In Wonder driver from Microsoft or ATI, the tuner and video capture drivers are still present, both nonfunctional and disabled. I can remove them by hand, but they are back again on the next boot.

> **Technical Note:** Windows 98 may in fact install multiple drivers for a single device as a perfectly normal and correct operation. The All In Wonder does in fact require multiple drivers, as does a Creative Labs AWE64. Windows 98 provides one driver per chip set on the card. The trick is to make sure that you have the right drivers for the chips on your card. A Diamond Video card, for example, can be mistaken for a generic S3 video card. The generic driver does not address the specific features of the card, and Windows 98 includes a better driver for the card. Plug and Play can be fooled by its own excellent logic. Always check your drivers in the Device Manager after installation to be certain that the best drivers for your devices are installed.

This is a fairly benign Plug and Play problem, because it allows the hardware and drivers to continue functioning. Imagine how frustrating it would be if Plug and Play created serious conflicts. To understand the kinds of problems you might experience with it, we need to examine its components to understand exactly how it works.

Plug and Play has three requirements:

- You must have a Plug and Play operating system (such as Windows 98).
- You must have a Plug and Play Basic Input/Output chip (BIOS) on your motherboard.
- You must have Plug and Play devices with appropriate drivers installed in the system.

If your system meets these requirements, Plug and Play can configure all the devices in your system. If you have the operating system and lack the other two components, a certain level of Plug and Play is possible, largely because Windows 98 knows how to sleuth out information about legacy devices. Without all three components, however, you cannot expect to swap hardware dynamically, as you do with PC Cards, or to configure hardware settings automatically. In the best of all possible worlds, you will meet all three requirements. (The machine with the All In Wonder card I mentioned meets all three.)

Plug and Play follows a specific process that involves nine different components (see Figure 28.1). The initial component in the process is the system BIOS chip. This chip powers up and engages in a certain amount of system configuration. Three devices must make up a minimum configuration before the Plug and Play process can continue. The BIOS must configure a display device, an input device, and a loading device for programs, typically a hard drive. After the BIOS has configured these devices, it possesses information about them. The last step in BIOS configuration is to transfer control to the Master Boot Record, MBR.EXE, which executes, providing additional information about the program-loading device. The Master Boot Record transfers control to the boot sector, which loads enough information about partitions and file systems to locate the operating system loader.

Peter's Principle: The Best Way to Work with Plug and Play Is to Upgrade Hardware

I often joke that the best way to optimize any version of Windows is to buy more hardware. Sadly, this joke is all too often true. You will have the least trouble with Plug and Play if you update your legacy devices to their Plug and Play equivalents. You will have the least trouble with PCI devices as opposed to ISA devices. You will have better configuration performance for devices that conform to the latest version of the Plug and Play standard, and with system BIOS chips that conform to the latest version of the standard and have been set to support Plug and Play. A good principle is to upgrade your hardware to Plug and Play devices if you are implementing Windows 98.

As the boot continues, the operating system carries out the following operations:

- Identifying the devices available on the system
- Identifying the resources required by the devices
- Arbitrating configurations for all the devices

- Programming any device settings necessary
- Loading and initializing the device drivers for the available devices
- Providing the operating system with all configuration details

Figure 28.1.
Plug and Play involves six different components, both software and firmware.

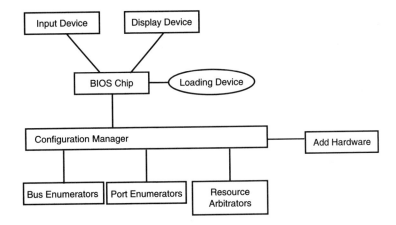

The central operating system component in this process is the Configuration Manager. It manages the entire process. After the BIOS initializes and the Configuration Manager loads, the Configuration Manager receives the initial hardware settings from the BIOS. The Configuration Manager also supervises device identification, device configuration, and recording of all settings in the Registry. The Configuration Manager receives help from other system components in this process.

An important component is the Registry—most specifically, the hardware tree. Your most direct view of the hardware tree is the Device Manager Properties sheet (see Figure 28.2). The actual hardware tree is stored in various nodes of the Registry key HKEY_LOCAL_MACHINE. As the system boots, the Configuration Manager stores all hardware information in the hardware tree. Any time that the hardware configuration changes, the Configuration Manager stores the revised settings in the hardware tree. This configuration information, along with software configuration information, can be loosely described as the *control set*. Windows 98 is always under the control of the *current control set*, the configuration currently loaded.

The Configuration Manager calls bus enumerators and port enumerators to identify the devices installed on the system. All currently available bus and port types are supported, as well as some that are just appearing. Each enumerator is familiar with the implementation of a given hardware type, so there is one enumerator for each bus and port type. The enumerators know how to find devices on the specific hardware type they are capable of enumerating. Plug and Play devices are not active when they power up. Enumerators query the device type and resource possibilities from the Plug and Play BIOS included on each device while the card is in the inactive state.

After identifying the list of devices available, the Configuration Manager calls resource arbitrators to resolve the configuration. The arbitrators examine the settings each device can take and assign nonconflicting settings to all devices. The resource arbitrators identify devices they cannot configure—the so-called legacy devices. The resource arbitrators work around the settings on the legacy devices in setting up the Plug and Play devices. After configuration, Plug and Play devices become active.

Figure 28.2.

The Device Manager displays the most direct view of the hardware tree.

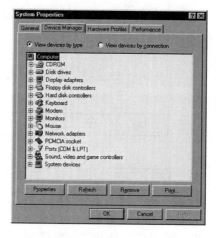

Note: Enumerators and resource arbitrators are implemented as separate components to allow the easy extension of Windows 98 to cover new hardware types using Service Packs.

After the resource arbitrators have finished their work, the Configuration Manager stores all the resolved settings in the Registry. Theoretically, you have a completely and correctly configured system. Sometimes, however, you may run into problems. In general, you will find the problems relate to either an enumerator or a resource arbitrator.

Enumerators can fail in one of three ways. They can fail to find a device, they can misidentify a device, or they can find a device that is not present. Each of these failures requires a different solution. If the enumerators fail to find a device, you can use the Add Hardware icon in the Control Panel to add the device, manually identifying the device if the aggressive search provided by the Add Hardware icon fails to identify the device. To add a device manually, follow these steps:

1. Open the Control Panel by selecting Start | Settings | Control Panel.
2. Double-click on the Add New Hardware icon.
3. Click on the Next button on the information page of the wizard.
4. On the page that announces Windows will search for Plug and Play devices, click Next to permit the search.
5. On the next screen, select the No option to manually select the hardware to add (see Figure 28.3). Then click Next. If a device that is not the one you want to configure is

found, or a device is found and labeled Unknown, select the No, the item is not on the list option. Otherwise, you will configure the device found rather than the one you intend to configure.

Figure 28.3.
Select No to manually select the device to install.

6. Select the type of device you want to add in the list presented, and then click Next.

7. Now select the manufacturer and the device in the Manufacturers and Models lists (see Figure 28.4). If you have a disk with drivers on it, click on Have Disk. You will be asked to insert the disk in the floppy drive, and it will be scanned for INF files. You will be presented with a list to select from. After you open the INF file, you will see a list like the one shown in Figure 28.4 that is drawn from the INF file. Select the appropriate device and click Next.

Figure 28.4.
Select the manufacturer and device to install.

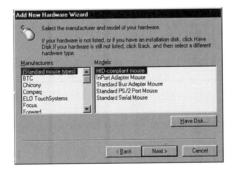

8. In the last wizard page, click on Finish. Windows 98 copies files into place for the new device. Depending on the device, you may be asked to restart the computer before it will be available.

Technical Note: Plug and Play has a rough relationship with legacy hardware and drivers. Sometimes a device will go unrecognized until after you install it manually. In some cases,

continues

you may have to install the 16-bit drivers for the device. After Plug and Play notices the manual installation, it may in fact offer to upgrade the drivers for you.

The reverse can also be true, however. Having an older driver, even a Windows 95 driver, in place may confuse Plug and Play. You will have an installed device, but it will have the older drivers. To get the device to work, you may have to remove the older drivers and let Plug and Play configure the device from a raw state.

If the device is misidentified, you have two options. You can use the Device Manager to remove the device, and use the Add Hardware icon to install the correct device. Or you can use the property sheet for that device, which you view by selecting the device in the Device Manager, and using the Change button found within the property sheet to change the driver for the device. To remove a device, follow these steps:

1. Open the Device Manager, either by opening the Control Panel and double-clicking the System icon or by right-clicking on My Computer and selecting Properties.

2. Select the Device Manager tab (see Figure 28.5).

Figure 28.5.
Select the Device Manager tab and navigate the tree to select the device to remove.

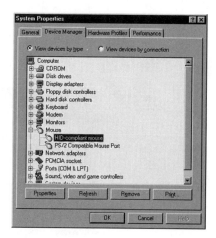

3. Navigate the tree by clicking on the plus and minus signs until you find the device you want to remove. Select the device.

4. Click Remove.

5. Click OK in the Confirmation dialog box that appears. Windows 98 removes the device.

Warning: Always remove the device from the Device Manager before powering down and removing the device from the machine. If you are removing a PC Card, use the PC Card utility in the System Tray to stop the card before removing it. If you don't stop the card, your system may freeze.

To change a device driver, follow these steps:

1. Open the Device Manager.

2. Select the device whose driver you want to change, and click on Properties.

3. Select the Driver tab (see Figure 28.6) and click Driver File Details. Write down the files associated with the driver, just in case you need to find one of these files to restore a failed upgrade.

Figure 28.6.
The Property sheet for any device provides you with a means for upgrading the driver.

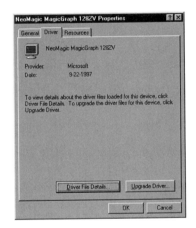

4. Click on Upgrade Driver.

5. Click Next on the first page of the Upgrade Device Driver Wizard.

6. You can now select to search for a driver or display a list of appropriate drivers (see Figure 28.7). Searching gives you more options. Displaying a list provides the list of drivers that Windows 98 currently has in its driver information database, as well as any drivers previously installed for the device. It also provides a Have Disk button if you need to install drivers from a disk. Select Search for a better driver, and then click Next.

7. Select the search options that you wish to invoke by checking the appropriate box (see Figure 28.8). You can search a specific path, Microsoft's Windows Update on the Internet, the CD, or a floppy disk. If you do not know that the driver you want is on a disk somewhere, be sure to check Windows Update. Click on Next.

8. Either you will be informed that the best driver is already installed or you will be informed of your driver options. Click Finish either to install the new driver or to keep the best driver. The method of installation depends, of course, on where the driver was located.

Figure 28.7.
Searching for a better driver provides more options than displaying a list of drivers.

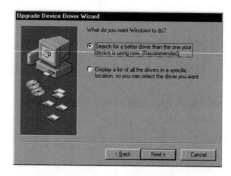

Figure 28.8.
You have several search options available to you.

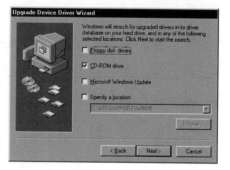

If an enumerator finds a device that is not present, usually you can do nothing. Normally such devices do not take resources away from existing devices and are a benign artifact of the Plug and Play process. If the device does interfere, you can remove it using the Device Manager. Very often, however, you will see the device reappear after the next boot.

Arbitrators can fail by providing a conflicting configuration for a device. A typical symptom of such a conflicting configuration is the absence of a particular device. You might find that the device is not present in the Device Manager tree, or you might just notice that you cannot use the device. You may find the device disabled in the Device Manager tree (shown by a No Entry symbol), or you may go to the device properties and discover that the device is listed as having a conflict (shown by an exclamation point in the tree and a text explanation in the first tab of the properties).

Under these circumstances, you can go to the device's properties and manually alter the settings for the device. Of course, you need to find what the proper settings are. You can check the device's manual, or you can check the configuration software that comes with the device. Sometimes possible settings are written on the device itself, especially if it can be configured with jumpers. Follow these steps after you know the possible settings:

1. Open the Device Manager and select the device for which you want to change settings.
2. Click on Properties and select the Resources tab.

Technical Note: On the Resources tab in the Device Manager, you may see several Base Configurations listed in a drop-down list box labeled Settings based on. Most devices present only one base configuration. However, some present multiple ones. When automatic settings are in force, they are based on a particular base configuration reported by the device as a part of its BIOS properties. If the arbitrator does not properly configure the device, you can try an alternative base configuration if one is available. It may in fact work. My experience has been, however, that most of the time the arbitrator failure occurs because a base configuration that yields appropriate settings in the arbitration process is not available. This might occur because too many devices are clamoring for the same resources, for example. In general, if arbitration fails, I strongly recommend that you manually configure the device using jumpers or its configuration software, and then let the arbitrators work around it. Set its resources manually in the Device Manager to match the resources you have assigned.

3. Select the resource for which you want to change the setting and click Change Setting (see Figure 28.9).

Figure 28.9.
Choose the resource to change and click Change Setting.

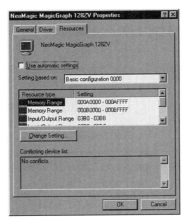

4. Use the dialog box that appears to change the setting, and click OK. You may be told that the setting cannot be changed, and you may have to uncheck the Use Automatic Settings box before you can make changes.

5. Click on OK to close the property sheet.

6. If Windows 98 cannot change the setting on the device by itself, run the configuration software to set the device to the settings you have just configured, or use jumpers to configure the device.

What do you do if you have a card that absolutely must have a certain DMA, IRQ, or I/O setting? You can reserve a setting for it by using the properties of the Computer icon in the Device Manager. Open the Device Manager, select the Computer icon, and click Properties. Use the Reserve Resources tab's Add button to reserve the resource. What this action does is take that resource out of the normal arbitration process, so it is free for you to assign. You should not take this action, however, unless the other options suggested in this section fail. You are interfering with the normal configuration process under Windows 98, and such interference can have unpredictable results.

You may be wondering whether you can disable Plug and Play for an individual device that is causing problems. That is up to the manufacturer of the device, mainly. Some devices—certain SMC network cards, for example—enable you to choose a dynamic or a static configuration. If you have the option, you can set the jumper on the card and let Plug and Play work around its static configuration. You might also be able to use the configuration software for the card to override Plug and Play configuration. In most cases, after you have overridden Plug and Play configuration, the settings for the device will be read from the Registry and used. Be aware, however, that no means are provided for shutting off Plug and Play.

Working with Legacy Hardware

Working with legacy hardware is usually a matter of setting up the hardware to a standard configuration and letting Plug and Play work around the static settings. If Plug and Play cannot work around the settings, you might have to reconfigure each legacy device through trial and error to find a configuration that will work. This procedure is in fact one of the troubleshooting procedures recommended when attaching a Windows CE handheld PC to your Windows 98 desktop. If you cannot communicate with your HPC through one serial port, you try another, and another, and another, until you find one that will work. When you have established communication with the HPC, you then reconfigure your other devices to use the free serial ports. (Compaq HPCs with Windows CE version 1.0 prefer COM1, by the way.)

This process can be extremely frustrating, especially because you normally have to open the case and pull cards to make the changes. Or you may have to boot into MS-DOS mode to run a DOS utility that configures the card. The process is slow and tedious. If you can successfully boot, printing a report of your configuration from the Device Manager can speed up the process. Just click the Print button on the Device Manager tab of the System Control Panel. You get a report that tells you what IRQ channels, DMA channels, and memory addresses are in use. This information can prove very helpful in finding the exact settings for a legacy card.

The most useful strategy is to locate free settings and set the problem card to known free values. If you have a heavily configured machine without a PCI bus, the process really is random. If you have a PCI bus, check your CMOS setup to see which IRQs have been allocated to the PCI bus. Try to locate legacy cards on the IRQs that the PCI bus has not been allocated by the CMOS setup. Then your PCI cards will self-configure using their allocated IRQ settings. If configuration seems absolutely impossible, try replacing the offending device with a Plug and Play PCI device. You may be able to reuse the legacy device in another machine with a less-intense configuration.

Using Microsoft System Information and Dr. Watson

After you have exhausted the troubleshooters—and more often than not you will—you are back to your native troubleshooting skills, your experience, and the need for information. Without information about the system, you cannot begin to guess what is wrong. You need to work through several questions to find the problem. You need to examine all the settings to see whether they are what you expect them to be. You need to raise questions about what would happen if you changed something. What would the implications be? And you need to look for conflicts.

Windows 98 provides two sources of information to help you work through these questions. One we have already seen, the Device Manager. The other is Microsoft System Information, a graphics system information utility shown in Figure 28.10. Using this window, you can acquire information about a variety of resources.

Figure 28.10.
Microsoft System Information provides detailed information about hardware and drivers.

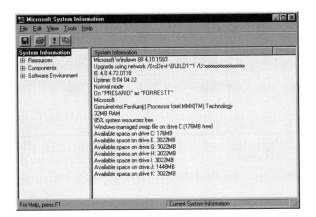

As you can see from the default screen, you can get information about the system itself and all drives it is attached to. If you open the Resources tree, you can get reports about hardware conflicts and device sharing. You can also get information about hardware that has to be forced, or have a resource assigned dynamically when it is in use. In addition, you can learn which regions of memory are claimed by devices, as well as how IRQs, DMA channels, and I/O ports are allocated.

The Components tree gives you complete information about every type of device attached to your system, basically a duplication of what you see in the Device Manager, but organized differently (see

Figure 28.11). System Information gives you the relevant Registry key for the device and reports, with explanatory labels, on all the Registry values associated with the device. Problem devices are also shown in a special report, along with all the information necessary to debug the problem if you have access to error code information for Windows 98. (For such information, check TechNet and the Developer's Library, as well as the Microsoft Web site.) Because a device history is also maintained, you can check when drivers were changed, what they changed from, and what they changed to.

Figure 28.11.
System Information gives you a slightly different view of the Device tree from that given in the Device Manager.

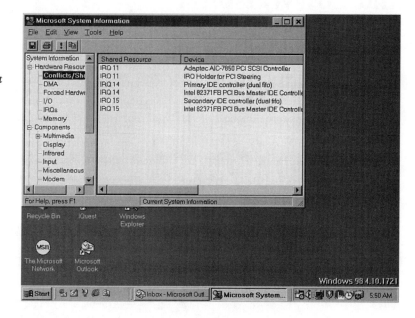

The Software Environment tree gives you access to a list of loaded modules, sorted into 16-bit code and 32-bit code. It provides a list of running tasks, startup programs, active system hooks, and all the OLE registration information. You can save all this information to a text file, so you can keep accurate records for your systems. You can also gain access to all the system tools.

Of some importance to debugging hardware problems is Dr. Watson. This tool has been around in varying forms since Windows 3.1. The latest version, however, gives you more access to information about your system (see Figure 28.12). Dr. Watson runs as an icon in your System Tray. Double-clicking the icon opens the program and takes a snapshot of your system. As you can see from the Advanced view in Figure 28.12, this is a very complete snapshot. Using the File menu, you can choose to save this to a log file; you can also force a new snapshot to be taken.

If your system crashes, Dr. Watson attempts to log the crash. In that log it provides by default a disassembly of the last 10 instructions and the last 100 stack frames. (You can adjust these parameters using View | Options.) Some crashes occur too catastrophically for the log to be completed. But when you get the log, you get a very precise description of what was happening on the system, including a diagnosis based on the error information. The user has an option to input what just happened as a part of the log. You may not be able to understand all that is in the log, but you can get a sense of what hardware devices were involved and what the good Dr. Watson estimates to be the problem. Your programmers for internally developed software may be able to make good use of this information to correct their source code. Extract what you can from the log, and use that information to help you focus your thinking.

Figure 28.12.

The Advanced view of Dr. Watson, showing the variety of information collected in a system snapshot.

The bottom line for hardware troubleshooting is that you can get access to all the information that you need to pin down at least a suspected source for the problem. You need to remember that hardware sometimes cannot report the exact problem back to you through software tools. Be prepared to think about what just happened on the hardware before the error took place, and what just happened afterward. Sometimes your tools may misreport the source of the error.

Using Third-Party Tools

All the preceding discussion assumes that you can boot Windows 98. Where are you left if you can't? With your Emergency Repair Disk (ERD). How do you discover system settings under those circumstances? You use somebody else's utility. In other words, don't throw that copy of DOS and Microsoft Diagnostics (MSD) away yet. You might need it.

Although Windows 98 provides you the capability of making Registry repairs from the ERD, you get no system information utility among the tools provided. Nor is there a copy lurking anywhere on the CD. As a result, you need to keep your favorite DOS system sleuth handy, just in case you need to investigate a system that cannot boot. Third-party vendors, most notably Symantec's Norton Utilities, provide command-line tools for examining systems and fixing all sorts of problems. Often they provide superior configuration backup and restore tools. Watch the market and definitely pick up the tools that meet your needs.

If you do a lot of hardware troubleshooting, you may wish to invest in a few tools. For example, you may want to purchase a board that you can insert into the computer that reads the results of the Power-On System Test (POST) in machines that will not boot. You can then investigate problems with the BIOS, CMOS setup, and low-level hardware even though you may not be able to have much of a functioning system. You might discover, for example, that the BIOS chip has gone bad and needs to be replaced, or that a memory board has gone bad. One such board is known as KickStart and is produced by Landmark International.

You may also want to purchase loopback plugs for all the types of ports that you have on the machines you install. You cannot effectively test a serial, parallel, or SCSI port unless you have a loopback plug. These plugs, available at most electronics stores, enable you to close the connection, just as if you had a device on the port. When you test, you receive ordinary responses back through the port, just as if a device were present.

> **Tip:** The equivalent of a loopback plug for a network cable is a crossover cable. It enables you to connect two computers directly through their network cards.

You may also find specialized debugging software useful. TouchStone Software produces CheckIt in several versions. Windsor Technologies produces PC-Technician. Others appear periodically, and all provide you with a platform for examining and testing the hardware on your system independently of the Windows 98 operating system. They provide suites of diagnostics for checking a variety of devices, and some packages enable you to build suites of tests that you can run sequentially to stress-test a machine.

Be sure to check your documentation and vendor-supplied disks. Often, vendors will provide either disk- or firmware-based diagnostics that enable you to test the hardware, diagnose problems, and take corrective action. Adaptec, for example, provides an excellent SCSI diagnostic tool with its SCSI adapters. Zenith provides a monitor program in its BIOS that enables you to test the machine without running an operating system. Compaq provides diagnostic tools that appear in the Control Panel for its laptops.

> **Tip:** You can learn more about specific troubleshooting tools in *Peter Norton's Complete Guide to Windows 98* (Sams Publishing, 1998).

Working Through the Thinking Process

When you are confronted with a machine that has a hardware problem, before you reach for your tools and rush to find a solution, you need to stop and carefully think through the problem. Most hardware problems manifest themselves as something not working. The user can't reach the network. The user can't print. The modem does not dial, and so forth. You need to follow a careful thinking procedure because hardware cannot communicate with you as easily as software can. You need to follow these sorts of steps:

1. Check for what I like to call the stupid problems. Are all the cables connected? Are all the power switches on? Does the offending device have all its appropriate supplies (paper, toner, and so forth)? Any kinks in the cables or other evidence of cable damage?

2. Power down the machine and open the case. Reseat the cards. Make sure all the internal connections are tight and all the cables are correctly seated.

3. Power the machine back up. If the problem persists, use a diagnostic tool—whichever one you can run—and check the hardware settings. Look for conflicts. If you find any, reset the appropriate setting to end the conflict.

4. Run diagnostic programs, either third-party or those provided by the hardware vendor. Verify that the device is working properly.

5. If the device is in fact working and configured without conflicts, try replacing the driver with a new one, or reinstall the driver. A corrupted or buggy driver could be the problem. Remember, with Windows 98, Microsoft is providing a single Web site to keep you up to date with the latest drivers. Check vendor Web sites as well, however, just in case.

6. Check the revision level of your BIOS. Older BIOS chips sometimes do not support newer devices. Upgrade the BIOS chip if necessary. The vendor can provide upgrade information. For some devices, most notably disk drives, software workarounds are supplied by the vendors.

7. If none of these steps work, replace the device with a similar one from a different vendor. Some devices just are not compatible, either with the operating system, with the software you run, or with other devices. You could have three devices in the machine that work fine independently but cause a failure when they are all three present.

To assist in debugging hardware problems, you may wish to set up a simple laboratory. In that lab, you should have a reference system, one that you know is in good working order. You should have a supply of devices that are known to be good and known to work with your software. You should have a supply of cables that you have verified to be good.

When you bring a machine into such a lab to evaluate a hardware problem, you can engage in simple swap testing. Want to know whether a network card is bad? Swap it into your reference system to see whether it works there. Want to evaluate whether you have a hardware incompatibility? Swap in a known good network card to see whether it works in the problem system. In such an environment, which can be built very cheaply, you can quickly evaluate hardware problems and deliver solutions to your users.

Tip: Remember, time to solution is what is most important to users and managers.

Summary

This chapter has looked at troubleshooting hardware. You have seen a description of the types of tools available to you—the Device Manager, System Information, and Dr. Watson. You have also seen some of the procedures you can apply. Windows 98 provides Plug and Play, and Plug and Play creates a special troubleshooting environment. We have looked at the remedies you can apply to Plug and Play problems. We have also worked through the general troubleshooting thinking process that you have to apply to hardware problems.

On Your Own

Open the Device Manager and examine your Hardware tree. Investigate the properties for each device. Try changing the settings for a device. Get a test machine and delete a couple of devices. Misconfigure a resource. Cause some general havoc on the machine in a controlled sort of way and see what happens. If you know what you did to cause a problem, when you see the problem, you will be more apt to know the cause. Open Microsoft System Information and explore the trees. Save a report of the System Information. Open Dr. Watson and configure its options to suit your needs.

29

Trouble-shooting Network Connections

Chapter 14, "Monitoring Network Performance," described how to monitor your network for problems. You may be wondering what else I might have to say about network troubleshooting. This chapter focuses on responding to network problems in a reactive way rather than the proactive way that monitoring suggests. This assumes that the problem has already occurred, and now your job is to track it down and solve it. It also assumes that you may not have monitoring logs to work from. You will assume in this chapter that the problem has been either sudden and catastrophic or that it has been intermittent and subtle. Both situations are ones where proactive monitoring may not help you see the problem.

To organize our thinking, I will approach troubleshooting from the point of view of the layers in the OSI Reference Model. Although many problems might cross the boundaries of these layers, the layers do represent different components that make up your network. Each set of components can cause unique sorts of problems. This chapter focuses on the following topics:

- Troubleshooting the Physical layer
- Dealing with the Data Link layer
- Working with the Transport and Network layers
- Working with the Session and Presentation layers
- Troubleshooting at the Application layer

Troubleshooting the Physical Layer

Because the Physical layer consists of physical objects and physical connections, strategies for troubleshooting focus on testing the physical equipment. The simplest way to test a physical component is to replace it with a component known to work correctly. If the working component does not experience the problem, you throw out the nonworking component and replace it.

Given the number of separate physical components in a network and their installation, however, this strategy may not work efficiently. A cable strung through a wall conduit is not a trivial thing to replace. You need to be able to separate whether the problem lies with the cable, the connector, the installation of the connector, or the installation of the plug into which you insert the connector. As a result, you often rely on test equipment when you troubleshoot at the Physical layer. The next few sections describe some of the equipment and strategies.

Cables

Cable problems tend to fall into two categories: interruption of service and slowdowns in service. A physically broken cable interrupts service. A cable with too much resistance because of fraying, crimping, or a badly attached connector can cause lost packets or retransmissions or just generally slow service. Cable problems can be very dramatic. Half your network could lose communication with the other half. Or they can be subtle. One workstation may wait an awfully long time to process logons and database transactions. Windows NT Servers might report that they have detected a slow network connection. In any case, you need to rely on the following strategies and tools:

- Physically trace the cable to see whether any breaks are visible. If the cable runs through ceilings or under floors, be sure you find all the surfacing points where connections can be made and broken. If you must rely on wiring diagrams, remember that they might be wrong. I recently watched a network operations crew desperately searching for a nonexistent port 501 on a cabling diagram. They never found the port, but they found a cable that dropped through the ceiling in roughly the correct location for port 501.

- Use a cable tester to verify the integrity of a cable segment. Such testers vary widely in price and features. Some even allow two-way voice communications between technicians at either end of the cable. Such a tester will check whether the cable has broken or shorted and whether its resistance is appropriate.

- Look for any sign of cable damage along the visible portions of the cable. Cables that have frayed, have been bent around sharp angles, or have been crimped may have experienced enough damage to affect signal strength.

- Ask what physical changes have occurred on the network, no matter how trivial. Someone may have moved a machine and disconnected the two ends of the coaxial cable from the T connector rather than disconnecting the T connector from the network interface card.

- Be sure to check run lengths to make sure that design specifications for the cable have not been exceeded (see the maximum run lengths listed in Table 29.1). The cable may not be the problem. Adding a repeater may be the solution.

- Make certain that the cables are appropriately terminated and that terminators are properly grounded. Pulling a terminator off a coaxial cable can cause nasty problems.

When you encounter a problem with interruption of service or slowdown in service, you are wisest to eliminate possible physical causes first. If you don't, you can spend hours troubleshooting only to discover that a cable has been unplugged. One of my current clients recently upgraded their network to switching 100-BaseT hubs. The work was completed over a weekend, and Monday afternoon the network went down. All the Windows 98 machines lost their Novell Client32 Logon dialog boxes and instead saw the Windows Logon dialog box. A flurry of individuals started searching the network, using nicely drawn network maps, trying to find out who did and did not have service. In about 15 minutes, we heard the question "Does anyone see port 501?" being shouted across the cubicles. Port 501 had been replaced by a drop line that ran between floors, not quite the original network plan and certainly representing a cable that had never been mapped. This cable became disconnected when technicians moved a PC they thought was no longer in use, because it belonged to a network administrator who had recently left the company. The machine was in his office, and it looked like his desktop machine. Actually, it was a server, and it had the switch that handled the drop cable. The cable was disconnected during this routine move of a "desktop" system, denying about 40 computers in the application-development area the services of the network.

Table 29.1. Cable types and run lengths.

Cable Type	Maximum Length
Thin coaxial	185 m (607 ft)
Thick coaxial	500 m (1,640 ft)
Unshielded twisted-pair	100 m (328 ft)
Fiber-optic	2 km (6,562 ft)

Network Interface Cards

Network interface cards fall into three categories for troubleshooting: the living, the dying, and the dead. Dead cards are easiest to recognize, because communication both in and out stops. If the card has lights to record link and transmit, both lights are off. At the other end of the connection, either the hub or another PC in the bus topology, the link light is probably out as well, although some cabling schemes may not cause the distant link light to go out. Some cards may show the traffic light on when they encounter a problem; others may show no lights at all. You need to be aware of the particular habits of your network interface cards. Replacing the dead card with a living card solves the problem.

Dying cards are a greater problem. Sometimes the card works intermittently. Sometimes the card can communicate only in one direction. When you face such a problem, you need to determine whether it is a hardware or a software problem. You may need to replace the card, you may need to replace the cable, or you may need to replace its driver. The easiest way to tell whether you have a hardware or a software problem is to see whether replacing the hardware with an identical component solves the problem. If the problem is resolved, you probably had a hardware problem. If the problem continues, you probably have a software problem. With cables, be sure to inspect the connectors. On 10Base-T and other RJ-45 connection schemes, stress on the cable can pull one of the strands in the twisted pairs loose from the connector. (Remember that replacing the cable may be a little more work than it seems if you are wired through the walls.)

In any case, before you pronounce a card either dead or dying, apply these strategies:

- Check all physical connections to the card to make certain they are good.
- Reseat the card in its slot. It may have lost a contact somewhere along its bus connection.
- Clean the dust off the card and out of its general vicinity. Ionized dust can cause problems.
- Make sure the card is receiving power. Cards with light emitting diodes on them always flash their lights when they power up. Remember that power supplies have been known to have bad cables that cause problems with the components they power.
- Check for conflicts between I/O ports and IRQ lines. You should make this inspection manually rather than relying on Plug and Play or the report in the Device Manager. You

must find out what the actual card settings are. The Device Manager places a pound sign (#) in front of the actual hardware settings (see Figure 29.1). You may indeed find that the hardware has one setting but the driver has another. The Device Manager may in fact report both settings accurately, but Plug and Play may not resolve the software settings to match the hardware settings. You may have to change the hardware settings manually.

Figure 29.1.
Windows 98 uses a pound sign to indicate the physical hardware settings.

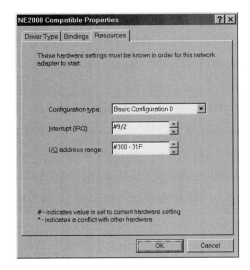

- Make sure that the card has been set to operate at the appropriate transmission speed for your network. Some cards may require manual adjustment to operate at a particular speed. A 100Mbps card that has been configured to function at 10Mbps certainly will appear to be slow.

- If you have a multihomed host, make certain that the network cards do not have conflicting settings, including incorrect bindings. If the cards have an I/O or IRQ conflict, they will not function. If the protocol for communication with the Novell network is bound to the UNIX network card and not the Novell network card, you won't communicate with the Novell network.

- Move the card to a different slot and away from other, potentially noisy components. You may have a bad slot or frequency interference.

Network card problems can be frustrating. PC Card NICs can be cranky devices. If your users are not careful, they can disable their machines by removing the card without first stopping it. (I have seen this error occur even in Microsoft presentations, so even the experts get caught off guard.) Users need to be aware of this matter if they are using docking stations as well. If the docking station cannot manage a hot dismount, you may have some very frustrated users on hand.

Hubs and Repeaters

Hubs are the components that connect one network cable to another in a star topology. The star topology gets its name from the cables radiating out from the hub like rays of starlight. Repeaters are used to strengthen attenuated signals over cable runs longer than the cable is rated for. Hubs and repeaters are combined in devices called repeating hubs, which both connect cables and strengthen the signals crossing among the ports. In general, hubs and repeaters will either work or not work. Ports and connectors on them will be either good or bad.

I have run into occasions where a hub was marginal and caused a significant slowdown of network traffic. On a small LAN (five workstations) the hub caused such slowdowns that Windows NT Workstations trying to make changes in the domain user database experienced timeout errors. The total cable length between the workstation and the server was no more than 64 feet. We diagnosed the problem by tracing the cables and verifying their integrity and then substituting a different hub.

When troubleshooting hubs and repeaters, you need to attend to these issues:

- Make certain that all components in the chain of links have power. Some hubs do not require power; they just serve as concentration points for connections on the network. Others have repeaters to ensure signal strength as packets cross from one port to another. If such repeating hubs lose power, you may encounter problems. Repeaters, of course, require power.

- If only one or two of the components on a hub are having problems, you probably have bad or marginal ports. Try connecting the devices to another port to see whether a new connection resolves the problem. If so, mark the port as bad and replace either the port or the hub when replacement is convenient.

- On laptops and green PCs, check to see whether the Ethernet port can power down. For some reason, perhaps beyond your control, it may not be able to power back up after it has been put to sleep. In such cases, disable the network port from powering down in your power management settings.

- Try substituting a good component to see whether a new component resolves the problem. If the substitution works, replace the old component.

Routers and Beyond

Routers, switches, and other connecting devices link cable segments on a network. Because of their complexity, we can cover only rudimentary troubleshooting for them in a book of this scope. From the point of view of a Windows 98 administrator, these components cause two types of problems: complete loss of service and loss of a few connections.

When you face complete loss of service, chances are the router is down. It has either lost power or its controlling software has crashed. You need to contact your WAN team and ask them to resolve the problem. Typically, they will restore power and reboot the router, or they will just reboot the router, whichever is appropriate. On some occasions, they must reload or reconfigure the routing software.

Partial loss of service relates to a different issue. Some devices send out so many packets that they can saturate a WAN link with nothing but command and control packets. NetWare servers broadcast a Server Advertising Protocol (SAP) packet once every 60 seconds. If you have enough NetWare servers on either side of a 56Kbps WAN line, you may never be able to push data across the line, because the SAP packets are hogging the line. The usual solution is to filter such packets at the router so that they do not cross the WAN link. Such packets do, however, have a purpose. If they do not cross the WAN link, a service available on one side may not be available on the other.

If you have a disappearing server or network service, ask your WAN team to determine what they are filtering and whether the filters are preventing the services from advertising themselves on your side of the WAN. The WAN team may have to allow a packet through on occasion to allow communication between your workstations and the network service. Or you may have to work out an alternative method of communicating with the server—such as an on-demand dial-up connection—if you cannot work out the control issues with the WAN team.

With WAN connections, you have an additional layer of possible problems in between you and the destination WAN—namely, the service provider that provides the telephone lines. Keep in mind that the service provider can change configuration or hardware and thereby introduce problems for you. Simultaneously as you work on the problem within your organization, you need to call your service provider to find out whether they have made any changes.

Dealing with the Data Link Layer

At the Data Link layer, you are dealing with two types of components: the NDIS layer provided by Microsoft to provide a uniform interface to network interface cards, and the mini drivers that link the network interface cards to the NDIS layer. You may also have to deal with configuring clients and servers to match the expectations that particular drivers impose. Primarily, you are concerned about three issues: packet types, because the Data Link layer packs the frames for transmission; access methods; and driver bugs. Symptoms will range from complete failure to connect to intermittent failures of varying types. Check the following issues if you are experiencing problems:

- If you have complete failure to communicate, and the Physical layer seems okay, check to make sure the access method of the network interface card matches that or your network. (Check the specifications to find out what type of card it is and how it accesses the network.) Token-ring cards will not communicate with Ethernet networks, for example.

- Make certain that the packet types are set correctly at the clients and servers. NetWare, for example, has used several different packet formats over its lifetime. You need to make certain that your clients and servers are trying to read the same packet format. You set the packet type using the property sheet for the NetWare client (see Figure 29.2). Check the documentation for your server software to see what the packet type is.

- If you are experiencing intermittent problems, check for driver upgrades, and upgrade the card driver to the latest version.

Figure 29.2.
Make sure that your clients and servers are trying to send and receive the same packet format.

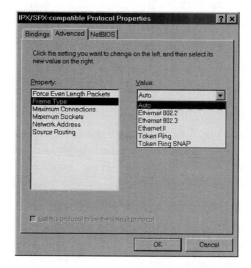

Working with the Transport and Network Layers

At the transport and network layers in the OSI model, you are working with the software that determines how packets will be created, and how they will be addressed for transmission and delivery. Because this is fairly high-level software, the kinds of failures you will experience are related to software corruption, absence of components, and duplicate addressing.

For two computers to communicate on a network, they must share at least one networking protocol. This requirement is often expressed as the statement that you must have a valid protocol path between two computers. The protocol must be bound to the network interface cards over which the communication must take place. Windows 98 handles bindings for you automatically. You need to make certain, however, that the protocols are installed. As you have seen, the first tab of the Network Control Panel applet enables you to install, remove, and configure protocols (see Figure 29.3). Check the list of installed protocols to make certain that an appropriate protocol is present. If not, click Add to install one.

Figure 29.3.

Check the Network Control Panel applet to make certain an appropriate protocol is installed.

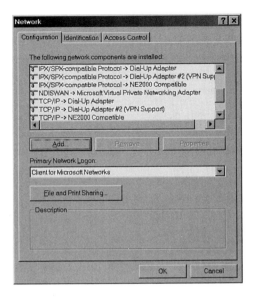

Windows 98 creates bindings automatically. You occasionally may need to adjust them manually. You do so by first inspecting the binding list in the Network Control Panel applet's Configuration tab. You need to see a binding between the network card for the communication under consideration and the protocol for that communication. If one does not exist, remove the protocol, reboot, and then again add the protocol to the list. If this action does not resolve the issue, check the Binding tab in the properties for the binding listed. Select the binding and click Properties, and then select the Binding tab. Verify that the check box for the client attempting the communication is checked. If this action does not resolve the problem, you probably face a problem at the Physical or Data Link layers.

Under some protocols, notably TCP/IP, you can experience address conflicts. They announce themselves either at the server or the client, or both, by presenting a dialog box or a text message that says you have an address conflict. Checking the address of the machine announcing the problem usually reveals the address of the problem machine. On Novell servers, the problem address is included in the address problem message. However, IP address conflicts are announced at a Windows NT Server even when the server does not participate in the conflict. Although the event log will reveal more information, including the problem address, resolving the conflict is not easy.

To resolve the conflict, you need to know where the offending address is on your network. Under most circumstances, the offending address has been mis-set during configuration. As a result, the records relating to the problem address will not show the problem address. Your records will show each machine addressed in a nonconflicting way. The only solution is a long Easter egg hunt, in which you visit each machine and check its address. You may be able to guide your search by checking the local subnet first, but you must remember that the offending address could be a router, a server, or some other such device. If you are extremely lucky, you will check the machine that announces the problem and find that it was set to an address that does not match the records. Resetting it to the correct address resolves the problem. If you are not lucky, you have a long effort of remapping all the addresses on your network. Woe be unto those who find multiple conflicting addresses on the network.

To limit addressing conflicts, you can use Dynamic Host Configuration Protocol (DHCP) to automatically assign nonconflicting addresses to the machines on your network. This is a wise step. You will need to maintain static addresses on routers and servers, but when you have an address conflict, you have far fewer machines to check.

> **Tip:** If you use DHCP on Windows NT Server 4.0, be sure to install Service Pack 3. A bug in the DHCP software can allow two machines to claim the same address at the same time. Service Pack 3 resolves this bug.

Working with the Session, Presentation, and Application Layers

Problems at the Session, Presentation, and Application layers can have many and mysterious causes. An application can fail because of lack of memory, lack of disk storage, a bug in an API, and a host of other reasons. Sessions can disconnect for similar reasons. (Because the Presentation layer is not implemented in most networks, we will have little to say about it in this section.) To troubleshoot at these levels, you work by ruling out what the problem is not in hopes of finding the culprit component or setting that has produced the problem. In general, you need to check these issues:

- **Hardware compatibility.** Your clients and servers need to be on the Hardware Compatibility Lists for both your operating systems and your applications.

- **Drivers.** You need to have the latest drivers installed for all devices, because these drivers will theoretically contain the fewest bugs. Sometimes this assumption does not hold, but in most cases you will find it correct.

- **Memory.** Your clients and servers need adequate supplies of both. Keep in mind that vendors often lowball their memory requirements. The best policy is to buy more than you think you need, and always make certain that you can add more.

- **Disk storage.** Your drives need enough storage space to handle both application and operating system needs. Always keep 100MB free for padding, because temporary files are always necessary. Having low free space can limit performance.

- **Processing power.** Your processor needs to be fast enough and have the instruction set that your applications and operating systems expect. For Windows 98, Pentium processors are adequate; an 80486 is a minimum. Some applications require particular revisions of the Pentium and compatible series—in particular, the MMX extensions. Make sure that you have what you need, and make it the fastest chip possible.

- **Client software.** You need to have appropriate clients loaded on all workstations. You may even need to have particular revisions of certain clients to meet application requirements.

If you are struggling with output devices such as printers or fax machines, look at these issues:

- **Power.** Make sure the device is in fact turned on. This is one of the most common causes of device failure, especially for user-accessible devices.
- **Device selection.** Make sure the user is choosing the correct device, or that the correct device has been mapped for the user's use.
- **Permissions.** Make certain that the correct permissions have been set for the device. Make sure the user is a member of the correct groups for using the device.
- **Firmware configuration.** Make sure the device firmware settings are correct. You can't expect to print on a device that has been told in the firmware it is a copy and fax machine only.
- **Drivers.** You need the latest driver for the device. Be aware, however, that on some occasions application software may demand a particular driver revision.
- **Protocols.** If the device requires a particular protocol for communication, make sure that the clients and servers, as well as the device, have the protocol installed.
- **Cables.** Make sure the cables are plugged in and in good shape.

In a multivendor environment, check these issues:

- Your computers need to have clients appropriate to each vendor network they access installed. Windows 98 computers, for example, communicate by default with Microsoft servers. You need to make certain that the NFS client is installed if you add UNIX servers to this environment.
- Your servers need to have the network services required by your clients installed and running. DOS NetWare clients cannot communicate with Windows NT Servers, for example, unless File and Printer Services for NetWare (FPNW) is installed and running on the server.
- If you have gateways, they must be correctly configured and running. If you are using the Windows NT Gateway Service for NetWare, for example, to make NetWare resources available, no one sees these resources when the gateway is not running.
- When you use client/server applications, you need to check that both ends of the software (the client and the server) are running and also correctly configured. You may have middleware software that must also be configured and running.

- In multivendor environments, users must more strictly meet operating procedures. Sometimes the procedures must be exact for software and hardware to work. Verify that users are meeting the necessary requirements.

In addition, a very important application runs at the Application layer: the network logon software. Troubleshooting logon problems can be frustrating, because so many different possibilities are involved. If users (or administrators) experience trouble with logging on, check these issues:

- **Typing.** Users often mis-type their account name or password.
- **Caps lock.** Passwords are often case-sensitive.
- **Account.** It must be present in the account database and enabled. In most cases, for a logon taking place from one machine to another over a network, requiring a user to change his password prior to logging on will functionally disable the account.
- **Rights, abilities, and permissions.** The user must have been granted the right to access the resource. The user must also have the operating system abilities, usually preassigned to specific groups, to use the resource. The user must also have the permissions appropriate for making use of the resource.

The Session, Presentation, and Application layers of your network are probably the most difficult to troubleshoot. They are the layers where problems can be poorly defined, where one problem can mask another, and where users interact with the software to create problems where problems probably should not exist. At these layers, troubleshoot carefully, making only one change at a time. Because of the complex interactions involved, making too many changes at once may just alter the characteristics of the problem in confusing ways rather than lead you toward a solution.

Working Through a Scenario

Networking problems can be very frustrating to troubleshoot. Imagine a user who comes to you and says that she cannot access the server named All_Home_Dir. She has effectively lost access to her data, because her home directory is on that server. She gets an error message when her logon script attempts to attach to the server, and the message states that a permanent connection to All_Home_Dir was not available.

Your instincts should tell you that this could be a physical problem, an addressing problem, or an application problem. The question of which it is can be very difficult to pin down. First, do yourself a favor and quickly check the physical connection between the user's computer and the network. Is the link light on her network card lit? You discover that it is. At this point, you should attempt a quick check of whether the server has a physical connection to the network. Try to attach to the server from another workstation in the same subnet. You find that you can, so the server probably has a valid connection to the network as well. You may have a cabling problem or a device problem somewhere between the two computers, but these quick checks enable you to discount that possibility.

Next, reboot the problem machine into MS-DOS mode. Press the F8 key during the boot, and choose Command Prompt from the menu. Depending on your protocols, you have a couple of tools that can help sort out the problem. If you are using IPX/SPX or NetBEUI, execute a NET USE command to map a drive to the server. If you can connect at this level, the problem is not with drivers or Kernel-level software—it is somewhere above. If you have TCP/IP, try pinging the server. Execute the PING command using the server's name first. If you get a response, you come to the same conclusion as you did with the NET USE command. If pinging the name fails, ping the IP address of the server. If you can ping the address but not the name, you have a name resolution problem. In this case, you find that you can connect to the server at the DOS prompt, and you can map a drive to it.

Next you try booting the machine and running the logon script. The same problem recurs. You check the Network Neighborhood and find that the server is present. If you double-click on the server, however, you discover that you cannot connect even to get a list of shares.

At this point, you have to suspect some component that loads after the network drivers and the core of the operating system, or you have to suspect a server problem. You have a sense that you are working at the Network, Session, or Transport protocol level, because the issue seems to be related to addressing or servicing connections. The software components at these levels are your redirectors and transport protocols. At this point, a practical strategy is to remove the redirector and reinstall it, making sure to reboot after the removal and after the reinstallation. You may have a corrupt network component. If replacing the redirector does not solve the problem, you can try replacing your protocols. If these actions fail, you need to check the server for problems.

In this case, replacing client-side software had no effect. The server in question is a Windows NT Server, so you begin investigating the configuration of its networking components. In the Server service properties, you discover that the server has been set to minimize the memory allocated to the Server service. (You check by opening the Network Properties, selecting Server in the component list, and clicking on the Properties button.) At this setting, the server can handle only about 10 connections. Unfortunately, you are expecting 70 users to do file sharing on this server. As a result, you reset the property to maximize throughput for file sharing. The problem goes away.

To troubleshoot on networks, you sometimes need a crystal ball. Problems don't always generate inherently informative symptoms or error messages. Experience is the only way you will learn to recognize problems for what they are. Just keep plugging away at the problems. Within a year, you will have a strong sense of where to look on your network when you see particular types of problems.

Summary

This chapter has focused on troubleshooting network problems. We have focused on problems that monitoring and proactive prevention are less likely to address. As a result, problems strike out of the blue, or they strike intermittently with few traces left in monitoring logs. We have focused on how to trace problems with the physical network, the Data Link layer, the protocols, and the applications and APIs that make up your networking software.

On Your Own

If you haven't got one, build a map of your network. Trace its cables and ports. Review the wiring closets and server rooms to see how things are connected. Learn how your LAN links to your WAN, which service providers are involved, and what hardware manages these connections. Try installing a Windows 3.x driver for a network device to see how it impacts network performance. Try removing a protocol to see what resources become unavailable to you. Change the firmware settings on a printer to see how they affect network printing. Change the rights and permissions for a dummy user to see how rights and permissions affect access to resources.

30 Investigating the Registry

Peter Norton®

For better or worse, with the advent of Windows for Workgroups, Microsoft invented the Registry. (In Windows for Workgroups, it was known as the registration database.) Users and system administrators have been frustrated by the change from INI files ever since. Just when you had mastered INI files, you had a new beast to get used to. Microsoft's official support policy is straightforwardly that, if you have a problem because you edited the Registry, you are on your own. In addition, neither the Windows 95 nor the Windows 98 Registries have been fully documented. Nevertheless, Registry tips, tricks, fixes, workarounds, and whatevers are recommended by all the gurus.

How you deal with the Registry is the subject of this chapter. Like it or not, we must understand the Registry structure in order to troubleshoot Windows 98 effectively. We need to know what is safe to edit, what is not safe to edit, and how to examine the Registry to find potential problems. Problems do occur that require Registry editing. Some piece of software ceases to show all of its menus. Or some set of functions in an application cease to respond. A file format ceases to be associated. On boot, Windows 98 reports that a file referenced in the Registry is no longer present. Or some similar problem that is obviously configuration related appears. You can enter the Registry and flip a single switch to restore a full menu structure in many cases. You can rebuild a file association using the Explorer's View | Options dialog box. You can delete references to the missing file, or restore the file, to solve the latter problem.

As you prepare to use the Registry to resolve problems, you need to be aware of certain issues. Making mistakes can have disastrous consequences. I will show you how to avoid costly mistakes and to edit the Registry safely. This chapter covers the following topics:

- The structure of the Registry
- Backing up the Registry
- Editing the Registry
- Software entries in the Registry
- Hardware entries in the Registry
- Solving Registry problems

Understanding the Registry Structure

Microsoft created the Registry because of the inadequacies of INI files. The main INI files were System.ini, which configured the Windows operating environment, and Win.ini, which configured applications and the user environment. These INI files are still with us for compatibility purposes. Sixteen-bit applications need to see them to properly initialize. And Windows 98 needs to see them to learn about certain devices necessary to 16-bit applications. In fact, Config.sys and Autoexec.bat are present for the same reason. Windows 98 reads them to learn which 16-bit drivers to install and what environment to set up for 16-bit compatibility. You can enter settings for the real-mode operating system in these files, so that when real-mode compatibility is required, the configuration is correct. However, INI file structure is inadequate for describing the configuration of Windows 98 as an operating system. Microsoft's solution to this inadequacy, the Registry, subsumed the function of `Autoexec.bat` and `Config.sys` as well.

The INI file structure functionally can have two levels of organization. Sections are denoted by entries enclosed in brackets, such as [386enh]. Within each section are entries of the form name=value (`run=clock.exe`, for example). This structure works well as long as each system has only one user. When you want two users to share a system, and one wants the Hot Dog Stand color scheme and the other wants Black Leather, you would need to have two sets of INI entries, one for each user. Or you would need separate INI files for each user. In either case, you are introducing at least a third level to the INI hierarchical structure, and plain-text INI files are not very good at handling that type of structure.

Microsoft also heard many complaints about the Windows INI files being slow to load. In addition to the goal of setting up a hierarchy of entries, they had the goal of speeding up access. One way to speed up access, of course, was to build a hierarchy. As you search a hierarchy, you start at the entry point. Your next search decision is which of the next level nodes to choose. As soon as you choose the appropriate node, you have limited your search by excluding the need to examine entries stored under other nodes. So long as the hierarchy is well structured so that information always appears under a particular node, searches can become very fast.

Microsoft solved its INI file problems in two ways. First, they structured the configuration information for Windows 95 as a binary tree database. That is, they built a hierarchy. They made it a binary code file as well to make it fast to search. Second, they divided the entries in the database into two files, one for the system and one for the user. The result was called the Windows 95 Registry. The files that comprised it were `system.dat` for the system entries and `user.dat` for the user settings. Each user had her own personal `user.dat` file. When the system started, the files were merged in memory to form the complete Registry.

Windows 98 continues to use the Registry structure introduced in Windows 95: nodes of keys that can hold values. What has changed is the number and kinds of settings under various nodes. Although it is nearly impossible to document every entry made in the Registry, I can give you a sense of its general structure. In most cases, having an understanding of the Registry structure is more important to troubleshooting than knowing individual value names and settings.

Technical Note: As a major step in moving toward a unified version of Windows, Microsoft has been promising to merge the code base for Windows 9x and Windows NT. With the advent of Win32, then Win32s, and then subsequent versions of the Windows Software Developer's Kit, the code that comprise Windows programs became unified. Opening a file in Windows 9x and Windows NT was accomplished with the same function, namely `FileOpen`, using the same parameters. Under Windows NT, however, the function checks for permission to read the file. Under Windows 9x it does not.

continues

The central obstacle in merging two versions of Windows was settling on a standard Registry structure. Windows 95 did not locate configuration information under the same key structure as Windows NT. Windows NT could contain different settings, permitting different functionality, than Windows 95. With Windows 98, Microsoft has generally provided the same key structure in the Registry. Functions that were available in Windows NT became available and documented in Windows 98, like automatic logon.

A few differences still exist, however, and I would expect that they will be resolved in Windows NT 5.0. The Windows 98 Registry contains a switch for disabling access to the command prompt, for example. The Windows NT Registry does not—at least not a documented switch. When these conflicts are resolved, Microsoft will configure multiple versions of Windows from identical Registries.

To see the Registry structure, you must use a tool called the Registry Editor. To run the Registry Editor, type **regedit** in the Run dialog box, which you open from the Start menu. When the editor starts, you see the display shown in Figure 30.1.

Figure 30.1.
The Registry Editor displays the internal structure of the Registry database.

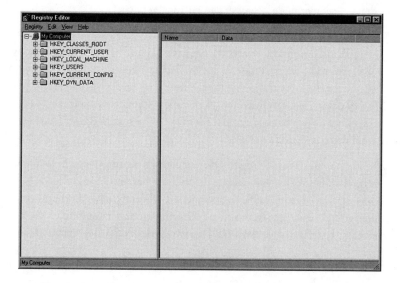

When you see the initial screen of the Registry Editor, you are viewing the highest level of organization within the Registry. The highest-level node is called My Computer. Below that node are six subnodes, each of which is formally called a key. These keys represent the highest-level entry points into the hierarchy of the Registry's settings.

Each key may contain two kinds of entries. It must contain at least one value, the equivalent of a setting in the old INI files. Every value has two parts: the name and the data. Very often the name will be (Default) and the value will be described as (Value Not Set). Most values, however, consist of a unique name assigned by the individual who created the value and data that represents the setting associated for the operating system or application software that reads the value.

Keys may also contain subkeys, which must contain a value and may also contain subkeys, as shown in Figure 30.2. The layering of keys and subkeys gives the Registry its hierarchical structure. As you navigate down through the subkeys, you head toward the destination value you seek. Because the keys are arranged into a hierarchy, only subkeys related to the parent key are located below a key. That is, the Registry has a semantic system that organizes it. Keys have meanings. They represent categories of related settings. If I need to search for all the keys for Microsoft Word, I begin at HKEY_CLASSES_ROOT, which represents all the software settings, look for the subkey that represents Word, and then look for the values that I need. You refer to a key and the hierarchy of keys and values below, a branch of the Registry tree, if you will, as a hive of keys.

Figure 30.2.
The Registry provides
a hive of keys and
subkeys to navigate.

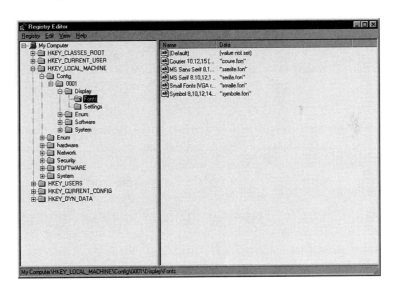

Table 30.1 presents the highest-level keys and the meanings associated with them. If you need to work in the Registry, you need to be aware of the basic categorizations these keys represent.

Table 30.1. The highest-level Registry keys and their categories.

Key	Category
HKEY_CLASSES_ROOT	Software settings (points to HKEY_LOCAL_MACHINE\Software\ Classes)
HKEY_CURRENT_USER	The logged on user's settings (points to HKEY_USERS\Username)
HKEY_LOCAL_MACHINE	The settings for the computer

continues

Table 30.1. continued

Key	Category
HKEY_USERS	List of users who have logged in
HKEY_CURRENT_CONFIG	The currently active system settings (points to a subkey of HKEY_LOCAL_MACHINE\Config)
HKEY_DYN_DATA	Statistics for the System Monitor

The structure of the Registry is not quite a simple hierarchy. Really, only two of the preceding keys hang directly below the My Computer node, HKEY_USERS and HKEY_LOCAL_MACHINE. The others point to particular nodes somewhere below these two nodes. They provide a convenient entry point, or alias, to that segment of the hierarchical tree structure.

In addition, the Registry contains linked sets of settings. Word, for example, places several sets of keys in at least three places in the Registry. Each set of these keys has a reference to the highest-level key in the other locations. As a result, any member of the ring can locate the other members by reaching out to these shared locations. If you are searching, after you find one set of Word settings, you can immediately find all the rest.

Both the operating system and applications access the Registry frequently. A good part of the operating system load procedure is to read the Registry and to set up interaction with the hardware according to the parameters found in the Registry. The Device Manager reads all its information from the Registry. Applications read the Registry when they load to locate their initialization settings. Each time you double-click a data file to launch an application and load the data, the Registry is checked. It stores all the instructions, for example, for what action to take when a file of a particular extension is double-clicked. When system policies are in effect, the Registry is written to as policy settings are applied.

Obviously, the Registry is a very busy set of files. Much of it is in memory constantly. One reason you need to shut a Windows 98 system down properly is that the Registry items in memory are flushed to disk as the system closes down. The Registry is also one very important database. You need to take very good care of it.

Using Registry Checker and Backing Up

Two kinds of problems face you routinely as your systems interact with the Registry. First, the Registry can grow to contain outdated entries. If you install software and delete it, chances are that you have left behind orphaned keys and values in the Registry. Uninstall programs usually end with a note that says some components could not be removed. Chances are they removed the files, but not the Registry entries. Or the software components are shared among other applications, and you now have references within its set of values to the software you just deleted.

For Windows 95, Windows 98, and Windows NT, Microsoft has created a free utility called Regclean to correct this problem. This utility searches your Registry, finds the outdated settings, and prompts you to adopt a solution, even suggesting a "best" solution. Regclean can even detect incorrect values and suggest the correct values. Regclean is available at the Microsoft Web site and as a part of TechNet. Make sure, however, that you have the most recent version. Recently, an update came out that caused Registry corruption. You want the latest, greatest release, as a result.

Be aware that Regclean has its limitations. First, it checks a set of predetermined keys and values. Regclean could never have appropriate knowledge about every key and value that could possibly be in your Registry. You could have created custom software, for example, that stores keys and values, and Microsoft would know nothing of how you have created these structures. As a result, it checks a predefined set of keys and values only. Also be aware that Regclean can create an undo file, just in case it leaves you worse off than before you ran it. You can return to your previous set of problems from your new set of problems.

The problem of corruption I just mentioned is the second problem that you routinely face with the Registry. Power outages, improper shutdowns, bad hair days, and similar events can cause Registry corruption. Keys can get deleted, values can be set to mysterious settings, and whole Registry files can be damaged so they won't load. Users can also accidentally delete Registry files, or open them in a programmer's editor and save them in the wrong file format.

For Windows 98, Microsoft has introduced Registry Checker as a system utility. If you need to run it manually, it is available from the Tools menu in the System Information utility. However, you should rarely need to run it. Registry Checker runs each time the operating system loads. It checks your current Registry for corruption. If it finds any, it loads a backup copy of your Registry. Then it once again backs up your Registry. Registry Checker will not remove orphaned keys and values, however. You should occasionally use Regclean on your systems, as a result.

Although the automatic Registry backup is a good feature, see Chapter 20, "Protecting Data," for other strategies that you should employ for backing up the Registry. The automatic backup can fail, especially when the corruption is caused by electrical or mechanical failure.

Editing the Registry Entries

Having shown you the Registry Editor, I have to admit that the purpose of the Registry Editor is to permit you to add, delete, rearrange, rename, or change Registry keys, values, and data. Having said that, I am going to participate in the bizarre duality that surrounds editing the Registry. Although you can edit the Registry, you should do so only as a last resort.

Warning: The Windows 98 Registry is at this time undocumented. Although you can study the Registry using the Registry Editor, although you can learn from what documentation exists, although you might get away with many innocent edits, you should edit the Registry only when there is absolutely no other choice. Editing the Registry can cause catastrophic system or application failure. You could lose data, and you could lose the operating system. Reinstallation is often the only recovery available.

Registry corruption can create very serious problems. Historically, even reinstallation has failed to repair all instances of Registry corruption. I had one Windows 95 system that, on boot, would throw up a text screen that announced a missing file. It said that The following file referenced in either SYSTEM.INI or the Registry is missing. Unfortunately, no filename appeared after the message tag. The remainder of the message told me that I had probably deleted an application or moved an application file. I should rerun the Uninstall program for that application, or I should reinstall the application that owns the file.

The only difficulty was that I had not deleted or moved files or applications. I tried Regclean. Actually, I ran it three times, until it reported absolutely no problems with the Registry. The same error message appeared when I rebooted. I went through SYSTEM.INI, commenting out each line and rebooting. The problem remained. I went through the Registry manually, verifying that each file referenced was in the path mentioned. Every reference was correct. The problem remained.

It was an innocuous problem. Pressing any key after the error appeared allowed the system to boot and function normally. The only complete solution I ever found, however, was to format the drive, reinstall Windows, and reinstall all applications. Sometimes Registry problems can be very difficult to solve.

Editing operations in the Registry Editor are very straightforward. Place the focus on a key name or value name at the entry-point key level or below. If the focus is on the My Computer node, you will not be able to edit. Then follow one of these basic procedures:

- To delete an object, press the Delete key and confirm by clicking Yes in the Confirmation dialog box.
- To add an object, select Edit | New on the menu, and select the type of object you want to add (Key, String Value, Binary Value, or Dword Value). The editor assumes that you know what data type you need if you are entering a value. (If you don't know, you should not be adding the item.) Type the name in the edit box after the new object is added.

Note: The data types in the Registry represent the storage of the data within the database of the Registry. A Key data type allocates space appropriate for the storage of a key name. String Value as a data type allocates space to store a sequence of ASCII characters and a terminating null character. A `Binary Value` allocates enough storage space to store a binary number. A `Dword Value` allocates enough storage to hold an unsigned long integer (32 bits).

- To set a value, choose Edit | Modify from the menu, or double-click on the value. Fill in the data in the editor that appears. You must enter the correct data type. The Registry Editor will not check to make sure that you have entered an appropriate value. Click OK.

Warning: All changes you make to the Registry in the Registry Editor are immediate and final. There is no Undo option, or exit without saving changes. If you do not remember what was there before you made the change, you are straightforwardly out of luck.

- To rearrange objects, use the Import and Export options on the File menu, with an intervening delete of a key. You will Export a key and its subkeys (also called a hive) to a text file with a `.REG` extension, edit the file to reflect the new key organization, delete the key you want to replace in the Registry Editor, and then Import the revised key structure.

  I have a very simple dictum in dealing with this process. If you are sure how the keys are represented in the text file without my help and dead certain about why you are attempting this operation, you may want to go ahead and try. If you are developing software and experimenting with different Registry configurations, this operation may be of value to you, and only when undertaken on a machine whose configuration you can afford to trash.

Remember, editing the Registry to solve a problem is the last-resort strategy. I see only four times when you should plan to undertake this strategy:

- Microsoft says you should do so and gives you a step-by-step procedure to follow.
- One of your application vendors says you should do so and gives you step-by-step instructions.
- One of your application developers, preferably the one who designed the Registry configuration for the application says you should do so, and preferably does it for you.
- You have a problem that is annoying enough that you have become desperate enough to try editing the Registry, no matter what the risks.

At the end of this chapter, I will walk you through one of the last types of problems.

Registering Software in the Database

If you are going to go mucking about in my Registry with me at the end of the chapter, you are going to need some background about how applications register themselves in the Registry. The first principle of understanding software registration is that Windows 98 must have a unique way of identifying each software component. Windows 98 does not trust text strings for this purpose. Windows 98 does not know Word 97 as "Word 97." Instead, it relies on a unique number, called a class ID, to identify Word. Programmers use a utility called UUGEN to create class IDs, or they get them assigned from Microsoft, in which case Microsoft uses the utility to generate the number. Because of the algorithm UUGEN uses to create the number, each software component is virtually guaranteed to have a unique number identifier assigned to it.

Software registers itself in at least five places in the Registry. One place is at HKEY_LOCAL_MACHINE\Software\Classes\CLSID. Here the software enters a key, the name of which is its class ID. Under this key, the software component registers additional keys (see Figure 30.3). Typically, two items appear, the server (either in process or out of process) that services the software and the program ID. The server is the code that runs as a part of this component. It may be the application program itself, or only a component of it. In addition, it may be an application designed only to run within the environment of another application. Typically the server entry is a path to an executable file or a dynamic link library. The server is identified as in process if it runs within the calling application's address space. The server is identified as out of process if it runs in its own address space as a separate program. The key name, for example, InProcServer, identifies this role. The program ID (typically stored under the ProgID key) is the string name associated with this program. This name serves as the name of this software component that is human readable and human rememberable. In addition, an application may store other keys here as its designers see fit.

Figure 30.3.

Software registers critical information under the class ID key.

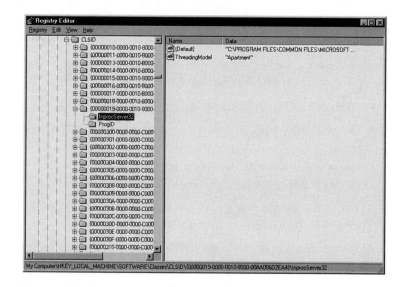

Under HKEY_LOCAL_MACHINE\Software\Classes, actually quite deeply buried in the Registry structure, you will find keys named after each program ID text string, as shown in Figure 30.4. Settings unique to this software component are stored here. Typically, one key identifies the default icon, if there is one. Another identifies a QuickView filter, if there is one. Typically, there is an entry for the associated class ID, and the shell commands available for the component, which define what happens when drag-and-drop or double-click operations take place. Typically, you see options for open and print, to handle the double-click of the application's icon, and dragging data from the application to a printer icon. Other settings may be located here as well. This entry has two links to others in the set associated with the software component: the program ID used as the key name and the class ID stored in a subkey.

Figure 30.4.
The program ID key defines typical behavior and associated software components.

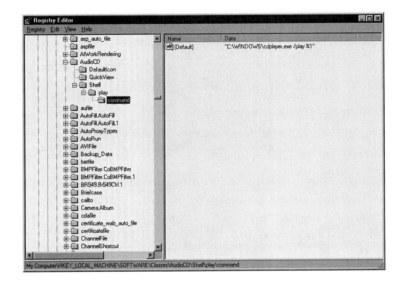

Also under HKEY_LOCAL_MACHINE\Software\Classes you find keys named after application extensions (see Figure 30.5). Here is where file associations are stored. The Registry maintains one such key for each file extension, and maintains subkeys underneath it that contain the association information for the file type identified by the extension. Typically in the .*xxx* key, you see values that are peculiar to managing that type of application file. The application designers have provided these values, and usually register them during application installation. You may find a Shell key, containing subkeys for the default commands associated with the software component. You will also find a ShellExt subkey that contains one subkey for each shell extension used by the program. In addition, you will find ShellNew subkeys. These keys contain information needed by the application to understand how to interpret applying the default actions to the file. For example, Word's registrations contain a key for each Word component type (in this case, actually different Word versions, including WordPad). These keys contain values that identify which file format to use in launching documents of that type.

Tip: A shell extension is a program that extends the functionality of the Explorer shell. The Explore from Here option for context menus provided in the Powertoys is a shell extension, for example.

Figure 30.5.

Additional keys identify file associations and related information.

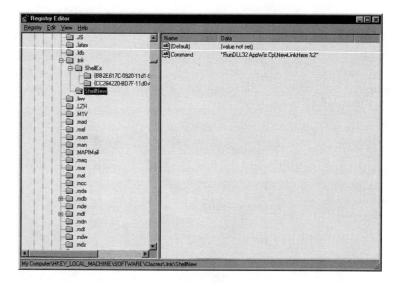

Before I explain the final type of information registered by applications, I would like to give you a sense of what the preceding linked sets of information do. Suppose I have Word 97 installed on my machine, and a friend gives me an old Word for Windows 2.0 document file as a gift. If I copy it to my drive and double-click on the file to open Word and load the document, here is roughly what happens:

1. Windows 98 receives the double-click message and processes it through its code.

2. During processing of the double-click message, Windows 98 retrieves the file extension of the Word 2.0 file (.doc) from the file and looks it up in the Registry.

3. If there are component-type registrations associated with the extension registration, Windows 98 returns to the file and queries it to obtain further information, if possible. In this case, Windows 98 discovers a Word.Document type, and looks it up in the Registry. It also queries the file for any other component information that might be available in the file.

4. If neither a component type nor more information is available, Windows 98 launches the application whose class ID is associated with the file in extension registration and passes the name of the file to the application launched so that the application might open the file and display its contents for editing. Windows 98 also locates any registered shell extensions and loads them as necessary.

5. When a component type is located, Windows uses the information there to continue loading the file. The CLSID key stored in this set of registrations for DOC files points to the CLSID registration for Word, whichever version is installed. The CurVer key identifies the current document type for this executable, which more than likely is not a Word 2.0 document. The presence of this key announces that a conversion must take place in this example.

6. Windows 98 uses the information stored under the CLSID registration for Word to find the executable file path, launch the application, set up the Word environment, locate the appropriate converter, and complete the Windows 98 portion of the load. Word also uses this information to control its processing of the file.

7. After all these steps are finished, I review my friend's file.

Having reviewed the linked set of Registry settings used by an application, you must remember that applications may store information in two other Registry locations. Users may have individual configurations for each application they use. These settings are stored under a software key below the username key for that user under HKEY_USERS. In addition, you may find another key for an application under HKEY_LOCAL_MACHINE\Software, equal in rank to both the Classes and CLSID subkeys. Applications typically store machine-specific facts about their installation, such as the path to the installation files, under such a key.

Registering Hardware in the Database

Hardware is registered under HKEY_LOCAL_MACHINE. What is registered and how largely depends on decisions made by the hardware manufacturer. Windows 98 itself stores the information it needs to be able to boot and to interrogate the hardware for Plug and Play purposes. Some of this information is stored under the Config subkey. More is stored under the Enum subkey, the purpose of which is to hold an enumeration of all the devices on the system. Other bits are stored in the System, Network, and Security subkeys.

By and large, your interaction with the hardware information on Plug and Play systems will be to plug the hardware in and let Windows 98 worry about storing Registry settings. For legacy devices, generally, Windows 98 sleuths out the information it needs during the installation process. When you install new hardware, Windows 98 references an INF file provided either by Microsoft or the hardware manufacturer to identify the driver to install. For installed devices, these files are copied to the \Windows\INF folder. Included in this INF file are the Registry settings for your hardware. To install a driver for a legacy device, therefore, you have to have an INF file. If you have an INF file, you have the Registry settings you need.

If you suspect that there are Registry problems with a hardware device, follow these steps:

1. Remove the driver and reinstall it using the appropriate Control Panel icon. Be sure to power off the machine for 20 seconds and reboot after the removal. This process should delete the Registry settings for that device and reinstall them.

2. If step 1 fails, log on to www.microsoft.com and search the Knowledge Base to see whether you can find the answer.

3. If step 2 fails to resolve the problem, call the manufacturer and get their assistance in editing the Registry to correct the problem.

4. If step 3 fails, screw up your courage. You are in dangerous territory, and you could hose the system. You can examine the INF file for the device to see what keys it installs and their correct values. You can find these keys and check their values. If you suspect corruption that editing will not correct, try exporting the highest-level key, deleting this key from the Registry Editor, and importing your exported file. If you can find an associated REG file on the setup disks for the device, try double-clicking on it. REG files are text descriptions of Registry settings. Their default action when double-clicked is to merge into the Registry.

Note: Sometimes a simple misspelling in a hardware registration can cause large headaches. I have a Practical Peripheral 28.8 modem, for example. By examining the modem's communication when trying to make a dial-up connection using a generic driver, I saw the firmware identify itself as "Practical Peripherals 28.8 PCMCIA." But, the INF was looking for a device response of "Practical Peripherals 28.8 EZ-CARD PCMCIA." Therefore, Windows 98 could never accurately identify it. Even if I forced the selection of the driver, when the card started up it announced itself incorrectly, as the INF information was now in the Registry. Windows 98 reports it got an unrecognized response from the device. I edited the Registry to correct the problem. The vendor suggested that buying a new modem card might help.

5. If step 4 fails, get out your credit card. It is time to call Microsoft for help. Backing up data, formatting the drive, and reinstalling everything is usually cheaper.

Solving Problems in the Absence of Documentation

One of the biggest problems is that the Windows 98 Registry is not fully documented. To what resources can you turn to get information about how it works and what it does? My favorites are the following:

- Search TechNet, the CD subscription service from Microsoft for support professionals. Articles on the Registry appear sporadically. Often you can glean the bits of information you need to solve the problem. If TechNet is not available, search the Microsoft Web site. Some of the information in TechNet is available there.

- Search the Developers Library, a part of the Microsoft Developers Network, the CD subscription service from Microsoft for developers. If you are not into C code, some of the information may be too technical. However, the parts that make sense to you may indeed help.

- Find the Windows NT Resource Kit, and open the file REGENTRY.HLP. This file documents the Windows NT Registry. Although the two Registries are not completely identical, they are close enough for your work. If you have an extra value here and there, Windows 98 ignores it. Don't fear adding the extraneous to the Registry. Fear changing what is already there.

- Check the msnews.microsoft.com newsgroups for any enlightening articles. Someone else may already have solved the problem for you and posted the solution.

- Read your Registry and await insight. Seriously, it is amazing what you can puzzle out. Most of the information I have presented I learned from a combination of reading the REGENTRY.HLP file and poking around in my own Registry. Of course, I have hosed a couple of systems that way. Be aware that you may, too.

Working Through the Thinking Process

Warning: This section presents how to solve a problem by editing the Registry. All those associated with this book take the same stance as Microsoft on editing the Registry. If you damage your machine because you have edited the Registry, the damage is not our responsibility. We can only assure you that these actions resolved a problem on one computer at one time. These methods may not work on your machine. If you attempt this solution, you may in fact damage your Windows 98 or your Office 97 installation. If you are going either to play or to try a fix, try it on a test machine first.

A common problem in Microsoft Outlook 97 is the appearance of extra sets of personal folders in the Folder view. Only one set is actually functional, the one Outlook is using at the moment and where it places all new items that you create. Selecting some of these folders, a perfectly possible action, may generate an error that the associated PST file cannot be found, as shown in Figure 30.6. Manipulating the options for Outlook using the menus and dialog boxes does not solve the problem. Going to the Mail and Fax icon in the Control Panel may reveal that several sets of Personal Folder services have been installed. Deleting all but one service sometimes does not solve the problem, although it should. This is definitely a Registry troubleshooting problem. Working with the ordinary means of changing settings is not solving the problem.

Note: Microsoft has just released Outlook 98 as a free upgrade to Outlook 97, available for download at www.microsoft.com. Whether Outlook 98 will exhibit the same behavior remains to be seen in production environments. The problem in Outlook 97 often took months to appear. One solution to avoid this Registry procedure, however, is to roll out Outlook 98.

Figure 30.6.

Outlook can report that extra personal folders have no related file.

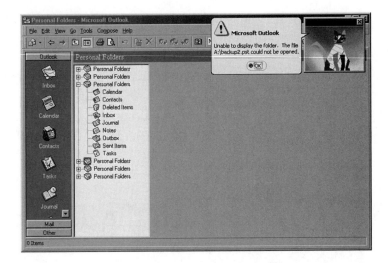

Tip: Back up the Registry before you attempt this operation. Do not use CFGBACK, because it is known to fail to restore from its backups. For the best method, see Chapter 20 on backup strategies.

How do you discover the nature of the problem? The reasoning steps are as follows:

1. You have several sets of personal folders showing in Outlook.

2. You do not recall installing the extra sets.

Note: Outlook 97 gets its extra lists of personal folders via a very normal action. The user has imported data, probably from a PST file. If the settings are not exactly correct—and I know many who would say even that when they are the problem still occurs—the information is not imported into the current set of personal folders only. An extra set of folders is created, apparently in addition to merging the data into the main set of folders. The problem also can occur when importing messages from cc:Mail folders.

3. No dialog box or menu command resolves the problem.

4. The information that populates the list of folders must be stored somewhere.

5. All settings for software are stored in the Registry.

6. The answer to the problem must, therefore, lie in the Registry.

By following this line of reasoning, you are forced to accept the possibility that the Registry is out of synchronization with the software. Something is registered that causes the extra folders to appear. However, it cannot be a totally spurious Registry entry. If it were, Windows 98 and Outlook would ignore the settings altogether. Their net effect would be to take up space in the Registry, nothing more. You need to find the spurious settings and either delete them or correct them to the expected values.

> **Tip:** Before you undertake any troubleshooting procedure that involves the Registry, take care to complete all the other possible actions that should solve the problem. In this case, delete the extra Personal Folder services using the Control Panel's Mail and Fax icon.

To pursue this hunch, use the search feature of the Registry Editor to discover where and how these settings might be stored. If you open the Registry Editor and choose Find from the Edit menu, search for *.pst in all keys, values, and data. Why this search string? You know that Outlook stores its data in files that end in .PST. You are looking for locations where those files might be referenced. What you find under a key named Exchange Settings is a set of class identifiers, each of which references one of the PST files associated with one of the folders that appears in the Personal Folders list (see Figure 30.7). You can tell that this list of folders is associated with the Folder list because the files that are reported as missing by Outlook are referenced in some of the entries. No other such list appears elsewhere in the Registry.

Figure 30.7.
Exchange maintains a set of keys that populate the Folder view in Outlook.

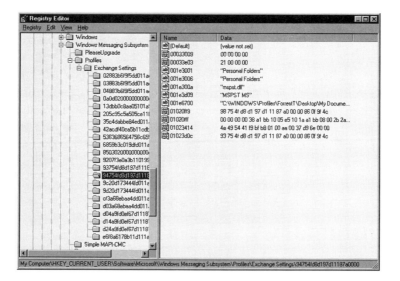

Troubleshooting can often be defined as the process of experimenting with options when you have no other choice. In this case, it is theoretically possible that this is not the list of personal folders to load. It is theoretically possible that deleting one of these class IDs could permanently damage your software, rendering Windows 98 unbootable or Outlook 97 unloadable. But if you want to solve the problem, you don't have any choice but to try deleting one of the keys to see what happens.

When I faced this problem, I chose to delete the key that identified the class ID of the missing folder set. I considered it the least likely to cause damage. I selected the key in the left pane of the Registry Editor, pressed the Delete key, and confirmed the delete operation (see Figure 30.8). I closed the Registry Editor and opened Outlook. I was greatly pleased to see that Outlook loaded. I was even more pleased to see that the list of folders had grown smaller. In addition, the missing folder was no longer referenced.

Figure 30.8.
Be very certain that you want to delete a key before you do.

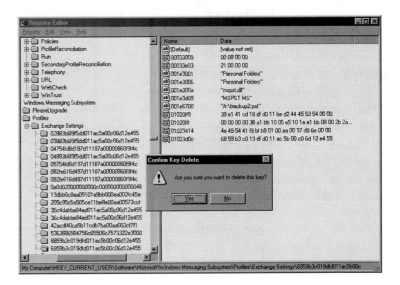

Having discovered what seemed like a solution, I counted the remaining number of similar entries in the Registry. There were six, exactly the number of personal folders showing in Outlook, and members of the set referenced two different PST files. I experimented again, deleting one of these six keys. The number of personal folders decreased again. By the time I was finished, I had one reference in the Registry to a set of personal folders, and Outlook was back to its normal look, feel, and behavior. The problem was solved.

Summary

This chapter has focused on the structure of the Registry. We have reviewed the importance of backing up the Registry, and examined how to edit the Registry. To prepare you for troubleshooting, this chapter discussed how software and hardware are registered. We have also walked through an actual case study in solving a software problem by editing the Registry.

On Your Own

I cannot recommend that you try any of this on your own. You could completely hose a machine or two if you do. We might as well end this tour of Windows 98 with some showstopper suggestions for activity on your own, however.

As you realize that no one associated with this book is responsible for what happens to you or your systems, try opening your Registry in the Registry Editor. Practice creating a bogus key, some values under the bogus key, and then delete this key and its associated values. Find a REG file to see how it is structured.

Search for the key HKEY_USERS\Control Panel and examine the subkeys and values there. Find the value Wallpaper and modify it to give yourself a new wallpaper. Find the keys Run, RunOnce, RunService, and RunServiceOnce. You should see familiar programs here. These keys control which programs and services run at startup, and which run only once to configure the system and then do not run again at startup. Note that these programs do not appear in the StartUp group on anyone's Start menu.

And then—most importantly—stay as far away from the Registry as you possibly can. That's the safest way to handle it.

VIII

Appendixes

A

System
Policy
Templates
and the
WINDOWS.
ADM File

Peter Norton®

Chapter 17, "Securing the Desktop," showed you how to use System Policies, and mentioned that policies are defined by templates that the System Policy Editor loads. You may find that you need to create custom policy templates for your organization. You may find Registry entries that you want to modify, but you do not wish to use the Registry Editor to modify them. You might not want to run the risk that an errant entry might be created. As a result, you need to know how the templates are structured and how to create one of your own.

Two files, WINDOWS.ADM and COMMON.ADM serve to build the template for the System Policy Editor in Windows 98. What few people realize is that these files are simply text files that describe how to present the book icons and check boxes on the screen. COMMON.ADM is a very short file that represents the entries in common between Windows 98 and Windows NT. WINDOWS.ADM represents the entries for Windows 98. You can read these files on your system using any editor, but you risk accidentally changing the files. So I have reproduced them here for your convenience.

> **Note:** Policies for Windows NT are defined by a third file named WINNT.ADM. This file contains the template for settings unique to Windows NT. WINDOWS.ADM contains settings that are relevant to both Windows 98 and Windows NT. All of these files are now stored in the INF subfolder in your Windows folder.

What is so interesting about WINDOWS.ADM? First, in the absence of complete documentation of the Windows 98 Registry, WINDOWS.ADM tips you off to important Registry keys and related sets of Registry keys. It is a sort of guided tour to important sections of the Registry and what they do. Second, you can edit the template and create custom templates for use with the System Policy Editor.

This appendix reproduces the templates in their entirety. In addition, using example sections, I explain how to create custom templates that could serve to modify any Registry entry. You can use this knowledge to build a template to load in the System Policy Editor so that its user can modify any Registry entry using the safety of the System Policy Editor. Finally, comments are inserted into the complete file so that you can get some clues as to how the Registry is organized and what keys are updated when you create system policies.

How to Read the Template

The WINDOWS.ADM file is structured into three parts. The first two parts relate to the two default icons that appear in the System Policy Editor: Default User and Default Computer (see Figure A.1). Two statements indicate the segment of the file that relates to each icon:

```
CLASS MACHINE
CLASS USER
```

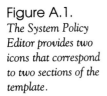

Figure A.1.
The System Policy Editor provides two icons that correspond to two sections of the template.

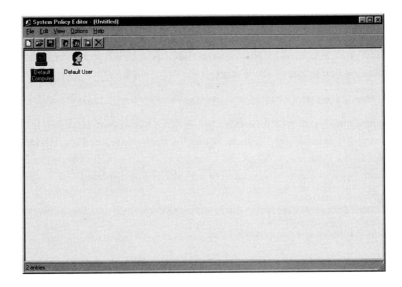

The lines following *CLASS MACHINE* relate to the Default Computer icon. The lines following *CLASS USER* relate to the Default User icon. When you create specific user and computer icons using the Edit menu, these icons are based on either the *CLASS USER* or *CLASS MACHINE* sections of WINDOWS.ADM, or the template that you are using at the time.

The third section of the file is identified by a line containing the text *[strings]*. This section contains lines of the following form:

```
identifier = string
```

The *identifier* represents text that you can use elsewhere in the file as shorthand for the *string*. In this way, if the exact string changes in some revision of the software, you do not need to update hundreds of strings in the file manually. You update the strings in the [strings] section of the file, and the identifiers in the file expand into those strings automatically.

Within the two CLASS sections are entries that define the book icons and check boxes that appear when you open either the User or Computer icons (see Figure A.2). The highest-level book icon is denoted as a category in the WINDOWS.ADM file. Such icons are created using a line like the following:

```
CATEGORY !!Network
```

The key word *CATEGORY* begins the line, followed by a space and two exclamation points. The text label for the book icon follows the exclamation marks. In this case, the identifier from a statement in the [strings] section appears, and the actual text used is the string associated with the identifier.

Following each *CATEGORY* line is a *KEYNAME* line. This line identifies the key in the Registry for use with the particular category. Keys for categories in CLASS MACHINE branch from HKEY_LOCAL_MACHINE. Those in the CLASS USER section branch from HKEY_USERS. The following line shows a sample entry:

```
KEYNAME Software\Microsoft\Windows\CurrentVersion\Policies\Network
```

Subordinate book icons are created by *CATEGORY* lines indented under the one that creates their superordinate book icon. The check box lines are created by *POLICY* keywords, which take a text label in the same way *CATEGORY* statements do. The following set of lines create the book icon shown open in Figure A.2, complete with the policy displayed:

```
CATEGORY !!Network
KEYNAME Software\Microsoft\Windows\CurrentVersion\Policies\Network
CATEGORY !!AccessControl
POLICY !!AccessControl_User
```

Figure A.2.
*The book icon is
created by lines of
code in the template.*

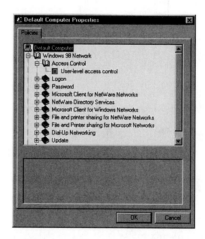

Three lines follow a *POLICY* line. First comes a *KEYNAME* line, which indicates the Registry key to modify when the checkbox associated with the policy changes. Second is a line that describes the value to modify, called a *VALUENAME* line. Third comes a line describing how to modify the value using the keywords *VALUEON* and *VALUEOFF*. The following lines illustrate:

```
POLICY !!AccessControl_User
KEYNAME System\CurrentControlSet\Services\VxD\FILESEC
VALUENAME Start
VALUEON NUMERIC 0 VALUEOFF DELETE
```

The *VALUEON* entry describes what to do when the check box is checked. In this case, the action is to insert the value if it is not present and give it the numeric value 0. The *VALUEOFF* entry describes what to do if the check box is cleared. In this case, the value is deleted from the key. (When the check box is grayed, no action takes place.) In these entries, you can see a variety of data types. Numeric data is indicated with the *NUMERIC* keyword. String data is placed between quotation marks.

Segments in the WINDOWS.ADM file named by keywords other than *CLASS* are paired with an *END* statement to indicate the last statement belonging to the scope of the keyword. *CATEGORY* is paired with *END CATEGORY*. *POLICY* is paired with *END POLICY*. The statements that appear between these two markers belong to the category or the policy identified.

Several other items can be included in the WINDOWS.ADM file. The first of these is called an *ACTIONLIST*. This element is basically a to-do list that describes what to do if the check box is either checked (on) or unchecked (off). The following *ACTIONLISTON* lines indicate to set a value if the check box is checked:

```
ACTIONLISTON
KEYNAME System\CurrentControlSet\Services\VxD\FILESEC
VALUENAME StaticVxD VALUE filesec.vxd
END ACTIONLISTON
```

In this case, the *FILESEC* key value *StaticVxD* is set to *filesec.vxd*. Paired with such a block of lines can be an *ACTIONLISTOFF*, as in the following:

```
ACTIONLISTOFF
KEYNAME Security\Provider
VALUENAME Platform_Type VALUE NUMERIC 0
KEYNAME System\CurrentControlSet\Services\VxD\FILESEC
VALUENAME StaticVxD VALUE DELETE
KEYNAME System\CurrentControlSet\Services\VxD\NWSP
VALUENAME Start VALUE DELETE
VALUENAME StaticVxD VALUE DELETE
KEYNAME System\CurrentControlSet\Services\VxD\MSSP
VALUENAME Start VALUE DELETE
VALUENAME StaticVxD VALUE DELETE
END ACTIONLISTOFF
```

In this case, a number of values are set to 0 or deleted when the check box is cleared.

In addition to action lists, the *PART* keyword can be used to identify items to display in the Settings box at the bottom of the System Policy Editor Properties windows. This block displays an edit box (described by *EDITTEXT*) and places the result in the value *Container* for the key *Security/Provider*:

```
PART !!AuthenticatorName EDITTEXT
KEYNAME Security\Provider
VALUENAME Container
END PART
```

PART blocks can be more complicated. For example, they can display a drop-down list box and fill it with values. For each possible selection in the list box, an action list can be defined, as in the following example:

```
PART !!AuthenticatorType DROPDOWNLIST
KEYNAME Security\Provider
VALUENAME Platform_Type REQUIRED
ITEMLIST
NAME !!AT_NetWare VALUE NUMERIC 3
ACTIONLIST
KEYNAME System\CurrentControlSet\Services\VxD\NWSP
VALUENAME StaticVxD VALUE nwsp.vxd
VALUENAME Start VALUE NUMERIC 0
```

```
KEYNAME Security\Provider
VALUENAME Address_Book VALUE nwab32.dll
END ACTIONLIST
NAME !!AT_NTAS VALUE NUMERIC 2
ACTIONLIST
KEYNAME System\CurrentControlSet\Services\VxD\MSSP
VALUENAME StaticVxD VALUE mssp.vxd
VALUENAME Start VALUE NUMERIC 0
KEYNAME Security\Provider
VALUENAME Address_Book VALUE msab32.dll
END ACTIONLIST
NAME !!AT_NT VALUE NUMERIC 1
ACTIONLIST
KEYNAME System\CurrentControlSet\Services\VxD\MSSP
VALUENAME StaticVxD VALUE mssp.vxd
VALUENAME Start VALUE NUMERIC 0
KEYNAME Security\Provider
VALUENAME Address_Book VALUE msab32.dll
END ACTIONLIST
END ITEMLIST
END PART
```

In this case, an *ITEMLIST* is appended to the *PART*. The *ITEMLIST* lists the possible values in the list box using *NAME* statements. On each such line is a string identifier providing the string to appear in the list box as well as a numeric value paired with the string. For each *NAME* statement there is an *ACTIONLIST* describing what to do if the user selects that name from the list box.

These elements are assembled together to form coherent policies. The elements that we have examined so far comprise the lines that display the User-Level Access Control check box under the Access Control book under the Network book in Figure A.2. The entire block that displays these lines follows:

```
CATEGORY !!Network
KEYNAME Software\Microsoft\Windows\CurrentVersion\Policies\Network
CATEGORY !!AccessControl
POLICY !!AccessControl_User
KEYNAME System\CurrentControlSet\Services\VxD\FILESEC
VALUENAME Start
VALUEON NUMERIC 0 VALUEOFF DELETE

ACTIONLISTON
KEYNAME System\CurrentControlSet\Services\VxD\FILESEC
VALUENAME StaticVxD VALUE filesec.vxd
END ACTIONLISTON
ACTIONLISTOFF
KEYNAME Security\Provider
VALUENAME Platform_Type VALUE NUMERIC 0
KEYNAME System\CurrentControlSet\Services\VxD\FILESEC
VALUENAME StaticVxD VALUE DELETE
KEYNAME System\CurrentControlSet\Services\VxD\NWSP
VALUENAME Start VALUE DELETE
VALUENAME StaticVxD VALUE DELETE
KEYNAME System\CurrentControlSet\Services\VxD\MSSP
VALUENAME Start VALUE DELETE
VALUENAME StaticVxD VALUE DELETE
END ACTIONLISTOFF
PART !!AuthenticatorName EDITTEXT
```

```
KEYNAME Security\Provider
VALUENAME Container
END PART

PART !!AuthenticatorType DROPDOWNLIST
KEYNAME Security\Provider
VALUENAME Platform_Type REQUIRED
ITEMLIST
NAME !!AT_NetWare VALUE NUMERIC 3
ACTIONLIST
KEYNAME System\CurrentControlSet\Services\VxD\NWSP
VALUENAME StaticVxD VALUE nwsp.vxd
VALUENAME Start VALUE NUMERIC 0
KEYNAME Security\Provider
VALUENAME Address_Book VALUE nwab32.dll
END ACTIONLIST
NAME !!AT_NTAS VALUE NUMERIC 2
ACTIONLIST
KEYNAME System\CurrentControlSet\Services\VxD\MSSP
VALUENAME StaticVxD VALUE mssp.vxd
VALUENAME Start VALUE NUMERIC 0
KEYNAME Security\Provider
VALUENAME Address_Book VALUE msab32.dll
END ACTIONLIST
NAME !!AT_NT VALUE NUMERIC 1
ACTIONLIST
KEYNAME System\CurrentControlSet\Services\VxD\MSSP
VALUENAME StaticVxD VALUE mssp.vxd
VALUENAME Start VALUE NUMERIC 0
KEYNAME Security\Provider
VALUENAME Address_Book VALUE msab32.dll
END ACTIONLIST
END ITEMLIST
END PART
END POLICY
END CATEGORY ; User-Level Security
END CATEGORY ; Network
```

The COMMON.ADM File

```
CLASS MACHINE

CLASS USER

[strings]
```

The WINDOWS.ADM File

```
CLASS MACHINE

CATEGORY !!Network
KEYNAME Software\Microsoft\Windows\CurrentVersion\Policies\Network

    CATEGORY !!AccessControl
        POLICY !!AccessControl_User
```

```
                    KEYNAME System\CurrentControlSet\Services\VxD\FILESEC
                    VALUENAME Start
                    VALUEON NUMERIC 0 VALUEOFF DELETE

                ACTIONLISTON
                    KEYNAME System\CurrentControlSet\Services\VxD\FILESEC
                    VALUENAME StaticVxD VALUE filesec.vxd
                END ACTIONLISTON
                ACTIONLISTOFF
                    KEYNAME Security\Provider
                    VALUENAME Platform_Type  VALUE NUMERIC 0
                    KEYNAME System\CurrentControlSet\Services\VxD\FILESEC
                    VALUENAME StaticVxD VALUE DELETE
                    KEYNAME System\CurrentControlSet\Services\VxD\NWSP
                    VALUENAME Start          VALUE DELETE
                    VALUENAME StaticVxD VALUE DELETE
                    KEYNAME System\CurrentControlSet\Services\VxD\MSSP
                    VALUENAME Start          VALUE DELETE
                    VALUENAME StaticVxD VALUE DELETE
                END ACTIONLISTOFF

                    PART !!AuthenticatorName EDITTEXT
                    KEYNAME Security\Provider
                    VALUENAME Container
                    END PART

                    PART !!AuthenticatorType DROPDOWNLIST
                    KEYNAME Security\Provider
                    VALUENAME Platform_Type REQUIRED
                    ITEMLIST
                        NAME !!AT_NetWare VALUE NUMERIC 3
                        ACTIONLIST
                            KEYNAME System\CurrentControlSet\Services\VxD\NWSP
                            VALUENAME StaticVxD VALUE nwsp.vxd
                            VALUENAME Start          VALUE NUMERIC 0
                            KEYNAME Security\Provider
                            VALUENAME Address_Book  VALUE nwab32.dll
                        END ACTIONLIST

                        NAME !!AT_NTAS  VALUE NUMERIC 2
                        ACTIONLIST
                            KEYNAME System\CurrentControlSet\Services\VxD\MSSP
                            VALUENAME StaticVxD VALUE mssp.vxd
                            VALUENAME Start          VALUE NUMERIC 0
                            KEYNAME Security\Provider
                            VALUENAME Address_Book  VALUE msab32.dll
                        END ACTIONLIST

                        NAME !!AT_NT  VALUE NUMERIC 1
                        ACTIONLIST
                            KEYNAME System\CurrentControlSet\Services\VxD\MSSP
                            VALUENAME StaticVxD VALUE mssp.vxd
                            VALUENAME Start          VALUE NUMERIC 0
                            KEYNAME Security\Provider
                            VALUENAME Address_Book  VALUE msab32.dll
                        END ACTIONLIST
                    END ITEMLIST
                    END PART
            END POLICY
    END CATEGORY  ; User-Level Security
```

```
CATEGORY !!Logon
    POLICY !!LogonBanner
    KEYNAME Software\Microsoft\Windows\CurrentVersion\Winlogon
        PART !!LogonBanner_Caption EDITTEXT
        VALUENAME "LegalNoticeCaption"
        MAXLEN 255
        DEFAULT !!LogonBanner_DefCaption
        END PART

        PART !!LogonBanner_Text EDITTEXT
        VALUENAME "LegalNoticeText"
         MAXLEN 255
        DEFAULT !!LogonBanner_DefText
        END PART
    END POLICY

    POLICY !!ValidatedLogon
    KEYNAME Network\Logon
    VALUENAME "MustBeValidated"
    END POLICY

    POLICY !!DontDisplayLastUserName
    KEYNAME Network\Logon
    VALUENAME "DontShowLastUser"
    END POLICY

END CATEGORY     ; Logon

CATEGORY !!Passwords
    POLICY !!HideSharePasswords
    VALUENAME "HideSharePwds"
    END POLICY

    POLICY !!DisablePasswordCaching
    VALUENAME "DisablePwdCaching"
    END POLICY

    POLICY !!RequireAlphaNum
    VALUENAME "AlphanumPwds"
    END POLICY

    POLICY !!MinimumPwdLen
        PART !!MPL_Length NUMERIC REQUIRED
        MIN 1 MAX 8 DEFAULT 3
        VALUENAME MinPwdLen
        END PART
    END POLICY
END CATEGORY     ; Password

CATEGORY !!NWClient
KEYNAME System\CurrentControlSet\Services\VxD\NWREDIR
    POLICY !!PrefServer
    KEYNAME System\CurrentControlSet\Services\NWNP32\NetworkProvider
        PART !!PrefServerName EDITTEXT REQUIRED
        VALUENAME "AuthenticatingAgent"
        MAXLEN 48
        END PART
    END POLICY
```

```
         POLICY !!SupportLFN
             PART !!SupportLFNsOn DROPDOWNLIST REQUIRED
             VALUENAME "SupportLFN"
             ITEMLIST
                 NAME !!LFN_No311    VALUE NUMERIC 1
                 NAME !!LFN_All        VALUE NUMERIC 2
             END ITEMLIST

             END PART
         END POLICY

         POLICY !!DisableAutoNWLogin
             KEYNAME System\CurrentControlSet\Services\NWNP32\NetworkProvider
             VALUENAME DisableDefaultPasswords
         END POLICY
END CATEGORY      ; Microsoft Netware-Compatible Network

CATEGORY !!NWClient4
     POLICY !!PrefTree
     KEYNAME System\CurrentControlSet\Services\VxD\NWREDIR
         PART !!PrefTreeName EDITTEXT REQUIRED
         VALUENAME "PreferredNDSTree"
         MAXLEN 32
         END PART
     END POLICY

     POLICY !!DefaultNameContext
     KEYNAME System\CurrentControlSet\Services\VxD\NWREDIR
         PART !!DefContextName EDITTEXT REQUIRED
         VALUENAME "DefaultNameContext"
         MAXLEN 250
         END PART
     END POLICY

     POLICY !!PreLoadNetWareRunTime
     KEYNAME System\CurrentControlSet\Services\NWNP32\NetworkProvider
         VALUENAME PreLoadNWRunTime
     END POLICY

     POLICY !!DisableNWAutoBootLogon
     KEYNAME System\CurrentControlSet\Services\NWNP32\NetworkProvider
         VALUENAME DisableDefaultLogon
     END POLICY

     POLICY !!EnableLogonPopup
     KEYNAME System\CurrentControlSet\Services\NWNP32\NetworkProvider
         VALUENAME EnableLogonPopup
     END POLICY

     POLICY !!DisableAdvLogonSettings
     KEYNAME System\CurrentControlSet\Services\NWNP32\NetworkProvider
         VALUENAME DisableAdvancedLogonSettings
     END POLICY

     POLICY !!DefaultLogonType
     KEYNAME System\CurrentControlSet\Services\NWNP32\NetworkProvider
         PART !!DefaultLogonType DROPDOWNLIST REQUIRED
         VALUENAME "LogonType"
         ITEMLIST
```

```
        NAME !!BinderyLogon      VALUE NUMERIC 0
        NAME !!TreeLogon          VALUE NUMERIC 1
    END ITEMLIST
    END PART
END POLICY


POLICY !!BrowseDisableBNDServers
    KEYNAME System\CurrentControlSet\Services\NWNP32\NetworkProvider
    VALUENAME BrowseDisableBNDServers
END POLICY


POLICY !!BrowseDisableWorkgroups
    KEYNAME System\CurrentControlSet\Services\NWNP32\NetworkProvider
    VALUENAME BrowseDisableWorkgroups
END POLICY


POLICY !!BrowseDisableServers
    KEYNAME System\CurrentControlSet\Services\NWNP32\NetworkProvider
    VALUENAME BrowseDisableServers
END POLICY


POLICY !!BrowseDisableContainers
    KEYNAME System\CurrentControlSet\Services\NWNP32\NetworkProvider
    VALUENAME BrowseDisableContainers
END POLICY


POLICY !!BrowseDisablePrinters
    KEYNAME System\CurrentControlSet\Services\NWNP32\NetworkProvider
    VALUENAME BrowseDisablePrinters
END POLICY


POLICY !!BrowseDisableQueues
    KEYNAME System\CurrentControlSet\Services\NWNP32\NetworkProvider
    VALUENAME BrowseDisableQueues
END POLICY


POLICY !!BrowseDisableVolumes
    KEYNAME System\CurrentControlSet\Services\NWNP32\NetworkProvider
    VALUENAME BrowseDisableVolumes
END POLICY
END CATEGORY      ; Microsoft Netware-Compatible Network

CATEGORY !!MSClient
    POLICY !!LogonDomain
    KEYNAME Network\Logon
    VALUENAME "LMLogon"
        PART !!DomainName      EDITTEXT REQUIRED
        MAXLEN 15
        KEYNAME System\CurrentControlSet\Services\MSNP32\NetworkProvider
        VALUENAME AuthenticatingAgent
        END PART

        PART !!DomainLogonConfirmation CHECKBOX
        KEYNAME Network\Logon
        VALUENAME DomainLogonMessage
        END PART

        PART !!NoDomainPwdCaching CHECKBOX
        KEYNAME Network\Logon
```

```
              VALUENAME NoDomainPwdCaching
              END PART
          END POLICY


          POLICY !!Workgroup
          KEYNAME System\CurrentControlSet\Services\VxD\VNETSUP
              PART !!WorkgroupName EDITTEXT REQUIRED
              VALUENAME "Workgroup"
              MAXLEN 15
              END PART
          END POLICY


          POLICY !!AlternateWorkgroup
          KEYNAME System\CurrentControlSet\Services\VxD\VREDIR
              PART !!WorkgroupName EDITTEXT REQUIRED
              VALUENAME "Workgroup"
              MAXLEN 15
              END PART
          END POLICY
      END CATEGORY     ; Microsoft Network


      CATEGORY !!NWServer
          POLICY !!DisableSAP
              KEYNAME System\CurrentControlSet\Services\NcpServer\Parameters
              VALUENAME Use_Sap
              VALUEON "0" VALUEOFF "1"
              ACTIONLISTON
                  KEYNAME
System\CurrentControlSet\Services\NcpServer\Parameters\Ndi\Params\Use_Sap
                  VALUENAME "" VALUE "0"
              END ACTIONLISTON
              ACTIONLISTOFF
                  KEYNAME
System\CurrentControlSet\Services\NcpServer\Parameters\Ndi\Params\Use_Sap
                  VALUENAME "" VALUE "1"
              END ACTIONLISTOFF
          END POLICY
      END CATEGORY


      CATEGORY !!VServer
          POLICY !!DisableFileSharing
              VALUENAME "NoFileSharing"
          END POLICY


          POLICY !!DisablePrintSharing
              VALUENAME "NoPrintSharing"
          END POLICY
      END CATEGORY


      CATEGORY !!RemoteAccess
          POLICY !!RemoteAccess_Disable
              VALUENAME "NoDialIn"
          END POLICY
      END CATEGORY     ; Remote Access


      CATEGORY !!Update
          POLICY !!RemoteUpdate
          KEYNAME System\CurrentControlSet\Control\Update
          ACTIONLISTOFF
```

```
            VALUENAME "UpdateMode" VALUE NUMERIC 0
        END ACTIONLISTOFF

            PART !!UpdateMode DROPDOWNLIST REQUIRED
            VALUENAME "UpdateMode"
            ITEMLIST
                NAME !!UM_Automatic VALUE NUMERIC 1
                NAME !!UM_Manual    VALUE NUMERIC 2
            END ITEMLIST
            END PART

            PART !!UM_Manual_Path EDITTEXT
            VALUENAME "NetworkPath"
            END PART

            PART !!DisplayErrors CHECKBOX
            VALUENAME "Verbose"
            END PART

            PART !!LoadBalance CHECKBOX
            VALUENAME "LoadBalance"
            END PART
        END POLICY
    END CATEGORY    ; Update
END CATEGORY    ; Network


CATEGORY !!System
KEYNAME Software\Microsoft\Windows\CurrentVersion\Setup

    CATEGORY !!UserProfiles
        POLICY !!EnableUserProfiles
            KEYNAME Network\Logon
            VALUENAME UserProfiles
        END POLICY
    END CATEGORY

    CATEGORY !!NetworkPaths
        POLICY !!NetworkSetupPath
            PART !!NetworkSetupPath_Path EDITTEXT REQUIRED
            VALUENAME "SourcePath"
            END PART
        END POLICY

        POLICY !!NetworkTourPath
            PART !!NetworkTourPath_Path EDITTEXT REQUIRED
            VALUENAME "TourPath"
            END PART
            PART !!NetworkTourPath_TIP TEXT END PART
        END POLICY
    END CATEGORY

    CATEGORY !!SNMP
        POLICY !!Communities
        KEYNAME System\CurrentControlSet\Services\SNMP\Parameters\ValidCommunities
            PART !!CommunitiesListbox LISTBOX
                VALUEPREFIX ""
            END PART
        END POLICY
```

```
        POLICY !!PermittedManagers
        KEYNAME System\CurrentControlSet\Services\SNMP\Parameters\PermittedManagers
            PART !!PermittedManagersListbox LISTBOX
                VALUEPREFIX ""
            END PART
        END POLICY


        POLICY !!Traps_Public
        KEYNAME
System\CurrentControlSet\Services\SNMP\Parameters\TrapConfiguration\Public
            PART !!Traps_PublicListbox LISTBOX
                VALUEPREFIX ""
            END PART
        END POLICY


        POLICY !!InternetMIB
        KEYNAME System\CurrentControlSet\Services\SNMP\Parameters\RFC1156Agent
            PART !!ContactName EDITTEXT REQUIRED
            VALUENAME sysContact
            END PART

            PART !!Location EDITTEXT REQUIRED
            VALUENAME sysLocation
            END PART
        END POLICY
    END CATEGORY


    CATEGORY !!ProgramsToRun
        POLICY !!Run
            KEYNAME Software\Microsoft\Windows\CurrentVersion\Run
            PART !!RunListbox LISTBOX EXPLICITVALUE
            END PART
        END POLICY

        POLICY !!RunOnce
            KEYNAME Software\Microsoft\Windows\CurrentVersion\RunOnce
            PART !!RunOnceListbox LISTBOX EXPLICITVALUE
            END PART
        END POLICY

        POLICY !!RunServices
            KEYNAME Software\Microsoft\Windows\CurrentVersion\RunServices
            PART !!RunServicesListbox LISTBOX EXPLICITVALUE
            END PART
        END POLICY
    END CATEGORY
END CATEGORY


CLASS USER

CATEGORY !!Network
KEYNAME Software\Microsoft\Windows\CurrentVersion\Policies\Network
    CATEGORY !!Sharing
        POLICY !!DisableFileSharingCtrl
        VALUENAME NoFileSharingControl
        END POLICY
```

```
        POLICY !!DisablePrintSharingCtrl
        VALUENAME NoPrintSharingControl
        END POLICY
    END CATEGORY  ; Sharing

END CATEGORY  ; Network

CATEGORY !!System
KEYNAME Software\Microsoft\Windows\CurrentVersion\Policies\System

    CATEGORY !!Shell
    KEYNAME "Software\Microsoft\Windows\CurrentVersion\Explorer\User Shell Folders"
        CATEGORY !!CustomFolders
            POLICY !!CustomFolders_Programs
                PART !!CustomFolders_ProgramsPath EDITTEXT REQUIRED
                VALUENAME "Programs"
                END PART
            END POLICY

            POLICY !!CustomFolders_Desktop
                PART !!CustomFolders_DesktopPath EDITTEXT REQUIRED
                VALUENAME "Desktop"
                END PART
            END POLICY

            POLICY !!HideStartMenuSubfolders
                KEYNAME Software\Microsoft\Windows\CurrentVersion\Policies\Explorer
                VALUENAME NoStartMenuSubFolders
                PART !!HideStartMenuSubfolders_Tip1 TEXT  END PART
                PART !!HideStartMenuSubfolders_Tip2 TEXT  END PART
            END POLICY

            POLICY !!CustomFolders_Startup
                PART !!CustomFolders_StartupPath EDITTEXT REQUIRED
                VALUENAME "Startup"
                END PART
            END POLICY

            POLICY !!CustomFolders_NetHood
                PART !!CustomFolders_NetHoodPath EDITTEXT REQUIRED
                VALUENAME "NetHood"
                END PART
            END POLICY

            POLICY !!CustomFolders_StartMenu
                PART !!CustomFolders_StartMenuPath EDITTEXT REQUIRED
                VALUENAME "Start Menu"
                END PART
            END POLICY
        END CATEGORY

        CATEGORY !!Restrictions
        KEYNAME Software\Microsoft\Windows\CurrentVersion\Policies\Explorer
            POLICY !!RemoveRun
            VALUENAME "NoRun"
            END POLICY

            POLICY !!RemoveFolders
            VALUENAME "NoSetFolders"
            END POLICY
```

```
                POLICY !!RemoveTaskbar
                VALUENAME "NoSetTaskbar"
                END POLICY

                POLICY !!RemoveFind
                VALUENAME "NoFind"
                END POLICY

                POLICY !!HideDrives
                VALUENAME "NoDrives"
                VALUEON NUMERIC 67108863      ; low 26 bits on (1 bit per drive)
                VALUEOFF NUMERIC 0            ;  *****
                END POLICY

                POLICY !!HideNetHood
                VALUENAME "NoNetHood"
                END POLICY

                POLICY !!NoEntireNetwork
                    KEYNAME Software\Microsoft\Windows\CurrentVersion\Policies\Network
                    VALUENAME "NoEntireNetwork"
                END POLICY

                POLICY !!NoWorkgroupContents
                    KEYNAME Software\Microsoft\Windows\CurrentVersion\Policies\Network
                    VALUENAME "NoWorkgroupContents"
                END POLICY

                POLICY !!HideDesktop
                VALUENAME "NoDesktop"
                END POLICY

                POLICY !!DisableClose
                VALUENAME "NoClose"
                END POLICY

                POLICY !!NoSaveSettings
                VALUENAME "NoSaveSettings"
                END POLICY

            END CATEGORY
        END CATEGORY     ; Shell


    CATEGORY !!ControlPanel
        CATEGORY !!CPL_Display
            POLICY !!CPL_Display_Restrict
            KEYNAME Software\Microsoft\Windows\CurrentVersion\Policies\System
                PART !!CPL_Display_Disable CHECKBOX
                VALUENAME NoDispCPL
                END PART

                PART !!CPL_Display_HideBkgnd CHECKBOX
                VALUENAME NoDispBackgroundPage
                END PART

                PART !!CPL_Display_HideScrsav CHECKBOX
                VALUENAME NoDispScrSavPage
                END PART
```

```
            PART !!CPL_Display_HideAppearance CHECKBOX
            VALUENAME NoDispAppearancePage
            END PART

            PART !!CPL_Display_HideSettings CHECKBOX
            VALUENAME NoDispSettingsPage
            END PART
        END POLICY
END CATEGORY    ; Display

CATEGORY !!CPL_Network
    POLICY !!CPL_Network_Restrict
    KEYNAME Software\Microsoft\Windows\CurrentVersion\Policies\Network
        PART !!CPL_Network_Disable CHECKBOX
        VALUENAME NoNetSetup
        END PART

        PART !!CPL_Network_HideID CHECKBOX
        VALUENAME NoNetSetupIDPage
        END PART

        PART !!CPL_Network_HideAccessCtrl CHECKBOX
        VALUENAME NoNetSetupSecurityPage
        END PART
    END POLICY
END CATEGORY    ; Network

CATEGORY !!CPL_Security
    POLICY !!CPL_Security_Restrict
    KEYNAME Software\Microsoft\Windows\CurrentVersion\Policies\System
        PART !!CPL_Security_Disable CHECKBOX
        VALUENAME NoSecCPL
        END PART

        PART !!CPL_Security_HideSetPwds CHECKBOX
        VALUENAME NoPwdPage
        END PART

        PART !!CPL_Security_HideRemoteAdmin CHECKBOX
        VALUENAME NoAdminPage
        END PART

        PART !!CPL_Security_HideProfiles CHECKBOX
        VALUENAME NoProfilePage
        END PART
    END POLICY
END CATEGORY    ; Security

CATEGORY !!CPL_Printers
    POLICY !!CPL_Printers_Restrict
    KEYNAME Software\Microsoft\Windows\CurrentVersion\Policies\Explorer
        PART !!CPL_Printers_HidePages CHECKBOX
        VALUENAME NoPrinterTabs
        END PART

        PART !!CPL_Printers_DisableRemoval CHECKBOX
        VALUENAME NoDeletePrinter
        END PART
```

```
                        PART !!CPL_Printers_DisableAdd CHECKBOX
                        VALUENAME NoAddPrinter
                        END PART
                END POLICY
        END CATEGORY     ; Printers

        CATEGORY !!CPL_System
                POLICY !!CPL_System_Restrict
                KEYNAME Software\Microsoft\Windows\CurrentVersion\Policies\System
                        PART !!CPL_System_HideDevMgr CHECKBOX
                        VALUENAME NoDevMgrPage
                        END PART

                        PART !!CPL_System_HideConfig CHECKBOX
                        VALUENAME NoConfigPage
                        END PART

                        PART !!CPL_System_NoFileSys CHECKBOX
                        VALUENAME NoFileSysPage
                        END PART

                        PART !!CPL_System_NoVirtMem CHECKBOX
                        VALUENAME NoVirtMemPage
                        END PART
                END POLICY
        END CATEGORY     ; System

END CATEGORY     ; Control Panel

CATEGORY !!Desktop
KEYNAME "Control Panel\Desktop"
        POLICY !!Wallpaper
                PART !!WallpaperName COMBOBOX REQUIRED
                SUGGESTIONS
                        !!Wallpaper1 !!Wallpaper2 !!Wallpaper3 !!Wallpaper4 !!Wallpaper5
                        !!Wallpaper6 !!Wallpaper7 !!Wallpaper8 !!Wallpaper9 !!Wallpaper10
                END SUGGESTIONS
                VALUENAME "Wallpaper"
                END PART

                PART !!TileWallpaper CHECKBOX DEFCHECKED
                VALUENAME "TileWallpaper"
                VALUEON "1" VALUEOFF "0"
                END PART
        END POLICY

        POLICY !!ColorScheme
                PART !!SchemeName DROPDOWNLIST
                KEYNAME "Control Panel\Appearance"
                VALUENAME Current REQUIRED
                ITEMLIST
                NAME !!Lavender VALUE !!Lavender
                        ACTIONLIST
                        KEYNAME "Control Panel\Colors"
                        VALUENAME ActiveBorder   VALUE "174 168 217"
                        VALUENAME ActiveTitle    VALUE "128 128 128"
                        VALUENAME AppWorkspace   VALUE "90 78 177"
                        VALUENAME Background     VALUE "128 128 192"
                        VALUENAME ButtonDkShadow VALUE "0 0 0"
```

```
        VALUENAME ButtonFace      VALUE "174 168 217"
        VALUENAME ButtonHilight   VALUE "216 213 236"
        VALUENAME ButtonLight      VALUE "174 168 217"
        VALUENAME ButtonShadow    VALUE "90 78 177"
        VALUENAME ButtonText      VALUE "0 0 0"
        VALUENAME GrayText        VALUE "90 78 177"
        VALUENAME Hilight         VALUE "128 128 128"
        VALUENAME HilightText     VALUE "255 255 255"
        VALUENAME InactiveBorder  VALUE "174 168 217"
        VALUENAME InactiveTitle   VALUE "90 78 177"
        VALUENAME InactiveTitleText VALUE "0 0 0"
        VALUENAME InfoText        VALUE "174 168 217"
        VALUENAME InfoWindow      VALUE "0 0 0"
        VALUENAME Menu            VALUE "174 168 217"
        VALUENAME MenuText        VALUE "0 0 0"
        VALUENAME Scrollbar       VALUE "174 168 217"
        VALUENAME TitleText       VALUE "255 255 255"
        VALUENAME Window          VALUE "255 255 255"
        VALUENAME WindowFrame     VALUE "0 0 0"
        VALUENAME WindowText      VALUE "0 0 0"
    END ACTIONLIST

    NAME !!Tan256 VALUE !!Tan256
    ACTIONLIST
        KEYNAME "Control Panel\Colors"
        VALUENAME ActiveBorder    VALUE "202 184 149"
        VALUENAME ActiveTitle     VALUE "0 0 0"
        VALUENAME AppWorkspace    VALUE "156 129 78"
        VALUENAME Background      VALUE "128 64 64"
        VALUENAME ButtonDkShadow VALUE "0 0 0"
        VALUENAME ButtonFace      VALUE "202 184 149"
        VALUENAME ButtonHilight   VALUE "228 220 203"
        VALUENAME ButtonLight      VALUE "202 184 149"
        VALUENAME ButtonShadow    VALUE "156 129 78"
        VALUENAME ButtonText      VALUE "0 0 0"
        VALUENAME GrayText        VALUE "156 129 78"
        VALUENAME Hilight         VALUE "0 0 0"
        VALUENAME HilightText     VALUE "255 255 255"
        VALUENAME InactiveBorder  VALUE "202 184 149"
        VALUENAME InactiveTitle   VALUE "156 129 78"
        VALUENAME InactiveTitleText VALUE "0 0 0"
        VALUENAME InfoText        VALUE "174 168 217"
        VALUENAME InfoWindow      VALUE "0 0 0"
        VALUENAME Menu            VALUE "202 184 149"
        VALUENAME MenuText        VALUE "0 0 0"
        VALUENAME Scrollbar       VALUE "202 184 149"
        VALUENAME TitleText       VALUE "255 255 255"
        VALUENAME Window          VALUE "255 255 255"
        VALUENAME WindowFrame     VALUE "0 0 0"
        VALUENAME WindowText      VALUE "0 0 0"
    END ACTIONLIST

    NAME !!Wheat256 VALUE !!Wheat256
    ACTIONLIST
        KEYNAME "Control Panel\Colors"
        VALUENAME ActiveBorder    VALUE "215 213 170"
        VALUENAME ActiveTitle     VALUE "0 0 0"
        VALUENAME AppWorkspace    VALUE "173 169 82"
        VALUENAME Background      VALUE "0 64 64"
```

```
      VALUENAME ButtonDkShadow VALUE "0 0 0"
      VALUENAME ButtonFace       VALUE "215 213 170"
      VALUENAME ButtonHilight  VALUE "235 234 214"
      VALUENAME ButtonLight      VALUE "215 213 170"
      VALUENAME ButtonShadow   VALUE "173 169 82"
      VALUENAME ButtonText       VALUE "0 0 0"
      VALUENAME GrayText         VALUE "173 169 82"
      VALUENAME Hilight          VALUE "0 0 0"
      VALUENAME HilightText      VALUE "255 255 255"
      VALUENAME InactiveBorder VALUE "215 213 170"
      VALUENAME InactiveTitle  VALUE "173 169 82"
      VALUENAME InactiveTitleText VALUE "0 0 0"
      VALUENAME InfoText         VALUE "174 168 217"
      VALUENAME InfoWindow       VALUE "0 0 0"
      VALUENAME Menu             VALUE "215 213 170"
      VALUENAME MenuText         VALUE "0 0 0"
      VALUENAME Scrollbar        VALUE "215 213 170"
      VALUENAME TitleText        VALUE "255 255 255"
      VALUENAME Window           VALUE "255 255 255"
      VALUENAME WindowFrame      VALUE "0 0 0"
      VALUENAME WindowText       VALUE "0 0 0"
END ACTIONLIST

NAME !!Celery VALUE !!Celery
ACTIONLIST
      KEYNAME "Control Panel\Colors"
      VALUENAME ActiveBorder   VALUE "168 215 170"
      VALUENAME ActiveTitle      VALUE "0 0 0"
      VALUENAME AppWorkspace   VALUE "80 175 85"
      VALUENAME Background       VALUE "32 18 46"
      VALUENAME ButtonDkShadow VALUE "0 0 0"
      VALUENAME ButtonFace       VALUE "168 215 170"
      VALUENAME ButtonHilight  VALUE "211 235 213"
      VALUENAME ButtonLight      VALUE "168 215 170"
      VALUENAME ButtonShadow   VALUE "85 175 85"
      VALUENAME ButtonText       VALUE "0 0 0"
      VALUENAME GrayText         VALUE "80 175 85"
      VALUENAME Hilight          VALUE "0 0 0"
      VALUENAME HilightText      VALUE "255 255 255"
      VALUENAME InactiveBorder VALUE "168 215 170"
      VALUENAME InactiveTitle  VALUE "80 175 75"
      VALUENAME InactiveTitleText VALUE "0 0 0"
      VALUENAME InfoText         VALUE "174 168 217"
      VALUENAME InfoWindow       VALUE "0 0 0"
      VALUENAME Menu             VALUE "168 215 170"
      VALUENAME MenuText         VALUE "0 0 0"
      VALUENAME Scrollbar        VALUE "168 215 170"
      VALUENAME TitleText        VALUE "255 255 255"
      VALUENAME Window           VALUE "255 255 255"
      VALUENAME WindowFrame      VALUE "0 0 0"
      VALUENAME WindowText       VALUE "0 0 0"
END ACTIONLIST

NAME !!Rose VALUE !!Rose
ACTIONLIST
      KEYNAME "Control Panel\Colors"
      VALUENAME ActiveBorder   VALUE "207 175 183"
      VALUENAME ActiveTitle      VALUE "128 128 128"
      VALUENAME AppWorkspace   VALUE "159 96 112"
```

```
        VALUENAME Background      VALUE "128 64 64"
        VALUENAME ButtonDkShadow  VALUE "0 0 0"
        VALUENAME ButtonFace      VALUE "207 175 183"
        VALUENAME ButtonHilight   VALUE "231 216 220"
        VALUENAME ButtonLight      VALUE "207 175 183"
        VALUENAME ButtonShadow    VALUE "159 96 112"
        VALUENAME ButtonText      VALUE "0 0 0"
        VALUENAME GrayText        VALUE "159 96 112"
        VALUENAME Hilight         VALUE "128 128 128"
        VALUENAME HilightText     VALUE "255 255 255"
        VALUENAME InactiveBorder  VALUE "207 175 183"
        VALUENAME InactiveTitle   VALUE "159 96 112"
        VALUENAME InactiveTitleText VALUE "0 0 0"
        VALUENAME InfoText        VALUE "174 168 217"
        VALUENAME InfoWindow      VALUE "0 0 0"
        VALUENAME Menu            VALUE "207 175 183"
        VALUENAME MenuText        VALUE "0 0 0"
        VALUENAME Scrollbar       VALUE "207 175 183"
        VALUENAME TitleText       VALUE "255 255 255"
        VALUENAME Window          VALUE "255 255 255"
        VALUENAME WindowFrame     VALUE "0 0 0"
        VALUENAME WindowText      VALUE "0 0 0"
END ACTIONLIST

NAME !!Evergreen VALUE !!Evergreen
ACTIONLIST
        KEYNAME "Control Panel\Colors"
        VALUENAME ActiveBorder    VALUE "47 151 109"
        VALUENAME ActiveTitle     VALUE "0 0 0"
        VALUENAME AppWorkspace    VALUE "31 101 73"
        VALUENAME Background      VALUE "48 63 48"
        VALUENAME ButtonDkShadow  VALUE "0 0 0"
        VALUENAME ButtonFace      VALUE "47 151 109"
        VALUENAME ButtonHilight   VALUE "137 218 186"
        VALUENAME ButtonLight      VALUE "47 151 109"
        VALUENAME ButtonShadow    VALUE "31 101 73"
        VALUENAME ButtonText      VALUE "0 0 0"
        VALUENAME GrayText        VALUE "31 101 73"
        VALUENAME Hilight         VALUE "0 0 0"
        VALUENAME HilightText     VALUE "255 255 255"
        VALUENAME InactiveBorder  VALUE "47 151 109"
        VALUENAME InactiveTitle   VALUE "31 101 73"
        VALUENAME InactiveTitleText VALUE "0 0 0"
        VALUENAME InfoText        VALUE "174 168 217"
        VALUENAME InfoWindow      VALUE "0 0 0"
        VALUENAME Menu            VALUE "47 151 109"
        VALUENAME MenuText        VALUE "0 0 0"
        VALUENAME Scrollbar       VALUE "47 151 109"
        VALUENAME TitleText       VALUE "255 255 255"
        VALUENAME Window          VALUE "255 255 255"
        VALUENAME WindowFrame     VALUE "0 0 0"
        VALUENAME WindowText      VALUE "0 0 0"
END ACTIONLIST

NAME !!Blues VALUE !!Blues
ACTIONLIST
        KEYNAME "Control Panel\Colors"
        VALUENAME ActiveBorder    VALUE "161 198 221"
        VALUENAME ActiveTitle     VALUE "0 0 0"
```

```
        VALUENAME AppWorkspace     VALUE "69 139 186"
        VALUENAME Background        VALUE "0 0 64"
        VALUENAME ButtonDkShadow VALUE "0 0 0"
        VALUENAME ButtonFace        VALUE "164 198 221"
        VALUENAME ButtonHilight    VALUE "210 227 238"
        VALUENAME ButtonLight       VALUE "164 198 221"
        VALUENAME ButtonShadow      VALUE "69 139 186"
        VALUENAME ButtonText        VALUE "0 0 0"
        VALUENAME GrayText          VALUE "69 139 186"
        VALUENAME Hilight           VALUE "0 0 0"
        VALUENAME HilightText       VALUE "255 255 255"
        VALUENAME InactiveBorder VALUE "164 198 221"
        VALUENAME InactiveTitle    VALUE "69 139 186"
        VALUENAME InactiveTitleText VALUE "0 0 0"
        VALUENAME InfoText          VALUE "174 168 217"
        VALUENAME InfoWindow        VALUE "0 0 0"
        VALUENAME Menu              VALUE "164 198 221"
        VALUENAME MenuText          VALUE "0 0 0"
        VALUENAME Scrollbar         VALUE "164 198 221"
        VALUENAME TitleText         VALUE "255 255 255"
        VALUENAME Window            VALUE "255 255 255"
        VALUENAME WindowFrame       VALUE "0 0 0"
        VALUENAME WindowText        VALUE "0 0 0"
END ACTIONLIST

NAME !!Teal VALUE !!Teal
ACTIONLIST
        KEYNAME "Control Panel\Colors"
        VALUENAME ActiveBorder      VALUE "192 192 192"
        VALUENAME ActiveTitle       VALUE "0 128 128"
        VALUENAME AppWorkspace      VALUE "128 128 128"
        VALUENAME Background        VALUE "0 64 64"
        VALUENAME ButtonDkShadow VALUE "0 0 0"
        VALUENAME ButtonFace        VALUE "192 192 192"
        VALUENAME ButtonHilight    VALUE "255 255 255"
        VALUENAME ButtonLight       VALUE "192 192 192"
        VALUENAME ButtonShadow      VALUE "128 128 128"
        VALUENAME ButtonText        VALUE "0 0 0"
        VALUENAME GrayText          VALUE "128 128 128"
        VALUENAME Hilight           VALUE "0 128 128"
        VALUENAME HilightText       VALUE "255 255 255"
        VALUENAME InactiveBorder VALUE "192 192 192"
        VALUENAME InactiveTitle    VALUE "192 192 192"
        VALUENAME InactiveTitleText VALUE "0 0 0"
        VALUENAME InfoText          VALUE "174 168 217"
        VALUENAME InfoWindow        VALUE "0 0 0"
        VALUENAME Menu              VALUE "192 192 192"
        VALUENAME MenuText          VALUE "0 0 0"
        VALUENAME Scrollbar         VALUE "192 192 192"
        VALUENAME TitleText         VALUE "0 0 0"
        VALUENAME Window            VALUE "255 255 255"
        VALUENAME WindowFrame       VALUE "0 0 0"
        VALUENAME WindowText        VALUE "0 0 0"
END ACTIONLIST

NAME !!TheReds VALUE !!TheReds
ACTIONLIST
        KEYNAME "Control Panel\Colors"
        VALUENAME ActiveBorder      VALUE "192 192 192"
```

```
        VALUENAME ActiveTitle    VALUE "128 0 0"
        VALUENAME AppWorkspace   VALUE "128 128 128"
        VALUENAME Background      VALUE "64 0 0"
        VALUENAME ButtonDkShadow VALUE "0 0 0"
        VALUENAME ButtonFace      VALUE "192 192 192"
        VALUENAME ButtonHilight  VALUE "255 255 255"
        VALUENAME ButtonLight     VALUE "192 192 192"
        VALUENAME ButtonShadow    VALUE "128 128 128"
        VALUENAME ButtonText      VALUE "0 0 0"
        VALUENAME GrayText        VALUE "128 128 128"
        VALUENAME Hilight         VALUE "128 0 0"
        VALUENAME HilightText     VALUE "255 255 255"
        VALUENAME InactiveBorder VALUE "192 192 192"
        VALUENAME InactiveTitle  VALUE "192 192 192"
        VALUENAME InactiveTitleText VALUE "0 0 0"
        VALUENAME InfoText        VALUE "174 168 217"
        VALUENAME InfoWindow      VALUE "0 0 0"
        VALUENAME Menu            VALUE "192 192 192"
        VALUENAME MenuText        VALUE "0 0 0"
        VALUENAME Scrollbar       VALUE "192 192 192"
        VALUENAME TitleText       VALUE "255 255 255"
        VALUENAME Window          VALUE "255 255 255"
        VALUENAME WindowFrame     VALUE "0 0 0"
        VALUENAME WindowText      VALUE "0 0 0"
END ACTIONLIST

NAME !!WindowsDefault VALUE !!WindowsDefault
ACTIONLIST
        KEYNAME "Control Panel\Colors"
        VALUENAME ActiveBorder    VALUE "192 192 192"
        VALUENAME ActiveTitle     VALUE "0 0 128"
        VALUENAME AppWorkspace    VALUE "128 128 128"
        VALUENAME Background       VALUE "0 128 128"
        VALUENAME ButtonDkShadow VALUE "0 0 0"
        VALUENAME ButtonFace       VALUE "192 192 192"
        VALUENAME ButtonHilight   VALUE "255 255 255"
        VALUENAME ButtonLight      VALUE "192 192 192"
        VALUENAME ButtonShadow     VALUE "128 128 128"
        VALUENAME ButtonText       VALUE "0 0 0"
        VALUENAME GrayText         VALUE "128 128 128"
        VALUENAME Hilight          VALUE "0 0 128"
        VALUENAME HilightText      VALUE "255 255 255"
        VALUENAME InactiveBorder VALUE "192 192 192"
        VALUENAME InactiveTitle   VALUE "192 192 192"
        VALUENAME InactiveTitleText VALUE "0 0 0"
        VALUENAME InfoText         VALUE "174 168 217"
        VALUENAME InfoWindow       VALUE "0 0 0"
        VALUENAME Menu             VALUE "192 192 192"
        VALUENAME MenuText         VALUE "0 0 0"
        VALUENAME Scrollbar        VALUE "192 192 192"
        VALUENAME TitleText        VALUE "255 255 255"
        VALUENAME Window           VALUE "255 255 255"
        VALUENAME WindowFrame      VALUE "0 0 0"
        VALUENAME WindowText       VALUE "0 0 0"
END ACTIONLIST

NAME !!BlueAndBlack VALUE !!BlueAndBlack
ACTIONLIST
        KEYNAME "Control Panel\Colors"
```

```
          VALUENAME ActiveBorder    VALUE "192 192 192"
          VALUENAME ActiveTitle     VALUE "0 0 0"
          VALUENAME AppWorkspace    VALUE "128 128 128"
          VALUENAME Background       VALUE "0 0 128"
          VALUENAME ButtonDkShadow  VALUE "0 0 0"
          VALUENAME ButtonFace       VALUE "192 192 192"
          VALUENAME ButtonHilight   VALUE "255 255 255"
          VALUENAME ButtonLight       VALUE "192 192 192"
          VALUENAME ButtonShadow    VALUE "128 128 128"
          VALUENAME ButtonText       VALUE "0 0 0"
          VALUENAME GrayText         VALUE "128 128 128"
          VALUENAME Hilight          VALUE "255 255 0"
          VALUENAME HilightText     VALUE "0 0 0"
          VALUENAME InactiveBorder  VALUE "192 192 192"
          VALUENAME InactiveTitle   VALUE "192 192 192"
          VALUENAME InactiveTitleText VALUE "0 0 0"
          VALUENAME InfoText         VALUE "174 168 217"
          VALUENAME InfoWindow      VALUE "0 0 0"
          VALUENAME Menu             VALUE "192 192 192"
          VALUENAME MenuText         VALUE "0 0 0"
          VALUENAME Scrollbar       VALUE "192 192 192"
          VALUENAME TitleText       VALUE "255 255 255"
          VALUENAME Window           VALUE "255 255 255"
          VALUENAME WindowFrame     VALUE "0 0 0"
          VALUENAME WindowText      VALUE "0 0 0"
      END ACTIONLIST

      NAME !!Wheat VALUE !!Wheat
      ACTIONLIST
          KEYNAME "Control Panel\Colors"
          VALUENAME ActiveBorder    VALUE "192 192 192"
          VALUENAME ActiveTitle     VALUE "128 128 0"
          VALUENAME AppWorkspace    VALUE "128 128 128"
          VALUENAME Background       VALUE "128 128 64"
          VALUENAME ButtonDkShadow  VALUE "0 0 0"
          VALUENAME ButtonFace       VALUE "192 192 192"
          VALUENAME ButtonHilight   VALUE "255 255 255"
          VALUENAME ButtonLight       VALUE "192 192 192"
          VALUENAME ButtonShadow    VALUE "128 128 128"
          VALUENAME ButtonText       VALUE "0 0 0"
          VALUENAME GrayText         VALUE "128 128 128"
          VALUENAME Hilight          VALUE "128 128 0"
          VALUENAME HilightText     VALUE "0 0 0"
          VALUENAME InactiveBorder  VALUE "192 192 192"
          VALUENAME InactiveTitle   VALUE "192 192 192"
          VALUENAME InactiveTitleText VALUE "0 0 0"
          VALUENAME InfoText         VALUE "174 168 217"
          VALUENAME InfoWindow      VALUE "0 0 0"
          VALUENAME Menu             VALUE "192 192 192"
          VALUENAME MenuText         VALUE "0 0 0"
          VALUENAME Scrollbar       VALUE "192 192 192"
          VALUENAME TitleText       VALUE "0 0 0"
          VALUENAME Window           VALUE "255 255 255"
          VALUENAME WindowFrame     VALUE "0 0 0"
          VALUENAME WindowText      VALUE "0 0 0"
      END ACTIONLIST

      END ITEMLIST
      END PART
```

```
            END POLICY
    END CATEGORY    ; desktop

    CATEGORY !!Restrictions
        POLICY !!DisableRegedit
        VALUENAME DisableRegistryTools
        END POLICY

        POLICY !!RestrictApps
        KEYNAME Software\Microsoft\Windows\CurrentVersion\Policies\Explorer
        VALUENAME RestrictRun
            PART !!RestrictAppsList LISTBOX
            KEYNAME
Software\Microsoft\Windows\CurrentVersion\Policies\Explorer\RestrictRun
                VALUEPREFIX ""
            END PART
        END POLICY

        POLICY !!DisableMSDOS
        KEYNAME Software\Microsoft\Windows\CurrentVersion\Policies\WinOldApp
        VALUENAME Disabled
        END POLICY

        POLICY !!DisableSingleMSDOS
        KEYNAME Software\Microsoft\Windows\CurrentVersion\Policies\WinOldApp
        VALUENAME NoRealMode
        END POLICY
    END CATEGORY

END CATEGORY

[strings]
System="Windows 98 System"
NetworkSetupPath="Network path for Windows Setup"
NetworkSetupPath_Path="Path:"
NetworkTourPath="Network path for Windows Tour"
NetworkTourPath_Path="Path:"
NetworkTourPath_Tip="Note: the path must end in TOUR.EXE"
EnableUserProfiles="Enable User Profiles"
Network="Windows 98 Network"
Logon="Logon"
LogonBanner="Logon Banner"
LogonBanner_Caption="Caption:"
LogonBanner_Text="Text:"
LogonBanner_DefCaption="Important Notice:"
LogonBanner_DefText="Do not attempt to log on unless you are an authorized user."
ValidatedLogon="Require validation from network for Windows access"
Sharing="Sharing"
VServer="File and Printer sharing for Microsoft Networks"
DisableFileSharing="Disable file sharing"
DisablePrintSharing="Disable print sharing"
AccessControl="Access Control"
AccessControl_User="User-level access control"
AuthenticatorName="Authenticator Name:"
AuthenticatorType="Authenticator Type:"
AT_NetWare="NetWare 3.x or 4.x"
AT_NT="Windows NT Server or Workstation"
AT_NTAS="Windows NT Domain"
Passwords="Password"
```

```
HideSharePasswords="Hide share passwords with asterisks"
DisablePasswordCaching="Disable password caching"
RequireAlphaNum="Require alphanumeric Windows password"
MinimumPwdLen="Minimum Windows password length"
MPL_Length="Length:"
RemoteAccess="Dial-Up Networking"
RemoteAccess_Disable="Disable dial-in"
Update="Update"
RemoteUpdate="Remote Update"
UpdateMode="Update Mode:"
UM_Automatic="Automatic (use default path)"
UM_Manual="Manual (use specific path)"
UM_Manual_Path="Path for manual update:"
DisplayErrors="Display error messages"
LoadBalance="Load-balance"
MSClient="Microsoft Client for Windows Networks"
NWServer="File and printer sharing for NetWare Networks"
LogonDomain="Log on to Windows NT"
DomainName="Domain name:"
Workgroup="Workgroup"
AlternateWorkgroup="Alternate Workgroup"
WorkgroupName="Workgroup name:"
NWClient="Microsoft Client for NetWare Networks"
PrefServer="Preferred server"
PrefServerName="Server name:"
SupportLFN="Support long file names"
SupportLFNsOn="Support long file names on:"
LFN_No311="NetWare 3.12 and above"
LFN_All="All NetWare servers that support LFNs"
SearchMode="Search Mode"
SearchMode1="Search Mode:"
DisableAutoNWLogin="Disable automatic NetWare login"
DisableSAP="Disable SAP Advertising"
ControlPanel="Control Panel"
CPL_Display="Display"
CPL_Display_Restrict="Restrict Display Control Panel"
CPL_Display_Disable="Disable Display Control Panel"
CPL_Display_HideBkgnd="Hide Background page"
CPL_Display_HideScrsav="Hide Screen Saver page"
CPL_Display_HideAppearance="Hide Appearance page"
CPL_Display_HideSettings="Hide Settings page"
CPL_Network="Network"
CPL_Network_Restrict="Restrict Network Control Panel"
CPL_Network_Disable="Disable Network Control Panel"
CPL_Network_HideID="Hide Identification Page"
CPL_Network_HideAccessCtrl="Hide Access Control Page"
CPL_Printers="Printers"
CPL_Printers_Restrict="Restrict Printer Settings"
CPL_Printers_HidePages="Hide General and Details pages"
CPL_Printers_DisableRemoval="Disable Deletion of Printers"
CPL_Printers_DisableAdd="Disable Addition of Printers"
CPL_System="System"
CPL_System_Restrict="Restrict System Control Panel"
CPL_System_HideDevMgr="Hide Device Manager page"
CPL_System_HideConfig="Hide Hardware Profiles Page"
CPL_System_NoFileSys="Hide File System button"
CPL_System_NoVirtMem="Hide Virtual Memory button"
CPL_Security="Passwords"
CPL_Security_Restrict="Restrict Passwords Control Panel"
```

```
CPL_Security_Disable="Disable Passwords Control Panel"
CPL_Security_HideSetPwds="Hide Change Passwords page"
CPL_Security_HideRemoteAdmin="Hide Remote Administration page"
CPL_Security_HideProfiles="Hide User Profiles page"
Desktop="Desktop Display"
Wallpaper="Wallpaper"
WallpaperName="Wallpaper name:"
Wallpaper1="Black Thatch.bmp"
Wallpaper2="Blue Rivets.bmp"
Wallpaper3="Bubbles.bmp"
Wallpaper4="Circles.bmp"
Wallpaper5="Egypt.bmp"
Wallpaper6="Houndstooth.bmp"
Wallpaper7="Pinstripe.bmp"
Wallpaper8="Straw Mat.bmp"
Wallpaper9="Tiles.bmp"
Wallpaper10="Triangles.bmp"
TileWallpaper="Tile wallpaper"
ColorScheme="Color scheme"
SchemeName="Scheme name:"
Lavender="Lavender 256"
Celery="Celery 256"
Rose="Rose 256"
Evergreen="Evergreen 256"
Blues="Blues 256"
WindowsDefault="Windows Default"
BlueAndBlack="Blue and Black"
Teal="Teal"
TheReds="The Reds"
Wheat="Wheat"
Wheat256="Wheat 256"
Tan256="Tan 256"
DisableFileSharingCtrl="Disable file sharing controls"
DisablePrintSharingCtrl="Disable print sharing controls"
Shell="Shell"
CustomFolders="Custom Folders"
CustomFolders_Programs="Custom Programs Folder"
CustomFolders_ProgramsPath="Path to get Programs items from:"
CustomFolders_Desktop="Custom Desktop Icons"
CustomFolders_DesktopPath="Path to get Desktop icons from:"
HideStartMenuSubfolders="Hide Start Menu subfolders"
HideStartMenuSubfolders_Tip1="Check this if you use a custom Programs Folder or"
HideStartMenuSubfolders_Tip2="custom Desktop icons."
CustomFolders_Startup="Custom Startup Folder"
CustomFolders_StartupPath="Path to get Startup items from:"
CustomFolders_NetHood="Custom Network Neighborhood"
CustomFolders_NetHoodPath="Path to get Network Neighborhood items from:"
CustomFolders_StartMenu="Custom Start Menu"
CustomFolders_StartMenuPath="Path to get Start Menu items from:"
Restrictions="Restrictions"
RemoveRun="Remove 'Run' command"
RemoveFolders="Remove folders from 'Settings' on Start Menu"
RemoveTaskbar="Remove Taskbar from 'Settings' on Start Menu"
RemoveFind="Remove 'Find' command"
HideDrives="Hide Drives in 'My Computer'"
HideNetHood="Hide Network Neighborhood"
HideDesktop="Hide all items on Desktop"
DisableClose="Disable Shut Down command"
NoSaveSettings="Don't save settings at exit"
```

```
DisableRegedit="Disable Registry editing tools"
DisableMSDOS="Disable MS-DOS prompt"
DisableSingleMSDOS="Disable single-mode MS-DOS applications"
Run="Run"
RunOnce="Run Once"
RunServices="Run Services"
RunListbox="Items to run at startup:"
RunOnceListbox="Items to run once at startup:"
RunServicesListbox="Services to run at startup:"
SNMP="SNMP"
Communities="Communities"
CommunitiesListbox="Communities:"
PermittedManagers="Permitted managers"
PermittedManagersListbox="Permitted managers:"
Traps_Public="Traps for 'Public' community"
Traps_PublicListbox="Trap configuration:"
NoEntireNetwork="No 'Entire Network' in Network Neighborhood"
NoWorkgroupContents="No workgroup contents in Network Neighborhood"
RestrictApps="Only run allowed Windows applications"
RestrictAppsList="List of allowed applications:"
DomainLogonConfirmation="Display domain logon confirmation"
InternetMIB="Internet MIB (RFC1156)"
ContactName="Contact Name:"
Location="Location:"
NoDomainPwdCaching="Disable caching of domain password"
NWClient4="NetWare Directory Services"
PrefTree="Preferred Tree"
PrefTreeName="Tree Name:"
DefaultNameContext="Default Name Context"
DefContextName="Default Name Context:"
DisableNWAutoBootLogon="Disable automatic tree login"
EnableLogonPopup="Enable login confirmation"
DisableAdvLogonSettings="Don't show advanced login button"
DefaultLogonType="Default type of NetWare login"
BinderyLogon="Log in to server in bindery mode"
TreeLogon="Log in to NDS tree"
BrowseDisableBNDServers="Don't show servers that aren't NDS objects"
BrowseDisableServers="Don't show server objects"
BrowseDisableContainers="Don't show container objects"
BrowseDisableWorkgroups="Don't show peer workgroups"
BrowseDisablePrinters="Don't show printer objects"
BrowseDisableQueues="Don't show print queue objects"
BrowseDisableVolumes="Don't show volume objects"
PreLoadNetWareRunTime="Load NetWare DLLs at startup"
DontDisplayLastUserName="Don't show last user at logon"
UserProfiles="User Profiles"
NetworkPaths="Network Paths"
ProgramsToRun="Programs to Run"
```

B

Using .INF Files for Windows 98 Setup

Peter Norton®

Chapter 2 introduced you to scripting Windows 98 setups. To do so, you used the Batch editor to create a script file and save it using the extension .INF. On occasion, you may need to manually modify this file to include lines that Batch could not insert, especially relating to hardware devices. To do so, you must locate lines in files supplied by device manufacturers that contain the settings you must insert into your scripts.

Windows 98 uses information files (those with the .INF extension) for two purposes, both having to do with setup. First, each manufacturer of a device must provide an .INF file to describe the device to the system. In this file is the setup information that allows the system to select the correct driver and set the hardware settings for a device. Second, you can create an .INF file that serves as an automation script for controlling setup.

The hitch, of course, is that to create good setup scripts, you have to know what is in the manufacturer's .INF files. As a result, this appendix shows you how to read both kinds of files, and how to create the second type. It is a what's where directory for the various settings that you might see or desire to use. For the manufacturer's file, the focus is on what you need to be able to read from the file. For the setup script file, the emphasis is on the settings you can use to control setup. It also shows you the editor that allows you to create setup scripts with ease.

The Device Information File

A device information file is a text file that describes the attributes of the device to the operating system. The information in the file is organized into sections that are identified by lines in the following format:

```
[Section]
```

The section headers serve as search keys that allow the operating system to quickly identify relevant settings that serve a particular purpose. They serve as entry points into the file that group the version information or the manufacturer information so that when this information is needed during setup, it can be retrieved efficiently.

The remaining lines in the file are written in the following format:

```
key=value
```

Each key serves as another search point. The value of the key is the information that the operating system needs to set up the detail identified by the key.

To locate the information necessary for any particular setup operation, Windows searches for a section and then a key. The first action very quickly locates the general region in the file where the key might reside. The second action locates the actual information. The next few sections identify the keys for each section of the device .INF file and provide a description of the information that the keys can provide.

The notation used to represent the syntax of the commands described in this appendix adheres to the standard used by Microsoft in its documentation and product descriptions.

[Version]

```
Signature="$CHICAGO$"
```

This line is required at the start of this section of the file. It shows that the device is designed to be used under Windows 98 and that this is the file for installing the device under Windows 98. In the event the device includes several files for installation under different versions of Windows, this line identifies that this is the file to use with Windows 98.

Class=class-name

In the Registry, information is stored about each type or *class* of device installed on your system. This line identifies the class to which the device described by this file belongs. Possible values include the following:

- Adapter—Identifies adapter cards not classified elsewhere.
- Cdrom—Identifies CD-ROM drives.
- Display—Identifies display adapters.
- EISADevices—Identifies devices designed for the EISA bus.
- fdc—Identifies floppy drive controllers.
- hdc—Identifies hard drive controllers.
- Keyboard—Identifies keyboards and their substitutes.
- MCADevices—Identifies Microchannel Architecture devices.
- Media—Identifies multimedia devices.
- Modem—Identifies modems.
- Monitor—Identifies display monitors and other types of screens.
- Mouse—Identifies your pointing device.
- MTD—Identifies memory technology drivers.
- Net—Identifies network devices.
- NetService—Identifies network services.
- Nodriver—Identifies devices that do not use a driver.
- PCMCIA—Identifies PC Cards.
- Ports—Identifies serial and parallel ports.

- Printer—Identifies printers and similar devices.
- SCSIAdapter—Identifies Small Computer System Interface adapters.
- System—Identifies system devices. (To identify what types of devices belong here, examine the System branch in the Device Manager display.)

Provider =INF_creator

This value identifies the creator of the file. The value is normally a string key placed between percentage characters, as in %MSFT%. (See the "[Manufacturer]" section for more information about string keys.)

LayoutFile=filename.inf

Associated with any device is a layout file, which describes the distribution media, its directory structure, and its file structure. The typical value for this key is LAYOUT.INF.

[Manufacturer]

This section consists of a single line that identifies the manufacturer of the device. This line has the following syntax:

manufacturer-name | %strings-key%=manufacturer-name-section

The *manufacturer-name* is any combination of printing characters that is uniquely paired with the manufacturer. It must be within double quotation marks. The *%strings-key%* is a set of characters that identifies a string in the [strings] section of the file. Character strings can be provided keys in the strings section by which they can be uniquely accessed. The percent characters enclosing the other characters identify the use of a string key as an alias for the full string, as in %MSFT% described in the "Provider=INF_creator" section earlier in this chapter. Either the *manufacturer-name* or the *%strings-key%* entry must be present. *Manufacturer-name-section* is the name of the section in the .INF file that marks the manufacturer name. This value includes the string that would appear between the square brackets ([]) that identify the [Manufacturer] section of the file.

[Manufacturer Name]

This section, which must be identified in the [Manufacturer] section, identifies the device description and names the [Install] section associated with the device. The syntax for the description required is as follows:

device-description=install-section-name, device-id[,compatible-device-id]...

The *device-description* is either a string of printable characters or a string key. The *install-section-name* is the name of the [Install] section, without the brackets, used for the device. The *device-id* is the unique identifier associated with the device, for example, *PNPA002*. Any number of compatible device identifiers, indicating devices compatible with this one, can follow, but they must be separated by commas. The descriptors and identifiers in this section build the Driver Description, Manufacturer Name, DeviceID, and Compatibility values for the Registry.

[Install]

The [Install] section contains lines that describe other sections used to configure the device and its drivers. Not all of the statements listed are required, only those necessary to the device in question. This section is essentially just a pointer to other critical sections in the file. Specifying the name of the section on a line associates the name used with the function described by the line.

LogConfig = log-config-section-name[,log-config-section-name]...

Indicates the logical configuration section or sections associated with the device. You can use multiple sections if there are alternate logical configurations the device can use, such as using or not using DMA or an onboard BIOS.

Copyfiles=file-list-section[,file-list-section]...

Indicates the copy files section or sections associated with the device.

Renfiles=file-list-section[,file-list-section]...

Indicates the rename files section or sections associated with the device.

Delfiles=file-list-section[,file-list-section]...

Indicates the delete files section or sections associated with the device.

UpdateInis=update-ini-section[,update-ini-section]...

Indicates the update .INI files section or sections associated with the device.

UpdateIniFields=update-inifields-section[,update-inifields-section]...

Indicates the update .INI fields section or sections associated with the device.

AddReg=add-registry-section[,add-registry-section]...

Indicates the add Registry section or sections associated with the device.

DelReg=del-registry-section[,del-registry-section]...

Indicates the delete Registry section or sections associated with the device.

Ini2Reg=ini-to-registry-section[,ini-to-registry-section]...

Indicates the .INI to Registry section or sections associated with the device.

UpdateCfgSys=update-config-section

Indicates the update CONFIG.SYS section associated with the device.

UpdateAutoBat=update-autoexec-section

Indicates the update AUTOEXEC.BAT section associated with the device.

Reboot | Restart

Causes the system to reboot or restart, depending on the keyword used, when the commands specified in the [Install] section are completed.

[ClassInstall]

The statements in this section define a class for the new device in the Registry. For each device on your system, there must be class listed in the Registry, even if that class is *Unknown*. For each class defined in the Registry, there is a class installer (defined as a section in an .INF file called *ClassInstall*). Only the entries actually used need to be included in this section. The class installer is processed only if the class does not currently exist in the Registry.

Copyfiles=file-list-section[,file-list-section]...

This statement specifies the name (or names) of the *CopyFiles* section (or sections) related to the class.

AddReg=add-registry-section[,add-registry-section]...

This statement specifies the name of the *AddRegistry* section or sections, which define the key names and values to add to the Registry for this class.

Renfiles=file-list-section[,file-list-section]...

This statement specifies the name of the rename files section or sections to be used in installing the class.

Delfiles=file-list-section[,file-list-section]...

This statement specifies the name of the delete files section or sections to be used in installing the class.

UpdateInis=update-ini-section[,update-ini-section]...

This statement specifies the name for the update .INI files section or sections to be used in installing the class.

UpdateIniFields=update-inifields-section[,update-inifield-section]...

This statement specifies the name for the update .INI fields section or sections to be used in installing the class.

DelReg=del-registry-section[,del-registry-section]...

This statement specifies the name of the delete Registry section, which specifies Registry entries to delete, to be used in installing the class. (See Chapter 30, "Investigating the Registry," for more information about the Registry.)

[Logical Configuration]

This section identifies the hardware resources to be allocated to the device. Only the lines specifying resources actually used are provided. Where multiple resources, such as two IRQ lines, are required, multiple lines are used to describe the device's needs.

ConfigPriority = priority-value

Describes the priority associated with the configuration, as shown in Table B.1. Only one such entry can appear in a logical configuration section.

Table B.1. ConfigPriority values.

Value	Meaning
HARDWIRED	You cannot reset the configuration.
DESIRED	Software configuration is preferable for the device.
NORMAL	Software configuration is acceptable for the device.
SUBOPTIMAL	Software configuration is least preferable for the device.
DISABLED	The hardware has been disabled.
RESTART	Windows must restart before the configuration takes effect.
REBOOT	The system must reboot before the configuration takes effect.
POWEROFF	Requires power cycle to take effect.
HARDRECONFIG	Requires Jumper setting to take effect.

MemConfig = mem-range-list

Identifies the memory address range used by the device.

I/OConfig = io-range-list

Describes the input/output ports used by the device.

IRQConfig = irq-list

Describes the interrupt request lines used by the device.

DMAConfig = dma-list

Describes the direct memory access channels used by the device.

[Update AutoExec]

Commands in this section describe how to update the AUTOEXEC.BAT file. Only the commands required should be present.

CmdDelete=command-name

Describes a command to delete.

CmdAdd=command-name[,command-parameters]

Describes a command to add.

UnSet=env-var-name

Describes an environment variable that should be unset in the file.

PreFixPath=ldid[,ldid]

Describes a string to prefix to the current path.

RemOldPath=ldid[,ldid]

Describes a string to remove from the path.

TmpDir=ldid[,subdir]

Describes the temporary directory to add.

[Update Config]

Commands in this section describe how to update the CONFIG.SYS file. Only the commands required should be used.

DevRename=current-dev-name,new-dev-name

Renames a device driver currently specified in the file.

DevDelete=device-driver-name

Deletes a device driver from the file.

DevAddDev=driver-name,configkeyword[,flag][,param-string]

Adds a device driver to the file.

Stacks=dos-stacks-values

Specifies the *Stacks* line to include in the file.

Buffers=legal-dos-buffer-value

Specifies the *Buffers* line to use in the file.

Files=legal-dos-files-value

Specifies the *Files* line to use in the file.

LastDrive=legal-dos-lastdrive-value

Specifies the *LastDrive* line to use in the file.

[Update INI]

These lines use the matching procedure specified by the *flags* entry to locate and replace .INI file entries. The syntax for the line is as follows:

ini-file, ini-section, [old-ini-entry], [new-ini-entry], [flags]

Ini-file identifies the file to search and *ini-section* indicates the section header to locate. *Old-ini-entry* indicates the key whose value should be updated, and *new-ini-entry* contains the new entry for the key. Table B.2 describes the effect of including a flag on the line.

Table B.2. UpdateINI flag values.

Flag Value	Meaning
0	Locates the value of the *old-ini-entry* and takes action dependent on the presence of the key described in *old-ini-entry*. If the key is present, it is replaced with the *new-ini-entry*. If the value of either *old-ini-entry* or *new-ini-entry* is NULL, an add or delete takes place. If the old value is NULL, the new entry is added. If the new value is NULL, the old entry is deleted. This is the default action.
1	Locates both the key and value for *old-ini-entry*. If both match, the value of *new-ini-entry* is inserted for the old value.
2	Searches for the key for *old-ini-entry* and replaces the value with *new-ini-entry* only if the key does not already exist.
3	Searches for both the key and value of *old-ini-entry* and replaces the entry only if both do not already exist.

You can use wildcard characters like the asterisk in the searches. The following line shows typical entries for this section:

```
%11%\app.ini, startup, maximize=*, ; deletes old entry
```

[Update IniFields]

This section includes statements that modify only a portion of an .INI file entry. The syntax for each line follows:

```
ini-file, ini-section, profile-name, [old-field], [new-field]
```

Ini-section is located in *ini-file*. For the entry named in *profile-name*, the *new-field* is substituted for *old-field*.

[Add Registry]

The statements in this section add keys to the registry using the following syntax:

```
reg-root-string, [subkey], [value-name], [Flag], [value]
```

Reg-root-string is one of the four registry entry points that begin with HKEY. *Subkey* identifies the subkey to add. *Value-name* provides the name of a value entry, whereas *value* provides the value to add. The values of *flag* are described in Table B.3.

Table B.3. AddRegistry flag values.

Binary Value	Meaning
0 0 (Default)	ANSI string.
0 1	Hexadecimal number.
1 0 (Default)	Replace existing key.
1 1	Do not replace existing key.

[Delete Registry]

This section contains lines that delete either subkeys or the value name specified from the registry. The statements adhere to the following syntax:

```
reg-root-string, subkey, [value-name]
```

[Ini to Registry]

This section contains lines that convert .INI file entries into settings in the Registry. The section name must be included under the *Ini2Reg* entry in the [Install] section of the .INF file. The statements take the following syntax:

```
ini-file, ini-section, [ini-key], reg-root-string, subkey, flags
```

The appropriate *ini-section* (and *ini-key*, if specified) is located and the entries there converted to registry entries under the Registry entry point and subkey specified. The *flags* field takes the values shown in Table B.4.

Table B.4. Values of the Ini to Registry flags.

Binary Value	Meaning
0 0 (Default)	Retain the INI entry in the INI file after adding the entry to the Registry.
0 1	Delete the INI entry after adding the entry to the Registry.
1 0	(Default) Do not replace existing subkey values in the Registry.
1 1	Replace existing subkey values in the Registry.

[DestinationDirs]

This section uses statements with the following syntax to describe the destination directory to be used with any file-list section described in the .INF file:

```
file-list-section=ldid[,subdir ]
```

File-list-section is the name of a file-list section in the .INF file. *Ldid* is a logical ID shown in Table B.5. *Subdir* names a subdirectory for use with the file-list section. Replacing *file-list* with *DefDestDir* specifies a default destination for each file copied directly by placing the @ symbol before its name.

Table B.5. LDIDs for DestinationDirs.

Value	Meaning
00	Null LDID. Use this entry to create a new LDID.
01	Source drive:\ pathname
02	For Windows 98 setup only. The temporary setup directory.
03	Uninstall directory
04	Backup directory
10	Windows directory
11	SYSTEM directory
12	IOSUBSYS directory
13	COMMAND directory
14	Control Panel directory
15	Printers directory

Value	Meaning
16	Workgroup directory
17	INF directory
18	Help directory
19	Administration
20	Fonts
21	Viewers
22	VMN32
23	Color directory
25	Shared directory
26	Winboot
27	Machine-specific
28	Host Winboot
30	Boot drive's root directory
31	Host drive's root directory (for virtual drives)
32	Existing old Windows directory
33	Existing old MS-DOS directory

[File-List]

The statements in this section define the names for files to be copied, renamed, or deleted. For copying files, the syntax is as follows:

```
destination-file-name,[source-file-name],[temporary-file-name]
```

The destination filename is the filename to copy to. The source filename is the filename to copy from. The temporary filename specifies a name to copy to temporarily between Windows 98 boots. Such files are copied to the temporary name. When Windows 98 reboots, they are copied to their destination filename.

For renaming, the syntax is as follows:

```
new-file-name,old-file-name
```

For deleting, the syntax is very simple:

```
filename
```

[SourceDisksFiles]

Pairs a filename with the ordinal number of a source disk using the following syntax:

```
filename=disk-number
```

To indicate that `detfile.exe` is on source disk one, you would use the following line:

```
detfile.exe=1
```

[SourceDisksNames]

Allows you to pair a disk ordinal number with a string description, a volume label, and a serial number for the disk, using the following syntax:

```
disk-ordinal="disk-description",disk-label,disk-serial-number
```

[Strings]

The entries in this section present a shorthand for referring to strings of printable characters used in the installation of the device. Because all of the strings are gathered into a single place in the file, they can be updated throughout the file by making changes in this section. The syntax for these entries takes the following form:

```
strings-key=value
```

The *strings-key* is a sequence of letters and numbers used to reference the string. *Value* is the string itself, enclosed in quotation marks. A reference to the string takes the form %*strings-key*% elsewhere in the file. A sample familiar entry is:

```
MSFT="Microsoft"
```

Miscellaneous Section

The device .INF file can contain several other sections. By and large, these sections are relevant only to device driver developers and not to those building setup scripts. A good rule of thumb is that if the section you see is not related to one of the sections named above, you can safely ignore the information it contains. If you are at all in doubt, complete documentation for all device .INF file sections is contained in the Device Driver Development Kit (DDK) provided by Microsoft.

The Setup Script File

The setup script file controls how setup executes. You can produce completely unattended setups, except for minor details, using such scripts. The settings substitute for user input during the setup process, and they are gathered into the file sections indicated hereafter. The run command for using a setup script looks like the following:

```
setup myscript.inf
```

[Setup]

Entries in this section determine how the setup program undertakes setup.

Devicepath

This setting controls whether Windows examines the source file path for .INF files or only the Windows .INF directory. A value of 0 causes Windows to examine only its own .INF path (the default). A value of 1 forces examination of the source path.

EBD

This setting directs setup to create the emergency startup disk. A value of 1 causes the disk creation (the default), whereas a value of 0 skips disk creation.

Express

This setting governs whether the values in MSBATCH.INF control setup or the user controls setup. A value of 0 allows user input (the default), whereas a value of 1 prevents user input.

InstallDir

This setting describes the directory for installation. The default is to use the existing Windows directory.

InstallType

This setting determines the type of setup that takes place. A value of 0 specifies compact, a value of 1 typical (the default), a value of 2 portable, and a value of 3 custom.

PenWinWarning

A value of 1 for this setting causes a warning message to be displayed if an unknown version of Pen Windows is installed (the default). A value of 0 skips this warning.

ProductID

This entry describes the product ID number for the installation. There is no default value. You must provide a product ID, which is printed on either the CD or Certificate of Authenticity.

SaveSUBoot

In server-based setup, a value of 0 causes the SUBOOT directory to be deleted (the default), whereas a value of 1 prevents deletion of the directory.

TimeZone

This entry provides a string that describes the time zone to use during setup. The following list provides the valid strings available for use:

- Afghanistan
- Alaskan
- Arabian
- Atlantic
- AUS Central
- Azores
- Bangkok
- Canada Central
- Cen. Australia
- Central
- Central Asia
- Central Pacific
- China
- Czech
- Dateline
- E. Europe
- E. South America
- Eastern

- Egypt
- Fiji
- GFT
- GMT
- Greenwich
- Hawaiian
- India
- Iran
- Israel
- Lisbon
- Warsaw
- Mexico
- Mid-Atlantic
- Mountain
- New Zealand
- Newfoundland
- Pacific
- Romance
- Russian
- SA Eastern
- SA Pacific
- SA Western
- Samoa
- Saudi Arabia
- South Africa
- Sydney
- Taipei
- Tasmania
- Tokyo
- US Eastern
- US Mountain
- W. Europe
- West Asia
- West Pacific

Uninstall (with BackupDir)

This entry governs whether compressed versions of the existing DOS and Windows directories are built for uninstall purposes. A value of 0 prevents their creation without user input, a value of 1 prompts the user to determine this issue, and a value of 5 causes their creation without user input. The default is 1.

Verify

This setting governs the use of verify mode, used mostly by OEMs. A value of 0 causes normal installation (the default), while a value of 1 invokes verify mode. In most cases you do not need to include this setting.

VRC

This setting governs the use of version checking. A value of 0 prompts the user before overwriting existing files (the default), while a value of 1 overwrites without prompting.

[System]

This section identifies the system settings. You can copy the relevant settings from the SETUPLOG.TXT file for a system that has already been installed with identical hardware. Simply find the identically named sections and items in this file.

Display

A triad of numbers indicating the color depth per pixel, number of lines horizontally, and number of lines vertically. The default value is 4640480.

DisplChar

Specifies the .INF section name in the file DISPLAY.INF or the equivalent file.

Keyboard

Specifies the .INF section name in the file KEYBOARD.INF or the equivalent file.

Locale

Specifies the .INF section name in the file LOCALE.INF or the equivalent file.

Machine

Specifies the .INF section name in the file MACHINE.INF or the equivalent file.

Monitor

Specifies the .INF section name in the file MONITOR.INF or the equivalent file.

Mouse

Specifies the .INF section name in the file MSMOUSE.INF or the equivalent file.

MultiLanguage

Identifies the type of multilanguage support. May be English (default), Greek, Cyrillic, or CE. CE adds support for Central European languages.

PenWindows

Specifies the .INF section name in the file PENWIN.INF or the equivalent file.

Power

Specifies the .INF section name in the file MACHINE.INF or the equivalent file.

Tablet

Specifies the .INF section name in the file PENDRV.INF or the equivalent file.

[NameAndOrg]

Identifies the name and organization the user would normally enter during setup.

Name

Contains the text string that gives the user's name. The default value is an empty string.

Org

Contains the text string describing the name of the user's organization. The default value is an empty string.

Display

Determines whether the name and organization dialog box is displayed during the setup operation. The default value of 1 displays the dialog. A value of 0 prevents the display.

[InstallLocationsMRU]

This section contains entries of the following type:

```
mruX=an install path
```

X represents a number, so that entries will begin at mru1 and continue in numerical sequence. Each entry gives a path from which users may select when prompted to provide the path to the Windows installation files. Instead you can use the CopyFiles= line in the [Install] section to specify this path exactly without user choice.

[OptionalComponents]

Each entry in this section specifies whether an optional Windows 98 component should be installed. The entries take the following form:

```
"Accessibility Options"=1
```

A value of 1 indicates to install the named components, a value of 0 not to install. The following list identifies the acceptable component names:

- Accessibility Options
- Accessories
- Audio Compression
- Backup
- Blank Screen
- Briefcase
- Calculator
- CD Player
- Character Map
- Clipboard Viewer
- Communications
- Curves and Colors
- Defrag
- Desktop Wallpaper

- Dial-Up Networking
- Direct Cable Connection
- Disk Compression Tools
- Disk Tools
- Document Templates
- Flying Through Space
- Games
- HyperTerminal
- Jungle Sound Scheme
- Media Player
- Microsoft Exchange
- Microsoft Fax
- Microsoft Fax Services
- Microsoft Fax Viewer
- Microsoft Mail Services
- Mouse Pointers
- Multimedia
- Musical Sound Scheme
- Mystify Your Mind
- Net Watcher
- Object Packager
- Online User's Guide
- Paint
- Phone Dialer
- Quick View
- Robotz Sound Scheme
- Sample Sounds
- Screen Savers
- Scrolling Marquee
- Sound Recorder
- System Monitor
- System Resource Meter
- The Microsoft Network

- Utopia Sound Scheme
- Video Compression
- Volume Control
- Windows 98 Tour
- WordPad

[Network]

This section identifies the settings for the network devices and components to be installed.

Clients

Contains a comma-separated list of device identifiers for network clients. If improperly specified, setup displays the network dialog box to allow the user to select the proper network clients. Table B.6 identifies the valid device identifiers.

Table B.6. Network client device identifiers.

Device Identifier	Meaning
LANT5	Artisoft® LANtastic® versions 5.x and 6.x
NETWARE3	Novell® NetWare® version 3.x
NETWARE4	Novell NetWare version 4.x
NWREDIR	Microsoft Client for NetWare Networks
PCNFS50	SunSoft® PC-NFS® version 5.x and greater
VINES552	Banyan® VINES® version 5.52 and greater
VREDIR	Client for Microsoft Networks

ComputerName

This entry provides the unique 15 character name that the computer uses to identify itself to the network. It may not contain spaces, but may contain these characters: ! @ # $ % ^ & ( ) - _ ' { } . ~.

Description

This statement provides a description that is presented along with the computer name in the browser. Often used to provide a description of the role of the computer or the shares it makes available, the description can contain up to 48 characters, but no commas.

DefaultProtocol

This entry contains a protocol name, as specified in *Protocol=*, and a network card ID, as specified in *NetCards=*, separated by a comma. This represents the default networking protocol for the system. The following example illustrates:

```
DefaultProtocol=netbeui,*pnp810d
```

Display

This entry governs whether the Network dialog box appears during setup. A value of 1 causes display (the default), while a value of 0 prevents display. The default value is 1.

DisplayWorkstationSetup

This entry governs whether the setup program interface appears during the setup of a diskless workstation. A value of 0 (the default) prevents display, while a value of 1 causes display.

HDBoot

If running from a shared copy on a server, a value of 0 (the default) for this entry causes Windows 98 to boot from the server or a floppy disk, while a value of 1 causes Windows 98 to boot from the local workstation hard drive.

IgnoreDetectedNetcards

A value of 1 tells setup to ignore the network cards detected during the hardware identification phase; a value of 0 (default) tells setup to use the detected cards.

NetCards

This entry provides a comma-separated list of network card driver identifiers in the form in which they are provided in the driver's .INF file. A typical entry looks like this:

```
NetCards= *PNP812D,*PNP80F3
```

PassThroughAgent

Under user-level security, this entry specifies the server or domain name for the security provider.

Protocols

This entry provides a comma-separated list of protocol identifiers which identify the protocols to be installed. Table B.7 provides the identifiers.

Table B.7. Protocol identifiers.

Identifier	Meaning
DEC40	DECnet™ version 4.1 Ethernet protocol
DEC40T	DECnet version 4.1 token ring protocol
DEC50	DECnet version 5.0a Ethernet protocol
DEC50T	DECnet version 5.0a token ring protocol
IPXODI	Novell-supplied IPXODI protocol
MSDLC	Microsoft DLC (real mode)
MSTCP	Microsoft TCP/IP
NDISBAN	Banyan VINES NDIS Ethernet protocol
NDTOKBAN	Banyan VINES NDIS token-ring protocol
NETBEUI	Microsoft NetBEUI
NFSLINK	Sun PC-NFS protocol
NWLINK	IPX/SPX-compatible protocol
NWNBLINK	NetBIOS support for IPX/SPX-compatible protocol

RemoveBinding

This entry contains a the device identifiers of two bound networking components. It indicates that the system should remove this binding.

RPLSetup

For remote boot workstations, a value of 0 (the default) for this entry causes Windows 98 not to create a remote boot image. A value of 1 causes setup to create a disk image on the server for booting a remote boot workstation and causes a boot from the server if *WorkstationSetup=1*.

Services

This entry contains a comma-separated list of identifiers for networking components to be installed. The identifiers are shown on Table B.8. Only the service VSERVER is installed by default.

Table B.8. Network service identifiers.

Identifier	Meaning	Related .INF file
BKUPAGNT	Arcada Backup Exec agent	BKUPAGNT.INF
CHEYAGNT	Cheyenne ARCserve agent	CHEYENNE.INF
JADM	HP Network Printer service for Microsoft	HPNETPRN.INF
JANW	HP Network Printer service for NetWare	HPNETPRN.INF
NMAGENT	Microsoft Network Monitor agent	NMAGENT.INF
NWSERVER	File and Printer Sharing for NetWare Networks	NETSRVR.INF
PSERVER	Microsoft Print Service for NetWare Networks	MSPSRV.INF
REMOTEREG	Microsoft Remote Registry service	REGSRV.INF
SNMP	Microsoft SNMP agent	SNMP.INF
VSERVER	File and Printer Sharing for Microsoft Networks	NETSRVR.INF

Security

This entry takes a value that determines the type of security used by Windows 98. *Share* specifies share-level security. *Domain*, *msserver*, and *nwserver* specify user level security, identifying the security provider as a Windows NT domain, a Windows NT server, or a Netware server, respectively. The default value is *share*.

ValidateNetcardResources

This entry governs the display of the wizard page if a resource conflict or incomplete installation of the network card is detected. A value of 1 causes the display while a value of 0 prevents the display. The default value is 1.

Workgroup

This entry provides the workgroup name for the workgroup the computer will join. The name may contain up to 15 characters. The illegal and legal characters are the same for *ComputerName*.

WorkstationSetup

This entry determines whether Windows 98 boots from the server. A value of 1 causes the server boot, while a value of 0 (the default) causes a local boot.

[netcard_ID]

This section contains entries derived from the. INF file for the network interface card. You should scan the file for the [netcard.NDI] section, where *netcard* is replaced by the actual name or device ID. You should check this segment for a section that specifies the Registry entries for the card. You should then construct lines in this section that provide a key with the same name as the Registry value set and a value that is the same set for the Registry key. For example, you might convert this Registry line:

```
HKR,NDI\params\DMAChannel,default,,1
```

to the following entry for this file:

```
DMAChannel=1
```

[MSTCP]

This section provides settings for the TCP/IP networking protocol that is provided with Windows 98.

DHCP

This entry governs the enabling of the Dynamic Host Configuration Protocol. A value of 1 (the default) enables dynamic configuration, while a value of 0 disables DHCP.

DNS

This parameter governs the use of the Domain Name System. A value of 1 enables DNS and requires the use of an LMHOSTS file. A value of 0 (the default) disables DNS.

DNSServers

This entry is a comma separated list of DNS server names, in the order to be tried, if DNS is enabled. The default is to provide no list.

Domain

The parameter provides the name of the DNS domain to which the computer belongs. The default is not to provide a name.

DomainOrder

This entry is a list of domain name system servers in the order to be tried, separated by commas. The default is not to provide such a list.

Gateways

This entry is a list of IP addresses for IP gateways (also called IP routers) in the order they are to be tried. The default is not to provide the list.

Hostname

This entry provides the DNS hostname for the computer, which is typically the computer's name on the network.

IPAddress

If DHCP is not enabled, this parameter contains the IP address for the computer.

IPMask

If DHCP is not enabled, this parameter contains the subnet mask for the computer.

LMHostPath

This entry provides the path to the LMHOST file for name resolution of distant hosts.

PrimaryWINS

This entry provides the IP address of the primary WINS server for use by this host.

ScopeID

This entry provides a string that identifies the scope of this computer. All computers with the same scope ID on a network running NetBIOS over TCP/IP are considered to have the same scope. Such computers communicate with each other but not with others outside the group defined by the scope ID.

SecondaryWINS

This entry provides the IP address of the secondary WINS server for use by this host.

WINS

This entry enables or disables the use of WINS for resolution of NetBIOS computer names. A value of 0 disables WINS, a value of 1 (the default) enables WINS, and a value of DHCP instructs the computer to enable WINS name resolution but also to use DHCP to get its addressing information.

[NWLink]

This section provides statements that configure the IPX/SPX protocol if it was specified on the *protocols=* line.

Frame_Type

This statement identifies the type of frame to use in communicating over IPX/SPX. Table B.9 provides the appropriate values, each of which is associated with a particular networking standard.

Table B.9. Values for the NWLink Frame_Type Parameter.

Value	Meaning
0	802.3
1	802.2
2	Ethernet II
4	Auto (the default, which allows Windows 98 to make the selection)
5	Token Ring
6	Token Ring SNAP

NetBIOS

This entry indicates whether to install NetBIOS support for IPX/SPX. A value of 0 (the default) indicates not to install the NetBIOS support; a value of 1 causes the installation to take place.

[NWRedir]

This section specifies the configuration for the client for Netware.

FirstNetDrive

This entry indicates the first drive letter for attachment when an attachment is specified in a login script overriding the value in Netwares NET.CFG file. Drive letters may be entered with or without the following colon. The default value is *F:*.

PreferredServer

This entry provides a string that identifies the name of the preferred Netware server for this computer, and it does not override the setting in the NET.CFG file.

ProcessLoginScript

This entry enables or disables the login script. A value of 0 disables script processing, while a value of 1 (the default) enables script processing.

SearchMode

This parameter provides a value ranging from 0 through 7, corresponding exactly with a Netware search mode value. Table B.10 identifies the meaning of these values.

Table B.10. Netware search mode values.

Value	Meaning
0	Use search drives after examining the default directory if no path is given.
1	Identical to mode 0.
2	Does not use search drives.
3	For read-only requests use search drives after examining the default directory if no search path is given.
5	Always use Netware search drives even if a path is specified.
7	Use search drives for read-only requests even if a path is specified.

[NWServer]

This section specifies the configuration of file and printer sharing for Netware networks.

BrowseMaster

This entry controls whether a computer with Netware file and print sharing installed can become the master browser. A value of 0 prevents the computer from becoming a master browser, a value of 1 (the default) allows selection as master browser, and a value of 2 makes the computer a preferred master browser.

Use_SAP

This entry determines whether the computer uses Server Addressing Protocol for browsing. Enabling SAP makes the computer visible to Netware clients, but leaves it invisible to the Network Neighborhood. A value of 0 disables SAP (the default), and a value of 1 enables it.

[Vredir]

This section specifies the configuration for the client for Microsoft networks.

LogonDomain

This statement indicates whether logons are validated by a Windows NT domain. A value of 0 indicates that the domain has no role in processing logons (the default), while a value of 1 indicates that the domain validates logons.

ValidatedLogon

This statement gives the name of the Windows NT domain used for processing logons. *LogonDomain* must be set to 1 for this value to be used.

[Vserver]

This section specifies the configuration of file and printer sharing for Microsoft networks.

Announce

This entry governs whether the computer broadcasts its presence to LAN Manager clients on the network. A value of 0 prevents the broadcast and makes browsing slower. A value of 1 (the default) makes browsing faster, but increases network traffic.

BrowseMaster

This entry governs whether the computer can participate in elections for master browser on the network. A value of 0 prevents the computer from participating, an values of 1 enables participation in elections and causes the computer to become master browser, and a value of 2 allows the computer to participate and become master browser if the election weightings allow it to do so. The default value is 2.

[Printers]

This section contains entries of the following form:

```
PrinterName=DriverModel,Port
```

The *PrinterName* is a string up to 31 characters long that does not contain the following characters: \ , ; =. It is called the friendly name, so you may choose what it is. The printer model name must be recognizable by Windows 98, which means the name must have a corresponding entry in the printer .INF files supplied with the operating system. *DriverModel* is the name of the driver to be used, and *Port* is a standard port name or a UNC path name of a printer queue. There is no default for these entries. The following entry serves as an example:

```
"My Laserjet"="HP Laserjet IIIsi",\\NTLONDON\HPSHARE
```

[Strings]

This section defines the string keys that you can use as a shorthand for strings elsewhere in the file. Wherever you use a string key, place it between percentage signs to indicate to Setup that the key should be expanded. Gathering frequently used strings into a [Strings] section allows you to revise the strings as necessary by editing only this section. Strings should be enclosed in quotation marks if the entry elsewhere in the file requires a string enclosed in quotation marks. Entries take the following form:

```
key=value
```

A widely seen string key is the following:

```
MSFT="Microsoft"
```

[Install]

This section allows you to specify additional files to copy for your installation and additional settings to merge into the registry. This section is formatted identically to the [Install] section described earlier in this appendix for device information files. In general, you use this section to accomplish one or more of the following goals:

- Copy custom shortcuts and bitmaps as part of the installation
- Update configuration entries
- Implement user profiles and remote administration

Copying custom files

Copying custom files is a matter of adding three entries. First, in the [Install] section, add a CopyFiles line that defines a section where the names of the files are defined. For example, you could include this entry:

```
[install]
CopyFiles=custfile.Copy
```

Next, create a section with the name *[custfile.Copy]* and list as entries the files to copy, as follows:

```
[CUSTFILES.Copy]
custfile.bmp      ;a bitmap, for example
custfile.lnk      ;a shortcut, for example
```

Finally, include a [DestinationDirs] section with an entry for the [custfile.Copy] section you just defined. The form of this entry is as follows:

```
[DestinationDirs]
custfile.copy=25
```

The values for each entry in this section indicate where the files should be copied. A value of 25 determines that files are copied to the Windows directory. A value of 11 copies files to the Windows SYSTEM directory. And a value of 10 causes files to be copied to the machine directory. (In shared installations, the machine directory is where Windows files are stored on the local machine, as opposed to the shared Windows directories on the network.)

Updating Configuration Entries

You may decide that you need to update entries in .INI files and configuration files prior to installing Windows 98 on a system. You can automate this task as a part of your setup script by adding entries to the [Install] section and creating related sections. In the [Install] section, add the following lines, which specify the sections where .INI files, CONFIG.SYS, and AUTOEXEC.BAT updates are defined:

```
[Install]
UpdateInis=Update_system.Ini
UpdateCfgSys=Update_config.sys
UpdateAutoBat=Update_autoexec.bat
```

Using the word *Update* in the section name is a useful reminder of the purpose of the section. Specifying the file updated as a part of the section name also clarifies the function of the section. For the .INI file updates, specify the file, the section, and the line to use, as in the following example:

```
[Update_system.Ini]
system.ini,386enh,"device=myvxd.386"
```

For the CONFIG.SYS and AUTOEXEC.BAT sections, use entries like the following:

```
[Update_config.sys]
DevRename=denon.sys,oldcd.sys
DevDelete=c:\dos\himem.sys
DevAddDev= c:\scsi\neccdr.sys /d:NECCD
Stacks=9,256
Buffers=20
Files=40
LastDrive=z

[Update_autoexec.bat]
CmdDelete=win
CmdAdd=doskey
UnSet=TEMP
```

The syntax for these entries is described for these sections in the description of the device information file provided earlier in this appendix.

Implementing User Profiles and Remote Administration

Preparing to use user profiles and remote administration in an automated install is a matter of adding some boilerplate lines to your script file. You must add the following lines to your .INF file to enable these two features:

```
[Install]
AddReg=User.Profiles,Remote.Admin
```

Throughout the following entries for these files, any line that begins with HK indicates a single line in the file. If possible, adjust the font to get each one of these entries on one line. If this is not possible, break the entries at a comma.

All Registry entries should appear as a single line in your .INF file. They have been broken into multiple lines here in order to fit them on a single page.

```
[User.Profiles]
HKLM,"Network\Logon","UserProfiles",1,1

[Remote.Admin]
HKLM,"Security\Access\Admin\Remote",%Server_Domain_Username%,1,ff,00

[Network]
Security=domain_or_server
PassThroughAgent=provider_name      ;These entries enable
;user-level security.
```

```
;See thefollowing text
;for how to set them.

services=remotereg

[strings]
; Names the server to provide user accounts or groups
; that will have the right to remotely administer systems
Server_Domain_Username = "server_or_domain\account"
```

The custom values you have to set in this block of entries must be set depending on whether you will use a Netware server or a Windows NT server as security provider. For the Netware scenario, provide these entries:

```
Security=server            ;indicates a server provides security
PassThroughAgent=NWSERV     ;indicates the name of the
;server providing security

;the following gives the user name or group that can
;remotely administer
Server_Domain_Username="NWSERV\HELPER
```

For the Windows NT scenario, the custom lines are the following:

```
Security=Domain            ;indicates a server provides security
PassThroughAgent=NTDOM      ;indicates the name of the
;server providing security

;the following gives the user name or group that can
;remotely administer
Server_Domain_Username="NTDOM\HELPER
```

In both scenarios, setup adds the user name or group to the list of groups and individuals allowed to administer computers remotely. It also sets permissions for these accounts to allow remote administration.

Enabling group policies is a matter of adding these boilerplate lines to the .INF file:

```
[Install]
Addreg=User.Profiles.Reg, Group.Policies.Reg
Copyfiles=Group.Policies.Copy

[User.Profiles.Reg]
HKLM,Network\Logon,UserProfiles,1,1

[Group.Policies.Reg]
HKLM,Network\Logon,PolicyHandler,,"GROUPPOL.DLL,ProcessPolicies"
HKLM,System\CurrentControlSet\Services\MSNP32\NetworkProvider,
 GroupFcn,,"GROUPPOL.DLL,NTGetUserGroups"
HKLM,System\CurrentControlSet\Services\NWNP32\NetworkProvider,
 GroupFcn,,"GROUPPOL.DLL,NWGetUserGroups"

[Group.Policies.Copy]
grouppol.dll

[DestinationDirs]
Group.Policies.Copy = 11
```

C

Building HOSTS and LMHOSTS

Peter Norton®

In Windows networking, names are a big issue. Each computer on the network has to have some sort of a name. To make matters worse, different networking protocols have different naming conventions. The protocol for Microsoft Networks, NetBEUI, assigns a unique text string to each computer. No two computers on the network may have the same name.

Under the TCP/IP protocol, each computer is assigned a numeric address consisting of four numbers separated by periods. An example is 144.84.22.9, and such addresses are called IP addresses. Each computer on the network must have a unique IP address.

IP addresses, unfortunately, are not memorable. As a result, text strings can also be assigned so that the humans operating the computers don't have to refer to the IP addresses. Such names have developed conventions, and you probably are most familiar with them as Internet addresses. The familiar *compuserve.com* or *aol.com* are simply the text strings paired with the IP addresses of the CompuServe and America Online computers.

To complicate matters even further, you can elect to run multiple networking protocols simultaneously. As a result, your network needs a mechanism for resolving the text string computer names to actual addresses when necessary. Many protocols, such as NetBEUI, provide their own mechanisms for name resolution. TCP/IP needs the help of a service that you set up.

Name Resolution Services

You have the option of using several name resolution services. The most popular require that you work with a server-based network. The most common in TCP/IP networking is probably a Domain Name System (DNS) server. In this scenario, a server, designated the DNS server, holds a master table of names and addresses. Whenever a workstation on the network needs to resolve a name, it requests that the server look up the name in its master table and provide the corresponding IP address. There may be multiple DNS servers functional for a given network. When you set up the TCP/IP protocol on each workstation, you provide the IP address of the DNS servers in the order to contact them so that the workstation knows which machine to query for names.

An alternative scheme when using a Windows NT server is to set up a Windows Internet Naming Service (WINS) server. A WINS server works much the same way as a DNS server, except that it runs under the Windows NT operating system and translates NetBIOS names to IP addresses, rather than the fully qualified domain names that DNS translates to IP addresses. The WINS server is responsible for maintaining a table of names and addresses, which it builds from the initial announcements the workstations broadcast when they join the network. When a workstation is powered up, it sends its name and address to the WINS server, which updates its table appropriately.

Under Windows NT 3.51 and earlier, you would choose a UNIX server as a DNS server and a Windows NT server as a WINS server because of incompatibilities in the two name services. However, with the release of Windows NT 4.0, WINS and DNS can both be run on Windows NT.

Another server-based option is the Dynamic Host Configuration Protocol (DHCP). Under TCP/IP, each computer on the network is called a host. Under DHCP, one computer is designated as the DHCP server. As each host joins the network, it queries the DHCP server to find out what address it should use, providing its name to the server as a part of the request. The DHCP server automatically assigns an IP address to the host, including its default gateway address, WINS server address, and DNS server address if necessary. The host receives the addressing information in a return broadcast and configures itself accordingly.

Windows 98, however, does not require a server-based network. In addition, you may not want to allocate a server to manage name resolution. Under either of these conditions, you can use local tables to provide name resolution. Two files, known as HOSTS and LMHOSTS, can perform these tasks.

Both HOSTS and LMHOSTS should not end in an extension. The default Windows 98 editor, Notepad, always adds a .TXT extension. To prevent Notepad from adding the extension, enclose the filename to be saved in quotation marks.

The HOSTS File

The purpose of a HOSTS file is to provide resolution of remote names. This is the equivalent of the UNIX HOSTS file, and is intended to translate fully qualified domain names to IP addresses. (However, any name you enter is resolved, even if it does not follow the domain naming convention.) The HOSTS file is not used internally on a Windows 98 computer. As a result, the Network Neighborhood is not based on the HOSTS file. The file is used when you invoke a TCP/IP utility, such as ping or ftp.

The HOSTS file consists of lines that contain two entries separated by a space. The first is an IP address; the second is a text string designating the name. The lines look like the following example:

```
144.84.32.2 ducksbreath.com
```

The string entry in a HOSTS file line is case sensitive. You may want to have one entry for the lowercase version and one entry for the uppercase version to avoid helpdesk questions motivated by a mispositioned Caps Lock key.

If you are using a HOSTS file, one such file must reside on each system. Each file should contain the following entry for the name *localhost*, which is paired with the loopback address for the local machine:

```
localhost 127.0.0.1
```

Microsoft provides an example HOSTS file, which is built when you install TCP/IP on a machine. The file is called HOSTS.SAM, and it contains the information shown here:

```
# Copyright (c) 1994 Microsoft Corp.
#
# This is a sample HOSTS file used by Microsoft TCP/IP for Chicago
#
# This file contains the mappings of IP addresses to host names. Each
# entry should be kept on an individual line. The IP address should
# be placed in the first column followed by the corresponding host name.
# The IP address and the host name should be separated by at least one
# space.
#
# Additionally, comments (such as these) may be inserted on individual
# lines or following the machine name denoted by a '#' symbol.
#
# For example:
#
#    102.54.94.97    rhino.acme.com      # source server
#    38.25.63.10     x.acme.com        # x client host

127.0.0.1    localhost
```

The only functional entry in this file is the last line, the address for localhost. The rest of the lines are interpreted as comments because the begin with the # character. You can use the # character after an entry to place an explanation of the entry on the same line, as shown in the file. Or you can place comments ahead of or behind an entry. You should include comments to note the purpose of the name assigned or the location of the computer given the name. To create your own HOSTS file, simply edit the sample with any text editor and add entries following the localhost entry.

To enable name resolution via the HOSTS file, you must select Enable DNS option button in the Configure DNS tab of the TCP/IP properties dialog. You reach this dialog from the Network icon in the Control Panel. Select the TCP/IP protocol in the list box and then click on the Properties button.

The LMHOSTS File

The purpose of an LMHOSTS file is to provide name resolution for remote systems when a WINS server is not available. Originally, it was designed to work with Microsoft's LAN Manager, hence the LM in its name. Specifically, LMHOSTS provides name resolution across gateways and routers. The entries in LMHOSTS identify the names for networked print, file, and remote access services. LMHOSTS also resolves names for domain services such as browsing, logon, and replication.

The LMHOSTS file is read whenever WINS name resolution fails. If WINS is available, some re-mote hosts may not be included in the WINS database because their name broadcasts cannot cross over subnetworks. If WINS is not available, LMHOSTS provides the sole means of locating remotes hosts. However, there are very few occasions when WINS would fail in this manner. You need to use LMHOSTS only when you have servers that cannot for some reason register a NetBIOS name with WINS. Examples might be UNIX servers that cannot function as WINS clients.

Microsoft provides the following sample LMHOSTS file, which is installed in the Windows directory when you install the TCP/IP protocol:

```
# Copyright (c) 1993-1995 Microsoft Corp.
#
# This is a sample LMHOSTS file used by the Microsoft TCP/IP for Windows
# NT.
#
# This file contains the mappings of IP addresses to NT computernames
# (NetBIOS) names. Each entry should be kept on an individual line.
# The IP address should be placed in the first column followed by the
# corresponding computername. The address and the computername
# should be separated by at least one space or tab. The "#" character
# is generally used to denote the start of a comment (see the exceptions
# below).
#
# This file is compatible with Microsoft LAN Manager 2.x TCP/IP lmhosts
# files and offers the following extensions:
#
#    #PRE
#    #DOM:<domain>
#    #INCLUDE <filename>
#    #BEGIN_ALTERNATE
#    #END_ALTERNATE
#    \0xnn (non-printing character support)
#
# Following any entry in the file with the characters "#PRE" will cause
# the entry to be preloaded into the name cache. By default, entries are
# not preloaded, but are parsed only after dynamic name resolution fails.
#
# Following an entry with the "#DOM:<domain>" tag will associate the
# entry with the domain specified by <domain>. This affects how the
# browser and logon services behave in TCP/IP environments. To preload
# the host name associated with #DOM entry, it is necessary to also add a
# #PRE to the line. The <domain> is always preloaded although it will not
# be shown when the name cache is viewed.
#
# Specifying "#INCLUDE <filename>" will force the RFC NetBIOS (NBT)
# software to seek the specified <filename> and parse it as if it were
# local. <filename> is generally a UNC-based name, allowing a
# centralized lmhosts file to be maintained on a server.
# It is ALWAYS necessary to provide a mapping for the IP address of the
# server prior to the #INCLUDE. This mapping must use the #PRE directive.
# In addition, the share "public" in the example below must be in the
# LanManServer list of "NullSessionShares" in order for client machines to
# be able to read the lmhosts file successfully. This key is under
# \machine\system\currentcontrolset\services\lanmanserver\parameters\nullsessionshares
# in the registry. Simply add "public" to the list found there.
#
# The #BEGIN_ and #END_ALTERNATE keywords allow multiple #INCLUDE
# statements to be grouped together. Any single successful include
# will cause the group to succeed.
#
# Finally, non-printing characters can be embedded in mappings by
# first surrounding the NetBIOS name in quotations, then using the
# \0xnn notation to specify a hex value for a non-printing character.
#
```

```
# The following example illustrates all of these extensions:
#
# 102.54.94.97    rhino       #PRE #DOM:networking #net group's DC
# 102.54.94.102   "appname \0x14"          #special app server
# 102.54.94.123   popular     #PRE      #source server
# 102.54.94.117   localsrv    #PRE         #needed for the include
#
# #BEGIN_ALTERNATE
# #INCLUDE \\localsrv\public\lmhosts
# #INCLUDE \\rhino\public\lmhosts
# #END_ALTERNATE
#
# In the above example, the "appname" server contains a special
# character in its name, the "popular" and "localsrv" server names are
# preloaded, and the "rhino" server name is specified so it can be used
# to later #INCLUDE a centrally maintained lmhosts file if the "localsrv"
# system is unavailable.
#
# Note that the whole file is parsed including comments on each lookup,
# so keeping the number of comments to a minimum will improve performance.
# Therefore it is not advisable to simply add lmhosts file entries onto the
# end of this file.
```

Because LMHOSTS is intended for use instead of a WINS server, the assumption is that you are running a Windows NT-based Microsoft network. As a result, the names that are resolved to IP addresses are the NetBIOS names you set for computers using the Network icon in the Control Panel. The reason these are NetBIOS names is that Windows NT runs NetBIOS atop TCP/IP in order to provide a browsing service for the network. Without NetBIOS included in this configuration, Windows NT would not provide a browsing service.

The most important property of the sample LMHOSTS file is that it provides no functional entries. Instead, it provides only the directions for creating such entries. The basic entry looks like the following example, which is the same as for the HOSTS file:

```
191.35.32.1    remserv
```

You should keep in mind that the entries in this file refer to your remote servers only. (Use the HOSTS file for hosts local to a subnetwork.) You should avoid comments if at all possible, because the entire file is parsed as it is read, including all of the comment lines. Avoiding comments improves the speed of name resolution, as a result. You should also follow these conventions in entering lines:

```
*Begin the address in column 1 of the file. Positioning of the address is critical.
*        Separate the address from the name with a space or tab. You can use multiple
spaces or tabs if you desire.
*Use the # character to indicate comments.
*Place each entry on a separate line.
```

In addition to address/name entries, your LMHOSTS file can contain several special directives. Table C.1 identifies these directives and provides examples.

- Begin the address in column 1 of the file. Positioning of the address is critical.

- Separate the address from the name with a space or tab. You can use multiple spaces or tabs if you desire.

- Use the # character to indicate comments.
- Place each entry on a separate line.

Table C.1. LMHOSTS directives.

Directive	Meaning	Example
#PRE	Preloads the entry into the NetBIOS name cache.	100.58.58.1 lclsrv #PRE
#DOM	Identifies the Windows NT domain associated with the address.	100.58.58.1 lclsrv #DOM:Boston
#INCLUDE	Provides the UNC name for a file whose entries should be included in the one being parsed.	#INCLUDE\\Boston\Public\lmhosts
#BEGIN_ALTERNATIVE	Marks the beginning of a group of #INCLUDE directives.	#BEGIN_ALTERNATIVE
#END_ALTERNATIVE	Marks the END of a group of #INCLUDE directives.	#END_ALTERNATIVE

To include nonprinting characters in a NetBIOS name, precede the character with a backslash and reference it using its hexadecimal value, as in \0x14, and enclose the entire name in blanks. You can have only one nonprinting character in the name, and you should make it the last character in the string.

The following example demonstrates a set of entries that you might have in your LMHOSTS file:

```
100.58.58.1 lclsrv #PRE #DOM:Boston
100.59.60.3 Boston #PRE
100.70.60.3 Paris #PRE
100.60.60.3 London #PRE
#INCLUDE \\Boston\Public\lmhosts
#BEGIN_ALTERNATIVE
#INCLUDE \\Paris\Public\lmhosts
#INCLUDE \\London\Public\lmhosts
#END_ALTERNATIVE
```

In this example, the first line identifies a name which is associated with the domain Boston and is preloaded into the NetBIOS name cache so that name resolution can occur without parsing the entire file. (For names that are not preloaded into the cache, the file must be read and parsed before resolution can occur. Also, the preloaded name takes precedence over the WINS entry for the name and any broadcast name for the server.) The fifth line identifies an LMHOSTS file in the Public directory of a system named Boston, in which the entries are treated as though they have been entered in this file. The name entry for Boston has been preloaded, as indicated on line 2 of the file, a requirement for including the name in the #INCLUDE directive.

The remaining lines in the files process a set of two #INCLUDE directives that are treated as a single unit. If one of them succeeds, they are treated as if all of them have succeeded, as indicated by the framing #BEGIN_ALTERNATIVE and #END_ALTERNATIVE directives. (Note that the names of the systems involved were preloaded into the cache by earlier lines.) Such a set of #INCLUDE directives is useful for loading names from a set of systems that may not all be switched on at the same time. In this case, if only Paris is up, the #INCLUDE succeeds and does not cause an error. The same is true if only London is up, or if both are up. The only case in which the #INCLUDE directive would fail is if both Paris and London are down. By contrast, the earlier #INCLUDE line fails if Boston is unavailable, since there are no alternative include locations specified.

The remaining lines in the files process a set of two #INCLUDE directives that are treated as a single unit. If one of them succeeds, they are treated as if all of them have succeeded, as indicated by the framing #BEGIN_ALTERNATIVE and #END_ALTERNATIVE directives. (Note that the names of the systems involved were preloaded into the cache by earlier lines.) Such a set of #INCLUDE directives is useful for loading names from a set of systems that may not all be switched on at the same time. In this case, if only Paris is up, the #INCLUDE succeeds and does not cause an error. The same is true if only London is up, or if both are up. The only case in which the #INCLUDE directive would fail is if both Paris and London are down. By contrast, the earlier #INCLUDE line fails if Boston is unavailable, since there are no alternative include locations specified.

To create and maintain an LMHOSTS file, follow these steps:

1. Create a new text file using Notepad or a similar editor containing the entries you need. Preload all names that you think will be accessed frequently.
2. Save the file as LMHOSTS in the Windows directory.
3. Update the file each time a system is added or removed from the network.

You should not create your LMHOSTS file by appending names to the sample file. In LMHOSTS, each line is read and parsed, including the comments. Each of the provided comments slows every effort at name resolution as a result.

Index